Information Systems Programming with Java™

SECOND EDITION

Andrew C. Staugaard, Jr.
College of the Ozarks

PEARSON
Prentice
Hall

Upper Saddle River, NJ 07458

Library of Congress Cataloging-in-Publication Data

Staugaard, Andrew C.
  Information systems programming with Java / Andrew C. Staugaard, Jr.—2nd ed.
    p.   cm.
  ISBN 0-13-101860-4
  1. Java (Computer program language) 2. Object-oriented programming (Computer
science) 3. Management information systems. I. Title.
  QA76.73.J38S788 2003
  005.13'3—dc21
                              2003051711

Vice President and Editorial Director, ECS: *Marcia J. Horton*
Acquisitions Editor: *Kate Hargett*
Editorial Assistant: *Michael Giacobbe*
Vice President and Director of Production and Manufacturing, ESM: *David W. Riccardi*
Executive Managing Editor: *Vince O'Brien*
Managing Editor: *Camille Trentacoste*
Production Editor: *Susan McClung*
Director of Creative Services: *Paul Belfanti*
Creative Director: *Carole Anson*
Art Director: *Jayne Conte*
Cover Designer: *Bruce Kenselaar*
Cover Image: *John S. Dykes/SIS* Inc.
Art Editor: *Greg Dulles*
Manufacturing Manager: *Trudy Pisciotti*
Manufacturing Buyer: *Lynda Castillo*
Marketing Manager: *Pamela Shaffer*
Marketing Assistant: *Barrie Reinhold*

Microsoft®, Windows®, MS-DOS®, and Visual Basic® are registered trademarks of the Microsoft
Corporation in the U.S.A. and other countries. This book is not sponsored or endorsed by or
affiliated with the Microsoft Corporation.

HotJava™, Java™, JavaBeans™, Java Database Connectivity™, and Sun™ are trademarks of Sun Microsystems, Inc., in the United States and other countries. Pearson Education and Prentice Hall are
independent of Sun Microsystems, Inc.

Apple®, Macintosh®, and Mac® are registered trademarks of Apple Computer, Inc., in the United
States and other countries.

JBuilder® is a registered trademark of Borland Software, Inc. UML™ is a trademark of Object
Management Group in the United States and other countries. UNIX® is a registered trademark of
The Open Group. Zip® disk is a registered trademark of Iomega Corporation.

 © 2004, 1999 by Pearson Education, Inc.
Pearson Prentice Hall
Pearson Education, Inc.
Upper Saddle River, New Jersey, 07458.

ISBN 0-13-101860-4

Pearson Education Ltd., *London*
Pearson Education Australia Pty. Ltd., *Sydney*
Pearson Education Singapore, Pte. Ltd.
Pearson Education North Asia Ltd., *Hong Kong*
Pearson Education Canada, Inc., *Toronto*

Pearson Educación de *Mexico*, S.A. de C.V.
Pearson Education—Japan, *Tokyo*
Pearson Education Malaysia, Pte. Ltd.
Pearson Education, Inc., Upper Saddle River, *New Jersey*

To my students, who continually inspire me to learn more and write more.

Preface

This second edition is a major rewrite from the first edition due to the movement of Java from an Internet language to a popular commercial language that is being used to develop all kinds of information systems (IS) software. Every chapter and appendix has been written with the IS student and industry in mind. After teaching programming to IS students since 1985 and Java since 1997, I know the kinds of difficulties and questions that IS students have in learning programming in general and Java programming in particular. This experience has allowed me to anticipate the problems and challenges a beginning programmer might have in order to head off questions and eliminate problems before they even arise. The overall presentation, along with the text examples, case studies, programming notes, *THINK!* boxes, debugging tips, and caution boxes are mostly the result of this teaching experience. A primary goal in all of my texts has been to write to the level of the student, making my texts extremely readable and user-friendly. This feature makes the material enjoyable and easier for students to learn. A special goal of this book is to get students writing object-oriented Java programs early using IS applications, while building essential problem solving and programming skills required for today's IS solutions. Here is what is new for this second edition:

- *Completely rewritten to conform to current Java technology emphasizing IS applications.*
- *Emphasis on problem solving throughout—Case study examples are developed and presented in a problem-solving style, beginning with a clear problem definition and proceeding through problem decomposition, algorithm and method design, Unified Modeling Language (UML) class diagrams, and Java coding. There are over 20 case studies on such topics as event-driven programming, e-commerce, inventory control, present value, payroll,*

consumer loan processing, data communications, professional baseball statistics, and easy equation solution.

- *Objects-First Approach: Begin developing classes and objects as well as compiling and running Java programs in Chapter 1. Classes and objects are used while developing essential programming skills, building up to in-depth coverage of classes and objects in two new chapters on object-oriented programming, also known as OOP (Chapters 8 and 9).*
- *Two new chapters on graphical user interfaces (GUIs) using Swing components (Chapters 11 and 12).*
- *New chapter on applets and graphics (Chapter 13).*
- *New chapter on multidimensional arrays (Chapter 15).*
- *New appendix on Sun ONE Studio and JBuilder to get students started with these integrated development environments, called IDEs.*
- *New appendix which provides a Systems Engineering tutorial with UML.*
- *New appendix on database connectivity using JDBC.*

Approach

The basic approach of the book is to provide an introductory programming experience in Java for courses offered in IS (CIS, MIS, BIS), IT, and CS programs at both the undergraduate and graduate (MBA) levels. The book provides a gentle but comprehensive introduction to both Java and object-oriented programming for the IS audience. It is specifically written for IS courses with an emphasis on business applications, although perfectly suitable for traditional CS programs. The text is very readable and engaging. It uses a classes/objects-first approach with no dependency on structured programming. OOP concepts are introduced early and expanded upon while building essential programming skills. Problem solving using classes, objects, and methods begins in Chapter 2 and provides a central theme throughout the text, as seen in the 22 case studies. All the basic concepts required for a first programming course are covered. Emphasis is placed on providing simple GUI input/output (I/O) from the beginning (in lieu of console I/O), culminating with two full chapters on GUIs followed by a chapter on applets and graphics. Key concepts for writing good code are presented. Programming is a core talent that many IT managers at least need to understand, if not master. It lends to the credibility of the manager and to his/her direct reports. This book is also tailored to this audience.

Pedagogical Features

- **Chapter Introduction** that provides a brief overview of what the chapter will cover.
- **Chapter Objectives** that provide a list of important concepts the student should understand after completing the chapter.

- **Tip and Note Boxes** throughout that eliminate questions before they even arise and draw attention to key concepts, including
  Programming Notes
  Debugging Tips
  Think! Boxes
  Style Tips
  Caution Boxes
- **Examples** that provide snippets of code that illustrate and reinforce the concepts being covered.
- **Quick-Check Questions** after each section for students to check their progress within a chapter. All answers are provided in an appendix.
- **Case Studies**, many of which are structured around IS applications, all of which follow proven problem solving and software engineering techniques.
- **Chapter Summary** that reviews the important material that the student should understand and retain.
- **Review Questions** at the end of each chapter for students to test their knowledge of the material presented within the chapter.
- **Graded Programming Problems** at the end of each chapter for students to apply and practice the material presented in the chapter.

To the Instructor

In today's market, it is imperative that IS students and managers know both OOP techniques and the Java language. In this text, students will understand the roles of, and relationship between, classes and objects early on, gradually building into in-depth coverage after they have mastered the language basics.

The text can be taught in one or two terms, depending on the ability of the students. In a two-term sequence, I would suggest coverage through the topic of methods (Chapters 1–7). Then, begin the second term with classes and objects in-depth and finish out the book (Chapters 8–15). In any event, make sure to get the students to the keyboard the first week of class to get familiar with their Java IDE (Appendix A) and doing the "Hello World" program in Chapter 1. After that, I would suggest that they do a programming assignment at least once every two weeks. The multitude of chapter problems are written specifically for this purpose and you have the Java solutions available at a password-protected Web site (see your local Prentice-Hall sales representative to obtain a password). I tell my students that learning how to program is like learning how to play a musical instrument. You do not learn how to play an instrument by reading a book and listening to your music teacher's lectures (although this is important to the learning process). You *must* sit down and practice, practice, practice one-on-one with the instrument. The same is true in learning how to program. Our instrument is simply the computer.

The first three appendices are important to teaching this course. Appendix A provides a "jump start" for students using the *Sun ONE Studio Community Edition* (formally *Forte*) IDE or *JBuilder Personal Edition* IDE. Both are free if your students do not mind filling out a survey and being placed on an e-mailing list. Otherwise, the enterprise editions are available at a modest cost. The *Sun ONE Studio Community Edition* IDE has been placed on the text CD for convenience. You can also download *Sun ONE Studio* at www.java.sun.com and *JBuilder* at www.borland.com. I suggest you download *Sun ONE Studio* as a bundle with the *Java SDK*. If you are using *JBuilder Personal*, make sure to download the document files since it is a separate download. I have found both to be very capable IDEs for what needs to be done in the first programming course sequence. I let my students choose which one they want to use. Some prefer one over the other and some use both. You and your students should be aware that these IDEs change versions quite frequently. You should periodically check the relevant Web site for the latest version.

Appendix B provides a tutorial on systems engineering. With this tutorial the student gets an understanding of the bigger systems engineering picture. The tutorial consists of a series of modules that follow the *Foo.com* company programming team from a disastrous build-it, fix-it, spaghetti code program, to a structured design, and finally an object-oriented design of their program using UML. In addition, the UML module prepares the student for planning and designing their own classes in Chapter 8. The UML has become the industry standard design tool for developing object-oriented systems and it is important that your students be familiar with it. I suggest that you begin assigning the tutorial modules early, making sure that all modules have been assigned prior to the first in-depth chapter on object-oriented programming (Chapter 8).

Appendix C provides a workshop on GUIs. In this appendix, the student is acquainted with the topic of graphical user interfaces through a series of hands-on *GUI10X* modules. These modules are designed to familiarize the student with GUI components and the related Java code so that they become familiar with the component behaviors and key concepts. This makes your job of teaching GUIs much easier in Chapters 11 and 12. There are prewritten Java programs that the student will use which are located on the text CD. The student will be asked to load a given program, execute the program, and exercise the GUI. In some cases they will be asked to modify the program code and observe the effect on the GUI and its components. I suggest that you begin assigning these experiment modules early, since they encourage the student to have fun with programming and tend to hold their interest while you are covering the more lackluster stuff, like loops and arrays. Make sure that you have assigned all the modules prior to covering the first in-depth chapter on GUIs (Chapter 11).

Appendix D provides a step-by-step procedure on how to connect to a Microsoft Access database using the JDBC (Java Database Connectivity) API and SQL (Structured Query Language). This important topic can be covered at any time, but preferably after the student has been exposed to exception handling in Chapter 14.

Finally, many instructors differ on when to do arrays in the first programming course sequence. Therefore, I have written the array material such that it can be done anytime after the chapter that covers methods (Chapter 7). A couple of alternatives are illustrated in the following dependency chart.

Chapter Dependency Chart

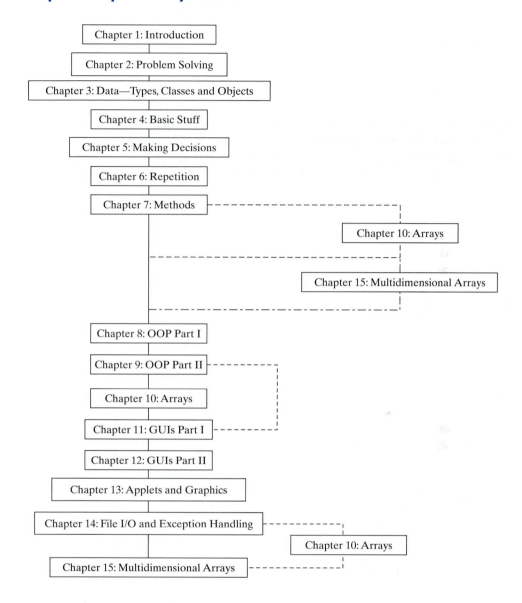

Instructor Resources

Password-protected Web site that contains:

- PowerPoint slides for each chapter
- Teaching tips based on my experience teaching Java to both CS and CIS students for many years

- Test bank with fill-in-the blank, true/false, and multiple-choice questions which includes chapter tests as well as comprehensive tests
- Answers to all chapter questions
- Coded solutions to all programming problems
- All example and case study code

Companion Web Site at www.prenhall.com/staugaard that provides:

- Objectives for each chapter
- Online quizzes for each chapter
- Assignment calendar and syllabus manager
- Downloads of text source code
- Answers to all section quick-check questions
- Links to valuable resources

To the Student

The market demands that IS students know the latest programming and systems engineering techniques to solve today's complex problems. This book has been written to do just that. It has been written to provide you with an introduction to problem solving using OOP techniques and the Java language. OOP allows you to solve problems in a more natural way—the way we humans tend to think of things, thus allowing you to deal with higher levels of complexity. Java is strictly an object-oriented language. In fact, Java is more than just a language—it is a technology in its own right because it allows you to solve problems across the entire computer spectrum, from small embedded applications for your cell phone and personal digital assistant, to commercial PC and mainframe applications, to Internet applications. By the end of the text, you will have the knowledge required to solve complicated problems using the object-oriented approach that these complex solutions require. In addition to learning OOP, you will learn about GUI and graphics programming. GUIs allow you to generate professional-looking windows for your program input and output. Graphics programming provides a means of adding graphical components, such as rectangles, ovals, arcs, and polygons, to your GUIs for added effect. Here you will find that programming is really fun, allowing you to create some really cool things.

Make sure that you go through all the examples and *Problem Solving in Action* case studies. These have been written in short, understandable modules that stress the fundamental concepts being discussed. These case studies are integrated into the text at key points in an effort to tie things together and present a methodical design approach to problem solving using the Java language.

Finally, get your hands dirty early and often! Just have some fun programming. Don't be afraid to try different things. A series of *GUI10X* experiment modules have been provided in Appendix C to let you do just that. In Appendix C you will be asked to load a given program, execute the program, and exercise the GUI. In some cases you will be asked to modify the program code and observe the effect on the GUI. Here you will become familiar with the individual GUI component behaviors and key concepts preparing you for in-depth coverage of GUI programming in Chapters 11 and 12. All the code for these modules is included on the accompanying CD.

Above all, become an *active learner*. You cannot become a competent programmer by just reading this book and listening to your instructor's lectures. You must get your hands dirty at the machine. Get started early by sitting down at a computer, getting acquainted with your Java integrated development environment, or IDE, in Appendix A, running the case study programs which are on the text CD as well as the GUI experiment modules in Appendix C. Start writing *your own* Java programs early and often. This is how you will really learn how to program in Java.

To the IT Manager

Programming is a core talent that many IT managers at least need to understand, if not master. It lends to the credibility of the manager and to his/her direct reports. This book is also tailored to this audience. The Java programming language has taken the commercial software development industry by storm. Much of today's Internet as well as application software is being developed using Java because of its portability and robust set of built-in classes. Java is more than a language—it is a technology of its own. Whether you are an experienced programmer or a novice, you will find that this book provides the "nuts and bolts" required to get you writing Java programs quickly. The text provides comprehensive coverage of both Java applications and applets, with an emphasis on business application programs and IT solutions using GUIs.

ACKNOWLEDGMENTS

This book represents years of accumulated writing efforts and has been extensively reviewed by many experts in both academic and industrial circles. For this particular edition, I would like to thank M. Brian Blake at Georgetown University, Rick Gibson at the American University, James Huddleston, Nitin Kale at the University of Southern California, Andrew J. Novobilski at the University of Tennessee–Chattanooga, Loran W. Walker at Lawrence Technological University, Umesh C. Varma at Campbell University, and Iyad A. Ajawa at Ashland University. They provided me with valuable feedback and insights which contributed greatly to this second edition.

I also would like to thank my students who, over the past 28 years, have made many valuable suggestions and have inspired the creation of this and many other texts.

From the publishing world of Prentice Hall, I would like to thank my editors Petra Recter and Marcia Horton, whose knowledge of the industry and attention to detail have contributed greatly to this text. Thanks also to my production editors Camille Trentacoste of Prentice Hall and Susan McClung of nSight, Inc. They know how to make a great book even better.

Enjoy!

Andrew C. Staugaard, Jr.

Contents

1

Computers, Programs, and Java

OBJECTIVES

When you are finished with this chapter, you should have a good understanding of the following:

- The hardware and software components of a typical computer system.
- The use of a compiler and an interpreter in translating and running Java programs.
- A short history of the Java language.
- The difference between a Java application and a Java applet.
- How several popular languages compare with each other.
- How to enter, compile, and execute your first Java program.
- The syntax of a typical Java program.
- The relationship between a Java package, class, and method.

Introduction

In this first chapter, you will begin your learning journey in the important topic of programming, using the Java™ programming language. This chapter has been written to provide you with an introduction to computers, computer programs, and Java in general. You will first review the hardware that makes up a typical computer system. Then, you will learn about the relationship between the computer system and the computer programs that operate the system. Most of the material in the first section of this chapter should be review.

You will begin to learn about Java in the second section of this chapter. You will first learn about different levels of software. Then you will learn where Java fits into the spectrum and how it compares to other popular programming languages.

The three major steps required to create a working Java program are *edit*, *compile*, and *run*. At the end of this chapter, you will be asked

1

to enter and execute your first Java program. At this time it's probably a good idea for you to familiarize yourself with the operation of your system. You should know how to launch the Java compiler, enter and edit programs, compile programs, and run programs. Refer to Appendix A for a tutorial on several popular Java development environments if need be.

1.1　The Hardware

You undoubtedly have seen some of the hardware components of a computer. These are the physical devices that you can see and touch, such as those shown in Figure 1-1a. This typical PC system obviously has a keyboard and mouse for user input, a display monitor for output, and disk drives for program and data storage. Two very important parts of the system that cannot be seen, because they are inside the console, are the *central processing unit* and its *primary memory.*

　　　The block diagram in Figure 1-1b shows all the major hardware sections that are inside the system box. From this figure, you see that the system can be divided into five functional parts: the central processing unit (CPU), primary memory, secondary memory, input, and output.

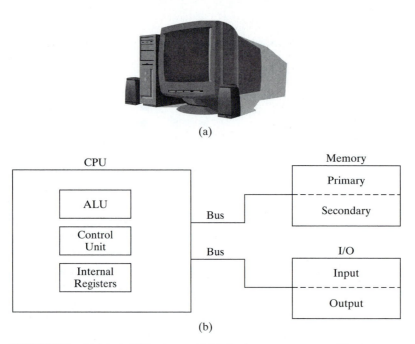

FIGURE 1-1　　(a) A typical PC system and (b) its hardware structure, or architecture.

The Central Processing Unit (CPU)

The central processing unit (CPU) is the brain and nerve center of the entire system. This is where all the calculations and decisions are made. In a PC system, the

entire CPU is contained within a single integrated circuit (IC) chip called a
microprocessor.

 A *microprocessor* is a single integrated-circuit (IC) chip that contains the entire central
processing unit (CPU).

In fact, a microprocessor is what distinguishes a PC from a minicomputer or
mainframe computer. In minicomputers and mainframe computers, several ICs make
up the CPU, not just one as in a PC. A typical microprocessor IC is pictured in Figure
1-2. There are three functional parts within the CPU. They are the *arithmetic and logic
unit (ALU)*, the *control unit*, and the *internal registers*, as shown in Figure 1-3.

FIGURE 1-2   A microprocessor chip is
the CPU of a PC system.

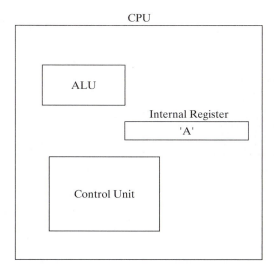

FIGURE 1-3   The CPU consists of an ALU, control unit,
and internal registers.

The Arithmetic and Logic Unit (ALU)   As its name implies, the arithmetic and logic unit (ALU) performs all the arithmetic and logic operations within the CPU. The arithmetic operations performed by the ALU include addition, subtraction, multiplication, and division. These four arithmetic operations can be combined to perform just about any mathematical calculation, from simple arithmetic to calculus.

Logic operations performed by the ALU are *comparison* operations that are used to *compare* numbers and characters. The three logic comparison operations are equality (==), less than (<), and greater than (>). Notice that two equals symbols (==) are used to denote the equality operation. From now on, we will use this to denote an equality operation because this is the *operator* that Java uses to denote the equality operation. These three operations can be combined to form the three additional logic operations of not equal (!=), less than or equal to (<=), and greater than or equal to (>=).

Take a look at Table 1-1. It summarizes the arithmetic and logic operations performed by the ALU. The symbols listed in the table are those that you will use later to perform arithmetic and logic operations when writing Java programs.

TABLE 1-1   A Summary of Arithmetic and Logic Operations Performed by the ALU Area of the CPU

Arithmetic Operation	Java Symbol
Addition	+
Subtraction	−
Multiplication	*
Division	/
Remainder	%

Logic Operation	Java Symbol
Equal to	==
Not equal to	!=
Less than	<
Less than or equal to	<=
Greater than	>
Greater than or equal to	>=

The Control Unit   The control unit area of the CPU directs and coordinates the activities of the entire system. This area interprets program instructions and generates electrical signals to the other parts of the system in order to execute those instructions. The control unit communicates with other sections of the CPU via internal signal paths called **buses**. The control unit often is likened to a traffic cop or orchestra leader because it directs the activity of the entire system.

Internal Registers   The internal register area of the CPU contains temporary storage areas for program instructions and data. In other words, these registers temporarily hold information while it is being processed by the CPU. In Figure 1-3, the internal register shown is holding the character 'A' in preparation for processing this character or as a result of some previous processing step. (Actually, the character 'A' is represented within the register by a series of binary 1's and 0's rather than the character symbol). Be aware that a CPU contains several internal registers, even though only one is shown in Figure 1-3.

Primary Memory

Primary memory often is called main working memory. The reason for this is that **primary** (or **main**) **memory** is used to store programs and data while they are being "worked on," or executed, by the CPU. As Figure 1-4 shows, primary memory is integrated into chips that are usually inserted into the PC motherboard. There are two types of primary memory: **random access memory (RAM)** and **read-only memory (ROM)**.

FIGURE 1-4   Primary memory is chip memory and consists of RAM and ROM.

Random-Access Memory (RAM)   Random-access memory is memory for you, the user, along with the programs and data that you are using at any given time. When you enter a program or data into the system, it goes into RAM. This is why the amount of RAM often is quoted when you buy a computer system. You most likely have heard the terms 256 megabyte (256 MB), 128 megabyte (128 MB), and so on, when describing a PC system. This is the amount of RAM, or user memory, that the system contains.

Bits and Bytes

Now, what is this megabyte stuff? Well, all digital computers operate on binary values. A binary value is a collection of bits, where a **bit** is simply a 0 or 1. Thus, we say the binary value 1010 is a 4-bit value. Likewise, the value 10101001 is an 8-bit value. The term **byte** is normally used to describe an 8-bit binary value. Thus, 100 bytes is 100×8, or 800 bits (0's and 1's). When describing large binary values we commonly use prefixes such as kilo (K), mega (M), and giga (G). Here, the letter K stands for the value 1024 (approximately one thousand), and M for the value K^2, or 1024×1024 (approximately one million), and the letter G stands for K^3, or $1024 \times 1024 \times 1024$, which is approximately one billion. Table 1-2 summarizes these quantities. Thus, a 256 MB system has $256 \times 1024 \times 1024 = 268,435,456$ bytes of RAM. The more bytes of RAM a system has,

TABLE 1-2   A Summary of Terms Associated with Binary Values

Term	Meaning
bit	0 or I
byte	8 bits
kilobyte (KB)	1024 bytes
megabyte (MB)	1,048,576 bytes
gigabyte (GB)	1,073,741,824 bytes

the more room there is for your programs and data. As a result, larger and more complex programs require larger amounts of RAM.

By definition, RAM is ***read/write memory***. This means that information can be written into, or stored, into RAM and read from, or retrieved, from it. When writing new information into a given area of RAM, any previous information in that area is destroyed. Fortunately, you don't have to worry about this when entering programs, because the operating system makes sure that the new program information is not written over any important old information.

Once information has been written into RAM, it can be read, or retrieved, by the CPU during program execution. A read operation is nondestructive. Thus, when data is read from RAM, the RAM contents are not destroyed and remain unchanged. Think of a read operation as a "copy" operation.

One final point about RAM: It is ***volatile***. This means that any information stored in RAM is erased when power is removed from the system. As a result, any programs that you have entered in main working memory (RAM) will be lost when you turn off the system. You must always remember to save your programs on a secondary memory device, such as a disk, before turning off the system power.

Also, be aware that RAM can be placed in other parts of the system, such as a printer. This allows the CPU to send large amounts of data to be printed to the printer and stored there without clogging up the system RAM.

You have probably heard the terms **cache memory**, or simply **cache**, and **virtual memory**. These are different than RAM but serve a similar purpose. Cache is high-speed RAM that is usually contained within the same chip as the CPU. Instructions waiting to be processed are fetched from primary memory and placed in the cache so that they are ready for execution when the CPU needs them. Virtual memory is hard-disk memory that is being used by the CPU as RAM when no more actual RAM is available. The term *virtual* means "illusion." Thus, when the CPU needs more memory space, it borrows hard-disk memory to create the illusion that it is reading/writing RAM. In this case, the apparent size of the system RAM is unbounded. However, system performance can be seriously degraded, since it takes much longer to access an electromechanical disk drive than it does actual semiconductor RAM.

Read-Only Memory (ROM)   Read-only memory often is called ***system memory*** because it stores system-related programs and data. These system programs and data take care of tasks such as reset, cursor control, binary conversions, input/output, and so on. All these system programs are part of a larger operating system program that is permanently stored in ROM or on a disk. In IBM PC and compatible systems, the system software stored in ROM is called **BIOS**. The operating system, **DOS** or **Windows**™, is stored on disk and works with BIOS to perform **transparent** system operations. The term **transparent** means that the user is not aware of the underlying system operations being performed.

As its name implies, read-only memory can only be read from and not written into. Consequently, information stored in ROM is permanent and cannot be changed. Because the information is permanent, ROM must be **nonvolatile**. This means that any information stored in ROM is not lost when power is removed from the system. Due to this feature, ROM programs often are called **firmware**.

Secondary Memory

Secondary memory, sometimes called **bulk** or **mass storage**, is used to hold programs and data on a semi-permanent basis. The most common type of secondary memory used in PC systems are disks, shown in Figure 1-5.

A floppy disk, like those shown in Figure 1-5a, gets its name because the actual disk is flexible, rather than rigid, or hard. The disk is coated with a magnetic material and enclosed within a $3^1/_2$-inch hard plastic cover. When inserted into a disk drive, the disk is spun on the drive at about 300 rpm. A read/write recording head within the drive reads and writes information on the disk through the access slot, or window, in the disk jacket. Virtually all systems today include a built-in hard disk drive like the one shown in Figure 1-5b. In fact, a hard drive system is a must when working with professional-level integrated program development software such as you find with most Java compilers. In today's world, any system must have a CD drive to process a CD (Figure 1-5c). As you probably know, CDs can store much more information than magnetic disks. Most systems today come equipped with a read-only CD drive, read/write CD drive (CD R/W), or both. In addition, many systems today include a Zip® disk drive. A Zip disk is a magnetic storage device similar to a floppy disk in construction, as you can see from Figure 1-5a, but stores much more information.

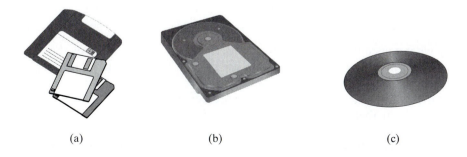

(a)   (b)   (c)

FIGURE 1-5   The common (a) $3^1/_2$-inch and Zip disks, (b) hard disk, and (c) CD.

When writing programs, you will first enter the program code into the system primary memory, or RAM. When **saving** Java programs, you must create a work file name for the program. This work file name creates an area, or file, on the disk where your program will be saved. As you enter and work with your program in RAM, you will periodically save the program on the disk so that it is permanently stored. When you save the program, the system simply copies the program from RAM and saves it on the disk under the work file name that you created. This process is illustrated in Figure 1-6a.

Saving a program on disk allows you to retrieve it later. To read a program from disk, you simply **load** the work file name assigned to the program. This tells the system to read the work file and transfer it into primary memory (RAM), as illustrated in Figure 1-6b. Once it is in working memory, the program can be compiled, executed (run), or changed (edited). Of course, if any changes are made, the program must be saved on disk again so that the changes are also made on the disk. By the way, all Java program files must have a file extension of *.java.*

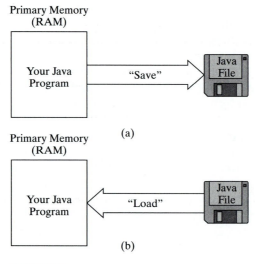

FIGURE 1-6   (a) Saving a program on disk, and (b) loading a program from disk.

Input

Input is what goes into the system. Input devices are hardware devices that provide a means of entering programs and data into the system. The major input devices for a PC system such as the one previously pictured in Figure 1-1a are the keyboard and mouse. The computer keyboard contains all the characters that you will need to write a program. In addition, there are also special control functions and special control keys that provide for system operations such as cursor movement.

The disk drive is another form of input device because it also provides a means of loading programs and data into the system. There are many other types of input devices used with computer systems, such as modems, network cards, and so on. However, the keyboard, mouse, and disk drive are the primary input devices that you will be using when learning how to write Java programs.

Output

Output is what comes out of the system. Output devices are hardware devices that provide a means of getting data out of the system. The four major output devices with which you will be concerned are the monitor, printer, disk drive, and modem. The monitor is just the screen in front of you. It allows you to view programs and data that are stored in primary memory (RAM).

A printer provides you with a hard copy of your programs and data. During a printing operation, the system actually copies information from primary or secondary memory to the printer. Thus, any information to be printed must be stored in primary or secondary memory.

A disk drive is also an output device because information stored in primary memory can be written to the disk. You could say that a disk drive is an input/output (I/O) device because it provides a means of getting information both in and out of the system.

Finally, a modem lets you communicate over the telephone or cable networks with other computers.

QUICK CHECK

1. List the three major areas of a PC's architecture.
2. A CPU contained within a single integrated circuit is called a(n) _____.
3. List at least three arithmetic and three logical operations performed by the ALU area of a CPU.
4. List three things that are found in a CPU.
5. A 128 MB system has _____ bytes of RAM.
6. Programs stored in ROM are often called_____.

1.2   Programming and Software

If computer hardware can be likened to an automobile, computer software can be likened to the driver of the automobile. Without the driver, nothing happens. In other words, the computer hardware by itself can do nothing. Therefore, computers are dumb. We have to tell them exactly what to do. The hardware system requires software that provides step-by-step instructions to tell the system what to do. A set of software instructions that tells the computer what to do is called a **computer program**. A **programmer** is a person who writes a computer program. One thing that a programmer must always keep in mind, even when programming in a high-level language, is that a computer always blindly follows orders. For example, take the instructions found on most shampoo bottles: *Wash, Rinse, Repeat.* As a human, you know that you only need to wash and rinse a second time if your hair really needs it, but a computer would wash and rinse forever. In programming terminology, this is known as an *infinite loop*. Programmers have to be careful to tell a computer when to stop in a case where instructions must be repeated.

Unfortunately computers don't speak English, so we have to use their language. That is where programming comes in. At the most basic level, computers communicate using binary codes (1's and 0's). Programmers don't generally use binary, though. Instead they use high-level languages. These high-level languages, such as Java, are translated to a series of 1's and 0's that the computer can understand. To communicate instructions to the computer, computer programs are written in different language levels. In general, computer languages can be categorized into one of three major levels: *machine language*, *assembly language*, and *high-level language*.

A **computer program** is a set of software instructions that tells the computer what to do.

Machine Language

All the hardware components in a computer system, including the CPU, operate in a language made up of binary 1's and 0's. A CPU does not understand any other language. When a computer is designed, the CPU is designed to interpret a given set of instructions, called its *instruction set*. Each instruction within the instruction set has a unique binary code that can be translated directly by the CPU. This binary code is called *machine code*, and the set of all machine-coded instructions is called the CPU's *machine language*.

A typical machine-language program is shown in Figure 1-7a. To write such a program, you must determine the operation to be performed and then translate the operation into the required binary machine code from a list of instruction set machine codes provided by the CPU manufacturer. As you might imagine, this is an extremely inefficient process. It is time-consuming, tedious, and subject to a tremendous amount of error. In addition, simple operations, such as multiplication and division, often require several lines of machine code. For these reasons, machine-language programming is rarely used. However, remember that a high-level language program must always be translated to machine language to enable the CPU to execute the program.

01001100	mov bx, offset value	x=2;
11101001	mov ax, [bx]	if(x<=y)
10101010	add ax, 5	x=x+1;
10001110	add bx, 2	else
00001111	add ax, [bx]	x=x-1;
(a)	(b)	(c)

FIGURE 1–7   (a) Machine language, (b) assembly language, and (c) high-level language.

Assembly Language

Assembly language is a step up from machine language. Rather than using 1's and 0's, assembly language employs alphabetic abbreviations called **mnemonics** that are easily remembered by you, the programmer. For instance, the mnemonic for addition is ADD, the mnemonic for move is MOV, and so forth. A typical assembly-language program is listed in Figure 1-7b.

The assembly-language mnemonics provide us with an easier means of writing and interpreting programs. Although assembly-language programs are more easily understood by us humans, they cannot be directly understood by the CPU. As a result, assembly-language programs must also be translated into machine code. This is the job of another program, called an **assembler**. The assembler program translates assembly-language programs into binary machine code that can be executed by the CPU.

Although programming in assembly language is easier than machine-language programming, it is not the most efficient means of programming. Assembly-language programming is also tedious and prone to error, because there is usually a one-to-one relationship between the mnemonics and corresponding machine code. The solution to these inherent problems of assembly-language programming is found in high-level languages.

This does not mean that assembly language is not useful. Because of its one-to-one relationship with machine language, assembly-language programs are very efficient relative to execution speed and memory utilization. In fact, many high-level-language programs include assembly-language routines, especially for those tasks requiring high-speed software performance as in hardware driver programs.

Operating Systems

An **operating system** is the "glue" that binds the hardware to the application software. Actually, an operating system is a collection of software programs dedicated to managing the resources of the system. These resources include memory management, file management, I/O management, monitoring system activity, system security, and system performance, just to mention a few.

In the early days, operating systems, such as MS-DOS™ and UNIX™, were text-based. Today, however, most operating systems are GUI-based. The acronym *GUI* stands for "graphical user interface," implying a window-based user interface. In today's world, new operating systems are developed using high-level languages, even Java.

Until not too long ago, assembly language was used to develop operating systems, due to its execution efficiency and its ability to access system components directly. Then, in the 1970s, Bell Telephone Laboratories developed a high-level language called C to write the UNIX operating system. The C language is sometimes referred to as a "mid-level" language since it contains many of the high-level commands of a high-level language, but also many of the "bit-level" commands of an assembly language.

High-Level Language

High-level languages overcome the programming tediousness inherent in assembly languages. Also, high-level languages are not CPU-dependent. Therefore, a high-level language program written for a PC that uses an Intel CPU will look the same as that written for a Mac that uses a Motorola CPU. However, the downside to high-level languages is that the programs they produce are not as fast and memory efficient as their assembly language counterparts.

A high-level language consists of instructions, or statements, that are similar to English and common mathematical notation. A typical series of high-level statements is shown in Figure 1-7c. High-level-language statements are very powerful. A typical high-level-language statement is equivalent to many machine-code instructions.

High-level programming languages are constructed so that ambiguities are not possible. This means that each program instruction has only one possible meaning. If a sentence can have more than one meaning, we say that it is ambiguous. Look at the following sentence: In the dark night crawlers roam. Does this sentence mean that *night crawlers roam in the dark* (whether the dark is a cellar, a closet, or the outdoors), or does it mean that *crawlers roam in the dark night* (which is almost definitely outdoors)? You will not find such ambiguity in high-level programming language instructions because they are constructed so that different interpretations are not possible.

High-level languages were developed in the early 1950s to take some of the work out of programming. When programming in a high-level language, you do not have to concern yourself with the specific instruction set of the CPU. Rather, you can concentrate on solving the problem at hand. Once you learn a given high-level language, you can program any computer for which a translator exists to translate your program into the CPU's machine language.

Why Java?

As you are probably aware, there are several popular high-level languages, including COBOL, Pascal, FORTRAN, BASIC, LISP, Ada, and C/C++. Each has been developed with a particular application in mind. For instance, COBOL, which stands for COmmon Business Oriented Language, was developed for business programming. FORTRAN, which means FORmula TRANslator, was developed for scientific programming. LISP was developed for artificial-intelligence programming, and Pascal was developed primarily for educators who wanted to teach the principles of software design. The C language is a structured/procedural language that allows complex problems to be solved using a modular, top/down approach. The C++ language contains the C language for structured/procedural programming, but in addition extends the C language to provide for **object-oriented programming (OOP)**. Object-oriented programming allows complex problems to be solved using a more natural approach, similar to the way in which we humans tend to look at the real world in terms of attributes and behavior. It allows complex programs to be developed using simpler constructs called **objects** that can communicate by exchanging messages. More about this later. Thus, C++ is a hybrid language, allowing for both structured and object-oriented programming.

The Java language was modeled after the C++ language. In fact, much of the Java language syntax is identical to C++. However, Java is strictly an object-oriented language. Java is taking the software development industry by storm as both a commercial application language and an Internet language. The main reason for this is that Java is totally portable across any system platform due to its compiler/interpreter method of translation, to be discussed shortly. This is why you can link to a given Internet site and run the same Java program through your browser whether you are using a PC or a Mac computer platform. Your Internet browser contains a Java interpreter that translates generic bytecodes into the machine language of that computer.

 Portability is that feature of a language that allows programs written for one type of computer to be used on another type of computer with few or no changes to the program source code. Java is totally portable, meaning that programs written and compiled on one computer can run on any other computer that has a Java interpreter. This is because the bytecodes generated by a Java compiler are totally generic and not specific to any CPU platform. These generic bytecodes are then translated and executed by a Java interpreter that is specific to the platform on which it is running.

Java Is Strictly Object-Oriented   Unlike most of its predecessors, Java was developed to be completely object-oriented. The idea behind OOP deals with ever increasing complexity by viewing the programming world much like we humans see the real world in terms of attributes and behavior. We see the real world as a collection of objects, each with its own attributes and behavior. For example, we can view an automobile as an object that has attributes of an engine, a transmission, tires, steering wheel, and so on, right down to the nuts and bolts that hold the thing together. We also see behavior in an automobile. An automobile can accelerate, decelerate, turn, start, stop, and so forth. As another example, consider a fish. A fish has attributes of eyes, fins, scales, etc. A fish also has behavior of swimming, eating, and reproducing. Get the idea? Real-world objects all have their own attributes and behavior. Object-oriented programming was developed to view programming in much the same way we view the real world, by allowing a programmer to create data objects that have their own attributes and behavior. These objects can be manipulated through their behaviors and made to work together to solve a problem. In addition, once an object is created for one application, it can easily be imported into another application. This is called *code reuse*. Why reinvent the wheel?

Java Is Relatively Simple   Compared to other programming languages, like C++, Java is considered to be relatively simple. Although Java was modeled after C++, it has been greatly simplified. As a programmer, you do not have to concern yourself with complicated things like pointers and garbage collection as you do in C++. Most of this complicated stuff is hidden from you and done for you behind the scenes in Java. In addition, Java has a rich set of classes you can use to build GUIs. The Java language supports graphics, animation, audio/video streaming, multithreading, database connectivity, and much more. Once you get the hang of it, you will find that building professional programs that employ these state-of-the-art features is a walk in the park as compared to building such programs with other languages, like C++.

Java Is Portable   We have already mentioned the idea of portability. Once a Java program is written, it only needs to be compiled once to create portable bytecodes that can be translated to any machine platform that has a Java interpreter. More about this later.

Java Is Secure   Hidden from the programmer, but built into every Java program, are certain security features. You do not have to worry about damaging your computer by running a Java program because of its built-in security. Have you ever heard of an applet destroying anyone's system files? Of course not! Java applets must be secure or they could not be used across the Internet.

Java Is a Network Language   The original reason that Java was developed was to support networks of embedded systems. An *embedded system* is one that is dedicated and "embedded" into a particular application, such as a cell phone, DVD player, PDA, and so on. When Java was expanded to support the Internet, this built-in support of networking made it easy to write programs that send and receive data to and from each other. And because of its portability, Java programs on different platforms can easily communicate with each other over a network.

Java Supports Multithreading   Multithreading, sometimes called multitasking, allows a program to perform several tasks (threads) simultaneously. Most of today's multimedia networked systems are multithreaded. For example, multithreading allows you to listen to a Web radio broadcast, while surfing the Web, while you are downloading and saving an album. Multithreading can be accomplished within a single Java program, whereas other languages might require several individual programs to support the individual tasks. These programs must communicate with a particular operating system to coordinate the multithreading activity. All this can be done within a single Java program.

Java Is Growing   Java is an ever-growing language. We therefore say that Java is a "dynamic language." New class libraries, called ***application program interfaces (APIs)***, are being added continually to support new applications. We should envision future APIs to support banking, insurance, financing, and tax accounting, just to mention a few applications. Once these libraries are developed they can be imported into any Java application. As a result, the potential applications for Java are unlimited!

Java Is Cheap   Yeah! In fact, Java is free. This is great for students. The Java programming language, development environment, and a host of class libraries are available free by download from Sun Microsystems, Inc. at *www.java.sun.com*. The Java language and associated class libraries are available by downloading and installing Sun's SDK (Software Development Kit). However, the SDK, by itself, is a command line compiler, meaning that compiling and execution must be done by typing in commands through a console window. A complete GUI-based IDE (Integrated Development Environment) is available for use with the SDK by downloading and installing the *Sun ONE Studio Community Edition*, formally called *Forte Community Edition*. It's all free, along with excellent documentation! However, *Sun ONE Studio* requires at least 128 MB of RAM to execute, so make sure your system can handle it. (The *Sun ONE Studio* IDE has been placed on the text CD for your convenience.) Another popular IDE for Java is *JBuilder*™, manufactured by the Borland Software Corporation. A free version of *JBuilder*, called *JBuilder Personal Edition*, is available for download at *www.borland.com*. A short tutorial on both *Sun*

ONE Studio and *JBuilder* is provided in Appendix A to help you get started with either of these IDEs.

Java Is for Business   As you will find out in this book, the Java language is ideal for business applications programming. It has a rich set of built-in classes that support easy development of GUIs, networking, multithreading, database connectivity, and e-commerce over the Internet. No other language can support business with all these built-in capabilities as Java can. One common feature of most business programs is that they must connect to and communicate with a database. Through its robust JDBC (Java Database Connectivity) API, Java supports connectivity to all popular databases, including Oracle, SQL, and Access. Database connectivity using the JDBC API is covered in Appendix D.

A Comparative Analysis of C, C++, C#, VB, J#, and Java

Before comparing these languages, let's take a minute to provide a brief description of each language.

The C Language   First, there was the BCPL language, then the B language, then C, and then C++. All were developed at Bell Telephone Laboratories (now a part of Lucent Technologies) and, like many high-level structured languages, have their roots in ALGOL. The B language was developed by Ken Thompson at Bell Labs in an effort to develop an operating system using a high-level language. Prior to B, operating systems were developed using the assembly language of the particular CPU on which the operating system was to run. Using the B language as a basis, Dennis Ritchie developed the C language at Bell Labs. The main purpose for the C language was to develop an operating system for the Digital Equipment Corporation (now part of Compaq/Hewlett-Packard) PDP-11 minicomputer. The resulting operating system became known as *UNIX*. In fact, most versions of UNIX today are written almost entirely in C. The C language was originally defined in the classic text *The C Programming Language*, written by Brian Kernighan and Dennis Ritchie (1977). In fact, the C language became such a popular commercial language that an ANSI standard for C was released in 1989.

The C++ Language   The C++, pronounced "C plus plus," language was developed at Bell Telephone Laboratories, now part of Lucent Technologies. The C++ language is an extension of the C language. Bjarne Stroustrup at Bell Labs enhanced the C language in the early 1980s by adding OOP capability. The stated goal of Dr. Stroustrup was to maintain the efficiency of C while providing the power of OOP to the language. The resulting language became known as C++. You will realize where the ++ came from when you learn about the Java *increment* operator later in this book. The C++ language has also become such a popular commercial language that an ANSI/ISO standard for C++ was released a few years ago. Because C++ is an enhancement of C, any C program is also a C++ program; however, the opposite is not true.

The C# Language   C#, pronounced "C sharp," was developed by Microsoft as an alternative to C/C++ and as competition for Java. Like C and C++, C# provides the power to access all the functionality of the underlying platform, but has been enhanced to allow for rapid development, especially Web development. Microsoft describes C# as a language that brings rapid Web development to the C and C++ programmer while maintaining the power and flexibility that those developers call for. C# is a modern, object-oriented language that enables programmers to quickly build a wide range of applications for Microsoft's .NET platform. The .NET platform provides tools and services that fully exploit both computing and communications for developing software within the Microsoft operating system environment.

The Visual Basic.NET (VB.NET) Language   Visual Basic.NET, commonly called "VB.NET," is a complete programming environment developed by Microsoft around the BASIC language. BASIC is an acronym that stands for Beginners All-purpose Symbolic Instruction Code. VB.NET contains a complete integrated development environment which contains "drag and drop" programming tools for development GUI programs. In addition, VB.NET contains the BASIC programming language.

The Java Language   The Java language was developed by Sun Microsystems, Inc. The early versions of Java were intended to be a programming language to program microprocessors for embedded applications such as VCRs and TVs, as explained earlier. James Gosling and his team at Sun realized that such applications were controlled by a variety of incompatible microprocessors. As a result, the language that they were developing needed to work on many different processors. This is where they developed the idea of using generic bytecodes that could be translated into any specific machine language using an interpreter. When the World Wide Web became popular around 1994, Gosling and his team thought that, due to its portability, Java would be an ideal language for Internet browsers. In 1995, Sun developed the HotJava™ Web browser. Then, also in 1995, Netscape announced that their Web browser would be Java-compliant. Since then, almost all the Web browser companies have followed Netscape's lead and made their browsers Java-compliant. As a result, Java programs have become a standard across the ever-growing and popular Web.

    As you might suspect, the name "Java" has its roots in coffee. Java coffee gets its name from a large island in Indonesia where the coffee is grown. At first, the language was called "Oak," supposedly named after an oak tree outside one of the office windows at Sun. As the story goes, the developers were agonizing over a better name for the language when they decided to go out for coffee. The rest is history. A quick comparison of these popular programming languages is provided in Table 1-3. As you can see, Java is very well suited to today's business programming needs.

The Art and Science of Programming

Once you decide that you want to learn how to program, the first step is to learn a programming language. With this book, you are well on your way to beginning the first step. In general, programming works like this: you type in the computer program instructions using a programming language, compile the program into machine readable form (called an executable), then you run the executable program. Additionally, most

TABLE 1-3   A Quick Language Comparison

Feature	C	C++	C#	VB.NET	Java
Object-Oriented	No	Yes	Yes	Yes	Yes
Easy GUIs	No	No	Yes	Yes	Yes
Portable	No	No	No	No	Yes
Internet Programming	No	No	Yes	No	Yes
Easy Multitasking	No	No	Yes	No	Yes
Easy Database Connectivity	No	No	Yes	Yes	Yes
Built-In Security	No	No	Yes	No	Yes
Simplicity	No	No	Yes	Yes	Yes
High Speed Execution	Yes	Yes	No	No	No
Low Level Coding	Yes	Yes	Yes	No	No
Widely Accepted	Yes	Yes	No	Yes	Yes

compilers have a built-in debugger that allows you to step through the code (i.e., run each instruction one at a time) to make sure everything is running correctly.

The way a program is designed and run can be loosely compared to the way a train travels. The train has a station where it begins, and it has to know where it is going. To get to where it's going, the track layout must be planned. Then the workers must lay out the track, taking care to make the track flow smoothly so that the train will not crash. The final step is to send a test train down the track to make sure the track is safe for general traffic. If the test train encounters any problems, they must be fixed.

The building of the track takes time. It must be planned out well, and any unforeseen problems must be worked around during construction. This is all very important because once the track has been built, every train that travels down the track will follow it blindly—they are not able to swerve around obstacles. They are limited to traveling the path defined by the train track.

Similarly, a programmer must decide what he or she wants the program to accomplish, plan out how the program will accomplish it, then actually sit down and *code* the program, working around any unforeseen problems encountered during the coding process.

Once a program is planned, it is built line by line by following the plan. The program begins at the first statement and flows through each statement, executing the instructions found on each line as it comes to them.

Shortly into the coding process, the programmer must begin ***debugging***. This is the process of searching for and fixing any errors in the program. There are two categories of errors in programming: *syntax* and *logical*. A ***syntax error*** is generally easy to find and correct. It is an error in following the rules of the programming language. A program with a syntax error will not compile. Most compilers will tell you exactly what and where the error is. For example, if you forget to put a semicolon at the end of a line of code in Java, the compiler will tell you and will point you to the line that is missing the semicolon. It will not, however, put the semicolon at the end of the line for you.

A ***logical error*** is harder to find. A program with a logical error will compile and run, but it will not act as expected. To correct a logical error, the programmer generally has to step through the program (run the code one line at a time in a debugger) to find the error, then rework the program design to fix the error. Once the program is working well (i.e., it compiles, and it runs correctly every time), it is finished except for future enhancements and maintenance. Like the finished train track, it is ready to be used. Just like any train can go down the track and end up where it wants to go, any user can run the program and accomplish the task that he or she wants to accomplish.

QUICK CHECK

  1. What is the major difference between Java and C++?
  2. What are the three levels of language used by computers?
  3. What is the purpose of an operating system?
  4. Briefly explain why Java has become such a popular language.
  5. True or false: Java was originally developed for networked embedded systems.
  6. Java was originally called _____.
  7. What company developed Java?

1.3   Java Programs

Applications versus Applets

Using Java, you can write many different kinds of programs, including *applications*, *applets*, *servlets*, *EJBs*, and *JavaBeans*™. In this book, we will focus on Java applications and applets. Java applications are designed to be run on your computer just like any other computer program written in any other language. Java applets are designed only to be run over the Internet using a Web browser. When you link to a Web site with your browser, the Web site transfers special Java code, called *bytecode*, over the Internet to your browser. Your browser then translates and executes the bytecode to produce the dynamic things, such as animation and moving messages, that you view on your browser. By the way, the word *applet* has nothing to do with apples. It simply denotes a "little application," just as the term *piglet* denotes a little pig. In this text, we will deal primarily with Java applications. Once you know how to program Java applications, it is easy to learn how to do Java applets. A complete chapter on applets is provided later in this book.

A Java **application** is designed to be run on a computer just like any other computer program written in any other language. A Java **applet** is a program designed only to be run over the Internet using a Web browser.

Compiling and Interpreting Java Programs

You must be aware that even when programming in a high-level language, the system must still translate your instructions into machine code that can be understood by the CPU. There are two types of system programs that can be employed for this purpose: a *compiler* and an *interpreter*. A compiler is a program that accepts a high-level-language

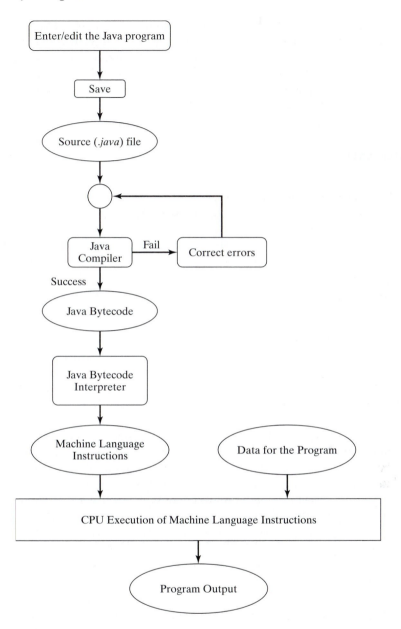

FIGURE 1-8   The Java compiler and bytecode interpreter translate source code into machine code that can be executed by the CPU.

program and translates the entire program into machine code all at one time, before it is executed by the CPU. On the other hand, an interpreter translates and executes one high-level instruction at a time. Once a given instruction has been executed, the interpreter then translates and executes the next instruction, and so on, until the entire program has been executed. Java employs both a compiler and an interpreter as shown in Figure 1-8. Here's how it works. Initially, you will type your program into a computer using an *editor* and save it in a file that must have a *.java* extension. The program that you enter is referred to as a *source code* program. After saving your program, you must invoke the Java compiler to translate your Java source code into Java *bytecode*.

 A **source program** is the one that you write in the Java language and, when saved on disk, must always have a file extension of *.java*.

 The **syntax** of a language is the set of grammatical rules required to write code for the language. Any violation of a syntax rule will always result in a compiler error.

As the program is being translated, the Java compiler checks for *syntax* errors. After the program is compiled, the compiler displays a list of error messages and warnings. You must correct all the syntax errors and recompile until you get a successful compilation. You may, however, encounter other *logic* errors later on when you actually run the program. The bytecode program generated by the compiler is a low-level program, similar to machine language. However, the Java bytecode is not associated with any specific CPU. In other words, Java bytecode is a generic code that can be executed by any computer that has a Java interpreter. This is what allows Java to be totally portable across many different operating system platforms. The Java interpreter translates the Java bytecode into machine language instructions specific to the CPU of a given computer. Since the translation is being performed by an interpreter, a given instruction is translated and executed before the next instruction is translated and executed, and so on.

 Java **bytecode** is generated by the Java compiler. The resulting bytecode is a low-level program similar to machine language, but generic and not specific to any particular CPU. Any given computer will have its own Java interpreter as part of a **Java Virtual Machine**, or **JVM**, which translates the generic bytecode into machine language for that CPU. This allows Java to be portable across many different computer platforms. For example, an Internet browser that is "Java-compliant" includes the Java bytecode interpreter. You can find more information on the JVM at *www.java.sun.com*.

Your First Program—Hello World!

It is now time to get your hands dirty by entering, compiling, and executing your first Java program. The program you will execute is the classic "Hello World!" program that all programming students have executed at some time in their early programming learning years. So, find yourself a computer with a Java compiler and read on. Here is the "Hello World!" program that you will execute:

```
1    /*
2    HelloWorld.java
3    *
4    Created on April 23, 2002, 7:47 AM
5    *
6    @author Andrew C. Staugaard, Jr.
```

```
7     @version 1.0
8     */
9
10
11    import staugIO.StaugIO;            //FOR INPUT/OUTPUT METHODS
12
13    public class HelloWorld
14    {//BEGIN CLASS
15
16        public static void main (String args[])
17        {//BEGIN main()
18            StaugIO io = new StaugIO();       //DEFINE INPUT/OUTPUT OBJECT
19
20            io.writeInfo("Hello World!");     //USE OBJECT TO CALL writeInfo()
21
22            //EXIT PROGRAM
23            System.exit(0);
24        }//END main()
25    }//END HelloWorld
```

It is now time to code, compile, and run the "Hello World!" program. But before you do, make sure you have installed the *staugIO* package on your system per the *staugIOReadMe.doc* file in the *TextSourceCode* directory of the text CD. Also, go through the tutorial on *Sun ONE Studio* or *JBuilder* in Appendix A if you are using one of these Integrated Development Environments (IDE's). Then, using your IDE, enter and save the foregoing program as *HelloWorld.java*. Do not enter the line numbers, because they are only there for discussion purposes and will create syntax errors if compiled as part of the program. Once saved, compile and run your program. If the program executes properly, you should see an information box containing the message "Hello World!" like that shown in Figure 1-9. Congratulations! You have just written and executed your first Java program. Now, let's learn "a bit" more about the program code.

First, take an overall look at the program. You see that we are using different colors to denote different things. This is called ***syntax highlighting*** and is a feature of most Java IDEs. Syntax highlighting allows you to easily identify key elements of the program. We have used gray to highlight comments within the program, dark blue to highlight Java keywords (special words recognized by Java), and light blue to highlight strings and numerical values within the program. All other code is in black.

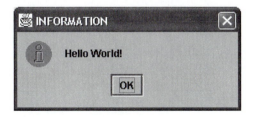

FIGURE 1-9   A screen print of the dialog box generated by the *HelloWorld.java* program.

SYNTAX HIGHLIGHTING USED IN THIS BOOK

```
//COMMENTS IN DARK GRAY
Keywords in dark blue
Strings and numerical values in light blue
All other code in black
```

The program code lines are numbered to facilitate our discussion. They are *not* normally part of a program and will *not* compile if present. Now for the details: Lines 1 through 8 provide an introductory **block comment** that shows the programmer, class, date, and purpose of the program. You should always include a comment at the top of your program to identify the programmer and explain the program's purpose. A block comment is two or more lines that provide the program reader with information. The comment block begins with a forward slash followed by a star (/*). The Java compiler will ignore any lines that appear after these symbols until it translates a star followed by a forward slash (*/) which ends the comment block. Next, in the remaining lines, you see the use of a **line comment**. Line comments are used for a single comment line and inserted into a program using double forward slashes (//). The double forward slashes tell the compiler to ignore the rest of that particular line. The double forward slashes can appear anyplace on a given line, but anything after // on a given line is ignored by the compiler. We will be making extensive use of comments within the programs in this book to self-document the Java code. We suggest that you do the same in your programs. Comments within your programs make them much easier to read and maintain.

A **block comment** begins with the symbols /* and is terminated with the symbols */. A **line comment** begins with the symbols // and is terminated at the end of the given line.

DEBUGGING TIP

Line comments in Java are inserted using double forward slashes, //. When the Java compiler encounters double forward slashes, it ignores the remainder of the line in which the slashes appear. Here's an example:

```
//THIS LINE IS A COMMENT AND IGNORED BY THE JAVA COMPILER
```

Block comments are used to comment a large area of the program. You can use a /* to begin the commented area and a */ to end the commented area like this:

```
/*****************************************************************

THIS IS ANOTHER WAY TO COMMENT IN JAVA, PARTICULARLY WHEN LARGE AREAS MUST
BE COMMENTED.

*****************************************************************/
```

Notice how we have used asterisks to "frame" the comment and make it stand out to anyone reading the program.

Program comments are an important part of the program documentation and should be used liberally. At a minimum, the program should include the following comments:

- The beginning of the program should be commented with the programmer's name, the date the program was written, the date the program was last revised, and the name of the person doing the revision. In other words, a brief ongoing maintenance log should be commented at the beginning of the program.
- The comments at the beginning of the program should explain the purpose of the program, which includes the problem definition and program algorithms. This provides an overall perspective by which anyone, including you, the programmer, can begin debugging or maintaining the program.
- Constants and variables should be commented as to their purpose.
- Major sections of the program should be commented to explain the overall purpose of the respective section.
- Individual program lines should be commented when the purpose of the code is not obvious relative to the application.
- All major procedures (methods in Java) should be commented just like the *main()* program method.
- The end of each program block (right brace) should be commented to indicate what the brace is ending.
- Commenting must be done as you write your code, not inserted later on when the code is complete. It is very easy to get lost in code. Commenting as you go helps you from getting lost.

In general, you should have enough comments so that someone unfamiliar with Java could read and understand the program the first time through. Remember, someone (including you) might have to debug or maintain the program in the future. A good commenting scheme makes these tasks a much more efficient and pleasant process.

The Import Section

The *import section* of a Java program does just what it says: it *imports* additional code into your Java program. Specifically, it imports any additional classes that are need for the proper execution of your program. All Java programs are collections of classes. Your program is a class. In addition, there are also *standard* classes provided by the Java language and classes developed by you or other programmers that you can import in order to make your programming task simpler. The `import` statement in line 11 tells the Java compiler to "import" the *StaugIO* class, which is contained in a ***package*** called *staugIO*, into your program. Notice that the keyword `import` is followed by the package name, *staugIO*, which is followed by a dot, **.**, which is followed by the class name, *StaugIO*. A semicolon terminates the statement. This is the required syntax for the `import` statement. Notice that the package name begins with a lowercase letter, while the class name begins with an uppercase letter. This is standard practice in Java. The Java language is ***case sensitive***. This means that Java "sees" *staugIO*, *StaugIO*, and *staugio* as three different names.

The *StaugIO* class contains the method necessary to display the information box with the message "Hello World!" as previously shown in Figure 1-9. The *StaugIO* class has been developed especially for this book to provide you an easy means of doing input/output (I/O) while learning the Java language. Later on we will "unwrap" this class and allow you to see how it works. Input and output can be a tricky proposition in Java. So, we have written this class to make it simple until you are ready to learn more advanced material.

The Java language itself contains many standard classes that are grouped into **packages**. A package is a set of related classes "packaged" together in a separate system directory. The set of all packages forms the Java class library, called the *Java Applications Program Interface*, or *Java API*. To use any of the API classes, you must make them available to your program using the `import` statement. For instance, later on you will be using the *Graphics* class in the *AWT* (*Abstract Windowing Toolkit*) package. The *Graphics* class will let you add some powerful graphics to your program. However, to use the *Graphics* class, it must be made available to your program using the `import` statement like this:

`import java.awt.Graphics;`

This statement tells Java to import the *Graphics* class of the *awt* (*abstract windowing toolkit*) package and compile it as part of your program. What do you suppose this statement does?

`import javax.swing.*;`

You're right if you thought to import all classes of the Java *swing* package. Here, the * is a wildcard character that means "all" classes.

 A **package** is a set of related classes "packaged" together in a separate system directory.

What makes Java a great language is the large number of prewritten classes available in the Java API. Why develop your own class if there is already one included in the API? Using the Java API means that programmers can reuse the code already developed, rather than "reinventing the wheel" to develop their own code. This is referred to as *code reuse* and facilitates developing new code from code that is already written. By the way, all standard packages in Java begin with the word *java* or *javax*, as you might have guessed from the above code.

The Class Section

The class is where access to all the executable Java code resides. A Java program is simply a collection of classes which interact with each other via class methods.

In our *HelloWorld.java* program, there are only a single class and a single method. As you begin to build more complex programs, your programs will contain many classes and many different methods. For now, we will keep things simple.

The program class name should be something that is related to the application for which the program was written. For example, the following code might be used to declare a class for a payroll program:

```
public class Payroll
```

The keyword `public` means that this class is accessible to the entire program and the keyword `class` means that *Payroll* is being declared as a class. Later on you will see the keywords `private` and `protected` which restrict the accessibility of classes and their contents. The name of the class will be determined by the specific application for which the class is developed, in this case a payroll application. However, once a `public` class name is determined, *the program must be saved using this class name as the file name with a .java extension.* Line 13 of our program declares our *HelloWorld* class. In line 14 you see that a left brace, {, must follow the first line of the class declaration, prior to any other statements. This brace defines the beginning of the class block. In line 25, you see a right brace, }. This brace is used to indicate the end of the class block. You must always use a set of braces, { }, to "frame" a block of code in Java.

A Java program file must have the same name as the program `public` class name plus a *.java* extension. Thus, if your program class name is *MyProgram*, the program must be saved with a file name of *MyProgram.java*. Class names always begin with a capital letter in Java. Multiple words within a class name are run together, with each subsequent word beginning with a capital letter.

Method *main()*

Java applications always begin execution with a method called *main()*. A **method** in Java is a procedure designed to perform a specific task. One way you can distinguish a Java application from a Java applet is that applets do not use *main()*. Only Java applications use *main()*.

The *main()* method must be declared inside the class and the first line of this method must be

```
public static void main(String args[])
```

The *main()* method identifier is preceded by the keywords `public, static,` and `void`. The reason for this will become apparent later on, so don't worry about it now. Here, the "main" task is your program, which displays the *Hello World!* message within an information box.

A **method** in Java is a procedure designed to perform a specific task. In other programming languages, methods might be referred to as *subprograms, functions,* or *subroutines.* By convention, method names always begin with a lowercase letter in Java. Multiple words within a method name are run together, with each subsequent word beginning with a capital letter. A set of parentheses after the name is used to denote a method. So *myMethod()* would be an acceptable method name in Java.

Some, but not all, methods require *arguments*. Method *main()* requires the argument *String args[]*. Notice that the argument is placed within the method parentheses. An **argument** is a value that is needed by a method in order to perform its designated task. For example, there is a standard method in Java called *sqrt()* which calculates the square root of a number. To do this, *sqrt()* needs a number, right? So, if we supply it with a number, say 4, we get *sqrt(4)* which calculates the square root of 4 to give us 2. Here we say that the number 4 is the method argument. The argument required by *main()* is *String args[]*. This is a standard argument that allows for command line execution of the program. We will always use parentheses to denote a method. In addition, a method always begins with a lowercase letter. So in a Java program, *Foo* would be used to denote a class while *foo()* would be used to denote a method.

An **argument** is a value that is passed to a Java method in order to perform its designated task.

Looking at the *HelloWorld.java* program, you see a set of beginning/ending braces to *frame* the *main()* method block. Notice that the ending braces are commented at the bottom of the program to indicate which brace ends method *main()* and which brace ends the *HelloWorld* class. It is always good practice to comment closing braces.

The body of *main()* is the executable part of the application. All the program instructions, or statements, go here except for the `import` statement. Each statement must be terminated with a semicolon. In line 18 you see an object called *io* being defined for the *StaugIO* class. This object is then used to "call" the *writeInfo()* method in line 20. In line 20 we have an executable statement which causes the message "Hello World!" to be displayed on the monitor. The *HelloWorld!* message is generated within an information box as previously shown in Figure 1-9. The information box is generated by method *writeInfo()*, which is part of the *StaugIO* class. Finally, the statement `System.exit(0);` is required to properly close the program when the *StaugIO* class methods are being used to generate GUI dialog boxes, as in this program.

QUICK CHECK

1. List the steps that must be performed to translate a Java source code program to an executable program.
2. What are bytecodes?
3. What makes Java an extremely portable language?
4. What is the difference between a Java application and a Java applet?
5. What is the difference between a compiler and an interpreter?
6. Your Java program code is referred to in general as _____code.
7. Any Java program consists of two sections, called the_____and _____ sections.
8. Write an `import` statement to make all classes in a package called *myPackage* available to a program.
9. A procedure that performs some specific task in Java is called a _____.

10. Suppose a Java application declares a `public` class called *Inventory* and this is the class in which *main()* resides. What must the source file be named for this program?

11. Comments are inserted into a Java program using
    a. left and right braces like this `{COMMENT}`.
    b. a semicolon like this `;COMMENT`.
    c. a star like this `*COMMENT`.
    d. double forward slashes like this `//COMMENT`.
    e. double backward slashes like this `\\COMMENT`.
    f. none of the above.

12. State at least four places where your program should include comments.

CHAPTER SUMMARY

Any computer system can be divided into two major components: hardware and software. Hardware consists of the physical devices that make up the machine, and software consists of the instructions that tell the hardware what to do.

There are five functional parts that make up the system hardware: the CPU, primary memory, secondary memory, input, and output. The CPU directs and coordinates the activity of the entire system as instructed by the software. Primary memory consists of user memory (RAM) and system memory (ROM). Secondary memory is usually magnetic or optical and is used to store programs and data on a semi-permanent basis. Input is what goes into the system via hardware input devices, such as a keyboard. Output is what comes out of the system via hardware output devices, such as a display monitor or printer.

There are three major levels of software: machine language, assembly language, and high-level language. Machine language is the lowest level, because it consists of binary 1's and 0's that can only be easily understood by the CPU. Assembly language consists of alphabetic instruction abbreviations that are easily understood by the programmer but must be translated into machine code for the CPU by a system program called an assembler. High-level languages consist of English-like statements that simplify the task of programming. However, to be understood by the CPU, high-level-language programs must still be translated to machine code using a compiler/interpreter. A bytecode program is generated by the Java compiler. This is a low-level program, similar to machine language. However, the Java bytecode is not associated with any specific CPU. In other words, Java bytecode is a generic code that can be executed by any computer that has a Java interpreter. This is what allows Java to be totally portable across many different operating system platforms. The Java interpreter translates the Java bytecode into machine-language instructions specific to the CPU of a given computer. Since the translation is being performed by an interpreter, a given instruction is translated and executed before the next instruction is translated and executed, and so on.

Java was developed at Sun Microsystems, Inc. by James Gosling and his team to be portable over a variety of incompatible microprocessors. When the World Wide Web became popular around 1994, Gosling and his team thought that, due to its portability, Java would be an ideal language for Internet browsers. In 1995, Sun developed the HotJava Web browser. Then, also in 1995, Netscape announced that their Web browser would be Java-compliant. Since then, almost all the Web browser companies have followed Netscape's lead and made their browsers Java-compliant. As a result, Java programs have become a standard across the ever-growing and popular Web.

Using Java, you can write many different kinds of programs, including applications and applets. Java applications are designed to be run on your computer just like any other computer program written in any other language. Java applets are designed only to be run over the Internet using a Web browser.

A Java application always contains at least one class. The class contains method *main()* where objects are created for other classes and used to call the other class methods. The program file name *must* always be the same as the application class name plus a file extension of *.java*.

Program comments are an important part of the program documentation and should be used liberally. In Java, a block comment begins with the symbols /* and is terminated with the symbols */. A line comment begins with the symbols // and is terminated at the end of the given line.

QUESTIONS AND PROBLEMS

Questions

1. Name the three operational regions of a CPU and explain their function.
2. Explain the term volatile as it relates to computer memory.
3. Another name for software located in read-only memory (ROM) is _____.
4. A floppy disk is a form of _____ memory.
5. Name the three levels of software and describe the general characteristics of each.
6. List at least four functions of an operating system.
7. Explain the operational difference between a compiler and an interpreter.
8. A Java compiler translates a source program into a(n) _____ program.
9. True or false: Java employs both a compiler and an interpreter to produce an executable program.
10. Explain how Java is portable across all computer platforms.
11. What is the difference between a Java application and a Java applet?
12. The Java language was developed by _____ and his team at _____.
13. Object-oriented programming allows complex programs to be developed using simpler programming constructs called _____.
14. The Java language evolved from the _____ language.
15. What is Java bytecode?
16. List at least three places where comments should occur in your Java program.

Problems

```
1    /*
2    HelloWorld.java
3    *
4    Created on April 23, 2002, 7:47 AM
5    *
6    @author Andrew C. Staugaard, Jr.
7    @version 1.0
8    */
9
10
11   import staugIO.StaugIO;    //FOR INPUT/OUTPUT METHODS
12
13   public class HelloWorld
```

```
14   {//BEGIN CLASS
15
16     public static void main (String args[])
17     {//BEGIN main()
18       StaugIO io = new StaugIO();       //DEFINE INPUT/OUTPUT OBJECT
19
20       io.writeInfo("Hello World!");     //USE OBJECT TO CALL writeInfo()
21
22       //EXIT PROGRAM
23       System.exit(0);
24     }//END main()
25   }//END HelloWorld
```

1. What do the /* and */ symbols accomplish in lines 1 and 8 of the program?
2. What is the purpose of the forward double slash, //, symbols in the program?
3. What is the purpose of the statement in line 18 of the program?
4. What is the purpose of the statement in line 20 of the program?
5. Enter the program using your Java IDE or load it if it was previously saved. Place the characters \n (a backward slash followed by n) between the word Hello and the word World in line 20. Compile and execute the program and observe the display. What did the \n cause the program to do?
6. Use your Java IDE to find and correct the syntax errors in the following program:

```
import staugIO.StaugIO;               //FOR INPUT/OUTPUT
public class Problem1_6
{
 public void main(String args[]
 {
   //DEFINE CONSTANT
   final double INTEREST_RATE = 10.0;   //ANNUAL INTEREST RATE

   //DEFINE VARIABLES
   double principal = 1000.0;   //PRINCIPAL LOAN VALUE
   term = 2;                    //TERM OF LOAN IN YEARS
   Double TotalAmount           //TOTAL AMOUNT OF LOAN
   StaugIO io = new StaugIO(); //DEFINE I/O OBJECT

   / GENERATE PROGRAM MESSAGE
   io.writeInfo("This program will calculate a total loan amount "
            + "given a principal of $1000, a term of 2 yrs. "
            + " and an interest rate of 10 percent."

   //CALCULATE TOTAL LOAN AMOUNT
   totalAmount = principal + ((principal * interestRate) * term)

   //DISPLAY RESULTS
   io.writeInfo("Given a principal amount of $" + principal
            + " a term of " + term " years "
            + " and an interest rate of " + interestRate "%"
            + " the total amount of the load is $" + totalAmount);
 }//END main()
```

7. Enter, compile, and run the following program. Does the output generated by the program make sense, especially if you were the customer? Of course not! There is a logic error in

the program. Use your Java debugger to locate and correct the logic error. (*Hint:* Watch the variable *tax* as you single-step the program with your debugger.)

```java
import staugIO.StaugIO;        //FOR INPUT/OUTPUT
public class Problem1_7
{
  public static void main(String args[])
  {
  //DEFINE CONSTANTS
  final double RATE = 7.0;       //INTEREST IN PERCENT FORM

  //DEFINE VARIABLES
  double cost = 0.0;             //COST OF ITEM
  double tax = 0.0;             //SALES TAX
  double totalCost = 0.0;       //TOTAL COST OF ITEM
  StaugIO io = new StaugIO();   //DEFINE I/O OBJECT

  //DISPLAY PROGRAM DESCRIPTION MESSAGE
  io.writeInfo("This program will calculate the total cost "
              + "\nof a $10.95 sales item.");

  //ASSIGN COST VALUE
  cost = 10.95;

  //CALCULATE TAX
  tax = RATE * cost;

  //CALCULATE TOTAL COST
  totalCost = cost + tax;

  //DISPLAY RESULT
  io.writeInfo("The total cost of the sales item with tax is: $"
              + totalCost);
  }//END main()
}//END Problem1_7 CLASS
```

2

Problem Solving

OBJECTIVES

When you are finished with this chapter, you should have a good understanding of the following:

- How to define a problem in terms of input, output, and processing
- How to plan a problem solution using algorithms and class diagrams
- The role of pseudocode in problem solution planning

- The concept of problem abstraction
- The steps required to test and debug a program
- What good program documentation must include

Introduction

Programming reduces to the art and science of problem solving. To be a good programmer, you must be a good problem solver. To be a good problem solver, you must attack a problem in a methodical way, from initial problem inspection and definition to final solution, testing, and documentation. In the beginning, when confronted with a programming problem, you will be tempted to get to the computer and start coding as soon as you get an idea of how to solve it. However, you *must* resist this temptation. Such an approach might work for simple problems but will *not* work when you are confronted with the complex problems found in today's real world. A good carpenter might attempt to build a doghouse without a plan but would never attempt to build your "dream house" without a good set of blueprints.

In this chapter, you will learn about a systematic method that will make you a good problem solver, and therefore a good programmer—it is called the ***program development life cycle,*** or ***PDLC***. In particular, you will study the steps required to solve just about any programming problem. You will be introduced to the concept of ***abstraction***, which allows problems to be viewed in general terms without agonizing over the implementation details required by a computer language. From an initial abstract solution, you will refine the solution step by step until it reaches a level that can be coded directly into a Java program. Make sure you understand this material and work the related problems at the end of the chapter. As you become more experienced in programming, you will find that the "secret" to successful programming is good planning through abstract analysis and stepwise refinement, which results in workable software designs. Such designs are supported by languages like Java. In the chapters that follow, you will build on this knowledge to create workable Java programs.

At the end of this chapter, you will be asked to write, enter, and execute your first Java programs. If you have not already done so, it's probably a good idea for you to familiarize yourself with the operation of your system at this time. You should know how to launch the Java compiler, enter and edit programs, compile programs, debug programs, and run programs. Refer to Appendix A for a tutorial on several popular Java development environments if need be.

2.1   The Program Development Life Cycle

Here is the life cycle in a nutshell:

THE PROGRAM DEVELOPMENT LIFE CYCLE

- Define the problem.
- Plan the problem solution.
- Code the program.
- Test and debug the program.
- Document the program.
- Maintain the program.

The life cycle is shown as a continuous process, or loop, in Figure 2-1.

Defining the Problem

You might suggest that defining the problem is an obvious step in solving any problem. However, it often is the most overlooked step, especially in computer programming. The lack of good problem definition often results in "spinning your wheels," especially in more complex computer programming applications.

Think of a typical computer programming problem, such as controlling the inventory of a large department store. What must be considered as part of the problem

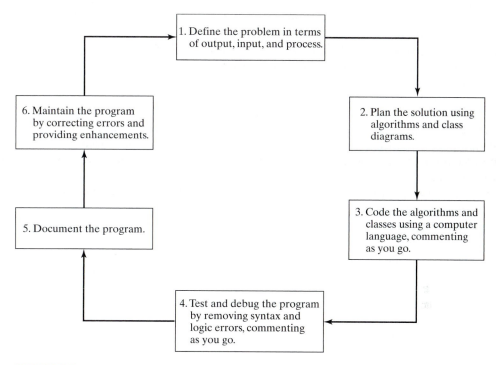

FIGURE 2-1 The program development life cycle, or PDLC.

definition? The first consideration probably is what you want to get out of the system. Will the output information consist of printed inventory reports or, in addition, will the system automatically generate product orders based on sales? Must any information generated by a customer transaction be saved permanently on disk, or can it be discarded? What type of data is the output to consist of? Is it numerical data, character data, or both? How must the output be formatted? All of these questions must be answered in order to define the output requirements.

Careful consideration of the output requirements usually leads to deciding what must be put into the system in order to obtain the desired system output. For instance, in our department store inventory example, a desired output most likely would be a summary of customer transactions. How are these transactions to be entered into the system? Are the data to be obtained from a keyboard, or is product information to be entered automatically via an optical character recognition (OCR) system that reads the bar code on the product price tags? Does the input consist of all numerical data, character data, or a combination of both? What is the format of the data?

The next consideration is processing. Will most of the customer processing be done at the cash register terminal, or will it be handled by a central store computer? What about credit card verification and inventory records? Will this processing be done by a local PC, a minicomputer located within the store, or a central mainframe computer located in a different part of the country? What kind of programs will be written to do the processing, and who will write them? What sort of calculations and decisions must be made on the data within individual programs to achieve the desired output?

All these questions must be answered when defining any computer programming problem. In summary, you could say that problem definition must consider the application requirements of input, processing, and output. The department store inventory problem clearly requires precise definition. However, even with small applications, you must still consider the type of input, processing, and output that the problem requires.

The reason this inventory problem lends itself to computer solution is that it deals with input, processing, and output, thus lending itself to an algorithmic approach to problem solving. Many real-world problems, such as long-range weather forecasting, do not lend themselves to this approach. So, when trying to define a problem you must first decide if it is a candidate for computer solution. To do this, you must ask yourself whether it lends itself to input and processing that input to produce useful information. Once a problem is identified as a candidate for computer solution, then you need to define the problem in terms of specific input, processing, and output.

When defining a problem, look for the nouns and verbs within a problem statement. The nouns often suggest input and output information, and the verbs suggest processing steps. The application will always dictate the problem definition. We will discuss problem definition later on in this chapter, as we begin to develop computer programs to solve real problems.

PROBLEM SOLVING TIP

Look for the nouns and verbs within a problem statement; they often provide clues to the required input, processing, and output. The nouns suggest input and output, and the verbs suggest processing steps.

Planning the Solution

The planning stage associated with any problem is probably the most important part of the solution, and computer programming is no exception. Imagine trying to build a house without a good set of blueprints. The results could be catastrophic! The same is true of trying to develop computer software without a good plan. When developing computer software, the planning stage is implemented using a collection of ***algorithms*** and ***class diagrams***. An algorithm is a series of step-by-step instructions, or recipe, that produces a solution to a problem. Algorithms are usually coded as methods within a Java class. A ***class diagram*** is a diagram that shows the data and methods which belong to a given class.

An ***algorithm*** is a series of step-by-step instructions that produces a solution to a problem. Algorithms are usually coded as methods within a Java class.

A ***class diagram*** is a diagram that shows the data and methods which belong to a given class.

Algorithms are not unique to the computer industry. Any set of instructions, such as those you might find in a recipe or a kit assembly guide, can be considered an algorithm. When planning computer programs, algorithms are used to outline the solution steps using English-like statements, called ***pseudocode***, that require less precision than a formal programming language. A good pseudocode algorithm should be independent of, but easily translated into, *any* formal procedural programming language.

Pseudocode is an informal set of English-like statements that denote common computer programming operations. Pseudocode is used to describe the steps in a computer algorithm.

Coding and Documenting the Program

Coding the program should be one of the simplest tasks in the whole programming process, provided you have done a good job of defining the problem and planning its solution. Coding involves the actual writing of the program in a formal programming language. The computer language you use will be determined by the nature of the problem, the programming languages available to you, and the limits of the computer system. Once a language is chosen, the program is written, or coded, by translating your algorithm and class diagram into the formal language code, commenting as you go. It is very easy to get lost in your own code. So insert your program comments as you write the code. Don't be tempted to write all the code in a hurry just to get the program working with the good intentions of going back and commenting later. What happens later is that we often forget what we did and why we did it. Commenting as you go will save you many future headaches and hours at the keyboard.

You should be cautioned, however, that coding is really a mechanical process and should be considered secondary to algorithm development. In the future, computers will generate their own program code from well-constructed algorithms and class diagrams. Research in the field of artificial intelligence has resulted in "code-generation" software. The thing to keep in mind is that computers might someday generate their own programming code from algorithms and class diagrams, but it takes the creativity and common sense of a human being to plan the solution and develop the algorithms and class diagrams.

Debugging the Program

You will soon find out that it is a rare and joyous occasion when a coded program actually "runs" the first time without any errors. Of course, good problem definition and planning will avoid many program mistakes, or "bugs." However, there always are a few bugs that manage to go undetected, regardless of how much planning you do. Getting rid of the program bugs (*debugging*) often is the most time-consuming job in the whole programming process. Industrial statistics show that often over 50 percent of a programmer's time is spent on program debugging.

There is no absolute correct procedure for debugging a program, but a systematic approach can help make the process easier. The basic steps of debugging are as follows:

- Realizing that you have an error
- Locating and determining the cause of the error
- Fixing the error

First of all, you have to realize that you have an error. Sometimes, this is obvious when your computer freezes up or crashes. At other times, the program might work fine until certain unexpected information is entered by someone using the program. The most subtle errors occur when the program is running fine and the results look correct, but when you examine the results closely, they are not quite right.

The next step in the debugging process is locating and determining the cause of the errors—sometimes the most difficult part of debugging. This is where a good programming tool, called a *debugger*, comes into play.

Fixing the error is the final step in debugging. Your knowledge of the Java language, this book, Java online help, a Java debugger, and your Java reference manuals are all valuable tools in fixing the error and removing the bug from your program.

When programming in Java, there are four things that you can do to test and debug your program: *desk-check* the program, *compile* the program, *run* the program, and *debug* the program.

Desk-Checking the Program   Desk-checking a program is similar to proofreading a letter or manuscript. The idea is to trace through the program mentally to make sure that the program logic is workable. You must consider various input possibilities and write down any results generated during program execution. In particular, try to determine what the program will do with unusual data by considering input possibilities that "shouldn't" happen. When desk-checking a program, always remember Murphy's Law: *Anything that can go wrong will go wrong—and at the worst possible moment!*

For example, suppose a program requires the user to enter a value whose square root must be found. Of course, the user "shouldn't" enter a negative value, because the square root of a negative number is imaginary. However, what will the program do if he or she does? Another possibility that should always be considered is an input of zero, especially when used as part of an arithmetic operation, such as division.

When you first begin programming, you will be tempted to skip the desk-checking phase, because you can't wait to run the program once it is written. However, as you gain experience, you soon will realize the time-saving value of desk-checking.

Compiling the Program   At this point, you are ready to enter the program into the computer system. Once entered, the program must be compiled, or translated, into machine code. Fortunately, the compiler is designed to check for certain program errors. These usually are syntax errors that you have made when coding the program. A *syntax* *error* is any violation of the rules of the programming language, such as using a period instead of a semicolon.

 A **syntax error** is any violation of the rules of the programming language.

During the compiling process, many Java compilers will generate error and warning messages as well as position the display monitor cursor to the point in the program where the error was detected. Once an error is corrected, you must attempt to compile the program again. If other errors are detected, you must correct them, recompile the program, and so on, until the entire program is successfully compiled.

Running the Program   Once the program has been compiled, you must execute, or run, it. However, just because the program has been compiled successfully doesn't mean that it will run successfully under all possible conditions. Common bugs that occur at this stage include *logic errors* and *run-time errors*. These are the most difficult kinds of errors to detect. A logic error will occur when a loop tells the computer to repeat an operation but does not tell it when to stop repeating. This is called an ***infinite loop***. Such a bug will not cause an error message to be generated, because the computer is simply doing what it was told to do. The program execution must be stopped and debugged before it can run successfully.

 A **logic error** occurs when the compiler does what you tell it to do but is not doing what you meant it to do.

A run-time error occurs when the program attempts to perform an illegal operation, as defined by the laws of mathematics or the particular compiler in use. Two common mathematical run-time errors are division by zero and attempting to take the square root of a negative number. A common error imposed by the compiler is an integer value out of range. Java limits byte-sized integers to a range of -128 to $+127$. Unpredictable results can occur if a byte value exceeds this range.

 A **run-time** error occurs when the program attempts to perform an illegal operation as defined by the laws of mathematics or the particular compiler in use.

Sometimes, the program is automatically aborted and an error message is displayed when a run-time error occurs. Other times, the program seems to execute properly but generates incorrect results, commonly called *garbage*, or *junk*. The error must be located and corrected before another attempt is made to run the program.

Using a Debugger   One of the most important programming tools that you can have is a debugger. A debugger provides a microscopic view of what is going on in your program. Many Java IDEs (integrated development environments) include a built-in, or *integrated*,

debugger that allows you to single-step program statements and view the execution results in the CPU and memory. Appendix A directs you to tutorials on how to use both the
Sun ONE Studio and *JBuilder* integrated debuggers.

 DEBUGGING TIP

A word from experience: Always go about debugging your programs in a systematic, common-
sense manner. Don't be tempted to change something just because you "hope" it will work and
don't know what else to do. Use your resources to isolate and correct the problem. Such resources include your algorithms, class diagrams, a program listing, your integrated Java debugger,
your reference manuals, this textbook, and your instructor, just to mention a few. Logic and run-
time errors usually are the result of a serious flaw in your program. They will not go away and
cannot be corrected by blindly making changes to your program. One good way to locate errors is to have your program print out preliminary results as well as messages that tell when a
particular part of the program is running.

Documentation

The documentation step in the program development life cycle often is overlooked,
but it probably is one of the more important steps, especially in commercial programming. Documentation is easy if you have done a good job of defining the problem,
planning the solution, coding, testing, and debugging the program. The final program
documentation is simply the recorded result of these programming steps. At a minimum, good documentation should include the following:

- A narrative description of the problem definition, which includes the type of
  input, output, and processing employed by the program.
- A set of algorithms.
- A set of class diagrams.
- A program listing that includes a clear commenting scheme. Commenting within
  the program is an important part of the overall documentation process. Each pro-
  gram should include comments at the beginning to explain what it does, any spe-
  cial algorithms that are employed, and a summary of the problem definition. In
  addition, the name of the programmer and the date the program was written and
  last modified should be included.
- Samples of input and output data.
- Testing and debugging results.
- Simple, clear, and readable user instructions.
- Software maintenance instructions and maintenance log.

The documentation must be neat and well organized. It must be easily understood by you as well as any other person who might have a need to use or modify your
program in the future. What good is an ingenious program if no one can determine
what it does, how to use it, or how to maintain it?

One final point: Documentation should always be an ongoing process. Whenever you work with the program or modify it, make sure the documentation is updated to reflect your experiences and modifications. Someday you might have to maintain a program written by yourself or somebody else. Without good documentation, program maintenance becomes a nightmare.

Maintenance

The maintenance step is where any future changes and enhancements to the system are made. Three types of maintenance are *corrective maintenance*, *enhancement maintenance*, and *forced maintenance*. Corrective maintenance is the removing of any software bugs found by the software developers or the user, without requiring any changes to the software specification developed in the planning phase. Enhancement involves updating the software with new or improved features. When enhancements are made, the software specifications are changed first, then the changes are implemented by changing or adding the required code. Forced maintenance occurs when an outside agency, like the local, state, or Federal government, makes changes in the law which require changes in the related software. By the way, studies have shown that over the complete life cycle of the software, the maintenance phase accounts for over 50% of the total cost of the software.

QUICK CHECK

1. English-like statements that require less precision than a formal programming language are called _____.
2. What questions must be answered when defining a computer programming problem?
3. What can be done to test and debug a program?
4. Why is commenting important within a program?
5. What is a syntax error?
6. What is a logic error?

2.2   Problem Solving Using Algorithms and Methods

In the previous section, you learned that an algorithm is a sequence of step-by-step instructions that solves a problem.

For instance, consider the following series of instructions:

Apply to wet hair.
Gently massage lather through hair.
Rinse, keeping lather out of eyes.
Repeat.

Look familiar? Of course, this is a series of instructions that might be found on the back of a shampoo bottle. But does it fit the technical definition of an algorithm? In other words, does it produce a result? You might say "yes," but look closer. The algorithm requires that you keep repeating the procedure an infinite number of times, so theoretically you would never stop shampooing your hair! A good computer algorithm must terminate in a finite amount of time. The repeat instruction could be altered easily to make the shampooing algorithm technically correct:

Repeat until hair is clean.

Now the shampooing process can be terminated. Of course, you must be the one to decide when your hair is clean.

The foregoing shampoo analogy might seem a bit trivial. You probably are thinking that any intelligent person would not keep on repeating the shampooing process an infinite number of times, right? This obviously is the case when we humans are executing the algorithm, because we have some common-sense judgment. But what about a computer; does it have common-sense judgment? Most computers do exactly what they are told to do by a program. As a result, a computer would repeat the original shampooing algorithm over and over an infinite number of times. This is why the algorithms that you write for computer programs must be precise.

Now, let's develop an algorithm for a process that is common to all of us—mailing a letter. Think of the steps that are involved in this simple process. You must first address an envelope, fold the letter, insert the letter in the envelope, and seal the envelope. Next, you need a stamp. If you don't have a stamp, you have to buy one. Once a stamp is obtained, you must place it on the envelope and mail the letter. The following algorithm summarizes the steps in this process:

Obtain an envelope.

Address the envelope.

Fold the letter.

Insert the letter in the envelope.

Seal the envelope.

If you don't have a stamp, then buy one.

Place the stamp on the envelope.

Mail the letter.

Does this sequence of instructions fit our definition of a good algorithm? In other words, does the sequence of instructions produce a result in a finite amount of time? Yes, assuming that each operation can be understood and carried out by the person mailing the letter. This brings up two additional characteristics of good algorithms: Each operation within the algorithm must be **_well defined_** and **_effective_**. By well defined, we mean that each of the steps must be clearly understood by people in the computer industry. By effective, we mean that some method must exist in order to carry out the operation. In other words, the person mailing the letter must be able to perform each of the algorithm steps. In the case of a computer program algorithm, the compiler must have the means of executing each operation in the algorithm.

In summary, a good computer algorithm must possess the following three attributes:

1. Employ well-defined instructions that are generally understood by people in the computer industry.

2. Employ instructions that can be carried out effectively by the compiler executing the algorithm.

3. Produce a solution to the problem in a finite amount of time.

In order to write computer program algorithms, we need to establish a set of well-defined, effective operations. The set of pseudocode operations listed in Table 2-1 will make up our algorithmic language. We will use these operations from now on whenever we write computer algorithms.

Notice that the operations in Table 2-1 are grouped into three major categories: *sequence*, *decision*, and *iteration*. These categories are called ***control structures***. The sequence control structure includes those operations that produce a single action or result. Only a partial list of sequence operations is provided here. This list will be expanded, as additional operations are needed. As its name implies, the decision control structure includes the operations that allow the computer to make decisions. Finally, the iteration control structure includes those operations that are used for looping, or repeating, operations within the algorithm. Many of the operations listed in Table 2-1 are self-explanatory. Those that are not will be discussed in detail as we begin to develop more complex algorithms.

QUICK CHECK

1. Why is it important to develop a set of algorithms prior to coding a program?

2. What are the three major control structure categories of pseudocode operations?

3. List three decision operations.

4. List three iteration operations.

5. Which pseudocode operation in Table 2-1 would be used for input of data from a user keyboard?

TABLE 2-1   Pseudocode Operations Used in This Text

Sequence	Decision	Iteration
Add (+)	If/Then	While
Calculate	If/Else	Do/While
Decrement	Switch/Case	For
Display		
Divide (/)		
Increment		
Multiply		
Read		
Set or assign (=)		
Subtract (−)		
Write		

2.3   Problem Abstraction and Stepwise Refinement

At this time, we need to introduce a very important concept in programming—
abstraction. Abstraction allows us to view a problem in general terms, without worrying
about the details. As a result, abstraction provides for generalization in problem solving.

Abstraction provides for generalization in problem solving by allowing you to view a
problem in general terms, without worrying about the details of the problem solution.

You might have heard the old saying, "You can't see the forest for the trees." This
means that it is very easy to get lost within the trees of the forest without seeing the big
picture of the entire forest. This saying also applies to problem solving and programming. When starting out to solve a problem, you need to get the "big picture" first.
Once you have the big picture of the problem solution, the "forest," you can gradually
refine the solution by providing more detail until you have a solution, the "trees," that
is easily coded in a computer language. The process of gradually adding more detail to
a general problem solution is called *stepwise refinement*.

Stepwise refinement is the process of gradually adding detail to a general problem solution until it can be easily coded in a computer language.

As an example, consider the problem of designing your own "dream house."
Would you begin by drafting the detailed plans of the house? Not likely, because you
would most likely get lost in detail. A better approach would be to first make an artist's
general-perspective rendition of the house; then make a general floor plan diagram,
and finally make detailed drawings of the house construction that could be followed by
the builders.

The concepts of problem abstraction and stepwise refinement allow you to *divide
and conquer* the problem and solve it from the *top down*. This strategy has been proven
to conquer all types of problems, especially programming problems. In programming,
we generate a general problem solution, or algorithm, and gradually refine it, producing more detailed algorithms, until we get to a level that can be easily coded using a
programming language.

In summary, when attacking a problem, always start with the big picture and begin
with a very general, or *abstract*, model of the solution. This allows you to concentrate on
the problem at hand without getting lost in the "trees" by worrying about the implementation details of a particular programming language. You then gradually refine the
solution until you reach a level that can be easily coded using a programming language
like Java. The *Problem Solving in Action* examples that follow illustrate this process.

QUICK CHECK

1. Explain why abstraction is important when solving problems.
2. Explain the process of stepwise refinement.
3. How do you know when you have reached a codable level of an algorithm when
   using stepwise refinement?

Problem Solving in Action: Sales Tax

Problem

Develop a set of algorithms and class diagram to calculate the amount of sales tax and the total cost of a sales item, including tax. Assume the sales tax rate is 7 percent and the user will enter the cost of the sales item.

Defining the Problem

When defining the problem, you must consider three things: *input, processing,* and *output* as related to the problem statement. Look for the nouns and verbs within the problem statement, as they often provide clues to the required input, processing, and output. The nouns suggest input and output, and the verbs suggest processing steps. The nouns relating to input and output are *sales tax, total cost,* and *cost.* The total cost is the required output, and the sales tax and item cost are needed as input to calculate the total cost of the item. However, the sales tax rate is given (7 percent), so the only data required for the algorithm is the item cost.

The verb *calculate* requires us to process two things: the amount of sales tax and the total cost of the item, including sales tax. Therefore, the processing must calculate the amount of sales tax and add this value to the item cost to obtain the total cost of the item. In summary, the problem definition in terms of input, processing, and output is as follows:

Input:	The cost of the sales item to be entered by the user on the system keyboard.
Processing:	$tax = 0.07 \times cost$
	$totalCost = cost + tax$
Output:	The total cost of the sales item, including sales tax, to be displayed on the system monitor.

Notice that we have indicated *where* the output is going (the system monitor), and *where* the input is coming from (the user). Where the output is going and the input is coming from should always be indicated for each item in the problem definition.

Planning the Solution

Now that the problem has been defined in terms of input, processing, and output, it is time to plan the solution by developing the required algorithms and class diagram. Using the foregoing problem definition, we are now ready to write the initial algorithm. We will call this initial algorithm *main()*. (*Note:* The parentheses after the algorithm name will be used from now on to indicate an algorithm, or method, to perform some given task.) Here is the required initial algorithm, main():

Initial Algorithm
main()
BEGIN
   Read the cost of the sales item from the user.
   Calculate the sales tax and total cost of the sales item.
   Write the total cost of the sales item, including sales tax, on the system monitor.
END.

Notice that, at this level, you are not concerned with how to perform the foregoing operations in a computer language. You are only concerned about the major program operations, without agonizing over the language implementation details. This is problem abstraction!

We have divided the problem into three major tasks relating to input, processing, and output derived directly from our problem definition. The next step is to refine repeatedly the initial

algorithm until we obtain one or more algorithms that can be coded directly in a computer language. This is a relatively simple problem, so we can employ the pseudocode operations listed in
Table 2-1 at this first level of refinement. Three major operations are identified by the preceding
algorithm: reading data from the user, calculating the tax and total cost, and displaying the results to the user. As a result, we will create three additional algorithms that implement these operations. First, reading the data from the user. We will call this algorithm *setCost()* as follows:

First Level of Refinement

setCost()
BEGIN
    Write a user prompt to enter the cost of the item (*cost*).
    Read *cost*.
END.

In Table 2-1, you will find two sequence operations called **Read** and **Write**. The *Read* operation is an input operation. We will assume that this operation will obtain data entered via the
system keyboard. The *Write* operation is an output operation. We will assume that this operation
causes information to be displayed on the system monitor. The *setCost()* algorithm uses the
Write operation to display a **prompt** to the user and a corresponding *Read* operation to obtain
the user input and assign it to the respective variable.

STYLE TIP

The *setCost()* algorithm illustrates some operations that result in good programming style. The
Write operation will display a message to tell the user to "Enter the cost of the item (*cost*)."
Without such a prompt, the user will not know what to do. You must write a user prompt message anytime the user must enter data via the keyboard. Such a message should tell the user
what is to be entered and in what format the information is to be entered.

The next task is to develop an algorithm to calculate the cost of the sales item, including
tax. We will call this algorithm *calculateTotalCost()* and employ the required pseudocode operations from Table 2-1, as follows:

calculateTotalCost()
BEGIN
    Set *tax* to $(0.07 \times cost)$.
    Set *totalCost* to $(cost + tax)$.
END.

Finally, we need an algorithm to display the results. We will call this algorithm
getTotalCost(). All we need here is a *Write* operation as follows:

getTotalCost()
BEGIN
    Write *totalCost*.
END.

That's all there is to it. The illustration in Figure 2-2 is called a **problem solution diagram**,
because it shows the overall structure of our problem solution. The problem solution diagram
shows how the problem has been divided into a series of subproblems, whose collective solution

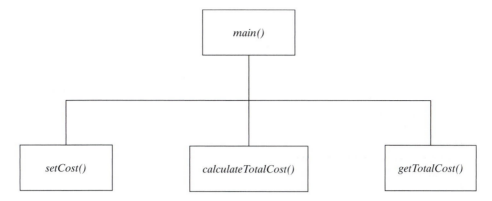

FIGURE 2-2   A problem solution diagram for the sales tax problem shows the abstract analysis and stepwise refinement required for solving complex problems.

will solve the initial problem. By using the above algorithms and problem solution diagram, this problem can be coded easily in any language, such as Java.

When you begin coding in Java, you will translate the preceding algorithms directly into Java code. Each of the algorithms will be coded as a Java **method**. Methods in Java are procedures designed to perform specific tasks, such as those performed by each of our algorithms. Thus, we will code a method called *setCost()* to read the data from the user, another method called *calculateTotalCost()* to calculate the total cost of the sales item, and a third method called *getTotalCost()* to display the final results to the user.

We will place these methods inside of a class along with the necessary class data, such as the *cost, tax,* and *totalCost*. Let's call our class *SalesTax*. Figure 2-3 shows a simplified **class diagram** for our *SalesTax* class. A class diagram is nothing more than an inside view of a class,

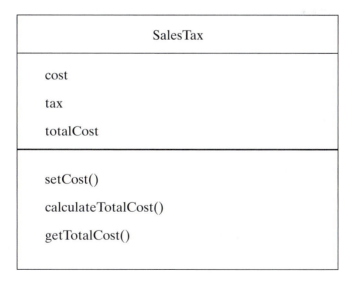

FIGURE 2-3   A class diagram for the *SalesTax* class shows the data and method members that make up the class.

showing the data and method members of the class. In addition, we will code a method called *main()* in our application to create an **object** for our *SalesTax* class and use this object to sequentially "call" our class methods as needed to produce the desired result.

A **method** in Java is a procedure designed to perform specific tasks, such as those performed by an algorithm. In other programming languages, methods might be referred to as *subprograms*, *functions*, or *subroutines*.

Coding the Solution

Here is the coded solution to the problem. Don't be overwhelmed by the code at this point. Let's just look at the overall structure of the program. We will fill in all the details in time. First, line numbers have been added to facilitate our discussion. These numbers are not part of the code and would not compile. So, if you enter this program into your own machine, just eliminate the numbers.

```
1    /*
2    TestSalesTax.java
3    *
4    Created on April 21, 2002, 7:20 AM
5    */

6    /**
7    *
8    @author Andrew C. Staugaard, Jr.
9    @version 1.0
10   */

11   import staugIO.StaugIO;               //FOR IO
12   class SalesTax
13   {
14      private double cost = 0.0;          //ITEM COST
15      private double tax = 0.0;           //SALES TAX VALUE
16      private double totalCost = 0.0;     //TOTAL COST OF SALES ITEM
17      private StaugIO io = new StaugIO(); //INPUT/OUTPUT OBJECT
18      //SalesTax() CONSTRUCTOR METHOD

19      public SalesTax()
20      {
21      }//END SalesTax()

22      //setCost() METHOD
23      public void setCost()
24      {
25         cost = io.readDouble("Enter the cost of the item");
26      }//END setCost()

27      //calculateTotalCost() METHOD
28      public void calculateTotalCost()
29      {
30         tax = 0.07 * cost;
31         totalCost = cost + tax;
32      }//END calculateTotalCost()

33      //getTotalCost() METHOD
34      public void getTotalCost()
```

```java
35     {
36       io.writeInfo("The total cost is: $" + totalCost);
37     }//END getTotalCost()
38   }//END SalesTax CLASS

39   public class TestSalesTax
40   {
41     public static void main (String args[])
42     {
43       SalesTax item = new SalesTax();
44       item.setCost();
45       item.calculateTotalCost();
46       item.getTotalCost();

47       //EXIT PROGRAM
48       System.exit(0);
49     }//END main()
50   }//END TestSalesTax CLASS
```

Now, lines 1 through 10 form a *block comment.* A block comment in Java begins with the /* symbols and ends with the */ symbols. This block comment simply shows the Java file name, date it was created, the program author, and the program version. In line 11 you see an `import` statement. The `import` statement is used to "import" a *package* into the program. A package is simply a collection of classes. The package imported here is the *staugIO* package which includes the *StaugIO* class. *(Notice that a package name begins with a lowercase letter, while a class name begins with an uppercase letter.)* The *StaugIO* class has been created especially for this text to provide a simple GUI for program input and output. We will "unwrap" the *staugIO* package and its classes in a later chapter so that you can see how it works.

Our *SalesTax* class begins in line 12. Inside the class, on lines 14 – 16, you find the three class data members *cost, tax,* and *totalCost* that appear in the class diagram previously shown in Figure 2-3. *(Notice that data members begin with a lowercase letter in Java.)* We have added a fourth data member at line 17. Here, we created an **object**, called *io*, of our *StaugIO* class to perform input and output operations. All classes that we create must have objects created for them in order to gain access to the class members.

In lines 18 through 21 you see a **constructor** for our *SalesTax* class. Don't worry about this for now. Just accept the fact that all classes in Java must contain a constructor.

> Package names, variable names, object names, and method names begin with a lowercase letter. Class names begin with an uppercase letter.

In lines 22 through 37 you find the three methods we decided upon for our *SalesTax* class: *setCost(), calculateTotalCost(),* and *getTotalCost(). (Notice that methods begin with a lowercase letter in Java.)* Look inside of each method and you will see that we have simply coded the method algorithm that we developed earlier. You might want to go back to compare the method code to its algorithm to see how each algorithm statement was coded in Java.

Our *SalesTax* class ends at line 38 with a closing right brace, }, as indicated by the *line comment.* A line comment begins with the // symbols. Anything appearing after the // symbols on a given line is ignored by Java. You will notice extensive use of line comments throughout the program to "self-document" the code.

Once we have coded our class, we need to write an application to test our class. An application is a class that will contain method *main()* which, as stated earlier, is used to call our *SalesTax* class methods as needed to produce the desired result. In other words, it is used to "test" our *SalesTax* class. Our application is called *TestSalesTax* and begins on line 39. Notice that it includes method *main()*. The first thing that is done in *main()* is to create an object, called *item,* for our *SalesTax* class in line 43. As you will soon discover, all classes that we create are programmer-defined classes which require that objects be created for them in order to have access to the class members. In lines 44 – 46 you see this object being used to call our methods in the order required to process the sales tax problem. Finally, method *main()* ends at line 49 and our application ends at line 50. Wow, that was quite a bit of information! Now, we have the rest of the book to fill in the details. Go ahead and code that program using your favorite Java IDE. In order for the program to work properly, you will have to place the *staugIO* package folder in your program working directory. The *staugIO* folder is available on the text CD and the text Web site. Instructions on how to install this package in your IDE are also available at these locations.

Here are the input and output windows that you would see when running the program:

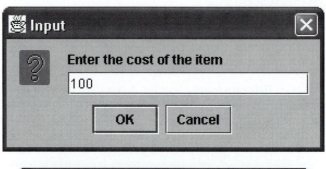

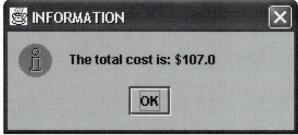

Problem Solving in Action: Student Payroll

Problem

Develop a set of algorithms and class diagram to calculate the gross pay for a student working part time (less than 40 hours a week). Assume that the student will enter his/her hourly rate of pay and number of hours worked in a given week. Make sure that the report shows the student name and date.

Defining the Problem

When defining the problem, you must consider three things: *input, processing,* and *output* as related to the problem statement. Identifying the nouns and verbs in the problem statement, you get the following:

    Nouns: gross pay, rate, hours, name, date.
    Verbs: calculate
    Remember, the nouns will relate to input and output, while the verbs relate to processing. Looking at the nouns you might suggest that all should appear on the output to provide the user with as much information as possible in the report. Thus the output will be:

Output: The *gross pay* for the week, the hourly *rate* of pay, the number of *hours* worked during the week, the student *name*, and the *date*.

Now, what data is needed to generate this output? Well, the *gross pay* can be calculated from the *rate* of pay and the *hours* worked. So, these two values must be input values to the program. In addition, the user must enter the student *name* and *date* in order for this information to appear on the report. So, the input must be:

Input: The *rate* of pay, the number of *hours* worked, the student *name,* and the *date*.

Finally, the processing simply involves *calculating* the *gross pay*. This can be done as follows:

Processing: gross pay = rate * hours

Now that the problem has been defined in terms of input, processing, and output, it is time to plan the solution by developing the required algorithms and a class diagram.

Planning the Solution

We will begin with an abstract model of the problem. This will be our initial algorithm, which we refer to as *main()*. At this level, we are only concerned with addressing the major operations required to solve the problem. These are derived directly from the problem definition. As a result, our initial algorithm is as follows:

Initial Algorithm
main()
BEGIN
    Read the *rate, hours, name,* and *date* from the user.
    Calculate the *gross pay*.
    Write the payroll report to the user.
END.

The next step is to refine repeatedly the initial algorithm until we obtain one or more algorithms that can be coded directly in a computer language. This is a relatively simple problem, so we can employ the pseudocode operations listed in Table 2-1 at this first level of refinement. Three major operations are identified by the preceding algorithm: reading data from the user, calculating the pay, and displaying the results to the user. As a result, we will create three additional algorithms that implement these operations. First, reading the data from the user. We will call this algorithm *setData()*.

First Level of Refinement
setData()
BEGIN
    Write a user prompt to enter the student *name*.
    Read *name*.
    Write a user prompt to enter the *date*.
    Read *date*.
    Write a user prompt to enter the hourly *rate* of pay.
    Read *rate*.
    Write a user prompt to enter the number of *hours* worked.
    Read *hours*.
END.

The next task is to develop an algorithm to calculate the *gross pay*. We will call this algorithm *calculatePay()* and employ the required pseudocode operations from Table 2-1, as follows:

calculatePay()
BEGIN
　　Set *gross pay = rate * hours.*
END.

The final task is to develop an algorithm to display the payroll report. We will call this algorithm *getData()*. All we need here are several *Write* operations as follows:

getData()
BEGIN
　　Write *name.*
　　Write *date.*
　　Write *rate* of pay.
　　Write *hours* worked.
　　Write *gross pay.*
END.

To summarize the problem solution, we generate a problem solution diagram as shown in Figure 2-4 and a class diagram as shown in Figure 2-5.

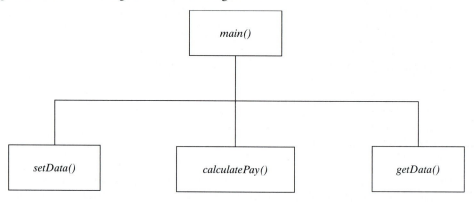

FIGURE 2-4　A problem solution diagram for the *Student Payroll* problem.

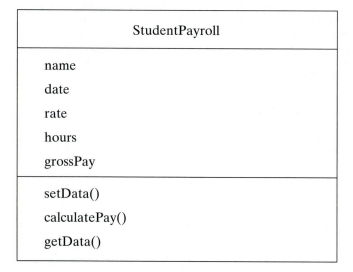

FIGURE 2-5　A class diagram for the *Student Payroll* problem.

Coding the Solution

Here is the coded solution to the problem. You will see that its structure is similar to the *Sales Tax* program discussed in the last case study. Again, don't be overwhelmed by the code. Just see if you can identify the class members and algorithms we developed for this problem.

```java
/*
 * TestStudentPayroll.java
 *
 * Created on April 21, 2002, 8:51 AM
 */

/**
 *
 * @author Andrew C. Staugaard, Jr.
 * @version 1.0
 */
import staugIO.StaugIO;                       //FOR IO
class StudentPayroll
{
     String name = "";                        //STUDENT NAME
     String date = "mm/dd/yyyy";              //PAYROLL DATE
     private double rate = 0.0;               //HOURLY RATE
     private double hours = 0.0;              //WEEKLY HOURS
     private double grossPay = 0.0;           //WEEKLY GROSS PAY
     private StaugIO io = new StaugIO();      //INPUT/OUTPUT OBJECT

   //StudentPayroll() CONSTRUCTOR METHOD
     public StudentPayroll()
     {
     }//END StudentPayroll()

   //setData() METHOD
     public void setData()
     {
         name = io.readString("Enter the student name");
         date = io.readString("Enter the date in mm/dd/yyyy format");
         rate = io.readDouble("Enter the hourly rate of pay");
         hours = io.readDouble("Enter hours that " + name + " worked");
     }//END setData()

   //calculatePay() METHOD
     public void calculatePay()
     {
         grossPay = rate * hours;
     }//END calculatePay()

   //getData() METHOD
     public void getData()
     {
         io.writeInfo("Student: " + name
                     + "\nDate: " + date
                     + "\nRate: $" + rate
                     + "\nHours: " + hours
                     + "\nGross Pay: $" + grossPay);
```

```
        }//END getData()
}//END StudentPayroll CLASS

public class TestStudentPayroll
{
    public static void main (String args[])
    {
        StudentPayroll student = new StudentPayroll();
        student.setData();
        student.calculatePay();
        student.getData();

    //EXIT PROGRAM
    System.exit(0);
    }//END main()
}//END TestStudentPayroll CLASS
```

Here is the output window that you would see after running the program:

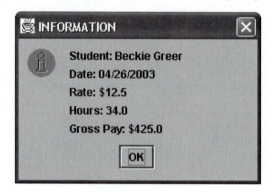

Problem Solving in Action: Credit Card Interest

Problem

The interest charged on a credit card account depends on the remaining balance according to the following criteria: Interest charged is 18 percent up to $500 and 15 percent for any amount over $500. Develop the algorithms and class diagram required to find the total amount of interest due on any given account balance.

Let's begin by defining the problem in terms of input, processing, and output.

Defining the Problem

Input:	We will assume that the user will enter the account balance via the system keyboard.
Processing:	Here is an application in which a decision-making operation must be included in the algorithm. There are two possibilities as follows: *If* the balance is less than or equal to $500, *then* the interest is 18 percent of the balance, or

$$interest = 0.18 \times balance$$

If the balance is over \$500, *then* the interest is 18 percent of the first \$500 plus 15 percent of any amount over \$500. In the form of an equation,

$$interest = (0.18 \times 500) + [0.15 \times (balance - 500)]$$

Notice the use of the two *if/then* statements in these two possibilities.

Output: According to the problem statement, the obvious output must be the total amount of interest due. We will display this information on the system monitor.

Planning the Solution

Our problem solution begins with the initial algorithm we have been calling *main()*. Again, this algorithm will simply reflect the problem definition as follows:

Initial Algorithm
main()
BEGIN
   Read the account balance from the user.
   Calculate the interest on the account balance.
   Write the calculated interest on the system monitor.
END.

Due to the simplicity of the problem, only one level of refinement is needed, as follows:

First Level of Refinement
setBalance()
BEGIN
   Write a user prompt to enter the account balance (*balance*).
   Read *balance*.
END.

calculateInterest()
BEGIN
   If *balance* <= 500 Then
     Set *interest* to (0.18 × *balance*).
   If *balance* > 500 Then
     Set *interest* to (0.18 × 500) + (0.15 × (*balance* - 500)).
END.

getInterest()
BEGIN
   Write *interest*.
END.

As you can see, the two decision-making operations stated in the problem definition have been incorporated into our *calculateInterest()* algorithm. Notice the use of indentation to show which calculation goes with which *if/then* operation. The use of indentation is an important part of pseudocode because it shows the algorithm structure at a glance.

How might you replace the two *if/then* operations in this algorithm with a single *if/else* operation? Think about it, as it will be left as a problem at the end of the chapter! A problem solution diagram and class diagram for this problem are shown together in Figure 2-6.

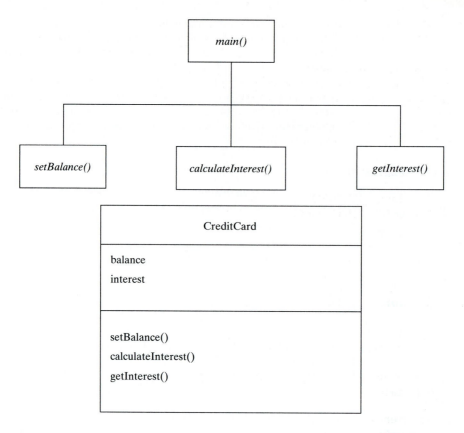

FIGURE 2-6   A problem solution and class diagram for the *CreditCard* problem.

Coding the Solution

Here is the coded solution to the problem. You will see that its structure is similar to the programs discussed in the last two case studies. Again, don't be overwhelmed by the code. Just see if you can identify the class members and algorithms we developed for this problem.

```
/*
 * TestCreditCard.java
 *
 * Created on April 21, 2002, 8:51 AM
 */

/**
 *
 * @author Andrew C. Staugaard, Jr.
 * @version 1.0
 */
```

```java
import staugIO.StaugIO;                        //FOR IO
class CreditCard
{
    private double balance = 0.0;             //ACCOUNT BALANCE
    private double interest = 0.0;            //CREDIT CARD INTEREST
    private StaugIO io = new StaugIO();       //INPUT/OUTPUT OBJECT

    //CreditCard() CONSTRUCTOR METHOD
    public CreditCard()
    {
    }//END CreditCard()

    //setBalance() METHOD
    public void setBalance()
    {
        balance = io.readDouble("Enter the credit card balance");
    }//END setBalance()

    //calculateInterest() METHOD
    public void calculateInterest()
    {
        if (balance <= 500)
          interest = 0.18 * balance;
        if (balance > 500)
          interest = (0.18 * balance) + (0.15 * (balance - 500));
    }//END calculateInterest()

    //getInterest() METHOD
    public void getInterest()
    {
        io.writeInfo("The credit card interest is: $" + interest);
    }//END getInterest()
}//END CreditCard CLASS

public class TestCreditCard
{
    public static void main (String args[])
    {
        CreditCard account = new CreditCard();
        account.setBalance();
        account.calculateInterest();
        account.getInterest();

        //EXIT PROGRAM
        System.exit(0);
    }//END main()
}//END TestCreditCard CLASS
```

Here are the input and output windows that you would see when running the program:

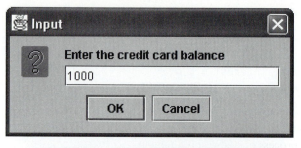

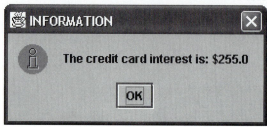

CHAPTER SUMMARY

The five major steps that must be performed when developing software are (1) define the problem, (2) plan the problem solution, (3) code the program, (4) debug the program, and (5) document the program. When defining the problem, you must consider the input, processing, and output requirements of the application. Planning the problem solution requires that you specify the problem solution steps via a set of algorithms and develop class diagrams. An algorithm is a series of step-by-step instructions that provides a solution to the problem in a finite amount of time. A class diagram shows the data and method members that make up the class.

Abstraction and stepwise refinement are powerful tools for problem solving. Abstraction allows you to view the problem in general terms, without agonizing over the implementation details of a computer language. Stepwise refinement is applied to an initial abstract problem solution to develop gradually a set of related algorithms that can be directly coded using a computer language, such as Java.

Once a codable algorithm is developed, it must be coded into some formal language that the computer system can understand. The language used in this text is Java. Once coded, the program must be tested and debugged through desk-checking, compiling, and execution. Finally, the entire programming process, from problem definition to testing and debugging, must be documented so that it can be easily understood by you or anyone else working with it.

Your Java debugger is one of the best tools that you can use to deal with bugs that creep into your programs. It allows you to do source-level debugging and helps with the two hardest parts of debugging: finding the error and finding the cause of the error. It does this by allowing you to trace into your programs and their methods one step at a time. This slows down the program execution so that you can examine the contents of the individual data elements and program output at any given point in the program.

QUESTIONS AND PROBLEMS

Questions

1. What is an algorithm?
2. List the five steps of the program development life cycle.
3. What three things must be considered during the problem-definition phase of programming?
4. What tools are employed for planning the solution to a programming problem?
5. Explain how problem abstraction aids in solving problems.
6. Explain the process of stepwise refinement.
7. The writing of a program is called _____.
8. State three things that you can do to test and debug your programs.
9. List the minimum items required for good documentation.
10. What three characteristics must a good computer algorithm possess?
11. The three major control structures of a programming language are _____, _____, and _____.
12. Explain why a single *if/then* operation in the credit card interest problem won't work. If you know the balance is not less than or equal to $500, the balance must be greater than $500, right? So, why can't the second *if/then* operation be deleted?

Problems

You should use the staugIO package to provide I/O in the problems that follow. See the staugIOReadMe.doc file in the TextSourceCode directory of the text CD for installation of this package on your system.

Least Difficult

1. Develop a set of algorithms to compute the sum, difference, product, and quotient of any two integers entered by the user.
2. Revise the solution you obtained in problem 1 to protect it from a divide-by-zero run-time error.
3. Code the *TestSalesTax.java* program given in this chapter. Compile and execute the program using your favorite Java IDE.
4. Code the *TestCreditCard.java* program given in this chapter. Compile and execute the program using your favorite Java IDE.
5. Code the *TestStudentPayroll.java* program given in this chapter. Compile and execute the program using your favorite Java IDE.

More Difficult

6. Develop a set of algorithms and class diagram to read in an employee's total weekly hours worked and rate of pay. Determine the gross weekly pay using "time-and-a-half" for anything over 40 hours.
7. Revise the solution generated in the credit card problem to employ a single *if/else* operation in place of the two *if/then* operations. As you will see later, an *if/else* operation does one thing "if" a condition is true, "else" it does something different if the same condition is false.

8. A dimension on a part drawing indicates that the length of the part is 3.00 ± 0.25 inches. This means that the minimum acceptable length of the part is $3.0 - 0.25 = 2.75$ inches and the maximum acceptable length of the part is $3.00 + 0.25 = 3.25$ inches. Develop a set of algorithms that will display "ACCEPTABLE" if the part is within tolerance and "UNACCEPTABLE" if the part is out of tolerance. Also, show your problem definition in terms of input, processing, and output.

9. Develop a problem definition and a set of algorithms to process a standard bank account. Assume that the user must enter the beginning bank account balance as well as any deposits or withdrawals on the account. The banking transactions that must be implemented are adding any deposits to the balance and subtracting any withdrawals from the balance. Of course, the program should display the account status, including the old balance, amounts of deposits, amounts of withdrawals, and the new balance.

10. Develop a problem solution diagram and a class diagram for the banking problem in problem 9.

11. Develop a problem definition and a set of algorithms to process a business inventory. Assume that the user must enter five inventory items for a local bait and tackle store. Each entry is to consist of the item name, quantity on hand, and item price. The program should calculate the expected profit on each item and total profit for all items, assuming a profit margin of 20%. The program should then display the expected profit on each item and total expected profit of all items.

12. Develop a problem solution diagram and a class diagram for the inventory problem in problem 11.

Most Difficult

13. Code a solution to the banking problem using the algorithms you developed in problem 9 and the class diagram you developed in problem 10. Look at the coded solutions given in the case studies in this chapter in order to develop your code.

14. Code a solution to the inventory problem using the algorithms you developed in problem 11 and the class diagram you developed in problem 12. Look at the code solutions given in the case studies in this chapter in order to develop your code.

3

Working with Data—Types, Classes, Objects, and I/O

OBJECTIVES

When you are finished with this chapter, you should have a good understanding of the following:

- The concepts of data abstraction and abstract data types (ADTs)
- The concept of object behavior
- The relationship between a class and its objects
- Methods and their use in Java programs
- The primitive data types in Java
- How to create constants and variables in a Java program
- How to code a programmer defined class and create objects for it
- How to use the *StauglO* class for GUI I/O
- How to use the *NumberFormat* class for currency formatting
- The purpose of an exception handler routine
- Console versus windows I/O

Introduction

You are now ready to begin learning the building blocks of the Java language. The Java language is what is called an ***object-oriented language***. Object-oriented programming (OOP) is built around ***classes*** and ***objects*** that model real-world entities in a more natural way than do procedural languages, such as C, BASIC, and COBOL. By natural we mean that OOP allows you to construct programs the way we humans tend to think about things in terms of their characteristics and behavior.

For example, we tend to classify real-world entities such as vehicles, airplanes, ATM machines, and so on. We learn about such things by studying their *characteristics* and *behavior*. Take a class of vehicles, for example. All vehicles have certain characteristics, or *attributes*, such as engines, wheels, transmissions, and so on. Furthermore, all vehicles exhibit *behavior*, like acceleration, deceleration (braking), and turning. In other words, we have a general abstract impression of a vehicle through its attributes and behavior. This abstract model of a vehicle hides all the "nuts and bolts" that are contained in the vehicle. As a result, we think of the vehicle in terms of its attributes and behavior rather than its nuts and bolts, even though a real-world vehicle could not exist without the nuts and bolts. How do objects relate to classes? Well, your car is an example, or instance, of the vehicle class. It possesses all the attributes and behavior of any vehicle but is an example of a specific vehicle. Likewise, in OOP, we create a class that describes the general attributes and behavior of a programming entity, then create objects of the class that will be actually manipulated within the program, just as your car is the thing that you actually drive, not your general abstract notion of a vehicle. You will begin learning about classes and objects in this chapter.

You will get your first exposure to the details of the Java language in this chapter as you learn about the various types of data contained in the Java language. *Data* is any information that must be processed by the Java program. However, before Java can process any information, it must know with what type of data it is dealing. As a result, any information processed by Java must be categorized into one of the legal *data types* defined for Java.

The *primitive data types* that you will learn about in this chapter are the *integer, floating-point, character*, and *Boolean* data types. It is important that you understand this idea of data classification because it is one of the most important concepts in any language. Once you learn the general characteristics and behavior of each data type, you will learn how to create constants and variables for use in a Java program.

In addition to the primitive data types employed by Java, this chapter will introduce you to the programmer-defined data type called a *class*. Here, the term *programmer-defined* refers to classes that you, the programmer, will create. Once you learn the general characteristics of the class, you will learn how to create class objects for use in a Java program. Classes and objects are particularly important for you to learn because they allow you to develop object-oriented programs.

Finally, this chapter concludes with a section on input/output (I/O). We have developed a simple class called *StaugIO* for use with this book. The class contains several methods that provide easy and convenient ways to perform I/O operations by using windowed dialog boxes. In this book it is not necessary to use console I/O. You will be doing graphical user interface (GUI) I/O from the start.

The chapter closes with two business-oriented case studies. Make sure you go through these case studies in detail because they illustrate many of the things covered in the chapter. The case study code is available on the text CD or can be downloaded from the text Web site at *www.prenhall.com/staugaard*. It might be a good idea to download the code and experiment with it, changing things and observing what happens.

3.1   The Idea of Data Abstraction and Classes

Just as Java programs are object-oriented, so is the data that the programs operate upon. You might be thinking: "Data is data, what's all this fuss about data?" First, you must think of data as any information that the computer might perform operations on or manipulate. So, let's define a ***data object*** to be any item of information that is manipulated or operated on by the computer. Many different types of data objects exist during the execution of a program. Some of these data objects will be programmer-defined while others will be system-defined.

Now, think about the types of information, or data objects, that a computer manipulates. Of course, a computer manipulates numbers, or ***numeric data***. One of the primary uses of a computer is to perform calculations on numeric data, right? But what about ***character*** data? Isn't the computer operating with character data when it prints out your name? Thus, numeric data and character data comprise two different ***classes*** of data. What makes them different? Well, numeric data consist of numbers, whereas character data consists of alphanumeric symbols. In addition, the operations defined for these two classes of data will be different.

 An ***abstract data type,*** or ***ADT,*** describes the data attributes and behavior of its objects.

Now, what's all this ADT stuff? Well, we say that an ADT describes the data characteristics, or ***attributes***, as well as legal operations, or ***behavior***, of its objects. Remember the vehicle analogy cited in the chapter introduction. The notion of a vehicle describes things such as engines and transmissions (the attributes), as well as acceleration and deceleration (the behavior), for any actual vehicle objects such as your own car. Well, we can look at data in the same natural way. Take integers as an example of an ADT. The attributes, or characteristics, of integers are that they include all the whole number data values between minus infinity and plus infinity. Furthermore, there is a set of operations specifically defined for the integers. These operations include addition, subtraction, multiplication, and division, among others, and define the behavior of the integers. Thus, the set of whole numbers from minus infinity to plus infinity, along with their related operations, form an ADT. Any integer value can only be a whole number and only be used in an operation specifically defined for integers just as any actual vehicle looks and behaves like a vehicle. In fact, we say that the set of integers forms an ***ADT***, as shown in Figure 3-1.

You were introduced to the idea of abstraction in Chapter 2. You found that abstraction, as applied to problem solving, allowed you to concentrate on solving the problem without worrying about the details of implementing the solution. The same is true with ADTs. ADTs allow you to work with data without concern for how the data is stored inside the computer or how the data operations are performed inside the computer. This is referred to as ***data abstraction***. Let's take the addition operation as an example. Integer addition, by definition, dictates that you must supply two integer values to be added, and it will return the integer sum of the two. Do you care about the details of how the computer implements addition or how the computer represents integers in memory? Of course not! All you care about is what information needs to be

```
┌─────────────────────────────────────────┐
│              Integer ADT                 │
│                                          │
│   Operations                             │
│   ─────────                              │
│        Add()                             │
│        Subtract()                        │
│        Multiply()                        │
│        Divide()                          │
│                                          │
│   Data Attributes                        │
│   ───────────────                        │
│      Whole Numbers                       │
│      - infinity to + infinity            │
│                                          │
└─────────────────────────────────────────┘
```

FIGURE 3-1   The integers can be considered an abstract data type, where the arithmetic operations on the integers define the behavior of any objects defined for the integer class.

supplied to the addition operation to perform its job and what information is returned by the operation. In other words, all you care about is *what* must be supplied to the addition operation and *how* the operation will respond. This is called ***behavior***—how the ADT will act and react for a given operation.

The term ***behavior***, as associated with ADTs and classes, has to do with how the ADT, or class, will act and react for a given operation.

The Java language supports several different ADTs, as shown in Figure 3-2.

The primitive data types are those that are simple and are predefined to, or built into, the Java language. These consist of integer numbers and floating-point (real, decimal) numbers, as well as character data. You will learn about these primitive data types shortly.

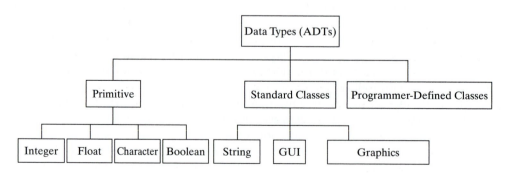

FIGURE 3-2   ADT hierarchy in the Java language.

The standard class category consists of classes that are also predefined by the Java language. These include the string, GUI, and graphics classes, among others. We say that these classes are complex data types, in the sense that they are made up of the other simpler primitive data types. As an example, your name is simply a collection of simple characters that are combined to form a *string*. Java supports strings with its standard *String* class. Other classes in this category include graphical component classes such as *Polygon*, *Rectangle*, *Button*, *Menu*, and *Checkbox*, just to mention a few. These standard classes allow you to create graphical images and windowed programs and are part of Java's *Abstract Windowing Toolkit (AWT)* package of classes. In fact, Java includes literally hundreds of built-in classes that allow you to do everything from taking a number's square root to generating graphics and windows. You will learn about many of these classes as you go through this book. One of the reasons OOP has been so popular is because of its support of **code reuse**. Code reuse allows commonly used code to be written just once, and then, using an OOP property called **inheritance**, the code can be reused and tailored to specific applications as required. In other words, code reuse eliminates the need for "reinventing the wheel" each time a common class or operation needs be coded. The standard classes in Java facilitate code reuse through inheritance.

Code reuse is an inherent feature of OOP that eliminates the need for "reinventing the wheel" each time a common class or operation needs to be coded. Code reuse is supported by the standard class library in Java.

Of particular interest is the programmer-defined class category previously shown in Figure 3-2. This category contains the **class** programming construct. (A construct is simply a programming entity.) The class provides the foundation for OOP in Java. You now know that the Java language includes standard classes via its standard class libraries. Well, the Java class allows you, the programmer, to create your own ADTs. For example, suppose that you have been hired to write an application to control an ATM machine. The ATM machine is required to handle various types of data with specific operations defined for that data, such as deposit and withdrawal. This is an ideal application for an ADT because an ADT is a collection of data along with a set of operations defined for that data. Obviously, there is no standard ATM machine ADT built into the Java language. However, the Java class allows you to build your own ATM ADT that will define all the data attributes and behavior associated with an ATM machine.

A Java class is composed of primitive data types. In addition, classes include methods that operate on the class data. Recall that a method is a procedure in Java usually associated with an algorithm of some kind. The data of the class provides the characteristics, or attributes, of the class, while the methods define the operations, or behavior, of the class. Thus, the Java class is ideal for implementing ADTs because it can be used to define ADT attributes and behavior.

A **class** in Java is a programming unit, or construct, that allows you to build your own ADTs. Classes contain data to provide the ADT attributes and methods to provide the ADT behavior.

QUICK CHECK

1. A(n) _____ describes the data attributes and behavior of its objects.
2. Classes that are predefined within a programming language are called _____ classes.
3. What is an ADT?
4. The three major data type categories in the Java programming language are the _____, _____, and _____ categories.
5. What is meant by the term *behavior* as applied to classes and ADTs?
6. What is a method?
7. Why is the Java class ideal for implementing your own ADTs?

3.2   Primitive Data Types in Java

Recall that primitive data types are built into the Java language. This built-in feature simply means that the Java compiler recognizes any legal data values contained in a primitive type. There are four primitive types of data that we need to discuss: *integer*, *floating-point, character*, and *Boolean*.

The Integer Types

As you know, integers are whole numbers. They may be positive, negative, or zero. In a math course, you most likely learned that there are no theoretical limits to the integers. They can range from minus infinity ($-\infty$) to plus infinity ($+\infty$). However, there are practical limits in the real world of computers. In Java, the largest and smallest possible integer values depend on the particular type of integer that is being used. So, you're thinking that integers are integers; how can there be different types of integers? Well, the Java language defines four separate integer types that define four separate ranges for integer data. They are: `byte`, `short`, `int`, and `long`. As you can see from Table 3-1, each integer type defines a legal range of integer values.

> The **range** of a data type specifies the largest and smallest values that can be stored for that type.

You might be wondering why there are different types of integers. Why not just define one type that will provide enough range for most applications? For instance, why not use the `long` type all the time because it provides the largest range of values? Well, each of the preceding integer types employs a predefined number of memory

TABLE 3-1   Java Integer Types and Corresponding Ranges

Integer Type	Range	Bytes
byte	−128 to +127	1
short	−32768 to +32767	2
int	−2147483648 to +2147483647	4
long	−9223372036854775808 to +9223372036854775807	8

bytes to represent an integer value. For example, `int` requires 4 bytes of memory to represent a value, and `long` requires twice as many, or 8 bytes, to represent a value. Thus, it takes twice as much memory space to represent `long` integers as it does `int` integers. Therefore, the idea is to use the type of integer that has enough range to satisfy a given application. For most applications, `int` will do the job and provide for efficient execution and memory utilization. In this text, we will always use `int`, unless we know we need a `long` to store a very big integer. The `byte` and `short` integer types are for more advanced programmers who will know best when to use them.

Example 3-1

Which of the following are *not* legal `short` integer values according to Table 3-1?

a. +35
b. 35
c. −247
d. 0
e. 3.14
f. 32,767
g. 32768

Solution

The values in a, b, c, and d are all legal `short` values in Java, because they are all whole numbers within the defined range of `short`. Notice that +35 and 35 are both legal representations of the integer value 35. The values in e, f, and g are not legal `short` values in Java. The value 3.14 is not an integer because it is not a whole number. The value 32,767 is an integer within the predefined range but is not legal in Java because it contains a comma. Commas are not allowed as part of numeric values in Java. Finally, the value 32768 is not a legal `short` value in Java, because it is outside the predefined `short` range.

 ## THINK!

You must be especially aware of the integer range limits imposed by Java when performing integer calculations within your Java programs. For example, multiplying two integers could easily produce an integer result beyond a given range, resulting in an incorrect result. This is called an ***overflow*** condition. Depending on where it occurs, an overflow condition often does not generate an error message during program compiling or execution. Even if no overflow error message is generated, the operation will always produce an incorrect result, commonly referred to as garbage.

Example 3-2

Which of the following `short` operations will generate an overflow condition in Java? (Use Table 3-1 to determine the legal `short` range, and assume that the ∗ symbol means multiplication and the / symbol means division.)

a. 32 ∗ 1000
b. 100 ∗ 1000

Solution

a. 32 * 1000 = 32000, which is within the predefined short range. No overflow condition exists.

b. 100 * 1000 = 100000, which is outside the predefined short range. The overflow condition will result in an incorrect integer result.

One final point: You probably have noticed that the word short is set in dark blue type. Such a word in Java is called a ***keyword***. Keywords have a specific meaning to the Java compiler and are used to perform a specific task. You cannot use a keyword for anything other than the specific operation for which it is defined. Java contains about 60 keywords, including short. See the quick reference on the inside of the back cover for a complete list of the Java keywords. You will learn about other keywords in subsequent chapters. In any event, all keywords will be printed in dark blue type in this book so that you can recognize them easily.

 A ***keyword*** is a word that has specific meaning to the Java compiler and cannot be used for anything other than the specific operation for which it is defined. In this text, keywords will be printed in dark blue type so that you can recognize them easily.

The Floating-Point Types

Floating-point data values include all the whole number integers as well as any value between two whole numbers that must be represented using a decimal point. Examples include the following:

$$-2.56$$
$$1.414$$
$$-3.0$$

All of the foregoing values have been written using ***fixed decimal point*** notation. Fixed decimal point notation requires a sign, followed by an unsigned integer, followed by a decimal point, followed by another unsigned integer. This format is as follows:

FIXED DECIMAL FORMAT FOR A FLOATING-POINT VALUE

(+ or - sign)(integer).(integer)

Another way to represent a very large or a very small floating-point value is with scientific notation, called ***exponential format***. With this notation, the floating-point value is written as a decimal-point value multiplied by a power of 10. The general format is as follows:

EXPONENTIAL FORMAT FOR A FLOATING-POINT VALUE

*(+ or - sign)(decimal-point value)**e**(exponent value)*

In both the foregoing formats, the leading + sign is optional if the value is positive. Examples of floating-point values using exponential format include 1.32e3, 0.45e–6, and −35.02e−4.

Here, the letter *e* means "times 10 to the power of." The letter *e* is used because there is no provision on a standard computer keyboard to type an above-the-line exponential value. Again, the + sign is optional for both the decimal point value and the exponential value when they are positive.

Example 3-3

Convert the following exponential values to fixed decimal values.

   a. 1.32e3

   b. 0.45e−6

   c. −35.02e−4

   d. −1.333e7

Solution

   a. $1.32\text{e}3 = 1.32 \times 10^3 = 1320.0$

   b. $0.45\text{e}{-}6 = 0.45 \times 10^{-6} = 0.00000045$

   c. $-35.02\text{e}{-}4 = -35.02 \times 10^{-4} = -0.003502$

   d. $-1.333\text{e}7 = -1.333 \times 10^7 = -13330000.0$

You might be wondering if there is any practical limit to the range of floating-point values that can be used in Java. As with integers, Java defines different types of floating-point data that dictate different legal value ranges. The floating-point types defined by Java are summarized in Table 3-2.

The greater the value range, the greater precision you will get when using floating-point values. However, as you can see from Table 3-2, it costs you more memory space to achieve greater precision when using a floating-point type. This might be a factor in small embedded systems where memory is limited. Again, the application will dictate the required precision, which, in turn, dictates which floating-point type to use. For most applications, we will use `double` to assure the proper precision.

The **precision** of a floating-point value is a measure of how many significant digits are used to store the value.

TABLE 3-2   Floating-Point Types and Corresponding Ranges in Java

Float Type	Range	Bytes
float	Roughly $\pm 3.40282347 \times 10^{\pm 38}$ (7 significant digits)	4
double	Roughly $\pm 1.79769313 \times 10^{\pm 308}$ (15 significant digits)	8

Example 3-4

In data communications and networks, you often see quantities expressed using the prefixes in Table 3-3.

TABLE 3-3 Common Prefixes Used in Data Communications and Networks

Prefix	Symbol	Meaning
pico	p	10^{-12}
nano	n	10^{-9}
micro	μ	10^{-6}
milli	m	10^{-3}
kilo	k	10^{3}
mega	M	10^{6}
giga	G	10^{9}

Given the following quantities:

220 picoseconds (ps)
1 kilohertz (kHz)
10 megahertz (MHz)
1.25 milliseconds (ms)
25.3 microseconds (µs)
300 nanoseconds (ns)

a. Express each of the listed quantities in exponential form.
b. Express each of the listed quantities in fixed decimal form.

Solution

a. To express in exponential form, you simply convert the prefix to its respective power of 10 using Table 3-3. Then, use exponential notation to write the value, like this:

220 ps = 220e−12 second
1 kHz = 1e3 hertz
10 MHz = 10e6 hertz
1.25 ms = 1.25e−3 second
25.3 µs = 25.3e−6 second
300 ns = 300e−9 second

b. To express each in its fixed decimal form, simply move the decimal point according to the exponent value.

220 ps = 220e−12 second = 0.000000000220 second
1 kHz = 1e3 hertz = 1000.0 hertz
10 MHz = 10e6 hertz = 10000000.0 hertz

$$1.25 \text{ ms} = 1.25\text{e}-3 \text{ second} = 0.00125 \text{ second}$$
$$25.3 \text{ μs} = 25.3\text{e}-6 \text{ second} = 0.0000253 \text{ second}$$
$$300 \text{ ns} = 300\text{e}-9 \text{ second} = 0.000000300 \text{ second}$$

Example 3-5

Java includes several ***standard methods*** that you can call upon to perform specific operations.

A ***standard method*** is a predefined operation that the Java compiler will recognize and evaluate to return a result.

One such method is the *sqrt()* method. The *sqrt()* method is part of the built-in *Math* class in Java and is used to find the square root of a floating-point number. As an example, execution of *Math.sqrt(2)* will return the value 1.414. Notice that the *Math* class *calls* the *sqrt()* method using the dot, •, operator. Now, given the standard *sqrt()* method, determine the result of the following operations:

a. `Math.sqrt(3.5)`
b. `Math.sqrt(-25)`
c. `Math.sqrt(4e-20)`

Solution

a. `Math.sqrt(3.5)=1.87`
b. `Math.sqrt(-25)` is imaginary and will generate a run-time error when encountered during a program execution.
c. `Math.sqrt(4e-20)=2e-10`

The Character Type

All of the symbols on your computer keyboard are characters. This includes all the upper and lowercase alphabetic characters, as well as the punctuation, numbers, control keys, and special symbols. Java employs the *Unicode* character code to represent characters inside the computer. Some of the more common codes are given in Table 3-4. As you can see from the table, each character has a unique numeric representation code because, in order for the CPU to work with character data, the individual characters must be converted to a numeric (actually, binary) code. Thus the character type is really an integer type. When you press a character on the keyboard, the CPU "sees" the binary representation of that character, not the character itself. Table 3-4 provides decimal equivalents of the Unicode characters. The table shows that there are ***printable*** as well as ***non-printable*** characters. Printable characters are the ones that you can see, while non-printable characters are the ones that you cannot see that are used for formatting and communications control purposes. The developers of Java decided to go with the Unicode character code because it is an international standard and is used to represent characters of many different languages. Unicode is a 2-byte code where the first 128 values of code represent the common ASCII character codes used in the U.S., Canada, and the U.K.

Example 3-6

Using Table 3-4, look up the decimal code for each of the following characters.

a.   'A'
b.   'Z'
c.   'a'
d.   'z'
e.   '#'

TABLE 3-4   Unicode/ASCII Character Code Table

Dec	Char	Dec	Char	Dec	Char	Dec	Char
0	Null	32	Space	64	@	96	`
1	Start of Header	33	!	65	A	97	a
2	Start of Text	34	"	66	B	98	b
3	End of Text	35	#	67	C	99	c
4	End of Trans	36	$	68	D	100	d
5	Enquiry	37	%	69	E	101	e
6	Acknowledge	38	&	70	F	102	f
7	Bell	39	'	71	G	103	g
8	Back Space	40	(	72	H	104	h
9	Horizontal Tab	41	)	73	I	105	i
10	Line Feed	42	*	74	J	106	j
11	Vertical Tab	43	+	75	K	107	k
12	Form Feed	44	,	76	L	108	l
13	Carriage Return	45	-	77	M	109	m
14	Shift Out	46	.	78	N	110	n
15	Shift In	47	/	79	O	111	o
16	Data Link Esc	48	0	80	P	112	p
17	Device Ctrl 1	49	1	81	Q	113	q
18	Device Ctrl 2	50	2	82	R	114	r
19	Device Ctrl 3	51	3	83	S	115	s
20	Device Ctrl 4	52	4	84	T	116	t
21	No Acknowledge	53	5	85	U	117	u
22	Sync. Idle	54	6	86	V	118	v
23	End of Block	55	7	87	W	119	w
24	Cancel	56	8	88	X	120	x
25	End of Medium	57	9	89	Y	121	y
26	Substitute	58	:	90	Z	122	z
27	Escape	59	;	91	[	123	{
28	File Separator	60	<	92	\	124		
29	Group Separator	61	=	93	]	125	}
30	Record Separator	62	>	94	^	126	~
31	Unit Separator	63	?	95	--	127	Delete

Solution

Using Table 3-4, you get the following:

a. `'A'=65`
b. `'Z'=90`
c. `'a'=97`
d. `'z'=122`
e. `'#'=35`

The foregoing example points out several characteristics of character data. First, each character has a unique numeric representation inside the computer. Because each character has a unique numeric representation, the characters are ordered, or scalar. For instance, 'A' < 'Z', because the numeric representation for 'A' (65) is less than the numeric representation for 'Z' (90). Likewise, '#' < 'a' < 'z', because 35 < 97 < 122. In general the uppercase alphabetic characters have a lower order than the lowercase alphabetic characters. Second, notice that whenever a character is specified, it is always enclosed in single quotes like this: 'a'. This is a requirement of the Java language.

Characters are stored in the machine as integer values, so you can perform arithmetic operations on character data. For instance, you can add 1 to the character 'A' and get the character 'B'. This is an example of the flexibility built into the Java language; however, *with this flexibility comes responsibility*. You must be able to predict the results you will get. Other languages, like Pascal, will not allow you to perform arithmetic operations on characters.

 **CAUTION**

Java will allow you to perform arithmetic operations on character data; however, be careful because the results can sometimes be difficult to predict. What do you get when you add the character 'A' to the character 'B' or when you multiply these two characters? If you tried to add these two characters, the computer would add their Unicode values of 65 and 66 to get a sum of 131, which is an undefined Unicode value. If you multiplied these two characters, the computer would multiply the values 65 and 66 to get a product of 4290, which might be a Unicode value for a character in some other language.

The Boolean Type

Boolean data, consisting solely of the values `true` and `false`, is the simplest type of data that can be employed in a program. Boolean data play an important role in a program's ability to make decisions because all program decisions are Boolean decisions, based on whether a given condition is `true` or `false`. You will learn this later when we discuss program decision making and iteration in Chapters 5 and 6.

Java specifies a Boolean data type called `boolean`. This type has two values, `true` and `false`. The `boolean` type is a scalar type, meaning that the elements within the type are ordered. By definition, `false` is defined to be less than `true`. The words `boolean`, `true`, and `false` are keywords and, therefore, cannot be used for any other purpose in a program.

QUICK CHECK

1. What is the range of values that can be provided via the standard `int` type?

2. What type of error occurs when, as a result of a calculation, a value exceeds its predefined range?

3. The two ways that floating-point values can be represented in a Java program are using either _____ or _____ format.

4. Which is greater, the character 'a' or the character 'z'?

5. Which is greater, the character 'a' or the character 'A'?

6. How many bytes of storage are required by the string "The United States of America"?

7. The primitive type that has only two values, `true` and `false`, is the _____ type.

3.3   Defining Constants, Variables, and String Objects

From mathematics, you know that a **constant** is a value that never changes, thereby remaining a fixed value. A common example is the constant *pi* (π). Here, the Greek symbol π is used to represent a floating-point value of approximately 3.14159. This value of π never changes, thus remaining constant regardless of where and how it might be used in a calculation.

> A **constant** is a data item that is defined when a program is coded and cannot change during program execution.

On the other hand, a **variable** is something that can take on different values. In mathematics, the symbols x and y are often used to denote variables. Using the equation $y = 3x + 2$, you can substitute different values of x to generate different values of y. Thus, the values of x and y in the equation are variable.

> A **variable** is a data item that is defined when a program is coded and used during program execution to store values. The value of a variable often changes during program execution, thereby making it "variable."

The values of variables are stored in main working memory of a computer for later use within a program. Each variable has a symbolic name, or **identifier**, that locates its value in memory. This idea is illustrated in Figure 3-3. The memory contents located by the identifiers *age*, *studentID*, and *gpa* might change during the execution of the program. As a result, these symbols are called variables.

All constants and variables used in a Java program must be defined prior to their use in the program. The reason that we must define constants and variables in a language is twofold. First, the compiler must know the value of a constant before it is used and must reserve memory locations to store variables. Second, the compiler must know the data type of the constants and variables so that it knows their attributes and behavior. Now, let's see how constants and variables are defined in Java.

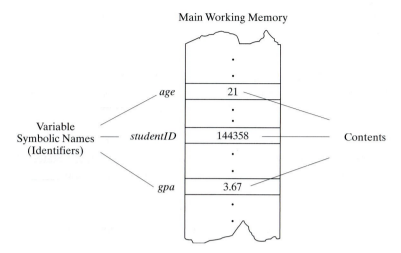

Main Working Memory

Variable
Symbolic Names
(Identifiers)

age

studentID

gpa

21

144358

3.67

Contents

FIGURE 3-3   Each variable has a symbolic name, or identifier, that locates its value in memory.

Defining Constants

To define a constant, you must use the keyword `final`, like this:

CONSTANT DEFINITION FORMAT

`final` *data type constant identifier* = *constant value;*

First, a word about how syntax will be formatted in this text. Words or symbols that must appear as part of the syntax will be shown outright in bold, such as the word `final` and the symbol = in the foregoing format box. If the word is a keyword, it will be shown in dark blue, like the word `final`. Those things that you must specify as a programmer, such as *data type, constant identifier,* and *constant value* in the foregoing format box, will be shown in italics.

Now, let's look at the syntax required to define a constant. The definition begins with the keyword `final`. The keyword `final` is used to signify that the value of the constant can never change within the course of the program execution. In other words, its value is "final." Next, you must specify the primitive data type of the constant, followed by a constant identifier. The identifier is the name of the constant that will be replaced by the constant value during compile time. By convention, you should always code your constant identifiers in capital letters. This way, it is clearer that no statement should attempt to alter the constant value. An equals sign (=) is used to separate the constant identifier from its defined value. Finally, each constant definition must end with a semicolon.

Example 3-7

Suppose you wish to use the price of 37 cents for a first-class postage stamp in your Java program. In addition, your program must calculate the sales tax required for a given sales item based on a sales tax rate of 7 percent. Define appropriate constants to represent the price of a stamp and the sales tax rate.

Solution

By using the format given before, the postage price and sales tax rate are defined as follows:

```
final double POSTAGE = 0.37;
final double TAX_RATE = 0.07;
```

With these definitions, you would simply use the words *POSTAGE* and *TAX_RATE* when performing calculations within the program. For instance, to find the total price of a sales item, you would write the expression:

```
totalPrice = price + (price * TAX_RATE);
```

When the program is compiled, the compiler simply substitutes the constant value 0.07 for the *TAX_RATE* identifier. What about the identifiers *price* and *totalPrice* in this expression? Are these constants or variables? You're right—they are both variables, because their values will change depending on the price of the item. What data type must *price* and *totalPrice* be? In other words, what type of data is required for this application: integer, floating-point, or character? Right again—floating-point, because you must provide for decimal quantities to allow for dollars and cents. Thus, *price* and *totalPrice* must be defined as floating-point variables. You will find out how to do this shortly.

 STYLE TIP

Always code your constant identifiers in all caps so that they are easily identified as constants within your program. Always code variable identifiers in lowercase. For a multiword variable identifier, the first letter of the first word should be lowercase, and the first letter of each succeeding word should be uppercase. For example, the two foregoing variable identifiers were *totalPrice* and *price*. This is the standard Java convention for variable identifiers.

Notice also in Example 3-7 that the constant identifier *TAX_RATE* is made up of two words, *TAX* and *RATE*. The Java compiler will not allow you to separate multiword identifiers using spaces. Thus, we have chosen to separate the two words with the underscore symbol (_). Also, notice that the variable identifier *totalPrice* is made up of two words. Here, the two words are run together with the first letter of the second word capitalized. These two techniques will be used throughout this book when using multiword identifiers:

1. Uppercase for constant identifiers, separating words within a multiword identifier with the underscore symbol, _.
2. Lowercase for variable identifiers, capitalizing the first letter of each word in a multiword identifier, except for the first word.

Here are some other rules that govern the use of identifiers in the Java language:

- Identifiers can contain the letters *a* to *z*, *A* to *Z*, the digits 0 to 9, and the underscore symbol, _. However, identifiers cannot begin with a digit (0 – 9).
- No spaces or punctuation, except the underscore symbol, _, are allowed.

- Identifiers in Java are *case-sensitive*. Thus, the identifiers *TAX*, *Tax*, and *tax* are seen as three unique identifiers by the compiler.

You are probably wondering why we should define constants using identifiers. Why not just insert the constant value into the expression whenever it is needed, like this:

```
totalPrice = price + (price * 0.07);
```

Have you ever known postage or sales tax rates to change? Of course you have! You might say that these types of "constants" are not constant forever. So, when using constants such as these that are subject to change in the future, it is much easier to define them in one single place. Then if they need to be changed, you only have to make a single change in your program. Otherwise, a change must be made in each place that you use the constant within the program.

Defining Variables

Before you can use a variable in a Java program, it must be defined. When you define a variable, the compiler reserves a location inside the computer memory for the variable value. When you define a variable, you are telling Java what type of data you will be storing for the variable. To define a variable, you must specify its data type, its name, and an optional initializing value. Here's the format:

VARIABLE DEFINITION FORMAT

```
data type identifier = optional initializing value;
```

The foregoing format requires that the variable data type be listed first. The data type is followed by the variable identifier, or name. The first word in a variable name should begin with a lowercase letter, with all subsequent words beginning with an uppercase letter. You can terminate the definition at this point with a semicolon, or you can add an optional equals symbol (=) followed by an initializing value, and then the semicolon to terminate the definition.

When defining constants and variables, your first task is to determine what type of data the constant or variable will be. The decision tree in Figure 3-4 should help you with this task. First, decide whether the constant or variable should be a numeric value, character value, or Boolean value. Sometimes deciding between numeric and character can be tricky. For example, should your student number be numeric or character? What about your age? What about your social security number or phone number? Well, a good rule of thumb is that if a value will never be added to, subtracted from, multiplied, or divided, then designate it as a character string. Thus, your student number, social security number, and phone number should be defined as strings. However, your age should be a numeric value, since we all get older, right? If you decide that the constant or variable must be numeric, then you need to decide if it should be an integer (whole number) or floating-point (decimal number) value. Your age would most likely be an integer, while your gpa would be a floating-point value. If an integer, then you must

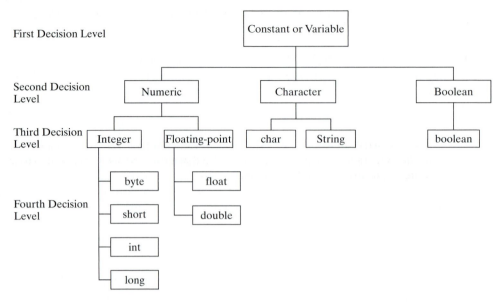

FIGURE 3-4   A decision tree to determine the data type of a constant or variable.

decide between byte, short, int, or long. If a floating-point value, you must decide between float and double. That's all there is to it!

 ## PROGRAMMING NOTE

You should initialize variables when they are defined. Generally, numeric variables will be initialized to the value 0 or 1, and character variables will be initialized with a space.

Example 3-8

Suppose you were asked to write a Java program to calculate the part-time hourly pay for an
employee, given his/her rate of hourly pay and number of hours worked over a given time
period. Define the necessary variables that will be used in the program for the calculation.

Solution

To solve this problem, you simply multiply the hourly rate by the number of hours
worked like this:

$p = h \times r$
where
       p is the pay, in dollars and cents.
       r is the hourly rate of pay, in dollars and cents.
       h is the number of hours worked.

Here, the variable identifiers are given to be p, r, and h. Now, the question is: What
data type must these variables belong to? You know that p, r, and h will be used to
represent numeric data, so your decision as to their type reduces to two choices:

integer or floating-point. If you define *p*, *r*, and *h* as integers, you will be limited to using whole number values for these variables within your program; however, this might create a problem because pay, rate of pay, and hourly values often are decimal values. So, let's define them as double floating-point variables, like this:

```
double p = 0.0;  //GROSS PAY
double r = 0.0;  //HOURLY RATE OF PAY
double h = 0.0;  //NUMBER OF HOURS WORKED
```

Notice that each variable is defined as a double floating-point type and initialized to the value 0.0. Of course, because these are variables their values will change during the execution of the program. Notice also that each variable is commented to indicate its purpose within the program.

 STYLE TIP

Java allows identifiers, or names, to be any length, where the first 32 characters are significant. Thus, your programs will become much more readable and self-documenting if you use words, rather than letters and symbols, to represent constants and variables. For instance, the variable definition in Example 3-8 would be much more readable to a user if you were to define pay, rate of pay, and hours worked like this:

```
double grossPay = 0.0;     //GROSS PAY
double hourlyRate = 0.0;   //HOURLY RATE OF PAY
double hoursWorked = 0.0;  //NUMBER OF HOURS WORKED
```

By using this definition, the actual words (*grossPay*, *hourlyRate*, and *hoursWorked*) would be used within your program when calculating payroll. So, the statement required to calculate the gross pay would appear in your program as follows:

```
grossPay = hourlyRate * hoursWorked;
```

Notice the use of the equals symbol (=) in this statement. This is the way that you must *set*, or *assign*, values in Java. Also, notice the use of the star symbol (*) for multiplication.

 CAUTION

When using names as variable identifiers, you cannot use any punctuation within the name. For instance, using the name *total Sales* to represent total sales is an illegal identifier in Java because of the space between the two words *total* and *Sales*. The name *total-Sales* is also illegal because of the hyphen. Acceptable identifiers would be *totalSales* or *total_Sales*. Notice that variable identifiers begin with a lowercase letter, then each subsequent word that makes up the identifier begins with an uppercase letter. The words are often run together to form a single word identifier, without using the underscore symbol. Java rejects spaces within an identifier because a space is seen as separating two identifiers and not as part of a single identifier.

Example 3-9

You must write a program to calculate the sales tax of an item using a sales tax rate of 7 percent. Define the appropriate constants and variables.

Solution

First, you must decide what identifiers to use. Always use word identifiers that best describe the related constant or variable. Let's use the word *salesTax* to identify the resulting calculation, the word *price* to identify the cost of the item, and the word *TAX_RATE* to identify the sales tax rate. So, using these identifiers, the sales tax calculation would be

```
salesTax = price * TAX_RATE;
```

Now, the question is: Which of these are variables and which are constants? Obviously, *salesTax* and *price* are variables, because they will change depending on the cost of the item. However, the *TAX_RATE* will be a constant, regardless of the cost of the item, and will not likely change during the execution of the program. So, we will define *salesTax* and *price* as variables and *TAX_RATE* as a constant, like this:

```
final double TAX_RATE = 0.07;      //CURRENT SALES TAX RATE
double price = 0.0;                //PRICE OF AN ITEM
double salesTax = 0.0;             //SALES TAX OF AN ITEM
```

Notice that both the variables are defined as double floating-point, because both will be decimal values. Suppose that you were to define the tax rate as a variable rather than a constant and initialize it to the value 0.07, like this:

```
double taxRate = 0.07;
```

There is no problem with this definition. The compiler will reserve storage for the variable *taxRate* and place the initial value of 0.07 at this storage location. However, the value of *taxRate* could be changed by the program, whereas it could not be changed if defined as a constant. Would this be desirable? Probably not, since the sales tax rate would not likely change during the course of the program execution.

Example 3-10

Place the variables and constants you defined in Example 3-9 into a Java class.

Solution

In Example 3-9, we used the following statement to calculate the sales tax:

```
salesTax = price * TAX_RATE;
```

where *salesTax* and *price* were defined as floating-point variables and *TAX_RATE* was defined as a constant with a value of 0.07.

Putting this information into a Java class, you get the following:

```
/****************************************************************
THIS CLASS WILL CALCULATE AND STORE THE SALES TAX OF A SALES ITEM
****************************************************************/

class SalesTax
{//BEGIN SalesTax CLASS

    //DEFINE CONSTANT
    private final double TAX_RATE = 0.07;   //CURRENT SALES TAX RATE
```

```
//DEFINE VARIABLES
private double price = 0.0;          //PRICE OF AN ITEM
private double salesTax = 0.0;       //SALES TAX OF AN ITEM

//calculateTax() METHOD
public void calculateTax()
{
  price = 1.95;                      //ASSIGN $1.95 TO price
  salesTax = price * TAX_RATE;       //CALCULATE TAX
}//END calculateTax()
}//END SalesTax CLASS
```

This simple class will calculate the sales tax of an item, given the item price of $1.95. The class is very readable, and everything used within the class is clearly defined. We decided to name this class *SalesTax*. Very appropriate, don't you think? Within the class you first find that the *TAX_RATE* constant is defined to be 0.07. Constants should always be defined after the opening brace of the class. Notice that the constant and variables are defined as `private` class members and the calculations are made within a `public` class method called *calculateTax()*. Most of the time, you will define your constants and variables as `private` and your methods as `public` inside of a programmer-defined class. The reason why variables are `private` and methods are `public` will be discussed later in this book.

Note that the class statements are always indented two or three spaces within the *SalesTax* class block. Such indentation is permissible because Java ignores spaces. In addition, the indentation clearly shows that the statements are part of the class block. Indentation is used to "set off" a block of code so that it is not confused with other blocks of code. We will make extensive use of indentation within our Java programs to make them easier to read and understand. Also, notice the use of commenting within the code. You always want to make liberal use of meaningful comments in order to self-document the code.

Example 3-11

Choose an appropriate name and define a variable that could be used to represent a day of the week. Assume that a day of the week is represented by the first letter of each day.

Solution

Let's pick a meaningful variable identifier, such as *dayOfWeek*. Now, because a day of the week will be represented by the first letter of a given day, the variable must be of the character data type. When defining character variables, you must use the keyword `char` in the variable definition, as follows:

```
char dayOfWeek = ' ';    //SINGLE CHARACTER FOR A DAY OF THE WEEK
                         //INITIALIZED WITH A SPACE
```

Notice that the character variable is initialized with a space character. To code a space character, simply type a single quote, a space, and then another single quote.

Do you see any problems with the definition in Example 3-11? There are no syntax errors, and it is perfectly legal as far as Java is concerned. But are there any problems associated with the usage of this variable? A character variable is limited to representing a *single* character at a given time. This is why each day of the week must be represented by a single letter. However, using the first letter of each day creates a problem. Does an 'S' represent Saturday or Sunday? Likewise, does a 'T' mean Tuesday or Thursday? The solution to this dilemma is found in the use of strings, the topic of the next section.

Boolean Variables   Variables can be defined for the `boolean` data type just as you define any other variable—by listing its data type followed by the variable identifier. Here's an example that illustrates this idea.

Example 3-12

Define a `boolean` variable called *decision* for use in a decision-making operation. Initialize the variable with a `boolean` value of `false`.

Solution

Boolean variables are often used in a program for decision-making operations. A `boolean` variable, called *decision*, can be defined for such a purpose as follows:

```
boolean decision = false;
```

With this definition, the variable *decision* can be used in a program, taking on the values of `true` or `false` as required by the program logic.

String Objects

A *string* is simply a collection of characters. Examples of strings include your name, address, and phone number, as well as the sentence you are now reading.

Strings in Java are always enclosed in double quotes, like this: "Java". Recall that individual characters are enclosed in single quotes. Thus, 'J' denotes an individual character, whereas "J" denotes a string of one character. Some methods, like *writeInfo()* require a string argument. If you want to display a single character, you would have to code it as a string, like this: *writeInfo("A")*.

A string is not a primitive data type in Java because, by definition, a string is a complex data type formed by combining simpler data types, namely characters. Also, there are special operations, or methods, defined for the specific purpose of manipulating strings. Doesn't this sound like a class (data combined with operations defined for that data)? For this reason, Java provides a *String* class that defines a string, (a collection of characters) as well as the operations, or methods, that can be used on a string.

 PROGRAMMING TIP

Double quotes around a number, such as "1234", indicate a string of characters and *not* numeric data. In fact, the string "1234" requires 8 bytes of storage, whereas the `int` 1234 requires only 4 bytes of storage. In addition, arithmetic operations cannot be performed on the string "1234". For these reasons, numeric data should be represented using a numeric type and not the *String* class.

Recall that a class describes the attributes (characteristics) and behavior (operations) for its objects. In other words, a class is a blueprint for any objects of the class. You *do not* manipulate a class within your program. Instead, you define an object of a given class, and then manipulate the object within your program, just as you define a variable of a primitive data type and manipulate the variable within your program.

To define an object of the *String* class, you simply list the class name, *String*, followed by a space, then the object name, followed by an = symbol, followed by an initializing string value within double quotes, like this:

String OBJECT DEFINITION FORMAT

String object name = "initializing string";

For example, suppose you need to create three string objects, one for your name, one for your address, and one for your phone number. Here is how these objects could be created:

```
String myName = "Andrew C. Staugaard, Jr.";
String myAddress = "999 Code Road, Java City, USA";
String myPhoneNumber = "(012)345-6789";
```

These definitions tell Java that *myName*, *myAddress*, and *myPhone* are objects of the *String* class. In addition, each object is initialized with a string value. Could the string values of these objects be changed? Of course they could, because each object is a variable object. Notice also that the string values are enclosed within double quotation marks.

Example 3-13

Using the character variable definition back in Example 3-12 presents a usage problem when representing a day of the week, because a character variable can only represent a single character at a time. Solve this problem by using a string object definition.

Solution

A string object can be used to represent any number of consecutive characters. So why not define *dayOfWeek* as a string object, like this:

```
String dayOfWeek = " ";   //DAY OF THE WEEK
```

With this definition, the object *dayOfWeek* can be used to represent the entire day of the week word ("Sunday," "Monday," "Tuesday," etc.). Notice that the string object is initialized with an empty string using empty double quotation marks. It is always good practice to initialize variables and objects when they are defined. Of course, during the execution of the program, an actual string value can be stored in *dayOfWeek* using an *assignment* statement, like this:

```
dayOfWeek = "Friday";
```

The assignment stores the string "*Friday*" in memory for the value of the *dayOfWeek* string object.

String Methods

Since *String* is a class, it includes operations, or methods, that are specifically written to manipulate string data. As a result, any object of the *String* class can call upon one of these methods to manipulate or provide information about its string. Some of the methods available in the *String* class are summarized in Table 3-5.

As you have seen before, a method is called with its object by placing a dot between the object name and the method. For example, suppose that you wish to calculate the length of a string in your program. Here is a code segment that will accomplish this task:

```
int stringLength = 0;
String teacher = "Grace Hopper";
stringLength = teacher.length();
```

Notice that our *teacher* string object is calling the *length()* method via the dot operator. This code would simply cause the length of the *teacher* string, 12, to be assigned to the integer variable, *stringLength*.

TABLE 3-5   String Methods

Method	Description	Use of
s1.compareTo(s2)	Returns 0 if s1 equals s2, else returns a negative value if s1 is less than s2 and a positive value if s1 is greater than s2.	String s1 = "Hello World"; String s2 = "hello world"; s1.compareTo(s2) returns a negative value
s1.equals(s2)	Returns **true** if s1 equals s2, else returns **false**.	String s1 = "Hello World"; String s2 = "hello world"; s1.equals(s2) returns **false**
s1.equalsIgnoreCase(s2)	Returns **true** if s1 equals s2, else returns **false**. Ignores case.	String s1 = "Hello World"; String s2 = "hello world"; s1.equalsIgnoreCase(s2) returns **true**
s.length()	Returns the length of s.	String s = "Hello World"; s.length() returns 11
s.toLowerCase()	Returns s with all characters converted to lowercase.	String s = "Hello World"; s.toLowerCase() returns "hello world"
s.toUpperCase()	Returns s with all characters converted to uppercase.	String s = "Hello World"; s.toUpperCase() returns "HELLO WORLD"
s.trim()	Returns s with leading and trailing whitespace removed.	String s = " Hello World "; s.trim() returns "Hello World"

Example 3-14

Write a Java code segment that will convert each of the *myName*, *myAddress*, and *myPhone* strings defined earlier to all uppercase characters.

Solution

To convert each string to uppercase, each string object must call the *toUpperCase()* method from Table 3-5. This can be done by calling the method and assigning the resulting uppercase string back to the string object like this:

```
myName = myName.toUpperCase();
myAddress = myAddress.toUpperCase();
myPhone = myPhone.toUpperCase();
```

 THINK!

Remember that Java is case-sensitive. Thus, using *ToUpperCase()* in place of *toUpperCase()* in the above code will cause a compile-time error.

You will have many occasions to manipulate strings within your Java programs using the string methods shown in Table 3-5. For now, just review each method in the table so that you get an idea of what can be done with strings. We will demonstrate the use of many of these methods as the need arises throughout the remainder of the book.

 QUICK CHECK

1. What are two reasons for defining constants and variables in a Java program?
2. Define a constant called *PERIOD* that will insert a period wherever it is referenced in a program.
3. Define a constant called *BOOK* that will insert the string: "Information Systems Programming using Java" wherever it appears in a program.
4. Define a variable called *age* that will store the age of an employee.
5. Define an object called *course* that will be initialized to a string value of "Accounting".
6. Write a statement to define a variable called *length* and set it equal to the length of the string in question 5.
7. Write a statement to convert the string in question 5 to all uppercase characters.
8. True or false: Data members of a class should be coded as `private` members.

3.4   Classes and Objects

In this section, we will take an introductory look at classes and objects. We will discuss them in depth in Chapters 8 and 9.

Classes

Earlier we defined a class as a programming unit, or construct, that allows you to build your own ADTs. Thus, we say that a class *encapsulates* the ADT attributes, or data, and behavior, or methods, into a single well-defined programming unit. You can think of a class as a model, or pattern, for its objects. If you have used a word processor, you are aware that most word processing programs include templates for business letters, personal letters, interoffice memos, press releases, and other common types of documents. The idea is to first open one of the built-in general-purpose template files when you want to generate a document such as an interoffice memo. An example of such a template is provided in Figure 3-5.

InterOffice Memo

To: Recipient

From: Sender

Date: May 16, 2003

Subject: The subject of the memo

CC:

FIGURE 3-5   A *class* can be thought of as a model, or pattern, like this memo template in a word processor.

As you can see, the template provides the accepted interoffice memo formatting, the memo type style, and any fixed information, such as headings and the date. Using this template, you fill in all the *object* information required for the memo, including the text of the memo as shown in Figure 3-6.

In other words, you provide the details that might make one memo different from another. You can think of a class as the memo template and the actual memo that you

---

InterOffice Memo

To: All Java Students

From: Prof. Andrew C. Staugaard, Jr.

Date: May 16, 2003

Subject: Classes and Objects

    This memo represents an object of the class shown in Figure 3-5. The class provides a general framework from which objects are created. It is important that you understand this concept.

CC:
    Your Instructor

FIGURE 3-6   An *object* is a particular instance, or occurrence, of a class, as this memo is an instance of the memo template of Figure 3-5.

generate as an object of that template. Different memos made from the same memo template would represent unique objects of the same class. The class template provides the framework for each of its object memos. All the object memos would have the same general format and type style defined by the class template but would have different text information defined by a given object memo. You could load in another template file, let's say for a business letter, that would represent a different class. Then using this class, you could construct different object business letters from the business letter template.

The word *class* in OOP is used to impart the notion of classification. Multiple objects defined for the same class share the fundamental framework of that class. Thus, the class is common to the set of objects defined for it. In the preceding example, the interoffice memo template defines the characteristics that are common to all interoffice memos created by the word processor. In fact, most current word processing programs employ classes and objects for this purpose. A given class provides the foundation for creating specific objects, each of which shares the general *attributes* and *behavior* of the class.

A class provides the foundation for creating specific objects, each of which share the same **attributes** and **behavior**.

As you can see from this example, classes and objects are closely related. In fact, it is difficult to discuss one without the other. The important difference is that, like an ADT, a class is only an ***abstraction***, or pattern, whereas an object is a real entity. The interoffice memo class is only an abstraction for the real memo object that can be physically created, printed, and mailed. As another example, think of a class of fish. The fish class describes the general characteristics and behavior of all fish. However, the notion of a fish only provides an abstraction of the real thing. To deal with the real thing, you must consider specific fish objects such as Charlie the tuna, my goldfish Skippy, and so on. A fish, in general, behaves as you would expect a fish to behave, but a particular *instance* of a fish has its own unique behavior and personality.

The implementation of a class consists of two types of ***members***: ***data members*** and ***method members***. Any item defined in a class is called a class ***member***. Consequently, to code a class we create data members and method members.

The Data Members

The data members of the class provide the class attributes, or characteristics. The data members of the class are the variables defined within the class. We say that these members are "private" because they are *accessible only by the method members declared for the same class*. This means that the data members can be changed only by the method members in the class.

The Method Members

The method members of the class consist of methods that often operate on the data members of the class. These methods are usually "public" because they can be accessed from outside the class.

There is nothing special about `public` member methods, except that they are used to operate on the data members of the class. The important thing to remember is that *no methods outside a given class can access the private data members of the class*.

The Class Declaration

The members of a class can be clearly seen by its declaration format as follows:

CLASS DECLARATION FORMAT

```
class ClassName
{
    //DATA MEMBERS
    private variable 1;
    private variable 2;
                •
                •
    private variable n;

    //METHOD MEMBERS
    public method 1()
    {
      //METHOD 1 STATEMENTS
    }
    public method 2()
    {
      //METHOD 2 STATEMENTS
    }
                •
                •
                •
    public method n()
    {
      //METHOD n STATEMENTS
    }
}//END CLASS
```

The declaration begins with the keyword `class`, followed by the class name. The class name should be a noun or a noun phrase that is descriptive of its purpose. The first letter of each word within the name should be capitalized. The entire class declaration is enclosed in a set of braces. Normally, the data members of the class are specified first, followed by the method members of the class. The data members of the class consist of `private` and `protected` *instance variables*. An instance variable is a variable that will be created for any given object of the class. Each instance variable is prefixed with the keyword `private` or `protected`. A `private` member of a class is visible within that class and, therefore, can only be accessed by methods within the same class. A `protected` member is used to implement *inheritance*, which is a key concept in OOP and will be covered in Chapter 9. For now, all our instance variables will be `private`. The method members of the class consist of `public` or `private` *instance methods*. An instance method is a method that will be available to any given object of the class. To declare a method as a class member, you list the method header line followed by the code for the method. Methods that can be accessed from outside the class are designated as `public`. Methods can also be `private` but then they are only accessible within the class and cannot be called outside the class. Such methods are referred to as ***utility methods***, since they are often used within the class to perform housekeeping, or utility, operations.

A `private` class member is accessible within the class only by methods of the same class. The `public` methods form the interface to the class and are accessible from outside the class. Public methods are used to manipulate and provide access to the `private` class members.

Objects

You should now have a pretty good grasp of objects. Here is a technical definition for your reference:

An **object** is an instance, or occurrence, of a given class. An object of a given class has the structure and behavior defined by the class that is common to all objects of the same class.

An object is a real thing that can be manipulated in a program. An object must be defined for a programmer-defined class to use the class, just as an object must be defined for the standard *String* class to use the class. An object defined for a class has the structure and behavior dictated by the class that is common to all objects defined for the class. You see from the foregoing definition that an object is an *instance* of a class. The word *instance* means an example or occurrence of something. If you have a class of dogs, then my dog *Randy* is an instance of a dog. The same idea applies to Java classes and objects.

Defining Objects   You define an object for a programmer-defined class using the `new` operator. When the object is defined, memory is allocated to store the object. Many different objects can be defined for a given class with each object made up of the data prescribed by the class and responding to methods defined by the class. However, the `private` member data is hidden from one object to the next, even when multiple objects are defined for the same class. Objects are usually nouns. This means that they are persons, places, or things, like a *box* object for a *Rectangle* class, a *myAccount* object for a *SavingsAccount* class, a *myMemo* object for a *Memo* class, and so on. Notice that the object names begin with a lowercase letter, while the class names begin with an uppercase letter. This will allow us to distinguish between classes and objects in our code. Now, here is the required object definition format:

FORMAT FOR DEFINING CLASS OBJECTS

```
ClassName objectName = new ClassName();
```

When defining objects for programmer-defined classes, you simply list the object name after the class name, followed by an = symbol, the keyword `new`, then the class name followed by a set of parentheses. The class name followed by a set of parentheses designates the class **constructor**. A constructor is a special class member that is used to initialize class data when an object is created. All classes must have a constructor. We will discuss constructors in detail in Chapter 8.

 A **constructor** is a special class member that is used to initialize class data when an object is created. All classes must have a constructor.

Example 3-15

Define a *square* object for a class called *Rectangle* and a *mySavings* object for a class called *SavingsAccount*.

Solution

The *square* object definition is

```
Rectangle square = new Rectangle();
```

The *mySavings* object definition is

```
SavingsAccount mySavings = new SavingsAccount();
```

Notice that the class name begins with an uppercase letter, while the object name begins with a lowercase letter. This is the accepted naming convention in Java. The constructor *always* has the same name as the class and, therefore, begins with an uppercase letter. Some objects require that you place things called *arguments* inside the parentheses of the constructor. The objects defined here do not require any constructor arguments within the parentheses. You will learn all about constructors in Chapter 8. Until then, we will define objects that do not require constructor arguments.

 ## DECLARATIONS VERSUS DEFINITIONS

The words *define* and *declare* are often used interchangeably in connection with programming languages. Actually, a declaration specifies the name and attributes of a programming entity, but does not reserve storage. On the other hand, a definition is a declaration that also reserves storage. Variables and objects are *defined* in Java, meaning that an identifier is specified and memory is reserved to store the variable or object values by the Java compiler. On the other hand, classes are *declared*. A class declaration only specifies what type of data and methods any objects defined for the class will contain. No memory is reserved until an object is actually defined for the class using the new operator. This again illustrates the idea that a class is a pattern or template for its objects, while an object is the real thing manipulated in the program.

 ## QUICK CHECK

1. What is a class?
2. How does a class differ from an object?
3. What do we mean when we say that a class defines the behavior of its objects?

4. True or false: `private` data can only be accessed from outside the class via `public` methods of the same class.

In questions 5 – 7, assume that no constructor arguments are required when the object is defined.

5. Define an object called *myAccount* for a class called *CheckingAccount*.

6. Define an object called *myPickUp* for a class called *Truck*.

7. Define an object called *myConvertible* for a class called *Automobile*.

3.5   Simple GUI I/O Using Dialog Boxes

In this section, you will begin learning the implementation details of the Java language. In particular, you will learn how to get information into and out of your system via Java objects and methods. Getting data into the system is called ***reading***, and generating data from the system is called ***writing***. You will discover how to write information to your display monitor and read information from your keyboard using a GUI (graphical user interface) dialog box. In Chapter 14, you will learn how to read and write disk files, since this requires more knowledge about classes and objects.

Armed with the knowledge gained from this section, you will be ready to write some *interactive* Java programs. By interactive, we mean programs that will interact with the user—writing user prompts and reading user input data. Make sure that you do the programming problems at the end of the chapter. You *must* get your hands dirty with some actual programming experience to learn how to program in Java.

We have developed a special class for I/O called *StaugIO*. The *StaugIO* class is contained within the *staugIO* package, which is available on the text CD or can be downloaded from the text web site. To use the *StaugIO* class, you must place the *staugIO* package folder in your working directory (see *staugIOReadMe.doc* on the text CD) and then import it into a Java program as follows:

```
import staugIO.StaugIO;
```

Then, you must create an object for the *StaugIO* class within your Java program like this:

```
StaugIO io = new StaugIO();
```

Here, we have named our object *io* for simplicity, but you can name the object anything you want.

The *StaugIO* class contains several methods for input and output that we need to discuss. These methods must be called by an object defined for the *StaugIO* class when they are needed to get user input and display information to the monitor.

Remember, the *staugIO* package is not a standard part of the Java language. It has been created specifically for this text and is available on the text CD or the text Web site at *www.prenhall.com/staugaard.* You will need to place the *staugIO* folder within your Java working directory before importing the *staugIO* package into your Java programs (see *staugIOReadMe.doc* on the text CD).

The StaugIO Output Methods

There are two methods in *StaugIO* that can be used for output: *writeInfo()* and *writeNumber()*. The *writeInfo()* method is used to write string information. To use it, you must call it with an object of the *StaugIO* class and provide it a string argument as follows:

```
io.writeInfo("Hello World!");
```

Here is what you would see when this statement is executed:

As you can see, the output information is displayed in a GUI dialog box. In the code, you see that the string to be displayed is enclosed within double quotation marks and inserted as the argument to the *writeInfo()* method. You can form a string using the concatenation operator, +. For example, the statement

```
io.writeInfo("My GPA is: " + 3.95 + " Wow!");
```

produces an output of

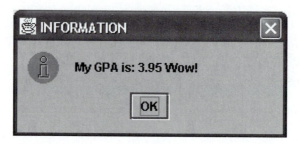

    The first output item is the string "My GPA is: ". The second item is the numeric *hard coded* value 3.95 which is *concatenated* to the first item using the + concatenation operator. Finally, the third item, " Wow!" is concatenated to the second item using the + concatenation operator. Notice the space at the end of the first string and the beginning of the second string. These spaces are necessary to provide the spacing around the hard coded value 3.95. In summary, to display several items using a single *writeInfo()* method, simply separate them as arguments within the *writeInfo()* method using the + concatenation operator.

    Next, suppose that you need to display the value of a variable. To do this, you can concatenate a variable to a string as part of the *writeInfo()* argument like this:

```
double gpa = 3.95;
io.writeInfo("My GPA is: " + gpa + " Wow!");
```

This code will display the same information as the earlier code that used a hard coded value for the *gpa*. As you can see here, the *gpa* variable is simply inserted into the output string using the concatenation operator in place of the hard coded value. It is important to note that no quotation marks are placed around the variable name. If quotation marks were used, Java would see the variable name as just another string and actually display the string "gpa" between the other two strings.

DEBUGGING TIP

Do not place quotation marks around a variable name. If you do, Java sees the name as a string and will treat it as such.

Example 3-16

Suppose your sales of widgets last month amounted to $5,346.75 but your cost for the widgets was $3,045.50. Write a code segment to calculate and display your profit.

Solution

Of course, you probably would not go to all the trouble of writing a Java program for such a simple chore. However, let's do it just to get some practice. Suppose we define three variables to represent the sale of widgets last month, the cost of the widgets, and the profit we made on selling the widgets. We will initialize the given sales and cost values and subtract the two to determine the profit we made. The resulting profit will then be displayed using the *writeInfo()* method. Here's the code:

```
//DEFINE AN I/O OBJECT
StaugIO io = new StaugIO();

//DEFINE AND INITIALIZE VARIABLES
double sales = 5346.75;   //SALES LAST MONTH
double cost = 3045.50;    //COST OF SALES LAST MONTH
double profit = 0.0;      //PROFIT MADE LAST MONTH

//CALCULATE PROFIT
profit = sales - cost;    //SUBTRACT COST FROM SALES TO GET PROFIT

//DISPLAY PROFIT
io.writeInfo("The profit of widgets last month was: $" + profit);
```

The output produced by this code segment is

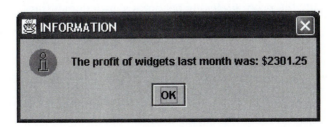

You must use the *writeNumber()* method if you want to display a numeric value all by itself, without an associated string. For example, the following two code segments will simply display the number 3.95 within a dialog box:

```
//DEFINE AN I/O OBJECT
StaugIO io = new StaugIO();

//WRITE A HARD CODED NUMERIC VALUE
io.writeNumber(3.95);

//WRITE A VARIABLE NUMERIC VALUE
double gpa = 3.95;
io.writeNumber(gpa);
```

In the first case, the number 3.95 is hard coded as the argument for the *writeNumber()* method. In the second case, the variable *gpa* is provided as the method argument. You cannot use a string as an argument for the *writeNumber()* method. The argument must be a hard coded number or numeric variable. Most of your output needs will require some sort of string to be associated with the data. Therefore, the *writeInfo()* method will normally be more useful. We just present the *writeNumber()* method here for your information.

Here is what you would see if either segment of code were executed:

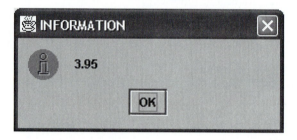

Formatting the Output   By formatting an output, we mean structuring it to meet a given application. Java allows output formatting using special commands within the output statements. These commands are referred to as *escape sequences*. Let's add a feature to the beginning of the program in Example 3-16 that will generate a window to tell the user what the program is going to do. Such a feature does two things:

1. It tells the user what the program is going to do.
2. It provides documentation within the program listing as to what the program will do. As a result, the program listing becomes self-documenting.

Suppose we use a *writeInfo()* method to generate such a window as follows:

```
io.writeInfo("This program will calculate monthly profit,\n"
            + "given the amount of sales and cost of sales.");
```

This one *writeInfo()* statement will generate the following output:

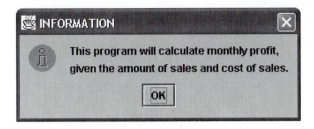

Observe that one *writeInfo()* statement is used to write two strings of character information. The trick is to divide the output sentence into two strings on two separate lines. Notice that each string item must be enclosed within double quotes. Also, notice the symbol '\n' (a backslash followed by the character *n*) at the end of the first string. The '\n' symbol is treated like a single character and is called an ***escape sequence***. When inserted into a string, a *newline* is generated wherever it appears, as illustrated in Figure 3-7. Thus, in the foregoing *writeInfo()* statement, the first string item is written on one line, a newline is generated to move the cursor to the beginning of the next line, and the second string item is written.

io.writeInfo("HELLO\nWORLD");

HELLO
WORLD

 |

'\n' character generates a newline
    within a string.

io.writeInfo("HELLO WORLD");

HELLO WORLD
     |

    Cursor remains at next position
    on current line without a newline

FIGURE 3-7   Using the '\n' escape sequence forces the cursor to the beginning of the next line, thus creating a "new line."

HISTORICAL NOTE

A newline is sometimes referred to as a carriage-return, line-feed, or CRLF. The term *carriage-return, line-feed* comes from the old typewriter days. Go to your local antiques shop or museum and look at a typewriter. There is a handle on the left side of the paper *carriage*. When you pull the handle from left to right, it returns the carriage to its beginning location to position the paper to type a new line. Thus the term "carriage-return." Also, when you pull the handle, a mechanical ratcheting device advances the paper roller so that the paper is positioned to begin typing on the next line. Thus the term *line feed*. This terminology is still used today to describe the action of positioning the monitor cursor to the beginning of the next line. We call it a *newline*.

Now, good style would dictate that the program output information should be as descriptive as possible. In other words, the output information should be self-documenting and easily understood by the user. Let's dress-up the Example 3-16 program output a bit by recoding the final *writeInfo()* statement as follows:

```
io.writeInfo("Given a monthly sales value of $" + sales + '\n'
        + "and a total cost value of $" + cost + ", the\n"
        + "resulting profit is $" + profit);
```

This one *writeInfo()* statement will generate the following output:

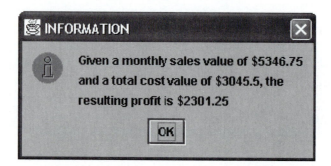

Let's analyze this output. First, observe that a '\n' escape sequence has been placed at the end of the first two lines in the *writeInfo()* statement. This generates a newline after each of these two lines, thereby creating three separate lines on the screen. Notice that the '\n' escape sequence is concatenated as a single character at the end of the first line but included as part of a string at the end of the second line. Single characters are enclosed in single quotes, while strings are enclosed in double quotes. You can treat '\n' as a single character, just as you would any other character.

Next, look at the output lines themselves. See how an output sentence is constructed using separate string items. The sentence is formed by separate character strings enclosed within double quotes. The monthly sales, cost of sales, and profit values are inserted into the output, between the string items, by concatenating the variables (*sales*, *cost*, and *profit*) when they are needed as part of the output. Notice that the character strings and variable items are concatenated to each other using the + operator.

It is important that you see that the quotation marks are around the string information and *not* around the variables.

To get a backslash (\), single quote ('), or double quote (") as part of your output you can use the \\, \', and \" escape sequences with a *writeInfo()* statement. These simple formatting escape sequences are summarized in Table 3-6.

TABLE 3-6   Formatting Escape Sequences for GUI Output

Sequence	Action
\n	Newline
\\	Backslash
\'	Single quote
\"	Double quote

Currency Output

Most business-related programs require some kind of currency output. Java has a built-in class called *NumberFormat* that you can use to generate professional-looking currency output. This class is in the standard *java.text* package, which must be imported into your program in order to use the class. Here's how it works:

1. Import the *NumberFormat* class at the beginning of your program like this:

   ```
   import java.text.NumberFormat;
   ```

2. Create an object for the *NumberFormat* class, like this:

   ```
   NumberFormat currency = NumberFormat.getCurrencyInstance();
   ```

   This statement creates an object called *currency*. Notice how the object is created by using the *NumberFormat* class to call its *getCurrencyInstance()* method. This provides the *currency* object with the attributes and behavior it will need to generate currency format.

3. Use your *NumberFormat* object to call its *format()* method. Use your currency variable as the argument for the *format()* method, like this:

   ```
   currency.format(sales)
   currency.format(cost)
   currency.format(profit)
   ```

4. Place this code in a *writeInfo()* statement, like this:

   ```
   io.writeInfo("Given a monthly sales value of "
               + currency.format(sales)
               + '\n'
               + "and a total cost value of "
               + currency.format(cost)
               + ", the \n"
               + "resulting profit is "
               + currency.format(profit));
   ```

This statement will generate the following output, using the *sales*, *cost*, and *profit* values calculated by the program in Example 3-16.

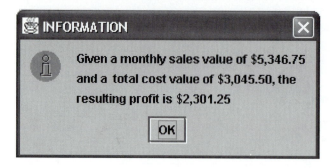

Notice that the currency values are generated in dollars/cents and include the $ symbol as well as commas where required to produce a complete currency format. You do not place any $ or commas in your *writeInfo* statement since the *format()* method does all this for you. Now that's cool! The *format()* method requires a double floating-point argument and returns a string. Since we have called it with our *currency* object, the string will be in currency format when appended to the string argument of the *writeInfo()* method. We will be using this technique in the future when we need to display currency values.

 The *NumberFormat* class, contained in the *java.text* package, contains several methods for formatting numeric data. One such method that is very useful for business applications is the *getCurrencyInstance()* method, which returns a currency format to a *NumberFormat* object. When this object is used to call the *format()* method, currency formatting will be applied to the numeric argument of the method, returning a string value that is pre-formatted in a dollars-and-cents format. The *NumberFormat* class provides for true currency formatting in dollars and cents which includes a $ sign, commas where required, and trailing 0's.

The StaugIO Input Methods

The *StaugIO* class contains several methods that allow you to obtain user input. These methods are summarized in Table 3-7.

TABLE 3-7   Keyboard Input Methods Used in This Text

Method	Description
readInt()	Returns the integer value entered by the user
readDouble()	Returns the double-float value entered by the user
readChar()	Returns a single character value entered by the user
readString()	Returns the string entered by the user
readBool()	Returns the Boolean value entered by the user

Each method accepts a string as its argument to generate a user prompt. There is a method to read each type of data that we discussed earlier in this chapter. Of course, each method must be called using a *StaugIO* class object. Each of these methods "returns" the data value that the user entered. Because the method returns a user entry value, it must have someplace to go. We will use a variable for this purpose. So, when using one of these methods, you must first define a variable of the same data type in order to store the user entry, like this:

```
//DEFINE AN I/O OBJECT
StaugIO io = new StaugIO();

//DEFINE AND INITIALIZE VARIABLE
double value = 0.0;

//ASSIGN USER ENTRY TO VARIABLE
value = io.readDouble("Enter a decimal value: ");

//ECHO USER ENTRY
io.writeInfo("The value you entered was " + value);
```

Here, we have first defined an object called *io* for the *StaugIO* class, then defined a `double` floating-point variable. We defined our variable as a `double`, because we are using the *readDouble()* method. The data type of the variable being used must match the data type returned by the input method. We then use this variable to store the `double` value returned by the *readDouble()* method. Notice our *value* variable is set, =, to the value returned by the *readDouble()* method, when called using our *io* object. The last line of code simply generates an output window which "echoes" the user input.

Here are the windows generated by the foregoing code:

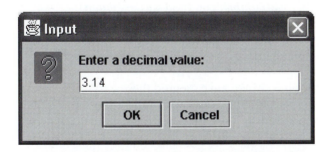

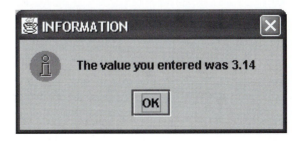

The two cardinal rules that apply when reading any data are as follows:

1. Any variable used in a read statement must be defined prior to its use in the statement.

2. The type of data entered for a given variable should match the data type defined for that variable.

To read numeric data, you will use *readInt()* to read integer values or *readDouble()* to read floating-point, or decimal, values. To read character data, you must use *readChar()* to read single characters, and *readString()* to read strings of multiple characters. You must use *readBool()* to read Boolean values of `true` or `false`. Again, the same rules apply. You must define a variable of the same data type that you are reading, then use this variable to store the value returned by the respective read method. Use a *StaugIO* class object to call the read method and provide a user prompt string as the method argument. Each of these methods contains an **exception handler** to "catch" any errors that the user might make when entering data. Exception handling is an advanced topic in Java and is covered in Chapter 14. When an error is caught, the method generates an exception window like this:

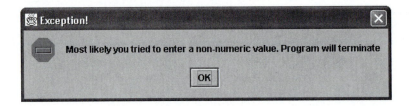

This window was generated when the user entered character data instead of numeric data when the *readDouble()* method was executed.

An **exception handler** is a Java program segment that is used to *catch* and handle errors as they occur during the execution of a Java program.

That's all there is to it! We have created these easy-to-use methods so that you do not have to worry about writing your own I/O routines at this time. Later on, we will "unwrap" the *staugIO* package and the *StaugIO* class to learn its secrets.

DEBUGGING TIP

When you initially code a program, it is usually wise to echo an input value to the display. This assures you that the program has performed the read operation and made the correct variable assignment. To echo an input value to the display, you simply insert a *writeInfo()* or *writeNumber()* statement after the read statement. Within the write statement, you list the same variable that is listed within the read statement. Once the program has been debugged and is completely operational, you can comment-out or remove the echoing write statements.

QUICK CHECK

1. Write a statement to define an object called *myIO* for the *StaugIO* class.

2. Write a statement to display the message "THIS STUFF IS GREAT!" as a single line in a GUI dialog box using the object you defined in question 1.

3. Write a statement to display the message "THIS STUFF IS GREAT!" as two lines within a dialog box using the object you defined in question 1.

4. Write a statement to define a variable called *gpa*. Write another statement to read your grade point average from the keyboard using the *myIO* object you defined in question 1 and assign it to the *gpa* variable.

5. Write a statement to echo your input in question 4 back to the display using the *myIO* object you defined in question 1.

6. Write statements to create a *NumberFormat* object called *currency* and display the value of a variable called *mySalary* within an information window in currency format.

7. What features does the *NumberFormat* class provide when it is used to format currency values?

3.6   Console Output

Console- vs. Window-Based Programming

Once upon a time all operating systems were text-based, sometimes referred to as ***CUI*** (character user interface) operating systems. All user I/O with these systems was character-based via the keyboard and a text screen. UNIX and DOS are two common examples of text-based operating systems. Then, with the development of graphical, called ***GUI*** (graphical user interface), operating systems, such as MacOS and Microsoft Windows, a mouse was introduced for navigation, and the keyboard used only when you actually needed to type. In a text-based environment, the mouse might as well not be there. Almost all commands are given through the keyboard. The screen you see in a text-based environment is called a ***console screen***. The typical console screen has a black background and a white (or light gray) prompt with a blinking cursor waiting for you to type in your command. The drawbacks to consoles are that they are not pretty and not intuitive. A black screen and a blinking cursor are a little daunting to the novice user. However, it is a good environment for learning to program because the I/O process (that is, the tasks of getting information from the user and writing information to the monitor) is relatively straightforward. All programmers should get experience in a console environment such as UNIX or DOS to get a basic idea of how console programming works.

Windows-based programs are graphical, or GUI, programs. Windows programming doesn't always refer to programs written for Microsoft Windows. Windows programming is a more generic term referring to programming that involves working with a graphical environment rather than a blank screen and a command prompt. Windows programs generally look better than console programs, and they are much less daunting for the novice user.

Java has limited support for console programming because it was primarily developed for graphical environments. In fact, console output is about the only thing you can easily do in Java. Keyboard input via a console screen is relatively difficult. As a result, we will cover only console output and ignore console input, using the *StaugIO* class for graphical input when input is needed. Most of our attention in the remainder of this book will be on window-based programming. However, we will cover console output using the *println()* and *print()* methods here, since some of the later text examples generate console output using these methods for testing programs when it is convenient to do so.

Using *println()*

You can display information to a console screen using the *println()* (pronounced "print line") method. The *println()* method is a standard method provided in Java and must be called using the *System.out* object, like this:

USING THE *println()* METHOD

```
System.out.println(items to be displayed);
```

The *println()* method automatically generates a newline after its items are displayed. Probably the simplest use of the *println()* method is to display fixed, or constant, text information. There are two types of fixed information that can be displayed: numeric and character.

Displaying Fixed Numeric Information   When you want to display fixed numeric information on a console screen, you simply insert the numeric values as arguments into the *println()* method. Thus, the statement

```
System.out.println(250);
```

generates an output of

```
250
```

The statement

```
System.out.println(-365);
```

generates an output of

```
-365
```

The statement

```
System.out.println(2.75);
```

generates an output of

```
2.75
```

Getting Out Fixed Character Information   To write character information, you must enclose the output information in quotes—single quotes for single characters and double quotes for strings. Consequently, the statement

```
System.out.println('A');
```

generates an output of

A

The statement

```
System.out.println("This text is great!");
```

produces an output of

This text is great!

The statement

```
System.out.println("My GPA is: " + 3.95 + " Wow!");
```

produces an output of

My GPA is 3.95 Wow!

Notice the use of the concatenation operator, +, to concatenate, or put together, the output items. The first output item is the string "My GPA is: ". The second item is the numeric value 3.95, which is concatenated to the first item using the + concatenation operator. Finally, the third item, "Wow!" is concatenated to the second item using the + concatenation operator. In summary, to display several items using a single *println()* statement, simply separate them as arguments within the *println()* method using the + concatenation operator.

Example 3-17

Construct *println()* statements to generate the following outputs:

a. 3.14
b. 1 2 3 4

Solution

a. `System.out.println(3.14);`
b. `System.out.println("1 2 3 4");`

To get spacing in a string, use spaces between the string characters. Remember that spaces are also characters. In fact, characters that you can't see, like spaces, tabs, newlines, and so on, are called ***non-printable***, or ***whitespace*** characters. Characters that you can see are called ***printable*** characters.

Getting Out Variable Information   The next thing you must learn is how to write variable information to the console screen. Again, this is a simple chore using the *println()* method. Simply insert the variable identifiers as arguments into the *println()* method. For instance, if your program has defined *sales*, *cost*, and *profit* as variables, you would write their respective values by inserting them as arguments into the *println()* method, like this:

```
System.out.println(sales);
System.out.println(cost);
System.out.println(profit);
```

The foregoing statements would write the values stored in memory for *sales*, *cost*, and *profit*, in that order, on separate lines.

Example 3-18

Suppose your sales of widgets last month amounted to $5,346.75 but your cost for the widgets was $3,045.50. Write a program to calculate and display your profit.

Solution

Remember that we did this example using *writeInfo()*? To generate the same output to the console screen you would use *println()*, like this:

```
//DEFINE AND INITIALIZE VARIABLES
double sales = 5346.75;    //SALES LAST MONTH
double cost = 3045.50;     //COST OF SALES LAST MONTH
double profit = 0.0;       //PROFIT MADE LAST MONTH

//CALCULATE PROFIT
profit = sales - cost;     //SUBTRACT COST FROM SALES TO GET PROFIT

//DISPLAY PROFIT
System.out.println(profit);
```

The output produced by the code is

```
2301.25
```

 STYLE TIP

The output generated in Example 3-18 is simply the number 2301.25. What a bore! Since console output is boring anyway, you need to be at least a little descriptive of the output meaning. Good style would dictate that output information should be descriptive. In other words, the output information should be self-documenting and easily understood by anyone looking at the screen, not just you. In Example 3-18, the profit output statement could be modified, like this:

```
//DISPLAY PROFIT
System.out.println("Sales: " + currency.format(sales)
             + "\nCost: " + currency.format(cost)
             + "\nProfit: " + currency.format(profit));
```

This one *println()* statement will generate the following output on the console screen:

```
Sales: $5,346.75
Cost: $3,045.50
Profit: $2,301.25
```

Let's analyze this output. First, observe that a '\n' escape sequence has been placed at the beginning of the second and third lines in the *println()* statement. This generates a newline before each of these two lines, thereby creating three separate lines on the screen. You can treat '\n' as a single character, just as you would any other character. However, it must appear within single quotations and surrounded by two concatenation operators, like this: + '\n' +. Here, we have included it as part of the output string to save some coding keystrokes.

Next, look at the output lines themselves. See how an output sentence is constructed using separate string items. The sentence is formed by separate character strings enclosed within double quotation marks. The monthly sales, cost of sales, and profit values are inserted into the output, between the string items, by concatenating the variables (*sales*, *cost*, and *profit*) when they are needed as part of the output. Notice that the character strings and variable items are concatenated to each other using the + operator. It is important that you see that the quotation marks are around the string information and *not* around the variables. Of course, we had to create the *currency* object from the *NumberFormat* class as discussed earlier to get a well formatted currency output.

The same thing could be accomplished with three separate *println()* statements, like this:

```
//DISPLAY PROFIT
System.out.println("Sales: "    + currency.format(sales));
System.out.println("Cost: "     + currency.format(cost));
System.out.println("Profit: "   + currency.format(profit));
```

We did not have to include the '\n' escape sequence character here because a newline is generated automatically at the end of each *println()* statement. If you did include the '\n' character, an additional newline would be generated.

You can utilize additional escape sequences with *println()* for formatting purposes. Table 3-8 provides a list of the escape sequences that can be used within *println()*. Notice that *println()* can utilize the \b, \r, and \t in addition to those that can be used for GUI I/O using *writeInfo()*.

TABLE 3-8   Escape Sequences for Console Output

Sequence	Action
\b	Backspace
\n	Newline
\r	CR, carriage return
\t	Horizontal tab
\\	Backslash
\'	Single quote
\"	Double quote

Using *print()*

There is another method called *print()* to display console information. The only difference between *print()* and *println()* is that *print()* does not generate a newline, thereby keeping the cursor on the same output line. Thus, the statements

```
System.out.print("Hello ");
System.out.println("World");
System.out.print("Goodbye ");
System.out.println("World");
```

will produce an output of

```
Hello World
Goodbye World
```

See how the *print()* method leaves the cursor on the existing line, while the *println()* method forces the cursor to the next line? (*Note:* The cursor would be left on a new line by the last *println()* statement. Thus, any subsequent output would begin on a new line.)

Now, let's close this chapter by looking at a couple of case studies that apply the material we just discussed.

QUICK CHECK

1. Write a *println()* statement to display your name as a fixed string of information.
2. Write a *println()* statement to display your name when it is stored in a string object called *name*.
3. The escape sequence that must be used to generate a tab within the console screen is the _____ escape sequence.
4. The escape sequence that must be used to generate a carriage return without a line feed on the console screen is the _____ escape sequence.
5. Explain the difference between using the *println()* and *print()* methods.

Problem Solving in Action: Bank Account Processing

Problem

Your local bank has contracted you to design a Java application that will process savings account data for a given month. Assume that the savings account accrues interest at a rate of 12% per year and that the user must enter the current account balance, amount of deposits, and amount of withdrawals. Develop a problem definition, set of algorithms, class diagram and Java program to solve this problem.

Defining the Problem

Input:	To process a savings account, you need to know the initial balance, amounts of deposits, amounts of withdrawals, and the interest rate. We will assume that these values will be entered by the program user, with the exception of the interest rate, which will be coded as a constant.
Processing:	The program must process deposits and withdrawals and calculate interest to determine the monthly balance.
Output:	The program must display a report showing the account transactions and balance for a given savings account in a given month.

We will divide the problem into individual sub-problems to solve the overall banking problem. Now, try to identify the separate tasks that must be performed to solve the problem. First, the user must enter the required transaction data, which will include the previous month's balance, current month's deposits, and current month's withdrawals. Once the transaction data is entered, the program must add the deposits to the account balance, subtract the withdrawals from the account balance, calculate the interest, and generate the required report. As a result, we can identify five program tasks as follows:

- Read the transaction data entered by the program user.
- Add the deposits to the account balance.
- Subtract the withdrawals from the account balance.
- Calculate the account interest.
- Generate the monthly account report.

The problem-solving diagram in Figure 3-8 shows the solution required for the program.

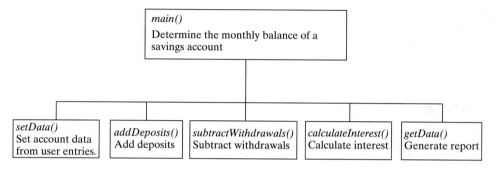

FIGURE 3-8   A problem-solving diagram for the banking problem.

Planning the Solution

Now we will employ stepwise refinement to develop the required set of algorithms. The initial algorithm level, *main()*, will reflect the problem definition and call the individual method modules as follows:

Initial Algorithm
main()
BEGIN
   Call the method to read the transaction data from user.
   Call the method to add the account deposits.
   Call the method to subtract the account withdrawals.
   Call the method to calculate the account interest.
   Call the method to generate the account report.
END.

The first level of refinement requires that we show a detailed algorithm for each method. They are as follows:

First Level of Refinement
setData()
BEGIN
   Write a prompt to enter the current account balance.
   Read *balance*.
   Write a prompt to enter the monthly deposits.
   Read *deposits*.

Write a prompt to enter the monthly withdrawals.
Read *withdrawals*.
END.

addDeposits()
BEGIN
   Calculate *balance = balance + deposits*.
END.

subtractWithdrawals()
BEGIN
   Calculate *balance = balance − withdrawals*.
END.

addInterest()
BEGIN
   Calculate *balance = balance + (balance * interest)*.
END.

getData()
BEGIN
   Write *deposits*.
   Write *withdrawals*.
   Write *interest*.
   Write *balance*.
END.

The last thing we need to do in our planning is to construct a class diagram, showing the required class members. We have chosen to call our class *Banking*, whose class diagram is shown in Figure 3-9.

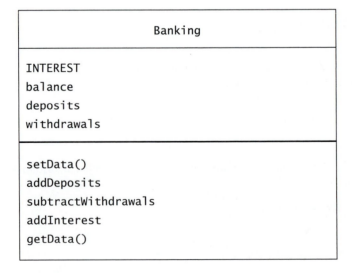

FIGURE 3-9   A class diagram for the *Banking* class shows the data and methods that make up the class.

Coding the Program

Here is how the foregoing class and algorithms are translated into Java application code:

```java
/*
 * Action03_01.java
 *
 * Created on April 23, 2002, 8:54 AM
 */

/**
 *
 * @author Andrew C. Staugaard, Jr.
 * @version 1.0
 */

import staugIO.StaugIO;        //FOR INPUT/OUTPUT
import java.text.NumberFormat;  //FOR CURRENCY FORMATTING

class Banking
{
    //DEFINE INTEREST CONSTANT
    private final double INTEREST = 0.01;   //MONTHLY INTEREST RATE

    //DEFINE VARIABLES AND OBJECTS
    private double balance = 0.0;          //ACCOUNT BALANCE
    private double deposits = 0.0;         //MONTHLY DEPOSITS
    private double withdrawals = 0.0;      //MONTHLY WITHDRAWALS
    private StaugIO io = new StaugIO(); //DEFINE INPUT/OUTPUT OBJECT

    //CONSTRUCTOR METHOD
    public Banking
    {
    }

    //setData() METHOD
    public void setData()
    {
     balance = io.readDouble("Enter the current balance of the account");
     deposits = io.readDouble("Enter the deposits this month");
     withdrawals = io.readDouble("Enter the withdrawals this month");
    }//END setData()

    //addDeposits() METHOD
    public void addDeposits()
    {
       balance = balance + deposits;
    }//END addDeposits()

    //subtractWithdrawals METHOD
    public void subtractWithdrawals()
    {
       balance = balance - withdrawals;
    }//END subtractWithdrawals()

    //addInterest() METHOD
    public void addInterest()
```

```
   {
     balance = balance + (balance * INTEREST);
   }//END addInterest()


   //getData() METHOD
   public void getData()
   {
     NumberFormat currency = NumberFormat.getCurrencyInstance();
     io.writeInfo("Deposits were "
                 + currency.format(deposits)
                 + "\nWithdrawals were "
                 + currency.format(withdrawals)
                 + "\nThe monthly interest is "
                 + currency.format(balance * INTEREST)
                 + "\n\nThe account balance is currently: "
                 + currency.format(balance));
   }//END getData()
}//END Banking

public class Action03_01
{
    public static void main (String args[])
    {
      //DEFINE BANKING OBJECT
      Banking account = new Banking();
      //CALL BANKING METHODS
      account.setData();
      account.addDeposits();
      account.subtractWithdrawals();
      account.addInterest();
      account.getData();
      //EXIT PROGRAM
      System.exit(0);
    }//END main()
}//END Action03_01
```

At this point, the code might look a little overwhelming. However, don't concern yourself with all the coding details; just observe the things that relate to what we discussed in this chapter. First, notice the overall structure of the program. A general program comment is at the top of the program, followed by two import statements, followed by the *Banking* class declaration. The *Banking* class is followed by the *Action03_01* application class, which includes method *main()*.

Now for the details: The first import statement makes the *StaugIO* class available to the program for GUI I/O. The second import statement makes the *NumberFormat* class available for currency formatting. The *Banking* class begins by defining the monthly *INTEREST* as a constant with the value 0.01. This is the decimal value required to calculate the monthly interest based on a 12% annual interest rate. Next, our variables are defined. The variables that need to be defined are *balance*, *deposits*, and *withdrawals*, which have been defined as private double floating-point variables. Lastly, we define an object, called *io*, for the imported *StaugIO* class. This object is required to call the I/O methods that are needed to read the user data and write the program results to the monitor. All the variables and the object are defined to be private class members. This means that they are only "visible", or accessible, by methods in the same class. More about this in Chapter 8.

Now we need to code the methods. All we have to do here is write a method header line and translate our pseudocode to Java method code within the body of the method. Now, notice the first line of each method. This is called the method **header** line. The first word in the header is the keyword `public`. This tells Java that the method will be a `public` method that can be called by an object of the class. The second word in the header is the keyword `void`. This tells Java that the method will not be returning any values outside the class. Then you see the method name, followed by a set of parentheses. Until you learn more about methods in Chapter 7, all of our method headers will follow this format. The first method is the *Banking()* constructor which has the same name as the class. Remember that a constructor is required for any class. There is no code inside this method since it is not being used to initialize any of the class data. Later on we will put code inside the constructor when we need to initialize the class data for a given application. Next you see the code for our *setData()* method. The implementation of *setData()* prompts the user for the required data and reads it from the keyboard. The *readDouble()* method is used to both prompt the user and assign the user entry to the respective variable. The *readDouble()* method is provided in the *StaugIO* class. Notice that we use our *io* object to call the *readDouble()* method and have provided the user prompt as its argument.

Next, our *addDeposits()* method is coded, followed by the *subtractWithdrawals()* method, followed by the *addInterest()* method. The coding of these methods should be straightforward. Finally, the *getData()* method is implemented by using our *io* object to call a *writeInfo()* method which writes the program results to the monitor. Notice how all the required information is put together to form a single string argument for the *writeInfo()* method. This will display the entire banking report within a single window. Also notice that we have defined a *NumberFormat* class object called *currency* within this method. This object calls its *format()* method within the *writeInfo()* method to provide currency formatting for our currency values.

Notice the use of comments. A comment is placed with each constant and variable definition to specify its purpose in the program. The comments are easily identified from the executable code, because they are coded in uppercase characters.

Once the *Banking* class ends, we must create a `public` application class, containing *main()*. Remember from Chapter 2 that *main()* is used to create an object for the class being tested. Here we have created an object called *account*. The *account* object is then used to call the methods in the order that they are needed to process the bank account just as we dictated in the *main()* algorithm. Finally, notice that the last statement in *main()* is `System.exit(0);` This statement is *always* required to close a program when using the dialog boxes generated by the *StaugIO* methods.

Always insert the statement *System.exit(0);* as the last statement in *main()* when using the *StaugIO* methods to generate dialog boxes.

That's all there is to it! Here is a sample output produced by the program:

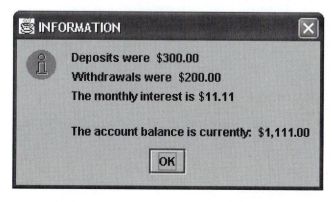

Problem Solving in Action: Inventory Control

Problem

The following is a partial inventory listing of items in the sporting goods department of the Java*Mart super-center:

Item	Beginning Quantity	Units Sold This Month
Fishing line	132 spools	66 spools
Fish hooks	97 packages	45 packages
Sinkers	123 packages	37 packages
Fish nets	12 ea.	5 ea.

Write a program that will display a monthly report showing the item name, beginning quantity, units sold this month, ending quantity, and percent of quantity sold. The problem solution begins with the problem definition phase.

Defining the Problem

Input: The sporting goods manager must enter the inventory item data shown in the table above.

Processing: The program must use the input information to calculate two things: the ending quantity and the percent sold. The ending quantity is found by simply subtracting the units sold from the beginning quantity, like this:

$$ending\ qty = begin\ qty - units\ sold$$

The percent sold is found by dividing the units sold by the beginning quantity and multiplying by 100%, like this:

$$\%\ sold = (units\ sold/begin\ qty) \times 100\%$$

Output: The program must generate a report of the item name, beginning quantity, units sold this week, ending quantity, and percent of quantity sold this week. Now is a good time to develop the output format. Suppose we create an output window that will display the item data using the following format:

ITEM: *item name*
BEGIN QUANTITY: *beginning quantity*
UNITS SOLD: *units sold*
ENDING QUANTITY: *ending quantity*
PERCENT SOLD: *percent sold*

Notice that we have shown the output heading information in regular type and the variable values in italicized type.

Planning the Solution

We must now construct a set of algorithms and class diagram from the problem definition. Using a modular program design, we will divide the problem into individual sub-problems to solve the overall problem. There are three major tasks that follow directly from the problem definition:

• Set the inventory data for a given item from the user.
• Calculate the ending quantity and percent sold for the given item.

- Get the item data and display a report.
- Repeat the above for all items in the inventory.

Because we do not yet have a way of telling Java to automatically repeat a task, the three tasks must be repeated for each item in the inventory. The diagram in Figure 3-10 shows the solution required for the program.

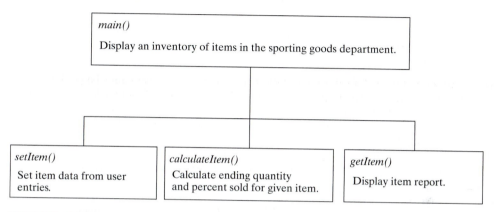

FIGURE 3-10 A problem-solving diagram for the inventory problem.

The initial algorithm level, *main()*, will reflect the foregoing analysis and call the individual method modules.

Initial Algorithm
main()
BEGIN
   Call method to set the inventory data for a given item from the user.
   Call method to calculate the ending quantity and percent sold.
   Call method to get the item data and display the item report.
   Repeat for each inventory item.
END.

In developing the algorithm, you would quickly realize that the processing is the same for each sales item. As a result, we have used a single *repeat* rather than actually repeating the algorithm statements three more times. This has been done to make the algorithm more efficient.

The first level of refinement requires that we show a detailed algorithm for each task, or method, that we have identified. They are as follows:

First Level of Refinement
setItem()
BEGIN
   Write a user prompt to enter the item name.
   Read *item*.
   Write a user prompt to enter the beginning quantity.
   Read *begin qty*.
   Write a user prompt to enter the number of units sold.
   Read *units sold*.
END.

calculateItem()
BEGIN
   Calculate *ending qty = begin qty − units sold*.
   Calculate *% sold = (units sold / begin qty)* × 100 %.
END.

getItem()
BEGIN
   Display *item name, begin quantity, units sold, ending quantity*, and *% sold* for each item.
END.

Given our problem definition, the foregoing collection of algorithms is straightforward. The three methods must be executed for each of the items in the inventory. The *setItem()* method prompts and reads the item information from the user and assigns it to the item variables. The *calculateItem()* method will make the required calculations. Finally, the *getItem()* method will display the item report.

We will place all the item data and methods in a class called *Inventory*, as shown in Figure 3-11.

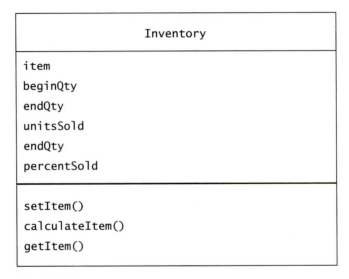

FIGURE 3-11 A class diagram for the *Inventory* class shows the data and methods that make up the class.

Coding the Program

Now the job is to code the class in Java. With your present knowledge of Java, coding most of this information should not present a problem. But what about the repeat statement at the end of the *main()* method algorithm? Well, notice that this statement requires that you go back and repeat many of the previous statements over and over until all the items are processed. Such a repeating operation is called an ***iteration***, or ***looping***, operation. To date, you do not have the Java tools to perform such an operation. So, we will have to repeat all of the processing steps for each of the sales items in the inventory. In Chapter 6 you will learn how to perform iterative operations in Java, thus making the code much more efficient.

Here's the code for the foregoing class:

```java
/*
 * Action03_02.java
 *
 * Created on April 23, 2002, 2:10 PM
 */

/**
 *
 * @author Andrew C. Staugaard, Jr.
 * @version 1.0
 */

import staugIO.StaugIO;          //FOR INPUT/OUTPUT
class Inventory
{
   //DEFINE AND INITIALIZE OBJECTS AND VARIABLES
   private String item = " ";               //SALES ITEM NAME
   private int beginQty = 0;                //BEGINNING QUANTITY
   private int unitsSold = 0;               //NUMBER OF UNITS SOLD
   private int endQty = 0;                  //ENDING QUANTITY
   private double percentSold = 0.0;        //PERCENT OF SALES
   private StaugIO io = new StaugIO();      //DEFINE INPUT/OUTPUT OBJECT

   //CONSTRUCTOR METHOD
   public Inventory()
   {
   }//END Inventory()

   //setItem() METHOD
   public void setItem()
   {
     item = io.readString("Enter the inventory item name");
     beginQty = io.readInt("Enter the begin quantity of " + item);
     unitsSold = io.readInt("Enter the number of units sold of " + item);
   }//END setItem()

   //calculateItem() METHOD
   public void calculateItem()
   {
     endQty = beginQty - unitsSold;
     percentSold = 100.0 * unitsSold / beginQty ;
   }//END calculateItem()

   //setItem() METHOD
   public void getItem()
   {
    io.writeInfo("ITEM: " + item
              + "\nBEGINNING QUANTITY: " + beginQty
              + "\nUNITS SOLD: " + unitsSold
              + "\nENDING QUANTITY: " + endQty
              + "\nPERCENT SOLD: " + percentSold + '%');
   }//END getItem
}//END Inventory
```

```
public class Action03_02
{
    public static void main (String args[])
    {
        //DEFINE INVENTORY OBJECT
        Inventory item = new Inventory();
        //CALL INVENTORY METHODS FOR FIRST ITEM
        item.setItem();
        item.calculateItem();
        item.getItem();
        //CALL INVENTORY METHODS FOR SECOND ITEM
        item.setItem();
        item.calculateItem();
        item.getItem();
        //CALL INVENTORY METHODS FOR THIRD ITEM
        item.setItem();
        item.calculateItem();
        item.getItem();
        //CALL INVENTORY METHODS FOR FOURTH ITEM
        item.setItem();
        item.calculateItem();
        item.getItem();

        //EXIT PROGRAM
        System.exit(0);
    }//END main()
}//END Action03_02
```

Again, notice how the *Inventory* methods are called four times, once for each inventory item. Wouldn't it be nice to simply code the processing steps once and then tell the computer to repeat these steps the required number of times? Such a repeating operation would make our coding much more efficient, wouldn't it?

You should be able to understand the above Java code, given the material presented up to this point in the text. Notice how our variables are coded as `private` members of the class and the methods are coded as `public` class members. The application class that contains *main()* simply creates an object of our *Inventory* class and uses this object to call the methods four times, once for each inventory item.

Here is what the sporting goods manager would see after entering the fishing line data:

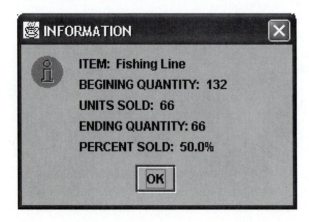

CHAPTER SUMMARY

Data abstraction allows us to work with a class without agonizing over the internal implementation details of the class; this gives rise to the term abstract data type, or ADT. The term *behavior* has to do with how an ADT, or class, will act and react for a given operation. As a result, all ADTs exhibit a given behavior, which is determined by the operations defined for the ADT.

Java is a strongly typed language. This means that all the data processed by a Java program must be part of a given data type or class that is defined within the program. We have identified three major data type/class categories: primitive, standard classes, and programmer-defined classes.

Primitive data types consist of the standard types built into the Java language. These include the integer, floating-point, character, and Boolean data types. The integer types in Java include byte, short, int, and long, each of which defines a given range of integers.

The floating-point data type consists of decimal values that can be represented in either fixed decimal or exponential form. Floating-point constants and variables can be defined as float or double, each of which defines a given precision of floating-point values.

Character data includes all of the symbols on your computer keyboard. Characters defined as char are ordered because they are represented internally using a numeric code (Unicode).

The Boolean data type, boolean, has only two values, true and false. Boolean values are used in programs to make decisions.

A string is a collection of characters. There is a standard *String* class built into the Java language that allows you to create string objects and manipulate string data using predefined string methods.

All constants and variables used in a Java program must be defined prior to their use in the program. Constants are defined using the keyword final. The constant identifier is set equal to its constant value. Variables are defined by listing the variable data type followed by the variable identifier. An initializing value should always be included in the definition.

String objects are defined as objects of the *String* class. The keyword *String* is listed first, followed by an appropriate object identifier. Like primitive variables, string objects should always be initialized when they are defined. Empty strings can be initialized with double quotation marks.

Java does not include any convenient methods for reading keyboard data or writing information through a GUI window. Therefore, we have developed a custom package, called *staugIO*, to read keyboard entries and write information using GUI dialog boxes. The *staugIO* package contains a *StaugIO* class which contains several methods to perform I/O within your Java program. To use any of the *StaugIO* methods you must:

- Import the *staugIO* package at the beginning of your program.
- Create an object for the *StaugIO* class using the new operator.
- Call an output method using your object and provide the information to be displayed as the method argument.
- Define variables to receive the data returned by the input methods. The data type of a given variable must be the same as that returned by a given method.
- Call an input method using your object as part of an assignment statement which assigns the value returned by the method to the input variable. Insert the user prompt as a string for the method argument.

You can use the *println()* and *print()* methods for text-based, console output. Both methods must be called by the *System.out* object. The information to be displayed on the console screen must be supplied as the argument for the method.

QUESTIONS AND PROBLEMS

Questions

1. What is an abstract data type, or ADT?

2. Give an example of an ADT.

3. What is meant by the term *behavior*, as related to classes and ADTs?

4. Why is the Java class ideal for implementing ADTs?

5. Name the four primitive types defined in Java.

6. Which of the following are *not* legal integer values in Java? Explain why they are not valid. Assume the `short` data type.
   a. −32.0
   b. +256
   c. 256
   d. 3,240
   e. 32000
   f. 40000

7. What is an overflow condition, and when will it generate incorrect results in Java?

8. Which of the following are not legal floating-point values in Java? Explain why they are not valid. Assume the `float` data type.
   a. 35.7
   b. −35.7
   c. 0.456
   d. 1.25e−9
   e. −2.5−e3
   f. −0.375e−3
   g. 25

9. Convert the following decimal numbers to exponential notation.
   a. −0.0000123
   b. 57892345.45
   c. 1.00004536
   d. +012.345

10. Convert the following exponential values to fixed decimal notation.
    a. 3.45e−7
    b. −2.25e−5
    c. 2.22e6
    d. −3.45e4

11. Three values in a data communications problem are 15.3 kHz, 2.2 MHz, and 10 ps.
    a. Express each as a floating-point value in fixed decimal form.
    b. Express each as a floating-point value in exponential form.
    c. Express each as an integer value.

12. The following current and voltage values are measured in a circuit: 1 milliampere, 32 millivolts, 100 microvolts, and 125 nanoamperes.
    a. Express each current and voltage value in fixed decimal form.
    b. Express each current and voltage value in exponential form.

13. What is the data type or class of each of the following?
    a. 250
    b. −250.0

    c. −16
    d. −3.5e−4
    e. 'x'
    f. '$'
    g. "2"
    h. "175"
    i. "1.25e−3"

14. True or false: An overflow condition always results in a compiler error.

15. State the difference between a character and a string.

16. Choose appropriate identifiers and define constants to represent each of the following:
    a. A maximum value of 100
    b. Your name
    c. Your student number
    d. Your age
    e. A period
    f. Your birth date
    g. Your school

17. Define a series of constants that would represent the months of the year.

18. Choose appropriate identifiers and define variables or objects for each of the following:
    a. Grade point average (GPA)
    b. Grade for a course
    c. Gross pay on a paycheck
    d. Student name

In questions 19–25, assume that io has been defined as an object of the StaugIO class.

19. Suppose that *name* is a string object. Explain what happens as the result of executing the following:

```
io.writeNumber(name.length());
```

20. What will be displayed by each of the following *writeInfo()* statements:

```
String s = "JAVA";
io.writeInfo(s.toLowerCase());
String s = "JAVA";
io.writeNumber(s.length());
```

21. Indicate the output for each of the following:

```
io.writeInfo("HELLO\nWORLD");
io.writeInfo("1\n2\n3\n4");
io.writeInfo("TEST SCORE\n97.5");
```

22. Suppose that you define a constant as follows:

```
final char SPACE = ' ';
```

What will the following statement do?

```
io.writeInfo("HELLO" + SPACE + "WORLD");
```

23. What is the difference between the output produced by the following two statements?

```
io.writeInfo("#\n#\n#");
io.writeInfo("###");
```

24. Create an object called *myIO* for the *StaugIO* class.

25. Consider the following program segment:

```
char char1 = ' ';
char1 = io.readChar("Enter a character" );
io.writeInfo("The value of char1 is: "+ char1);
```

What will be displayed for each of the following user entries?
   a. A↵
   b. AB↵
   c. 3.14↵

26. What package must be imported in order to use the *readChar()* method in question 25?

27. What method in the *StaugIO* class must be used to obtain string data?

28. Define the appropriate variables and objects and write statements to read and then display your school name.

29. What is the relationship between *staugIO*, *StaugIO*, and *readInt()*?

30. True or false: The *StaugIO* class is a standard class in the Java language.

31. List and explain at least two commonly used escape sequences.

32. Write the statements required to display the following table headings in an information box:

EMPLOYEE NAME   EMPLOYEE NUMBER   ANNUAL SALARY

33. The Java operator used to concatenate items within a *writeInfo()* method is the _____ operator.

34. Explain the difference between a declaration and a definition.

35. What is the standard convention for naming constants, variables, packages, methods, objects, and classes in Java?

36. What are the two things that make up a class declaration?

37. What is meant by the term *behavior* relative to a class object?

38. What operator must an object use to call one of its methods?

Use the following class declaration to answer questions 39 – 43:

```
class Student
{
  //DATA MEMBERS
  private String name = " ";              //STUDENT NAME
  private String major = " ";             //STUDENT MAJOR
  private String studentNumber = " "; //STUDENT NUMBER
  private double gpa = 0.0;               //STUDENT GPA

  //METHOD MEMBERS
  //CONSTRUCTOR
  public Student()
  {
  }//END Student()
```

```
        //SET STATS FROM USER ENTRIES
        public void setStats()
        {

        }//END setStats()

        //DISPLAY STUDENT DATA
        public void getStats()
        {

        }//END getStats()
    } //END Student
```

39. Write a statement to define a student named Isaac Newton as an object of the *Student* class.

40. Write statements for the *setStats()* method that will allow the user to enter the data values using a dialog box.

41. Write a statement that will call the *setStats()* method for the Isaac Newton object.

42. Write statements for the *getStats()* method, assuming that this method will display the student data within an information window.

43. Write a statement that will call the *getStats()* method for the Isaac Newton object.

Problems

In problems 1 – 10 place your solution code inside the single main() application class shell shown below. Name your application PXX_YY, where XX is the chapter number (03 in this chapter) and YY is the problem number. Note: Do not define your variables as private or create separate methods when placing your solution inside of main().

```
/*
 * PLACE THE PROBLEM NUMBER HERE
 *
 * PLACE THE DATE AND TIME HERE
 */

/**
 *
 * @author PLACE YOUR NAME HERE
 * @version 1.0
 */

import staugIO.StaugIO;          //FOR GUI I/O IF NEEDED
import java.text.NumberFormat;   //FOR CURRENCY FORMATTING IF NEEDED

public class PXX_YY
{
  public static void main(String[] args)
  {

    //PLACE YOUR SOLUTION CODE HERE

    //EXIT PROGRAM
    System.exit(0);
  }//END main()
}//END PXX_YY APPLICATION
```

Least Difficult

1. Write a program to display your name within a dialog box.

2. Write a program that will display a rectangle within a dialog box. Construct the rectangle using X's.

3. Write a program that will display the following within a dialog box:

STUDENT	SEMESTER AVERAGE
1	84.5
2	67.2
3	77.4
4	86.8
5	94.7

More Difficult

In the problems that follow, you will need to employ several arithmetic operations. In Java, a plus symbol (+) is used for addition, a minus symbol (−) is used for subtraction, a star symbol (*) is used for multiplication, and a slash symbol (/) is used for division.

4. Design and code a program that will find the sum of three test score values and display the sum within a dialog box. Call the variables *score1*, *score2*, and *score3*, and assume that they have initial values of 95.3, 78.5, and 85.2, respectively. Compile and run your program using your Java compiler.

5. Expand the program you wrote in problem 4 to calculate and display the average of the three scores. (*Note*: The / symbol is used for division in Java.) Compile and run your program.

6. Design and code a Java program that will generate a weekly payroll report for Bill Gates. Assume that Bill worked 22.5 hours this week at a rate of $1,000,000 per hour. Also, assume that Bill's payroll deductions were 35% of his gross pay. The report should show the employee name, number of hours worked, hourly rate, gross pay, payroll deduction amount, and net pay.

7. Write a program to calculate simple interest on a $2000 loan for 2 years at a rate of 12.5 percent. Format your output appropriately, showing the amount of the loan, time period, interest rate, and interest amount.

8. Write a program that will prompt the user to enter any four-letter word one character at a time. Then display the word backwards. (Keep it clean!)

9. Write a program that will display an information box showing a monthly utility invoice from the Java Electric Company to a customer named "Joe Foo". Assume that Joe used 2300 KWH (kilowatt hours) during the month and the Java Electric Company charges 10.125¢ per KWH.

10. Write a program that will display a monthly utility invoice described in problem 9 assuming that the customer name and monthly power usage is entered by an employee of the Java Electric Company.

Most Difficult

In the problems that follow, code your solution in a separate class using private variables and public methods like you observed in the chapter case studies. Give this class a name that describes its purpose. Then, create an application and define an object in main() to call your public functions as needed to solve the problem. Name your application PXX_YY where XX is the chapter number and YY is the problem number as you did for the earlier problems.

11. The rumor mill at the Java*Mart super-center is saying that employees are about to get a 5.5% raise. Write a program for the employees that will allow them to determine their new annual, as well as monthly, gross salary if the rumor is true. Assume that the user will enter his/her current monthly salary.

12. Write a program that will calculate the weekly gross pay amount for an employee from user entries of the employee's rate of pay and number of hours worked. Assume the employee is part-time and, therefore, works less than 40 hours per week. Generate a dialog box showing the employee's name, rate of pay, hours worked, and gross pay.

13. Write a program to calculate the circumference and area of a circle from a user's entry of its radius. Generate a tabular display showing the circle's radius, circumference, and area. (*Note*: Circumference of a circle $= 2 \times pi \times r$. Area of a circle $= pi \times r^2$)

14. Write a program that will allow a student to calculate his/her test average of four test scores. Generate a display of the student's name, course name, individual test scores, and test average.

15. The "Alley Cats" bowling team has four bowlers. On a given bowling night, each team member bowls three games. Write a program that will read the date, each bowler's name, and the individual game scores for each bowler. Using the input information, display a bowling report. The report should show the date at the top of the window, and then a listing showing each bowler's scores, total, and average.

16. Write a program to act as an electronic cash register. The program must display a receipt showing four sales items, their price, a subtotal of the four sales items, the sales tax at a rate of 7%, the total amount due, the amount tendered, and the amount of change returned similar to the screen shot shown below.

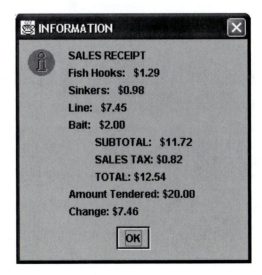

4

Nuts and Bolts—Basic Stuff in Java

OBJECTIVES

When you are finished with this chapter, you should have a good understanding of the following:

- The standard arithmetic operations in Java
- The standard mathematical methods provided by the *Math* class in Java
- The increment/decrement operators in Java

- Preincrement/predecrement versus postincrement/postdecrement when used within arithmetic expressions
- Simple and compound assignment operations in Java

Introduction

This short chapter will familiarize you with several standard, or built-in, operations available to you in Java. The simplest of these are the arithmetic operations. By definition, an arithmetic operation generates a numeric result. Such operations are the topic of the first section of this chapter. Pay particular attention to the division (/), remainder (%), and increment/decrement (++, −−) operators. Java also has a standard *Math* class that includes several commonly used mathematical methods. These methods simplify the chore of programming because they can be called via the standard *Math* class. Several of these methods will be discussed in this chapter.

The second section deals with the Java assignment operators. Assignment operators assign a value to a variable in memory. There are compound assignment operators in Java that allow you to combine an arithmetic operation with the assignment operation.

The chapter closes with three *Problem Solving in Action* case studies. Make sure you go through these problems in detail, since each focuses on how to use the operations discussed in this chapter.

4.1   Arithmetic Operations

Arithmetic operations in Java include the common add, subtract, multiply, and divide operations, as well as increment/decrement operations. By definition, an arithmetic operation generates a numeric result. The basic add, subtract, multiply, and divide operations can be performed on any numeric data type. Recall that the standard numeric data types in Java are the integers and floats.

Table 4-1 lists the five basic arithmetic operations and the Java symbols used to represent those operations. The Java symbol for an operation is called an **operator**. The addition (+), subtraction (−), and multiplication (*) operators are straightforward and do not need further explanation. However, you might note that an asterisk (*) is used for multiplication rather than a times symbol (×) so that the computer does not get multiplication confused with the character 'x'.

The division operator needs some special attention. This operator will generate a result that is the same data type as the operands used in the operation. (*Note:* An **operand** is a value used in an operation.) Thus, if you divide two integers, you will get an integer result. If you divide *one or more* decimal floating-point values, you get a decimal result. Thus, 10/3 = 3 and 10.0/3 = 3.333333. Here, the former is integer division and generates an integer result. The latter is floating-point division and generates a floating-point result.

Finally the *remainder*, sometimes called *modulus*, operator (%) simply generates the remainder that occurs when you divide two integer values. For example, the result of 5 % 3 is 2, 5 % 4 is 1, and 5 % 5 is 0.

THINK!

The remainder operator (%) is only defined for integers. So, what happens if you use a floating-point value with %? Well, nothing critical. You will *not* get a compile or run-time error, just bad data, or garbage. For example, the statement

`value = 2.0%2.9;`

produces a totally unpredictable value of 2.0. The lesson to be learned here is *never* use the remainder operator with floating-point values, since the results can be unpredictable.

Let's look at a couple of examples that illustrate these operations. Example 4-1 shows several arithmetic operations on integers, and Example 4-2 deals with arithmetic operations on floating-point values.

TABLE 4-1 Arithmetic Operators Defined in Java (Listed in Precedence Order)	
Operation	**Operator**
Multiplication	*
Division	/
Remainder	%
Addition	+
Subtraction	−

Example 4-1

What value will be returned as the result of each of the following operations?

   a.   3*(−5)
   b.   4*5−10
   c.   10/3
   d.   9%3
   e.   −21/(−2)
   f.   −21%(−2)
   g.   4*5/2+5%2

Solution

   a. 3*(−5) returns the value −15.
   b. 4*5−10 returns the value 10. Note that the multiplication operation is performed before the subtraction operation.
   c. 10/3 returns the value 3, because this is integer division.
   d. 9%3 returns the value 0, because there is no remainder.
   e. −21/(−2) returns the integer quotient 10.
   f. −21%(−2) returns the remainder −1.
   g. 4*5/2+5%2 = (4*5)/2+(5%2) = 20/2+(5%2) = 10+1 = 11

Notice that the multiplication (*), division (/), and remainder (%) operators are performed first, from left to right. The addition operation is performed last. Aside from showing how the individual operators work, the previous example illustrates the priority, or ordering, of the operators. When more than one operator is used in an expression, you must know the order in which they will be performed to determine the result. Java performs operations in the following order:

- All operators within parentheses are performed first.
- If there are nested parentheses (parentheses within parentheses) the innermost operations are performed first, from the inside out.
- The *, /, and % operators are performed next, from left to right within the expression.
- The + and − operators are performed last, from left to right within the expression.

This order of precedence is summarized in Table 4-2.

THINK!

Beginning programmers—and even experienced programmers for that matter—often forget that the Java division operator produces a floating-point result only if one or both of the operands are floating-point. For example, consider the problem of converting degrees Fahrenheit to degrees Celsius. The equation you all learned in high school for this is $C = 5/9 \times (F−32)$,

TABLE 4-2   Order of Precedence for Java Arithmetic Operators

Operator(s)	Operation	Precedence
( )	Parentheses	Evaluated first, inside-out if nested, or left-to-right if same level.
*, /, or %	Multiplication Division Remainder	Evaluated second, left-to-right.
+, −	Addition Subtraction	Evaluated last, left-to-right.

where *F* is degrees Fahrenheit and *C* is degrees Celsius. Now, suppose you were to code this equation as you see it, as follows:

```
C = 5/9*(F−32);
```

What do you suppose would happen? You're right. The resulting value for C would always be 0, regardless of the value of F, because Java always produces a 0 for 5/9. How could this be corrected? Yes, by coding either the numerator or denominator of the fractional value as a floating-point value, like this:

```
C = 5.0/9*(F−32);
```

There is another way to correct this problem. What if you coded the statement like this:

```
C = (F−32)*5/9;
```

Here, if *F* is defined as a floating-point value then the expression $(F - 32)$ produces a floating-point value. This value is then multiplied by 5 to produce another floating-point value, which is divided by 9 to produce the final floating-point result.

Example 4-2

Evaluate each of the following expressions:

a. `4.6 − 2.0 + 3.2`
b. `4.6 − 2.0 * 3.2`
c. `4.6 − 2.0 / 2 * 3.2`
d. `−3.0 * ((4.3 + 2.5) * 2.0) − 1.0`
e. `−21.0/−2`
f. `−21.0 % −2`
g. `10.0/3`
h. `((4*12)/(4+12))`
i. `4*12/4+12`
j. `grossPay = rate*40+(hours−40)*(1.5*rate)`

Solution

a. `4.6 − 2.0 + 3.2 = (4.6 − 2.0) + 3.2 = 2.6 + 3.2 = 5.8`
b. `4.6 − 2.0 * 3.2 = 4.6 − (2.0 * 3.2) = 4.6 − 6.4 = −1.8`

c. $4.6 - 2.0/2 * 3.2 = 4.6 - ((2.0/2) * 3.2) = 4.6 - (1.0 * 3.2) = 4.6 - 3.2 = 1.4$

d. $-3.0 * ((4.3 + 2.5) * 2.0) - 1.0 = -3.0 * (6.8 * 2.0) - 1.0 = -3.0 * 13. 6 - 1.0 = -40.8 - 1.0 = -41.8$

e. $-21.0/-2 = 10.5$

f. $-21.0\%-2 = -1$

g. $10.0/3 = 3.333333$

h. $((4*12)/(4+12)) = 48/16 = 3$

i. $4*12/4+12 = 48/4+12 = 12+12 = 24$

j. This is how you might code an hourly gross pay value, based on "time and a half" for any hours over 40. To do this calculation, the overtime rate must be added to the regular 40-hour rate. Does this expression accomplish this task? Well, let's see. The expressions within the parentheses are evaluated first, from left to right. Therefore, 40 is first subtracted from *hours*, then *rate* is multiplied by 1.5. Next, the multiplication is performed, from left to right, so *rate* is multiplied by 40, and then the results from the two parenthetical expressions are multiplied together. Finally, the addition operation is performed, adding the overtime calculation to the regular pay calculation, the result being assigned to *grossPay*. Adding some parentheses, as follows, might clarify the calculation; however, the result would be the same. Here you definitely see that the overtime calculation is added to the regular pay calculation.

```
grossPay=(rate*40)+((hours-40)*(1.5*rate))
```

DEBUGGING TIP

When using parentheses within an arithmetic expression, the number of left parentheses must equal the number of right parentheses. When coding your programs, always count each to make sure that this equality holds.

Notice that we have used parentheses in the solutions for the preceding examples to indicate the order of operations. As you can see, the parentheses clarify the expression. For this reason, we suggest that you use parentheses liberally when writing arithmetic expressions. This way, you will always be sure of the order in which the compiler will execute the operators within the expression. Keep in mind, however, that the compiler will always perform the operations within parentheses from inside out, as shown in part d of Example 4-2. In particular, notice how the evaluation of part h of Example 4-2 differs from part i. The parentheses in part h force Java to perform the division last, after the addition. In part i, the division is performed prior to the addition, generating a completely different result. This is why you should use parentheses liberally when writing expressions. It is better to be safe than sorry! You might have also noticed that spacing around an operator is ignored. In other words, 2 % 3 produces the same result as 2%3. In this text, we will often use spacing when we feel it is necessary to make the code easier to interpret. Just remember that the compiler ignores any spacing when it evaluates the expression.

Standard Arithmetic Methods

To perform more advanced mathematical operations, you can use any of the standard methods contained in the Java *Math* class. Some of these standard mathematical methods are listed in Table 4-3. Many of these operations should be familiar to you from your

TABLE 4-3   Some Standard Mathematical Methods Available in Java

Method Name	Operation
abs(x)	Returns the absolute value of x.
acos(x)	Returns the arc cosine of x (radians).
asin(x)	Returns the arc sine of x (radians).
atan(x)	Returns the arc tangent of x (radians).
ceil(x)	Rounds x up to the next highest integer.
cos(x)	Returns the cosine of x (radians).
exp(x)	Returns e^x.
floor(x)	Rounds down to the next lowest integer.
log(x)	Returns the natural log of x.
min(x,y)	Returns the smallest of x and y.
max(x,y)	Returns the largest of x and y.
pow(x,y)	Returns x raised to the power of y.
random()	Generates a random number between 0 and 1.
round(x)	Rounds x to the nearest integer value.
sin(x)	Returns the sine of x (radians).
sqrt(x)	Returns the square root of x.
tan(x)	Returns the tangent of x (radians).
E	Value of e (2.718281828459045)
PI	Value of π (3.141592653589793)

background in mathematics. When using any of these methods in Java, you must make sure that the argument is the correct data type as specified by the method definition. In addition, any variable to which the method is assigned must be defined as the same data type returned by the method.

The methods in Table 4-3 must be called using the *Math* class name. For example, to call the *sqrt()* method, you must use the code *Math.sqrt(x)*.

   Use the *Math* class name to call a method in the *Math* class.

Thus, the statement

```
Math.sqrt(9);
```

returns the value 3.0.

You can raise any value to the power of any other value using the *pow()* method. As a result, the statement

```
Math.pow(2, 3);
```

returns the value 8.0.

Notice that the *Math* class also includes the standard trig operations. However, be careful when using these because they evaluate radians, not degrees. For example, the statement

```
Math.sin(90*Math.PI/180);
```

returns the value 1.0.

Let's take a closer look at this last statement. First, you see that the *sin()* method is being called. The intent here is to return the sine of 90 degrees. However, notice from Table 4-3 that the *sin()* method requires radians, rather than degrees, as its argument. To convert degrees to radians, you must multiply the degrees by π/180. The *Math* class includes a constant called *PI* that can be called upon for this operation. Thus, we multiply 90 by *Math.PI/180* to convert 90 degrees to radians as required by the *sin()* method.

 The standard trig methods in the Java *Math* class evaluate radians, not degrees. Multiply degrees by *Math.PI/180* within the trig method argument to convert degrees to radians.

Rounding Decimal Output   The *Math.floor()* method can be conveniently used to round a decimal number to a specific number of decimal places. For example, the statement

```
netPay = Math.floor(netPay*100+.5)/100;
```

will round the *value* to the nearest 100th, thus providing for two decimal places. Look at the argument provided for the *Math.floor()* method. The *netPay* variable is multiplied by 100 and .5 is added to this value, all within the *Math.floor()* argument. The value returned by *Math.floor()* is then divided by 100. The value 100 being used two places in the calculation is referred to as a *scaling factor*. If you change the scaling factor value, you can round to different decimal places. For example, using a scaling factor of 10 will round to the nearest 10th, providing one decimal place, while using a scaling factor of 1000 will round to the nearest 1000th, providing three decimal places. What do you suppose the .5 does in the above calculation? Well, if you think about how rounding works, you know that anything below .5 is rounded down and anything of .5 or above is rounded up. The .5 is used in the calculation to provide proper rounding, regardless of the scaling factor.

Increment and Decrement Operators

There are many times in a program when you will need to increment (add 1) or decrement (subtract 1) a variable. The increment and decrement operators shown in Table 4-4 are provided for this purpose.

Increment/decrement can be applied to both integer and floating-point variables, as well as character variables. An increment operation adds 1 to the value of a variable. Thus, $++x$ or $x++$ is equivalent to the statement $x = x + 1$. Conversely, a decrement operation subtracts 1 from the value of a variable. As a result, $--x$ or $x--$ is equivalent

TABLE 4-4   Increment and Decrement Operators

Operation	Operator
Increment	++
Decrement	--

to the statement $x = x - 1$. As you can see, you can *pre*increment/*pre*decrement a variable, or *post*increment/*post*decrement a variable. What follows is a short example to illustrate increment/decrement.

Example 4-3

Determine the output generated by the following program:

```
StaugIO io = new StaugIO();
int x = 5;
int y = 10;

io.writeInfo("x = " + ++x
        + "\nx = " + --x
        + "\ny = " + (y = ++x - 2));
x = 5;
io.writeInfo("\ny = " + (y = x++ - 2)
        + "\nx = " + x);

x = 0;
io.writeInfo("\ny = " + (y = x-- - 2)
        + "\nx = " + x);
```

Solution

Here is the output that you will see on the monitor:

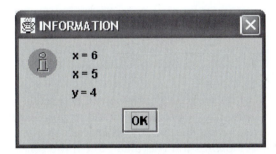

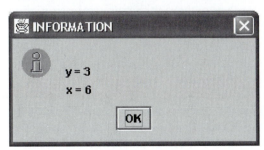

Notice that the variable x is initialized with the value 5 at the start of the code. Here is what happens within the first *writeInfo()* statement. The value of x is preincremented from 5 to 6 and displayed. Then the value of x is predecremented from 6 back to 5 and displayed. Next, the value of x is preincremented and 2 is subtracted from this value. This value is then assigned to y. We say that x is preincremented because the increment symbol appears before x and the increment operation is performed *before x is used in* the expression. Thus, the expression reduces to $y = x + 1 - 2 = 5 + 1 - 2 = 4$. Observe that the arithmetic operations are performed first, and then the result is assigned to y via the assignment operator. Thus, the value displayed by the *writeInfo()* statement is the value of y, or 4.

Now, look at the second *writeInfo()* statement. This involves a postincrement operation on x. A postincrement operation is indicated by the increment symbol following x. So, what's the difference between a preincrement and a postincrement operation? Well, a preincrement operation increments the variable *before any expression involving the variable is evaluated*. On the other hand, a postincrement operation increments the variable *after any expression involving the variable is evaluated*. Now, looking at the code, you find that x starts out with the value 5. Thus, the expression reduces to $y = x - 2 = 5 - 2 = 3$. *After* the expression is evaluated, x is incremented to the value 6. This is verified in the second output window. Finally, the last *writeInfo()* statement shows the result of a postdecrement operation. Here, x is first assigned the value 0 to be used in the expression. Thus, $y = 0 - 2 = -2$. *After* the expression is evaluated, the value of x is decremented to -1, as shown by the last output window.

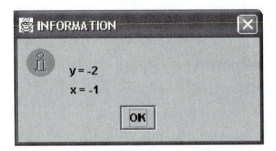

From Example 4-3, you see that a variable can be preincremented or postincremented. Likewise, a variable can be predecremented or postdecremented. If a variable is preincremented or predecremented within an expression, the variable is incremented/decremented *before* the expression is evaluated. On the other hand, if a variable is postincremented or postdecremented within an expression, the variable is incremented/decremented *after* the expression is evaluated.

THINK!

There is often confusion about pre- versus post-increment/decrement. Just remember that it doesn't matter *unless* the increment/decrement operation is part of an expression. Within an expression a pre-increment/decrement is executed *before* the expression is evaluated, while a post-increment/decrement is executed *after* the expression is evaluated. As a further example, suppose we define two integer variables called *number* and *value*. Then the statements

```
++value; and value++;
```

will produce the same value for *value*. However, the statements

```
number = ++value; and number = value++;
```

will produce two different values for *number*. Of course, the value of *value* would be incremented by 1 after executing any of the foregoing statements. To avoid potential problems, we suggest that you *do not* use ++ or −− within expressions, even within simple assignment and output statements. Use the more readable and predictable longer form of adding or subtracting 1 from a variable. Only use ++ or −− when a variable is being incremented/decremented as a statement by itself.

QUICK CHECK

1. List the order in which Java performs arithmetic operations. Be sure to mention how parentheses are handled.
2. What can be said about *x* if *x* % 2 returns the value 0?
3. What can be said about *y* if *y* % 17 returns the value 0?
4. What is returned by the expression 1 / 2 % 5?
5. What is returned by the expression (2 − ++x), assuming that *x* has the value 1 before the expression is evaluated?
6. What is returned by the expression (2 − x++), assuming that *x* has the value 1 before the expression is evaluated?
7. Write a statement using the decrement operator that is equivalent to the statement x = x − 1.
8. True or false: The division operator will produce an integer result when either of the operands is an integer.
9. What is the difference between using the preincrement operator versus the postincrement operator on a variable, especially when the variable is used as part of an expression?
10. What is the result of 10/100?
11. Write a statement to display a random number between 0 and 100.
12. Write a statement that will display the tangent of 45 degrees.
13. Write a statement that will return the value of π.
14. Explain how you can get an online description of a standard method using your IDE.

4.2   Assignment Operations

An assignment operation stores a value in memory. The value is stored at a location in memory that is identified by the variable on the left-hand side of the assignment operator. As a result, a Java assignment operator *assigns* the value on the right side of the operator to the variable appearing on the left side of the operator. Another way to say this is that the variable on the left side of the operator is *set* to the value on the right side of the operator. The Java assignment operators are listed in Table 4-5.

First, let's say a word about the simple assignment operator, =. Although an equals symbol is used for this operator, you cannot think of it as "equals." Here's why. Consider

TABLE 4-5   Assignment Operators Used in Java

Operation	Symbol	Example	Equivalent to
Simple assignment	=	value = 1	value = 1
Addition/assignment	+=	value += 1	value = value + 1
Subtraction/assignment	-=	value -= 1	value = value - 1
Multiplication/assignment	*=	value *= 2	value = value * 2
Division/assignment	/=	value /= 2	value = value / 2
Remainder/assignment (integers only)	%=	value %= 2	value = value % 2

the statement $x = x + 1$. If you put this expression in an algebra exam, your professor would mark it as incorrect, because x cannot be equal to itself plus 1, right? However, in Java, this expression means to add 1 to x, and then assign the resulting value back to x. In other words, set x to the value $x + 1$. This is a perfectly legitimate operation. As you will soon find out, equals is a Boolean operator and uses two equals symbols, ==, in Java.

The compound assignment operators shown in Table 4-5 simply combine the assignment operator with an arithmetic operator. Suppose that we define x and y as integers; then the following holds:

x +=y is equivalent to $x = x + y$
x -=y is equivalent to $x = x - y$
x *=y is equivalent to $x = x * y$
x /=y is equivalent to $x = x/y$
x %=y is equivalent to $x = x \% y$

As you can see, both the increment/decrement operators and the compound assignment operators provide a shorthand notation for writing arithmetic expressions. This shorthand notation takes a bit of getting used to. These are simply syntactic shortcuts which you don't have to use. In fact, many instructors prefer the regular notation because it is more readable and less cryptic than the shorthand notation. Ask your instructors which notation they prefer.

 QUICK CHECK

1. Write a statement using the compound addition assignment operator that is equivalent to the statement x = x + 5.
2. Write a statement using the compound division assignment operator that is equivalent to the statement x = x/10.
3. Write a statement using the compound division assignment operator that is equivalent to the statement x = 10/x.
4. Why does the statement x = x + 5 make sense in Java, but not in your math class?

Problem Solving in Action: Consumer Loan

Problem

Your local bank has hired you to write a consumer loan program. The banker tells you that this program will be run by their loan officers, who will enter the date, customer name, loan amount, term of the loan, and annual interest rate. The program must then display this data, along with the monthly payment for the loan. The banker gives you the following formula to calculate the monthly payment.

$$payment = principal * rate/(1\text{-}(1 + rate)^{-term})$$

Let's first define the problem in terms of input, processing, and output as follows:

Defining the Problem

Input:	The input must be the date, customer name, and values for the loan principal, interest rate, and term.
Processing:	$payment = principal * rate/(1\text{-}(1 + rate)^{-term})$
	where: *principal* is the amount of the loan.
	rate is a monthly interest rate in decimal form.
	term is the number of months of the loan.
Output:	The final program output must show the calculated monthly loan payment along with the date, customer name, loan principal, interest rate, and term used in the calculation.

Planning the Solution

The next step is to construct a set of algorithms from the problem definition. Now, try to identify the separate tasks that must be performed to solve the problem. First, the program must obtain the required data from the user. Once the data is entered, the program must calculate the payment. Finally, the program must display the results. Thus, we can identify three program tasks, or methods, as follows:

- Read the user's name, date of program run, loan principal, interest rate, and term from the user.
- Calculate the monthly payment using the equation
    $$payment = principal * rate/(1\text{-}(1 + rate)^{-term})$$
- Display the customer name, date the program was run, the loan data, and monthly payment.

The problem-solving diagram in Figure 4-1 shows the structure required for the program.

Now, we must employ stepwise refinement to develop the algorithms. The initial algorithm level, *main()*, will simply reflect the problem definition and call the individual methods, as follows:

Initial Algorithm

main()
BEGIN
   Call method to obtain the input data from the user.
   Call method to calculate the loan payment.
   Call method to get the data and display the results.
END.

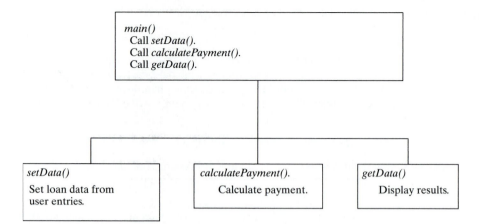

FIGURE 4-1   A problem solution diagram for the loan problem.

The first level of refinement requires that we show a detailed algorithm for each method. They are as follows:

First Level of Refinement

setData()
BEGIN
    Write a user prompt to enter the user's name.
    Read *name*.
    Write a user prompt to enter the date.
    Read *date*.
    Write a user prompt to enter the loan principal.
    Read *principal*.
    Write a user prompt to enter the annual interest rate of the loan.
    Read *rate*.
    Write a user prompt to enter the term of the loan, in months.
    Read *term*.
END.

calculatePayment()
BEGIN
    Calculate *decRate* = *rate*/12/100.
    Calculate *payment* = *principal* $*$ *decRate*/$(1-(1+decRate)^{-term})$.
END.

getData()
BEGIN
    Display user's name and date of program run.
    Display the principal, rate, term, and payment values.
END.

Notice that *rate* is converted to a monthly value in decimal form. Why? Because the user entry is an annual value in percentage form; however, the banker informs you that the payment calculation formula requires a monthly value in decimal form. The next step is to construct the

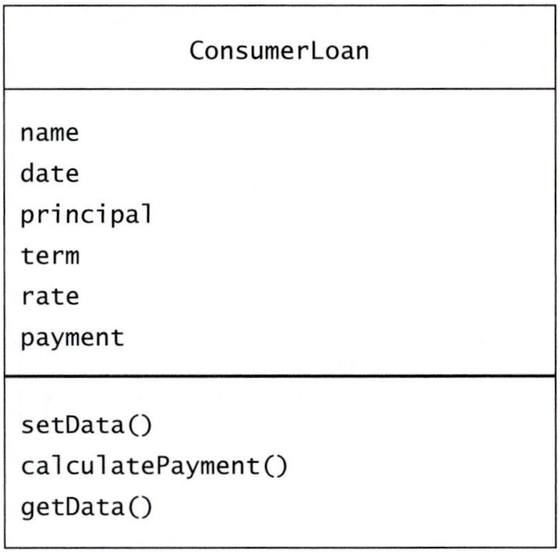

FIGURE 4-2   A class diagram for the *ConsumerLoan* class shows the data and method members that make up the class.

class diagram. We will call this class *ConsumerLoan* and fill it with the data and methods discussed above and shown in Figure 4-2.

Coding the Program

Here is how the foregoing class is translated into Java code. Compare the program code to the corresponding output seen by the user. Make an effort to look at each of the coding details. Note in particular how the *pow()* method is used to code the exponential equation that calculates the payment.

```
/*
 * Action04_01.java
 *
 * Created on April 25, 2002, 12:26 PM
 */

/**
 *
 * @author Andrew C. Staugaard, Jr.
 * @version 1.0
 */

import staugIO.StaugIO;          //FOR INPUT/OUTPUT
import java.text.NumberFormat;   //FOR CURRENCY FORMATTING

class ConsumerLoan
{
  //DEFINE VARIABLES AND OBJECTS
```

```java
    private String name = " ";              //CUSTOMER NAME
    private String date = " ";              //DATE OF REPORT
    private double principal = 0.0;         //LOAN PRINCIPAL
    private double term = 0;                //TERM OF LOAN IN MONTHS
    private double rate = 0.0;              //ANNUAL INTEREST IN PERCENT FORM
    private double payment = 0.0;           //MONTHLY PAYMENT
    private double decRate = 0.0;           //MONTHLY INTEREST IN DECIMAL FORM
    private StaugIO io = new StaugIO();     //FOR INPUT/OUTPUT

    //CONSTRUCTOR METHOD
    public ConsumerLoan()
    {
    }//END CONSTRUCTOR

    //setData() METHOD
    public void setData()
    {
      name = io.readString("Enter your name: ");
      date = io.readString("Enter the date in mm/dd/yyyy format: ");
      principal = io.readDouble("Enter the amount of the loan: ");
      term = io.readDouble("Enter the duration of the loan in months: ");
      rate = io.readDouble("Enter the annual interest rate in percent: ");
    }//END setData()

    //calculatePayment() METHOD
    public void calculatePayment()
    {
      payment=principal*(rate/12/100)/(1-Math.pow((1+(rate/12/100)),-term));
    }//END calculatePayment()

    //getData() METHOD
    public void getData()
    {
      NumberFormat currency = NumberFormat.getCurrencyInstance();
      io.writeInfo(name + " " + date
                        + "\nAMOUNT: " + currency.format(principal)
                        + "\nRATE: " + rate + '%'
                        + "\nTERM: " + term + " months"
                        + "\nPAYMENT: " + currency.format(payment));
    }//END getData()
}//END ConsumerLoan

public class Action04_01
{
    public static void main(String args[])
    {
      ConsumerLoan myLoan = new ConsumerLoan();
      myLoan.setData();
      myLoan.calculatePayment();
      myLoan.getData();
```

```
      //EXIT PROGRAM
      System.exit(0);
   }//END main()
}//END Action04_01
```

Here is what the loan officer would see after running the program for a sample consumer loan:

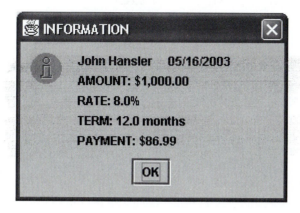

Notice how the payment is expressed in dollars and cents. This is made possible by using the *format()* method of the *NumberFormat* class to convert the calculated payment to currency format. You now should have no trouble understanding this program with the material presented in this chapter.

Problem Solving in Action: Present Value

Problem

Suppose that you want to buy a new car in 5 years and you plan on spending $30,000. Something you might want to know is what that same expenditure would cost you in today's dollars. Present value (*PV*) is a measure of the value of a future expenditure in today's dollars. Knowing the future value (*FV*) of an expenditure and an expected interest rate over the period between the present and future, you can calculate how much the expenditure would be in today's dollars using the following equation:

$$PV = FV/(1 + r)^n$$

where
  PV is the present value in today's dollars.
  FV is the future value in future dollars.
  r is the periodic interest rate.
  n is the number of periods between the *PV* and *FV*.

Write a program to find the present value of a future expenditure.

Defining the Problem

Input:　　　　　　　The user must enter the following information:
- The future value (*FV*) of the expenditure.
- The periodic interest rate (*r*) as an annual percentage.
- The number of periods (*n*) in years.

Processing:　　　　The program must calculate the present value using the equation

$$PV = FV/(1 + r)^n$$

Output:　　　　　　The program must display the present value in a dialog box along with the future value, interest rate and period used in the calculation.

Planning the Solution

Using a modular approach to solving this problem, we will divide the problem into three sub-problems that reflect the problem definition. The three major tasks that follow directly from the problem definition are

- Read the user entries for *FV*, *r*, and *n*.
- Calculate the present value, *PV*.
- Display the calculated present value, along with the future value, interest rate, and period used in the calculation within a dialog box.

Here are the respective algorithms:

Initial Algorithm
main()
BEGIN
　　Call a method to read the user entries for *FV*, *r*, and *n*.
　　Call a method to calculate the present value, *PV*.
　　Call a method to display the present value, *PV*, along with the values used to calculate the present value.
END.

First Level of Refinement
setData()
BEGIN
　　Write a user prompt to enter the expenditure in future dollars, *FV*.
　　Read *FV*.
　　Write a user prompt to enter the annual interest rate, *r*.
　　Read *r*.
　　Write a user prompt to enter the number of years, *n*.
　　Read *n*.
END.

calculatePresentValue()
BEGIN
　　Calculate $PV = FV/(1 + r)^n$.
END.

getData()
BEGIN
   Write *PV, FV, r,* and *n.*
END.

The problem solution diagram is shown in Figure 4-3.

Next, we will put our variables and methods in a class called *PresentValue* as shown in the class diagram in Figure 4-4.

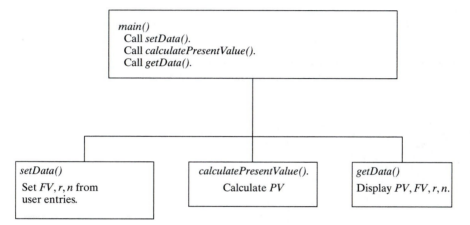

FIGURE 4-3 A problem solution diagram for the present value problem shows the stepwise refinement of the algorithms.

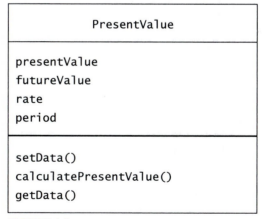

FIGURE 4-4 A class diagram for the *PresentValue* class shows the data and methods that make up the class.

Coding the Program

The implementation of the above set of algorithms and class is as follows:

```
/*
 * Action04_02.java
 *
```

```java
 * Created on April 25, 2002, 12:26 PM
 */

/**
 *
 * @author Andrew C. Staugaard, Jr.
 * @version 1.0
 */

import staugIO.StaugIO;         //FOR INPUT/OUTPUT
import java.text.NumberFormat;  //FOR CURRENCY FORMATTING

class PresentValue
{
  //DEFINE VARIABLES AND OBJECTS
  private double futureValue = 0.0;    //FUTURE VALUE OF EXPENDITURE
  private double presentValue = 0.0;   //PRESENT VALUE OF EXPENDITURE
  private double period = 0;           //YEARS TO COMPOUND
  private double rate = 0.0;           //ANNUAL INTEREST IN PERCENT FORM
  private StaugIO io = new StaugIO();  //FOR INPUT/OUTPUT

 //CONSTRUCTOR METHOD
  public PresentValue()
  {
  }//END CONSTRUCTOR

  //setData() METHOD
  public void setData()
  {
    futureValue = io.readDouble("Enter the future expenditure amount");
    period = io.readDouble("Enter the number of years to compound");
    rate = io.readDouble("Enter the annual interest rate in percent");
  }//END setData()

  //calculatePresentValue() METHOD
  public void calculatePresentValue()
  {
    presentValue = futureValue/Math.pow(1+rate/100,period);
  }//END calculatePayment()

  //getData() METHOD
  public void getData()
  {
    NumberFormat currency = NumberFormat.getCurrencyInstance();
    io.writeInfo("FUTURE VALUE: " + currency.format(futureValue)
                + "\nPRESENT VALUE: " + currency.format(presentValue)
                + "\nRATE: " + rate + '%'
                + "\nTERM: " + period + " years");
  }//END getData()
}//END PresentValue
```

```
public class Action04_02
{
  public static void main(String args[])
  {
    PresentValue myMoney = new PresentValue();
    myMoney.setData();
    myMoney.calculatePresentValue();
    myMoney.getData();

    //EXIT PROGRAM
    System.exit(0);
  }//END main()
}//END Action04_02
```

Again, we have used the standard *pow()* method to make the $(1 + r)^n$ calculation. Here is the sequence of dialog boxes the user would see for a sample run of the program:

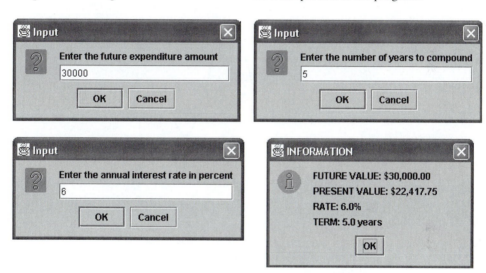

What the final output shows is that if you invest the present value of approximately $22,417 today, it will be worth $30,000 in 5 years if invested at an interest rate of 6%. Study the program code to make sure you understand how it is working.

Problem Solving in Action: Data Communications

Problem

In the field of data communications, binary digital computer data is converted to analog sine wave data for transmission over long distances via the telephone and cable networks. Hardware devices that perform this operation are called ***modems***. As you know, digital data is composed of binary 1's and 0's. On the other hand, analog data is composed of sine waves. Thus, a modem converts binary 1's and 0's to a series of sine waves for communication over the telephone or cable systems. Since binary data is represented using sine waves, the study of data communications often requires the analysis of a sine wave. One such analysis is to find the amplitude, in volts, of a sine wave at any given point in time.

This is called the ***instantaneous value*** of the sine wave and is found using the equation

$$v = V_{peak} \sin(2\pi ft)$$

where

    v is the instantaneous voltage at any point in time t on the waveform, in volts.
    V_{peak} is the peak amplitude of the waveform, in volts.
    π is the constant 3.14159.
    f is the frequency of the waveform, in hertz.
    t is the time, in seconds, for v.

Write a program to find the instantaneous voltage value of the sine wave in Figure 4-5. Have the user enter the peak voltage in volts, the frequency in kilohertz, and the time in milliseconds.

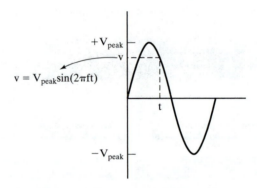

FIGURE 4-5   A sine wave for the data communications problem.

Defining the Problem

Input: The user must enter the following information:
- The peak amplitude of the waveform, V_{peak}, in volts.
- The frequency of the waveform, f, in kilohertz.
- The point in time, t, in milliseconds, for which the instantaneous voltage must be calculated.

Processing: The program must calculate the instantaneous voltage value using the equation $v = V_{peak} \sin(2\pi ft)$

Output: The program must display the instantaneous voltage value, v, resulting from the previous equation.

Planning the Solution

Using the modular approach to solving this problem, we will divide the problem into three sub-problems that reflect the problem definition. The three major tasks that follow directly from the problem definition are

- Read the user entries for V_{peak}, f, and t.
- Calculate the instantaneous voltage, v.
- Display the instantaneous voltage value, v, resulting from the calculation.

Here are the respective algorithms:

Initial Algorithm

main()
BEGIN
    Call method to read the user entries for V_{peak}, f, and t.
    Call method to calculate the instantaneous voltage, v.
    Call method to display the instantaneous voltage value, v.
END.

First Level of Refinement

setData()
BEGIN
    Write a user prompt to enter the peak amplitude of the waveform, V_{peak}, in volts.
    Read V_{peak}.
    Write a user prompt to enter the frequency of the waveform, f, in kilohertz.
    Read f.
    Write a user prompt to enter the time, t, in milliseconds.
    Read t.
END.

calculateVoltage()
BEGIN
    Calculate $v = V_{peak} \sin (2\pi ft)$.
END.

getVoltage()
BEGIN
    Write the instantaneous voltage value, v.
END.

The problem solution diagram is shown in Figure 4-6.

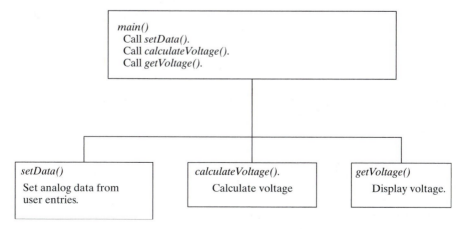

FIGURE 4-6 A problem solution diagram for the analog voltage problem shows the stepwise refinement of the algorithms.

Next, we will put our variables and methods in a class called *AnalogVoltage* as shown in the class diagram in Figure 4-7.

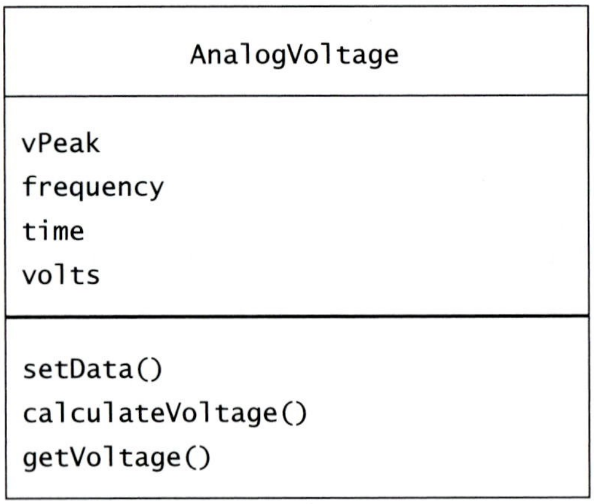

<table>
<tr><td align="center">AnalogVoltage</td></tr>
<tr><td>vPeak
frequency
time
volts</td></tr>
<tr><td>setData()
calculateVoltage()
getVoltage()</td></tr>
</table>

FIGURE 4-7   A class diagram for the *AnalogVoltage* class shows the data and method members that make up the class.

Coding the Program

The implementation of the above set of algorithms and class is as follows:

```java
/*
 * Action04_03.java
 *
 * Created on April 25, 2002, 1:58 PM
 */

/**
 *
 * @author Andrew C. Staugaard, Jr.
 * @version 1.0
 */

import staugIO.StaugIO;                  //FOR INPUT AND OUTPUT
class AnalogVoltage
{
    //DEFINE AND INITIALIZE OBJECTS AND VARIABLES
    private double vPeak = 0.0;           //PEAK VOLTAGE IN VOLTS
    private double frequency = .0;        //FREQUENCY IN KILOHERTZ
    private double time = 0.0;            //TIME IN MILLISECONDS
    private double volts = 0.0;           //INSTANTANEOUS VOLTAGE IN VOLTS
    private StaugIO io = new StaugIO();   //INPUT/OUTPUT OBJECT
```

```
      //CONSTRUCTOR
      public AnalogVoltage()
      {
      }//END CONSTRUCTOR

      //setData() METHOD
      public void setData()
      {
        vPeak = io.readDouble("Enter the peak voltage in volts");
        frequency = io.readDouble("Enter the frequency in kilohertz");
        time = io.readDouble("Enter the time in milliseconds");
      }//END setData()

      public void calculateVoltage()
      {
         volts = vPeak * Math.sin(2 * Math.PI * frequency * time);
      }//END calculateVoltage()

    //getVoltage() METHOD
      public void getVoltage()
      {
         io.writeInfo("Peak Voltage: " + vPeak + " volts"
                      + "\nFrequency: " + frequency + " kilohertz"
                      + "\nTime: " + time + " milliseconds"
                      + "\nInstantaneous voltage: " + volts + " volts.");
      }//END getVoltage()
}//END AnalogVoltage

public class Action04_03
{
      public static void main (String args[])
      {
        //DEFINE DataComm OBJECT
        AnalogVoltage voltage = new AnalogVoltage();

        //CALL METHODS
        voltage.setData();
        voltage.calculateVoltage();
        voltage.getVoltage();

        //EXIT PROGRAM
        System.exit(0);
      }//END main()
}//END Action04_03
```

Here is the sequence of dialog boxes the user would see for a sample run of the program:

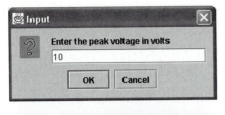

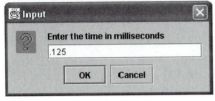

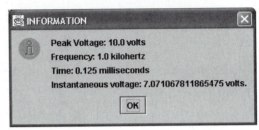

It's probably a good idea to take a closer look at some of the features of this program. An observation from the above output is that the user had to enter the waveform frequency in kilohertz and the time in milliseconds. These are typical units found in data communications. Notice that the user prompts indicate this entry requirement.

The calculation of the output voltage, *volts*, is performed with the following program statement:

```
volts = vPeak * Math.sin(2 * Math.PI * frequency * time);
```

Notice that the standard *Math* class is used to call the *sin()* method required for the equation. Within the *sin()* method argument, the value of *PI* is obtained from the *Math* class as required by the voltage equation. The equation does not have to be altered to accommodate frequency in kilohertz and time in milliseconds, because the product of these two units cancel each other out (10^{+3} cancels 10^{-3}). One final point: The *sin()* method in Java is defined to evaluate angles in *radians*. Fortunately, the quantity $(2 * PI * f * t)$ produces radians and not degrees. This is why there is no conversion factor within the equation. If the value to be evaluated by the *sin()* method is in degrees, it must be converted to radians to obtain a correct result.

Now, make a serious effort to complete all of the questions and problems that follow. It is time to get your hands dirty and write some of your own programs. This is where you will really begin learning how to program in Java.

CHAPTER SUMMARY

Arithmetic operations in Java include the common add, subtract, multiply, and divide operations that can be performed on any numeric data type. Addition, subtraction, multiplication, and division are basically the same for both the integer and floating-point data types. However, when you divide two integers, you will get an integer result. If you need a floating-point result, at least one of the operands must be defined as a floating-point value. The remainder (%) operator is defined for integers only and will generate unpredictable results if used with floating-point values.

There are increment/decrement operators defined in Java. The increment operator, ++, adds one to a variable, and the decrement operator, −−, subtracts one from a variable. You can preincrement/predecrement a variable or postincrement/postdecrement a variable. There's a big difference when the increment/decrement is used as part of an expression to be evaluated by

Java. A preincrement/predecrement operation on a variable is performed *before* the expression is evaluated, and a postincrement/postdecrement operation is performed on the variable *after* the expression is evaluated.

The simple assignment operator in Java is the = operator. A value on the right side of the = operator is assigned to a variable on the left side of the operator. There are compound assignment operators, such as +=, *=, and so on, that combine an arithmetic operation with the assignment operation. These operators are used as a form of shorthand notation within a Java program.

Finally, Java includes several standard methods that can be used to perform common tasks. There are mathematical methods, conversion methods, and string methods, just to mention a few categories.

QUESTIONS AND PROBLEMS

Questions

1. What value will be returned for each of the following integer operations:
   a. 4-2*3
   b. -35/6
   c. -35%6
   d. -25 * 14 % 7 * -25/-5
   e. -5 * 3+9-2 * 7
   f. (-13/2) % 6

2. Evaluate each of the following expressions:
   a. 0.5+3.75/0.25*2
   b. 2.5-(1.2+(4.0-3.0)*2.0)+1.0
   c. 6.0e-4*3.0e+3
   d. 6.0e-4/3.0e+3

3. Evaluate each of the following expressions:
   a. 5.0-(6.0/3)
   b. 200*200
   c. 5-6/3
   d. (5-6)/3
   e. 1+25%5
   f. -33000+2000

4. Determine what will be displayed by each *writeInfo()* method. Assume that *io* has been defined as an object of the *StaugIO* class.
   a. int i = 0;
      int j = 10;
      io.writeInfo(++i + j++);
   b. double k = 2.5;
      io.writeInfo (k-- * 2);
   c. char character = 'a';
      io.writeInfo(++character);
   d. int x = 1;
      int y = -1;
      int z = 25;
      io.writeInfo(++x + ++y - --z);

5. Determine the output generated by the following. Assume that *io* has been defined as an object of the *StaugIO* class.
   a. io.writeInfo((2%5)/(5%2));

   b. io.writeInfo(3*6/3+6);
   c. io.writeInfo((3*6)/(3+6));
 6. Explain how to get information on how to use a standard method available in your compiler.
 7. Determine the value returned by the following methods. Use your compiler reference manual or online help feature to make sure that you understand how the method operates.
   a. Math.abs(−5)
   b. Math.sin(1.57)
   c. Math.log(2.73)
   d. Math.pow(2,5)
   e. Math.cos(0)
   f. Math.random()*10
   g. Math.sqrt(25)
   h. Math.sqrt(Math.sqrt(5))
   i. Math.sqrt(2)

Problems

Least Difficult

*In problems 1 – 3 place your solution code inside the single main() application class shell shown
below. Name your application PXX_YY, where XX is the chapter number (04 in this chapter) and
YY is the problem number. Note: Do not define your variables as private or create separate methods when placing your solution inside of main().*

```
/*
 * PLACE THE PROBLEM NUMBER HERE
 *
 * PLACE THE DATE AND TIME HERE
 */

/**
 *
 * @author PLACE YOUR NAME HERE
 * @version 1.0
 */
import staugIO.StaugIO;          //FOR GUI I/O IF NEEDED

public class PXX_YY
{
   public static void main(String[] args)
   {
      //PLACE YOUR SOLUTION CODE HERE

      //EXIT PROGRAM
      System.exit(0);
   }//END main()
}//END PXX_YY APPLICATION
```

   1. Write a program that will allow a user to convert a temperature in degrees Fahrenheit to
   degrees Centigrade using the following relationship:

$$C = 5/9 \times (F - 32)$$

2. Write a program that will allow a user to convert a measurement in inches to centimeters.

3. Write a simple test program that will demonstrate what happens when you use an illegal argument within a method. For example, what happens when you use a character argument in an mathematical method?

More Difficult

In the problems that follow, code your solution in a separate class using private variables and public methods like you observed in the chapter case studies. Give this class a name that describes its purpose. Then, create an application class and define an object in main() to call your public functions as needed to solve the problem.

4. Write a program for the Java-Mart Company accounting department to determine the gross margin, in percent, for the an input of net sales and cost of goods sold. Gross margin, in percent, can be found by subtracting the cost of sales from the net sales, then dividing by the net sales and multiplying this result by 100.

5. Here is a partial inventory and price list for the Java-Mart coffee shop.

Item	Price
Java of the Day	$1.49
Decaf Java of the Day	$1.59
Cappuccino	$2.29
Espresso	$3.35
Java Mocha	$2.99
Hot Chocolate	$1.29

Java-Mart wants to run a big sale and reduce all these items by 5 percent. Write a program that will print a listing of all the inventory items showing both the regular and sale prices. Assume that a Java-Mart employee will enter the given price list.

6. Revise the program in problem 5 to allow the employee to enter any percentage sales discount.

Most Difficult

7. Employees at the Java-Mart coffee shop just received a 5.5% pay increase retroactive for seven months. Write a program that accepts the employee name, employee number, and current annual salary. The program must then display the employee's name, number, amount of retroactive pay due, the new annual salary and new monthly salary in a tabular format.

8. The Java-Mart management was elated with the programs you have written. They want you to expand their computer operations to the payroll department. Write Java-Mart a payroll program that will calculate an employee's net pay given the following information:

Employee's name
Number of weekly hours worked
Hourly rate of pay
FICA (7.15%)
Federal withholding (28%)
State withholding (10%)

Assume that a Java-Mart payroll employee will be required to enter only the first three items when running the program. Generate a report using the following format:

Employee Name: XXXXXXXXXXXXXXXXXXXXXXXXX
Rate of Pay: $XXX.XX
Hours Worked: XX.XX
Gross Pay: $XXXX.XX
Deductions:
    FICA: $XXX.XX
    Fed. Withholding: XXX.XX
    State Withholding: XXX.XX
                                       ————————
    Total Deductions: $XXX.XX
Net Pay: $XXXX.XX

9. The diagram in Figure 4-8 illustrates how triangulation is used to find the distance to an object. Here's the idea: Two triangulating devices are positioned a certain distance apart, and both devices get a "fix" on an object as shown in the figure. The two triangulating devices and the object form a triangle whose one leg, d, and two angles $\theta 1$ and $\theta 2$ are known. The third angle is easily found by subtracting the two known angles from 180 degrees. The distance from each triangulating device to the object is then found using the Law of Sines, which states:

$$r_1/\sin \theta_1 = r_2/\sin \theta_2 = d/\sin[180 - (\theta_1 + \theta_2)]$$

Write a program to find the distance that the object is from each triangulation device. Assume that the user will enter the distance (d) between the devices and the two angles (θ_1 and θ_2) that the object makes with the triangulating devices.

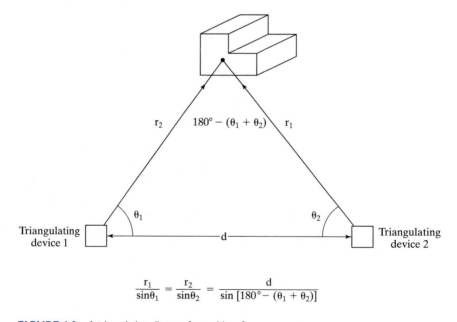

$$\frac{r_1}{\sin\theta_1} = \frac{r_2}{\sin\theta_2} = \frac{d}{\sin\,[180° - (\theta_1 + \theta_2)]}$$

FIGURE 4-8   A triangulation diagram for problem 9.

5

Making Decisions

OBJECTIVES

When you are finished with this chapter, you should have a good understanding of the following:

- The common Boolean relational operators and logical operators used in Java
- The Java decision control structures of if, if/else, and switch
- How to compare strings
- Nested if and if/else structures

- How to write menu-driven programs
- How to test for invalid user entries in a menu-driven program
- When to use the break and default options in a switch statement

Introduction

At the basic level of any programming language there are three fundamental patterns called *control structures*. A control structure is simply a pattern for controlling the flow of program execution. The three fundamental control structures of a programming language are *sequence*, *decision* (sometimes called *selection*), and *iteration*. The sequence control structure is illustrated in Figure 5-1. As you can see, there is nothing fancy about this control structure because program statements are executed sequentially, one after another, in a straight-line fashion. This is called *straight-line programming* and is what you have been doing in Java up to this point.

FIGURE 5-1   The sequence control structure is a series of sequential step-by-step statements.

 A **control structure** is a pattern for controlling the flow of program execution. The three fundamental control structures of any programming language are **sequence**, **decision**, and **iteration**.

The second two control structures, decision and iteration, allow the flow of the program to be altered, depending on one or more conditions. The decision control structure is a decision-making control structure. It is implemented in Java using the `if`, `if/else`, and `switch` statements. These are the topics of this chapter. The iteration control structure is a repetition control structure. It is implemented in Java using the `while`, `do/while`, and `for` statements. These operations are discussed in the next chapter. Both the decision and iteration control structures force the computer to make decisions based on the result of a Boolean operation. So, let's first explore the Boolean operations available in Java.

5.1   Boolean Operations

The real intelligence of a computer comes from its ability to make decisions. All computer decisions, no matter how complex, reduce to Boolean decisions because of the digital nature of the CPU. A Boolean decision is one that is based on a Boolean result of `true` or `false`. That's pretty simple, right? Remember, no matter how complex or sophisticated a digital computer system seems to be, it is only making simple Boolean decisions: `true`/`false`. Decisions in a computer program are made by testing one value against another, such as *if* $x < y$. Here, the value of x is tested against the value of y. If x is in fact less than y, the test result is `true`. However, if the value of x is greater than or equal to the value of y, the test is `false`. Thus, the result of such a test will be a Boolean result of `true` or `false`. Boolean operators in Java can be categorized as either *relational* or *logical* operators.

Relational Operators

Relational operators allow two quantities to be compared. The six common relational operators available in Java are listed in Table 5-1. The relational operators in Table 5-1 can be used to compare any two variables or expressions. In general, you should only compare data of the same data type. This means that integers should be compared to integers, floating-point to floating-point, and characters to characters. The one exception to this rule is that floating-point values can be compared to integers, because an integer can be expressed as a floating-point value by adding a decimal point and a 0. In all cases, the operation generates a Boolean result of `true` or `false`. Let's look at some examples.

TABLE 5-1 The Six Relational Operators Used in Java

Mathematical Symbol	Java Operator	Meaning
$=$	$==$	Equal to
$\neq$	$!=$	Not equal to
$<$	$<$	Less than
$\leq$	$<=$	Less than or equal to
$>$	$>$	Greater than
$\geq$	$>=$	Greater than or equal to

Example 5-1

Evaluate the following relational operations:

a. `5 == 5`

b. `0.025 >= 0.333`

c. `3 != 3`

d. `-45.2 < -3`

e. `'A' < 'Z'`

f. `x = 25, y = -10`
     `x <= y`

Solution

a. `true`, because 5 equals 5.

b. `false`, because 0.025 is not greater than or equal to 0.333.

c. `false`, because 3 equals 3.

d. `true`, because −45.2 is less than −3.

e. `true`, because Java is actually comparing the Unicode value of 'A' to the Unicode value of 'Z'.

f. `false`, because the value assigned to x (25) is not less than or equal to the value assigned to y (−10).

Relational operators can also be combined with arithmetic operators, like this:

$$5 + 3 < 4$$

Now the question is: How does the computer evaluate this expression? Does it perform the addition operation or the relational operation first? If it performs the addition operation first, the result is `false`. However, if it performs the relational operation first, 3 is less than 4 and the result is `true`. As you might suspect, the addition operation is performed first, and then the relational operation. Consequently, the result is `false`, because 8 is not less than 4. Remember, when relational operators are combined with arithmetic operators within an expression, the *relational operators are always performed last*.

Example 5-2

Both arithmetic and relational operators can be part of an output statement to evaluate an expression. Determine the results generated by the following expressions:

a.   `System.out.println('J' > 'K');`

b.   `System.out.println(3*10%3 - 2 > 20/6 + 4);`

Solution

The results generated by the above expressions are:

a. `false`
b. `false`

These values are Boolean values based on the evaluation of the respective relational operations. The result of 'J' > 'K' is `false` because the Unicode value for 'J' is not greater than the Unicode value for 'K'. The result is also `false` in the second case. Here, the evaluation process goes like this:

```
(((3*10)%3)-2) > ((20/6)+4) =
((30%3)-2) > (3+4) =
0-2 > 7 =
-2 > 7 is false
```

Notice that the multiplication operation is performed first, followed by the % and / operations, from left to right. Then the addition/subtraction operations are performed, and finally the greater-than operation is performed.

DEBUGGING TIP

To avoid execution problems, it is *not* a good idea to use the == or != operators to test floating-point values. Rather, you should use <, >, <=, or >= when testing floating-point values. The reason is due to the way that the computer represents floating point values in memory. Unless you have infinite precision, two floating-point values cannot, theoretically, ever be equal.

THINK!

The relational operators of <, >, <=, and >= in Table 5-1 are used to test simple data types such as integer and character. However, you cannot use them to test the relationship between two string objects. Remember that an object has data as well as methods associated with it. So, to test the relationship between two string objects you must have an operation that only looks at the relationship between the object data. The required method in Java is the *compareTo()* method. You saw this method in Chapter 3 when you learned about string objects. The *compareTo()* method tests the relationship between its calling string object and its argument string object, like this:

`s1.compareTo(s2)`

Think of *compareTo()* as a subtraction operation. If the string data within the two string objects are equal, *compareTo()* returns the value 0 because subtracting two equal quantities produces a 0 result, right? If the calling string (*s1*) is less than the argument string (*s2*), *compareTo* returns a negative quantity because subtracting a larger value from a smaller value produces a negative result. However, if the calling string (*s1*) is greater than the argument string (*s2*), *compareTo* returns a positive quantity because subtracting a smaller value from a larger value produces a positive result. For example, suppose we define two string objects like this:

```
String myName = "Andy";
String yourName = "Sandy";
```

Then, to test the relationship between these two objects you would call the *compareTo()* method like this:

```
myName.compareTo(yourName)
```

Here, the result would be negative, since the string "Andy" is less than the string "Sandy".

 When testing the relationship between two string objects, you must use the *compareTo()* method, not the Boolean relational operators.

Logical Operators

Logical operations also generate Boolean results. The three most common logical operators used in Java are given in Table 5-2. You see from the table that the exclamation symbol (!) is used for NOT, the double vertical bar symbols (‖) for OR, and the double ampersand symbols (&&) for AND.

The NOT (!) operator is used to negate, or invert, a Boolean value. Because there are only two possible Boolean values (`true` and `false`), the negation of one results in the other. For example, suppose we define a Boolean variable *A*. Then the variable *A* can take on only two values, `true` or `false`. If *A* is `true`, then !*A* is `false`. Conversely, if *A* is `false`, then !*A* is `true`. This operation can be shown using a ***truth table***. A truth table simply shows the result of a logic operation on a Boolean value. Here is the truth table for the simple NOT operation:

```
A        !A
true     false
false    true
```

TABLE 5-2	Logical Operators Used in Java	
Operation Name	**Symbol**
NOT	!
OR	‖
AND	&&

The OR operator ($\parallel$) is applied to two or more Boolean values. For instance, suppose that *A* and *B* are both defined as Boolean variables. Then *A* and *B* can be either true or false. The OR operation dictates that if either *A* or *B* is true, the result of the operation is true. Another way to say this is that "*any* true results in true." In terms of a truth table, the result is as follows:

A	B	A $\parallel$ B
true	true	true
true	false	true
false	true	true
false	false	false

Notice from the table that *A* $\parallel$ *B* is true whenever *A* is true or *B* is true. Of course, if both *A* and *B* are true, the result also is true.

The AND operator (&&) also operates on two or more Boolean values. Here, if *A* and *B* are Boolean variables, then the expression *A* && *B* is true only when both *A* and *B* are true. Another way to say this is that "*any* false results in false." In terms of a truth table, the result looks like this:

A	B	A && B
true	true	true
true	false	false
false	true	false
false	false	false

The Boolean logical operators can also be applied to logical expressions. For example, consider the following:

(-6<0) && (12>=10)

Is this expression true or false? Well, $-6 < 0$ is true and $12 >= 10$ is true. Consequently, the expression must be true. How about this one?

((3-6)==3)$\parallel$(!(2==4))

You must evaluate both sides of the expression. If either side is true, then the result is true. On the left side, $3 - 6$ is equal to -3, which is not equal to 3. Thus, the left side is false. On the right side, $2 == 4$ is false, but $!(2 == 4)$ must be true. Consequently, the right side of the expression is true. This makes the result of the ORing operation true.

Observe in the two foregoing expressions that parentheses are used to define the expressions being operated upon. Remember to do this whenever you code a logical operator to evaluate two or more expressions. In other words, *always* enclose the things you are ORing and ANDing within parentheses.

You will see in the next section how these logical operators are used to make decisions that control the flow of a program. For example, using the AND operator, you can test to see if two conditions are true. If both conditions are true, the program will execute a series of statements, while skipping those statements if one of the test conditions is false.

PROGRAMMING NOTE

You should be aware that the single vertical bar, ¦, and single ampersand symbol, &, also have meaning to Java. So, always be sure to use two vertical bars and two ampersand symbols when you code the logical OR and AND tests, respectively.

QUICK CHECK

1. Operators that allow two values to be compared are called _____ operators.
2. What is the difference between the = operator and the == operator in Java?
3. What value is generated as a result of the following operation?
   4 > 5 − 2
4. What value is generated as a result of the following operation?
   (5! = 5) && (3==3)
5. Why should the *compareTo()* method be used instead of Boolean relational operators when comparing string objects?

5.2   The if Statement

The operation of the if statement is illustrated by the diagram in Figure 5-2.

The diamond symbol in Figure 5-2 is used to denote a Boolean decision operation, while the rectangles are used to denote processing statements. Observe that the flow of the program is altered, depending on the result of a test expression. The if test can be true or false. If the test expression is true, the if statements, sometimes collectively referred to as the "if clause," are executed. However, if the result of the test is false, the if statements are bypassed and the program flow continues. This is known as a ***decision-making***, or ***selection***, operation, because the program selects, or decides, between one of two possible routes, depending on the conditions that are tested. In summary, the if operation can be stated in words like this: "If the test is true, execute the if statements." Of course, this implies that if the test is false, the if statements are not executed and are then bypassed.

One way of looking at the if statement is as a program "detour." The program must "detour" its route of execution and execute the if statements if the Boolean test is true, before going on to the next sequential program statement.

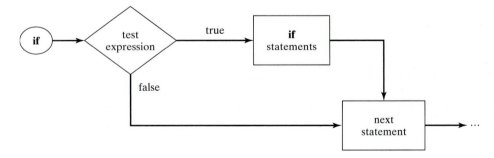

FIGURE 5-2   The flow of the if operation.

Before we look at the Java format for the if statement, let's take a closer look at the test expression. The test expression is a conditional test. This means that one or more conditions are tested to generate a true or false result. To test a single condition, you will use the relational Boolean operators of ==, !=, <, >, <=, and >=. For instance, a typical test might be if(x == y). Here, the single condition, x == y, is tested. If x does in fact equal y, the result of the test is true, and the associated if statements will be executed. If x does not equal y, the if statements are bypassed, and the next sequential statement is executed.

To test multiple conditions, you must use the Boolean logical operators of OR and AND. For example, a test such as if((x != y) && (a < b)) tests two conditions. If x does not equal y *and* if a is less than b, the test result is true, and the associated if statements will be executed. On the other hand, if x equals y *or* if a is *greater than or equal to b*, then the if statements are bypassed.

The Java format for the if statement is as follows:

if *STATEMENT FORMAT*

```
if(test expression)
{
    statement 1;
    statement 2;
         •              //COMPOUND STATEMENT
         •
         •
    statement n;
}//END IF
```

First, notice the overall structure of this format. The keyword if and its associated test expression are written on the first line of the statement. The test expression follows the if keyword and *must* be enclosed within parentheses. The first line is followed by the statements that will be executed if the test is true. This statement block is "framed" by braces. A left brace ({) signals the beginning of the statement block, and a right brace (}) denotes the end of the block. Notice that the beginning brace is placed on a separate line, directly below the keyword if. The ending brace is placed on a separate line, immediately after the last statement in the block and in the same column as the beginning brace. In addition, you should always indent all the block statements two or three spaces in from the braces for readability. When this structure is part of a complex program, there is no question which statements belong to the if operation. If there is more than one statement to be executed within this block, the entire group of statements is referred to as a ***compound statement***. When a compound statement is encountered within a Java program, the entire group of statements is treated like a single statement. Compound statements must always be framed with braces. However, framing is optional when there is only a single statement within the block.

Finally, look at the punctuation syntax of the if statement. Notice that there is no semicolon after the test expression in the first line. However, each statement within the statement block is terminated by a semicolon.

PROGRAMMING NOTE

The framing of statements into a block within the **if** control structure using left and right braces ({ }) is always required when there is more than one statement, but optional when there is only a single statement. However, framing is a good habit to get into, even when there is only a single statement. Many good programmers will, as a matter of habit, place beginning and ending braces for their **if** statements before entering the statements themselves. This way, if you need to add a statement within the body of an **if** later on, you will not forget to add the framing. This prevents any "framing errors" from occurring. A framing error might not generate a compiler error and can be difficult to find. For example, how would the compiler "see" the following code?

```
if(balance < 500)
   monthlyInterest = balance * .02;
   balance = balance + monthlyInterest;
```

Here, the indentation shows that there are two statements within the **if**. However, the compiler only "sees" one **if** statement. The second statement, which adds the *monthlyInterest* to the *balance*, is not part of the **if** statement at all. This statement would always be executed, even when the *balance* is >= 500. To get the desired result, the correct syntax must be

```
if(balance < 500)
{
   monthlyInterest = balance * .02;
   balance = balance + monthlyInterest;
}
```

DEBUGGING TIP

A common error when coding an **if** statement is to place a semicolon at the end of the first line, like this:

```
if(balance < 500);    //A SEMICOLON HERE IS AN ERROR
{
   monthlyInterest = balance * .02;
   balance = balance + monthlyInterest;
}
```

Here, the compiler does not connect the two framed **if** statements with the Boolean test expression. The **if** statement simply compares the value of *balance* to the value of 500 and generates a Boolean result that is not used for anything. The result is that the two statements are always executed, even when the *balance* is >= 500. This will not produce a compiler error, just bad data, or garbage. Such errors can be very difficult to find, even with a trained eye.

THINK!

A mistake when coding an "equals" test in an `if` statement is to use the assignment symbol, =, rather than the Boolean equals test symbol, ==. Thus, the statement `if(x = y)` will cause a compiler error (unless *x* and *y* are Boolean variables) and must be corrected to `if(x == y)`.

It's probably a good idea to look at some example exercises and programs at this time to get a sense for the `if` operation.

Example 5-3

Determine the output on the console screen for each of the following program segments. Assume that *x* and *y* have been defined and take on the following assignments prior to the execution of *each* `if` operation:

```
x = 2;
y = 3;
```

a. `if(x < y)`
        `System.out.println("x = " + x + "\ny = " + y);`

b. `if(x != 0)`
        `System.out.println("The value of x is nonzero");`

c. `if(x < y)`
    `{`
        `int temp = y;`
        `y = x;`
        `x = temp;`
        `System.out.println("x = " + x +  "\ny = " + y);`
    `}//END IF`

d. `if((x < y) && (y != 10))`
    `{`
        `int sum = x + y;`
        `System.out.println("x = " + x + "\ny = " + y + "\nsum = " + sum);`
    `}//END IF`

e. `if((x > y) || (x - y < 0))`
    `{`
        `++x;`
        `--y;`
        `System.out.println("x = " + x + "\ny = " + y);`
    `}//END IF`

f. `if((x > y) || (x * y < 0))`
    `{`
        `++x;`
        `--y;`
        `System.out.println("x = " + x + "\ny = " + y);`
    `}//END IF`
    `System.out.println("x = " + x + "\ny = " + y);`

g. `if(x % y == 0)`
        `System.out.println("x is divisible by y");`
        `System.out.println("x is not divisible by y");`

Solution

a. The value of *x* is less than the value of *y*. Thus, the output is:

```
x = 2
y = 3
```

b. Here, the test is on the value of *x*. If *x* is zero, the test is `false`. When *x* is a nonzero value, the test is `true` and the *println()* statement is executed, producing an output of:

```
The value of x is nonzero
```

c. The value of *x* is less than *y*, so the compound statement is executed and the output is:

```
x = 3
y = 2
```

Notice that the values of *x* and *y* have been swapped using a temporary variable called *temp*. This temporary variable is required so that the value of *y* is not lost in the first assignment.

d. The value of *x* is less than *y* *and* the value of *y* is not equal to 10. As a result, the two values are added and the output is:

```
x = 2
y = 3
sum = 5
```

e. Here, the value of *x* is not greater than the value of *y*, but *x* – *y* is less than 0. Thus, the test result due to the OR operator is `true`, and the `if` statements are executed, resulting in an output of

```
x = 3
y = 2
```

f. This time the test is `false`. Thus, the compound statement is bypassed. As a result, the values of *x* and *y* remain unchanged, and the output is:

```
x = 2
y = 3
```

g. This is a tricky one. Here, the test is `false`, because *y* does not divide evenly into *x*. So, what happens? There are no braces framing the block, so the compiler takes only the first *println()* statement to be the `if` statement. As a result, the first *println()* statement is bypassed, and the second one is executed to produce an output of:

```
x is not divisible by y
```

Remember, the logical flow of the program always goes to the next statement outside the `if` when the test is `false`. What would happen if the test expression were `true`? In this case, both *println()* statements would be executed, generating an output of:

```
x is divisible by y
x is not divisible by y
```

But, this logic doesn't make sense. You want only one of the *println()* state-ments executed, not both. To solve this dilemma, we need a different decision control structure called the `if/else` control structure. The `if/else` control structure is discussed next.

QUICK CHECK

1. True or false: The logical opposite of greater-than is less-than.
2. True or false: When a test expression in an `if` statement evaluates to `true`, the related statements are bypassed.
3. What is wrong with the following `if` statement?

    ```
    if(x = y)
       System.out.println("There is a problem here");
    ```
4. What Boolean operator must be employed to test if all conditions are `true`?
5. What Boolean operator(s) must be employed to test if one or more of several conditions is `false`?
6. What Boolean operator must be employed to test if one of several conditions is `true`?
7. For what values of *x* will the *println()* statement in the following code be skipped?

    ```
    if(x > 50)
       System.out.println("Hello World");
    ```

5.3   The `if/else` Statement

The operation of the `if/else` statement is illustrated by the diagram in Figure 5-3. Here, you see that there are two sets of statements that can be executed, depending on whether the test expression is `true` or `false`. If the test result is `true`, the `if` state-ments, collectively referred to as the "if clause", are executed. Conversely, if the test re-sult is `false`, the `else` statements, collectively referred to as the "else clause", are executed. In other words, if the test expression is `true`, then execute the `if` statements;

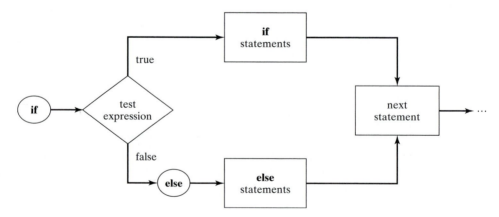

FIGURE 5-3   The flow of the if/else operation.

otherwise, execute the else statements. As compared to the if operation, you could say if/else is a two-way decision process, and if is a one-way decision process.

The if/else statement *always* requires the program to detour its execution before going on to the next sequential program statement. Here, there are two possible detours. Which detour is taken depends on the Boolean test result.

The Java format for the if/else operation is as follows:

if/else *STATEMENT FORMAT*

```
if(test expression)
{
    statement 1;
    statement 2;
        •
        •
        •
    statement n;
}//END IF
else
{
    statement 1;
    statement 2;
        •
        •
        •
    statement n;
}//END ELSE
```

As you can see, the else option is included after the if statement. If the test expression is true, the if statements are executed, and the else statements are ignored. However, if the test expression is false, the if statements are ignored, and the else statements are executed.

Note the syntax. First, observe that both the if and else statements are "framed" using braces. However, you can eliminate the braces in either section when only a single statement is required. (Again we recommend, as a matter of habit, that you always frame your if and else statements.) Second, notice the indentation scheme. Such a scheme makes your programs self-documenting and readable, even though the indentation has no meaning to the compiler.

 DEBUGGING TIP

Always remember to frame your if/else statements with braces ({ }) when you have more than one statement to execute. If the braces are missing, only the first statement will execute. This could cause a logic error that is very difficult to find. For example, consider the following:

```
if(x < y)
    --x;
```

```
    System.out.println("x is less than y");
else
    System.out.println("x is greater than or equal to y");
```

Here, the compiler "sees" three separate statements, one of them illegal. The first statement is the if statement that decrements the value of x if the test is true. The second statement is a *println()* statement. Even though this statement is indented under the if, the compiler does *not* consider it to be part of the if statement, because it is not framed as part of the if. Remember, the compiler *does not* recognize indentation. The only statement that the compiler recognizes as part of the if is the $--x$ statement. This is a logic error and *would not* be caught by the compiler. Finally, the else is all by itself and, therefore, is referred to as a **dangling**, or **misplaced**, else. An else must *always* be associated with a corresponding if. This is a syntax error and would be caught by the compiler. The dangling else problem often occurs when improper framing is used within if/else logic.

Example 5-4

Determine when the if statements will be executed and when the else statements will be executed in each of the following program segments.

```
a.  if(x < y)
        sum = x + y;
    else
        difference = x - y;
b.  if(x != 0)
        sum = x + y;
    else
        difference = x - y;
c.  if(x = 0)
        sum = x + y;
    else
        difference = x - y;
d.  if((x < y) && (2*x - y == 0))
        sum = x + y;
    else
        difference = x - y;
e.  if((x < y) ‖ (2*x - y == 0))
        sum = x + y;
    else
        difference = x - y;
f.  if(x > 2*y)
        sum = x + y;
        product = x * y;
    else
        difference = x - y;
```

Solution

a. The if statement is executed when x is less than y, and the else statement is executed when x is greater than or equal to y. Remember, the opposite of less than is greater than *or equal to*.

b. The `if` statement is executed when *x* is nonzero. The `else` statement is executed when the value of *x* is zero.

c. This is a syntax error, because the Boolean test is coded as *x* = 0 and must be coded as *x* == 0.

d. This segment employs the Boolean AND (`&&`) operator. Here, the `if` statement is executed when the value of *x* is less than the value of *y and* the value of 2*x* − *y* is equal to zero. The `else` statement is executed when the value of *x* is *greater than or equal to* the value of *y or* the value of 2*x* − *y* is not equal to zero.

e. This segment employs the Boolean OR (⁞) operator. Here, the `if` statement is executed when the value of *x* is less than the value of *y or* the value of 2*x* − *y* is equal to zero. The `else` statement is executed when the value of *x* is *greater than or equal to* the value of *y and* the value of 2*x* − *y* is not equal to zero.

f. This segment of code will not compile because of a dangling, or misplaced, `else`. The `if` statements must be framed in order for the segment to compile. When the `if` statements are framed, they will be executed when the value of *x* is greater than the value of 2*y*. The `else` statement will execute when the value of *x* is *less than or equal to* the value of 2*y*.

THINK!

You learned earlier that the standard string compare method, *compareTo()*, should always be used when comparing strings rather than Boolean relational operators because Boolean relational operators do not give you what you expect when comparing strings. For example, the following code will generate a compiler error:

```
String s1 = "Andy";
String s2 = "Sandy";

if(s1 < s2)
    System.out.println("String s1 is less than string s2");
else
    System.out.println("String s1 is not less than string s2");
```

To prevent a compiler error, you must use the *compareTo()* method within the `if/else` statement like this:

```
String s1 = "Andy";
String s2 = "Sandy";
if(s1.compareTo(s2) < 0)
    System.out.println("String s1 is less than string s2");
else
    System.out.println("String s1 is not less than string s2");
```

This code is valid because the *compareTo()* method actually subtracts the individual Unicode values of the two strings one character at a time from left to right until an unequal condition occurs, or it runs out of characters. If all the characters in the two strings are the same, the result of subtracting character-by-character is zero. If a given character in the first string is larger than the corresponding character in the second string, the subtraction result is positive. If a given character in the first string is smaller than the corresponding character in the second string, the subtraction result is negative. Thus, in the foregoing code, if strings *s1* and *s2* are equal, *compareTo()* returns a 0. If string *s1* is less than string *s2*, *compareTo()* returns a negative value. If string *s1* is greater than string *s2*, *compareTo()* returns a positive value. Here, the string "Andy" is less than the string "Sandy", since the character 'A' is less than the character 'S' in the Unicode table. Thus, the *compareTo()* method generates a negative result, making the Boolean test `true`.

If you are just interested in string equality, use the standard *equals()* method like this:

```
String s1 = "Andy";
String s2 = "Sandy";
if(s1.equals(s2))
    System.out.println("The strings are equal");
else
    System.out.println("The strings are not equal");
```

Here, by definition, the *equals()* method returns a Boolean result of `true` or `false`. As a result, you do not have to test it against zero.

 Use *compareTo()* to see if one string is alphabetically less than or greater than another string. The *compareTo()* method returns an integer value that must be tested against zero. Use *equals()* to test if two strings are equal or not equal. The *equals()* method returns a Boolean value and, therefore, must not be tested against zero.

 QUICK CHECK

1. True or false: An **else** must always have a corresponding **if**.
2. Why does the following pseudocode need an **else** statement?
   If Day is Friday
      Write("It's pay day")
   Write("It's not pay day")
3. True or false: Framing with braces can be eliminated when an **if** or **else** statement section has only a single statement.
4. The *compareTo()* method actually performs a(n) _____ operation on two strings.
5. True or false: The *compareTo()* method returns a Boolean value.
6. True or false: The *equals()* method returns a Boolean value.

5.4 Nesting `if/else`'s

Until now, you have witnessed one-way and two-way decisions using the `if` and `if/else` statements, respectively. You can achieve additional decision options by using nested `if/else` statements. A nested `if/else` statement is simply an `if/else` statement within an `if/else` statement. To illustrate this idea, consider the diagram in Figure 5-4. Here, a temperature is being tested to see if it is within a range of 0 to 100 degrees Celsius. If it is within this range, you get water. However, if it is outside the range, you get steam or ice, depending on whether it is above or below the range, respectively.

Let's follow through the diagram. The first test-expression operation checks to see if the temperature is greater than 0 degrees. If the test result is `false`, the temperature must be less than or equal to 0 degrees, resulting in ice. However, if the test result is `true`, a second test is made to see if the temperature is greater than or equal to 100 degrees. If this test result is `true`, you get steam. However, if this second test result is `false`, you know that the temperature must be somewhere between 0 degrees and 100 degrees, resulting in water. Notice how the second test is "nested" within the first test. The first test result must be `true` before the second test is performed.

Let's develop a program to implement the nested decision-making operation illustrated in Figure 5-4. We begin with the problem definition.

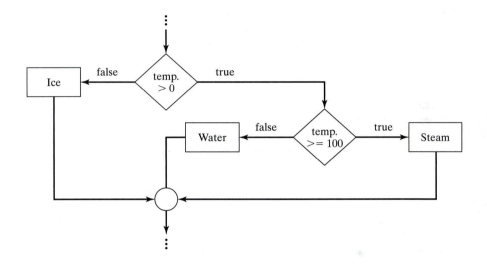

FIGURE 5-4   A nested `if/else` operation.

Defining the Problem

Input:	Temperature in degrees Celsius from the user keyboard.
Processing:	Determine if the temperature constitutes water, steam, or ice.
Output:	The word "WATER", "STEAM", or "ICE".

Now for the algorithm. Here is one that will work.

Planning the Solution

```
BEGIN
    Write a user prompt to enter the temperature in degrees Celsius.
    Read temperature.
    If temperature > 0
      If temperature >= 100
         Write "STEAM."
      Else
         Write "WATER."
```

```
        Else
           Write "ICE."
        END.
```

This algorithm is constructed by simply following the diagram in Figure 5-4. Notice how the second `if/else` statement is nested within the first `if/else` statement. If the *temperature* is not greater than 0 degrees, the nested `if/else` operation is not performed. However, if the *temperature* is greater than 0, the nested `if/else` operation is performed to see if the *temperature* results in steam or water.

To code the program, you simply follow the algorithm, like this:

Coding the Program

```java
/*      OUTPUT:        DISPLAY THE WORD "STEAM", "ICE", OR "WATER",
                       DEPENDING ON TEMPERATURE TO BE ENTERED
                       BY THE USER.

        INPUT:         A CELSIUS TEMPERATURE FROM THE USER.

        PROCESSING:    TEST TEMPERATURE VALUE AGAINST
                       A RANGE OF 0 TO 100 DEGREES CELSIUS.
*/
import staugIO.StaugIO;                    //FOR GUI I/O

public class Test
{
   public static void main(String[] args)
   {
   //DEFINE VARIABLES
   double temperature = 0.0;   //TEMPERATURE VALUE FROM USER

   //CREATE I/O OBJECT
   StaugIO io = new StaugIO();

   //READ THE TEMPERATURE FROM USER
   temperature = io.readDouble("Enter a temperature in degrees Celsius:");

   //TEST IF TEMPERATURE IS WATER, STEAM, OR ICE
   if (temperature > 0)
      if (temperature >= 100)
         io.writeInfo("STEAM");
      else
         io.writeInfo("WATER");
   else
      io.writeInfo("ICE");

   //EXIT PROGRAM
   System.exit(0);
   }//END main()
}//END temperature
```

Notice how the program flow can be seen by the indentation scheme. However, you do not see any brace pairs framing the `if` or `else` blocks. Remember that you do not need to frame a code block when it consists of only a single statement. But the first if block looks as if it consists of several statements. Well, the first if block contains a single if/else statement. Because the compiler sees this as a single statement, it does not need to be framed. Of course, if you are in doubt, it does no harm to completely frame things, like this:

```
//TEST IF TEMPERATURE IS WATER, STEAM, OR ICE
if (temperature > 0)
{
    if (temperature >= 100)
    {
        io.writeInfo("STEAM");
    }//END IF "STEAM"
    else
    {
        io.writeInfo("WATER");
    }//END ELSE "WATER"
} //END IF TEMPERATURE > 0
else
{
    io.writeInfo("ICE");
}//END ELSE "ICE"
```

PROGRAMMING NOTE

There are different ways to construct nested *if/else* logic. For example, some might see the temperature algorithm logic as follows:

> If *temperature* <= 0
>   Write "ICE"
> Else
>   If *temperature* > = 100
>   Write "STEAM."
>   Else
>   Write "WATER."

Here you see the inner *If/Else* operation nested inside of the outer *Else* operation. This logic will also accomplish the required decision task. Both methods are correct and adhere to good programming style. We will refer to this method as the *If-Else-If-Else* form and the earlier method as the *If-If-Else-Else* form. It's simply a matter of personal choice and how you view the logic of the problem. In general, the *If-Else-If-Else* form should be used when a number of *different* conditions need to be satisfied before a given action can occur, and the *If-If-Else-Else* form should be used when the *same* variable is being tested for different values and a different action is taken for each value. This latter reason is why we first chose to use the *If-If-Else-Else* form. Notice also that indentation is extremely important to determine the nested logic.

Example 5-5

Determine when "Red", "White", and "Blue" will be written to the console screen in each of the following program segments.

a.
```
if(x < y)
    if(x == 0)
        System.out.println("Red");
    else
        System.out.println("White");
else
    System.out.println("Blue");
```
b.
```
if(x >= y)
    System.out.println("Blue");
else
    if(x == 0)
        System.out.println("Red");
    else
        System.out.println("White");
```
c.
```
if((x < y)&&(x == 0))
    System.out.println("Red");
if((x < y)&&(x != 0))
    System.out.println("White");
if(x >= y)
    System.out.println("Blue");
```

Solution

All three segments of code will produce the same results. "Red" will be written when the value of x is less than the value of y and the value of x is zero. "White" will be written when the value of x is less than the value of y and the value of x is not equal to zero. "Blue" will be written when the value of x is greater than or equal to the value of y regardless of whether or not the value of x is zero. Desk-check the logic of each code segment to see if you get these results.

Example 5-6

Convert the following series of `if` statements to nested `if/else` statements using the `if-else-if-else` form and the `if-if-else-else` form.

```
if(year == 1)
    System.out.println("Freshman");
if(year == 2)
    System.out.println("Sophomore");
if(year == 3)
    System.out.println("Junior");
if(year == 4)
    System.out.println("Senior");
if(year > 4)
    System.out.println("Graduate");
```

Solution

a. To convert to the `if-else-if-else` form, we use the logic that if the year is greater than 4, then we know to write "Graduate"; else we test to see if the year is greater than 3. If the year was not greater than 4 but is greater than 3, its value must be 4, so we write "Senior"; else we test to see if the year is greater than 2. If it passes this test, you know that the year was not greater than 4 and not greater than 3 but is greater than 2, so its value must be 3, and we write "Junior". We continue this logic to produce "Sophomore" and "Freshman" for year values of 2 and 1, respectively. Here's the resulting code:

```java
if(year > 4)
    System.out.println("Graduate");
else
    if(year > 3)
        System.out.println("Senior");
    else
        if(year > 2)
            System.out.println("Junior");
        else
            if(year > 1)
                System.out.println("Sophomore");
            else
                System.out.println("Freshman");
```

b. To convert to the `if-if-else-else` form, we use the logic that if the year is greater than 1, we test to see if the year is greater than 2, then 3, then 4. If it passes all of these tests, we know to write "Graduate". However, if the year was not greater than 1 in the first test, we know to write "Freshman", which forms the `else` part of the first `if` test. Next, if the year is greater than 1, but fails the second `if` test (>2), we know to write "Sophomore", which forms the `else` part of the second `if` test. This logic continues to produce "Junior" and "Senior" for year values of 3 and 4, respectively. Here's the resulting code:

```java
if(year > 1)
    if(year > 2)
        if(year > 3)
            if(year > 4)
                System.out.println("Graduate");
            else
                System.out.println("Senior");
        else
            System.out.println("Junior");
    else
        System.out.println("Sophomore");
else
    System.out.println("Freshman");
```

QUICK CHECK

1. Explain why indentation is important when operations are nested.

2. An `else` that cannot be associated with a corresponding `if` is called a(n) _____.

Consider the following pseudocode to answer questions 3 – 6:

```
If value < 50
    If value > –50
        Write ("Red")
    else
        Write ("White")
else
    Write ("Blue")
```

3. What range of values will cause "Red" to be written?
4. What range of values will cause "White" to be written?
5. What range of values will cause "Blue" to be written?
6. Convert the *If-If-Else-Else* logic to *If-Else-If-Else* logic.

5.5   The `switch` Statement

This last category of decision enables the program to select one of many conditions, or *cases*. The operation of the `switch` statement is illustrated by the diagram in Figure 5-5. The selection of a particular `case` is controlled by a matching process. A *selector variable* is first evaluated to produce a value. The selector value is then compared to a series of `cases`. If the selector value *matches* one of the `case` values, the corresponding `case` statements are executed. If no match is made, the program simply continues in a straight-line fashion, with the first statement following the `switch` statement. Using the detour analogy, the `switch` statement provides multiple detour routes (the `cases`) for the program execution, before going on to the next sequential program statement. Here's the Java format for `switch`:

`switch` *STATEMENT FORMAT*

```
switch(selector variable)
{
    case case 1 value : case 1 statements;
                        break;
    case case 2 value : case 2 statements;
                        break;

        •
        •
        •

    case case n value : case n statements;
}//END SWITCH
```

The format requires the selector variable to follow the keyword `switch`. The selector variable must be enclosed within parentheses and must be an integral data type. By an *integral data type*, we mean a data type that is stored as an integer. This basically means that the selector variable must be defined as either an integer or a character, and *not* a floating-point variable or string object. Defining the selector variable as a floating-point variable or string object will cause a compiler error.

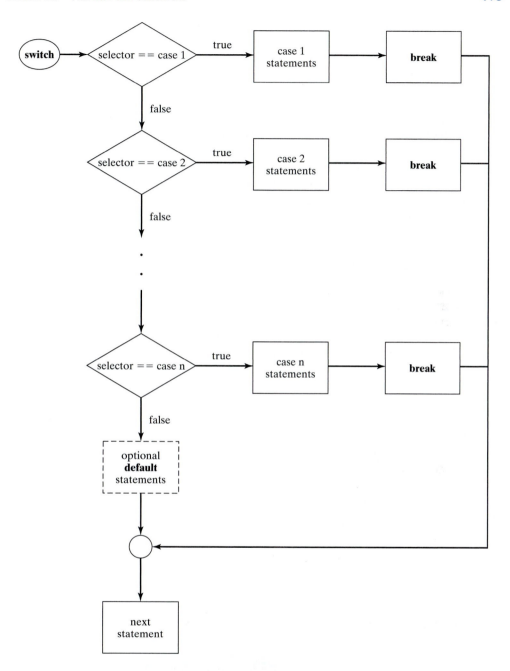

FIGURE 5-5   The flow of the switch operation.

DEBUGGING TIP

When coding a `switch` statement, the selector variable and `case` values must be the same data type. Only the integral data types (integer or character) are allowed. Any other data type will cause a compiler error.

The `switch` syntax requires the use of braces to open and close the `switch` block of `case` statements as shown. The `switch` block is comprised of several `case`s that are identified using the keyword `case`. An integral `case` value must be supplied with each `case` for matching purposes. The `switch` statement attempts to match the value of the selector variable to a given `case` value. If a match occurs, the corresponding `case` statements are executed. Note that a colon separates the `case` value from the `case` statements. A given `case` statement block can be any number of statements in length, and does not require framing with braces. However, the keyword `break` is usually inserted as the last statement in a given `case` statement block. If `break` is not used, any subsequent `case`s will be executed after a given `case` match has occurred, until a `break` is encountered. This may be desirable at times, especially when multiple `case` values are to "fire" a given set of `case` statements. Notice that a `break` is not required for the last `case`, since once this `case` is executed, the `switch` ends naturally. Again, the idea behind the `switch` statement is easy if you simply think of it as a matching operation. The following examples will demonstrate this idea.

Suppose the selector variable is the letter grade you made on your last quiz. Assuming that the variable *letterGrade* is defined as a character variable, a typical `switch` statement might go something like this:

```
switch(letterGrade)
{
    case 'A' :  io.writeInfo("Excellent");
                break;
    case 'B' :  io.writeInfo("Superior");
                break;
    case 'C' :  io.writeInfo("Average");
                break;
    case 'D' :  io.writeInfo("Poor");
                break;
    case 'F' :  io.writeInfo("Try Again");
}//END SWITCH
```

Here, the selector variable is *letterGrade*. The `case` values are 'A', 'B', 'C', 'D', and 'F'. The value of the selector variable is compared to the list of `case` values. If a match is found, the corresponding `case` statements are executed. For instance, if the value of *letterGrade* is 'B', the code generates an output of

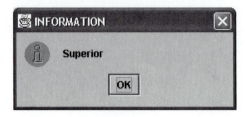

Now, suppose you leave out the keyword break in each of the previous cases, like this:

```
switch(letterGrade)
{
    case 'A' : io.writeInfo("Excellent");
    case 'B' : io.writeInfo("Superior");
    case 'C' : io.writeInfo("Average");
    case 'D' : io.writeInfo("Poor");
    case 'F' : io.writeInfo("Try Again");
}//END SWITCH
```

This time, assuming that *letterGrade* has the value 'B', the code generates an output in four consecutive information boxes, like this:

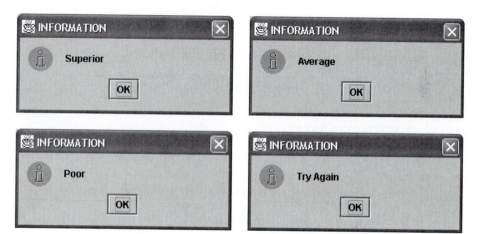

As you can see from the output, case 'B' was matched and its case statement executed. However, all of the case statements subsequent to case 'B' were also executed. Surely, you can see the value of using break in this application.

Are there times where you might want to eliminate the break command? Of course! Consider the following switch statement:

```
switch(letterGrade)
{
    case 'a' :
    case 'A' :  io.writeInfo("Excellent");
                break;
    case 'b' :
    case 'B' :  io.writeInfo("Superior");
                break;
    case 'c' :
    case 'C' :  io.writeInfo("Average");
                break;
    case 'd' :
    case 'D' :  io.writeInfo("Poor");
                break;
```

```
    case 'f' :
    case 'F' :  io.writeInfo("Try Again");
}//END SWITCH
```

Here, multiple `case` values need to "fire" the same `case` statement. So, if *letterGrade* has the value 'b', then a match is made with `case` 'b'. No `break` is part of this `case`, so the next sequential `case` is executed, which will write the word "Superior". Because `case` 'B' contains a `break`, the `switch` statement is terminated after the output is generated.

What happens if no match occurs? As you might suspect, all the `case`s are by-passed, and the next sequential statement appearing after the `switch` closing brace is executed.

The default Option

The last thing we need to discuss is the use of the `default` option within a `switch` state-ment. The `default` option is normally employed at the end of a `switch` statement, like this:

default *OPTION FORMAT*

```
switch(selector variable)
{
    case   case 1 value : case 1 statements;
                          break;
    case   case 2 value : case 2 statements;
                          break;

               •
               •
               •

    case   case n value : case n statements;
                          break;
    default: default statements;
}//END SWITCH
```

The `default` option allows a series of `default` statements to be executed if no match occurs within the `switch`. On the other hand, if a match does occur, the `default` statements are skipped. The keyword `default`, followed by a colon and the default statements, must appear after the last `case` as shown. In addition, a `break` statement must be added to the last case in order for the default to work properly when this `case` is executed. The `default` option provides a valuable protection feature within your program. For instance, suppose that you ask the user to enter a letter grade to be used in a `switch` statement. But the user presses the wrong key and enters a character that is not a valid `case` value. Well, you can use the `default` option to protect against such invalid entries, like this:

```
switch(letterGrade)
{
    case 'a' :
    case 'A' : io.writeInfo("Excellent");
               break;
    case 'b' :
    case 'B' : io.writeInfo("Superior");
               break;
    case 'c' :
    case 'C' : io.writeInfo("Average");
               break;
    case 'd' :
    case 'D' : io.writeInfo("Poor");
               break;
    case 'f' :
    case 'F' : io.writeInfo("Try Again");
               break;

    default  : io.writeInfo("No match was found for the entry "
                              + letterGrade);
}//END SWITCH
```

Here, the default statement is executed if *letterGrade* is anything other than the listed case characters. For example, if the user enters the character 'E' for *letterGrade*, the foregoing switch statement will produce an output of

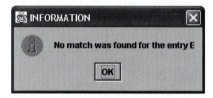

You will find that the default option in the switch statement is extremely useful when displaying menus for user entries.

Example 5-7

A switch statement is simply a convenient way to code a series of nested if/else statements. Convert the following series of if/else statements to a single switch statement that employs the default option.

```
if (year == 1)
    io.writeInfo("Freshman");
else
  if (year == 2)
      io.writeInfo("Sophomore");
  else
    if (year == 3)
        io.writeInfo("Junior");
    else
```

```
if (year == 4)
    io.writeInfo("Senior");
else
    io.writeInfo("Graduate");
```

Solution

All that needs to be done to convert a series of `if/else` statements to a single `switch` statement is to use the `if` test variable as the selector variable and the `if` test values as `case`s within the `switch`. Here's the converted code:

```
switch(year)
{
    case 1: io.writeInfo("Freshman");
            break;
    case 2: io.writeInfo("Sophomore");
            break;
    case 3: io.writeInfo("Junior");
            break;
    case 4: io.writeInfo("Senior");
            break;
    default: io.writeInfo("Graduate");
}//END SWITCH
```

Notice how the `default` option is used to write "Graduate". You know to write "Graduate" if no match is made to the previous four `case`s, right? So, the `else` part of the inner-most `if/else` test is converted to the `default` in the `switch` statement.

PROGRAMMING NOTE

Be aware that a `switch` statement can only be used to code simple equality tests and *not* relational tests. For instance, you cannot use a `switch` statement to determine if a test score is within a range of values. You must use nested `if/else` logic for such an application.

QUICK CHECK

1. The selection of a particular `case` in a `switch` statement is controlled by a(n) _____ process.
2. Suppose that you have *n* `case`s in a `switch` statement and there are no `break` statements in any of the `case`s. What will happen when a match is made on the first `case`?
3. True or false: There are never any times when a `case` should not contain a `break` statement.
4. A statement that can be inserted at the end of a `switch` statement to protect against invalid entries is the _____ statement.
5. A common application for a `switch` statement is _____.

Problem Solving in Action: Menu-Driven Programs

Problem

The `switch` statement is often used to create menu-driven programs. We're sure you have seen a menu-driven program. It's one that asks you to select different options during the execution of the program. For instance, suppose you must write a menu-driven consumer loan calculator program that will allow the user to determine several things about a loan. The idea will be to generate a menu similar to the one shown in Figure 5-6 that gives the user four options as follows:

- An option to calculate monthly loan payment
- An option to calculate the total interest of the loan
- An option to calculate the total amount of the loan
- An option to quit the program

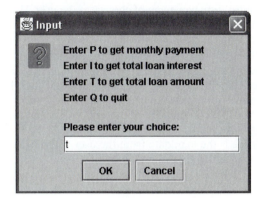

FIGURE 5-6   A sample menu for the loan program.

We will assume that the user will enter the amount of the loan, the annual interest rate of the loan, and the term of the loan. The program should reject invalid menu entries.

Defining the Problem

Input: A user response to the menu (P, I, T, or Q).
If P is selected: User enters the loan amount, interest rate, and term.
If I is selected: User enters the loan amount, interest rate, and term.
If T is selected: User enters the loan amount, interest rate, and term.
If Q is selected: Terminate program.

Processing: Calculate the selected option as follows:
Case P: $payment = principal * rate/(1 - (1 + rate)^{-term})$
Case I: $interest = term * payment - principal$
Case T: $total = principal + interest$
Case Q: Terminate program.
where: *principal* is the amount of the loan.
rate is a monthly interest rate in decimal form.
term is the number of months of the loan.

Output: A program menu that prompts the user to select a monthly payment, total interest, or total loan amount calculation option.
The monthly loan payment, total loan interest, or total loan amount, depending
on the program option that the user selects.
Invalid entry messages as required.

Planning the Solution

Using a modular program design, we will divide the problem into individual subproblems to solve
the overall problem. There are four major tasks that follow directly from the problem definition:

- Display the menu and read the user choice
- Read the loan principal, interest rate, and term from the user
- Perform the chosen calculation
- Display the chosen calculation

First, the program must display a menu of choices to the user. The user will enter his or her
choice from the menu, and, depending on this choice, one of three calculations will be made to determine the required quantity. The problem solving diagram in Figure 5-7 illustrates the design.

Here you see two levels of refinement after *main()*. At the initial level, *main()* simply calls
two methods, *displayMenu()* and *loanCalculator()*. The job of *displayMenu()* is to display the
menu and read the user's choice. This accomplishes the first task listed above. The job of
loanCalculator() will be three-fold to accomplish the latter three tasks listed above. First it calls
the *setData()* method to set the loan data from user entries. Second it performs the chosen calculation. Third it displays the result of the chosen calculation. At the last level of refinement, the
setData() method simply reads the loan data from the user when called by the *loanCalculator()*
method. Here is the required set of algorithms.

Initial Algorithm
main()
BEGIN
  Call *displayMenu()* method.
  Call *loanCalculator()* method.
END.

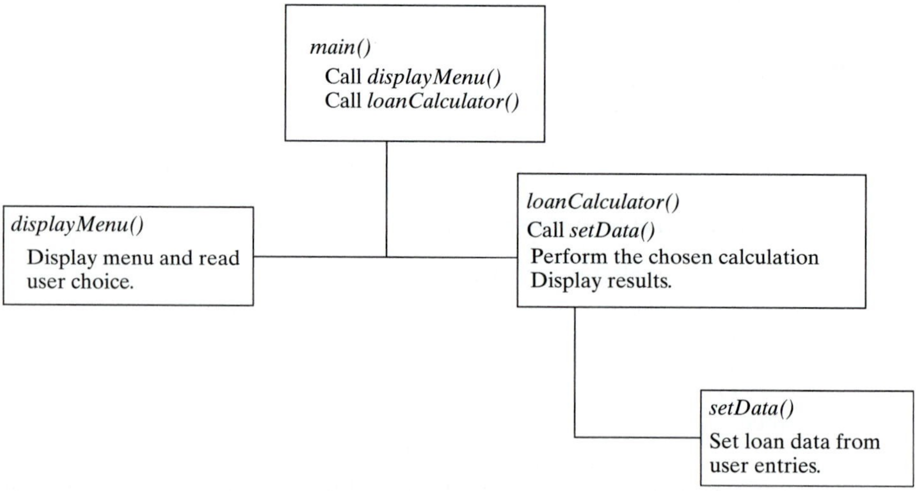

```
main()
    Call displayMenu()
    Call loanCalculator()
```

```
displayMenu()
    Display menu and read
    user choice.
```

```
loanCalculator()
    Call setData()
    Perform the chosen calculation
    Display results.
```

```
setData()
    Set loan data from
    user entries.
```

FIGURE 5-7   A problem-solving diagram for the loan problem.

First Level of Refinement

The first level of refinement shows the contents of the *displayMenu()* and *loanCalculator()* methods, as follows:

displayMenu()
BEGIN
    Display a program menu that prompts the user to choose a monthly payment (P), total interest (I), total loan amount (T), or quit (Q) option.
    Read *choice.*
END.

loanCalculator ()
BEGIN
    Switch on *choice*
    Case P: Call *setData()*
            Calculate payment.
            Display payment.
    Case I: Call *setData()*
            Calculate interest.
            Display interest.
    Case T: Call *setData()*
            Calculate total amount.
            Display total amount.
    Case Q: Terminate program.
    Default: Write an invalid entry message and ask the user to select again.
END.

Notice that the *loanCalculator()* method simply uses a *Switch* statement to make the chosen calculation and display the result depending on the user's choice. Also, observe that within each *Case*, *loanCalculator()* calls *setData()* to obtain the data required for the calculation. In addition, the *loanCalculator()* method terminates the program if the user chooses to quit, and writes an invalid entry message if the user's choice does not reflect one of the choice options.

Second Level of Refinement

The second level of refinement shows the contents of the *setData()* method, as follows:

setData()
BEGIN
    Write a user prompt to enter the loan principal.
    Read *principal.*
    Write a user prompt to enter the annual interest rate of the loan.
    Read *rate.*
    Write a user prompt to enter the term of the loan, in months.
    Read *term.*
END.

The next step is to construct the class diagram that shows the data and methods required for our class. Let's call this class *ConsumerLoanMenu* and fill it with the data and methods discussed above as shown in Figure 5-8.

```
+-------------------------------------------------------+
|                   ConsumerLoanMenu                    |
+-------------------------------------------------------+
|                                                       |
|     principal                                         |
|                                                       |
|     term                                              |
|                                                       |
|     rate                                              |
|                                                       |
|     payment                                           |
|                                                       |
|     interest                                          |
|                                                       |
|     total                                             |
|                                                       |
|     choice                                            |
|                                                       |
+-------------------------------------------------------+
|                                                       |
|     displayMenu()                                     |
|                                                       |
|     loanCalculator()                                  |
|                                                       |
|     setData()                                         |
|                                                       |
+-------------------------------------------------------+
```

FIGURE 5-8   A class diagram for the *ConsumerLoanMenu* class shows the data and methods that make up the class.

Coding the Program

Here is how the foregoing class is translated into Java code:

```java
/*
 * Action05_01.java
 *
 * Created on June 20, 2002, 10:09 AM
 */

/**
 *
 * @author  Andrew C. Staugaard, Jr.
 * @version 1.0
 */
import staugIO.StaugIO;          //FOR INPUT AND OUTPUT
import java.text.NumberFormat;   //FOR CURRENCY FORMATTING

class ConsumerLoanMenu
{
    //DEFINE VARIABLES AND OBJECTS
    private double principal = 0.0;    //LOAN PRINCIPAL
    private double term = 0;           //TERM OF LOAN IN MONTHS
    private double rate = 0.0;         //ANNUAL INTEREST IN PERCENT FORM
    private double payment = 0.0;      //MONTHLY PAYMENT
    private double interest = 0.0;     //TOTAL LOAN INTEREST
```

```java
    private double total = 0.0;              //TOTAL LOAN AMOUNT
    private char choice = 'Q';               //USER MENU CHOICE
    private StaugIO io = new StaugIO();      //FOR INPUT/OUTPUT

//displayMenu()
public void displayMenu()
{
    //DISPLAY A MENU AND READ USER'S CHOICE
    choice = io.readChar("Enter P to get monthly payment"
                    + "\nEnter I to get total loan interest"
                    + "\nEnter T to get total loan amount"
                    + "\nEnter Q to quit"
                    + "\n\nPlease enter your choice:  ");
}//END displayMenu()

//setData() METHOD
private void setData()
{
    principal = io.readDouble("Enter the amount of the loan: ");
    term = io.readDouble("Enter the duration of the loan in months: ");
    rate = io.readDouble("Enter the annual interest rate in percent: ");
    rate = rate/12/100;
}//END setData()

//loanCalculator() METHOD
public void loanCalculator()
{
    //CREATE CURRENCY OBJECT
    NumberFormat currency = NumberFormat.getCurrencyInstance();

    //SWITCH ON CHOICE
    switch(choice)
    {
        case 'p': //CALCULATE AND DISPLAY PAYMENT
        case 'P' : setData();
                    payment = principal * rate/(1-Math.pow((1+rate), -term));
                    io.writeInfo("The monthly payment is "
                            + currency.format(payment));
                    break;
        case 'i':  //CALCULATE AND DISPLAY INTEREST
        case 'I' : setData();
                    payment = principal * rate/(1-Math.pow((1+rate), -term));
                    interest = term * payment - principal;
                    io.writeInfo("The total interest is "
                            + currency.format(interest));
                    break;
        case 't':  //CALCULATE AND DISPLAY TOTAL LOAN AMOUNT
        case 'T':  setData();
                    payment = principal * rate/(1-Math.pow((1+rate), -term));
                    interest = term * payment - principal;
                    total = principal + interest;
                    io.writeInfo("\n\nThe total loan amount is "
                            + currency.format(total));
                    break;
```

```
      case 'q': //TERMINATE PROGRAM
      case 'Q': io.writeInfo("Program terminated");
                break;

      //DISPLAY INVALID ENTRY MESSAGE
      default : io.writeInfo("\n\nThis is an invalid entry"
                           + "\nPlease run the program again");
    }//END SWITCH
  }//END loanCalculator()
}//END ComsumerLoanMenu CLASS
public class Action05_01
{
  public static void main (String args[])
  {
    //CREATE LOAN OBJECT
    ConsumerLoanMenu myLoan = new ConsumerLoanMenu();

    //CALL METHODS
    myLoan.displayMenu();
    myLoan.loanCalculator();

    //EXIT PROGRAM
    System.exit(0);
  }//END main()
}//END Action05_01
```

Now look at the program closely and you will find that it demonstrates many of the things that you have learned in the last few chapters. In general, you will find a `switch` statement that contains a `default` option. In particular, you should observe the beginnings and endings of the various sections, along with the associated indentation and commenting scheme. As you can see, the program is very readable and self-documenting.

Now for the details. There are eight `case`s, two for each user-selected option. Notice that the first `case` in each option allows the user to enter a lowercase character. These `case`s do not have a `break` statement and, therefore, permit the program to "fall through" to the uppercase character `case`. This is done to allow the user to enter either a lower or an uppercase character for each option. Notice that there is a `break` statement at the end of each uppercase `case` to terminate the `switch` once the `case` statements are executed.

If the user enters an invalid character from the main menu, the `default` statement is executed which displays an error message and asks the user to run the program again. Finally, notice how the standard *pow()* and *format()* methods are called within the payment calculation. The following screenshots show the menu generated by the program, as well as a sample execution:

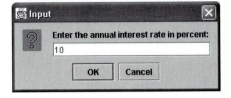

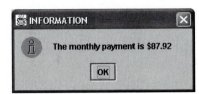

STYLE TIP

As you begin to frame more operations using braces, it often becomes difficult to determine what a closing brace is actually closing. The indentation scheme helps, but a commenting technique is also important. When several closing braces appear in succession, you should insert a comment after the brace, as shown at the end of the foregoing program, to indicate what a given brace is closing. Commenting helps both you and anyone reading your program to readily see the program framing.

CHAPTER SUMMARY

Boolean operators are those that generate a logical result of `true` or `false`. The two categories of Boolean operators in Java are relational and logical operators. Relational operators allow two quantities to be compared. These operators include ==, !=, >, <, <=, and >=. Logical operators perform logic operations on Boolean values to generate Boolean results. The standard logical operators available in Java are NOT (!), OR (¦¦), and AND (&&). Boolean operators are used within your program to test conditions as part of the decision and iteration control structures in Java.

In this chapter, you learned about the decision-making, or selection, control structure available in Java. It includes the `if`, `if/else`, and `switch` statements. Each of these operations alters the flow of a program, depending on the result of a Boolean test expression or matching condition.

The `if` statement executes its statements, or *clause*, "if" its test expression is `true`. If the test result is `false`, the `if` statements are bypassed and the program continues in a straight-line fashion. The `if` clause can be a single-line statement or a compound statement composed of a series of single-line statements. When using a compound statement, you must frame the entire statement block within braces.

The `if/else` statement consists of two separate clauses: an `if` clause and an `else` clause. If the associated test expression is `true`, the `if` clause is executed; otherwise, the `else` clause is executed when the test result is `false`. Thus, you could say that `if/else` is a two-way decision operation. Again, compound statements can be used within the `if` or `else` clauses; however, they must be framed within braces. Additional selection options can be achieved using nested `if` or `if/else` statements.

The `switch` statement achieves decision using a matching process. Here, the value of an integral selector variable is compared to a series of `case` values. If the selector value matches one of the `case` values, the corresponding `case` statements are executed until a `break` statement is encountered, or the `switch` statement terminates. If no match is made, the program simply continues in a straight-line fashion. In addition, Java provides a `default` option with the `switch` statement. When using the `default` option, the `default` statements are executed if no match is made. However, if a match does occur, the corresponding `case` statements are executed, and the `default` statements are skipped. Remember, you must always frame the body of the `switch` statement using braces.

QUESTIONS AND PROBLEMS

Questions

1. Evaluate each of the following relational expressions:

   a. `7!=7`

   b. `-0.75 <= -0.5`

   c. `'m'>'n'`

   d. `2*5%3-7<16/4+2`

   e.
   ```
   String s1;
   String s2;
   s1 = "Andy";
   s2 = "ANDY";
   s1.equals(s2);
   ```

   f.
   ```
   String s1;
   String s2;
   s1 = "Andy";
   s2 = "ANDY";
   s1.compareTo(s2);
   ```

2. Determine the result generated by the following expression:

   ```
   int x = -7;
   int y = 3;
   !(3*x<4*y)&&(5*x>=y)
   ```

3. Java also provides the *exclusive OR*, XOR logic operation. The caret, ^, symbol is used as syntax for this operation. Given any two Boolean variables, A and B, here is how the XOR operation is defined:

A	B	$A \wedge B$
true	true	false
true	false	true
false	true	true
false	false	false

   Do you see a pattern in the table that gives a hint to how XOR works? Well, the XOR operation will always produce a `true` result if there is an odd number of `true` values. Now for the question: Which of the following logical expressions will produce the XOR operation?

   a. !A ‖ !B
   b. (A && !B) ‖ (!A && B)
   c. !(A && !B) ‖ (!A && B)
   d. !(!A && !B)

4. What standard logical operation is performed by the expression in question 3d?

5. Develop a truth table for the following logical expression:
   !A ‖ !B

6. Which of the following is equivalent to the logic operation in question 5?
   a. !(A && B)
   b. !(A ‖ B)
   c. !A && !B
   d. None of these

7. When will x be incremented as a result of the following if statement?

```
if((x <= 0)&&(x % 5 == 0))
    ++x;
```

8. Convert the single if statement in question 7 into two nested if statements.

9. Consider the following program segment:

```
StaugIO in = new StaugIO();
int x = 0;
int y = 0;
x = in.readInt("Enter a value for x ");
y = in.readInt("Enter a value for y ");
if x > 0
{
   if y > 0
      --y;
}//END IF x > 0
else
   ++x;
```

   a. Are there any syntax errors in this code? If so, where are they?
   b. Assuming any syntax errors are corrected, when will y be decremented?
   c. Assuming any syntax errors are corrected, when will x be incremented?

10. Consider the following segment of code:

```
StaugIO in = new StaugIO();
int x = 0;
int y = 0;
x = in.readInt("Enter a value for x ");
y = in.readInt("Enter a value for y ");
```

```
if(x > 0)
{
  if(y > 0)
     --y;
  else
     ++x;
}//END IF x > 0
```

a. Are there any syntax errors in this code? If so, where are they?

b. Assuming any syntax errors are corrected, when will *y* be decremented?

c. Assuming any syntax errors are corrected, when will *x* be incremented?

11. True or false: You must always frame the body of a `switch` statement.

12. Which `if` does the `else` belong to in the following code segment?

```
if(x > 0)
   if(y > 0)
      --y;
else
   ++x;
```

13. True or false: When using a `switch` statement in Java, a no-match condition results in an error.

14. Consider the following segment of code:

```
if(x >= 0)
   if(x < 10)
   {
       y = x * x;
       if(x <= 5)
          x = Math.sqrt(x);
   }//END if x < 10
   else
       y = 10 * x;
else
   y = x * x * x;
io.writeInfo("x = " +  x + "\ny = " +  y);
```

What will be displayed by the program for each of the following initial values of *x*?

a. X = 0;

b. X = 4;

c. X = -5;

d. X = 10;

15. Consider the following `switch` statement:

```
int x = 2;
switch(power)
{
   case 0 : io.writeInfo('1');
            break;
   case 1 : io.writeInfo(x);
            break;
```

```
case 2 : io.writeInfo(x * x);
          break;
case 3 : io.writeInfo(x * x * x);
          break;
case 4 : io.writeInfo(x * x * x * x);
          break;
default : io.writeInfo("No match exists for this power");
}//END SWITCH
```

What will be displayed by the code for each of the following values of power?

a. power = 0;
b. power = 1;
c. power = 2;
d. power = 3;
e. power = 4;

16. Consider the following nested switch statements:

```
switch(x)
{
  case 2 :
  case 4 :
  case 6 : switch(y)
           {
             case 1 :
             case 2 :
             case 3 :   x = x + y;
                        break;
             case -1 :
             case -2 :
             case -3 : x = x - y;
           }//END SWITCH(y)
             break;
  case 1 :
  case 3 :
  case 5 : switch(y)
           {
             case 2 :
             case 4 :
             case 6 : x = x * y;
                        break;
             case -1 :
             case -4 :
             case -6 : x = y * y;
           }//END SWITCH(y)
}//END SWITCH(x)
io.writeInfo("x = " +  x + "\ny = " +  y);
```

What will be displayed by the code for each of the following values of x and y?

a. x = 4;
  y = -2;

b. x = 3;
  y = 6;

c. x = 1;
  y = -4;

d. x = 7;
  y = -2;

e. x = 2;
  y = 5;

17. Prove or disprove via truth tables that:

!A && !B == !(A && B)

Problems

Least Difficult

1. A part drawing indicates that the length of the part is 3.00 ± 0.25 inch. This means that the minimum acceptable length of the part is 2.75 inches and the maximum acceptable length of the part is 3.25 inches. Write a simple program in *main()* to display "ACCEPT-ABLE" if the part is within tolerance or "UNACCEPTABLE" if the part is out of tolerance. (Note: In Chapter 2, problem 8, you developed an algorithm for this problem. Why not use this algorithm to code the Java program?)

2. Write a program that will calculate weekly gross pay for an employee, given the employee's hourly rate and hours worked. Assume that overtime is paid at "time and a half" for any hours worked in excess of 40 hours. Place your data and methods inside a class called *GrossPay* and create an application to test your class.

3. Write a program that will display the corresponding name of a month for an integer entry from 1 to 12. Protect for invalid entries. Place your data and methods inside a class called *Month* and create an application to test your class.

4. Write a simple program in *main()* that will display two integer values in numerical order, regardless of the order in which they are entered.

5. Write a simple program in *main()* to sort two strings entered by the user in alphabetical order. Assume that the strings are student names that will be entered last name first followed by a comma followed by the first name. The program is to display an information box showing the names in alphabetical order.

More Difficult

6. Write a program in *main()* that employs nested if/else statements to convert a numerical grade to a letter grade according to the following scale:

90–100 : A
80–89 : B
70–79 : C
60–69 : D
Below 60: F

Place your solution inside *main()* in an application.

7. Write a program that will determine monthly credit card interest when interest is charged at a rate of 18% for the first $500 balance, and 12% for any balance amount over $500. Assume that the user will enter the account number, customer name, and current balance. Display a statement in a businesslike format. Place your data and methods inside a class called *CreditCard* and create an application to test your class.

Most Difficult

8. Java-Mart is at it again. This time they need a program that will project the profit of their inventory. The items in the department are coded with a 1, 2, or 3, depending on the amount of profit for the item. An item with a profit code of 1 produces a 10-percent profit, a code of 2 produces a 12-percent profit, and a code of 3 generates a 15-percent profit. Write a program that will project the profit of the following inventory:

Item	Quantity	Price	Profit Code
Java of the Day	532 cups	$1.49	1
Decaf Java of the Day	450 cups	$1.59	2
Cappuccino	323 cups	$2.29	2
Espresso	259 cups	$3.35	1
Java Mocha	256 cups.	$2.99	3

The program should generate a report of the item, quantity, expected profit in dollars per item, and total expected profit for all items. Place your data and methods inside a class called *ProfitProjection* and create an application to test your class.

9. Besides getting a regular salary, the employees at Java-Mart also receive a commission on what they sell. Their commission is based on the total dollar sales they make in one week according to the following schedule:

Sales	Commission
Below $250	0%
$250–$499	5%
$500–$1000	7.5%
Over $1000	10%

Develop a class called *Commission* that will determine a given employee's sales commission from a user entry of his or her weekly sales. The program should display the total sales dollars and corresponding sales commission in dollars. Write an application to test your class.

10. Write a menu-driven application that uses a class called *MetricConversion* to allow the user to convert between the following units. Provide for invalid user entries.

a. Degrees Fahrenheit to degrees Centigrade
b. Degrees Centigrade to degrees Fahrenheit
c. Inches to centimeters
d. Centimeters to inches
e. Pounds to kilograms.
f. Kilograms to pounds.

6

Repetition

OBJECTIVES

When you are finished with this chapter, you should have a good understanding of the following:

- Pretest, posttest, and fixed repetition iteration control structures
- The Java iteration control structures of `while`, `do/while`, and `for`
- How to detect an infinite loop condition
- How to desk-check a loop for correct number of iterations and termination

- How to construct loop-controlled menu-driven programs
- How to test for invalid user entries in a program using loops
- Nested loop structures
- When to use one Java loop structure over another

Introduction

In Chapter 5, you learned about the decision control structure. It is now time to explore the third and final control structure employed by Java: *repetition*, also called *iteration*. Iteration simply means doing something repeatedly. In programming, this is called *looping* because the iteration control structure causes the program flow to go around in a loop. Of course, there must be a way to get out of the loop, or the computer would loop forever! Such a situation is called an *infinite loop*. To prevent infinite looping, all iteration control structures test a condition to determine when to exit the loop. *Pretest* loops test a condition *before* each loop is executed. *Posttest* loops test a condition *after* each loop execution.

And, finally, ***fixed repetition*** loops cause the loop to be executed a *predetermined number of times.*

The three iteration control statements employed by Java are while, do/while, and for. As you will learn in this chapter, each provides a means for you to perform repetitive operations. The difference between them is the means by which they control the exiting of the loop. The while is a pretest loop, the do/while is a posttest loop, and the for is a fixed repetition loop. Let's begin our discussion with the while loop.

6.1   The while Loop

You can see from Figure 6-1 that a while loop is a pretest loop because a Boolean test is made *before* the loop body can ever be executed. If the test expression is true, the loop body is executed. If the test expression is false, the loop body is bypassed and the next sequential statement after the loop is executed. As long as the test expression is true, the program continues to go around the loop. In other words, the loop is repeated "while" the test expression is true. To get out of the loop, something must change within the loop that makes the test expression false. If such a change does not take place, you have an infinite loop. In addition, the diagram shows that *if the test expression is false the first time it is encountered, the loop body will never be executed.* This is an important characteristic of the while control structure.

The Java format for the while statement is as follows:

while **STATEMENT FORMAT**

```
while(test expression)
{
    statement 1;
    statement 2;
        •
        •        //LOOP BODY
        •
    statement n;
}//END WHILE
```

The first line of the statement contains the keyword while followed by a test expression within parentheses. To test a single condition, you will often use the Boolean

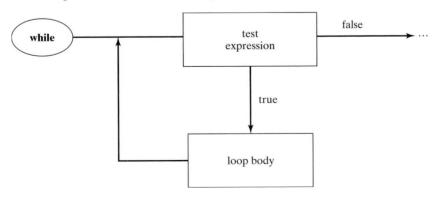

FIGURE 6-1   The while loop operation.

operators of ==, !=, <, >, <=, >=, and !. To test multiple conditions, you must use the logical operators of OR (||) and AND (&&). Notice that the loop body is framed using braces. This forms a compound statement, which consists of the individual loop body statements. An indentation scheme is also used so that the loop body can be easily identified. Finally, you should be aware that the loop body does not have to be framed if it consists of only a single statement. However, the CPU will execute just this single statement during the loop. Any additional statements are considered to be outside the loop structure.

Two things are important to remember when constructing a `while` loop:

- The variable(s) being tested in the test expression must have a legitimate value(s) *before* the `while` statement is encountered.
- The variable(s) being tested in the test expression must be changed within the body of the loop so that the test expression eventually becomes `false`. Otherwise you have an infinite loop.

For these reasons, the variable(s) being tested in the test expression are often referred to as the ***loop control variable(s)***.

Always remember to desk-check your loop structures for these two requirements *before* you try to execute the code. Now, let's look at a few examples to get the idea.

Example 6–1

What will be displayed on the console screen for each of the following segments of code?

```
a.  int number = 5;
    int sum = 0;
    while(number > 0)
    {
       sum += number;
       --number;
    }//END WHILE
    System.out.println("The sum is " + sum);
```

Here, the loop control variable, *number*, is first assigned the value 5, and the variable *sum* is assigned the value 0. The `while` loop body will be executed as long as *number* is greater than 0. Observe that each time the loop is executed, the value of *number* is added to *sum*. In addition, the value of *number* is decremented by 1. Let's desk-check the code by tracing through each iteration to see what is happening. To desk-check a loop, we suggest that you set up a table, recording the values of variables affected by the loop for each iteration. Here, we will set up a table to track the values of *number* and *sum* after each iteration:

Iteration	number = 5	sum = 0
1	4	5
2	3	9
3	2	12
4	1	14
5	0	15

Notice that the looping stops when *number* reaches 0 because the test expression *number* > 0 becomes `false`. As a result, the loop body is bypassed and the *println()* statement is executed, producing a display of:

```
The sum is 15
```

In summary, you could say that the program segment computes the sum of integers from 1 through 5.

DEBUGGING TIP

Always initialize a variable that is accumulating a sum to 0. On the other hand, always initialize a variable that is accumulating a product to 1 *not* 0. What will be the result if such a product variable is initialized to 0? Well, 0 times anything is still 0, so your result will always be 0.

b.
```
int number;
int sum = 0;
while(number > 0)
{
   sum += number;
   --number;
}//END WHILE
System.out.println("The sum is " + sum);
```

What has been changed in this segment of code versus the previous segment in part a? Well, notice that the loop control variable, *number*, has not been initialized prior to the loop test. As a result, *number* will initially have some arbitrary value from memory. This condition will result in an indeterminate number of looping iterations, often producing an infinite loop for all practical purposes. *Never* assume that a variable starts at 0 unless it is initialized to 0.

THINK!

Make sure the loop control variable always has a meaningful value prior to entering the `while` loop statement. The `while` loop is a pretest loop and, therefore, must have a legitimate value to test the first time the loop test is executed.

c.
```
int number = 5;
int sum = 0;
while(number > 0)
{
   if(number % 2 != 0)
        sum += number;
   --number;
}//END WHILE
System.out.println("The sum is " + sum);
```

Here, an `if` statement has been included within the loop so that *number* is added to *sum* only if *number* is odd. Why will the calculation be performed when *number* is odd? Well, the remainder of any odd number divided by 2 is 1, right? Since 1 is not equal to 0, the test is `true` and *number* is added to *sum*. If *number* is even, the remainder operation generates a 0 result. This makes the `if` test `false` and the calculation statement is bypassed. This program segment computes the sum of odd integers from 1 through 5, resulting in a display of:

```
The sum is 9
```

d.
```java
int number = 5;
int sum = 0;
while(number > 0)
{
   if(number % 2 == 0)
        sum += number;
   --number;
}//END WHILE
System.out.println("The sum is " + sum);
```

This time, the program computes the sum of even integers from 1 through 5, because *number* is added to *sum* only if *number* is even. As a result, the display is:

```
The sum is 6
```

e.
```java
int maxNumber = 5;
int number = 0;
double sum = 0;
while(number < maxNumber)
    sum += number;
System.out.println("The average of the first " + maxNumber
                   + "positive integers is : " + sum/maxNumber);
```

This is an infinite loop. Notice that the loop is executed as long as *number* is less than *maxNumber*. The initial value of *number* is 0, and the initial value of *maxNumber* is 5. However, these values are never changed within the loop. Thus, *number* is always less than *maxNumber*, resulting in an infinite loop. No display is generated, and with many systems you must turn off the computer in order to get out of the loop. To correct this problem, you must change the loop control variable somewhere within the loop so that the loop test will eventually become `false`. In this segment of code, you need to increment *number* within the body of the loop, like this:

```java
int maxNumber = 5;
int number = 0;
double sum = 0;
while(number < maxNumber)
{
    ++number;
    sum += number;
}//END WHILE
System.out.println("The average of the first " + maxNumber
                   + " positive integers is " + sum/maxNumber);
```

The loop will now produce a result of:

```
The average of the first 5 positive integers is 3.0
```

By the way, why was *sum* defined as a floating-point value?

f.

Suppose we changed the test expression from *number < maxNumber* to *number !=maxNumber*. Would this have any effect on the outcome? No, the result would be the same. However, what would happen if *number* were incremented by 2 rather than 1 using this test expression? This would result in an infinite loop, because the value of *number* would skip over the value of *maxNumber* and the two would always be unequal. For this reason, it is often more desirable to use the < or > operators within the test expression rather than == and != when testing numeric values.

THINK!

Remember, an infinite loop is the result of a logical error in your program. The loop test variable(s) *must* change within the loop body so that the test expression eventually becomes `false`. **The compiler will not detect an infinite loop condition**. For this reason, you should always **desk-check** your loop structures very closely prior to coding and execution. A little time desk-checking will save you a lot of time at the keyboard.

g.
```java
StaugIO io = new StaugIO();       //FOR I/O
boolean positive = true;          //DEFINE BOOLEAN FLAG VARIABLE
int number = 0;
int sum = 0;
while(positive == true)
{
   //GET A NUMBER
   number = io.readInt("Enter an integer value: ");

   //SET FLAG TO FALSE IF NUMBER < 0
   if(number < 0)
   {
     positive = false;
     io.writeInfo("Loop terminated");
   }//END IF

   //ELSE ADD NUMBER TO SUM AND DISPLAY
   else
   {
     sum = sum + number;
     io.writeInfo("The sum is now: " + sum + "\n\n");
   }//END ELSE
}//END WHILE
```

This is an example of a *flag controlled loop*. A *flag* is a Boolean variable that is used to control the flow of a program. We first initialize the flag to `true`, then change it to `false` when a given event has occurred within the program. Here, we have started out by defining a variable for the `boolean` data type called *positive*. This will be our Boolean flag. The variable *positive* is then initialized to the value `true`. The loop will continue to execute as long as the value of *positive* remains `true`. With each iteration, the program will display the sum of the integers entered by the user. However, when the user enters a negative number, *positive* is set to `false`, and the loop will terminate. Here is a typical output produced by the loop:

```
Enter an integer value: 1
The sum is now 1

Enter an integer value: 2

The sum is now 3

Enter an integer value: 3

The sum is now 6

Enter an integer value: –1

Loop terminated
```

Of course, the above I/O would be displayed within dialog boxes using our *StaugIO* class. We have just shown it as text here to save the publisher some paper.

DEBUGGING TIP

Always remember to frame the body of a loop with braces, { }, if it contains more than one statement. For example, consider the following:

```
int count = 0;
while(count < 10)
    System.out.println(count);
    ++count;
```

The body of this loop looks as if it consists of two statements, as shown by the indentation. However, the loop body is not framed and the compiler only "sees" a single statement within the loop body. This means that *count* is not incremented within the loop, resulting in an infinite loop.

Data Entry Using `while`

There are many situations in which you will want to use a looping operation to read data. One common example is to read strings of data. The idea is to read a single data element, such as a character, each time the loop is executed. Then break out of the loop when the data string is terminated. For instance, consider the following code segment:

```
StaugIO io = new StaugIO();                  //FOR I/O
char inChar = ' ';                           //USER ENTRY VARIABLE
int charCount = 0;                           //CHARACTER COUNT

io.writeInfo("Enter several characters"
            + "\nTerminate the input with a period");
//READ A CHARACTER
inChar = io.readChar("Enter a character (period to quit)");
while(inChar !='.')                          //CHARACTER A PERIOD?
```

```
{
  ++charCount;                              //INCREMENT CHARACTER COUNT

  //READ ANOTHER CHARACTER
  inChar = io.readChar("Enter a character (period to quit)");
}//END WHILE
io.writeInfo("The number of characters entered was "+ charCount);
```

The general idea of this program is to read a string of characters, one character at a time, until a period, '.', is encountered. The period is called a ***sentinel value***, because it ends the input string but is not part of that string. The input variable is *inChar*. The while loop is executed as long as *inChar* is not equal to a period. With each iteration, a counter is incremented to count the number of characters that were entered before the period. Here is what you will see, in text form, when the program is executed:

```
Enter several characters
Terminate the input with a period

Enter a character (period to quit) a

Enter a character (period to quit) b

Enter a character (period to quit) c

Enter a character (period to quit) d

Enter a character (period to quit) .

The number of characters entered was 4
```

Here the user has entered five characters, including the sentinel. The program counts the number of characters entered, excluding the sentinel value.

Now, let's look at the program a bit closer. First, notice that a character is read just prior to the while statement because the while statement tests the variable *inChar* to see that it is not a period. Without the first read operation, *inChar* would not have a value and, therefore, could not be tested. Remember that the variable being tested in the while statement must always have a value prior to the first test. This is a common source of error when writing while loops. Why didn't the program count the period? Well, the loop is broken and *count* is not incremented for the period character.

A ***sentinel***-controlled loop is a loop that terminates when a given sentinel value is entered by the user.

PROGRAMMING TIP

When using a sentinel-controlled loop, always provide a prompt that instructs the user what to enter as the sentinel value. The prompts for data entry must continually remind the user of the sentinel value in a clear, unambiguous manner. Never use a sentinel value that the user could confuse with the normal data items being entered.

QUICK CHECK

1. True or false: A `while` loop repeats until the test expression is `true`.
2. True or false: The `while` loop is a posttest loop.
3. What is wrong with the following code?

```
int x = 10;
while(x > 0)
   System.out.println("This is a while loop.");
   --x;
```

4. Correct the code in question 3.
5. How many times will the following loop execute?

```
int x = 1;
while(x <= 0)
{
   System.out.println("How many times will this loop execute?");
   ++x;
}//END WHILE
```

6. How many times will the following loop execute?

```
int x = 1;
while(x >= 0)
{
   System.out.println("How many times will this loop execute?");
   ++x;
}//END WHILE
```

6.2 The do/while Loop

The flow of the do/while loop can be seen in Figure 6-2.

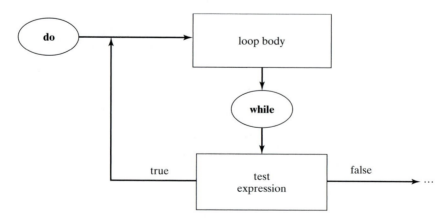

FIGURE 6-2 The do/while loop operation.

If you compare Figure 6-2 to the flow of while in Figure 6-1, you will find that the test is made at the end of the loop, rather than the beginning of the loop. This is the main difference between the while and the do/while loops. Because the do/while is a posttest loop, *the loop body will always be executed at least once.* To break the loop, the test expression must become false. Thus, if the test condition is initially true, something must happen within the loop to change the condition to false; otherwise, you have an infinite loop. Here's the required Java syntax:

do/while **STATEMENT FORMAT**

```
do
{
    statement 1;
    statement 2;
        .
        .        //LOOP BODY
        .
    statement n;
}//END DO/WHILE
while(test expression);
```

This format shows that the operation must begin with the single keyword do. This is followed by the loop body, which is followed by the keyword while and the test expression enclosed within parentheses. You must always frame the loop body with braces if it contains multiple statements. However, no framing is required when there is only a single loop statement within the body of the loop. In addition, notice that there is no semicolon after the keyword do in the first line, but a semicolon is required after the test expression in the last line. Look at the program segments in Example 6-2 and see if you can predict their result.

Example 6-2

What will be displayed by the following segments of code?

```
a.  int number = 5;
    int sum = 0;
    do
    {
      sum += number;
      --number;
    }//END DO/WHILE
    while(number > 0);
    System.out.println("The sum is " + sum);
```

In this segment, the value of *number* is initially set to 5, and the value of *sum* to 0. Each time the loop is executed, the value of *number* is added to *sum*. In addition, the value of *number* is decremented by 1. The looping will end when *number* has been decremented to 0. The resulting display is:

```
The sum is 15
```

Notice that this do/while loop computes the sum of integers 1 through 5, as did the while loop in Example 6-1a.

b.
```
int number = 0;
int sum = 0;
do
{
   sum += number;
   ++number;
}//END DO/WHILE
while(number < 5);
System.out.println("The sum is " + sum);
```

In this segment, both *number* and *sum* are initially 0. Again, you might suspect that the loop computes the sum of the integers 1 through 5. But, it actually computes the sum of integers 1 through 4. Notice that *number* is incremented after the *sum* is calculated. Thus, when *number* increments to 5, the loop is broken, and the value 5 is never added to *sum*. Desk-checking this code would reveal this result. The resulting display is:

```
The sum is 10
```

How would you change the loop to sum the integers 1 through 5? One way is to change the test expression to while (*number* <=5). Another way is to reverse the two loop statements so that *number* is incremented prior to the *sum* calculation.

THINK!

It is easy to introduce an *off-by-one* error into a loop. To prevent off-by-one errors, always desk-check the last few loop iterations before executing the code.

c.
```
int maxNumber = 5;
int number = 0;
double sum = 0;
do
{
   --number;
   sum += number;
}//END DO/WHILE
while(number < maxNumber);
System.out.println("The average of the first " + maxNumber
                 + " positive integers is :  " + sum/maxNumber);
```

In this segment, *maxNumber* begins with the value 5, and both *number* and *sum* are initialized to 0. The loop is broken when the value of *number* is greater than or equal to the value of *maxNumber*. How many times will the loop execute? If you said "five," you are wrong! Notice that *number* is decremented each time the loop is executed. Theoretically, the loop will execute an infinite number of times. However, because the range of integers in Java is normally from −2,147,483,648 to +2,147,483,647 the loop will execute 2,147,483,649 times.

How did we get this figure? Well, 2,147,483,648 loops will have executed when number reaches −2,147,483,648. The next looping operation will actually decrement number to +2,147,483,647, because binary values "wrap-around" inside the computer. This value is obviously greater than 5 so the loop will break. Notice that 2,147,483,648 + 1= 2,147,483,649. Of course, this is infinite for all practical purposes! However, this loop will eventually (after a long, long time) produce the following output:

```
The average of the first 5 positive integers is −4.611686...
```

Of course this is erroneous, because the average of the first 5 positive integers is 3.0. Bad data like this is often what you get when you do not thoroughly desk-check your loop logic. Such errors often become very difficult to find in a large program, especially were one result is used to calculate another result, which is used to calculate something else, and so on. Again, a few minutes of desk-checking saves a few hours debugging.

d.
```java
int maxNumber = 5;
int number = 0;
double sum = 0;
do
{
    ++number;
    sum += number;
}//END DO/WHILE
while(number < maxNumber);
System.out.println("The average of the first " + maxNumber
                    + " positive integers is :  " + sum/maxNumber);
```

Here, the loop in part c has been corrected so that the value of *number* is incremented by 1 with each iteration. When *number* reaches 5, it is no longer less than the value of *maxNumber*, and the loop is broken. The resulting display is:

```
The average of the first 5 positive integers is 3.0
```

e.
```java
StaugIO io = new StaugIO();           //FOR I/O
char inChar = ' ';                     //DEFINE USER ENTRY VARIABLE
int charCount = 0;                     //DEFINE CHAR COUNTER

io.writeInfo("Enter several characters"
            + "\nTerminate the input with a period");
do
{
    ++charCount;

    //READ A CHARACTER
    inChar = io.readChar("Enter a character (period to quit)");
}//END DO/WHILE
while(inChar != '.');                  //CHARACTER A PERIOD?
io.writeInfo("The number of characters entered was " + --charCount);
```

This program segment shows how a sentinel value can be employed to break a do/while loop. Notice that each iteration reads a single character from the keyboard until a period is entered. When this operation was performed using a while loop, you had to read the first character prior to the loop structure, so there was an initial value to test. This is because the Boolean test is made at the beginning of while. On the other hand, a do/while loop performs the Boolean test at the end of the loop. As a result, you do not have to read the first character prior to the loop structure, because the loop body will always be executed at least once and *inChar* will have a legitimate value before the loop test is made. Now, look at the *writeInfo()* statement. The value being displayed is $--charCount$. Why? Observe that *charCount* will be incremented, even for the last loop iteration that reads the period sentinel value. Therefore, *charCount* must be decremented to get the correct number of characters entered, excluding the sentinel value. This is required because of the post-test nature of do/while.

Here is a sample text dialog of the program execution. Of course, this text would actually be seen within dialog boxes.

```
Enter several characters
Terminate the input with a period

Enter a character (period to quit) a

Enter a character (period to quit) b

Enter a character (period to quit) c

Enter a character (period to quit) d

Enter a character (period to quit) .

The number of characters entered was 4
```

Problem Solving in Action: Loop-Controlled Menu-Driven Programs

Problem

In the last chapter, you saw that the switch statement is used to create menu-driven programs. It is often desirable to allow the user to select a menu option, perform the task associated with that option, then return to the menu to select another option without terminating the program until a quit option is chosen. Such a program would require the menu to be displayed repeatedly until the quit option is chosen. This is an ideal application for looping. We will encase our menu within a loop so that the menu and associated tasks will keep repeating until the user chooses to terminate the program. We will apply this technique to the menu-driven loan program developed in the last chapter. Let's revisit the problem.

Defining the Problem

Input:	A user response to the menu (P, I, T, or Q), as follows:
	If P is selected: User enters the loan amount, interest rate, and term.
	If I is selected: User enters the loan amount, interest rate, and term.
	If T is selected: User enters the loan amount, interest rate, and term.
	If Q is selected: terminate program.
Processing:	Calculate the selected option as follows:
	Case P: $payment = principal * rate/(1-(1+rate)^{-term})$
	Case I: $interest = term * payment - principal$

Case T: *total = principal + interest*
Case Q: terminate program.

where: *principal* is the amount of the loan.
         rate is a monthly interest rate in decimal form.
         term is the number of months of the loan.

Output: A program menu that prompts the user to select a monthly payment, total interest, or total loan amount calculation option.
The monthly loan payment, total loan interest, or total loan amount, depending on the program option that the user selects.
Invalid entry messages as required.

Planning the Solution

Using the program design developed in the last chapter, we divided the problem into four subproblems to solve the overall problem. They were:

- Display the menu and read the user choice.
- Read the loan principle, interest rate, and term from the user.
- Perform the chosen calculation.
- Display the chosen calculation.

The problem-solving diagram for this solution is shown again in Figure 6-3.

Now, the process description requires that we add a loop control feature to the program. To accomplish this, all we need to do is embed our method calls within a do/while loop, like this:

Initial Algorithm

main()
BEGIN
  do
    Call *displayMenu()* method.

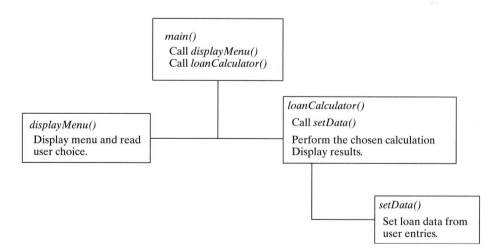

FIGURE 6-3   A problem-solving diagram for the loan problem.

Call *loanCalculator()* method.
        while *choice* ≠ 'q' AND *choice* ≠ 'Q'
END.

That's all there is to it! The *displayMenu()*, *loanCalculator()*, and *setData()* algorithms have not changed from our earlier solution. So, let's focus on the loop control in *main()*. Now, recall that the *displayMenu()* method obtains the user's menu choice. If the user enters a 'q' or 'Q' to quit the program, the loop will break, and the program will terminate. But, is there something wrong here? We said if the "user enters a 'q' *or* 'Q' to quit the program, the loop will break"; however, the loop test employs the AND operation. So, why have we used the Boolean AND operation rather than the OR operation to perform this test? This is a classic candidate for desk-checking the algorithm logic *before* coding the program. Ask yourself: "When will the loop break?" Any Java loop breaks when the condition tested is `false`, right? Remember that the result of an AND operation is `false` when any one of its conditions is `false`. As a result, the loop will break when *choice* is a 'q' *or* a 'Q'. The loop will continue when both sides of the AND operation are `true`. Therefore, the loop will continue as long as *choice* is not a 'q' *and choice* is not 'Q'. Isn't this what we want to do? What would happen if you mistakenly used the OR operation in the foregoing loop test? An OR operation produces a `true` result when any one of its conditions is `true`. One of these conditions would always be `true` because *choice* cannot be both a 'q' and a 'Q'. The result of this oversight would be an infinite loop.

Another point needs to be made here. This application is a classic candidate for a `do/while` loop rather than a `while` loop because you always want the menu to be displayed at least once to allow for a user choice.

 THINK!

A common mistake when developing loop control logic is to use an OR operation rather than an AND operation, or vice versa. This mistake almost always results in an infinite loop. The lesson to be learned here is to *always* desk-check your loop control logic before coding the program.

We will not repeat the additional levels of refinement or the class diagram because they have not changed from the solution developed in the last chapter. We are now ready to code the program.

Coding the Program

Here is the implementation of the foregoing program design:

```
/*
 * Action06_01.java
 *
 * Created on June 20, 2002, 10:09 AM
 */

/**
 *
 * @author  Andrew C. Staugaard, Jr.
 * @version 1.0
 */
```

```java
import staugIO.StaugIO;           //FOR INPUT AND OUTPUT
import java.text.NumberFormat;    //FOR CURRENCY FORMAT
class ConsumerLoanLoop
{
    //DEFINE VARIABLES AND OBJECTS
    private double principal = 0.0;      //LOAN PRINCIPLE
    private double term = 0;             //TERM OF LOAN IN MONTHS
    private double rate = 0.0;           //ANNUAL INTEREST IN PERCENT FORM
    private double payment = 0.0;        //MONTHLY PAYMENT
    private double interest = 0.0;       //TOTAL LOAN INTEREST
    private double total = 0.0;          //TOTAL LOAN AMOUNT
    private StaugIO io = new StaugIO();  //FOR INPUT/OUTPUT
    private char choice = 'Q';           //USER MENU CHOICE

    //displayMenu()
    public void displayMenu()
    {
        //DISPLAY A MENU AND READ USER'S CHOICE
        choice = io.readChar("Enter P to get monthly payment"
                            + "\nEnter I to get total loan interest"
                            + "\nEnter T to get total loan amount"
                            + "\nEnter Q to quit"
                            + "\n\nPlease enter your choice:  ");
    }//END displayMenu()

    //setData() METHOD
    private void setData()
    {
      principal = io.readDouble("Enter the amount of the loan: ");
      term = io.readDouble("Enter the duration of the loan in months: ");
      rate = io.readDouble("Enter the annual interest rate in percent: ");
      rate = rate/12/100;
    }//END setData()

    //loanCalculator() METHOD
    public void loanCalculator()
    {
        //CREATE CURRENCY OBJECT
        NumberFormat currency = NumberFormat.getCurrencyInstance();

        switch(choice)
        {
          case 'p': //CALCULATE AND DISPLAY PAYMENT
          case 'P' : setData();
                  payment = principal * rate/(1-Math.pow((1+rate), -term));
                  io.writeInfo("The monthly payment is "
                               + currency.format(payment));
                  break;

          case 'i':  //CALCULATE AND DISPLAY INTEREST
          case 'I' : setData();
                  payment = principal * rate/(1-Math.pow((1+rate), -term));
                  interest = term * payment - principal;
```

```
                io.writeInfo("The total interest is "
                                + currency.format(interest));
            break;

    case 't':   //CALCULATE AND DISPLAY TOTAL LOAN AMOUNT
    case 'T':   setData();
                payment = principal * rate/(1-Math.pow((1+rate), -term));
                interest = term * payment - principal;
                total = principal + interest;
                io.writeInfo("\n\nThe total loan amount is "
                                + currency.format(total));
            break;

    case 'q':   //TERMINATE PROGRAM
    case 'Q':   io.writeInfo("Program terminated");
            break;

    //DISPLAY INVALID ENTRY MESSAGE
    default : io.writeInfo("\n\nThis is an invalid entry");
  }//END SWITCH

 }//END loanCalculator()
//getChoice() METHOD
public char getChoice()
{
  return choice;
 }//END getChoice()
}//END ComsumerLoanLoop CLASS

public class Action06_01
{
  public static void main (String args[])
  {
    //CREATE LOAN OBJECT
    ConsumerLoanLoop myLoan = new ConsumerLoanLoop();
    do
    {
    //CALL METHOD
    myLoan.displayMenu();
    myLoan.loanCalculator();
    }//END do/while
    while ((myLoan.getChoice() != 'q') && (myLoan.getChoice() != 'Q'));

    //EXIT PROGRAM
    System.exit(0);
  }//END main()
}//END Action06_01
```

The major change here is the do/while loop control feature that we added in our solution planning. Notice how the conditional loop test is coded at the end of the program. The entire test must be within parentheses. The variable *choice* is tested twice; both tests must be enclosed within parentheses. The results of both tests are combined via the Boolean AND (&&) operation. There is another small, but significant addition. We have added a method called *getChoice()* to return the value of *choice* in order to make the do/while loop test. Since *choice* is a private class member, it cannot be accessed outside of the *ComsumerLoanLoop* class. A public method must be called using the class object, *myLoan*, to return its value. This is the job of *getChoice()*. These concepts will become more clear when you learn more about methods and classes in the next two chapters.

THINK!

A common mistake when coding a compound Boolean test on a variable is to forget to code it so that each side of the compound test produces a Boolean result. For example, suppose that we coded the foregoing loop test as:

```
while(choice != 'q' && 'Q');
```

This code will always produce a compiler error because the right side of the AND operation does not produce a Boolean result. It might make sense for you to code it this way, but it doesn't make sense to the compiler!

QUICK CHECK

1. True or false: A do/while repeats until the loop test is true.
2. True or false: The do/while loop is a posttest loop.
3. What is wrong with the following code?

```
int x = 10;
do
    System.out.println("This is a do/while loop");
while(x > 0);
```

4. Correct the code in question 3.
5. How many times will the following loop execute?

```
int x = 1;
do
    System.out.println("This is a do/while loop");
    ++x;
while(x <= 0);
```

6. How many times will the following loop execute?

```
int x = 1;
do
{
    System.out.println("This is a do/while loop");
    ++x;
}//END DO/WHILE
while(x >= 0);
```

6.3   The for Loop

The for loop is called a ***fixed repetition*** loop because the loop is repeated a fixed number of times. You would use it in place of a while or do/while loop when it is

known in advance, by you or the program, exactly how many times the loop must repeat itself.

You can see from Figure 6-4 that the first thing that takes place before the loop
body is executed is the initialization of a loop counter. Initialization means setting a
counter variable to some initial, or beginning, value. A test expression is then executed
to test the counter value. If the result of this test is `true,` the loop body is executed.
Each time the loop body is executed, the counter value is *automatically* incremented or
decremented. The test expression is evaluated again before the loop body is executed
another time. The loop is repeated as long as the result of the test expression is `true.` In
other words, the counter is incremented/decremented, tested, and the loop is repeated
until the test expression is `false.` When this occurs, the loop body is not executed
again, and the loop is broken. Control of the program then goes to the next sequential
statement following the loop.

Here's the Java syntax:

for *STATEMENT FORMAT*

```
for(int count=initial value; count test expression;
                       increment/decrement count)
{
   statement 1;
   statement 2;
      •
      •      //LOOP BODY
      •
   statement n;
}//END FOR
```

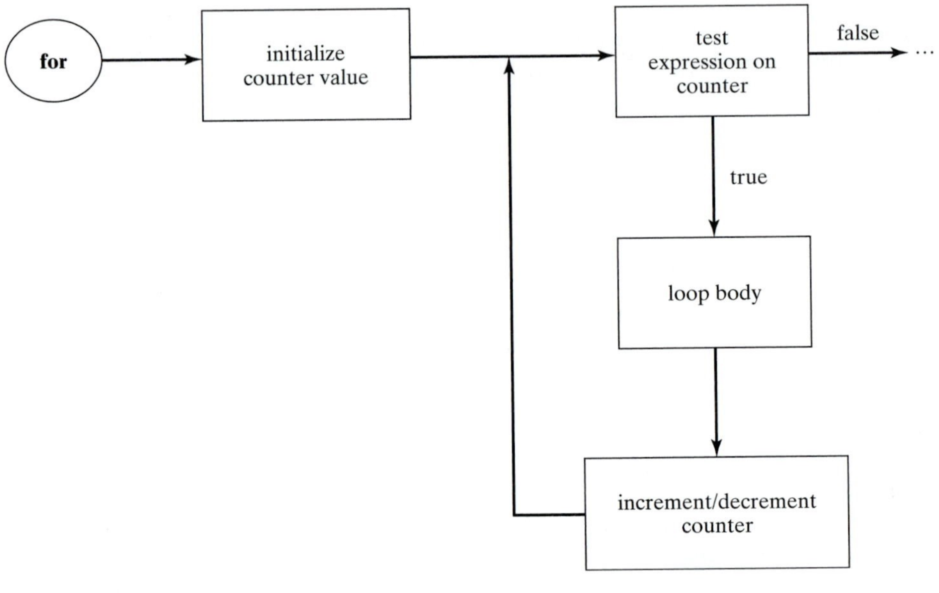

FIGURE 6-4   The for loop operation.

The statement begins with the keyword for. This is followed by *three* separate statements: an *initialization* statement, a *test expression*, and an *increment/decrement* statement, all enclosed within a single set of parentheses. The loop counter is initialized by assigning an initial value to the counter variable. The counter variable will almost always be an int but can be any simple data type, except a floating-point type. The counter variable can be defined before the for statement or within the for statement as part of the initialization step, like this:

```
for(int count = 1; ...
```

If defined within the for statement, it is only valid within the for statement in which it is defined. Thus, as far as Java is concerned, the counter variable doesn't exist outside of the for statement in which it is defined.

The test expression is used to test the value of the loop counter against some predetermined value. The loop body will be executed until the result of the test expression becomes false.

The increment/decrement statement is used to change the value of the loop counter so that the test expression becomes false after a fixed number of iterations. It is important to note that the increment/decrement statement is executed *automatically after* the loop body is executed in a given iteration. Thus, *if the initial test expression is true, the loop body will be executed at least once*. However, *if the initial test expression is false, the loop body is never executed*. This means that the for loop acts very much like the while loop. In fact, a for loop and a while loop are really one and the same looping structure, just coded differently. Think about it!

One last point about the loop counter variable: *Never* alter the counter variable within the body of the loop. The counter variable can be used within the body of the loop, but its value should not be altered because it is *automatically* altered according to the increment/decrement statement in the first line of the for. In other words, never use the counter variable on the left side of the assignment symbol (=) within the loop.

 ## DEBUGGING TIP

A common programming error is to increment the loop counter inside a for loop like this:

```
for(int count = 0; count != 5; ++count)
{
    System.out.println(count);
    ++count;
}//END FOR
```

This code will not produce a compiler error, but will produce an infinite loop. Why? Because *count* is incremented twice during each loop, thereby skipping completely over the value 5 and creating an infinite loop condition. The lesson to be learned here is: Don't mess with the loop counter inside a for loop.

Finally, notice from the above format that the loop body is framed within the braces. This is always required when there is more than one loop statement. The framing can be eliminated when there is only a single loop statement. Here are a few examples; see if you can predict the results.

Example 6-3

What will be displayed by the following segments of code?

a.
```
for(int count = 1; count < 11; ++count)
      System.out.println("The value of count is now " + count);
```

The loop counter variable, *count*, ranges from 1 to 11. How many iterations will there be? Eleven, right? Wrong! The ++ *count* statement increments the value of *count after* each loop iteration. When the value of *count* reaches 11, the test expression is `false` and the loop is broken. As a result, there is no eleventh iteration. With each loop iteration, the *println()* statement displays the value of *count* in a console window like this:

```
The value of count is now 1
The value of count is now 2
The value of count is now 3
The value of count is now 4
The value of count is now 5
The value of count is now 6
The value of count is now 7
The value of count is now 8
The value of count is now 9
The value of count is now 10
```

 THINK!

When desk-checking a loop, always check the *loop boundaries*. The loop boundaries occur at the initial and final value of the loop control variable. Checking these values will help prevent *off-by-one* errors, where the loop executes one time more or one time less than intended. Also, when desk-checking a loop, try to imagine circumstances where the loop might execute 0 times, 1 time, or *n* times.

b.
```
for(int count = 10; count > 0; --count)
      System.out.println("The value of count is now " + count);
```

Here, the value of *count* ranges from 10 to 0. The −−*count* statement decrements the value of *count* after each loop iteration. When the value of *count* reaches zero, the loop is broken. This type of loop is sometimes referred to as a "down-to" loop. The output generated by this loop will appear in a console window as follows:

```
The value of count is now 10
The value of count is now 9
```

```
The value of count is now 8
The value of count is now 7
The value of count is now 6
The value of count is now 5
The value of count is now 4
The value of count is now 3
The value of count is now 2
The value of count is now 1
```

c. ```
for(int count = 0; count != 5; ++count)
{
    sum = sum + count;
    System.out.println("The sum in the first iteration is " + sum);
    ++count;
}//END FOR
```

This is an infinite loop! Notice that the loop counter is incremented within the body of the loop. What actually happens is that the loop counter is incremented twice, once within the body of the loop by the increment statement, and then automatically by the `for` statement. As a result, the value of *count* skips over the value 5, creating an infinite loop. The lesson to be learned here is this: *Never change the loop counter within the body of a `for` loop*.

**d.**  ```
for(int count = -5; count < 6; ++count)
    System.out.println("The value of count is now " + count);
```

Here, *count* ranges from −5 to 6. Because the loop is broken when *count* reaches 6, the *println()* loop statement is executed for values of *count* from –5 to 5. How many times will the loop be executed? Ten, right? Wrong! There are 11 integers in the range of −5 to 5, including 0. As a result, the loop is executed eleven times, producing eleven output lines in a console window as follows:

```
The value of count is now -5
The value of count is now -4
The value of count is now -3
The value of count is now -2
The value of count is now -1
The value of count is now 0
The value of count is now 1
The value of count is now 2
The value of count is now 3
The value of count is now 4
The value of count is now 5
```

e. ```
for(int count = 1; count < 11; ++count)
    System.out.println("Number   Square   Cube\n"
                        + count
                        + "   " + count * count
                        + "   " + count * count * count);
```
```

This **for** loop is being used to generate a table of squares and cubes for the integers 1 through 10. Notice how the counter variable *count* is squared and cubed within the *println()* loop statement. However, observe that at no time is the value of *count* altered within the loop. The resulting console output is:

Number	Square	Cube
1	1	1
Number	Square	Cube
2	4	8
Number	Square	Cube
3	9	27
Number	Square	Cube
4	16	64
Number	Square	Cube
5	25	125
Number	Square	Cube
6	36	216
Number	Square	Cube
7	49	343
Number	Square	Cube
8	64	512
Number	Square	Cube
9	81	729
Number	Square	Cube
10	100	1000

f.
```
for(char character = 'A'; character <= 'Z'; ++character)
     System.out.print(character);
```

The counter variable in this loop is the character variable *character*. Recall that the character data type is ordered so that 'A' is smaller than 'Z'. Notice that the test expression, *character* <= 'Z' forces the loop to execute for the last time when the value of *character* is 'Z'. Consequently, the loop is executed 26 times as *character* ranges from 'A' to 'Z'. The value of *character* is displayed each time within the same console window, producing a single line containing the alphabet like this:

ABCDEFGHIJKLMNOPQRSTUVWXYZ

g.
```
StaugIO io = new StaugIO();       //FOR I/O
final int MAX_COUNT = 100;
double sum = 0.0;
double average = 0.0;
for(int count = 1; count <= MAX_COUNT; ++count)
   sum = sum + count;
```

```
average = sum/MAX_COUNT;
io.writeInfo("The average of the first " + MAX_COUNT
            + "\npositive integers is:  " + average);
```

Here, the counter value is being added to the floating-point variable *sum* each time through the loop. Thus, the loop adds all the positive integers within the defined range of the counter variable. The range of *count* is from 1 to *MAX_COUNT*. Notice that *MAX_COUNT* has been defined as a constant with a value of 100. Therefore, *count* will range from 1 to 100 + 1, or 101. However, because the loop is broken when *count* reaches the value 101, this value is never added to *sum*. This results in a summing of all integers within the range of 1 to *MAX_COUNT*. After the loop is broken, the value of *sum* is divided by *MAX_COUNT* to calculate the *average* of all integers from 1 to 100. Here's what you would see:

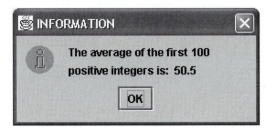

Notice that the variable *sum* was defined as a floating-point value, so that the division operator, /, produces a floating-point quotient. If both *sum* and *MAX_COUNT* were defined as integer values, the division operator would produce an erroneous integer result of 50. Also, you should be aware that constants like *MAX_COUNT* are often used as shown here for the initial or final counter values in a for loop. The reason is this: If the constant value needs to be changed for some reason, you need to change it in only one place, within the final definition. This changes its value any place it is used within the block of code in which it is visible.

h.
```
final int MAX_COUNT = 100;
for(int i = 1; i <= MAX_COUNT; ++i)
{
    if(i % 17 == 0)
        System.out.println("The value " + i + " is divisible by 17.");
}//END FOR
```

An if statement is used in this loop to determine when the counter value, *i*, is divisible by 17. Thus, the loop displays all the values between 1 and *MAX_COUNT* (100) that are divisible by 17. Do you understand how the test expression is working in the if statement? Here is the output that you would see in a console window when it is executed:

```
The value 17 is divisible by 17.
The value 34 is divisible by 17.
The value 51 is divisible by 17.
The value 68 is divisible by 17.
The value 85 is divisible by 17.
```

PROGRAMMING TIP

Suppose that a loop must execute *n* times and you create a loop control variable called *count*. In Java, if the loop control variable begins with the value 0, the loop test would use the *less than* (<) operator, like this: *count < n*. If the application requires you to begin the loop control variable with the value 1, the test would use the *less than or equal to* (<=) operator, like this: *count <= n*. When the application does not require otherwise, it is standard practice to initialize Java loop control variables with the value 0 and use the *less than* test.

Nested Loops

Many applications require looping operations within loops. This is called ***nested looping***. To get the idea, think about the hours, minutes, and seconds of a 12-hour digital timer that ranges from 00:00:00 to 11:59:59. Isn't each unit of time a simple counter? The seconds count from 0 to 59, the minutes from 0 to 59, and the hours from 0 to 11. For every 60 seconds, the minutes counter is incremented. Likewise, for every 60 minutes, the hours counter is incremented. Thus, the seconds count is "nested" within the minutes count, and the minutes count is "nested" within the hours count. Here's how a digital timer might be coded in a Java program using nested `for` loops:

```java
for(int hours = 0; hours < 12; ++hours)
   for(int minutes = 0; minutes < 60; ++minutes)
      for(int seconds = 0; seconds < 60; ++seconds)
         System.out.println(hours + " : " + minutes + " : " + seconds);
```

As you can see, the seconds loop is part of the minutes loop, which is part of the hours loop. The *outer* `for` loop begins by initializing the *hours* counter to 0. The statement within this loop is another `for` loop that begins by initializing the *minutes* counter to 0. This leads to the seconds loop, where the *seconds* counter is initialized to 0. Once the *seconds* counter is initialized, the seconds loop is executed 60 times, as *seconds* ranges from 0 to 59. Each time the seconds loop is executed, the *hours*, *minutes*, and *seconds* count values are displayed. After the seconds loop is executed 60 times, the *minutes* count is incremented, and the seconds loop is entered again and executed 60 more times. So, the seconds loop is executed 60 times for each iteration of the minutes loop. Likewise, because the minutes loop is nested within the hours loop, the minutes loop is executed 60 times for each iteration of the hours loop. After 60 iterations of the minutes loop (3600 iterations of the seconds loop), the *hours* count is incremented and displayed. The hours loop is not broken until it has been executed 12 times, from 0 to 11. Of course, this requires 12 × 60 = 720 iterations of the minutes loop and 12 × 60 × 60 = 43,200 iterations of the seconds loop. We say that the seconds loop is the *innermost* loop, and the hours loop is the *outermost* loop. It is important to observe that the index of an outer loop controls how many times its inner loop statement is entered. For instance, since the hours loop executes 12 times, the minutes loop statement is entered 12 times. Since the minutes loop executes 60 times, the seconds loop statement is entered 60 times. Notice that *no* framing is required for any of the loops because the hours loop consists of a single `for` statement, which is the minutes loop, the minutes loop consists of a single `for` statement, which is the seconds loop, and the seconds loop consists of a single statement which is the *println()* statement. An indentation scheme becomes important here, because it is the indentation that really shows the nesting, even though the compiler ignores the indentation.

To make the digital timer work, the *seconds* counter must be incremented precisely, once every second. This requires a time delay routine within the seconds loop to slow down the seconds count accordingly. This will be left as an exercise at the end of the chapter.

Aside from counting, nested `for` loops are commonly used in graphics applications for line drawing, pattern drawing, and graphing things like histograms.

Before we leave the topic of nested loops, you should be aware that `while` and `do/while` loops can also be nested. You will find examples of this in the questions at the end of the chapter.

DEBUGGING TIP

A common error when coding a `for` loop is to place a semicolon at the end of the `for` statement like this:

```
int count = 0;
int sum = 0;
for(count = 1; count <= 5; ++count);
    sum = sum + count;
io.writeInfo("The sum is " + sum);
```

Here, the programmer obviously wanted to sum the integers from 1 to 5. However, the sum is calculated once, resulting in a value of 6. Why? Well, if you were to single step this code with your debugger and place a watch on *count*, you would find that it increments from 1 to 6 as expected. (Remember that the value of the loop counter is automatically incremented after the loop body. So, the value of *count* actually increments to 6, which causes the loop to break.) Now the erroneous semicolon at the end of the `for` statement terminates the `for` statement and the *sum = sum + count* statement is seen as a single statement all by itself. So, it adds the *count* value of 6 to the *sum* value of 0 to produce a *sum* of 6. The `for` loop actually executes through its entire cycle but does not do anything since the compiler sees it with no statement section. It just sits there and "spins its wheels."

There might be an application where this is desirable within a program. Can you think of one? How about creating time delays within a program? You could simply use a very large test value and force the program to loop enough times to create a noticeable delay. Of course, the precise amount of delay would depend on your system performance, right? Maybe you could use this idea to create a time delay within the seconds loop of the preceding timer program.

Now, rather than defining *count* prior to the `for` loop, if you were to define *count* within the `for` loop like this:

```
int sum = 0;
for(int count = 1; count <= 5; ++count);
    sum = sum + count;
io.writeInfo("The sum is " + sum);
```

you would get a compile error. Why? Because remember that when the loop counter is defined within the `for` statement, it is only valid within that statement. Since the compiler sees the *sum* = *sum* + *count* statement as a separate statement outside the `for` loop, it sees *count* as an undefined variable within this statement. Thus, the lesson here is to define your loop control variable inside the `for` loop. Then if you mistakenly add a semicolon at the end of the `for` statement, the compiler will generate an undefined variable message when you try to use the variable outside of this statement. This just might help you find the erroneous semicolon.

Coding versus Pseudocoding for Loops

The pseudocode of a `for` loop looks quite different from the Java code. For example, the pseudocode for the earlier timer program might look something like this:

> For *hours* = 0 to 11
> > For *minutes* = 0 to 59
> > > For *seconds* = 0 to 59
> > > > Write *hours* : *minutes* : *seconds*.

Wow! This is quite a bit different from the Java code and, on the surface, seems to be quite simple. Remember that one of the reasons for pseudocode is to ignore detail and concentrate on solving the problem at hand. Now, look at the *hours* loop. The pseudocode indicates that *hours* starts at 0 and goes up to 11. The *hours* loop will break when the value of *hours* exceeds 11. Notice, however, that there is nothing that indicates the testing operation or the incrementing operation. We say that the testing and incrementing of *hours* are both ***implicit***, or understood, within this pseudocode statement. However, when you code this loop in Java, the testing and incrementing of *hours* must be ***explicit***, or actually coded, within the equivalent Java statement.

Down-to for Loops

In most of the `for` loops you have seen so far, the loop counter has been incremented from some initial value to some final value. You can also begin the loop counter at some value, then decrement it down to a final value. Such a loop is called a "down-to" loop. The digital timer program segment could be easily revised to employ down-to loops. Here is the required pseudocode:

> For *hours* = 11 down to 0
> > For *minutes* = 59 down to 0
> > > For *seconds* = 59 down to 0
> > > > Write *hours*, *minutes*, *seconds*.

The pseudocode clearly shows why these are called down-to loops. Notice that, for example, *hours* begins at 11 and goes down to 0. Here is the corresponding Java code:

```java
for(int hours = 11; hours >= 0; --hours)
   for(int minutes = 59; minutes >= 0; --minutes)
      for(int seconds = 59; seconds >= 0; --seconds)
         System.out.println(hours + " : " + minutes + " : " + seconds);
```

The differences here are that the initial and final values of the respective loop counters have been changed so that the timer counts down from 11:59:59 and times out when the count reaches 00:00:00. The test expressions are simply the counter values, and the counters are being decremented rather than incremented. When a given counter value reaches −1, the loop test becomes `false` and the respective loop is broken. The net effect is still the same: There are 60 iterations of the seconds loop for each iteration of the minutes loop, and 60 iterations of the minutes loop for each iteration of the hours loop. Of course, the timer counts down rather than counting up as in the previous program.

QUICK CHECK

1. List the three things that must appear in the first line of a `for` loop structure.
2. True or false: The loop counter in a `for` loop is altered after the loop body is executed in a given iteration.
3. True or false: A `for` loop can always be replaced by a `while` loop, because both are basically the same looping structure, just coded differently.
4. How many times is the following loop executed?

```
for(int x = 0; x > 0; ++x)
   System.out.println("How many times will this loop execute?");
```

5. How many times is the following loop executed?

```
for(int x = 0; x <= 10; ++x)
   System.out.println("How many times will this loop execute?");
```

6. When must the body of a `for` loop be framed?
7. Suppose that you have two nested loops. The inner loop executes five times and the outer loop executes ten times. How many total iterations are there within the nested loop structure?
8. In a down-to loop, the loop counter is always _____.

6.4   The break and continue Options

The `break` and `continue` statements can be used to alter the execution of predefined control structures, such as loops, when certain conditions occur. In general, the `break` statement is used to immediately terminate a loop, and the `continue` statement is used to skip over a single loop iteration.

The break Statement

You observed the use of the `break` statement within the `switch` statement in the last chapter. Recall that the `break` statement forced the `switch` statement to terminate. The same is true when you use the `break` statement inside a loop structure. When Java executes the `break` statement within a loop, the loop is immediately terminated and control is passed to the next statement following the loop. The `break` statement is usually used as part of an `if` statement within the loop to terminate the loop structure if a certain condition occurs. The action of the break statement within a `while` loop can be illustrated like this:

THE break OPTION

```
while(test expression)
{
    statement;
    statement;
        •
        •
        •
    if(test expression)
        break;
    statement;
    statement;
        •
        •
}//END WHILE
Next statement after while;
```

Consider the following program segment:

```
int number = 1;                    //LOOP CONTROL VARIABLE
while(number < 11)
{
    if(number == 5)
        break;

    System.out.println("In the while loop, number is now " + number);
    ++number;

}//END WHILE
System.out.println("The loop is now terminated "
                  + "and the value of number is "
                  + number);
```

This `while` loop employs a break statement to terminate the loop when *number* reaches the value of 5. Here are the output lines that you would see in a console window as a result of the loop execution:

```
In the while loop, number is now 1
In the while loop, number is now 2
In the while loop, number is now 3
In the while loop, number is now 4
The loop is now terminated and the value of number is 5
```

As you can see, even though the final value of *number* is 5, the *println()* statement within the loop is not executed when *number* reaches 5, because the break statement forces the loop to terminate for this value. Normally, you would not break out of a loop as a result of a natural loop counter value. Doing so would indicate that you have coded your loop test incorrectly. This was done only to illustrate how the break statement works. You will use the break statement primarily to break out of a loop when the potential for an infinite loop exists. Such an application could be to interrupt the digital timer loops given in the last section as the result of a user entry to stop the timer.

The continue Statement

You have not seen the use of the continue statement before because it is used primarily to skip a single iteration within a loop if a certain condition occurs. Like the break statement, the continue statement is normally employed within a loop as part of an if statement. We can illustrate the operation of continue within a for loop, like this:

THE continue OPTION

```
for(int count=initial value; count test expression;
                          increment/decrement count)
{
   statement;
   statement;
      •
      •
      •
   if(test expression)
       continue;
   statement;
   statement;
      •
      •
      •
}//END FOR
Next statement after for;
```

Here you see that when the if statement test expression is true, the continue statement is executed, forcing the current iteration to terminate. It is important to remember that *only the current iteration is terminated* as the result of continue. All subsequent iterations will be executed, unless, of course, they are terminated by executing a break or continue. The following program segment demonstrates how continue works:

```
int value = 0;
for(int counter = 1;counter < 11; ++counter)
{
   if(counter == 5)
       continue;

   System.out.println("In the for loop, the counter value is now "
                    + counter);
   value = counter;
}//END FOR

System.out.println("The loop is now terminated "
                  + "with a counter value of "
                  + value);
```

Here is what you would see in a console window as the result of executing the program segment:

```
In the for loop, the counter value is now 1
In the for loop, the counter value is now 2
In the for loop, the counter value is now 3
In the for loop, the counter value is now 4
In the for loop, the counter value is now 6
In the for loop, the counter value is now 7
In the for loop, the counter value is now 8
In the for loop, the counter value is now 9
In the for loop, the counter value is now 10
The loop was terminated with a counter value of 10
```

You see here that the fifth iteration is skipped because of the execution of the `continue` statement. All subsequent iterations are performed, and the loop is broken naturally when *counter* reaches the value of 11.

The foregoing program segment also illustrates something you need to remember about a `for` loop counter. That is, when a `for` loop counter is actually defined within the `for` loop, it has no meaning outside the `for` loop in which it is defined. This is why we defined the integer variable *value* prior to the loop. *value* acts as a placeholder for *counter* during the loop execution. This way, the final value of *counter* can be displayed via the variable *value* after the loop terminates. You could not display *counter* after the loop terminates, because *counter* is not defined outside of the `for` loop. Of course, you could have defined *counter* prior to the loop statement, not within the loop statement, to avoid the need for an extra variable in this situation.

PROGRAMMING TIP

We *strongly* urge you to only use a **break** or **continue** statement within a loop as a last resort. If your loops are well thought out, there should be very few times that you would need to use **break** or **continue**. If you find yourself using **break** or **continue** too often, you might not be thoroughly thinking through the loop logic. Overuse of **break** and **continue** makes the logic hard to follow.

QUICK CHECK

1. The statement that will cause only the current iteration of a loop to be terminated is the
_____ statement.

2. The **break** and **continue** statements are normally used as part of a(n) _____
statement within a loop structure.

3. How many times will the following loop execute?

```
int x = 0;
while(x < 10)
{
```

```
     System.out.println("How many times will this loop execute?");
     if(x > 0)
        break;
     ++x;
}//END WHILE
```

Problem Solving in Action: Computing Your Test Average

Problem

Let's close this chapter by writing a program that will allow a user to compute his or her test average. We will solve the problem using the `while` loop structure. Then you will be asked to convert the solution to a `do/while` and a `for` loop solution in the problems at the end of the chapter. As usual, let's define the problem in terms of input, processing, and output.

Defining the Problem

Input:	The number of test scores to average and the individual test score values.
Processing:	Each time a test score value is entered, a new test total will be recalculated as follows:

$$testTotal = testTotal + score$$

Then, the average of all the test scores will be calculated as follows:

$$average = testTotal/number$$

Output:	The program must first prompt the user to enter the number of test scores to average. A prompt will then be generated to enter each test score value separately. The final output will be a display of the test average.

Now, using this problem definition, we are ready for the algorithm. Let's employ the `while` iteration control structure to repeatedly calculate the test total each time a score value is entered.

Planning the Solution

So as not to distract from concentrating on iteration, we will not stepwise refine the problem solution. Rather, we will employ one main algorithm, as follows:

```
main()
BEGIN
    Set count = 0.
    Set testTotal = 0.
    Write a user prompt to enter the number of test scores to be averaged.
    Read number.
    While (number <= 0)
        Write an invalid entry message.
        Write a user prompt to enter the number of test scores to be averaged.
        Read number.
    While (count < number)
        Set count = count + 1.
```

> Write prompt to enter test score #*count.*
> Read *score.*
> While (*score* < 0) OR (*score* > 100)
>   Write an invalid entry message.
>   Write prompt to enter test score #*count.*
>   Read *score.*
> Calculate *testTotal* = *testTotal* + *score.*
> Calculate *average* = *testTotal/number*
END.

Wow! Here you see three loops. Why three loops? Well, one loop is used to calculate the test total as expected, and two additional loops are used to force the user to provide valid entries. The first loop is used to force the user to enter a valid number for the number of scores. If the value of *number* entered by the user is less than or equal to zero, the loop will repeat until the user enters a value which is greater than zero. A negative value for *number* is not reasonable and a value of zero will cause a divide-by-zero error later in the program. In other words, we keep the user trapped inside the loop until he or she enters an acceptable value.

The second loop is used to add up the individual test scores. Each time the loop is executed, an additional score value is entered, and the test total is calculated. However, a nested loop is provided which forces the user to enter valid scores. Notice how the OR test is employed to test the score value. If the entered score value is less than 0 or greater than 100, the user is prompted again and must enter a value between 0 and 100 to get out of the loop. Remember this loop trick to force the user to enter correct values—it often comes in handy.

Observe that a loop counter (*count*) was initialized to 0 at the beginning of the algorithm. The value of *count* must then be incremented with each loop iteration to prevent an infinite loop. The looping continues until the value of *count* equals the number of test scores (*number*). When this happens, the loop body is not executed again and control is passed to the next sequential statement which calculates the average. Also notice how the value of *count* is used as part of the prompt to instruct the user which score to enter. Next, it is important to initialize the value of *testTotal* to zero prior to the second loop. (Why?) Finally, notice that the pseudocode indentation clearly shows which statements go with which loop.

Following the algorithm, you can easily code a Java program, like this.

Coding the Program

```
/*
 * Action06_02.java
 *
 * Created on June 20, 2002, 12:46 PM
 */

/**
 *
 * @author  Andrew C. Staugaard, Jr.
 * @version 1.1
 */

import staugIO.StaugIO;          //FOR GUI I/O

public class Action06_02
{
  public static void main (String args[])
```

```java
{
  //DEFINE VARIABLES AND OBJECTS
  int count = 0;                 //LOOP COUNTER
  int number = 0;                //NUMBER OF TEST SCORES TO AVERAGE
  double score = 0.0;            //INDIVIDUAL TEST SCORE VALUES
  double testTotal = 0.0;        //TOTAL OF TEST SCORES ENTERED
  double average = 0.0;          //FINAL TEST AVERAGE
  String info = "TEST SCORE SUMMARY\n"; //OUTPUT STRING
  StaugIO io = new StaugIO();    //FOR I/O

  //OBTAIN NUMBER OF SCORES TO AVERAGE
  number = io.readInt("Please enter the number of scores to average");

  //LOOP UNTIL VALID NUMBER IS ENTERED
  while (number <= 0)
  {
    number = io.readInt("Invalid entry"
                   + "\nPlease enter the number of scores to average");

  }//END INVALID ENTRY WHILE

  //READ IN THE SCORES AND ADD THEM UP USING WHILE
  while (count < number)
  {
      ++count;
      score = io.readDouble("Enter the value for score #" + count);

      //LOOP UNTIL VALID SCORE IS ENTERED
      while ((score < 0) || (score > 100))
      {
        score = io.readDouble("Invalid entry"
                       + "\nEnter the value for score #" + count);
      }//END INVALID ENTRY WHILE

      //ADD SCORE TO TEST TOTAL
      testTotal = testTotal + score;

      //CONCATENATE SCORE TO OUTPUT STRING
      info += score + "\n";
  }//END TEST TOTAL WHILE

  //CALCULATE THE TEST AVERAGE
  average = testTotal/number;

  //CONCATENATE AVERAGE TO OUTPUT STRING
  info += "\nThe average of the scores you entered is "
      + Math.round(average);

  //DISPLAY RESULTS
  io.writeInfo(info);

   //EXIT PROGRAM
   System.exit(0);
  }//END main()
}//END Action06_02 CLASS
```

Here is a series of screen shots for a typical program execution. Notice how our `while` loop caught the invalid number of scores entry.

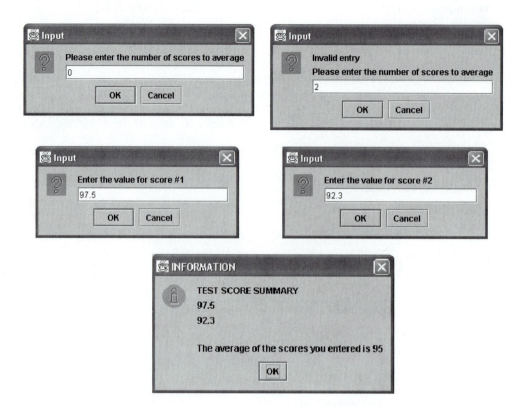

You should now have no problem understanding the foregoing code, given the algorithm discussion. However, you might be interested in the way we generated the final output screen. Our *writeInfo()* method that generates an information box needs a string argument. So, all we need to do is build a single string that contains all test scores, and then pass this string to our *writeInfo()* method. The string we will build is defined as *info* at the beginning of the program. The *info* string object is initialized to a heading for a table that will list the test scores vertically under the heading. Now, look at the loop that sums the test scores. The last statement in the loop concatenates the score value and a newline to the *info* string, like this:

```
//CONCATENATE SCORE TO OUTPUT STRING
info += score + "\n";
```

After the loop is terminated, the average of the scores is calculated and concatenated to the *info* string this way:

```
//CONCATENATE AVERAGE TO OUTPUT STRING
info += "\nThe average of the scores you entered is "
        + Math.round(average);
```

Notice how we called the *Math* class *round()* method to round the test average to the nearest whole number. Finally, the *info* string is used as the argument for the *writeInfo()* method. Remember this technique because it comes in handy when you need to display multiple values within an information box.

CHAPTER SUMMARY

In this chapter, you learned about the three iteration control structures employed by Java: `while`, `do/while`, and `for`. The `while` is a pretest looping structure, the `do/while` a posttest looping structure, and the `for` a fixed repetition looping structure. As a result, the following general guidelines should be considered when deciding which looping structure to use in a given situation:

- Use `while` whenever there is a possibility that the loop body will not need to be executed.
- Use `do/while` when the loop body must be executed at least once.
- Use `for` when it can be determined exactly how many times the loop body must be executed. Thus, if the number of loop iterations is predetermined by the value of a variable or constant, use a `for` loop.

The `break` and `continue` statements can be used to interrupt loop iterations. Execution of the `break` statement within a loop forces the entire loop structure to terminate immediately and pass control to the next statement following the loop structure. Execution of the `continue` statement within a loop terminates only the current loop iteration.

QUESTIONS AND PROBLEMS

Questions

1. Name the three iteration control structures employed by Java.
2. Which iteration control structure(s) will always execute the loop at least once?
3. Which iteration control structure(s) evaluate(s) the test expression before the loop is executed?
4. Which iteration control structure(s) should be employed when it can be determined in advance how many loop repetitions there should be?
5. What will the following loop do?

```
while(count < 10)
    System.out.println("Hello");
```

6. Explain the difference between the execution of `break` and `continue` within a loop.

In questions 7–17, determine the output generated by the respective program segment. Assume that io has been defined as an object of the StaugIO class, if needed.

```
7. int a = 1;
   while(17 % a != 5)
   {
       System.out.println(a + "  " + 17 % a );
       ++a;
   }//END WHILE
```

```
 8.  int b = 2;
     do
     {
         System.out.println(b + "   "  + b / 5);
         b *= 2;
     }//END DO/WHILE
     while(b != 20);
 9.  int b = 2;
     do
     {
         System.out.println(b + "   "  +  b / 5);
         b *= 2;
     }//END DO/WHILE
     while(b != 32);
10.  int number = 1;
     int product = 1;
     do
     {
       ++number;
       product *= number;
     }//END DO/WHILE
     while(number < 5);
     io.writeInfo("The product is:  " + product);
11.  int count = -3;
     while(count < 3)
     {
         if(count == 0)
            continue;
         System.out.println(count + "    ");
         ++count;
     }//END WHILE
12.  int count = -3;
     while(count < 3)
     {
         ++count;
         if(count == 0)
            continue;
         System.out.println(count + "    ");
     }//END WHILE
13.  int count = -3;
     while(count < 3)
     {
         ++count;
         if(count == 0)
            break;
         System.out.println(count + "    ");
     }//END WHILE
```

14.
```java
System.out.println("Angle\tSin\t\t\tCos");
for(int angle = 0; angle <= 90; angle += 5)
      System.out.println(angle
                                   + "\t" + Math.sin(angle * Math.PI/180)
                                   + "\t" + Math.cos(angle * Math.PI/180));
```

15.
```java
for(int row = 1; row < 6; ++row)
{
   for(int col = 1; col < 11; ++col)
           System.out.print(row + "," + col + "\t");
   System.out.println();
}//END FOR
```

16.
```java
int count = 0;
final int MAX_COUNT = 5;
while(count < MAX_COUNT)
{
   for (int i = 1; i < MAX_COUNT + 1; ++i)
      System.out.print(i);
   System.out.println();
   ++count;
}//END WHILE
```

17.
```java
final int MAX_COUNT = 5;
int times = 3;
do
{
   int count = 0;
   while (count < MAX_COUNT)
   {
       for (int j = 1; j < count + 1; ++j)
          System.out.print(j);
       ++count;
       System.out.println();
   }//END WHILE
   System.out.println();
   --times;
}//END DO/WHILE
while (times != 0);
```

18. When will the following loop terminate?
```java
StaugIO io = new StaugIO();    //CREATE KEYBOARD OBJECT
boolean flag = true;           //DEFINE BOOLEAN VARIABLE
int number = 0;                //INPUT VARIABLE
int sum = 0;                   //SUM VARIABLE
char query = 'n';              //QUERY VARIABLE

while(flag == true)
{
   number = io.readInt("Enter an integer number: ");
   query = io.readChar("Want to continue (y/n)? ");
   if ((query == 'n') || (query == 'N'))
```

```
    {
        flag = false;
        io.writeInfo("Loop terminated");
    }//END IF
    else
    {
        sum = sum + number;
        io.writeInfo("The sum is now " + sum);
    }//END ELSE
}//END WHILE
```

Problems

Least Difficult

1. Revise the *Action06_02.java* program to employ do/while loops.

2. Revise the *Action06_02.java* program to employ for loops.

3. Expand the *Action06_02.java* program to include an average for lab scores and a composite average which weights tests at 70% and labs at 30%.

4. Write a Java program in *main()* that will ask the user for a number, then display a box of asterisks whose dimension is the number entered. Place the routine within a loop that allows the user to repeat the task until he or she wants to quit.

5. In Chapter 5, problem 8, you wrote a program for the Java-Mart coffee shop that would calculate expected profit based on profit codes for each item in the inventory. The items in the inventory are coded with a 1, 2, or 3, depending on the amount of profit for the item. An item with a profit code of 1 produces a 10 percent profit, a code of 2 produces a 12 percent profit, and a code of 3 generates a 15 percent profit. Rewrite the program to allow the user to enter sales item information until the user decides to quit. The required sales item information includes an item description, quantity on hand, price, and profit code. For example, a typical entry dialog might appear as follows:

   Enter Item Name: **Java of the Day** ↵
   Enter Quantity on Hand: **532** ↵
   Enter Price: **1.49** ↵
   Enter Profit Code: **1** ↵
   Have another item to enter? (y/n) **y** ↵

   The program should generate a tabular report of the item, quantity, expected profit in dollars per item, and total expected profit for all items at the end of the report.

6. Using the formula $C = 5/9(F - 32)$, generate a Celsius conversion table for all even temperatures from 32 degrees to 212 degrees Fahrenheit. Write a simple program in *main()* to display a new information box for each 20 temperature values in this range.

7. The subway system in Java City, USA has three fee classifications: student (17 years old or less), adult, and senior (65 years old or more). Write a program that counts how many of each fee classification rode the subway on a given day. Assume that the subway conductor has a laptop PC that runs your program. The conductor enters the age of each customer as the subway is under way. Your user instructions tell the conductor to enter a sentinel value of −1 at the end of the day to terminate the entry process. After the sentinel value is entered,

the program must display the number of customers in each fee category. Develop a class called *Subway* to accomplish this task and write an application to test the *Subway* class.

More Difficult

8. Write a program in *main()* that will obtain any two integers between 2 and 10 from the user and display a multiplication a table. For example, if the user enters the values 4 and 5, the table would be:

1	2	3	4	5
2	4	6	8	10
3	6	9	12	15
4	8	12	16	20

9. Write a program in *main()* that will calculate the mean ($\overline{x}$) and standard deviation (σ) of a series of numbers. The arithmetic mean of a series of numbers is the same as the average of the numbers. The standard deviation of a series of numbers is found using the following formula:

$$\sigma = \sqrt{\frac{(x_1 - \overline{x})^2 + (x_2 - \overline{x})^2 + \cdots + (x_n - \overline{x})^2}{n}}$$

10. Some programming languages, like BASIC, allow you to use a STEP command within a `for` statement, like this:

FOR counter = <initial value> TO <final value> STEP N

The *STEP* command allows the loop counter to increment by some value (N), other than the value 1, with each loop iteration.

Write a `for` loop in *main()* that will emulate this STEP operation. Provide for user entry of any desired step value. To demonstrate its operation, use your step loop to display every fifth integer, from 1 to 100.

11. To make the digital timer program given in this chapter work properly, you must insert a time delay within the seconds loop so that the seconds counter is incremented precisely once every second. To do this, you can insert a `for` loop that simply decrements a large counter, like this:

```
for(long timer = 4000000; timer > 0; --timer);
```

This loop will not do anything but waste time. However, the amount of the time delay is dependent on the initial counter value and the clock speed of your system CPU. Insert such a delay loop into the timer program given in this chapter, and, by trial and error, determine a counter value that will provide a one-second delay for your system. Compile, execute, and observe the program output.

12. Develop a class called *Depreciation* that will figure depreciation using the *straight-line* method. With the straight-line method, the cost of the item is depreciated each year by $1/n$, where *n* is the number of years to depreciate. Assume that the user will enter the original cost of the item and the number of years to depreciate the item. The program should display a table showing the depreciated value at the end of each year, the amount depreciated for each year, and the total accumulated depreciation at the end of each year. Write an application to test your *Depreciation* class.

Most Difficult

13. Develop a class called *CompoundInterest* that will determine the value of a bank account balance that is compounded monthly. Assume that the user will enter the beginning balance, annual interest rate, and number of years to compound. As an example, suppose that the beginning balance was $1000 and the annual interest rate is 12%. Then, at the end of the first month, the balance would be $1010. At the end of the second month, the balance would be $1020.10, and so on. Notice that at the end of each month, the interest is added to the old balance to form a new balance that will be used in the next month's calculation. Write an application to test your *CompoundInterest* class. The class should generate an information box similar to the following:

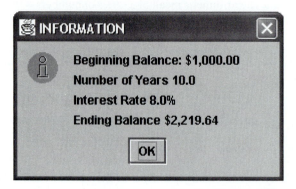

14. The Java City First National Bank has asked you to write a program for their loan department. The program is to read the loan amount from the user and, using an interest rate of 1% per month, display a table showing the monthly payment, amount of principal, amount of interest, and remaining loan balance for each month over the number of months specified by the user. Develop a *Loan* class to solve this problem and write an application to test your class.

7

Class Behavior—Methods

OBJECTIVES

When you are finished with this chapter, you should have a good understanding of the following:

- How to construct your own `void` and non-void methods in Java
- The difference between a non-void method and a `void` method
- How to call non-void versus void methods
- How to develop method headers
- The significance of a method interface

- The scope, or visibility, of a variable
- The difference between an argument and a parameter
- Overloaded methods and the concept of polymorphism
- The concept of recursion

Introduction

Methods are a major part of programming in Java. Recall from Chapter 3 that a class provides the foundation for creating specific objects, each of which shares the general attributes, or characteristics, and behavior of the class. As you already know, classes in Java contain methods that provide for the behavior of the class. In addition, the methods provide the only way of communicating with the class. The methods of the class typically operate on the data members of the class. These methods are usually "public" so they can be accessed from outside the class. The important thing to remember is that *no methods outside a given class can access the private data members of the class*.

You have already used built-in, or standard, methods in your programs. All of these methods are part of the various classes included

233

with Java. In addition, we have implemented our algorithms using methods to provide the behavior for the various classes developed in the problem solving case studies and programming problems. Now it is time to learn the details of building your own methods.

In this chapter and the next chapter, you will begin building true object-oriented programs as collections of classes employing methods to control the behavior of the program. Commercial object-oriented programs are written as a collection of classes, with each class containing its own collection of data and methods. Writing programs this way has several advantages, as follows:

- Methods eliminate the need for duplicate statements within a program. Given a task to be performed more than once, the statements are written just once for the method. Then, the method is called each time the task must be performed.

- Methods make the program easier to design, since the program activities and class behaviors (algorithms) are modularized as individual methods, whose combined execution solves the problem at hand.

- Methods make the program easier to code and test, since you can concentrate on a single method at a time, rather than one big *main()* method.

- Methods allow for *software reusability*, where existing methods can be reused by new classes.

- Methods make the program clearer and more readable, thus making the program easier to maintain.

- And most important, the use of methods provides the basis for us to construct classes in object-oriented programming.

The bottom line is that without methods, a class has no behavior, and therefore, is useless. In fact, without methods you cannot even access the `private` class data from outside the class. So this chapter is crucial to your learning about object-oriented programming in general, and programming in the Java language in particular.

This chapter will end with a discussion of a very powerful language capability known as ***recursion***. Recursion is a process whereby an operation keeps "cloning" itself until a terminating condition is reached. Although the process of performing recursion is rather complex, it is relatively simple for the programmer, because most of the work is done by the compiler. Many problems are recursive in nature, such as calculating compound interest, among others. This chapter will introduce you to recursion via a practical compound interest example.

In Java, a method can be made to serve two roles. A method can be made to return a single value to the calling program. This type of method is referred to as a ***non-void*** method. In addition, methods can also be written to perform specific tasks or operate on class data. This type of method is called a *void* method. Most of the methods that you have written so far have been `void` methods.

7.1   Non-Void Methods

You have already had some experience with methods that return a single value in Java. Recall some of the standard methods that you have already learned, such as *compareTo()*, *sqrt()*, *sin()*, and *length()*, just to mention a few. You found that Java included several predefined mathematical, string, and I/O methods that are part of standard classes in the Java language. However, suppose you want to perform some operation that is not a predefined method in Java, such as calculating the gross pay for an hourly employee. Because Java does not include any standard method for such an operation, you could code the operation as a statement in your program, like this:

```
if(hours <= 40)
   grossPay = rate * hours;
else
   grossPay = rate * 40 + (hours - 40) * (1.5 * rate);
```

Here, we have used an `if/else` statement to take into account overtime at "time and a half" when the number of hours exceed 40. Of course, the code assumes that *rate*, *hours*, and *grossPay* have been previously defined, most likely as floating-point variables. Now, you could insert this `if/else` statement into your program each time the gross pay of an hourly employee needed to be calculated. However, wouldn't it be a lot easier simply to insert the command *returnGrossPay(rate,hours)* each time the gross pay is to be calculated, where Java knows what to do just as it knows how to execute *sqrt(x)* to calculate the square root of *x*? You can do this by defining your own *returnGrossPay()* method. Thus, if *returnGrossPay()* is a method that will return the gross weekly pay of an hourly employee, given the employee's hourly rate (*rate*) and number of hours worked (*hours*), the statement

```
grossPay = myPay.returnGrossPay(rate,hours);
```

will call the method and cause the gross pay of the *myPay* object to be calculated and assigned to the variable *grossPay*. Now you need to learn how to create such methods. Here is the format that you must use when defining your own methods.

METHOD FORMAT

```
//METHOD HEADER
modifier return type method name(parameter list)
{//BEGIN METHOD BODY
   method statement;
   method statement;
         •
         •                       //METHOD BODY
         •
   method statement;
   return a single value;
}//END METHOD BODY
```

The method definition format consists of two main parts: a ***method header*** and a ***method body***. Here is the *returnGrossPay()* method code that we are about to develop. Take a look at the code to identify its header and body. The sections that follow will analyze this code.

```
/***************************************************************
THIS METHOD RETURNS THE WEEKLY GROSS PAY OF AN EMPLOYEE
GIVEN HIS/HER HOURLY RATE OF PAY AND NUMBER OF HOURS WORKED
***************************************************************/
public double returnGrossPay(double rate, double hours)
{
  if(hours <= 40)
    return rate * hours;
  else
    return rate * 40 + (hours - 40) * (1.5 * rate);
}//END returnGrossPay()
```

The Method Header

The *method header* provides a data *interface* for the class in which the method resides. What is an interface? Well, the door in your classroom is an interface between the hallway and the classroom. It allows you to enter the room and leave the room. You cannot enter or leave the room through the classroom wall. Likewise, a method header provides an interface for the class in which it resides. You cannot get data in or out of the class without going through a method interface. It controls what will be accepted from outside the class when the method is called, and what will be returned by the method to its calling program.

 A **method header**, or **interface**, is a statement that forms a common boundary between the class in which the method resides and its calling program.

This idea is illustrated by Figure 7-1. Notice that the header dictates what data the method will *accept* from the calling program and what data the method will *return* to the calling program, if any. When developing method headers, your perspective

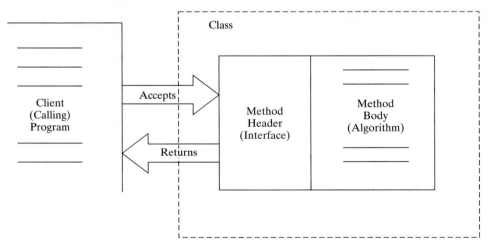

FIGURE 7-1   The method header forms the interface between the calling program and the class in which the method resides.

needs to be relative to the calling program and the class in which the method resides. You must ask yourself two things:

- What data must the method *accept* from *outside its class* in order to perform its designated task?
- What data, if any, must the method *return outside its class* in order to fulfill its designated task?

One thing to always consider is what the method accepts and returns. However, the point of reference is always between the calling program and the class in which the method resides.

In general, the method header consists of the following four parts:

- A modifier that declares the scope of the method
- The data type of the value to be returned by the method, if any
- The name of the method
- A parameter listing

The Modifier   The first thing that appears in the method header is the modifier. The modifier determines the *scope* of the method. The scope of a method defines to what extent the method can be used within the program. This is sometimes referred to as *visibility*, since the scope of a method determines the portion of a program in which the method is visible.

The **scope**, or **visibility**, of a method defines to what extent the method can be used within the program.

The methods that we will create will be part of a class which will have objects defined for it. Because an object is an instance of a class, such methods are called *instance methods*. An object is always required to call an instance method. Thus, to call an instance method, an object (instance) must be created; then this object must be used to call the method. An example is the *length()* method of the *String* class. To call this method you must create a string object, say *s*, and then call the method like this: `s.length()`.

Instance methods are part of a class and must be called by an object of either the class in which they are defined, or a subclass of the class in which they are defined in the case of inheritance (Chapter 9).

An instance method can be `public`, `private`, or `protected`. These are called *modifiers* that control the scope of the method. A `public` method can be called anywhere outside of its class using an object of that class, while a `private` method can only be called within its class by another method of that class. A `protected` method is visible to its class as well as any subclasses of its class when using inheritance. More about this in Chapter 9.

TABLE 7-1   Method Modifiers

Modifier	Description
`private`	Visible only in its class
`protected`	Visible to its class as well as any subclasses of its class (inheritance)
`public`	Visible anywhere outside of its class within the scope of the class

A summary of these method modifiers is provided in Table 7-1.

In this chapter, the only modifier that we will be using is `public`. We will use the `private` and `protected` modifiers in later chapters.

The Return Type   The return type can be `void` or non-void. A `void` return type indicates that that method does not return anything. This type of method is called a *void method* and is discussed in the next section.

A *void **method*** has a return type of `void`, which means it does not return anything to its calling program. A ***non-void*** method has a return type such as `double`, `int`, `char`, etc., which indicates the type of data returned by the method. Non-void methods always return a *single value* to the calling program.

If a method is non-void, the return type indicates the type of data the method will return. A non-void method, such as our *returnGrossPay()* method, *will always return a single value*. Thus, the return type will be any of the simple data types discussed earlier, such as `int`, `double`, `char`, and so on. Because gross pay must be in dollars and cents, our *returnGrossPay()* method must return a floating-point value. As a result, the return type must be `float` or `double` and specified in the method header, like this:

```
public double returnGrossPay(parameter listing)
```

The Method Name   The method name should be a verb or a verb phrase in mixed lower and uppercase. Like a variable name, the first letter of the name should be lowercase and the first letter of any subsequent word, uppercase. The method name should be descriptive of the operation that the method performs, just as *returnGrossPay* describes what it does. You will use this name when you call, or invoke, the method within your calling program. However, you need to remember one thing:

- The method name can never be used on the left side of the assignment symbol anywhere in the program, whether it be inside of the method or outside of the method. Therefore, the following statement will cause an error anyplace it is encountered in the program:

```
returnGrossPay = hours * rate;
```

The Parameter Listing   The method parameter listing includes variables called ***parameters***, which will be received from the calling program and evaluated by the method. Think of a parameter as a method variable waiting to receive a value from the calling program when the method is called. To determine the method parameters, ask yourself: What data must the method *accept from outside the class* to perform its designated task? Now, our *returnGrossPay()* method needs the employee's rate of pay and number of hours worked in order to do its job. If these values are not available within its class, it must accept them from the calling program. If this is the case, our method requires two floating-point variables, one for the rate of pay and one for the number of hours worked. Likewise, we will assume that our method is returning the calculated gross pay to its calling program. With this in mind, our *method interface* can be described as follows:

returnGrossPay():   Returns the weekly gross pay of an hourly employee
Accepts: Two floating-point values, one for the rate of pay and one for the hours worked
Returns: A floating-point value for the calculated weekly gross pay

Let's designate *rate* and *hours* as the floating-point values that the method must accept. In Java, something that the method accepts, called a ***parameter***, must be specified in the method header by indicating its data type followed by its identifier. As a result, the appropriate parameter listing for the *returnGrossPay()* method would be *(double rate, double hours)*. Putting everything together, the complete header would be

 A ***parameter*** is a variable in the method header used to accept a data item during a method call.

The Method Body

The body of the method includes those statements that the method must execute to perform its designated task. In other words, the method body is the coded algorithm for the method. The entire method body must be framed with braces. After the opening brace, you should begin by defining any variables and objects that will be used only within the method. Any variables listed here are called ***local*** because they are defined only for local use within the method itself. Local variables have no meaning outside of the method in which they are defined. *Do not duplicate any of your method parameters here.* You list only additional variables that the method might require during its execution that are in addition to the method parameter variables. A common example of a local variable is a loop counter that is employed as part of a `while`, `do/while`, or `for` loop within the method.

A ***local variable*** is a variable that is defined within a given block of code, such as a `for` loop or a method. In general, variables should be defined as locally as possible.

 THINK!

Do not confuse local variables with method parameters. A local variable is defined after the opening brace of a method for use within that method to temporarily store values during the method execution. A method parameter is defined in the method header as a place holder for argument values passed to the method when the method is called. It is used within the method to supply data from the calling program to the method.

The executable statements of the method follow any local definitions. A non-void method must always return a value to the calling program using a `return` statement. Thus, all possible logical paths within a non-void method must lead to a `return` statement. This is why there is a `return` statement in both the `if` and the `else` clauses of the *returnGrossPay()* method code, like this:

```
if(hours <= 40)
    return rate * hours;
else
    return rate * 40 + (hours - 40) * (1.5 * rate);
```

 DEBUGGING TIP

A non-void method *must always* return a value, or a compiler error will result. So, regardless of the path of execution a non-void method takes, it must lead to a `return` statement.

Combining the method header with the method body gives us the complete *returnGrossPay()* method, as follows:

```
/*****************************************************************
THIS METHOD RETURNS THE WEEKLY GROSS PAY OF AN EMPLOYEE
GIVEN HIS/HER HOURLY RATE OF PAY AND NUMBER OF HOURS WORKED
*****************************************************************/
public double returnGrossPay(double rate, double hours)
{
   if(hours <= 40)
      return rate * hours;
   else
      return rate * 40 + (hours - 40) * (1.5 * rate);
}//END returnGrossPay()
```

Our *returnGrossPay()* method is a relatively simple method that doesn't require any local variables or additional logic.

DEBUGGING TIP

A possible source of error in coding a non-void method is to make an assignment to the method name within the method, as follows:

```
/****************************************************************
THIS METHOD RETURNS THE WEEKLY GROSS PAY OF AN EMPLOYEE
GIVEN HIS/HER HOURLY RATE OF PAY AND NUMBER OF HOURS WORKED
****************************************************************/
public double returnGrossPay(double rate, double hours)
{
  if(hours <= 40)
    return returnGrossPay = rate * hours;
  else
    return returnGrossPay = rate * 40 + (hours - 40) * (1.5 * rate);
}//END returnGrossPay()
```

This will always cause a compiler error because you are attempting to return the method name. You must return a value, which, in this case, is a calculation involving *hours* and *rate*.

Example 7-1

Write a method to return the sum of all integers from 1 to some maximum integer value, called *max*. The method must obtain the value of *max* from the calling program.

Solution

Let's call this method *returnSum()*. Now, the method must *accept* an integer value, called *max*, from the calling program. Because the method is to sum all the integers from 1 to *max*, it must return an integer value. Thus, our method interface can be described as follows:

Method *returnSum()*:	Returns the sum of all integers from 1 to *max*
Accepts:	An integer value, *max*
Returns:	An integer value

Using this information, the method header becomes

```
public int returnSum(int max)
```

The next step is to determine what control structures are needed within the method. You can use a loop to calculate the sum of integers from 1 to *max* because it is a simple repetitive process to sum consecutive values. We will use the for loop. Why a for loop? Because the method knows exactly how many values it needs to sum via the parameter, *max*. In addition, the for statement requires a local counter variable. We will call this variable *count*. Next, we also need a temporary variable within the for loop to keep a running subtotal of the sum each time the loop executes. Let's call this local variable *subTotal*. Using these ideas, the complete method becomes

```
/******************************************************
THIS METHOD RETURNS THE SUM OF ALL INTEGERS
FROM 1 TO MAX
******************************************************/
```

```
public int returnSum(int max)
{
   int subTotal = 0;        //LOCAL SUBTOTAL VARIABLE
   for(int count = 1; count <= max; ++count)
      subTotal = subTotal + count;
   return subTotal;
}//END returnSum()
```

Notice that *subTotal* is defined as a local variable for the method, *count* is defined locally inside the `for` loop, while *max* is a parameter variable.

Calling a Non-void Method—Sending Messages

A method is given a name and ***called***, or ***invoked***, using its name each time the task is to be performed within the program. We will refer to the code in which a method call is made as the ***calling program***. The term ***message*** is used to describe a call to an instance method with the idea that when we are calling a method, we are sending a message to the class object in which it is defined. In other words, the calling program is communicating with the object via the method call.

A ***message*** is a call to an instance method.

The object responds to the calling program by performing some operation (behavior) and possibly sending back a return value. This concept is illustrated in Figure 7-2. We say that objects communicate with each other using messages. As you have seen earlier, to generate a message, or method call, you must use the dot operator. The required syntax is

object name . method name(argument listing)

You call, or invoke, a non-void method by using an assignment operator or an output statement, like this:

```
double grossPay = 0.0;
grossPay = myPay.returnGrossPay(8.75, 20);
```

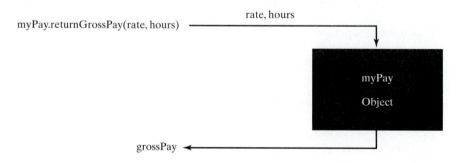

FIGURE 7-2 Messages are the means of communicating with an object.

or

```
System.out.println(myPay.returnGrossPay(8.75,20));
```

or

```
StaugIO io = new StaugIO();
io.writeNumber(myPay.returnGrossPay(8.75,20));
```

Here we have assumed that an object called *myPay* has been defined for the class that contains our *returnGrossPay()* method. In each call, the value 8.75 is *passed* as an argument to the method for the hourly rate and the value 20 is *passed* as an argument to the method for the hours worked. Thus, in our *returnGrossPay()* method, the parameter *rate* takes on the value 8.75 and the parameter *hours* takes on the value 20. The method will return the gross pay value of 175.0. How did we get a return value of 175.0? Well, if an employee's hourly rate of pay is $8.75 and he/she worked 20 hours, the gross pay would simply be the product of the two, or $175.00, right? With the assignment statement, the variable *grossPay* will be assigned the value 175.0. The *println()* statement causes the value 175.0 to be displayed in a console window. The *writeNumber()* statement causes the value 175.0 to be displayed in an information box. The foregoing assignment call is illustrated in Figure 7-3.

Here are three other ways that our *returnGrossPay()* method could be called:

```
double r = 10.00;
double h = 52.5;
double grossPay = 0.0;
StaugIO io = new StaugIO();

grossPay = myPay.returnGrossPay(r,h);

System.out.println(myPay.returnGrossPay(r,h));

io.writeNumber(myPay.returnGrossPay(r,h));
```

In these cases, we are using arguments of *r* for the rate of pay and *h* for the hours worked. Thus, the value of *r*, or 10.00, is passed to the method. In our *returnGrossPay()* method, the parameter *rate* takes on the value of *r*. Likewise, the value of *h*, or 52.5, is passed to the method. In our *returnGrossPay()* method, the parameter *hours* takes on

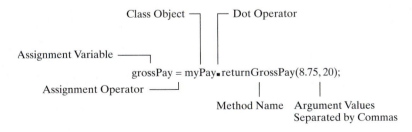

FIGURE 7-3 The anatomy of an instance method call.

the value of *h*. Notice that the arguments have different names than the parameters. There is no requirement that they be the same nor that they be different.

A non-void method always returns a single value. You can think of this return value as replacing the method call wherever the call appears in a calling program. For example, the statement

```
grossPay = myPay.returnGrossPay(8.75,20);
```

is actually seen as the statement

```
grossPay = 175.0;
```

Likewise, the statements

```
double r = 10.00;
double h = 52.5;
System.out.println(myPay.returnGrossPay(r,h));
```

are actually seen as the statement

```
System.out.println(587.5);
```

which would display the value 587.5 within a console window. The value that replaces the method call in the calling program is referred to as the ***return value***.

Arguments versus Parameters

Some terminology is appropriate at this time. In the foregoing *returnGrossPay()* code, the variables *r* and *h* used in the method call are referred to as ***arguments***. On the other hand, the corresponding variables *rate* and *hours* used in the method header are called ***parameters***.

Arguments are values/variables used within the method call, and ***parameters*** are variables used within the method header that receive the argument values. There is no requirement that an argument variable have the same name as its corresponding parameter, nor that they be different. The parameter variable simply takes on the value of the argument when the method is called. We say that a copy of the argument value is *passed* to the parameter when the method is called.

Here are some things that you will want to remember about arguments and parameters:

- Variables used as arguments must be defined in the calling program.
- The data type of the corresponding arguments and parameters should be the same.
- Parameters are place holders for the arguments passed to the method.
- The number of arguments used during the method call must be the same as the number of parameters listed in the method header.

- The correspondence between arguments and parameters is established on a one-to-one basis according to the respective listing orders.
- Although the argument and parameter variables often have different variable names, they can be the same. When this is the case, the respective variables must still be defined in the calling program and must also appear in the parameter listing of the method.

DEBUGGING TIP

A very common error made by beginning programmers when using arguments during a method call is to list the argument data type in front of the argument identifier during the call, like this:

```
double r = 10.00;
double h = 52.5;
double grossPay = 0.0;
grossPay = myPay.returnGrossPay(double r, double h);
```

This will always generate a compiler error. You only list the data type in the method parameter list, not the method call. The correct call is simply

```
grossPay = myPay.returnGrossPay(r,h);
```

DEBUGGING TIP

Always remember to check that the number and data types of the arguments in a method call match the number and data types of the method's parameter list on a one-to-one basis, according to their respective listing orders. Each argument in the method call *must* correspond to one and only one parameter in the list, and the respective ordering *must* be the same. You will always get a compiler error if the number of arguments does not match the number of parameters. However, you may not get a compiler error if their data types do not match or the respective ordering is different. The result here will be garbage, and its source might be very difficult to locate.

The names of the arguments do not have to match the names of the parameters and often do not match. For instance, suppose we have a method header as follows:

```
public double foo(int a, int b, int c)
```

Then, a method call of

```
System.out.println(myObject.foo(x,y,z));
```

is perfectly legal. Here, *a* takes on the value of *x*, *b* takes on the value of *y*, and *c* takes on the value of *z* within the body of the method. Of course, the variables *x*, *y*, and *z* must be defined as `int` prior to the method call.

Non-void methods can also be called as part of arithmetic expressions or relational statements. For instance, our *returnGrossPay()* method can be called as part of an arithmetic expression, like this:

```
double r = 8.75;
double h = 20.0;
double grossPay = 0.0;
double bonus = 100.00
grossPay = myPay.returnGrossPay(r,h) + bonus;
```

What will be assigned to *grossPay*? Well, Java evaluates the *returnGrossPay()* method first to get 175.0, then adds the *bonus* amount of 100.0 to get 275.0. You also can use non-void methods as part of relational operations, like this:

```
if(returnGrossPay(r,h) > 1000)
    grossPay = myPay.returnGrossPay(r,h) + bonus;
else
    grossPay = myPay.returnGrossPay(r,h);
```

When will the relationship be `true`? When *returnGrossPay(r,h)* is greater than 1000. Here, if the calculated gross pay is greater than 1000, a bonus is added, or else no bonus is added. Just remember that when a non-void method is called, the *return value replaces the method call wherever the call appears in the calling program.*

THINK!

You will normally call non-void methods within your program using an assignment statement, as part of an output statement, as part of an arithmetic expression, or as part of a test expression. Remember to think of the non-void method call as a *value*. That is, a value replaces the method call where it appears in the program. Ask yourself: "Does a *value* make sense here?" For example, the following statements all make sense because a value can easily be substituted for the method call. The call

```
grossPay = myPay.returnGrossPay(8.75,20) + 100;
```

is seen as

```
grossPay = 175.0 + 100;
```

The call

```
System.out.println(myPay.returnGrossPay(8.75,20));
```

is seen as

```
System.out.println(175.0);
```

On the other hand, the following statement makes absolutely no sense and would cause a compile error, because the compiler sees just a single value coded as an executable statement. The call

```
myPay.returnGrossPay(8.75,20);
```

is seen as

```
175;
```

QUICK CHECK

1. List four advantages of using methods in a Java program.
2. The two different kinds of methods provided by Java are _____ and _____ methods.
3. The two parts of a method are the method _____ and the method _____.
4. All logical paths in a non-void method must lead to a(n) _____ statement.
5. What two things must be considered when developing a method header?
6. What is the purpose of the method header in a Java program?
7. List the four parts of a method header.
8. A method variable, waiting to receive a value from the calling program, is called a(n) _____.
9. What is the purpose of a `return` statement in a method?
10. Explain the difference between an argument in a calling program and a parameter in a method header.
11. Write a header for a non-void method called *loanPayment()* that will return a monthly loan payment, given the loan amount, interest rate, and term.
12. Write a header for a method called *wheels()* that will return the number of wheels from a class called *Truck*. Assume that the number of wheels is a private member of the class.
13. Why is the term *message* associated with a call to a method of an object?

7.2   Void Methods

Methods that do not return a value to the calling program are often written to perform some procedural task or operate directly on class data. These are called *void methods*.

A *void method* does not return a value to the calling program.

A void method does not return anything to the calling program. To indicate this, Java requires that the return type be void, like this:

```
modifier void voidMethod(parameter listing)
```

PROGRAMMING NOTE

You should be aware that any method, upon completion, always returns control back to the calling program. Non-void methods return a value along with control, while void methods only return control to the calling program when they are finished executing. No `return` statement is required for a void method.

When a method is not returning a value to the calling program, you must use the keyword void as the return type. In addition, these methods may or may not require parameters. When no parameters are required, you simply leave the parameter listing blank to indicate to the compiler that the method does not need to receive any values from the calling program. Methods that do not return a value and do not require any parameters are the simplest type of methods in Java. For example, suppose that you need a method that will display the following heading in a console window each time it is called:

NAME   STREET   ADDRESS   STATE   CITY   ZIP
_____   _____   _____   _____   ____   ___

Let's call this method *displayHeading()*. To develop the method header, ask yourself what the method must *accept* to perform its designated task and what it must *return*. In this case, the method is simply displaying constant header information and does not need to accept any data or return any data to the calling program because it is simply displaying information to the console window. Thus, our method interface can be described as follows:

Method *displayHeading()*:   Displays fixed heading information
Accepts: Nothing
Returns: Nothing

Using this information, the method header becomes

```java
public void displayHeading()
```

Look at the method header and you will see the keyword void used as the method return type. The keyword void used here indicates to the compiler that there is no return value. Furthermore, notice that there are no parameters required by this method because the parameter listing is left blank. In other words, the method does not return a value and does not require any arguments to evaluate. It simply performs a given task, in this case displaying a heading. To display the heading in a console window, all you need are a couple of *println()* statements in the body of the method. Putting everything together, the method becomes

```java
public void displayHeading()
{
 System.out.println("\tNAME\tSTREET ADDRESS\tCITY\tSTATE\tZIP");
 System.out.println("\t____\t_____\t____\t____\t____\t___");
}//END displayHeading()
```

Finally, you do not see a return statement at the end of the method, because no single value is being returned by the method.

How would you call this method in your program? Simple; just use the method name as a statement within the calling program each time the heading must be displayed. Again, the method must be called by an object of the class in which the method resides. So, let's assume that we define an object called *myObject* for the class in which *displayHeading()* resides. Then, the method is called like this:

```java
myObject.displayHeading();
```

No arguments are listed in the method call, because no arguments need to be evaluated by the method.

THINK!

When calling a `void` method, simply list the method name and required arguments as a single statement within your program. You *cannot* call a `void` method with an assignment operator, output statement, arithmetic statement, or test expression as you do a non-void method. The following calls on *displayHeading()* would, at best, cause a compiler error:

```
heading = myObject.displayHeading();            //ERROR
System.out.println(myObject.displayHeading());  //ERROR
```

The correct call is simply

```
myObject.displayHeading();
```

Example 7-2

Write a method called *displayAddr()* that could be used to display a name, address, and telephone number obtained from the calling program within a console window. Write a statement to call the *displayAddr()* method, assuming an object called *myObject* has been defined for the class in which *displayAddr()* resides.

Solution

The first chore in writing a method is to write the method header. To do this, you must decide what the method accepts and returns. Here is a description of the required interface:

Method *displayAddr()*:   Displays a name, address, and telephone number accepted from the calling program

Accepts: Three strings representing a name, address, and telephone number

Returns: Nothing

To pass a string to a method, you simply define a string object in the method parameter listing. Our method requires that three strings be passed to it. Thus, the method header becomes

```
public void displayAddr(String nam, String addr, String ph)
```

Notice that the method return type is `void`. Why? Once the method header is determined, the method body is developed. This method only requires *println()* statements. The complete method then becomes

```
/************************************************************
DISPLAY MY NAME ADDRESS AND PHONE NUMBER
*************************************************************/
public void displayAddr(String nam, String addr, String ph)
{
    System.out.println(nam);
    System.out.println(addr);
    System.out.println(ph);
}//END displayAddr()
```

How do you suppose this method will be called? Well suppose we define three string objects in the calling program, like this:

```
String name = "Andrew C. Staugaard, Jr.";
String address = "Java City, USA";
String phone = "(123) 456-7890";
```

Then, to call the method you simply use the string identifiers as arguments, and call the method with the *myObject* object as follows:

```
myObject.displayAddr(name, address, phone);
```

Notice that the string object identifiers in the method call are different from those used in the parameter listing. Is there a problem here? No! In fact, the argument identifiers used in a method call are often different from the identifiers employed in the method parameter listing. This allows the method parameters to be more general, as you will see shortly. The only requirement is that the number and types of the arguments be the same and that they be listed in the same respective order.

PROGRAMMING NOTE

Is it possible to place a `return` statement within a `void` method to return control to the calling program? Yes! For instance, consider the following method:

```
public void processIfEven(int value)
{
  //IS value ODD?
  if(value % 2 == 1)
      return;            //YES, RETURN CONTROL TO CALLING PROGRAM
  else                   //NO, VALUE IS EVEN, PROCESS VALUE
  {
      //PROCESS value
        •
        •
        •
  }//END else
}//END processIfEven()
```

This method will only process the value that it receives if *value* is even. If *value* is odd, control is *returned* to the calling program via the `return` statement without processing the value.

QUICK CHECK

1. What must be used as the return type when a method does not return a value to the calling program?
2. What two things must be considered when developing a method header?
3. How must you call a `void` method?
4. True or false: A `void` method can be called with an assignment operator.

5. When might you want to use a `return` statement within a `void` method?
6. Write a header for a method called *displayEmployee()* that would display an employee's name, social security number, number of years employed, and annual salary, all obtained from the class in which the method resides.

7.3   Locating Methods Within Your Classes

From the case studies and programming problems in earlier chapters, you have a good idea of how methods are used within a class so most of this section should be review. Recall that when writing Java applications where your methods are instance methods and called by *main()*, you will locate your methods within the class in which they reside, just before *main()* as shown in Figure 7-4. Here, we have only shown one class containing one method. However, there is no limit on the number of classes within a given program or the number of methods that can be used in a given class. First, notice that the program contains two classes. The class at the bottom is the *application class* that contains *main()*. It must be designated as a `public` class as you have seen in the past. The class above the application class is a programmer defined class, called *MyClass*, which is usually not designated as a `public` class, unless it is part of a package (packages are discussed in the next chapter). There can only be one `public` class in a given Java source file. *MyClass* contains a programmer defined method, called *myMethod()*. You must place the entire method (header and body) inside the class.

```
class Myclass
{
      public return type myMethod(parameters)
      {
          _____
          _____
          _____

      }//END myMethod( )
} //END Myclass

public class MyApplicationClass
{
   public static void main (String [] args)
   {
    MyClass myObject = new Myclass();

    myObject.myMethod(arguments);
   }//END main()
}//END MyApplicationClass
```

FIGURE 7-4   The structure of a Java application with a programmer-defined class and residing method.

Now, look at *main()* and you will find an object, called *myObject*, defined for *MyClass*. Note the syntax. This is the same syntax that you have been using in past chapters to define objects for the imported *StaugIO* class. The difference here is that *MyClass* is contained in the application, while the *StaugIO* class was imported in past programs. However, the object definition syntax is the same, whether the class is a resident class of the program or has been imported into the program. One final note: when saving this program, you must name the file the same name as the application class name, with a *.java* extension. So, the program file for Figure 7-4 must be named *MyApplication-Class.java*. That's it for now. You have enough information to begin writing some simple object-oriented programs that employ instance methods. In the next chapter, you will study classes and objects in more detail.

QUICK CHECK

1. Where is an instance method normally located in an application when the method is called within *main()*?
2. Where must variables be defined when used as arguments for methods being called within *main()*?
3. Where must variables be defined when used locally by a method?
4. At a minimum, how many classes must be provided in an application that calls instance methods?
5. What name must you give a Java source file?

7.4   Method Overloading

The idea of method overloading is important to programming in Java. When a method is overloaded, it is designed to perform differently than when it is supplied with a different number of arguments or argument data types. In other words, the same method exhibits different *behavior* with a different number of arguments or argument data types. Thus, a given method might *behave* one way when supplied one argument, and an entirely different way when supplied two arguments. For example, consider the following program:

```java
import staugIO.StaugIO;  //FOR GUI I/O

class Overload
{
   //THIS METHOD FINDS THE AREA OF A SQUARE
   public int returnArea(int s)
   {
      return s * s;
   }//END returnArea(int)

   //THIS METHOD FINDS THE AREA OF A RECTANGLE
   public int returnArea(int l, int w)
   {
      return l * w;
   }//END returnArea(int,int)
```

```
    //THIS METHOD FINDS THE AREA OF A CIRCLE
    public double returnArea(double r)
    {
        return 3.14159 * r * r;
    }//END returnArea(double)
}//END CLASS Overload

public class OverloadTest
{
  public static void main(String[] args)
  {
    //DEFINE I/O OBJECT
    StaugIO io = new StaugIO();

    //DEFINE CLASS OBJECT
    Overload over = new Overload();

    //DEFINE METHOD ARGUMENT VARIABLES
    int side = 3;
    int length = 4;
    int width = 5;
    double radius = 6.25;

    //CALL METHODS
    io.writeInfo("Area of the square is "
                + over.returnArea(side)
                + "\nArea of the rectangle is "
                + over.returnArea(length,width)
                + "\nArea of the circle is "
                + over.returnArea(radius));

    //EXIT PROGRAM
    System.exit(0);
  }//END main()
}//END CLASS OverloadTest
```

Look at the method headers. The first thing you see are three different headers for the same method, *returnArea()*. In the first header, *returnArea()* requires a single integer argument and returns an integer value. In the second header, *returnArea()* requires two integer arguments and returns an integer value. In the third header, *returnArea()* requires a single floating-point argument and returns a floating-point value. Thus, the single method *returnArea()* is defined three different times to do three different things. The way *returnArea()* will *behave* is determined by the number and types of the arguments supplied when it is called. If a single integer argument is provided when *returnArea()* is called, it will return the area of a square. If two integer arguments are supplied in the call, *returnArea()* will return the area of a rectangle, which is not square. However, if a single floating-point argument is supplied in the call, *returnArea()* will return the area of a circle. Here is the result of the program execution:

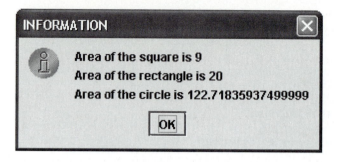

You could say that *returnArea()* is *overloaded* with work, because it is performing three different tasks, depending on the number and data types of the arguments used in its call. Overloading is used where the tasks are very similar, differing only in the number of arguments required by the method or the data types of the arguments. Without overloading, you would have to invent different names for each similar task instead of just one, thus requiring you and your program users to remember all of them.

Overloaded methods cannot be distinguished by their return type. Two methods with the same name that have the same parameter list but different return types are not overloaded and will cause a compiler error. For example, suppose that we change the parameter for the area of a square method to be a floating-point value, the same as the area of a circle method, like this:

```
public int returnArea(double s);
public double returnArea(double r);
```

Here, both *returnArea()* methods have a floating-point parameter but have different return types. The corresponding method calls might be

```
io.writeInfo("The area is:  " + over.returnArea(x)
          + "\nThe area is: " + over.returnArea(x));
```

The argument *x* must be defined as a floating-point variable. Could *you* decide from the method calls which *returnArea()* method to execute, the area of a square or the area of a circle? Of course not, since both methods operate on a floating-point value. Well, if you can't decide which method to execute, neither can the compiler. As a result, the compiler will generate an error message. Thus, overloaded methods must have different parameter listings.

Method overloading is related to the concept of **polymorphism**, which is one of the cornerstones of object-oriented programming (OOP), as you will find out in Chapter 9. Polymorphism is used extensively in commercial programs. A common example is the print method used in a word processor. The print button on the tool bar of a typical word processor invokes a polymorphic print method to perform the printing task. Do you have a separate print button for a memo document, one for a fax document, one for a text document, and so on? Of course not! A single print button is provided for printing any type of document. You expect the single print button to print the document, regardless of the document format. Thus, we say that the printing operation is polymorphic. We are introducing polymorphism here so that you are aware of the concept. You will see how it is applied when you learn more about OOP in the next two chapters.

QUICK CHECK

1. When overloading a method, what determines how the method will behave?
2. Why is method overloading important in commercial programs?
3. True or false: Method overloading can be distinguished by the method return type as well as parameter listings.
4. Method overloading relates to an important concept in object-oriented programming called _____.

Problem Solving in Action: Programming with Methods

Problem

In previous chapters, we developed a loop-controlled, menu-driven loan program for a consumer loan application. We employed methods in the solution without much discussion of the details. The diagrams shown in Figure 7-5 and Figure 7-6 represent our last solution to the problem.

Here you see that we employed three methods: *displayMenu()*, *setData()*, and *loanCalculator()*. All were void methods and did not require any parameters. As you know, these are the simplest types of methods. However, you might be wondering why no return values or parameters are required for these methods. Well, in the case of *displayMenu()*, the method is simply displaying a fixed menu and reading a menu choice from the user. So, you say that it must return the menu choice, right? No, since the menu choice, *choice*, is a class member. Remember, a method only needs to accept and return data from *outside* the class. Data

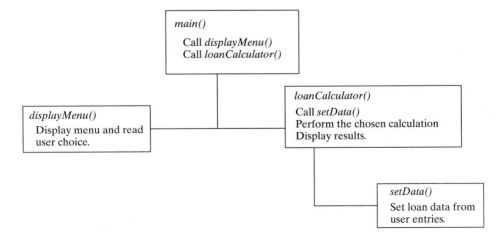

FIGURE 7-5 A problem-solving diagram for the loan problem.

```
┌───────────────────────────────────────┐
│              ConsumerLoan              │
├───────────────────────────────────────┤
│  principal                            │
│  term                                 │
│  rate                                 │
│  payment                              │
│  interest                             │
│  total                                │
│  choice                               │
├───────────────────────────────────────┤
│  displayMenu()                        │
│  setData()                            │
│  loanCalculation()                    │
└───────────────────────────────────────┘
```

FIGURE 7-6   A class diagram for the
ConsumerLoan class shows the data and method
members that make up the class.

within the class are not passed to/from methods of the class. OK, what about the *setData()* method? Doesn't it accept data from the user to set the loan principal, interest rate, and term? Yes, this is true, but the point of reference is always between the method and its calling program, not the method and the user. If the loan principal, interest rate, and term were being received from the calling program, then the method would require three parameters to accept the data. However, these data are being accepted directly from the user within the method. Therefore, no parameters are required. What about return values? None are required here either because all three variables are members of the class in which this method resides. Finally, the *loanCalculator()* method does not require any parameters either. But, you say that it needs the values of *principal*, *rate*, and *term* to perform its calculations, and you are right. But these values are class members and, therefore, are not passed to the method. In addition, the method does not need to return the *payment*, *interest*, or *total* loan values because these are also members of the same class.

So, how can we make our program better? Well, one way is to refine the program more. Good programmers will refine as much as possible. For example, the *setData()* method can be refined into three methods: *setPrincipal()*, *setTerm()*, and *setRate()* for each of the three loan variables. Each method will simply prompt and read its respective variable. Do these methods require any parameters or return values? No, because they will be getting their values directly from the user, not the calling program, and the variables they are setting are already part of the class.

 THINK!

When deciding what a method must accept or return in an object-oriented program, you only consider those data items that need to be accepted or returned outside its class, relative to the *calling program*, not the program user.

Another way we might improve our program is to give the user the option of seeing a loan summary at the end of the program. This requires that we display all the loan values in summary format. The most likely place to do this is in *main()*, after we have let the user run the menu portion of the program. All the values that must be displayed for a loan summary are private members of the class. To get access to a private class member, we must use a public method. Such a method is often referred to as a *get*, or *accessor* method, for obvious reasons. A get method simply returns the value of a private class member. Notice we said "returns." Therefore, a get method is usually a non-void method that returns a single private member value to its calling program. In our case, the calling program is *main()*. So let's add six get methods to our class, one to return each of the loan values. Now, our class diagram must be expanded, as shown in Figure 7-7.

```
┌─────────────────────────────────────┐
│            ConsumerLoan             │
├─────────────────────────────────────┤
│  principal                          │
│  term                               │
│  rate                               │
│  payment                            │
│  interest                           │
│  total                              │
│  choice                             │
├─────────────────────────────────────┤
│  displayMenu()                      │
│  setPrincipal()                     │
│  setTerm()                          │
│  setRate()                          │
│  loanCalculator                     │
│  getPrincipal()                     │
│  getTerm()                          │
│  getRate()                          │
│  getPayment()                       │
│  getInterest()                      │
│  getTotal()                         │
└─────────────────────────────────────┘
```

FIGURE 7-7 An expanded class diagram for the *ConsumerLoan* class shows additional refinement using set and get methods.

Observe that we have replaced our one *setData()* method with three set methods and added six get methods. It looks like our class is becoming a bit crowded. Not really. Many actual commercial business classes have hundreds of methods. Again, the idea is to refine things as much as possible. This makes the class easier to revise and maintain.

 A **get**, or **accessor** method is a method that returns the values of one or more private class members.

Here is the modified code:

```java
/*
 * Action07_01.java
 *
 * Created on June 21, 2002, 1:07 PM
 */

/**
 *
 * @author  Andrew C. Staugaard, Jr.
 * @version 1.0
 */

import staugIO.StaugIO;           //FOR INPUT AND OUTPUT
import java.text.NumberFormat;    //FOR CURRENCY FORMATTING

class ConsumerLoan
{
    //DEFINE VARIABLES AND OBJECTS
    private double principal = 0.0;      //LOAN PRINCIPAL
    private double term = 0;             //TERM OF LOAN IN MONTHS
    private double rate = 0.0;           //ANNUAL INTEREST IN PERCENT FORM
    private double payment = 0.0;          //MONTHLY PAYMENT
    private double interest = 0.0;         //TOTAL LOAN INTEREST
    private double total = 0.0;            //TOTAL LOAN AMOUNT
    private StaugIO io = new StaugIO();    //FOR INPUT/OUTPUT
    private char choice = 'Q';             //USER MENU CHOICE

  //displayMenu()
  public void displayMenu()
  {
    //DISPLAY A MENU AND READ USER'S CHOICE
    choice = io.readChar("Enter P to get monthly payment"
                    + "\nEnter I to get total loan interest"
                    + "\nEnter T to get total loan amount"
                    + "\nEnter Q to quit"
                    + "\n\nPlease enter your choice:  ");
  }//END displayMenu()

  //setPrincipal() METHOD
  private void setPrincipal()
  {
    principal = io.readDouble("Enter the amount of the loan: ");
  }//END setPrincipal()

  //setTerm()
  private void setTerm()
  {
    term = io.readDouble("Enter the duration of the loan in months: ");
  }//END setTerm()
```

```
//setRate()
private void setRate()
{
    rate = io.readDouble("Enter the annual interest rate in percent: ");
    rate = rate/12/100;
}//END setRate()

//getPrincipal()
public double getPrincipal()
{
    return principal;
}//END getPrincipal()

//getTerm()
public double getTerm()
{
    return term;
}//END getTerm()

//getRate()
public double getRate()
{
    return rate;
}//END getRate()

//getPayment()
public double getPayment()
{
    return payment;
}//END getPayment()

//getInterest()
public double getInterest()
{
    return interest;
}//END getInterest()

//getTotal()
public double getTotal()
{
    return total;
}//END getTotal()

//loanCalculator() METHOD
public void loanCalculator()
{
    //CREATE CURRENCY OBJECT
    NumberFormat currency = NumberFormat.getCurrencyInstance();

    //SWITCH ON CHOICE
    switch(choice)
    {
```

```
      case 'p': //CALCULATE AND DISPLAY PAYMENT
      case 'P':  setPrincipal();
                 setTerm();
                 setRate();
                 payment = principal * rate/(1-Math.pow((1+rate), -term));
                 interest = term * payment - principal;
                 total = term * payment;
                 io.writeInfo("The monthly payment is "
                                    + currency.format(payment));
                   break;


      case 'i':  //CALCULATE AND DISPLAY INTEREST
      case 'I':  setPrincipal();
                 setTerm();
                 setRate();
                 payment = principal * rate/(1-Math.pow((1+rate), -term));
                 interest = term * payment - principal;
                 total = term * payment;
                 io.writeInfo("The total interest is "
                                    + currency.format(interest));
                 break;


      case 't':  //CALCULATE AND DISPLAY TOTAL LOAN AMOUNT
      case 'T':  setPrincipal();
                 setTerm();
                 setRate();
                 payment = principal * rate/(1-Math.pow((1+rate), -term));
                 interest = term * payment - principal;
                 total = term * payment;
                 io.writeInfo("\n\nThe total loan amount is "
                                    + currency.format(total));
                 break;


      case 'q': //TERMINATE PROGRAM
      case 'Q': io.writeInfo("Click OK to continue");
                 break;

      //DISPLAY INVALID ENTRY MESSAGE
      default : io.writeInfo("\n\nThis is an invalid entry");
     }//END SWITCH
    }//END loanCalculator()

   //getChoice() METHOD
   public char getChoice()
   {
     return choice;
   }//END getChoice()
}//END ComsumerLoanLoop CLASS

public class Action07_01
{
  public static void main (String args[])
  {
```

```java
//Y/N USER RESPONSE TO LOAN SUMMARY QUERY
char query = 'Y';

//CREATE I/O OBJECT
StaugIO io = new StaugIO();

//CREATE CURRENCY OBJECT
NumberFormat currency = NumberFormat.getCurrencyInstance();

//CREATE LOAN OBJECT
ConsumerLoan myLoan = new ConsumerLoan();
do
{
//CALL METHOD
 myLoan.displayMenu();
 myLoan.loanCalculator();
}//END do/while
while ((myLoan.getChoice() != 'q') && (myLoan.getChoice() != 'Q'));

query = io.readChar("Do you want to see a loan summary? Y/N");
if ((query == 'y') || (query == 'Y'))
    io.writeInfo("LOAN SUMMARY"
                + "\nPrincipal: "
                + currency.format(myLoan.getPrincipal())
                + "\nAnnual Interest Rate: "
                + myLoan.getRate()*12*100 + '%'
                + "\nTerm of Loan: "
                + myLoan.getTerm() + " months"
                + "\nMonthly Payment: "
                + currency.format(myLoan.getPayment())
                + "\nTotal Loan Interest: "
                + currency.format(myLoan.getInterest())
                + "\nTotal Loan Amount: "
                + currency.format(myLoan.getTotal()));
else
    io.writeInfo("Program Terminated");
//EXIT PROGRAM
System.exit(0);
}//END main()
}//END Action07_01
```

You see that we have refined our earlier *setData()* method into three separate set methods, one for each of the loan variables. Notice that each set method is a void method that does not require any parameters. In addition, we have added six get methods to return each of the loan variables and resulting loan values. Each of the get methods is a non-void method requiring no parameters. Now, look at *main()*. Here you see the do/while loop developed in the last chapter that repeats the menu until the user quits the program. What we have added here is a query statement and associated if/else statement after the loop which queries the user as to whether or not he/she wants a loan summary report. If the user enters a "y" or "Y" in response to the query, a loan summary report is generated by calling the object get methods. Here is the query screen and sample summary report generated by this new code:

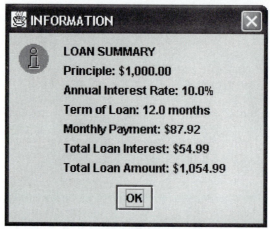

One last point: you see that the *currency* object has been defined in two places: *loanCalculator()* and *main()*. Why? The reason is that the *currency* object defined in *loanCalculator()* is local to that method and cannot be seen by *main()*. Therefore, it had to be defined again in *main()* to provide the currency formatting for the summary report. So, you say to make it a `private` member of the *ConsumerLoan* class. Then it can be seen by all methods within the class. You're right, but *main()* is not a member of this class. The remaining parts of the program have not changed from our solution in the last chapter. That's it! You should now have a good grasp of developing your own methods.

7.5   Recursion

The Java language supports a very powerful process called ***recursion***.

Recursion is a process whereby an operation calls itself until a terminating condition is reached.

A recursive method is a method that calls itself. That's right, with the power of recursion, a given method can actually contain a statement that calls, or invokes, the same method, thereby calling itself. By calling itself, the method actually "clones" itself into a new problem which is one step closer to a terminating condition. A recursive method keeps calling, or cloning, itself until the terminating condition is reached.

To understand the idea of recursion, consider a typical compound interest problem. Suppose you deposit $1,000 in the bank at a 12 percent annual interest rate, but it is compounded monthly. What this means is that the interest is calculated and added to the principal on a monthly basis. Thus, each time the interest is calculated, you get interest on the previous month's interest. Let's analyze the problem a bit more closely.

Your initial deposit is $1,000. Now, the annual interest rate is 12 percent, which translates to a 1 percent monthly rate. Because interest is compounded monthly, the balance at the end of the first month will be

$$\text{month 1 balance} = \$1,000 + (0.01 \times \$1,000) = \$1,010$$

As you can see, the interest for month 1 is $0.01 \times \$1,000$, or $10.00. This interest amount is then added to the principal ($1,000) to get a new balance of $1,010. Using a little algebra, the same calculation can be made like this:

$$\text{month 1 balance} = 1.01 \times \$1,000 = \$1,010$$

Now, how would you calculate the interest for the second month? You would use the balance at the end of the first month as the principal for the second month calculation. So, the calculation for month 2 would be

$$\text{month 2 balance} = 1.01 \times \$1,010 = \$1,020.10$$

For month 3, the calculation would be

$$\text{month 3 balance} = 1.01 \times \$1,020.10 = \$1,030.30$$

Do you see a pattern? Notice that to calculate the balance for any given month, you must use the balance from the previous month. In general, the calculation for any month becomes:

$$balance = 1.01 \times previous\ balance$$

Let's let *balance(n)* represent the balance of any given month, *n*, and *balance(n − 1)* the previous month's balance. Using this notation, the balance for any month, *balance(n)* is

$$balance(n) = 1.01 \times balance(n - 1)$$

Let's use this relationship to calculate what your balance would be after four months. Here's how you must perform the calculation:
First, the balance for month 4 is

$$balance(4) = 1.01 \times balance(3)$$

However, to find *balance(4)* you must find *balance(3)* like this:

$$balance(3) = 1.01 \times balance(2)$$

Then *balance(2)* must be found like this:

$$balance(2) = 1.01 \times balance(1)$$

Finally, *balance(1)* must be found like this:

$$balance(1) = 1.01 \times balance(0)$$

Now, you know that *balance*(0) is the original deposit of $1,000. This is really the only thing known, aside from the interest rate. Therefore, working backwards using substitution, you get:

$$balance(1) = 1.01 \times \$1,000 = \$1,010$$
$$balance(2) = 1.01 \times \$1,010 = \$1,020.10$$
$$balance(3) = 1.01 \times \$1,020.10 = \$1,030.30$$
$$balance(4) = 1.01 \times \$1,030.30 = \$1,040.60$$

This is a classic example of recursion, because in order to solve the problem, you must solve the previous problem condition using the same process, and so on, until you encounter a known condition (in our case, the initial $1,000 deposit). This known condition is called a **terminating condition**. Thus, a **recursive operation** is an operation that calls itself until a terminating condition is reached. Likewise, a **recursive method** is one that calls, or invokes, itself until a terminating condition is reached.

Now, suppose we wish to express the preceding compound interest calculation as a recursive method. The mathematical expression would be

$$balance(0) = 1,000 \text{ and } balance(n) = 1.01 \times balance(n-1) \text{ (for } n > 0)$$

This mathematical expression can be expressed in pseudocode form, like this:

> If *n* is 0
> > *balance*(*n*) = 1,000
>
> Else
> > *balance*(*n*) = 1.01 × *balance*(*n* − 1)

Notice that the terminating condition is tested first. There must *always* be a test for a terminating condition. If the terminating condition exists, the cloning process is halted and the substitution process begins; or else, another recursive call is made to the method. Do you see the recursive call in the `else` clause? To calculate *balance(n)* the algorithm must call itself and calculate *balance*(*n* − 1). This is recursion!

Next, let's assume that we use a variable called *deposit* to represent the initial deposit, and a variable called *rate* to represent the annual interest rate. Then, our balance could be calculated using recursion, as follows:

> If *n* is 0
> > *balance*(*n*) = *deposit*
>
> Else
> > *balance*(*n*) = (1 + *rate* / 12 / 100) × *balance*(*n* − 1)

If a programming language supports recursive operations, a method can be coded directly from the above algorithm. Because Java employs the power of recursion, the Java method is simply

```java
public double balance(int n)
{
   if(n == 0)
      return deposit;
   else
      return (1 + rate / 12 / 100) * balance(n - 1);
}//END balance()
```

Here, the number of months, n, to compound is listed as a parameter for the method. Without this parameter, the recursive calls would not be possible because the previous month, $n - 1$, must be passed to the method with each recursive call. That's all there is to it! This method will calculate the balance at the end of any month, n, passed to the method. Notice how the method calls itself in the `else` clause. Here's how it works. When the computer encounters the recursive call in the `else` clause, it must temporarily delay the calculation to evaluate the recursive method call just as we did as part of the compounded interest calculation. When it encounters the `else` clause a second time, the method calls itself again, and keeps calling itself each time the `else` clause is executed until the terminating condition is reached. When this happens, the `if` clause is executed (because n is zero), and the recursive calling ceases.

Now, let's insert this method into a class and write an application to calculate compounded interest, as follows:

```java
/*
 * CompoundInterestTest.java
 *
 * Created on July 3, 2002, 10:04 AM
 */

/**
 *
 * @author  Andrew C. Staugaard, Jr.
 * @version 1.0
 */
import staugIO.StaugIO;         //FOR GUI I/O
import java.text.NumberFormat;  //FOR CURRENCY FORMATTING

class CompoundInterest
{
   //DATA MEMBERS
   private double deposit = 0.0;      //INITIAL DEPOSIT
   private double rate = 0.0;         //ANNUAL INTEREST RATE
                                      //DEPOSIT TO DETERMINE BALANCE
   private StaugIO io = new StaugIO(); //FOR GUI I/O

   //METHOD MEMBERS
   //setData() GET DEPOSIT, NUMBER OF MONTHS, AND INTEREST RATE
   public void setDeposit()
   {
     deposit = io.readDouble("Enter the initial deposit");
   }//END setDeposit()

   public void setRate()
   {
     rate = io.readDouble("Enter the annual interest rate");
   }//END setRate()

   public double getDeposit()
   {
     return deposit;
   }//END getDeposit()
```

```java
   public double getRate()
   {
      return rate;
   }//END getRate()

   //*********************************************************
   //
   //THIS RECURSIVE METHOD WILL CALCULATE A BANK BALANCE
   //BASED ON A MONTHLY COMPOUNDED INTEREST RATE
   //
   //*********************************************************
   public double balance(int n)
   {
      if (n == 0)
         return deposit;
      else
         return (1 + rate / 12 / 100) * balance(n - 1);
   }//END balance()
}//END CompoundInterest CLASS

public class CompoundInterestTest
{
   public static void main (String args[])
   {
      //DEFINE VARIABLES AND OBJECTS
      int months = 0;                  //NUMBER OF MONTHS TO COMPOUND
      StaugIO io = new StaugIO();      //FOR GUI I/O

      //CREATE COMPOUND INTEREST OBJECT
      CompoundInterest myBalance = new CompoundInterest();
       //CALL METHODS
      myBalance.setDeposit();
      myBalance.setRate();
      months = io.readInt("Enter the number of months to compound");

      //CREATE CURRENCY OBJECT
      NumberFormat currency = NumberFormat.getCurrencyInstance();

      //DISPLAY RESULTS, MAKING RECURSIVE METHOD CALL
      io.writeInfo("With an initial deposit of "
            + currency.format(myBalance.getDeposit())
            + " and an interest rate of "
            + myBalance.getRate()
            + "%\nthe balance at the end of "
            + months
            + " months would be "
            + currency.format(myBalance.balance(months)));

      //EXIT PROGRAM
      System.exit(0);
   }// END main()
}//END CompoundInterestTest
```

First you see that our *CompoundInterest* class contains two `private` members to store the initial deposit and rate of interest. There are two set methods to set the values of these members, and two get methods to return their values. Our recursive *balance()* method is the only other method in the class. Our *CompoundInterestTest* application defines an object called *myBalance* for the *CompoundInterest* class, then uses this object to set the initial deposit and interest rate. The user is then prompted in *main()* to enter the number of months to compound. The entry variable, called *months*, is passed to the recursive *balance()* method as part of a *writeInfo()* statement that produces the final output report. Note that we must use the *myBalance* object to call the *balance()* method because it is part of the *CompoundInterest* class.

Here is the sequence of dialog boxes the user would see for a sample run:

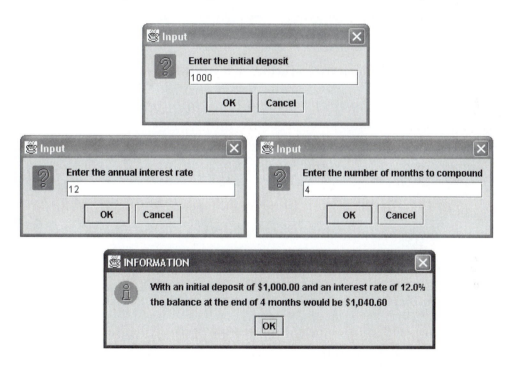

During any recursive call, all information required to complete the calculation after the recursive call is saved by the computer in a memory area called a **stack**. As the recursive calls continue, information is saved on the memory stack until the terminating condition is reached. Then the computer works backward from the terminating condition, retrieving the stack information to determine the final result. The process that the computer goes through is identical to what we did when working the compound interest problem and is illustrated in Figure 7-8. The values shown in the figure assume a $1,000.00 initial deposit and an interest rate of 12% per year, compounded monthly. Notice that the last thing placed into the stack is the first thing retrieved from the stack when recursion begins to "unwind." This principle is known as **last-in-first-out**, or **LIFO**. All stacks operate using the LIFO

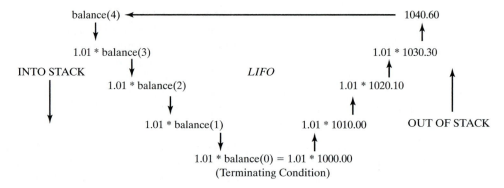

FIGURE 7-8   As recursion winds up, calculation information is placed into a memory stack until a terminating condition is reached. Recursion then unwinds by retrieving the calculation information out of the stack and using substitution to generate the final result.

principle. A stack is a classic data structure that you will most likely study in a more advanced course.

 **CAUTION**

A recursive method must always reach a terminating condition. If it does not, the method will keep calling itself forever, resulting in a memory overflow run-time error.

Example 7-3

Write a recursive method to find the sum of all integers from 1 to some number, n.

Solution

Think about this operation for a minute. Isn't it a classic recursive operation? To find the sum of integers 1 to, say, 5, couldn't you add 5 to the sum of integers from 1 to 4? Then, to find the sum of integers from 1 to 4, you add 4 to the sum of integers from 1 to 3, and so on, right? Expressed in symbols:

$sum(5) = 5 + sum(4)$
$sum(4) = 4 + sum(3)$
$sum(3) = 3 + sum(2)$
$sum(2) = 2 + sum(1)$
$sum(1) = 1$

Notice that $sum(1)$ is the terminating condition because its value is known. Now, translating this process to a recursive expression, you get:

$$sum(1) = 1 \text{ and } sum(n) = n + sum(n - 1) \text{ (for } n > 1)$$

This expression can be translated to pseudocode, like this:

> If n is 1
> > $sum(n) = 1$
>
> Else
> > $sum(n) = n + sum (n - 1)$

The recursive Java method is then coded directly from the algorithm as

```java
public int sum(int n)
{
  if(n == 1)
    return 1;
  else
    return n + sum(n - 1);
}//END sum()
```

We say that recursion is ***elegant*** when it comes to problem solving because it is relatively simple to express via an `if/else` statement in an algorithm or code. However, as you have just discovered, there is a lot of work going on behind the scenes. Although recursion is a very powerful feature of any language, you should be aware that it is not always the most efficient method of solving a problem. Whenever we talk about computer efficiency, we must consider two things: *execution speed* and *memory usage*. When using recursion, the computer must keep track of each recursive call in a stack so that it can work backward to obtain a solution. This requires large amounts of both memory and time. As a result, a recursive solution to a problem may not always be the most efficient solution. *All* recursive problems can also be solved non-recursively using iteration. For instance, consider the sum of integers from 1 to *n* done recursively in Example 7-3. This problem can be solved using an iterative method, like this:

```java
public int sum(int n)
{
  int subTotal = 0;      //SUM SUBTOTAL
  for(int count = 1; count <= n; ++count)
    subTotal = subTotal + count;
  return subTotal;
}//END sum()
```

So, why use recursion? Probably the main reason is that many recursive solutions are much simpler than their iterative counterparts. In addition, there are some problems in data structures, such as when working with linked lists and binary trees, where recursion isn't a mere convenience, and it is essential to keep the code manageable. Here are two guidelines that should help you decide when to use recursion:

1. Consider a recursive solution only when a *simple* iterative solution is not possible.
2. Use a recursive solution only when the execution and memory efficiency of the solution is within acceptable limits, considering the system limitations.

 QUICK CHECK

1. True or false: There is no way that a Java method can call itself.
2. Explain why we can describe recursion as a "winding" and "unwinding" process.
3. What terminates a recursive method call?
4. A factorial operation, *factorial(n)*, finds the product of all integers from 1 to some positive integer *n*. Thus, 5! = 5 * 4 * 3 * 2 * 1. Write the pseudocode required to find *factorial(n)*, where *n* is any integer. (*Note:* By definition, *factorial(1)* = 1.)
5. True or false: An advantage of recursion is that it does not require a lot of memory to execute.

6. True or false: All recursive problems can also be solved using iteration.

7. Recursion employs a memory data structure called a(n) _____ to save information during recursive calls.

8. Stacks operate on the _____ principle.

CHAPTER SUMMARY

In this chapter, you learned how to write and use methods in Java. A method is created by writing a method header, which includes the method modifier, the return type, the method name, and a parameter list. The body, or statement section, of the method then follows the method header. Methods in Java can be ***non-void*** methods which return a single value to the calling program, or *void* methods which do not return any values. When a non-void method is designed to return a single value to the calling program, the value returned replaces the method call wherever the call is made within the calling program. Thus, the method call can appear as part of an assignment operation, an output statement, an arithmetic operation, or a conditional test statement. When a *void* method is designed to perform a specific task, the method is called by using the method name (followed by a list of arguments) as a statement in the program.

     Arguments are data passed to the method when the method is called. Parameters are defined within the method header and take on the value(s) of the arguments when the method is called.

     In addition to parameters, methods can operate with local variables that are defined within the method body. Such local variables are visible only for use within the method in which they are defined. Local variables are destroyed once the method execution is terminated. The scope of a constant or variable refers to the largest block in which it is visible. Variables always should be defined as locally as possible, whereas constants should be declared as globally as possible.

     A recursive method is a method that calls itself until a terminating condition is reached. There must always be a terminating condition to terminate a recursive method call; otherwise, a memory (stack) overflow error will occur. Recursive operations are performed as part of an `if/else` statement. The terminating condition forms the `if` clause, and the recursive call is part of the `else` clause of the statement. All recursive operations also can be performed using iteration. Because recursion eats up time and memory as compared to iteration, you should consider recursion only when a simple iterative solution is not possible and when the execution and memory efficiency of the solution are within acceptable limits.

QUESTIONS AND PROBLEMS

Questions

1. What four things must be specified in a method header?

2. Three possible modifiers for Java methods are _____, _____, and _____.

3. Explain the difference between a `void` method and a non-void method.

4. Explain the difference between an argument and a parameter.

5. Which of the following are invalid method headers? Explain why they are invalid.
     a. `public double average(num1, num2)`
     b. `public int largest(x,y : int)`
     c. `public double smallest(double a,b)`
     d. `public String display(String name)`

6. Write the appropriate headers for the following methods:
   a. Inverse of x: $1/x$
   b. *tan* (x)
   c. Convert a decimal test score value to a letter grade.
   d. Convert degrees Fahrenheit to degrees Celsius.
   e. Compute the factorial of any integer n ($n!$).
   f. Compute the average of three integer test scores.
   g. Display the average of three integer test scores.

7. True or false: When a method does not have a return type, you must indicate this with the keyword `null`.

8. When passing an argument to a method parameter,
   a. the argument takes on the parameter value.
   b. the parameter takes on the argument value.
   c. the argument reflects any changes to the parameter after the method execution.
   d. a and b
   e. b and c
   f. a and c

9. When using an assignment operator to call a method, the method must include a(n) _____ statement.

10. Which of the following are invalid method headers? Explain why they are invalid.
    a. `public void print()`
    b. `public boolean error(float num1, char num2)`
    c. `public void getData(int amount, char date)`
    d. `public double average (int number, float total)`
    e. `public char sample (int, char, float);`

11. True or false: A variable defined in *main()* has visibility in all methods called by *main()*.

12. Explain the difference between calling a non-void method and calling a `void` method.

13. Write the appropriate headers for the following methods:
    a. a method called *sample()* that must return a floating-point value and receive an integer, a floating-point value, and a character (in that order) when it is called.
    b. a method called *skip()* that will cause the printer to skip a given number of lines where the number of lines to skip is obtained from the calling program.
    c. a method called *myMethod()* that accepts a string and returns a Boolean value.
    d. a method called *hypot()* that will return the hypotenuse of a right triangle, given the values of the two sides from the calling program.
    e. a method called *yourMethod()* that accepts a Boolean value and returns a string value.

14. Write Java statements that will call the methods in question 13.

15. What is a local variable?

16. What is meant by the scope of a variable or method?

17. True or false: Variables should be defined as locally as possible and constants as globally as possible.

18. Suppose that a method must have access to a variable defined in *main()*. How must this be accomplished?

19. Explain recursion.

20. When should you consider a recursive solution to a problem?

21. Recursion employs a data structure called a(n) _____.

Problems

Least Difficult

In problems 1 – 9, develop `public` *non-void methods to perform the required task. Place the method inside a class whose name is descriptive of its purpose. Write a Java application to test your method. Obtain any unknown quantities that the method needs to evaluate from the user in main() and pass them to the method for evaluation. (Reference Figure 7-4)*

   1. A method that returns a temperature in degrees Fahrenheit to degrees Celsius.

   2. Find the inverse $(1/x)$ of any real value x.

   3. Return the maximum of two integer values. Make sure to account for the case when the two values are equal.

   4. Return the minimum of two integer values. Make sure to account for the case when the two values are equal.

   5. Examine a range of values and return the Boolean value `true`, if a value is within the range, and `false` if the value is outside of the range.

   6. Return your bank balance after one year, given user entries of an initial deposit and annual simple (not compounded) interest rate.

More Difficult

   7. Return the *tan(θ)* for some angle θ in degrees. (*Hint: Use the tan() method in the Math class but remember that tan() evaluates radians, not degrees, so you must convert degrees to radians in order to return the correct value.*)

   8. Return x^y, where x is a real value and y is an integer value. (*Hint: x^y is simply x multiplied by itself y times. You can use a loop to accomplish this task.*)

   9. Find the height at which the ladder in Figure 7-9 makes contact with the wall, given the length of the ladder and the distance the base of the ladder is from the wall.

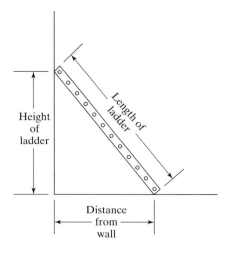

FIGURE 7-9   A ladder for problem 9.

TABLE 7-2 Federal Taxable Income Rates for Single Tax Payers

If the amount on Form 1040, line 38, is: Over –	But not over	Enter on Form 1040, line 39		of the amount over -
$0	$24,650		15%	$0
24,650	59,750	3,697.50+	28%	24,650
59,750	124,650	13,525.50+	31%	59,750
124,650	271,050	33,644.50+	36%	124,650
271,050		86,348.50+	39.6%	271,050

Most Difficult

10. Table 7-2 provides a federal income tax schedule for single tax payers. Write a program that calculates the federal income tax, given the taxable income from the user. Use three methods: one to obtain the taxable income from the user, one to calculate the income tax, and one to display the taxable income and corresponding income tax. Place your methods and associated data in a class called *FedTax* to accomplish this task. Then, write an application to test the class.

11. McJava's coffee shop sells espresso coffee for $1.25 a cup, bagels for $1.50, and Danish pastries for $2.25. Write a cash register program to compute a customer's bill. Use methods to obtain the quantity of each item ordered, calculate the subtotal of the bill, calculate the total cost of the bill including a 7% sales tax, and display an itemized bill as follows:

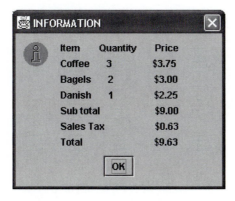

Place your methods and associated data in a class called *CustomerReceipt* to accomplish this task. Then, write an application to test the class.

12. Develop an algorithm and code a method to find $n!$ using iteration. Write an application to test your method. Recall that $n! = n * (n-1) * (n-2) * (n-3) * \ldots * 1$. Example: $5! = 5*4*3*2*1$

13. Develop an algorithm and code a method to find $n!$ using recursion. Write an application to test your method.

14. A Fibonacci sequence of numbers is defined as follows:

$$F_0 = 0$$
$$F_1 = 1$$
$$F_n = F_{n-1} + F_{n-2}, \text{ for } n > 1$$

This says that the first two numbers in the sequence are 0 and 1. Then, each additional Fibonacci number is the sum of the two previous numbers in the sequence. Thus, the first 10 Fibonacci numbers are:

$$0, 1, 1, 2, 3, 5, 8, 13, 21, 34$$

Here, we say that the first number occupies position 0 in the sequence, the second number position 1 in the sequence, and so on. Thus, the last position in a 10-number sequence is position 9. Develop a program that employs a recursive method to generate a Fibonacci sequence of all numbers up to some position n entered by the user.

15. Develop a program that employs an iterative method to generate a Fibonacci sequence of all numbers up to some position n entered by the user.

16. Measure the amount of time it takes each of the programs in problems 14 and 15 to generate a Fibonacci sequence of 50 elements. What do you conclude about the efficiency of recursion versus iteration? Why does the recursive program take so long?

8

Object-Oriented Programming—Part I

OBJECTIVES

When you are finished with this chapter, you should have a good understanding of the following:

■ UML™ class diagrams

■ Encapsulation and information hiding

■ Private versus public class members

■ Constructors

■ Overloaded constructors

■ Accessor methods

■ How to develop your own class packages

Introduction

This chapter will introduce you to object-oriented programming (OOP). With OOP, you construct complex programs from simpler program entities called *objects*, which are instances, or occurrences, of *classes*. Object-oriented programs are organized as a collection of objects that cooperate with each other. Thus, OOP employs objects as the fundamental building blocks for program development.

OOP facilitates the extension and reuse of general-purpose classes in new applications with minimal modification to the original code. Although this can be accomplished with ordinary methods in procedural programming, OOP provides an important feature called *inheritance*, which is a mechanism for deriving new classes from existing ones. As a result, classes are related to each other to create a hierarchy of classes through inheritance. This inheritance feature also allows new classes to "inherit" code from existing classes, thereby making the programming chore much more productive. Inside-out expansion is possible through the use of inheritance in OOP.

In summary, the goals of OOP are to improve programmer productivity by managing software complexity via the use of classes and their associated objects that provide for reusable code via the class inheritance feature.

Up to this point you have been using classes and objects to write simple programs involving a single class. We have used a top-down design to design algorithms and implemented them as methods of our classes. Although the overall design of any software is a top-down process, writing object-oriented programs requires a different approach. You create object-oriented programs from the inside out by expanding on classes. For example, you might approach a banking problem by creating a bank account class that defines the basic data that all accounts must contain (account number, balance, etc.), as well as the fundamental operations that are performed on bank accounts (deposit, withdrawal, etc.). This basic bank account class can then be expanded into classes that define specific types of bank accounts, such as checking accounts, interest checking accounts, savings accounts, and so on.

OOP has its own unique terminology. Be sure to grasp the terminology as you progress through the chapter. A glossary of OOP terms is provided at the end of this text for quick reference.

There are three concepts central to OOP: ***encapsulation***, ***inheritance***, and ***polymorphism***. You have already had experience with polymorphism when you learned about overloaded methods. In this chapter, you will be exposed to the idea of encapsulation and information hiding. Chapter 9 is devoted entirely to inheritance.

In this chapter, we will apply the ***Unified Modeling Language***, or ***UML***, as a design tool when developing our class diagrams. The UML is becoming a widely accepted standard for designing object-oriented software. Therefore, you should have a general understanding of its use. There is a learning module on UML in Appendix B. You should read this module now or when instructed to do so within the first section of this chapter.

8.1   Classes and Objects—A Deeper Perspective

A thorough understanding of classes and objects is essential to developing object-oriented code. You have been working with classes and objects since Chapter 2, so you should have a good feeling for the class/object concept. Let's now take time to gain a deeper understanding of classes and objects.

Classes

In order to completely understand the nature of a class, we must consider two levels of definition: the ***abstract*** level and the ***implementation*** level.

The Abstract Level   The abstract level of a class provides the outside, or ***client***, view of the class without concern for the inner structure and workings of the class. Here's how we define a class at the abstract level.

At the abstract level, a **class** can be described as an *interface* that defines the behavior of its objects.

An *interface* is something that forms a common boundary, or barrier, between two systems. The interface for a class is provided by its methods. The method headers of a class define how data must be presented to the class. At the abstract level, all you need to be concerned with are the method interfaces, or headers, and not the inner workings of the class. A good analogy of this idea would be the postal system. You do not have to know how the postal system works to mail a letter and get it to its destination. All you need to know is how to present the required data (address and a stamp) and place the letter in a mail box. The postal system defines how the letter must be addressed (data presentation) just as the method headers of a class define how data must be presented to the class. The class methods also define the behavior of the class through their designated operations. In this way, we say a class defines the behavior common to all of its objects. By behavior, we mean how an object of a given class acts and reacts when it is accessed via one of its methods. Another analogy is your DVD remote control. It acts as an interface between you and the DVD. Do you care what goes on inside the control? Of course not! All you care about is the "behavior" of the buttons. You interact with the DVD through the button interface which provides a set of behaviors defined for the DVD.

The abstract view of a class as an interface provides its *outside* view while hiding its internal structure and behavioral details. Thus, an object of a given class can be viewed as a black box, as shown in Figure 8-1. As you can see, the operation, or method,

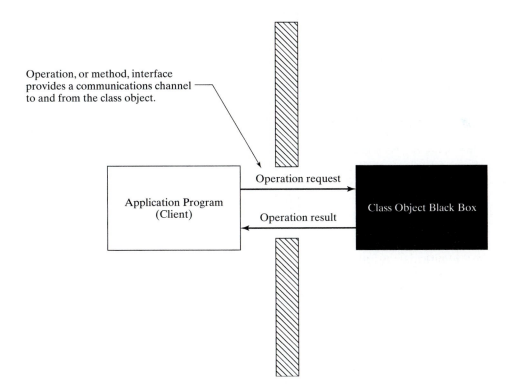

FIGURE 8-1   At the abstract level, a class is an interface that defines the behavior of its objects.

interface provides a communications channel to and from the class object. The application, or client, program generates an operation request to the object, and the object responds with the desired result. The interface dictates *what* must be supplied to the object and *how* the object will respond. As a result, a class, through its method interfaces, defines how its objects will behave. At the client application level, you treat the class object as a black box because you do not care about what goes on inside the object. All you care about is how to work with the object.

The Implementation Level   The class implementation provides its *inside* view, showing the secrets of its data organization and method implementation. As a result, the class implementation reveals the secrets of its behavior because it is primarily concerned with the operations that define the abstract level, or interface.

 At the implementation level, a **class** is a syntactical unit that describes a set of data and related operations that are common to its objects.

The implementation of a class consists of two types of **members**: (1) **data members** and (2) **method members**. Any item declared in a class is called a class **member**. Consequently, to implement a class we create data members and method members.

The Data Members   The data members of the class provide the class attributes, or characteristics. The data members of the class are usually the variables defined within the class. We say that these members are "private" because they are *accessible only by the method members declared for the class*. This means that the data members can be changed only by the method members in the class.

The Method Members   The method members of the class consist of methods that operate on the data members of the class. These methods are usually "public" because they can be accessed anywhere within the scope of a given class. In other words, method members can be called from outside the class, as long as the class is visible at the time of access. As you might suspect, it is the public method members that form the interface and exhibit the behavior of the class objects.

There is nothing special about public member methods, except that they are used to operate on the data members of the class. The important thing to remember is that *no methods outside a given class can access the private data members of the class*.

The Class Declaration   The implementation level of a class can be clearly seen by its declaration format, as follows:

CLASS DECLARATION FORMAT

```
class class name
{

  //DATA MEMBERS
  private data type  variable;
  private data type  variable;
```

```
        •
        •
  private data type  variable;

   //METHOD MEMBERS
  public return type method name (parameter listing)
  {
   //METHOD STATEMENTS
  }

  public return type method name (parameter listing)
  {
     //METHOD STATEMENTS
  }

        •

        •

  public return type method name (parameter listing)
  {
   //METHOD STATEMENTS
  }

}//END CLASS
```

The declaration begins with the keyword `class`, followed by the class name. The class name should be a noun or a noun phrase that is descriptive of its purpose. The first letter of each word within the name should be capitalized. The entire class declaration is enclosed in a set of braces. Normally, the data members of the class are specified first, followed by the method members of the class. The data members of the class usually consist of ***private instance variables***. An instance variable is a variable that will be created for any given object of the class. Each instance variable is prefixed with the keyword `private`. A `private` member of a class is visible within that class and, therefore, can only be accessed by methods within the class. The method members of the class consist of `public` and `private` ***instance methods***. An instance method is a method that will be available to any given object of the class. To declare a method as a class member, you list the method header, followed by the code for the method. The access modifier for a class method is usually `public`. Public methods form the interface to the class because they can be accessed, or called, from outside the class. Methods can also be `private` but then they are only accessible within the class and cannot be called outside the class. Such methods are referred to as ***utility methods***, since they are often used within the class to perform housekeeping, or utility, operations.

A `private` class member is only accessible within the class by methods of the same class. The `public` class methods form the interface to the class and are accessible from outside the class. It is the `public` methods that are used to provide access to and manipulate the `private` class members.

The diagram in Figure 8-2 illustrates the idea of the `public` class methods providing the interface, or boundary, to access the `private` class members. The data members of a class should always be designated as `private`. Why? Because making the data members private enforces ***encapsulation*** with ***information hiding***.

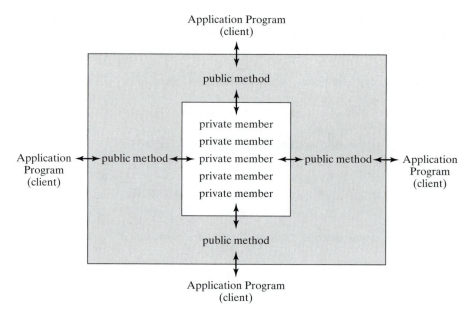

FIGURE 8-2   The `private` class members can only be accessed from outside the class via the `public` class methods, which provide the interface, or boundary, between the class and its application, or client, program.

Encapsulation and Information Hiding

Encapsulation is simply the idea of packaging things together in a well-defined programming unit. A record, or table, in a database program is encapsulated because it is a collection of data that are combined into a well-defined unit, the record, or table. The class in Java obviously provides for encapsulation by packaging both data and methods into a single class unit.

 Encapsulation means to package data and/or operations into a single well-defined programming unit.

The idea of encapsulation can be enhanced with *information hiding*.

 Information hiding means that there is a binding relationship between the information, or data, and its related operations so that operations outside the encapsulated unit cannot affect the information inside the unit.

With information hiding, there is a *binding* relationship between the information and the operations that are performed on that information. The class provides for information hiding in Java. The public methods provide the class interface that is accessible from outside the class, and the private data members provide the information that is accessible only from within the class itself. Only the methods declared for the class can operate on the private class members. Thus, the private data members of a class provide the information hiding. Without encapsulation and information hiding, there is no such binding relationship. In programming languages that do not support information hiding, you define data structures and the methods that operate on those data structures separately. Then, you place both in a single source code file while attempting to treat the data and methods as separate modules within the file. Although such an approach seems reasonable, it can create problems. Because there is no defined, or explicit, binding relationship between the data and the methods, another programmer could write methods to access and inadvertently change the data.

For instance, suppose that you are writing a program for a bank that calculates bank account interest. To write such a program, you would define an account balance variable, among others, and write methods to change the balance based on deposits, withdrawals, interest earned, and so on. These methods would be written according to the policies dictated by the bank—and the government, for that matter. Would you want another programmer to be able to write methods that would affect the account balances differently than yours? Even worse, would you want the transactions of one account to affect the balance of another account? Of course not!

With information hiding, you can truly separate the account data and the methods operating on those data into two separate categories, private and public, but bind them tightly together in an encapsulated class unit. Only public methods can operate on the private account data. This means that outside methods written by another programmer cannot corrupt the data. Thus, only the operations that you have defined for a given type of account can be applied to that type of account and no others. In addition, these same operations applied to one account cannot affect another account of the same type. The class dictates the data format and legal operations for all accounts of a given type. Then, individual accounts of the same type are created as objects of the account class. A class in Java inherently enforces information hiding.

There is a cost, however. You must use a method call to access the private data. This reduces the efficiency of the code slightly. On the other hand, using the compiler to enforce the rules that relate data to methods can pay off in a big way when it comes time to debug a large program. In addition, object-oriented code is much easier to maintain because the classes and their objects closely match the application. Finally, once object-oriented code is developed for a given application, it can be easily reused in another program that has a similar application. Consider a windows program. All windowing programs employ the same window classes. To create a new windows application, you simply "inherit" the general window classes and customize them to the new application.

The ideas of encapsulation and information hiding are not new. Only languages like Ada, Modula II, C++, and Java, which easily and efficiently provide for encapsulation and information hiding, are new. These concepts have been around as long as computers. Common examples of information hiding include those data and routines that are part of BIOS to control a PC keyboard, monitor, and file access. Also, the file handling routines built into most commercial programs employ information hiding. Imagine what would happen if you could inadvertently corrupt these data and routines (system crash, lost unrecoverable files, etc.). You can use these built-in routines just by knowing how to operate them, but you cannot get at the inner workings of the routines. Likewise, you can operate your CD player via its controls without worrying about the inner workings of the player. Imagine what might happen if a non-technical user could get to the inner workings of your CD player. This is why it is so important to think of a class in the abstract sense of an interface.

Encapsulation is the mechanism that implements information hiding in an object-oriented language. Each language permits various parts of a programming entity to be accessible to the outside world. Those parts that are not visible to the outside world represent the information hiding aspect of encapsulation. COBOL records, for example, are encapsulated and permit all member data to be visible and manipulated by outside operations and, therefore, do not provide any information hiding. Java classes are encapsulated, but in addition, provide information hiding through the private members of the class.

Problem Solving in Action: Banking

Suppose you are working for a bank, and they want you to convert an old COBOL program to a Java application. The program is a savings account program that contains an account balance and account interest rate. The operations within that program allow the user to add deposits, subtract withdrawals, add interest, and return the current balance.

The first thing you should do when writing an object-oriented program is to develop a problem statement and look for the nouns and verbs within the statement. The nouns will suggest classes as well as data members for those classes. The verbs will suggest methods, or interfaces, for the classes. Here is the foregoing problem statement again, with the applicable noun and verb phrases underlined.

Convert an old COBOL program to a Java application. The program is a <u>savings account</u> program that contains an <u>account balance</u> and <u>account interest rate</u>. The program allows the user to <u>add deposits</u>, <u>subtract withdrawals</u>, <u>add interest</u>, and <u>return the current balance</u>.

Now, there are three noun phrases: *savings account*, *account balance*, and *account interest*. Do you see a hierarchy within these? Of course, the main noun phrase is *savings account*. The other two, *account balance* and *account interest*, are part of the *savings account*, right? Thus, the class will be a savings account class, which includes data members of account balance and account interest.

The four verb phrases within the problem statement are: *add deposits*, *subtract withdrawals*, *add interest*, and *return balance*. Each of these phrases suggests an action to be performed on the account data and therefore will form the method members of the class. So here is the class specification:

Class: *SavingsAccount*
   Data Members: *balance*
                 interest rate

   Method Members: *addDeposit()*
                 subtractWithdrawal()
                 addInterest()
                 getBalance()

The **Unified Modeling Language**, or **UML**, is a technique for analyzing and designing object-oriented software. Read the UML module in Appendix B for an introduction to UML before going on, if you have not already done so. You need to learn how to construct UML class diagrams.

Now, let's consider the method interfaces. The *addDeposit()* and *subtractWithdrawal()* methods both need to accept an amount from outside the class to add to or subtract from the account *balance*. These methods will not return anything because they are simply operating on the private member, *balance*. This gives us enough information to write the UML interface descriptions as follows:

+addDeposits(in amount:double)
+subtractWithdrawals(in amount:double)

Do you remember what this means in UML? Well, both methods are public, as indicated by the + sign, and both methods accept (*in*) a double floating-point value as a parameter. Nothing is returned by either method, indicated by the lack of any return type after the parameter listing.

Next, the *addInterest()* method will simply operate on the private account *balance* member using the private *interest rate* member. Thus, no parameters or return types are required. When method members of a class operate directly on private data members of the same class, you *do not* pass the member data to the methods. Therefore, the resulting UML description is simply:

+addInterest()

PROGRAMMING NOTE

Remember, when method members of a class operate directly on private data members of the class, you *do not* pass the member data to the methods. The reason is that the method and data members are so tightly bound within the class that passing of class data is not necessary.

Finally, the job of the *getBalance()* method is to return the value of *balance* outside the class. Because *balance* is a private class member, you must use a method to obtain its value. Does *getBalance()* need any parameters? No, because *balance* is a class member and, therefore, does not have to be passed. Any of the class methods have direct access to the private class members. Thus, the UML description is:

+getBalance():double

This says that *getBalance()* is a public method , +, that does not require any parameters, (), and returns a double, *:double*.

Finally, the UML descriptions of the private members are:

−balance:double = 1000.00
−INTEREST_RATE:double = 2.0

As you can see, each is a private member, as indicated by the − symbol. Both the *balance* and *INTEREST_RATE* members will be double floating-point values which will be initialized to 1000.00 and 2.0, respectively. Thus, we have assumed that the beginning balance is $1000.00 and the interest rate is a 2% annual rate. The interest rate identifier is in all caps to indicate that it will be coded as a constant.

We now have addressed all the class members. The resulting UML class diagram is shown in Figure 8-3.

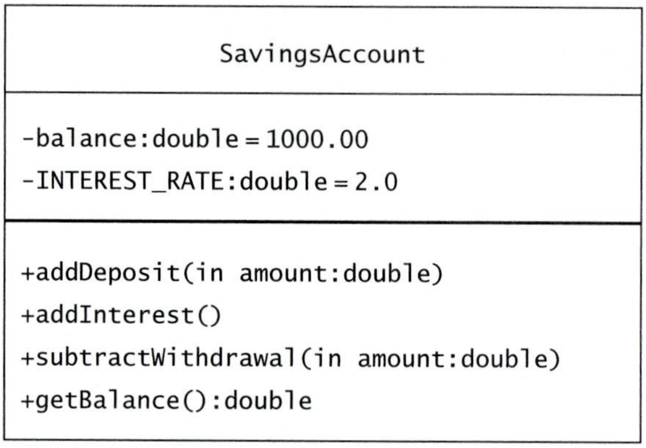

```
                    SavingsAccount

  -balance:double = 1000.00
  -INTEREST_RATE:double = 2.0


  +addDeposit(in amount:double)
  +addInterest()
  +subtractWithdrawal(in amount:double)
  +getBalance():double
```

FIGURE 8-3   The *SavingsAccount* class consists of private *balance* and *INTEREST_RATE* members which are hidden inside the class, and public *addDeposit()*, *subtractWithdrawal()*, *addInterest()*, and *getBalance()* methods that form the class interface, or boundary.

Once you develop the method algorithms and UML class diagram showing all the class members, the class can be coded. We will forgo writing the method algorithms for this problem, since they are so simple. Here is the required class code:

```
class SavingsAccount
{
  //DATA MEMBERS
  private final double INTEREST_RATE = 2.0;    //ANNUAL INTEREST RATE
  private double balance = 1000.0;             //ACCOUNT BALANCE

  //METHOD MEMBERS

  //ADD DEPOSITS
  public void addDeposit(double amount)
  {
     balance = balance + amount;
  } //END addDeposit()

  //SUBTRACT WITHDRAWAL
  public void subtractWithdrawal(double amount)
  {
     balance = balance - amount;
  }//END subtractWithdrawal()

  //ADD MONTHLY INTEREST
  public void addInterest()
  {
     balance = balance + balance * INTEREST_RATE/12/100;
  }//END addInterest

  //GET BALANCE
  public double getBalance()
```

```
    {
        return balance;
    }//END getBalance()
} //END SavingsAccount
```

The class declaration begins with the keyword `class`, followed by our class name, *SavingsAccount*. First, you find a listing of the private class members. There are two private floating-point members, *balance* and *INTEREST_RATE,* each initialized with a beginning value.

Next, you find a listing of the public member methods of the class. Each method header has been coded directly from the UML class diagram. This class contains four public method members. All the methods operate on the private data members. The *addDeposit()* method adds an amount received from its calling program to the account balance. The amount to be added must be supplied as an argument when the method is called. The *subtractWithdraw()* method subtracts an amount received from its calling program from the account balance. The amount to be subtracted must be supplied as an argument when the method is called. The *addInterest()* method calculates a new balance from the current private member values and, therefore, does not require any parameters. The *getBalance()* method returns the value of the account balance to the calling program. Again, because of encapsulation, this is the only way the *balance* can be accessed for reporting purposes.

Example 8-1

Develop a UML class diagram and code a class declaration for the following:

a. A rectangle class that consists of the rectangle length and width with methods to calculate the perimeter of the rectangle and calculate the area of the rectangle

Solution

a. The two private members must be the rectangle length and width, so let's call them *length* and *width.* These will be defined as private floating-point members of the class. The rectangle class requires two public methods, one to calculate the area, and another to calculate the perimeter of the rectangle. Let's call them *area()* and *perimeter().* Now, how about the method interfaces? Well, both methods need the private rectangle length and width members to perform their task. Thus, because they are private members, they do not have to be passed, right? What about return values? Each method must return its calculated value outside the class so *area()* will return the area of the rectangle and *perimeter()* will return the perimeter of the rectangle. The resulting method interfaces can be described as follows:

Method *area()*: Returns the area of a rectangle
Accepts: Nothing
Returns: Area

Method *perimeter()*: Returns the perimeter of a rectangle
Accepts: Nothing
Returns: Perimeter

Notice that both methods do not receive data from outside the class. The rectangle length and width are private members of the class and, therefore, do not need to be passed to the methods. Because the private data and public methods are so tightly bound within the class, you *do not pass the private data to or from the public methods*. We now have enough information to write the UML specifications as follows:

+area():double

+perimeter():double

Next, the two private members are *length* and *width*. We will define these as double floating-point variables. We now have enough information to construct the UML class diagram shown in Figure 8-4.

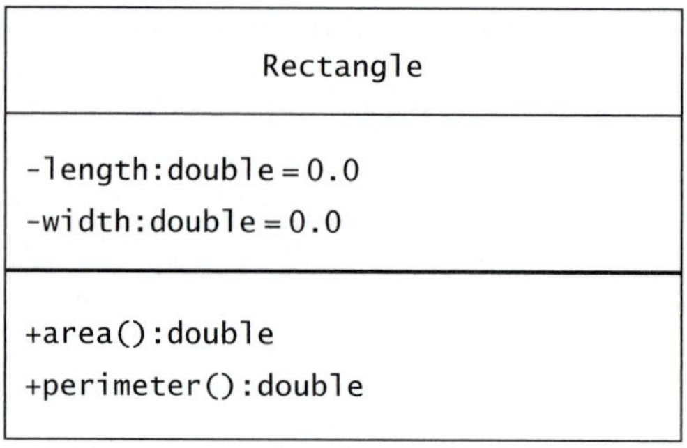

```
                 Rectangle

    -length:double = 0.0
    -width:double = 0.0

    +area():double
    +perimeter():double
```

FIGURE 8-4   A UML class diagram for the *Rectangle* class.

The class is then coded directly from the UML class diagram as follows:

```
class Rectangle
{
    //DATA MEMBERS
    private double length = 0.0;      //RECTANGLE LENGTH
    private double width  = 0.0;      //RECTANGLE WIDTH

    //METHOD MEMBERS
    public double perimeter()         //RETURN PERIMETER
    {
        return 2*(length + width);
    }//END perimeter()

    public double area()         //RETURN AREA
    {
        return length * width;
    }//END area()
}//END Rectangle
```

Example 8-2

Define a *mySavings* object for our *SavingsAccount* class, and a *square* object for our *Rectangle* class.

Solution

The *mySavings* object definition is:

```
SavingsAccount mySavings = new SavingsAccount();
```

The *square* object definition is:

```
Rectangle square = new Rectangle();
```

Neither of these object definitions require any constructor arguments within the parentheses. You will learn all about constructors in the next section. Then, we will define objects that require constructor arguments.

Be aware that not all classes require objects to be defined in order to access the class methods. Remember the standard *Math* class in Java? You access methods of this class by referencing the class name as in *Math.sqrt(x)* rather than first creating an object and then using the object to access the class methods. However, our programmer-defined classes will always require that objects be defined for them.

QUICK CHECK

1. What do we mean when we say that a class defines the behavior of its objects?
2. True or false: Encapsulation ensures information hiding in any language.
3. True or false: The private members of a class can only be accessed from outside the class via the public methods of the same class.
4. Combining data with the operations that are dedicated to manipulating the data so that outside operations cannot affect the data is known as _____.
5. True or false: A class is an encapsulated unit.
6. Information hiding is provided by the _____ members of a class.
7. The behavioral secrets of a class are revealed at the _____ level.

8.2   Special Class Methods

The method members of a class provide the interface to the class objects because the private data within an object can only be manipulated by calling the class methods. Recall that to include a member as part of a class declaration, you list the method header followed by the method body, or ***implementation***. Class methods are generally designated as `public` so they can be called from code outside their resident class. However, class methods can be `private` when they perform special "housekeeping" tasks for the class. Such tasks normally support the operation of a public method. The private class methods are referred to as ***utility methods***, sometimes called ***helper methods***. You will see an example of such a method shortly. Another special type of class method that needs to be discussed now is the ***constructor***.

Constructors

A constructor is a special class method that is used to initialize an object automatically when the object is defined. It is most commonly used to set the private data of the class to initial values, but can also be used to open files, call any special utility methods, and generally get an object ready for processing. The advantage of using a constructor is that the constructor is *called automatically* when an object is defined for the class in which the constructor resides.

 A **constructor** is a special class method that is used to initialize an object automatically when the object is defined.

Here are the rules governing the creation and use of constructors:

- The name of the constructor is always the same as the name of the class.
- The constructor cannot have a return type, not even `void`.
- A class cannot have more than one constructor; however, the constructor is often overloaded.
- Constructors should *not* be developed for tasks other than to initialize an object for processing.

To illustrate how to set up a constructor, we have modified our *SavingsAccount* class declaration as follows:

```
class SavingsAccount
{
  //DATA MEMBERS
  private final double INTEREST_RATE = 2.0;    //ANNUAL INTEREST RATE
  private double balance = 0.0;                //ACCOUNT BALANCE

  //METHOD MEMBERS
  //CONSTRUCTOR
  public SavingsAccount(double bal)
  {
    balance = bal;
  }//END SavingsAccount()

  //ADD DEPOSITS
  public void addDeposit(double amount)
  {
      balance = balance + amount;
  } //END addDeposit()

  //SUBTRACT WITHDRAWAL
  public void subtractWithdrawal(double amount)
  {
      balance = balance - amount;
  }//END subtractWithdrawal()
```

```
//ADD MONTHLY INTEREST
public void addInterest()
{
   balance = balance + balance * INTEREST_RATE;
}//END addInterest

//GET BALANCE
public double getBalance()
{
   return balance;
}//END getBalance()
}//END SavingsAccount
```

This is the declaration for the *SavingsAccount* class that we developed earlier, with one big difference: It includes a constructor. Aside from the comment, you can recognize the constructor because it has the same name as the class and does not have any return type, not even void. The format of the *SavingsAccount()* constructor header is illustrated in Figure 8-5.

Notice the implementation within the body of the constructor. The code shows that the private class member *balance* is being initialized to a value received by the constructor parameter, *bal*.

Now, the next question is: How is the constructor called? Well, the reason for using a constructor over a regular method to initialize an object's data is that the constructor is called automatically when an object is defined. So, let's define two objects for the *SavingsAccount* class and therefore automatically call the constructor.

```
SavingsAccount myAccount = new SavingsAccount(2000.00);
SavingsAccount yourAccount = new SavingsAccount(1000.00);
```

Here, *myAccount* and *yourAccount* are defined as objects of the *SavingsAccount* class. Notice the argument values are passed to each object constructor. What do you suppose happens with these arguments? You're right, the argument values are passed

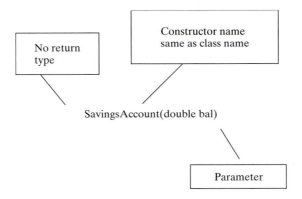

FIGURE 8-5   The format of the *SavingsAccount* class constructor header.

to the constructor, which is automatically called to set the *balance* of *myAccount* to 2000.00, and *yourAccount* to 1000.00.

Example 8-3

Rewrite the *Rectangle* class declaration from Example 8-2 to include a constructor that will initialize the *length* and *width* of the class.

Solution:

Here is the required class code:

```
class Rectangle
{
    //DATA MEMBERS
    private double length = 0.0;          //RECTANGLE LENGTH
    private double width = 0.0;           //RECTANGLE WIDTH

    //METHOD MEMBERS
    //CONSTRUCTOR
    public Rectangle(double l, double w)
    {
        length = l;
        width = w;
    }//END Rectangle()

    //PERIMETER METHOD
    public double perimeter()
    {
        return 2 * (length + width);      //RETURN PERIMETER
    }//END perimeter()

    //AREA METHOD
    public double area()
    {
        return length * width;            //RETURN AREA
    }//END area()
} //END Rectangle
```

Here, the constructor is called *Rectangle()*, which has the same name as the class. The body of the *Rectangle()* constructor shows that the two private class members, *length* and *width*, are being initialized to the values received by the constructor parameters, *l* and *w*, respectively.

Example 8-4

Define two objects for the *Rectangle* class in Example 8-3. Call one object *smallBox* and initialize its length to 4 and width to 3. Call the second object *largeBox* and initialize its length to 20 and its width to 10.

Solution:

```
Rectangle smallBox = new Rectangle(4,3);
Rectangle largeBox = new Rectangle(20,10);
```

Here, *smallBox* and *largeBox* are defined as objects of the *Rectangle* class. Notice that two argument values are passed to each object constructor. The *smallBox* constructor receives the argument values (4,3) and the *largeBox* constructor receives the argument values (20,10). What do you suppose happens with these arguments? You're right; the argument values are passed to the constructor, which is automatically called to set the *length* and *width* of the *smallBox* object to 4 and 3, respectively. Likewise, the *length* and *width* of the *largeBox* object are initialized to the values 20 and 10, respectively. So, the idea is to list the constructor arguments in parentheses after the class name when the object is defined. This passes the arguments to the constructor, which is automatically called to perform its initializing task.

PROGRAMMING NOTE

In the foregoing *Rectangle* class example, the constructor was only used to initialize the private members, *length* and *width*, of the object. It was not used to calculate the perimeter or area of the object. Separate methods were developed for these tasks. Good practice dictates that constructors only be used to initialize the object prior to additional processing by other object methods.

Overloaded Constructors Any method, even a constructor, can be overloaded. Recall from Chapter 7 that an overloaded method is one that performs different tasks depending on the number and/or type of arguments that it receives. Let's overload our *Rectangle()* constructor as follows:

```
class Rectangle
{
    //DATA MEMBERS
    private double length = 0.0;      //RECTANGLE LENGTH
    private double width = 0.0;       //RECTANGLE WIDTH

    //METHOD MEMBERS
    //CONSTRUCTORS
    //THIS CONSTRUCTOR REQUIRES NO ARGUMENTS
    public Rectangle()
    {
    } //END Rectangle()

    //CONSTRUCTOR FOR A SQUARE, REQUIRES ONE ARGUMENT
    public Rectangle(double s)
    {
        length = width = s;
    } //END Rectangle(double)

    //CONSTRUCTOR FOR A RECTANGLE, REQUIRES TWO ARGUMENTS
    public Rectangle(double l, double w)
    {
        length = l;
        width = w;
    }//END Rectangle(double,double)
```

```
    //PERIMETER METHOD
    public double perimeter()
    {
        return 2 * (length + width);    //RETURN PERIMETER
    }//END perimeter()

    //AREA METHOD
    public double area()
    {
        return length * width;          //RETURN AREA
    }//END area()
}//END Rectangle CLASS
```

You are probably thinking that there are three constructors in the foregoing declaration. No, there is a single constructor called *Rectangle()*, which is overloaded. You can tell that the *Rectangle()* constructor is overloaded because it has three different sets of parameters. The first version of the constructor does not have any parameters and, therefore, does not initialize the *length* and *width* members. Such a constructor is sometimes referred to as a **parameterless**, or **default**, constructor. When this constructor is called, the *length* and *width* members each remain at their default values of 0. The second version of the constructor is for a square and the third for a non-square rectangle. The square version of the constructor sets the *length* and *width* members of the rectangle equal to the same value, *s*, that is received when the constructor is called. The non-square version of the constructor sets the *length* and *width* to two different values, *l* and *w*, when the constructor is called. What determines which version of the constructor is used? Well, if an object is created with no arguments, the first version is executed. If an object is created with a single argument, the square constructor is executed. If an object is created with two arguments, the non-square version of the constructor is executed. Here are some sample object definitions:

```
Rectangle box1 = new Rectangle();       //box1 OBJECT DEF
Rectangle box2 = new Rectangle(2);      //box2 OBJECT DEF
Rectangle box3 = new Rectangle(3,4);    //box3 OBJECT DEF
```

Here, three objects, *box1*, *box2*, and *box3*, are defined. Notice that no argument is passed to *box1*, a single argument of 2 is passed to *box2*, and a double argument of 3,4 is passed to the *box3* object. What do you suppose happens? When the *box1* object is defined, its *length* and *width* remain at 0. When the *box2* object is defined, the second constructor is executed, setting the *length* and *width* of the *box2* object to the same value, 2. When the *box3* object is defined, the third constructor is executed, setting its *length* to 3 and the *width* to 4.

Scoping Inside Methods

There can be a problem using a constructor, or any class method for that matter, when the private member names are the same as the method parameter names. For instance, suppose that we declare a simple *Circle* class that contains a private member called *radius*. You then decide to use the *radius* name as a parameter for the constructor. Here is the appropriate class declaration:

```
class Circle
{
    //DATA MEMBERS
    private double radius = 0.0;   //CIRCLE RADIUS

    //CONSTRUCTOR
    public Circle(double radius)   //CONSTRUCTOR
    {
        radius = radius;
    }//END Circle()
}//END Circle
```

The problem arises in the constructor implementation. The implementation will compile; however, it will initialize *radius* to garbage! Look at the statement within the constructor implementation and you will see ambiguity in the use of the *radius* name. It appears that *radius* is being assigned to itself. How does the compiler know what *radius* to use? Is *radius* the variable defined as the private class member, or is *radius* the value received by the constructor, or both? We must tell the compiler that the *radius* on the left side of the assignment operator is the private class member and the *radius* on the right side of the assignment operator is the value received by the constructor. There is a simple way to solve this problem: by using the `this` reference.

The " this" Reference   All objects carry with them a reference to themselves, called `this`, that locates the object that called the method. The use of the `this` reference can be used to prevent ambiguity problems like the one in the foregoing *Circle()* constructor. Here is how the `this` reference is employed in the constructor implementation to solve an ambiguity problem:

```
public Circle(double radius)   //CONSTRUCTOR
{
    this.radius = radius;
}//END Circle()
```

 Every object has an associated `this` reference to itself which is a pointer to the object's address in memory. A pointer is a reference to a physical memory address. Therefore, a given object's `this` pointer locates the object in memory.

The compiler knows that `this` references the object that called the constructor, and it knows what class the object belongs to from the class reference in the object definition. As a result, `this.radius` references the private member *radius* of the *Circle* class. Now there is no ambiguity between the two *radius* names. Notice that the dot operator is employed to apply the `this` reference to the class member.

PROGRAMMING TIP

A simple solution to the use of duplicate names in a program is to make sure that you employ different names to avoid any ambiguity. For instance, the radius of a circle could be named *radius*, *rad*, or *r*, depending on where it is used in the program. Thus, the *Circle()* constructor could be coded like this:

```
public Circle(double r)        //CONSTRUCTOR
{
    radius = r;
}//END Circle()
```

This represents better overall programming style and is less confusing to anyone looking at the code. However, this solution is not always possible in order to keep the code readable and self-documenting. This is why we have introduced the `this` reference at this time. In addition, `this` will become more useful later on when we do more advanced OOP.

Example 8-5

Develop a UML class diagram and declare a *Point* class that defines an (*x,y*) coordinate for a cursor position on the console screen. Provide a constructor to initialize the coordinate when an object is defined for *Point*. The default coordinate should be (0,0). Include a method, called *plot()*, as part of the class that will display the string "Java" at the (*x,y*) coordinate location on the console screen. Finally, code a statement to define an object, *p*, of the *Point* class, and initialize this object to point to the middle of the console screen. Also, write a statement to call the *plot()* method.

Solution

From the problem description the class must contain two private data members, *x* and *y*, along with two public methods: a constructor called *Point()* to initialize the (*x,y*) values, and a method called *plot()* to plot a string at the coordinate location specified by the *x* and *y* data members. First, let's address the method interfaces. The *Point()* constructor must initialize the (*x,y*) values. We must use a default coordinate of (0,0), but we will also allow the constructor to receive a different set of coordinate values when an object is defined. Thus, our constructor interface can be described as follows:

Method *Point()*: Initializes the (*x,y*) coordinate values

Accepts: A value for *x* and a value for *y*

Returns: Nothing

In terms of UML, the specification of this method would be:

+*Point(in x : int, in y : int)*

Remember what this specification means from the UML module in Appendix B? Well, the + means that *Point()* is a public class member. It has two parameters, *x* and *y*, which are both being accepted (*in*) by the method. Both parameters are *int* and there is no return value because this method is a constructor.

Next, the *plot()* method must display a string at a position on the screen specified by the private *x* and *y* values. Since *x* and *y* are members of the class, they are not passed to the method. Also, the method is not returning any values outside the class because it is simply writing to the console screen. The appropriate interface description is simply:

Method *Plot()*:   Displays a string at a given (*x,y*) coordinate on the console screen
Accepts: A value for *x* and a value for *y*
Returns: Nothing

This translates to a UML specification of:

+ plot()

The corresponding UML class diagram is shown in Figure 8-6. Notice that the constructor is listed as the first method in the method section of the diagram.

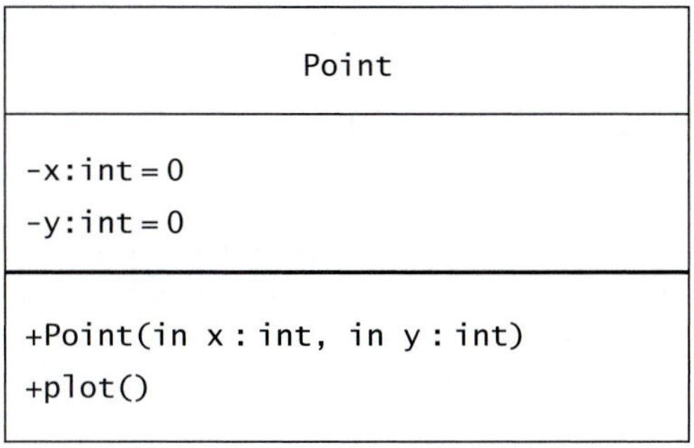

```
                        Point

  -x:int = 0
  -y:int = 0

  +Point(in x : int, in y : int)
  +plot()
```

FIGURE 8-6   A UML class diagram for the *Point* class.

Now, the class can be coded directly from the UML diagram, like this:

```java
//Point CLASS DECLARATION
class Point
{
  //DATA MEMBERS
  private int x = 0;              //X-COORDINATE
  private int y = 0;              //Y-COORDINATE

  //METHOD MEMBERS

  //CONSTRUCTOR
  public Point(int x, int y)
  {
    this.x = x;
    this.y = y;
  }//END Point()

  //PLOT POINT(x,y)
  public void plot()
  {
    for(int i = 0; i < y; ++i)        //MOVE CURSOR DOWN y LINES
      System.out.println();
    for (int i = 0; i < x; ++i)       //MOVE CURSOR OVER x LINES
      System.out.print(' ');
    System.out.println("Java");       //DISPLAY "Java"
  }//END plot()
}//END Point
```

This declaration should be straightforward. The *Point* class consists of two private integer members, *x* and *y*, that will form the coordinate. The default coordinate is (0,0). A constructor is included to initialize the *x* and *y* values to a coordinate received when an object is defined for the class. Notice that the constructor implementation uses the `this` reference to prevent ambiguity between the *x,y* class members and the *x,y* constructor parameters. The *plot()* method uses the *x,y* class members within `for` loops to position the cursor at the (*x,y*) position within the console window. Once the cursor is positioned, the final *println()* statement within the method displays the string "Java" at the cursor position.

A statement to define an object, *p*, of the *Point* class and initialize *p* to point to the middle of the console window is:

```
Point  p = new Point(40,12);
```

This statement defines an object, *p*, and calls the constructor to initialize the (*x,y*) coordinate to (40,12), which is the approximated middle of the console screen. The following statement will call the *plot()* method to move the cursor to the (*x,y*) coordinate position and display the string

```
p.plot();
```

Of course, the *plot()* method doesn't require any arguments because it operates directly from the private members of the object.

Accessor, or *get()*, Methods

Remember that the only way to access the private members of a class are with a public method member of the same class. Even if we simply want to examine the private members of a class object, we need to use a public method that is declared within the same class. Such a method needs to return only the private member(s) to the calling program. Accessor methods, sometimes called **get** methods, are used for this purpose.

 An **accessor**, or **get**, method is a method that returns only the value of a private data member of an object.

Let's revisit one of our earlier *Rectangle* class declarations, adding accessor methods to it, as follows:

```
class Rectangle
{
    //DATA MEMBERS
    private double length = 0.0;    //RECTANGLE LENGTH
    private double width = 0.0;     //RECTANGLE WIDTH

    //METHOD MEMBERS
    //CONSTRUCTORS
    //THIS CONSTRUCTOR REQUIRES NO ARGUMENTS
    public Rectangle()
    {
    }//END Rectangle()
```

```
//CONSTRUCTOR FOR A SQUARE, REQUIRES ONE ARGUMENT
public Rectangle(double side)
{
   length = width = side;
}//END Rectangle(double)

//CONSTRUCTOR FOR A RECTANGLE, REQUIRES TWO ARGUMENTS
public Rectangle(double l, double w)
{
   length = l;
   width = w;
}//END Rectangle(double,double)

//PERIMETER METHOD
public double perimeter()
{
   return 2 * (length + width);        //RETURN PERIMETER
}//END perimeter()

//AREA METHOD
public double area()
{
   return length * width;       //RETURN AREA
}//END area()

//LENGTH ACCESSOR METHOD
public double getLength()
{
   return length;              //GET LENGTH
}//END getLength()

//WIDTH ACCESSOR METHOD
public double getWidth()
{
   return width;               //GET WIDTH
}//END getWidth()
}//END Rectangle
```

Two new accessor methods called *getLength()* and *getWidth()* have been added here to return the *length* and *width* private member values, respectively. The only purpose of an accessor method is to return the value of a private data member, so the implementation requires only a `return` statement as shown. When either of these methods is executed, the respective private member value is returned to the calling program. So, if we define *box* to be an object of *Rectangle*, you can call either accessor method using the dot operator to examine the private data members. For instance, to display the member values of *box*, the accessor methods could be called as part of *println()* statements, like this:

```
System.out.println("The length of the box is:  " + box.getLength());
System.out.println("The width of the box is:  " + box.getWidth());
```

Putting Everything Together in a Complete Program

We now have all the ingredients to build a complete application to test our *Rectangle* class. Here it is:

```java
import staugIO.StaugIO;              //FOR GUI I/O
//Rectangle CLASS DECLARATION
class Rectangle
{
   //DATA MEMBERS
   private double length = 0.0;      //RECTANGLE LENGTH
   private double width = 0.0;       //RECTANGLE WIDTH

   //METHOD MEMBERS
   //CONSTRUCTORS
   //THIS CONSTRUCTOR REQUIRES NO ARGUMENTS
   public Rectangle()
   {
   }//END Rectangle()

   //CONSTRUCTOR FOR A SQUARE, REQUIRES ONE ARGUMENT
   public Rectangle(double side)
   {
     length = width = side;
   }//END Rectangle(double)

   //CONSTRUCTOR FOR A RECTANGLE, REQUIRES TWO ARGUMENTS
   public Rectangle(double l, double w)
   {
      length = l;
      width = w;
   }//END Rectangle(double,double)

   //PERIMETER METHOD
   public double perimeter()
   {
      return 2 * (length + width);        //RETURN PERIMETER
   }//END perimeter()

   //AREA METHOD
   public double area()
   {
      return length * width;       //RETURN AREA
   }//END area()

   //LENGTH ACCESSOR METHOD
   public double getLength()
   {
      return length;               //GET LENGTH
   }//END getLength()

   //WIDTH ACCESSOR METHOD
   public double getWidth()
   {
```

```
        return width;                           //GET WIDTH
    }//END getWidth()
}//END Rectangle
//APPLICATION CLASS DECLARATION
public class RectangleTest
{
  public static void main(String[] args)
  {
  //DEFINE OBJECTS
  Rectangle box1 = new Rectangle();            //box1 OBJECT DEF
  Rectangle box2 = new Rectangle(2);           //box2 OBJECT DEF
  Rectangle box3 = new Rectangle(3,4);         //box3 OBJECT DEF
  StaugIO io = new StaugIO();                  //FOR I/O

  //DISPLAY LENGTH, WIDTH, PERIMETER, AND AREA OF BOX1 OBJECT
  io.writeInfo("The length of box1 is " + box1.getLength()
            + "\nThe width of box1 is " + box1.getWidth()
            + "\nThe perimeter of box1 is " + box1.perimeter()
            + "\nThe area of box1 is " + box1.area());

  //DISPLAY LENGTH, WIDTH, PERIMETER, AND AREA OF BOX2 OBJECT
  io.writeInfo("The length of box2 is " + box2.getLength()
            + "\nThe width of box2 is " + box2.getWidth()
            + "\nThe perimeter of box2 is " + box2.perimeter()
            + "\nThe area of box2 is " + box2.area());

  //DISPLAY LENGTH, WIDTH, PERIMETER, AND AREA OF BOX3 OBJECT
  io.writeInfo("The length of box3 is " + box3.getLength()
            + "\nThe width of box3 is " + box3.getWidth()
            + "\nThe perimeter of box3 is " + box3.perimeter()
            + "\nThe area of box3 is " + box3.area());
  //EXIT PROGRAM
  System.exit(0);
 }//END main()
}//END RectangleTest
```

First, notice the overall structure of the program. Two classes are declared: *Rectangle* and *RectangleTest*. Method *main()* resides within the *RectangleTest* class. Our *Rectangle* class is declared first which includes two private members and five public method members (the single *Rectangle()* constructor is overloaded). The method members consist of an overloaded constructor, a method to return the perimeter of the rectangle, a method to return the area of the rectangle, and two accessor methods to return the length and width of the rectangle. Next, a class called *RectangleTest* is declared. The *RectangleTest* class has a single method, *main()*. Within *main()* you see our *Rectangle* class objects defined and used to call the various methods. Three objects are defined for the *Rectangle* class, and then messages are sent to the objects by calling all their respective methods. Here are the information boxes generated by the program:

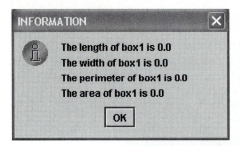

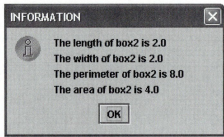

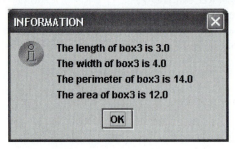

QUICK CHECK

1. A class member that is used specifically to initialize object data is called a(n) _____.

2. How do you know which member of a class is the constructor?

3. True or false: The return type of a constructor is optional.

4. How is a constructor called?

5. True or false: A constructor cannot be overloaded.

6. A method that returns only the values of the private class members is called a(n) _____ method.

7. Write a header for a constructor of a class called *MyClass* that initializes two integer members of the class.

8. Write a statement to define an object called *myObject* for *MyClass* in question 7. Assume that the two integer members of the class must be initialized to the values 5 and 6.

Problem Solving in Action: Baseball Stats

Professional baseball has heard about Java and they have hired you to write a simple program for their pitchers. The program must store the pitcher's name, team, wins, losses, winning percentage, and earned run average (ERA). In addition, a provision must be provided for the user to enter a given pitcher's stats, as well as display a given pitcher's stats. Develop such a program using classes and objects.

The first thing to be done when developing an object-oriented program is to identify the nouns and verbs in the problem statement. Remember, the nouns suggest private data for the class, and the verbs suggest methods for the class. Here is the problem statement again with the important nouns and verbs underlined:

The program must store the pitcher's <u>name</u>, <u>team</u>, <u>wins</u>, <u>losses</u>, <u>winning percentage</u>, and <u>ERA</u>. In addition, provision must be provided for the user to <u>enter</u> a given pitcher's data as well as <u>display</u> a given pitcher's data. Develop such a program using classes and objects.

From the nouns and verbs, we develop a class specification as follows:

Class: *Pitcher*
   Data Members: *name*
                 team
                 wins
                 losses
                 winningPercentage
                 era

   Method Members: *setStats()*
                  getStats()

After analyzing the class members, a UML diagram can be constructed as shown in Figure 8-7.

Notice how the UML diagram shows an overloaded constructor, one parameterless version, one version to initialize just the pitcher's name, and another to initialize all the private member variables. This version of the constructor will initialize all the private members, with the exclusion of *winPercent* which will be calculated by the private *calculateWinPercent()* method shown at the bottom of the diagram. More about this shortly.

```
                              Pitcher

-name:string = ""
-team:string = ""
-wins:int = 0
-losses:int = 0
-winPercent:double = 0.0
-era:double = 0.0

+Pitcher()
+Pitcher(in name:string)
+Pitcher(in name:string, in team:string,
            in wins:int, in losses:int,
            in era:double)
+setStats()
+getStats()
-calculateWinPercent()
```

FIGURE 8-7   A UML class diagram for the *Pitcher* class.

Now, we are ready to code the class. Here it is:

```java
/*
 * Action08_02.java
 *
 * Created on June 28, 2002, 1:37 PM
 */

/**
 *
 * @author  Andrew C. Staugaard, Jr.
 * @version 1.0
 */
import staugIO.StaugIO;           //FOR GUI I/O
class Pitcher
{
  //DATA MEMBERS
  private String name = " ";        //PITCHER'S NAME
  private String team = " ";        //PITCHER'S TEAM
  private int wins = 0;             //NUMBER OF WINS
  private int losses = 0;           //NUMBER OF LOSSES
  private double winPercent = 0.0;  //WIN PERCENTAGE
  private double era = 0.0;         //EARNED RUN AVERAGE
  private StaugIO io = new StaugIO();  //FOR I/O

  //METHOD MEMBERS
  //PARAMETERLESS CONSTRUCTOR
  public Pitcher()
  {
  }//END Pitcher()

  //CONSTRUCTOR THAT INITIALIZES ONLY PITCHER NAME
  public Pitcher(String n)
  {
      name = n;
  }//END Pitcher(String)

  //CONSTRUCTOR THAT INITIALIZES ALL PITCHER DATA EXCEPT WIN %
  public Pitcher(String n,String t, int w, int l, double era)
  {
      name = n;
      team = t;
      wins = w;
      losses = l;
      this.era = era;
      calculateWinPercent();
  }//END Pitcher(String,String,int,int,double)

  //UTILITY METHOD TO CALCULATE winPercent
  private void calculateWinPercent()
  {
      if ((wins + losses) == 0)
          winPercent = 0.0;
```

```
            else
                winPercent = (double)wins/(wins + losses) * 100;    //CASTING
        }//END calculateWinPercent

        //SET PITCHER STATS TO USER ENTRIES
        public void setStats()
        {
            //PROMPT AND READ PITCHER STATS
            name = io.readString("Enter the pitcher's name ");
            team = io.readString("Enter the team for " + name);
            wins = io.readInt("Enter the number of wins for " + name);
            losses = io.readInt("Enter the number of losses for " + name);
            era = io.readDouble("Enter the ERA for " + name);
            calculateWinPercent();
        }//END setStats()

        //GET AND DISPLAY STATS
        public void getStats()
        {
            io.writeInfo("Pitcher name: " + name
                    + "\nTeam: " + team
                    + "\nNumber of wins: " + wins
                    + "\nNumber of losses: " + losses
                    + "\nWinning percentage: " + winPercent
                    + "\nERA: " + era);
        }//END getStats()
}// END pitcher

public class Action08_02 {
    public static void main (String args[])
    {
        Pitcher rogerClemens = new Pitcher();
        rogerClemens.setStats();
        rogerClemens.getStats();

        //EXIT PROGRAM
        System.exit(0);
    }//END main()
}//END Action08_02
```

First, look at the data members of the class. Here you see all the data members that we found in the problem statement. Each member is initialized with a default value and designated as private to enforce information hiding. We have also defined *io* as a private member of the class, since it is used to call the *StaugIO* methods within the *setStats()* and *getStats()* methods.

Next, look at the method members of the class. The first thing you see is an overloaded constructor. The first version of the constructor does not have any arguments and, therefore, will allow an object to be defined without supplying constructor arguments. Of course, if no arguments are supplied, the class data are initialized with their default values. The second version of the constructor requires only the pitcher's name. Notice that the single constructor parameter is a string object. The third version of the constructor requires arguments for each of the data members, except the winning percentage. Thus, values for each argument must be supplied when an object is defined in order for this constructor to execute. When the constructor is executed, the argument values are assigned to their respective data members. But what about the *winPercent* member? Well, the winning percentage is calculated from the *wins* and *losses* members. To accomplish this task, we have created a ***utility*** method called *calculateWinPercent()*. This method calculates the winning percentage using the *wins* and *losses* data members. This is an ideal application for a utility method because it will only be called within the class to calculate the *winPercent* data member and does not need to be called from outside the class. Once values have been assigned to *wins* and *losses* the constructor calls the *calculateWinPercent()* method to initialize the *winPercent* data member.

A ***utility***, or ***helper***, method is a private class method that is called by other class methods to perform internal class "housekeeping" chores.

Now, look at the *calculateWinPercent()* method itself. First, you see that it is a `private` method and, therefore, cannot be called from outside the class. Second, you see that it contains an `if/else` statement. Why? Because if both *wins* and *losses* were zero, a run-time error would occur and the program would crash. So, the `if/else` statement protects against division by zero. Last, you see something that you have not seen before. The statement

```
winPercent = (double)wins/(wins + losses) * 100;     //CAST
```

includes what is called a *cast*. A cast temporarily converts data of one type to a different type. The cast is created by the code `(double)` in the preceding statement. Without the cast to double, the calculation would always be 0. Why? Because *wins* and *losses* are both integers. When you divide two integers, you get an integer. Since `(wins + losses)` will always be greater than *wins*, integer division will always give you a result of 0. The cast forces a double floating-point result, which is what we need for our *winPercent* member. Remember this little trick because it often comes in handy. We should caution you, however, that casting should only be used when completely necessary as in the above application. If you find yourself doing a lot of casting, then you probably have not data-typed your variables properly when they were defined. This is why we have not discussed casting until now.

PROGRAMMING NOTE

A ***cast*** converts data of one type to a different type, temporarily. You can convert data of one type to another type by preceding the data variable/expression with the type to convert to within parentheses like this: `(double)`. The conversion is not permanent since it is only in effect for the statement in which it resides. Casting should be used sparingly, when a legitimate need for its use arises. Too much casting within a program indicates a problem in the way in which the program variables have been typed when they were defined.

The next method, *setStats()*, prompts the user and reads the user entries for the private members. Again, notice that the *calculateWinPercent()* method is called to determine *winPercent* member value after the values for *wins* and *losses* have been entered.

Finally, you see an application class, called *Action08_02*, that includes *main()*. Here is where we test our *Pitcher* class by defining an object for the class and using the object to call methods *setStats()* and *getStats()*. That's it! Now you are ready to build your own object-oriented programs.

This case study summarizes most of what has been covered in the last two sections. Before going on, study the program to make sure that you understand everything in it. Many important OOP concepts are demonstrated here.

Problem Solving in Action: Building OO Programs Using Packages

You have been importing Java packages, such as *staugIO*, into your programs when prewritten classes are needed to perform some task. Java provides packages as a way to group related classes together.

All files that make up a given package must be stored in a directory whose name is the same as the package name. So, the *StaugIO.class* file must be stored in a directory called *staugIO*.

All files that make up a given package must be stored in a directory whose name is the same as the package name.

As you build your programs, it is convenient to create your own packages to hold related classes, just as we created the *staugIO* package to hold the GUI classes. You can compile the classes independently and import them when needed into an application or applet. For example, you might want to create a *SavingsAccount* class and a *CheckingAccount* class and place them in a *banking* package. Well, we're about to do just that! Together, we will create a *banking* package that includes the *SavingsAccount* class that we developed in an earlier case study, and a *CheckingAccount* class to process those types of banking transactions. However, before getting into the details, let's learn a "bit" more about Java packages in general.

Recall that the name of the package directory must be the same name as the package. So, our *banking* package will be placed in a directory called *banking*. This way, when you reference the *SavingsAccount* class of the *banking* package, Java knows to look in the *banking* directory.

As you know, Java was designed to be totally platform independent. To support platform independence, Java requires that the operating system set a *CLASSPATH* variable to determine where to begin looking for user-defined packages. Setting the *CLASSPATH* variable differs between operating systems, such as UNIX versus Windows. In Windows, for example, a *set classpath* statement is required in the *autoexec.bat* file. The parameters for the statement are the path where the user-defined packages will be found. For instance, the statement:

```
set classpath= C:\myPackages
```

would tell Windows to look in the *myPackages* directory for the user-defined package directories. Thus, you would locate your *banking* directory within the *myPackages* directory.

Check your operating system's help for details on setting the *CLASSPATH* variable because the requirements differ between operating systems. Also, check your IDE help since your IDE installation might automatically set the *CLASSPATH* variable for you.

Once we create a package directory, the separate *.java* files will be compiled in the normal way from within this directory. The compiler will produce *.class* files and store them in the package directory. Thus, we will save our *SavingsAccount.java* and *CheckingAccount.java* source files in a *banking* directory and compile these class files independently. The compiler will produce byte-code files called *SavingsAccount.class* and *CheckingAccount.class* and place them in the *banking* directory. We can then write an application or applet program and import these classes using an `import` statement at the beginning of the program.

Package Naming

Sun Microsystems has recommended certain naming conventions for packages in order to encourage consistency within the industry. They are as follows:

- The first word in a package name should begin with a lowercase letter; all subsequent words should begin with an uppercase letter.

- Package names must not begin with the word *java* or *javax* because this is reserved for naming standard Java packages.

- For Internet programs, package names should begin with the Internet domain name, only reversed. Thus, if your Internet domain name is *domain.COM*, your package name should begin with *COM.domain*. So, if you have a package called *myPackage* on your Internet server, the complete package name would be *COM.domain.myPackage*. Notice that *COM* is capitalized. It is suggested that domain categories, such as *COM*, *EDU*, *GOV*, and the like always be capitalized. However, if a package is only for local system use, such a prefix would be inappropriate.

- Always be consistent with case when naming and referring to packages. Windows systems are not case sensitive, but other operating systems, such as UNIX, are case sensitive.

These are only guidelines and the Java compiler does not enforce them. However, when used consistently in developing your programs, you are likely to avoid naming conflicts, especially across multiple systems and platforms.

Now, let's get back to our *banking* package. First we will create two separate classes, *SavingsAccount* and *CheckingAccount*. Each will be placed within its own separate *.java* file within the *banking* directory and compiled independently. The class diagram in Figure 8-8 shows our earlier *SavingsAccount* class. Notice that we have added an overloaded constructor to the interface.

```
                   SavingsAccount

    -balance:double = 0.0
    -INTEREST_RATE:double = 2.0

    +SavingsAccount()
    +SavingsAccount(in balance:double)
    +addDeposit(in amount:double)
    +subtractWithdrawal(in amount:double)
    +addInterest()
    +getBalance():double
```

FIGURE 8-8 The *SavingsAccount* class consists of private *balance* and *INTEREST_RATE* members and public *addDeposit()*, *subtractWithdrawal()*, *addInterest()*, and *getBalance()* methods, as well as a constructor, all of which form the class interface.

Here is the corresponding class code:

```java
package banking;
public class SavingsAccount
{
  //DATA MEMBERS
  private final double INTEREST_RATE = 2.0;   //ANNUAL INTEREST RATE
  private double balance = 0.0;                //ACCOUNT BALANCE

  //METHOD MEMBERS
  //PARAMETERLESS CONSTRUCTOR
  public SavingsAccount()
  {
  }//END SavingsAccount()

  //CONSTRUCTOR TO INITIALIZE BALANCE
  public SavingsAccount(double bal)
  {
    balance = bal;
  }//END SavingsAccount(double)

  //ADD DEPOSITS
  public void addDeposit(double amount)
  {
      balance = balance + amount;
  } //END addDeposit()

  //SUBTRACT WITHDRAWAL
  public void subtractWithdrawal(double amount)
  {
      balance = balance - amount;
  }//END subtractWithdrawal()

  //ADD MONTHLY INTEREST
  public void addInterest()
  {
    balance = balance + balance * INTEREST_RATE/12/100;
  }//END addInterest

  //GET BALANCE
  public double getBalance()
  {
    return balance;
  }//END getBalance()
} //END SavingsAccount
```

There are three major differences between this code and the code we developed earlier. First, and most important, you see the statement

```java
package banking;
```

as the first line in the program. This statement tells Java that the *SavingsAccount* class is part of the *banking* package. Second, you see that we have declared the class public. This allows the class to be accessible outside the package in which it resides. Third, we have an overloaded *SavingsAccount()* constructor. Notice that the first version does not require any arguments, and the second version requires a single argument to initialize *balance*. The remaining parts of the code are the same as the code we used earlier.

 Classes that are part of packages must be declared `public` so that they can be accessed from outside of the package. Declaring a class `public` allows the class to be visible outside the package in which the class resides.

Next, we will "spec-out" our *CheckingAccount* class as follows:

Class: *CheckingAccount*
　　Data Members:　*balance*
　　　　　　　　　　minimum
　　　　　　　　　　charge

　　Method Members:　*addDeposit()*
　　　　　　　　　　　cashCheck()
　　　　　　　　　　　getBalance()

The class has three data members: *balance*, *minimum*, and *charge*. The *balance* is self-explanatory. The *minimum* data member will be the minimum account balance required to avoid a check cashing charge. If the balance goes below this minimum, an additional charge will be added to cash a check. The amount of the charge is stored in the *charge* data member.

The *addDeposit()* method does exactly what is says: adds a deposit to the balance. The *cashCheck()* method subtracts the amount of the check from the balance and also subtracts a check cashing charge, if applicable. Finally, the *getBalance()* method will return the current account balance. The class diagram in Figure 8-9 specifies the *CheckingAccount* class members and interface.

```
+-------------------------------------------------+
|                CheckingAccount                  |
+-------------------------------------------------+
| -balance:double = 0.0                           |
| -minimum:double = 500.00                        |
| -charge:double = 0.5                            |
+-------------------------------------------------+
| +CheckingAccount()                              |
| +CheckingAccount(in balance:double)             |
| +addDeposit(in amount:double)                   |
| +cashCheck(in amount:double)                    |
| +getBalance():double                            |
+-------------------------------------------------+
```

FIGURE 8-9　The *CheckingAccount* class consists of private *balance*, *minimum*, and *charge* members along with public *addDeposit()*, *cashCheck()*, and *getBalance()* methods, as well as a constructor, all of which form the class interface.

Here's the corresponding class code:

```java
package banking;
import staugIO.StaugIO;        //FOR StaugIO CLASS
public class CheckingAccount
{
  //DATA MEMBERS
  private double balance = 0.0;        //ACCOUNT BALANCE
  private double minimum = 500.00;     //MINIMUM BALANCE TO
                                       //AVOID CHECK CHARGE
  private double charge = 0.5;         //PER-CHECK CHARGE
  private StaugIO io = new StaugIO();   //FOR I/O

  //METHOD MEMBERS
  //CONSTRUCTORS
  //PARAMETERLESS CONSTRUCTOR
  public CheckingAccount()
  {
  }//END CheckingAccount()

  //INITIALIZE balance
  public CheckingAccount(double bal)
  {
      balance = bal;
  }//END CheckingAccount(double)

  //INITIALIZE balance, minimum, AND charge
  public CheckingAccount(double bal, double min, double chg)
  {
      balance = bal;
      minimum = min;
      charge = chg;
  }//END CheckingAccount(double,double,double)

  //ADD DEPOSIT
  public void addDeposit(double amount)
  {
      balance = balance + amount;
  } //END addDeposit()

  //CASH A CHECK
  public void cashCheck(double amt)
  {
    //TEST FOR OVERDRAW
    if (amt > balance)
      io.writeInfo("Cannot cash check, account overdrawn.");

    //CASH CHECK
    else
      //CHECK FOR MINIMUM BALANCE
      if (balance < minimum)
        balance = balance - (amt + charge);        //DEBIT BALANCE WITH
```

```
                                                    //CHECK AMOUNT
                                                    //AND CHARGE
        else                                        //DEBIT BALANCE WITH
            balance = balance - amt;                //CHECK AMOUNT
   } //END cashCheck()

   //RETURN BALANCE
   public double getBalance()
   {
     return balance;
   }//END getBalance()
} //END CheckingAccount
```

Most of this code should be self-explanatory by now. Again you see the package statement as the first line in the program. You also see that the class is declared as a public class. Why? Look at the *cashCheck()* method. Notice that it receives an amount (*amt*) from the calling object and generates an error message if this amount exceeds the account balance. Otherwise, the check is cashed, and the account balance is debited accordingly. Notice that a check-cashing charge is applied if the amount of the check is less than the required minimum balance.

Once the *banking* package classes are coded, they must be compiled to produce byte-code *.class* files in the package folder so that they can be imported into other applications. The last thing we need to do is create an application that tests our banking classes. In this program, we must import the *banking* package and create objects of the banking classes. We can then write statements to process banking transactions and generate a report using the class methods. Here is such a program:

```
/*
 * Action08_03.java
 *
 * Created on July 1, 2002, 8:20 AM
 */

/**
 *
 * @author  Andrew C. Staugaard, Jr.
 * @version 1.0
 */
import banking.CheckingAccount;      //FOR  CheckingAccount CLASS
import banking.SavingsAccount;       //FOR  SavingsAccount CLASS
import staugIO.StaugIO;             //FOR I/O CLASS
import java.text.NumberFormat;      //FOR CURRENCY FORMATTING

public class Action08_03
{
  public static void main(String[] args)
  {

    //CREATE BANKING OBJECTS
    SavingsAccount GraceHopper1 = new SavingsAccount(5000);
    CheckingAccount GraceHopper2 = new CheckingAccount(2000);
```

```
                 //CREATE KEYBOARD OBJECT
                 StaugIO io = new StaugIO();

                 //PROCESS TRANSACTIONS
                 GraceHopper1.subtractWithdrawal(501.25);
                 GraceHopper1.addDeposit(300.52);
                 GraceHopper2.cashCheck(200);
                 GraceHopper2.addDeposit(352.90);
                 GraceHopper2.cashCheck(25.37);

                 //CREATE CURRENCY OBJECT
                 NumberFormat currency = NumberFormat.getCurrencyInstance();

                 //GENERATE STATEMENT
                 io.writeInfo("Your savings account balance is: $"
                             + currency.format(GraceHopper1.getBalance()));
                 io.writeInfo("Your checking account balance is: $"
                             + currency.format(GraceHopper1.getBalance()));

               //EXIT PROGRAM
               System.exit(0);
         }//END main()
}//END Action08_03 CLASS
```

The first thing you see are import statements that import our two classes from the *banking* package. The application class name is *Action08_03* and, therefore, the application file name is *Action08_03.java*. The class has one method, *main()*. Within *main()* you see that we have defined two objects, *GraceHopper1* and *GraceHopper2*, as objects of our imported *SavingsAccount* class and *CheckingAccount* class, respectively. When each object is defined, a single argument is provided which will initialize the respective account balances. Then, several transactions are made by calling the various class methods. Finally, each object calls its *getBalance()* method to report the balance after the account transactions were processed. Here is the output produced by the program:

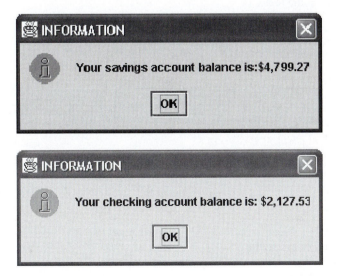

As you can now see, method *main()* simply acts as a coordinator, or control panel, for objects within a Java application. Objects are created in *main()* and messages are sent to those objects via calls to the object methods. Make sure to review the foregoing package and application code to assure that you understand all the coding details. From now on, many of our applications will be built using packages.

 The real purpose of method *main()* in a Java application is to act as a coordinator, or control panel, for objects that make up the program. It is the entry point for the execution of the application.

Project Managers

Most commercial Java IDEs on the market today allow you to build your own multifile programs easily. By a multifile program, we mean one which links several packages and classes together to build a complete workable program using a ***project manager***. When using a project manager, you specify the files required to build an application. This information is kept by the compiler in a ***project file***.

 A ***project file*** identifies the files that need to be compiled and linked to create a workable Java program.

In the foregoing banking program we had three separate source files: *SavingsAccount.java*, *CheckingAccount.java*, and *Action08_03.java*. Using a project manager, you code and compile the banking account class files separately, then open a project. Once a project is open, you can add and delete class files and packages to and from the project. For this project, all we did was add the *Action08_03.java* application file. When the project manager detected the `import` statement in this file, it added the *banking* package class files to the project. Figure 8-10 illustrates the composition of our project.

At this point, it might be a good idea to build, compile, and execute your own project for the banking program, using the code we developed and your IDE project manager. The source code can be found on the text CD.

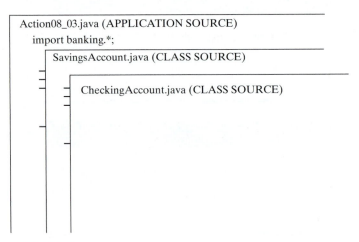

FIGURE 8-10   A project includes all the files needed to create a workable Java program.

CHAPTER SUMMARY

Object-oriented programs are developed from the inside out by using inheritance to expand simple classes. The fundamental components of any object-oriented program are the class and its objects. At the abstract level, a class can be described as an interface because its methods provide a boundary and define the behavior common to all of its objects. At the implementation level, a class is a syntactical programming construct that describes a set of data and related operations that are common to its objects. The abstract level provides an outside view of a class, whereas the implementation level provides the inside view of the class, disclosing its behavioral secrets. At the implementation level, a class is comprised of public and private members. The private class members are hidden from the outside, because they can only be accessed using the public method members. This provides for information hiding within the class.

Encapsulation is the idea of packaging things together in a well-defined programming unit. A COBOL record is encapsulated because it consists of a collection of data members. A class in Java is also encapsulated, because it consists of a collection of data members and related methods. However, a COBOL record does not provide information hiding, whereas a Java class does enforce information hiding through its private members.

An object is an instance, or occurrence, of a class. Thus, an object of a given class has the attributes and behavior defined by the class. The private data of a given object provide for the object attributes, while the public methods of the object provide for the behavior of the object.

There are various types of class methods, including constructors, utility methods, and accessor methods. It is the class methods that provide a means of communication with objects defined for the class. Messages are sent to an object by calling its methods to perform a given task on the hidden object data. The object responds via the values returned by the method members. A constructor is a special class method that is called automatically when an object is defined for the class. Constructors are used to initialize class data. A utility method is a private method that is called by other class methods in order to perform "housekeeping" chores for the class. An accessor method is a *get* method used to gain access to the private data of an object.

Java object-oriented programs are normally constructed using packages. A package is a directory where related classes are stored. To designate a class as part of a package you must place a `package` statement that provides the package name as the first line in the class source code. The class file must then be placed in the package folder. To include a package in a Java program, you simply use the `import` statement. Once a package is imported, you can create and manipulate objects for the classes declared within the package.

Most commercial Java IDEs include a project manager that makes it easier to build Java programs. When using the project manager, you specify all the files required to build an application. This information is kept in a project file. A project file identifies the files that need to be compiled to create a workable Java program. Typically, the project file will identify the application and class source files required for the program.

QUESTIONS AND PROBLEMS

Questions

1. Define the following OOP terms:

   Class at the abstract level
   Class at the implementation level
   Encapsulation
   Information hiding
   Object

> Instance
> Member
> Instance variable
> Instance method
> Set method
> Get method
> Constructor
> Accessor method
> Utility method
> Overloaded constructor
> Message

2. What are the two things that make up a class declaration?

3. What is the scope of a `private` class member?

4. What is the scope of a `public` class member?

5. The concept of combining data with a set of operations that are dedicated to manipulating the data so tightly that outside operations cannot affect the data is called _____.

6. A computer window can be considered an object of a window class. What data and operations might be part of this object?

7. True or false: Only `public` members of a given class can access the `private` members of that class.

8. Why are classes *declared* and objects *defined*?

9. True or false: Utility methods are declared as `private` methods.

10. At the abstract level, a class can be described as a(n) _____ that defines the behavior of its objects.

11. At the implementation level, a class consists of _____ and _____ members.

12. True or false: The abstract view of a class provides its inside view, showing the secrets of its data organization and method implementation.

13. What is meant by the term "behavior" relative to a class object?

14. OOP provides an important feature called _____, which is a mechanism for deriving new classes from existing ones.

15. A method that simply returns the value of a class data member is called a(n) _____ method.

16. What is the purpose of a constructor?

17. Write a constructor for a class called *MyClass* that does not initialize any members of the class.

18. Define an object called *myObject* for the class in question 17.

19. How do you provide default values for the `private` data members of a class?

20. A `private` method of a class is often called a(n) _____ method.

Use the following class declaration to answer questions 21–27:

```
class Student
{
  //DATA MEMBERS
  private String name = " ";          //STUDENT NAME
  private String major = " ";         //STUDENT MAJOR
```

```
  private String studentNumber = 0;    //STUDENT NUMBER
  private double gpa = 0.0;             //STUDENT GPA

  //METHOD MEMBERS
  //CONSTRUCTOR WITH NO INITIALIZING VALUES
  public Student()
  {
  }//END Student()

  //CONSTRUCTOR WITH INITIALIZING VALUES
  public Student(String nam, String maj, String num, double gpa)
  {
    name = nam;
    major = maj;
    studentNumber = num;
    this.gpa = gpa;
  }//END Student

  //INITIALIZE FROM USER ENTRIES
  public void setStats()
  {

  }//END setStats()

  //ACCESSOR STUDENT DATA
  public void getStats()
  {

  }//END getStats()
} //END Student
```

21. What is the name of the constructor?

22. Write a statement to define a student named John Doe as a student object that will be initialized to the default values in the class.

23. Jane Doe (student #456) is a Computer Information Systems major with a GPA of 3.58. Write a statement to define Jane Doe as a student object that will be initialized to the proper data values.

24. Write statements for the *setStats()* method that will allow the user to enter the data values from the keyboard.

25. Write a statement that will allow the user to initialize the Jane Doe object from the keyboard.

26. Write statements for the *getStats()* method, assuming that this method will display the student data.

27. Write a statement that will display the data in a Jane Doe student object.

28. Why does defining a data member of a class as public defeat the concept of information hiding?

29. True or false: A constructor never has a return type, not even void.

30. Suppose that you have a class called *Circle*. What will be the corresponding constructor name?

31. Given the following method implementation:

```
public Dogs(int legs)
{
   legs = legs;
}//END Dogs()
```

   a. What special type of method is this?
   b. What problem would the compiler encounter when attempting to compile this method?
   c. Rewrite the method to correct any problems.

32. What operator is used to send a message to an object?

33. Explain why you should use packages when developing Java programs.

34. A package called *accounting* must be stored in a directory called _____.

Problems

Least Difficult

   1. Write an application to test the *SavingsAccount* class developed in this chapter.

   2. Develop a class called *Address* to store a person's name and address. The address should be divided into separate fields of street, city, state, and zip code. In addition, a provision must be provided for the user to enter a given person's name and address as well as display a given person's data. Write an application program to test your *Address* class.

   3. Professional basketball has heard about Java and they have hired you to write a program for their players' statistics. The program must store the player's name, team, total points scored, number of games played, average points per game, number of assists, number of rebounds, and average field goal percentage. In addition, a provision must be provided for the user to enter a given player's stats as well as display a given player's stats. Develop a class called *Basketball* to accomplish this task. Write an application program to test your *Basketball* class.

More Difficult

   4. The Java-Mart CEO was reading the latest issue of *The Wall Street Journal* and ran across an article on OOP. She became so excited that she contracted you to write an object-oriented payroll program. She wants the program to include an *Employee* class to store the employee's name, hourly rate, and hours worked. The class is to have operations that perform the following tasks:

   - An operation to initialize the hourly rate to a minimum wage of $6.00 per hour and the hours worked to 0 when an employee object is defined

   - An operation to get the employee's name, hourly rate, and hours worked from the user

   - An operation to return weekly pay, including overtime pay, where overtime is paid at a rate of time-and-a-half for any hours worked over 40

   - An operation to display all the employee information, including the employee's pay for a given week

   Develop the class and write an application to test it.

Most Difficult

5. Develop a class called *Invoice* to process one line of an invoice. Assume that the invoice must include the following data and operations:

> *Data*:
>> Quantity Ordered
>> Quantity Shipped
>> Part Number
>> Part Description
>> Unit Price
>> Extended Price (Qty. Ordered * Unit Price)
>> Sales Tax rate
>> Sales Tax amount
>> Shipping
>> Total

> *Operations*:

> - An operation to initialize all the data items to 0, except the sales tax rate, which should be initialized to 7%
> - An operation to allow the user to initialize all the data items from the keyboard
> - An operation to calculate the extended price of the item
> - An operation to calculate the sales tax amount of the item
> - An operation to calculate the total amount of the invoice
> - An operation to display the invoice data with header information in a businesslike format in an information window

Write an application to test your *Invoice* class.

6. Develop a class called *Clock* that provides a 12-hour clock to store hours, minutes, seconds, A.M., and P.M. Provide methods to perform the following tasks:

- Set hours, minutes, seconds to 00:00:00 by default.
- Initialize hours, minutes, seconds, A.M., and P.M. from user entries.
- Allow the clock to tick by advancing the seconds by one and at the same time correcting the hours and minutes for a 12-hour clock value of A.M. or P.M.
- Display the time in hours:minutes:seconds A.M./P.M. format.

Write an application that allows the user to set the clock and tick the clock at 1-second intervals while displaying the time.

7. Add an *InterestChecking* class to the *banking* package developed in this chapter. An interest checking account is simply an interest-bearing checking account. Assume that interest will be credited to the account at the end of each month if the balance exceeds $1000. Write an application to test your *InterestChecking* class.

Object-Oriented Programming—Part II

OBJECTIVES

When you are finished with this chapter, you should have a good understanding of the following:

- The concepts of inheritance, polymorphism, and dynamic binding
- Why inheritance is important to OOP
- How to build class families within Java packages
- When to declare a class as a `public` class
- How to call a superclass constructor within a subclass constructor
- The difference between static and dynamic binding
- The difference between overloaded methods and polymorphic methods
- When and how to use `abstract` classes and methods

Introduction

One of the most important properties of OOP is *inheritance*. In fact, some believe that a program that doesn't employ inheritance is not an object-oriented program.

Inheritance is that property of OOP that allows one class, called a **subclass**, to share the structure and behavior of another class, called a **superclass**.

The natural world is full of inheritance. All living things inherit the characteristics, or traits, of their ancestors. Although you are different in many ways from your parents, you are also the same in many ways because of the genetic traits that you have inherited from them. In OOP, inheritance allows newly created classes to inherit members from existing classes. These new **subclasses** will include their own members and members inherited from the **superclass**. You can view a collection of classes with common inherited members as a *family* of classes, just like the family to which you belong. Classes are related to each other through inheritance. Such inheritance creates a class family hierarchy.

This chapter will focus mostly on the concept of inheritance. We will first explain why inheritance is important and then illustrate its use via a practical example. Finally, we will discuss two more important aspects of OOP: *polymorphism* and *dynamic binding*.

9.1   Why Use Inheritance?

One reason to use inheritance is that it allows you to reuse the code from a previous programming project without starting from scratch to reinvent the code. Many times the code developed for one program can be reused in another program. Although the new program might be slightly different from the old, inheritance allows you to build on what was done previously. Why reinvent the wheel?

Another reason for using inheritance is that it allows you to build a *hierarchy* among classes. The classes that include those things that are most commonly inherited are at the top of the hierarchy, just as your ancestors are at the top of your genetic family hierarchy. Take a banking situation, for example. A general bank account class is used to define variables, such as an account number and account balance, and methods, such as deposit, that are common to all bank accounts. Then, classes that define a regular checking account, an interest-bearing checking account, and savings account can all be derived from the bank account *superclass*. This way, they will inherit the account number and balance members as well as the deposit method of the general bank account class. Although the subclasses may have their own unique members, they all include the bank account superclass as part of their structure and behavior. Thus, a general bank account class would be at the top of a banking class hierarchy. This idea is illustrated by the UML hierarchy diagram in Figure 9-1. In fact, the left side of the hierarchy diagram

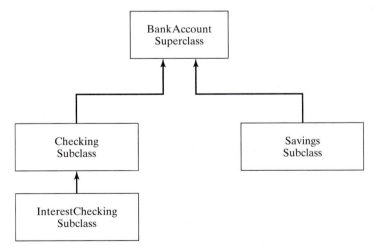

FIGURE 9-1   The *Checking* and *Savings* classes are extended from the *BankAccount* superclass, which has data and methods common to both of these subclasses. The *InterestChecking* class is derived from the *Checking* class and will inherit data and methods from both the *Checking* and *BankAccount* classes.

in Figure 9-1 shows two levels of inheritance. The *BankAccount* class is inherited by both the *Checking* class and the *Savings* class. In addition, the *Checking* class is inherited by the *InterestChecking* class. Notice that the *InterestChecking* class inherits the *BankAccount* class indirectly through the *Checking* class. A family of classes related like this is referred to as a ***class hierarchy***.

THINK!

The important relationship between a subclass and its superclass is the IS-A relationship. The IS-A relationship must exist if inheritance is used properly. For instance, a checking account IS-A bank account. An interest-bearing checking account IS-A checking account. However, a savings account IS **NOT** A checking account; it IS-A banking account. Thus, a savings account should not be derived from a checking account but from a more general bank account class. Always consider the IS-A relationship when creating inheritance. If there is no IS-A relationship, inheritance should not be used.

QUICK CHECK

1. A class which is inherited is called a(n) _____ class.
2. A class which inherits another class is called a(n) _____ class.
3. A collection of classes with common inherited members is called a(n) _____.
4. List at least two reasons for using inheritance.
5. The important link between a subclass and its superclass is the _____ link.
6. True or false: The proper use of inheritance would allow a line class to be derived from a point class.
7. True or false: The proper use of inheritance would allow a pixel class to be derived from a point class.
8. True or false: The proper use of inheritance would allow a pick-up truck class to be derived from a truck class.

9.2   Building a Class Family

A subclass is declared using the following format:

FORMAT FOR DECLARING SUBCLASSES

```
class subclass name extends superclass name
{
    Subclass Data Members

    Subclass Method Members
}//END CLASS
```

Let's illustrate inheritance via the classes of bank accounts shown in Figure 9-1. Look at the figure again. You see that the *Checking* and *Savings* classes are derived directly from the *BankAccount* superclass, and the *InterestChecking* class is derived indirectly from the *BankAccount* superclass through the *Checking* class. Here is how we will set up the various account classes.

BankAccount Class

The *BankAccount* class is at the top of the hierarchy diagram and, therefore, will be the superclass for the entire family. It will contain data and methods that are common to all types of bank accounts. The composition of this class will be as follows:

Data Members
- An account number
- The account holder's name
- An account balance

Method Members
- A constructor to initialize the account data members
- A method to make deposits
- A method to access the account number
- A method to access the account holder's name
- A method to access the account balance

Why do you suppose a deposit method is included in the superclass? Well, any type of bank account allows for a deposit where the deposit amount is simply added to the balance, right? Thus, a deposit operation is common to all bank accounts, just as an account number, account holder's name, and balance are common to all accounts. When developing a superclass, you include those data and operations that are common to all classes within the family. So, you're thinking that a withdrawal operation is also common to all types of bank accounts? Well, it is but each different type of account might withdraw funds a different way. For instance, a checking account withdrawal might add a check cashing charge, whereas a savings account withdrawal might not. Thus, each derived bank account class will have its own unique withdrawal method.

 Look for *commonality* across a class family when deciding what attributes (data) and behaviors (methods) need to be members of a superclass. The things that are common to all class members should be in the superclass.

Checking Account Class

The *Checking* account class will inherit the *BankAccount* class members. In addition, it will contain the following members:

Data Members
- A minimum balance value that will dictate when a per check charge is to be made
- A value that will be charged on each check cashed when the account balance is less than the minimum required balance

Method Members

- A constructor to initialize the *Checking* account data members
- A method that will cash a check by receiving a check amount and debit the account balance accordingly

Interest-Bearing Checking Account Class

An interest-bearing checking account is a checking account which earns interest when its balance remains above a certain minimum requirement. As a result, this class will inherit the *Checking* account class members and therefore will also inherit the *BankAccount* class members. In addition, the *InterestChecking* account class will contain the following members:

Data Members

- An annual interest rate value that is credited to the account balance on a monthly basis, if the account balance remains above a minimum required level

Method Members

- A constructor to initialize the *InterestChecking* checking account data members
- A method that will credit interest to the account if the balance is above the required minimum

Savings Account Class

The savings account class is derived from the original *BankAccount* superclass. In addition to the *BankAccount* class members, the *Savings* account class will contain the following:

Data Members

- An annual interest rate value that is credited to the account balance on a monthly basis

Method Members

- A constructor to initialize the *Savings* account data members
- A method that will credit interest to the account
- A method that will debit the account for a withdrawal

Now, we begin our program construction by developing the UML *BankAcccount* class diagram shown in Figure 9-2.

The data members of the class are *accountNumber*, *name*, and *balance*. Notice that they are designated as **protected members** by the leading # symbol as required by the UML.

A **protected member** of a class is a member that is accessible to both the superclass and any subclasses of the superclass in which it is declared. Thus, a protected member of a class is accessible to any descendent subclass within the class family, but not accessible to non-descendent classes in the family or classes outside the class family.

```
                          BankAccount

 #accountNumber:string
 #name:string
 #balance:double

 +BankAccount(in acctNum:string, in name:string, in bal:double)
 +deposit(in amount:double)
 +getName():string
 +getAcctNum():string
 +getBalance():double
```

FIGURE 9-2   The UML class diagram for the *BankAccount* superclass shows that the class consists of protected *accountNumber*, *name*, and *balance* members along with a public constructor, and public *deposit()*, *getNumber()*, *getName()* and *getBalance()* methods that form the class interface.

You could say that a protected member of a superclass has accessibility that is somewhere between that of a private member and a public member. If a member is a private member of a class, it is *not* accessible to a subclass. However, a protected member of a class is accessible to any descendent subclasses. On the other hand, a protected member is "protected" from being accessed by non-descendent subclasses of the same family or by classes outside of the class family, thereby preserving information within a family line.

The public methods are *BankAccount()*, *deposit()*, *getAcctNum()*, *getName()* and *getBalance()*. The *BankAccount()* constructor has three parameters which will be used to initialize the three data members. The *deposit()* method will be used to make a deposit to the account. It has a single parameter which is the amount to be deposited. The *getAcctNum()*, *getName()*, and *getBalance()* methods are accessor methods that are used to return the account number, name, and balance, respectively.

The class declaration is now easily coded from the UML diagram, as follows:

```java
package bankAccounts;

//SUPERCLASS FOR ALL BANK ACCOUNTS
public class BankAccount
{
  //DATA MEMBERS
  protected String accountNumber;    //ACCOUNT NUMBER
  protected String name;             //ACCOUNT HOLDER
  protected double balance;          //ACCOUNT BALANCE

  //METHOD MEMBERS

  //CONSTRUCTOR TO INITIALIZE DATA MEMBERS
  public BankAccount(String acctNum,String nam,double bal)
  {
```

```
      accountNumber = acctNum;
      name = nam;
      balance = bal;
   } //END BankAccount(String,String,double)

   //deposit() METHOD
   public void deposit(double amount)
   {
      balance = balance + amount;
   } //END deposit()

   //getAcctNum() ACCESSOR METHOD
   public String getAcctNum()
   {
      return  accountNumber;      //RETURN ACCOUNT NUMBER
   } //END getAcctNum()

   //getName() ACCESSOR METHOD
   public String getName()
   {
      return name;                //RETURN ACCOUNT NAME
   }//END getName()

   //getBalance() ACCESSOR METHOD
   public double getBalance()
   {
      return  balance;            //RETURN ACCOUNT BALANCE
   } //END getBalance()
} //END BankAccount
```

First, you see that the class declaration is part of a package called *bankAccounts*. The *bankAccounts* package will be used to hold all of our bank account classes. Notice that our *BankAccount* class is declared as a public class. When a class is public, it can be inherited outside the package in which it resides. To provide maximum inheritance flexibility, we will designate all our package classes as public. This way they can be inherited by any class outside the *bankAccounts* package so that a client application programmer using this package could create his/her own subclasses if needed. Now, looking inside the class declaration, you see that it contains the three protected data members and five public method members specified in the UML diagram.

 THINK!

You will avoid confusion about when to use the keywords private, protected, and public relative to inheritance if you remember the following points:

- Use the keyword private when declaring a member of a class if you do not want that member of the class to be inherited by another class. A private class member is only accessible from outside the class by public methods of the same class.

- Use the keyword protected when declaring a member of a class if you want to allow access to that member by a subclass. A protected member will be accessible within all descendent subclasses of the class in which it is defined but not to non-descendent family classes or classes outside the class family.

- Use the keyword `public` when declaring a member if you want that member to be accessible anywhere the class is visible. Of course, data members should never be declared `public`; otherwise, the whole purpose of information hiding is defeated.
- Use the keyword `public` when declaring a class if you want the class to be inheritable outside the package in which it resides.

The `private`, `protected`, and `public` options in Java are provided for flexibility during inheritance and packaging. With the proper use of these options, you can specify precisely which class members are to be inherited by other classes. If you *do not* want a member of a class inherited, declare it as `private`. If you *do* want a member of a class inherited, declare it as `protected` or `public`. If you *do not* want a class in a package to be inheritable outside the package, do not use the keyword `public` in the class declaration. If you *do* want a class to be inheritable outside its package, declare it as `public`.

Another option that you will have for both classes and class members relative to inheritance is declaring them as `final`. A `final` class cannot be extended by another class even in the same class family, or package. A `final` data or method member cannot be overridden in a subclass. In other words, you can redefine a non-final member of a class in a subclass and the subclass method will override the superclass definition. However, a `final` member of a class can never be redefined, or overridden, in a subclass.

Now, let's declare our first subclass. This class, called *Checking,* will be derived from the *BankAccount* class. The UML diagram in Figure 9-3 describes the class. Here you see two protected data members, *minimum* and *charge,* as well as an overloaded *Checking()* constructor and the *cashCheck()* method.

```
                              Checking

   #minimum:double = 500.0
   #charge:double = 0.5

   +Checking()

   +Checking(in acctNum:string, in name:string, in bal:double)

   +Checking(in acctNum:string, in name:string, in bal:double,
             in min:double, in chg:double)

   +cashCheck(in amount:double)
```

FIGURE 9-3 The *Checking* subclass inherits the *BankAccount* superclass members and adds its own protected members of *minimum* and *charge* as well as an overloaded constructor and a public method called *cashCheck().*

The UML class diagram leads to the Java code, as follows:

```java
package bankAccounts;
//SUBCLASS Checking INHERITS BankAccount CLASS
public class Checking extends BankAccount
{
  //DATA MEMBERS
  protected double minimum = 500.0;   //MINIMUM BALANCE TO
                                      //AVOID CHECK CHARGE
  protected double charge = 0.5;      //PER CHECK CHARGE

  //METHOD MEMBERS
  //PARAMETERLESS CONSTRUCTOR
  public Checking()
  {
   super("0000"," ",0.0);
  }//END Checking()

  //CONSTRUCTOR TO INITIALIZE ACCOUNT NUMBER, NAME, AND BALANCE
  public Checking(String acctNum, String nam, double bal)
  {
   super(acctNum,nam,bal);
  }//END Checking(String,String,double)

  //CONSTRUCTOR TO INITIALIZE ALL PRIVATE DATA
  public Checking(String acctNum, String nam, double bal,
                  double min, double chg)
  {
    super(acctNum,nam,bal);
    minimum = min;
    charge = chg;
  } //END Checking(String,String,double,double,double)

  //cashCheck() METHOD
  public void cashCheck (double amt)
  {
    if (amt > balance)                 //TEST FOR OVERDRAW
      System.out.println("Cannot cash check, account overdrawn.");
    else                               //CASH CHECK
      if (balance < minimum)           //CHECK FOR MIN BALANCE
        balance = balance - (amt + charge);
      else
        balance = balance - amt;
  } //END cashCheck()
}//END Checking
```

First, you see that this class is part of our *bankAccounts* package because of the statement package bankAccounts; . Now, looking at the class declaration, you see that the *Checking* class is derived from the *BankAccount* class. This is indicated by the class header line which includes the code extends BankAccount. The keyword extends is used to tell Java that this class is to be derived from the *BankAccount class*. You see that the *Checking* class has two protected data members, *minimum* and *charge*. The *minimum* data member will be used to store a minimum balance value, whereby no per-check charge is made if the account balance is greater than or equal to the stored minimum value. The *charge* data member will be used to store a per-check charge for writing checks if the account balance is less than *minimum*. Notice that both *minimum* and *charge* are designated as protected members, because they will be inherited by the *InterestChecking* class (see Figure 9-1). Also, observe that each data member has a default value. Of course, because *Checking* is derived from *BankAccount*, the protected *BankAccount* class members of *accountNumber*, *name*, and *balance* are inherited by the *Checking* class. Thus, *Checking* actually has five data members, *accountNumber*, *name*, and *balance*, which are inherited from *BankAccount*, as well as *minimum* and *charge* which are declared in *Checking*.

Two method members are declared for the *Checking* class: *Checking()* and *cashCheck()*. The *Checking()* method is an overloaded constructor. The first version is a ***parameterless*** constructor. The parameterless constructor is executed when an object is created without supplying any arguments in the object definition. You see that its body contains a statement that you haven't seen before, as follows:

```
super("0000"," ",0.0);
```

This statement tells the compiler to call the superclass constructor. The keyword `super` calls the superclass constructor, which requires three arguments to initialize the *accountNumber*, *name*, and *balance*. Here, we have supplied arguments of "0000", " ", and 0.0 to initialize *accountNumber*, *name*, and *balance*, respectively. Maybe you noticed in the *BankAccount* class declaration that we did not initialize its data members. This is because they will be initialized automatically by a call to the superclass constructor within a subclass constructor when any object is created for a subclass. The superclass constructor is not inherited by the subclass but can be called by the subclass constructor using the keyword `super`. One thing you need to remember is that the call to the superclass constructor must be the first statement in the subclass constructor.

A superclass constructor is called by a subclass constructor using the keyword `super` and supplying the argument values required by the superclass constructor. The call to the superclass constructor must be the first statement in the subclass constructor.

Now, look at the second version for the *Checking()* constructor. Do you see what it is doing? You're right if you thought that it is initializing the *accountNumber*, *name*, and *balance* data members with values received by the constructor. Notice that these values are passed on to the superclass constructor via the `super(acctNum,nam,bal)` call. How about the third version of the constructor? Here you see the *accountNumber*, *name*, and *balance* being initialized by calling the superclass constructor, followed by assignments to *minimum* and *charge* to initialize these data members. Of course, the constructor requires five parameters to initialize all five data members. Why does this class have five data members, when only two are shown in the foregoing declaration? Because three of the members are being inherited from the superclass. Now, we have three different versions of the *Checking()* constructor, so we can define an object for the *Checking* class three different ways. Here are some examples:

```
Checking NoName = new Checking();
Checking TedWilliams = new Checking("0010", "Ted Williams",10000);
Checking MickeyMantle = new Checking("0020", "Mickey Mantle",
                                      100000,100,0.25);
```

With what values have each of the five data members been initialized in the fore-going definitions? Think about it, since this will be left as an exercise at the end of this section.

Finally, the *cashCheck()* method is used to debit the account balance by cashing a check. It receives an amount (*amt*) from the calling object and generates an error message if this amount exceeds the account balance. Otherwise, the check is cashed, and the account balance is debited accordingly. Notice that a check-cashing charge is applied if the amount of the check is less than the required minimum balance.

Looking back at Figure 9-1, you see that the *InterestChecking* class is derived from the *Checking* class. This type of checking account adds interest to an account balance only if a certain minimum balance is maintained. In addition, no per-check charge is made if the balance stays at or above the minimum. This is a perfect place to declare a subclass of the *Checking* class because the *InterestChecking* class can inherit the *minimum* and *charge* data members, as well as the *cashCheck()* method of the *Checking* class. The UML class diagram in Figure 9-4 shows the *InterestChecking* subclass structure and interface.

```
┌─────────────────────────────────────────────────────────────┐
│                      InterestChecking                        │
├─────────────────────────────────────────────────────────────┤
│  #interestRate:double = 2.0                                  │
├─────────────────────────────────────────────────────────────┤
│  +InterestChecking()                                         │
│  +InterestChecking(in acctNum:string, in name:string, in bal:double) │
│  +InterestChecking(in acctNum:string, in name:string, in bal:double  │
│                in min:double, in chg:double, in rate:double) │
│  +addInterest()                                             │
└─────────────────────────────────────────────────────────────┘
```

FIGURE 9-4   The *InterestChecking* subclass inherits the *Checking* class members and adds its own protected member of *interestRate*, as well as an overloaded constructor and a public method called *addInterest()*.

The UML class diagram leads to the Java code, as follows:

```
package bankAccounts;

//SUBCLASS InterestChecking INHERITS Checking CLASS
public class InterestChecking extends Checking
{

  //DATA MEMBERS
  protected double interestRate = 2.0;   //ANNUAL INTEREST RATE

  //METHOD MEMBERS
  //PARAMETERLESS CONSTRUCTOR
```

```java
public InterestChecking()
{
    super("0000"," ",0.0);
}//END InterestChecking()

//CONSTRUCTOR TO INITIALIZE ACCOUNT NUMBER AND BALANCE
public InterestChecking(String acctNum, String nam, double bal)
{
    super(acctNum,nam,bal);
}//END InterestChecking(String,String,double)
//CONSTRUCTOR TO INITIALIZE ALL DATA
public InterestChecking(String acctNum,
                        String nam,
                        double bal,
                        double min,
                        double chg,
                        double rate)
{
    super(acctNum,nam,bal);
    minimum = min;
    charge = chg;
    interestRate = rate;
} //END InterestChecking(String,String,double,double,double,double)

//IMPLEMENTATION FOR addInterest() METHOD
public void addInterest()
{
    double interest = 0.0;      //LOCAL VARIABLE TO CALC. INTEREST
    if (balance >= minimum)
    {
        interest = balance * (interestRate/12/100);
        balance = balance + interest;
    } //END IF
} //END addInterest()
}//END InterestChecking
```

Again, this class is part of our *bankAccounts* package because of the statement package bankAccounts; . As you can see, this class inherits the *Checking* class, which inherits the *BankAccount* class. The only data member unique to this class is *interestRate*, which specifies the annual interest rate to be applied to the account. However, through inheritance, there are five additional data members. What are they? Well, *accountNumber*, *name*, and *balance* are inherited from the *BankAccount* class via the *Checking* class, and *minimum* and *charge* are inherited directly from the *Checking* class.

There are two additional methods declared for this class: the overloaded *InterestChecking()* constructor, which initializes the data members of the class, and the *addInterest()* method, which will credit the account balance with interest at a rate specified by the *interestRate* data member. As you can see, the *InterestChecking()* constructor is overloaded three ways. Observe how each version of the constructor uses super to call the superclass constructor. The *addInterest()* method adds monthly interest to the account if the account balance is greater than or equal to the minimum required balance.

The last class we need to declare is the *Savings* account class. The UML diagram in Figure 9-5 describes this class.

Savings
#interestRate:double = 2.0
+Savings()   +Savings(in acctNum:string, in name:string, in bal:double)   +Savings(in acctNum:string, in name:string, in bal:double   in rate:double)   +addInterest()   +withdraw(in amount:double)

FIGURE 9-5 The *Savings* subclass inherits the *BankAccount* superclass members and adds its own protected member of *interestRate*, as well as an overloaded constructor and public methods called *withdraw()* and *addInterest()*.

The class code follows from the UML diagram, as follows:

```
package bankAccounts;

//SUBCLASS Savings INHERITS BankAccount CLASS
public class Savings extends BankAccount
{
  //DATA MEMBERS
  protected double interestRate = 2.0;          //ANNUAL INTEREST RATE

  //METHOD MEMBERS
  //PARAMETERLESS CONSTRUCTOR
  public Savings()
  {
    super("0000"," ",0.0);
  }//END Savings()

  //CONSTRUCTOR TO INITIALIZE ACCOUNT NUMBER AND BALANCE
  public Savings(String acctNum, String nam, double bal)
  {
    super(acctNum,nam,bal);
  }//END Savings(String,String,double)

  //CONSTRUCTOR TO INITIALIZE ALL PRIVATE DATA
  public Savings(String acctNum, String nam, double bal, double rate)
  {
    super(acctNum,nam,bal);
    interestRate = rate;
  }//END Savings(String,String,double,double)
```

```
  //withdraw() METHOD
  public void withdraw(double amt)
  {
    balance = balance - amt;
  }//END withdraw()

  //IMPLEMENTATION FOR addInterest() METHOD
  public void addInterest()
  {
    double interest;
    interest = balance * (interestRate/12/100);
    balance = balance + interest;
  } //END addInterest()
}//END Savings
```

As you can see, the *Savings* class extends the *BankAccount* superclass. Therefore, it inherits the *accountNumber*, *name*, and *balance* data members from the *BankAccount* class. In addition, an *interestRate* data member is defined for this class. The *interestRate* data member will store an annual savings account interest rate value. There are three additional methods defined for the *Savings* class. The overloaded *Savings()* constructor is used to initialize the class data members. The *addInterest()* method is used to credit the account balance with monthly interest earnings. The *withdraw()* method is used to debit the account balance when a savings withdrawal is made. Moreover, because the *Savings* class is derived from the *BankAccount* class, it inherits the *deposit()* method. The method implementations should be self-explanatory by now. Notice, however, that this *addInterest()* method differs from the *addInterest()* method in the *InterestChecking* class. The *Savings* class *addInterest()* method does not depend on a minimum balance, whereas the *InterestChecking* class *addInterest()* method does.

We can use the **Venn diagram** shown in Figure 9-6 to summarize the bank account class family hierarchy. Notice how the class inheritance patterns can be seen by

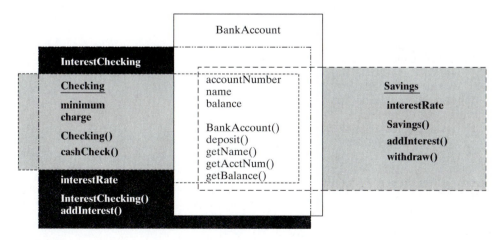

FIGURE 9-6   A Venn diagram shows the shared members of a class family hierarchy.

the intersections between the classes. You might have studied Venn diagrams in an algebra course and wondered what practical application they had. Well, now you can tell your math professor you have found a "real world" application for a Venn diagram.

Finally, we need an application to exercise our class family. Here is one that will demonstrate most of the family features:

```java
/*
 * Transactions.java
 *
 * Created on July 5, 2002, 10:14 AM
 */

/**
 *
 * @author  Andrew C. Staugaard, Jr.
 * @version 1.0
 */

import bankAccounts.*;              //FOR BANKING ACCOUNT CLASSES
import staugIO.StaugIO;            //FOR GUI I/O
import java.text.NumberFormat;     //FOR CURRENCY FORMATTING

public class Transactions
{
  public static void main(String[] args)
  {
    //DEFINE GUI I/O OBJECT
    StaugIO io = new StaugIO();

    //DEFINE BANKING ACCOUNT OBJECTS
    Checking BillGates = new Checking("0001","Bill Gates",0);
    InterestChecking StevenJobs = new InterestChecking("0002",
                                               "Steven Jobs",1050);
    Savings GraceHopper1 = new Savings("0003-1","Grace Hopper", 2500);
    Checking GraceHopper2 = new Checking("0003-2","Grace Hopper",0);

    //MONTHLY CHECKING ACCOUNT TRANSACTIONS
    BillGates.deposit(2500);
    BillGates.cashCheck(500.00);
    BillGates.cashCheck(500.00);
    BillGates.cashCheck(700.75);
    BillGates.cashCheck(200.00);
    GraceHopper2.deposit(2500);
    GraceHopper2.cashCheck(25.75);
    GraceHopper2.cashCheck(75.25);

    //MONTHLY INTEREST CHECKING ACCOUNT TRANSACTIONS
    StevenJobs.deposit(2000.00);
    StevenJobs.cashCheck(200.00);

    //MONTHLY SAVINGS ACCOUNT TRANSACTIONS
    GraceHopper1.deposit(2000.00);
```

```
GraceHopper1.withdraw(350);

//CREATE CURRENCY OBJECT
 NumberFormat currency = NumberFormat.getCurrencyInstance();

//MONTHLY REPORT OF ACCOUNT BALANCES
StevenJobs.addInterest();
GraceHopper1.addInterest();
io.writeInfo("ACCOUNT STATEMENT"
            + "\nAccount number: " + BillGates.getAcctNum()
            + "\nName: " + BillGates.getName()
            + "\nBalance: " + currency.format(BillGates.getBalance()));

io.writeInfo("ACCOUNT STATEMENT"
            + "\nAccount number: " + StevenJobs.getAcctNum()
            + "\nName: " + StevenJobs.getName()
            + "\nBalance:" + currency.format(StevenJobs.getBalance()));

io.writeInfo("ACCOUNT STATEMENT"
          + "\nAccount number: " + GraceHopper1.getAcctNum()
          + "\nName: " + GraceHopper1.getName()
          + "\nBalance: " + currency.format(GraceHopper1.getBalance()));

io.writeInfo("ACCOUNT STATEMENT"
          + "\nAccount number: " + GraceHopper2.getAcctNum()
          + "\nName: " + GraceHopper2.getName()
          + "\nBalance: " + currency.format(GraceHopper2.getBalance()));

   //EXIT PROGRAM
   System.exit(0);
 } //END main()
}//END Transactions
```

The application class is called *Transactions* and begins by importing all of the bank account classes contained in the *bankAccounts* package. Looking at method *main()* within the class, you see that several objects are defined for the various banking account classes. The object name corresponds to the customer name. A suffix is added to the customer name if the same customer has more than one bank account. For instance, you see that *GraceHopper1* is a checking account object, and *GraceHopper2* is a savings account object. Notice also that a unique account number, name, and an initial account balance are specified when each object is defined. As a result, the customer account number, name, and balance are initialized with these values. All other data members will take on their respective default values.

Next, monthly transactions are listed for each type of account. Can you determine what should happen in each transaction? Finally, a monthly balance report of each account is generated in an information window for each account. Using the indicated transactions in the order they appear, what will be the balance for each account at the end of the month? Well, here is what you would see if you ran the program:

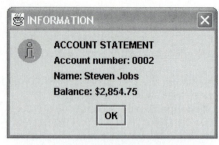

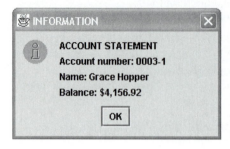

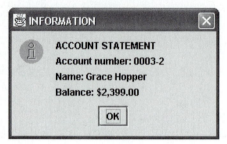

QUICK CHECK

1. True or false: When declaring a subclass, the subclass name is listed first, followed by the keyword `extends`, followed by the superclass name.
2. You must use the keyword _____ to call the superclass constructor in a subclass constructor.
3. True or false: A protected superclass member is protected from any use by the subclasses of that superclass.
4. Explain the difference between a `private`, `protected`, and `public` member of a class.
5. What would be wrong with deriving the *Savings* class from the *InterestChecking* class in the program discussed in this section?
6. Given the following object definitions for the *Checking* class declared in this section:

   ```
   Checking AndrewStaugaard = new Checking();
   Checking MichaelJordan = new Checking("0010",
                                     "Michael Jordan",10000);
   Checking PaulAllen = new Checking("0020",
                                     "Paul Allen",100000,100,0.25);
   ```

   To what values will each of the object data members be initialized?

9.3   Polymorphism and Dynamic Binding

In the introduction to Chapter 8, it was stated that there are three concepts central to OOP: encapsulation, inheritance, and polymorphism. We have thoroughly explored the first two. For completeness, we will now briefly discuss the last concept of polymorphism. You will see uses of these concepts in the chapters that follow.

Polymorphism

The term "polymorphic" is Greek, meaning "of many forms." Polymorphism is associated with methods, as indicated in the following definition:

A **polymorphic** method is one that has the same name for different classes of the same family, but has different implementations, or behavior, for the various classes.

As you can see, polymorphism allows methods of the same name to behave differently within a class family. You have just seen an example of a polymorphic method in our bank account class family. Can you identify which method it is from the class declarations? You're right if you thought the *addInterest()* method. Notice that this method is defined in both the *InterestChecking* and *Savings* classes. The method interface is identical in both classes; however, the implementation is different in each class. In effect, we are hiding alternative operations behind the common *addInterest()* interface. This means that two objects defined for these classes will respond to the common operation, *addInterest()*, in different ways. Languages that do not support polymorphism, such as BASIC, COBOL, and C, require large `switch/case` statements to implement this effect.

Polymorphism allows objects to be more independent, even though they are members of the same class family. Moreover, new classes can be added to the family without changing existing ones. This allows systems to evolve over time, meeting the needs of a changing application. Consider a word processing program where the system is required to print many different types of documents. Recall from Chapter 3 that many such programs employ classes to define the structure and behavior of a given type of document. Each document class will have a *print()* method to print a specific document in its correct format. Such a method would be a polymorphic method because it would have a common interface but behave differently for different document objects. Polymorphism allows one method name to be shared throughout the class family, with each class implementing the method in a way that is appropriate to its own purpose. Another example would be a *weeklyPay()* method in a family of employee classes. In this family, different employee classes (hourly, salary, etc.) would implement the same *weeklyPay()* method differently.

Polymorphism is accomplished using **overloaded methods** or **polymorphic methods**. Overloaded methods were discussed earlier in Chapter 7. However, polymorphic methods are something new. The difference between the two has to do with the different techniques that are used by Java to call the method. Overloaded methods are called using **static binding**, and polymorphic methods are called using **dynamic binding**.

Dynamic versus Static Binding

Binding relates to the actual time when the code for a given method is attached, or bound, to the method.

Dynamic, or **late**, **binding** occurs when a method is defined for several classes in a family, but the actual code for the method is not attached, or bound, until execution time. Such a method is called a **polymorphic method**.

Dynamic binding is used in Java to support ***polymorphism***. With dynamic binding, the selection of code to be executed when a method is called is delayed until execution time. This means that when a method is called, the executable code determines at run time which version of the method to call.

As an example of dynamic binding consider what happens when you double-click a mouse. The double-clicking action generates an *event*, which calls upon a polymorphic method. If you double-click on a file folder, a directory listing opens. If you double-click on an application icon, a program is executed. If you double-click on a document, a word processing program is launched and the document is opened. So, the double-clicking event resulted in a different behavior each time. This is polymorphism and it surely happens at execution time.

 Static binding occurs when a method is defined with the same name but with different headers and implementations. The actual code for the method is attached, or bound, at compile time. Static binding is used to support overloaded methods in Java.

Static binding, on the other hand, occurs when the method code is "bound" at compile time. This means that when an overloaded method is called, the compiler determines at compile time which version of the method to call. Overloaded methods are statically bound, whereas polymorphic methods are dynamically bound. With overloaded methods, the compiler can determine which method to call based on the number and data types of the method arguments. However, polymorphic methods have the same header within a given class family. Therefore, hidden ***pointers*** must be used during run time to determine which method to call. Fortunately, you don't have to worry about how the binding is accomplished, because this is taken care of automatically by the compiler.

 A **pointer** is a direct program reference to an actual physical address in memory. Java uses pointers extensively to implement programs, but does not allow you, the programmer, to use pointers. This can be an advantage or a disadvantage. Languages that allow the use of pointers, such as C and C++, provide more flexibility for the programmer because the programmer can create a pointer to point to anything in memory, even the operating system memory. But, of course, this could be very hazardous to your system if not used properly. Because pointers can be dangerous when used improperly, Java simply does not support them, providing you protection from errors commonly associated with pointers. Another reason Java does not support pointers is that Java was meant to be a totally portable language across all platforms.

Abstract Classes and Methods

You have probably noticed that with inheritance, superclasses are very abstract and become more concrete as subclasses are created. In other words, a superclass starts off as very general while its subclasses become more specific, or refined, with each succeeding subclass in the class hierarchy. In fact, when inheritance is used properly, there should never be any objects defined for the superclass, since the superclass is too general, or abstract. When no objects can be created for a class, the class is called an *abstract class*. A subclass of an abstract class is referred to as a ***concrete class*** since objects can be created for the subclass.

An ***abstract*** class is a superclass for which objects will never be created.

A ***concrete class*** is a subclass for which objects will always be created.

To declare a superclass as abstract in Java, you must use the keyword `abstract` in the class header line. When would you want to declare a superclass as abstract? Well, when you have a situation where no objects will ever be created for the superclass. When a class is declared `abstract`, the compiler will not allow any objects to be created for that class. Actually, our *BankAccount* class is a good candidate for an abstract class since no objects would ever be created for this class. A given bank account can only be a checking, savings, or some other type of account, right? As another example, consider an employee package. Such a package would most likely have one class for hourly employees, and another class for salaried employees. Both classes would have common data members, such as the employee's name and number, and both classes would have common operations, or methods, such as one to determine weekly pay. Thus, you would likely create an employee superclass with two subclasses as shown in Figure 9-7.

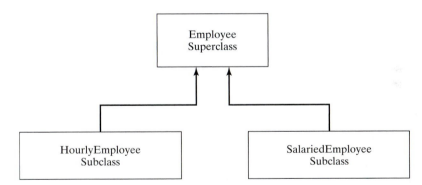

FIGURE 9-7   This employee class family consists of an abstract superclass called *Employee* and two concrete subclasses called *HourlyEmployee* and *SalariedEmployee*.

So, let's specify an *Employee* superclass like this:

Class: *Employee*
    Data Members: *employeeName*
                            employeeNumber

    Method Members: *getName()*
                            getNumber()

The UML class diagram in Figure 9-8 illustrates this superclass. Should the *Employee* class be an abstract class? Of course it should, because no object will ever be created for this class. An employee must either be an hourly employee or a salaried employee.

Employee
#employeeName:string #employeeNumber:string
+Employee() +getName():string +getAcctNum():string +weeklyPay():double

FIGURE 9-8   The *Employee* superclass consists of protected *employeeName* and *employeeNumber* members along with public accessor methods of *getName()* and *getNumber()*, as well as a *weeklyPay()* method and constructor.

So, let's declare an abstract class called *Employee* as follows:

```
package employees;

//ABSTRACT SUPERCLASS FOR ALL EMPLOYEES
public abstract class Employee
{
  //DATA MEMBERS
  protected String employeeName;      //EMPLOYEE NAME
  protected String employeeNumber;    //EMPLOYEE NUMBER

  //METHOD MEMBERS

  //CONSTRUCTOR
  public Employee(String name, String number)
  {
     employeeName = name;
     employeeNumber = number;
  }//END Employee(String,String)

  //ACCESSOR METHOD FOR name
  public String getName()
  {
    return employeeName;                //RETURN EMPLOYEE NAME
  }//END getName()

  //ACCESSOR METHOD FOR employeeNumber
  public String getNumber()
  {
```

```
    return employeeNumber;                 //RETURN EMPLOYEE NUMBER
 }//END employeeNumber()

 //ABSTRACT METHOD TO RETURN WEEKLY PAY
 public abstract double weeklyPay();
}//END Employee CLASS
```

Most of the *Employee* class code should be familiar to you by now. The class is part of a package called *employees*. Notice that the class is declared as an abstract class by including the keyword `abstract` in the class header line. This means that no objects can ever be created for this class. The class has two protected data members, *employeeName* and *employeeNumber*, to store the employee's name and number, respectively. The class has four methods: an *Employee()* constructor, two accessor methods that return the employee's name and number, and an **abstract method** called *weeklyPay()* that will return the weekly pay for a given employee. An abstract method is a polymorphic method whose header is placed in the superclass, along with the keyword `abstract`. Notice that only the header for the *weeklyPay()* method is provided in the *Employee* class declaration. A semicolon follows the header with no implementation provided. The implementation will be provided in the subclass declarations. Why? Because the process of determining the weekly pay for an hourly employee differs from that of determining the weekly pay for a salaried employee, right? Observe that we have added the keyword `abstract` within the method header to specify it as an abstract method. This tells the compiler to look for the method implementation in the subclasses. By the way, an `abstract` method can never be `static`, `final`, or `private`.

An **abstract method** is a polymorphic method in a superclass whose behavior will be defined in the subclasses.

DEBUGGING TIP

It is a syntax error to create an object for an abstract class. Thus, the statement

```
Employee BobJones = new Employee();
```

will not compile. An employee object must be either an hourly employee object, or a salaried employee object in this example.

Now, let's declare our two subclasses. First, the *HourlyEmployee* class needs to have the following members:

    Class: *HourlyEmployee*
      Data Members: *rate*
                  hours

      Method Members: *weeklyPay()*

```
                        HourlyEmployee
-rate:double = 0.0

-hours:double = 0.0

+HourlyEmployee()
+HourlyEmployee(in name:string, in number:string)
+HourlyEmployee(in name:string, in number:string, in rate:double,
               in hours:double)
+weeklyPay():double
```

FIGURE 9-9 The *HourlyEmployee* superclass consists of *rate* and *hours* data members, an overloaded constructor, and a *weeklyPay()* method member, in addition to the members inherited from the *Employee* superclass.

The UML class diagram in Figure 9-9 illustrates this subclass. Following the class specification, the class code becomes:

```java
package employees;
public class HourlyEmployee extends Employee
{
  //DATA MEMBERS
  private double rate = 0.0;           //HOURLY PAY RATE
  private double hours = 0.0;          //WEEKLY HOURS WORKED

  //METHOD MEMBERS

  //PARAMETERLESS CONSTRUCTOR
  public HourlyEmployee()
  {
    super(" ","0000");
  }//END HourlyEmployee()

  //CONSTRUCTOR TO INITIALIZE EMPLOYEE NAME AND NUMBER
  public HourlyEmployee(String name, String number)
  {
    super(name,number);
  }//END HourlyEmployee(String,String)

  //CONSTRUCTOR TO INITIALIZE ALL PRIVATE DATA
  public HourlyEmployee(String name, String number,
                        double rate, double hours)
  {
    super (name,number);
    this.rate = rate;
    this.hours = hours;
  }//END HourlyEmployee(String,String,double,double)

  //METHOD TO RETURN WEEKLY PAY
  public double weeklyPay()
```

```
{
   if (hours <= 40)
      return rate * hours;
   else
      return 40 * rate + ((hours - 40) * 1.5 * rate);
  }//END weeklyPay()
}//END HourlyEmployee
```

This class has two additional private members for the hourly rate and weekly hours. There are two methods: an overloaded constructor which should be self-explanatory at this point, and our polymorphic *weeklyPay()* method. This is where you find the implementation required to calculate the weekly pay of an hourly employee.

Next we have the *SalariedEmployee* class specification as follows:

Class: *SalariedEmployee*
   Data Members: *annualSalary*

   Method Members: *weeklyPay()*

The UML class diagram in Figure 9-10 specifies this subclass.

SalariedEmployee
-annualsalary:double = 0.0
+SalariedEmployee() +SalariedEmployee(in name:string, in number:string) +SalariedEmployee(in name:string, in number:string, in salary:double) +weeklyPay():double

FIGURE 9-10   The *SalariedEmployee* superclass consists of an *annualSalary* data member and *weeklyPay()* method member, in addition to the members inherited from the *Employee* superclass.

Here's the class code:

```
package employees;

public class SalariedEmployee extends Employee
{
   //DATA MEMBERS
   private double annualSalary = 0.0;   //ANNUAL SALARY

   //METHOD MEMBERS

   //PARAMETERLESS CONSTRUCTOR
   public SalariedEmployee()
   {
      super(" ","0000");
   }//END SalariedEmployee()
```

```
//CONSTRUCTOR TO INITIALIZE EMPLOYEE NAME AND NUMBER
public SalariedEmployee(String name, String number)
{
  super(name,number);
}//END SalariedEmployee(String,String)

//CONSTRUCTOR TO INITIALIZE ALL PRIVATE DATA
public SalariedEmployee(String name, String number, double salary)
{
  super (name,number);
  annualSalary = salary;
}//END SalariedEmployee(String,String,double)

//METHOD TO RETURN WEEKLY PAY
public double weeklyPay()
{
  return annualSalary/52;
}//END weeklyPay()
}//END SalariedEmployee
```

Here you see an additional data member called *annualSalary*. Again, we have an overloaded constructor and the *weeklyPay()* method. However, the implementation of this *weeklyPay()* method is that which is required to calculate the weekly pay of a salaried employee from an annual salary figure, versus that of an hourly employee.

How do you suppose that the compiler knows which *weeklyPay()* method to use? You're right if you thought that it doesn't until an object is defined in an application class. If an object is defined as an *HourlyEmployee* object, the hourly implementation is executed, while a *SalariedEmployee* object will cause the salary implementation to be executed. This will happen at run time, making the *weeklyPay()* method truly a polymorphic method. Here is the application class that we used to test the *Employee* class family:

```
import employees.*;        //FOR EMPLOYEE CLASSES
import staugIO.StaugIO;    //FOR GUI I/O
import java.text.NumberFormat;  //FOR CURRENCY FORMATTING

public class Payroll
{
  public static void main(String[] args)
  {
    //DEFINE GUI I/O OBJECT
    StaugIO io = new StaugIO();

    //DEFINE EMPLOYEE OBJECTS
    HourlyEmployee BobJones= new HourlyEmployee("Bob Jones","0001",
                                                10.00,45.0);

    SalariedEmployee JoeDileo = new SalariedEmployee("Joe Dileo","0002",
                                                100000.00);

    //CREATE CURRENCY OBJECT
    NumberFormat currency = NumberFormat.getCurrencyInstance();
```

```
    //DISPLAY WEEKLY PAY
    io.writeInfo("The weekly pay for " + BobJones.getName()
                + " is "
                + currency.format(BobJones.weeklyPay()));

    io.writeInfo("The weekly pay for " + JoeDileo.getName()
                + " is "
                + currency.format(JoeDileo.weeklyPay()));

    //EXIT PROGRAM
    System.exit(0);
  }//END main()
}//END Payroll
```

Here is the output produced by the program:

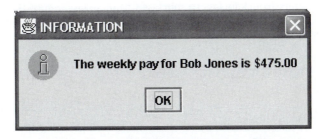

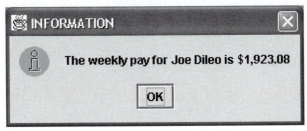

QUICK CHECK

1. True or false: An overloaded method is polymorphic.
2. True or false: All overloaded methods are dynamically bound.
3. True or false: A polymorphic method interface is identical for each version of the method in a given class family.
4. Overloaded methods are _____ bound.
5. Polymorphic methods are _____ bound.
6. The implementation code for a dynamically bound method is determined at _____.
7. What is the difference between an abstract class and a concrete class?
8. True or false: An `abstract` method is always polymorphic.
9. Where is the implementation found for an `abstract` method?

CHAPTER SUMMARY

Inheritance is an important property of OOP that allows one class, called a subclass, to share the structure and behavior of another class, called a superclass. The subclass should always be related to its superclass via the IS-A relationship. You control the amount of inheritance by designating the members as `private`, `protected`, or `public` in the class declarations. Classes are designated as subclasses in Java by using the keyword `extends` within the class header line.

Polymorphism has to do with methods and objects that have the same name but different behavior within a class family. Polymorphism allows methods and objects to be more independent and class families to be more flexible. Overloaded methods and polymorphic methods are both polymorphic. Overloaded methods are statically bound to their code during compile time, whereas polymorphic methods are dynamically bound to their code during run time.

When inheritance is used properly, there should never be any objects defined for a superclass, since the superclass is too general, or abstract. When no objects can be created for a class, the class is called an abstract class. A subclass of an abstract class is referred to as a concrete class since objects are normally created for subclasses. An abstract method is truly polymorphic since its implementation differs from subclass to subclass within a class family. Both abstract classes and methods are designated as such in Java by using the keyword `abstract` within the class header line or method header.

QUESTIONS AND PROBLEMS

Questions

 1. Define the following terms:

    Superclass
    Subclass
    Inheritance
    IS-A
    Polymorphism
    Abstract class
    Concrete class
    Abstract method
    Dynamic binding
    Static binding

 2. Suggest several real-world applications for the use of inheritance.
 3. What relationship must be considered between a potential subclass and its superclass when developing inheritance?
 4. Given a superclass called *Point*, write the class declaration header line for a subclass called *Pixel*. Assume that the *Pixel* class is to be accessible outside of its package.
 5. Why doesn't Java support pointers?
 6. Explain the difference between a `private`, `protected`, and `public` member of a class.
 7. When should you use the keyword `public` in a subclass declaration?
 8. Why is an overloaded method polymorphic?
 9. Explain the difference between static binding and dynamic binding.
 10. Draw a Venn diagram for the employee class family developed in this chapter.
 11. When should a superclass be declared as an `abstract` superclass?

12. When should a method be declared as an `abstract` method?

13. Where are the implementations found for an `abstract` method?

Problems

Least Difficult

1. Code the files for the banking program given in this chapter. Then, write your own application to exercise the class family in different ways. See if you can predict the results of your banking transactions.

2. Rewrite the *BankAccount* class given in this chapter as an abstract class. This class can be found in the *BankAccount.java* file of the *bankAccounts* package on the CD that came with this book. Make the *deposit()* method an abstract method and define its implementation in the respective subclasses that employ its use. Then, write your own application to exercise the class family in different ways. See if you can predict the results of your banking transactions.

3. Code the files for the employee program given in this chapter. The *Employee* class family is within the *employees* package on the CD that accompanies this book. Then, write your own application class to exercise the class family in different ways.

More Difficult

4. Add a *CreditCard* class to the *BankAccount* class family developed in this chapter. The *BankAccount* class family is within the *bankAccounts* package on the CD which accompanies this book. The *CreditCard* class should inherit the *BankAccount* class directly. Provide methods to debit monthly charges and interest from the account balance. Write an application to exercise a *CreditCard* class object and report the balance due.

5. Add a *PartTimeEmployee* class to the *Employee* class family developed in this chapter. The *Employee* class family is within the *employees* package on the CD that accompanies this book. The *PartTimeEmployee* class should have a *weeklyPay()* method that does not calculate overtime. Write an application to exercise a *PartTimeEmployee* class object and report the weekly pay for this object.

6. Create a *persons* package that contains a family of classes of persons. Think of the persons that make up your institution. For example, a student is a person, a staff member is a person, a faculty member is a person, and an administrator is a person (some of the time). Each of these persons has common as well as unique attributes and behaviors. For instance, both a student and a faculty member have a name and address. However, a student has a GPA, while a faculty member has a rank.

   Build, compile, and test your person family using an application. Be creative and try different things—this is when you really learn how to program in Java, as well as any other language for that matter.

Most Difficult

7. Declare an *Insurance* superclass that contains the following members:

Class: *Insurance*

Data Members
- An insurance account number
- An insurance policy number
- The name of the insured
- Annual premium

Method Members

- A set method that will allow the user to enter the values of the data members
- A get method that will display the data member values

8. Declare two subclasses called *Automobile* and *Home* that inherit the *Insurance* superclass declared in problem 7. Provide the following methods in these subclasses:

Class: *Automobile*

Data Members

- Make of automobile
- Model of automobile
- Automobile VIN number
- Amount of liability coverage
- Amount of comprehensive coverage
- Amount of collision coverage

Method Members

- Set and get methods for the specific automobile data members

Class: *Home*

Data Members

- House square footage
- Amount of dwelling coverage
- Amount of contents coverage
- Amount of liability coverage

Method Members

- Set and get methods for the specific home data members

9. Write an application that defines an automobile and home insurance object from the classes declared in problem 8. Include statements in the program that will exercise the object methods.

10

One-Dimensional Arrays

OBJECTIVES

When you are finished with this chapter, you should have a good understanding of the following:

- How to define one-dimensional arrays in Java
- How to access one-dimensional arrays using direct assignment, reading/writing, and loops
- How to pass arrays and array elements to methods
- How to search an array for a given element using sequential search
- How to search an array for a given element using binary search
- How to sort an array using insertion sort

Introduction

This chapter will introduce you to a very important topic in any programming language: *arrays*. The importance of arrays cannot be overemphasized because they lend themselves to so many applications.

An **array** is an *indexed* data structure that is used to store data elements of the same data type or class.

Arrays simply provide an organized means for locating and storing data, just as the post office boxes in your local post office lobby provide an organized means of locating and storing mail. This is why an array is referred to as a **data structure**. The array data structure can be used to store just about any type or class of data, including integers, floats, characters, arrays, and objects. In addition, arrays are so versatile that they can be used to implement other data structures like stacks and queues. In fact, in some languages like FORTRAN, the array is the only data structure available to the programmer because most other structures can be implemented using arrays.

We will cover **one-dimensional** arrays in this chapter because they are the most commonly used arrays in Java programs. You will learn about arrays of more dimensions, called **multidimensional arrays**, in Chapter 15.

10.1   The Structure of a One-Dimensional Array

An array is a data structure. In other words, an array consists of data elements that are organized, or structured, in a particular way. This array data structure provides a convenient means of storing large amounts of data in primary, or user, memory. There are both one-dimensional and multidimensional arrays.

To get the idea of an array, look at the illustration in Figure 10-1. Here you see a single row of post office boxes as you might find in any common post office lobby. As you know, each box has a post office (P.O.) box number. In Figure 10-1, our P.O. box numbers begin with 0 and go up to some finite number N. How do you locate a given box? By using its P.O. box number, right? However, the P.O. box number has nothing to do with what's inside the box. It is simply used to locate a given box. Of course, the contents of a given box is the mail delivered to that box. The reason the postal service uses the P.O. box method is that it provides a convenient, well-organized method of storing and accessing the mail for its postal customers. An array does the same thing in a computer program; it provides a convenient, well-organized method of storing and accessing data for you, the programmer. By the way, how many post office boxes are there in Figure 10-1? Because the first box number is 0 and the last is N, there must be $N + 1$ boxes.

You can think of a one-dimensional array, like the one shown in Figure 10-2, as a row of post office boxes. The one-dimensional array consists of a single row of storage

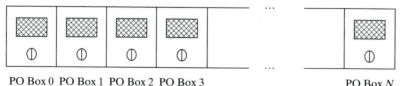

PO Box 0 PO Box 1 PO Box 2 PO Box 3   PO Box N

FIGURE 10-1   A one-dimensional array is like a row of post office boxes.

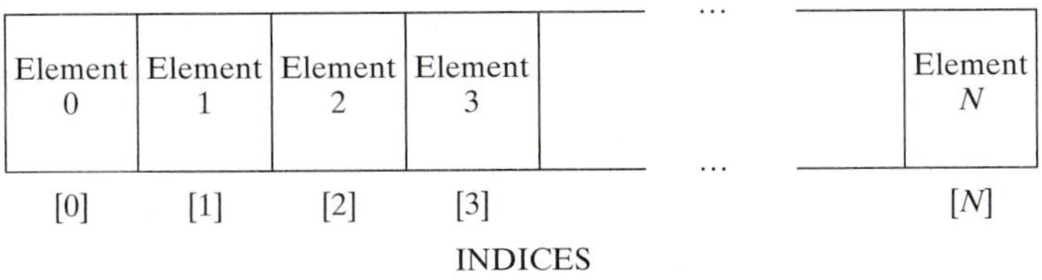

FIGURE 10-2   A one-dimensional array, or list, is a sequential list of storage locations that contain data elements that are located via indices.

locations, each labeled with a number called an ***index***. The data stored at a given index location is referred to as an array ***element***. Thus, a one-dimensional array is a sequential list of storage locations that contain individual data elements that are located, or accessed, via indices.

The two major components of any array are the elements stored in the array and the indices that locate the stored elements. Don't get these two array components confused! Although array elements and indices are related, they are completely separate quantities, just as the contents of a post office box is something different from its P.O. box number. With this in mind, let's explore array elements and indices a bit further.

The Array Elements

The elements of an array are the data stored in the array. These elements can be any type of data that you have seen so far. Thus, a given array can store integer elements, floating-point elements, character, and Boolean elements. In addition to these primitive data-type elements, an array can also be used to store objects. In fact, the elements in an array even can be other arrays. However, there is one major restriction that applies to the array elements: *The elements in a given array must all be of the same type.*

As you will see shortly, arrays must be defined before they can be used to store data in a Java program. Part of the definition specifies the type or class of the elements that the array will store. Once a given array is defined for a certain data type or class, only elements of that type or class can be stored in that array.

The Array Indices

The array indices locate the array elements. In Java, the compiler automatically assigns integer indices to the array element list beginning with index [0]. So, the first element of the array shown previously in Figure 10-2 is located at index [0], and the last element is located at index [N]. The indices begin with 0 and go to N, so there must be $N + 1$ elements in the array. Also, because this is a one-dimensional array, or ***list***, we say that it has a ***dimension*** of $1 \times (N + 1)$, meaning that there is one row of $N + 1$ elements. The dimension of an array indicates the size of the array, just as the dimension of a piece of lumber indicates its size.

QUICK CHECK

1. The two major components of an array are the _____ and _____.

2. True or false: The elements within a given array can be any combination of data types.

3. Suppose the last element of a Java array is located at index [10]. What is the dimension of the array?

10.2   Defining One-Dimensional Arrays in Java

All arrays in Java must be defined. In order to define an array, you must specify three things:

1. The data type or class of the array elements

2. The name of the array

3. The size of the array

Here's the general format:

ONE-DIMENSIONAL ARRAY DEFINITION FORMAT

```
elementType arrayName[] = new elementType[size];
```

The first thing you see in the definition is the data type (or class) of the array elements. Then comes the array identifier, or name, which is followed by empty square brackets, [], to indicate an array definition. This is followed by an assignment operator and the keyword new. After the keyword new, the element data type (or class) must be specified again, followed by the number of elements that the array will store enclosed within square brackets. We will refer to the number of elements that an array will store as its size. A semicolon terminates the definition. For instance, the following code defines an array of 10 characters whose name is *characters*:

```
char characters[] = new char[10];
```

Example 10-1

Write definitions for the following arrays:

a. An array called *integers* that will store 10 integers

b. An array called *reals* that will store 5 double floating-point values

c. An array called *characters* that will store 11 characters

d. An array called *strings* that will store 15 string objects

Solution

```
a.   int integers[] = new int[10];
b.   double reals[] = new double[5];
c.   char characters[] = new char[11];
d.   String strings[] = new String[15];
```

Each definition should be fairly self-explanatory, except perhaps the *strings* array definition. In this definition, the class of the array is *String*. Thus, the definition specifies that the *strings* array will store 15 string objects.

Initializing Arrays

Arrays, like variables, can be initialized when they are created. The initializing values can be supplied for any array, wherever the array is defined in the program. Let's consider some example array definitions to illustrate how arrays can be initialized.

```
int integers[]  = {10,20,30};
```

In this definition, an integer array of three elements has been defined. The three integer elements have been initialized to the values 10, 20, and 30, respectively. Notice the syntax. The empty array brackets, [], are followed by an assignment operator, which is followed by the initialization values enclosed within braces. Notice that you *do not* see the keyword new in this definition. Here is what you would see if you inspected the array using a typical debugger:

 DEBUGGER RESULTS

integers[]

```
integers[0] = 10
integers[1] = 20
integers[2] = 30
```

As you can see, the first initialization value, 10, is placed at index [0] of the array, the value 20 is placed at index [1], and the value 30 is placed at the last index position, which is [2]. With this definition, the compiler will set aside enough storage to hold all the initialization values.

Next, let's consider character arrays. Suppose that you define a character array with initializing values, like this:

```
char characters[]  = {'H','E','L','L','O'};
```

Again you see that the initialization values are enclosed in braces after an assignment operator. Here is what a typical debugger would reveal:

 DEBUGGER RESULTS

characters[]

```
characters[0] = 'H'
characters[1] = 'E'
characters[2] = 'L'
characters[3] = 'L'
characters[4] = 'O'
```

You see here that the five initialization characters are placed in the array starting at index [0] and ending at the last index position, [4].

Finally, let's consider how to initialize string arrays with string values. Here is how a string array can be initialized with string values:

```
String strings[]= {"Bob","Sally","Gayle","Andy"};
```

Here is what you would see stored in memory via a debugger:

 DEBUGGER RESULTS

strings[]

```
strings[0] = "Bob"
strings[1] = "Sally"
strings[2] = "Gayle"
strings[3] = "Andy"
```

Default Initialization of Arrays

If you define an array and don't provide any initialization values, Java will initialize the array with the respective default value (zeros for integer and floating-point arrays, and spaces for character arrays). For instance, suppose you define an integer array and a character array as follows:

```
int integers[] = new int[5];
char characters[]= new char[5];
```

Inspecting these arrays with a debugger would reveal the following:

 DEBUGGER RESULTS

integers[]   *characters[]*

```
integers[0] = 0        characters[0] = ' '
integers[1] = 0        characters[1] = ' '
integers[2] = 0        characters[2] = ' '
integers[3] = 0        characters[3] = ' '
```

Here is a summary of the foregoing discussion:

- Integer, floating-point, and character arrays are initialized by using an assignment operator after the array definition, followed by a listing of the individual initializing values within braces.
- String arrays can be initialized with strings by enclosing the strings within double quotes.
- Arrays are always initialized with the respective default values when no initialization values are supplied in the array definition. The default value for integer and floating-point arrays is zero. The default value for character arrays is a space.

QUICK CHECK

1. Define an array called *testScores* that will store up to 15 decimal test scores.
2. What is the dimension of the array in question 1?
3. What is the index of the first element of the array in question 1?
4. What is the index of the last element of the array in question 1?
5. Suppose that the index of the last element in an array is [25]. How many elements will the array store?
6. Define an array called *values[]* and initialize it with the integer values −3 through +3.
7. What is the dimension of the array that you defined in question 6?
8. Define an array called *family[]* and initialize it with the first names of your family members.
9. Suppose that you define a floating-point array without any initializing values. What does the compiler store in the array?
10. Suppose that you define a character array without any initializing values. What does the compiler store in the array?

10.3   Accessing One-Dimensional Arrays

Accessing the array means to insert elements into the array for storage or to copy stored elements from the array.

Inserting Elements into One-Dimensional Arrays

There are basically three major ways to insert elements into an array: by using a *direct assignment* statement, by *reading*, or by using *loops*.

Direct Assignment   Here's the general format for inserting an element into an array using a direct assignment:

INSERTING ARRAY ELEMENTS USING DIRECT ASSIGNMENT

```
arrayName[arrayIndex] = elementValue;
```

Using the following array definitions,

```
char characters[] = new char[6];
int integers[] = new int[3];
```

direct assignments might go something like this:

```
characters[0] = 'H';
characters[5] = '$';
integers[0] = 16;
integers[2] = -22;
```

In each of these instances, an element is placed in the first and last storage positions of the respective array. The character 'H' is placed in the first position of the *characters* array, and a dollar sign is placed in the last position of this array. Recall that the first position of an array is always [0], and the last array position is always one less than the array size. The integer 16 is placed in the first position of the *integers* array, and the integer −22 placed in the last position of this array.

Observe that the respective array name is listed, followed by the array index within brackets. An assignment operator (=) is then used, followed by the element to be inserted. The data type or class of the element being inserted should be the same as the data type or class defined for the array elements; otherwise, you could get unpredictable results when working with the array elements.

CAUTION

Be careful not to specify an array index that is out of bounds. Such an index would be one that is less than zero or greater than the maximum index value. For example, suppose that you define an array like this:

```
int array[] = new int[SIZE];
```

A common mistake using this definition would be to attempt to access the element *array[SIZE]*. However, remember that array indices in Java begin with 0; therefore, *SIZE* specifies one position beyond the maximum index value of the array. The maximum index in this array is [*SIZE* − 1]. So, both of the following statements would create an error:

```
array[SIZE] = 55;       //ARRAY OUT OF BOUNDS ERROR
array[-1] = 25;         //ARRAY OUT OF BOUNDS ERROR
```

The Java compiler will not detect such an error because arrays are defined *dynamically* using the **new** operator. This means the array storage is not created and the compiler does not determine the size of the array until run time. However, during run time an *ArrayIndexOutofBounds* exception would be generated which might crash the program. We will discuss how to handle such exceptions in Chapter 14.

THINK!

Remember that Java array indices are integer values. This means that any specified index is converted to its integer equivalent. For instance, you can specify an index as a character, like this: *array['A']*; however, Java sees this as *array[65]*, because the integer equivalent of the character 'A' is 65 from the UNICODE/ASCII character set. To avoid confusion and potential problems, we suggest that you always use integer values for your indices, unless the application specifically dictates otherwise.

Reading Elements into the Array   You can also use any of the methods found in the *StaugIO* class to insert array elements from a keyboard entry, like this:

```
characters[1] = io.readChar("Enter a single character");
integers[0] = io.readInt("Enter an integer");
```

Here, the user must enter the respective array element value in the dialog box. A character must be entered for the first statement and an integer for the second statement. The character entered from the keyboard will be stored in the second position (index [1]) of the *characters* array, whereas the integer entered from the keyboard will be stored in the first position (index [0]) of the *integers* array.

Inserting Array Elements Using Loops   The obvious disadvantage to using direct assignments to insert array elements is that a separate assignment statement is required to fill each array position. You can automate the insertion process by using a loop structure. Although any of the three loop structures (while, do/while, for) can be employed, the for structure is the most common. Here's the general format for using a for loop:

INSERTING ARRAY ELEMENTS USING A for LOOP

```
for(int index = 0; index < arraySize; ++index)
   assign or read into array[index]
```

Consider the following segment of code:

```
//DEFINE GUI OBJECT
StaugIO io = new StaugIO();

//DEFINE ARRAY SIZE
final int SIZE = 10;

//DEFINE ARRAY
int sample[] = new int[SIZE];

//READ ELEMENTS FROM DIALOG BOX
for(int index = 0; index < SIZE; ++index)
   sample[index] = io.readInt("Enter an integer");
```

First, you see a constant called *SIZE* defined. Notice where *SIZE* is used in the program. It is the array-size value and the final counter value in the for loop. Using a constant like this allows you to change the size of the array easily. Here, the array size is 10 elements. To change the size of the array, you only need to make a change one place in the program, at the constant definition.

Next, look at the array definition. The array *sample* is defined as an array of integer elements. The program then enters a for loop. The loop counter variable is *index*, which ranges from 0 to *SIZE*. When the loop counter reaches the value of *SIZE*, the loop is broken because the loop test is *index* < *SIZE*. It is important to use the "less than" (<) test here rather than the "less than or equal to" (<=) test; otherwise, the loop will execute one too many times. The loop counter is employed as the index value for the array. With each loop iteration, a single *readInt()* statement is executed to insert an element into the array at the respective position specified by the loop counter, *index*.

Let's analyze the *readInt()* statement. First, the array name *sample* is listed with the loop counter variable *index* as the array index in brackets. What does *index* do with each loop iteration? It increments from 0 to *SIZE*, right? As a result, the first loop iteration reads a value into *sample*[0], the second iteration reads a value into *sample*[1], and so on, until the last loop iteration reads a value into the last array position *sample*[*SIZE* − 1]. When the loop counter increments to the value of *SIZE* at the end of the last loop iteration, the loop is broken and no more elements are inserted into the array. That's all there is to it! The array is filled!

You can also use loops for assigning values to array elements. For instance, using the foregoing definitions, consider this loop:

```
for(int index = 0; index < SIZE; ++index)
    sample[index] = 2 * index;
```

This time, the array elements are assigned twice the loop counter value with each loop iteration. What values are actually inserted into the array? How about the 10 even integers from 0 through 18?

CAUTION

It is easy to specify an array index that is out of bounds when using a loop. For example, suppose that you define an array like this:

```
final int SIZE = 10;
int array[] = new int[SIZE];
```

In a loop situation, the following loop statement would create an *ArrayOutofBounds* exception during run time, which might crash the program:

```
for(int index = 0; index <= SIZE; ++index)
    sample[index] = 2 * index;
```

Again, the last loop iteration specifies an array index of [*SIZE*], which is out of the index range. To prevent this error, the test must be *index < SIZE*. Of course, the test could also be *index <= SIZE − 1*, but this is a bit more awkward. When an array index is out of bounds, you *will not* get a compiler error. Java will throw an exception and, if not caught, your program might crash. So, be safe and make sure that your indices are always within their specified bounds.

Copying Array Elements

As with insertion, you can copy array elements using one of three general methods: *direct assignment*, *writing*, or *looping*.

Direct Assignment   Copying array elements using assignment statements is just the reverse of inserting elements using an assignment statement. Here's the general format:

COPYING ARRAY ELEMENTS USING DIRECT ASSIGNMENT

variableName = arrayName[arrayIndex];

As an example, suppose we make the following definitions:

```
final int SIZE = 10;
int sample[] = new int[SIZE];
int value = 0;
```

As you can see, the array *sample[]* consists of 10 integer elements. Now, assuming the array has been filled, what do you think the following statements do?

```
value = sample[0];
value = sample[SIZE-1];
value = sample[3] * sample[5];
value = 2 * sample[2] - 3 * sample[7];
```

The first statement assigns the element stored in the first array position to the variable *value*. The second statement assigns the element stored in the last array position to the variable *value*. The third statement assigns the product of the elements located at indices [3] and [5] to *value*. Finally, the fourth statement assigns two times the element at index [2] minus three times the element at index [7] to *value*. The last two statements illustrate how arithmetic operations can be performed using array elements.

In all of the foregoing cases, the array element values are not affected by the assignment operations. The major requirement is that *value* should be defined as the same data type as the array elements so that you don't get unexpected results.

As a final example, consider these assignment statements:

```
sample[0] = sample[SIZE-1];
sample[1] = sample[2] + sample[3];
```

Can you determine what will happen here? In the first statement, the first array element is replaced by the last array element. Is the last array element affected? No, because it appears on the right side of the assignment operator. In the second case, the second array element at index [1] is replaced by the sum of the third and fourth array elements at indices [2] and [3]. Again, the third and fourth array elements are not affected by this operation because they appear on the right side of the assignment operator.

Writing Array Elements   The *print()/println()* or *writeNumber()/writeInfo()* methods can be used to display array elements. Let's use the same array to demonstrate how to write array elements. Here's the array definition again:

```
final int SIZE = 10;
int sample[] = new int[SIZE];
StaugIO io = new StaugIO();
```

Now what do you suppose the following statements will do?

```
System.out.println(sample[0]);
System.out.println(sample[SIZE-1]);
io.writeNumber(sample[1] * sample[2]);
io.writeNumber(Math.sqrt(sample[6]));
```

The first statement will display the element contained at index [0] of the array on the console screen. The second statement will display the last element of the array, located at index $[SIZE - 1]$ on the console screen. The third statement will multiply the element located at index [1] by the element located at index [2] and display the integer product in an information box. Finally, the fourth statement will display the square root of the element located at index [6] in an information box. None of the array element values is affected by these operations.

Copying Array Elements Using Loops   As with inserting elements into an array, copying array elements using loops requires less coding, especially when copying multiple elements. Again, any of the loop structures can be used for this purpose, but `for` loops are the most common.

Consider the following program segment:

```
final int SIZE = 10;

//DEFINE ARRAY
int sample[] = new int[SIZE];

//FILL ARRAY WITH SQUARE OF INDEX
for(int index = 0; index < SIZE; ++index)
    sample[index] = index * index;

//DISPLAY ARRAY ACROSS MONITOR
for(int index = 0; index < SIZE; ++index)
    System.out.print(sample[index] + "\t");
```

Here again, the array is defined as an array of *SIZE* (10) integer values. The array name is *sample*. Notice that the loop counter variable *index* is used as the array index in both `for` loops. The first loop will fill the array locations with the square of the loop counter. Then, the second loop will display each of the array elements located from index [0] to index $[SIZE - 1]$. A *print()* statement is used to display the array elements horizontally across the face of the console screen. Notice also that each time an element is displayed, a tab is written after the element to separate it from the next sequential element. Here is what you would see on the display:

0	1	4	9	16	25	36	49	64	81

As a final example, consider this segment of code:

```
//DEFINE VARIABLES AND OBJECTS
StaugIO io = new StaugIO();
final int SIZE = 10;
int sample[] = new int[SIZE];

//FILL ARRAY WITH SQUARE OF INDEX
for(int index = 0; index < SIZE; ++index)
  sample[index] = index * index;

//DISPLAY ARRAY IN INFO BOX
String info = "Array Elements\n";
for(int index = 0; index < SIZE; ++index)
    info += sample[index] + "\n";
io.writeInfo(info);
```

Here we are using a *writeInfo()* method to display the contents of an array. Remember that our *writeInfo()* method needs a string argument. So, all we need to do is build a single string that contains all the array elements, then pass this string to the *writeInfo()* method. The string we will build is defined as *info* and is initialized to a heading for a table that will list the array elements vertically under the heading. Then a for loop is executed that concatenates the *sample[]* array elements to the *info* string. Do you see how this is done using the statement:

```
info += scores[index] + "\n";
```

inside the loop? With each loop iteration, an array element is concatenated to the *info* string along with a newline. When the loop terminates, the *info* string is used as the argument for the *writeInfo()* statement. That's all there is to it! Here is the information box generated by the code:

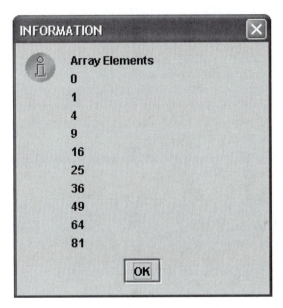

QUICK CHECK

1. Write a for loop that will fill the following array from user entries:

    ```
    char characters[] = new char[15];
    ```

2. Write a for loop that will display the contents of the array in question 1 vertically within an information box.

Problem Solving in Action: Array Processing

The object-oriented approach to solving this problem will employ a class to hold the array and its associated methods, then use *main()* to define a class object and call the required class methods.

Problem

Write a program that uses an array to store a maximum of 25 test scores and calculate their average. Use one method to fill the array with the scores from user entries, a second method to calculate the average, and a third method to display all the scores along with the calculated average.

Defining the Problem

We will place the array and its methods within a class. The specification for such a class is as follows:

> Class: *Scores*
>> Data Members: *scores array*
>>> *number of scores*
>
>> Method Members: *setScores()*
>>> *average()*
>>> *displayResults()*

Our *Scores* class will contain an array to hold the test scores and a value that stores the number of scores stored in the array. The methods include a method to fill the array with scores from user entries, *setScores()*, a method to calculate the average of the scores, *average()*, and a method to display the scores along with the average, *displayResults()*.

Once the class composition is established, we need to determine the method interfaces, or headers. First, *setScores()* simply gets scores from the user and places them in the private array member of the class. Here is its interface description:

Method *setScores()*:   Obtains test scores from user and places them in an array
Accepts: Nothing
Returns: Nothing

Wow, what a simple interface! Why is nothing being passed to or from the method? Well, the array itself is a private class member, as well as the number of scores held in the array. Remember, if a method operates directly on a private member of its class, the private member does not get passed to or from the method. This is the great thing about classes! Because of the tight binding between the data and methods of a class, you do not need to pass the data to or from the methods.

So, based on the method interface description, our *setScores()* header becomes

```
void setScores()
```

The body of the method must obtain the number of scores and the scores themselves from the user, setting the class members to these values. Here's the entire method code:

```
public void setScores()
{
  //GET NUMBER OF SCORES FROM USER
  number = io.readInt("How many scores do you have to average? ");

  //FILL ARRAY WITH USER ENTRIES
  for(int index = 0; index < number; ++index)
    scores[index] = io.readDouble("Enter score #" + (index+1));
}//END setScores()
```

Within the method, we have used a *StaugIO* class object, *io*, to read the data entered by the user through a GUI dialog box. We then read the number of scores the user has to enter. The scores are then entered and placed in the array via a call to the *readDouble()* method within a `for` loop. Notice that the value received by the method for *number* is employed to terminate the `for` loop.

The next method we need to develop is the *average()* method. Suppose we call this method by the *displayResults()* method when the average needs to be calculated and displayed. If this is the case, the method does not have to be accessible from outside the class and, therefore, can be a private utility method, right? So, its interface description becomes:

Method *average()*:   Computes the average of the test scores
Accepts: Nothing
Returns: A single value that is the average of the test scores

Again, the array is not passed (accepted) because it is a private member of the same class as the method. However, the method must return a value to its calling method, *displayResults()*, since the test average value is not a member of the class. The body of the method simply adds up all the test scores in the array and divides by the number of test scores. Here is the complete method header and body:

```
//METHOD TO CALCULATE AVERAGE
private double average()
{
  double total = 0.0;
  for(int index = 0; index < number; ++index)
     total += scores[index];
  return total/number;
}//END average()
```

There are two local method variables defined: *total* and *index*. The variable *total* will act as a temporary variable to accumulate the sum of the scores, and the variable *index* is a loop counter variable. The variable *total* is first initialized to 0.0. Then the loop is used to obtain the array elements, one at a time, and to add them to *total*. Observe that the loop counter (*index*) acts as the array index within the loop. Thus, the array elements, from index [0] to [*number* − 1], are sequentially added to *total*. The last test score is located at index [*number* − 1]. Once the loop calculates the sum total of all the test scores, a `return` statement is used to return the calculated average.

The last method we need to define is the *displayResults()* method. This method displays the scores contained in the private scores array and will call the *average()* utility method to determine the average of the scores. Here is its interface description:

Method *displayResults()*   Displays the individual test scores and their average
Accepts: Nothing
Returns: Nothing

Again, there is nothing to accept because the method has direct access to the *scores[]* array. Also, there is nothing to return because the method is simply displaying the values. Here is the resulting method header and body:

```
public void displayResults()
{
  String info = "Test scores\n";
```

```
    for(int index = 0; index < number; ++index)
        info += scores[index] + "\n";
    info += "\nThe average of the above scores is " + average();
    io.writeInfo(info);
}//END displayResults()
```

Notice that we are displaying the *scores[]* array contents and the average in an information box. A *for* loop is used to concatenate the array elements to a string called *info*. Then, the *average()* utility method is called to concatenate the test score average to the *info* string.

When using an object-oriented solution to a problem, we always try to first visualize the class composition, then develop its interface, and finally specify everything in a UML class diagram, like the one shown in Figure 10-3.

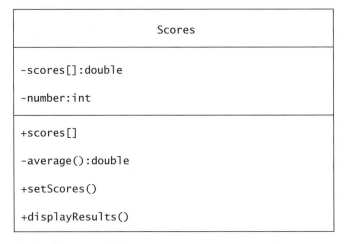

```
                            Scores

    -scores[]:double

    -number:int

    +scores[]

    -average():double

    +setScores()

    +displayResults()
```

FIGURE 10-3   The *Scores* class consists of a private *scores[]* array, number of scores in the array, *number*, and utility method, *average()*, to determine the average of the scores in the array. The public interface consists of a constructor, a method to set the scores from user entries, *setScores()*, and a method to display the scores and their average, *displayResults()*.

Here, you see a *Scores* class which consists of a private *scores[]* array, a private member to store the number of scores in the array, *number*, and a private utility method, called *average()*, to determine the average of the scores in the array. The public interface consists of a class constructor, a method to set the scores from user entries, *setScores()*, and a method to display the scores and their average, *displayResults()*. Now that we have determined the class data and method implementations, the class code becomes

```
class Scores
{
    //DATA MEMBERS
    private final int SIZE = 25;                    //MAXIMUM ARRAY SIZE
    private double scores[] = new double[SIZE]; //ARRAYS OF TEST SCORES
    private int number = 0;                         //NUMBER OF ARRAY SCORES
    private StaugIO io = new StaugIO();             //FOR GUI I/O
```

```
//METHOD MEMBERS
//PARAMETERLESS CONSTRUCTOR
public Scores()
{
}//END Scores()

//METHOD TO SET THE ARRAY VALUES TO SCORES ENTERED BY USER
public void setScores()
{
  //GET NUMBER OF SCORES FROM USER
  number = io.readInt("How many scores do you have to average? ");

  //FILL ARRAY WITH USER ENTRIES
  for(int index = 0; index < number; ++index)
     scores[index] = io.readDouble("Enter score #" + (index+1));
}//END setScores()

 //METHOD TO CALCULATE AVERAGE
 private double average()
 {
   double total = 0.0;
   for(int index = 0; index < number; ++index)
      total += scores[index];
   return total/number;
 }//END average()

//METHOD TO DISPLAY RESULTS
 public void  displayResults()
 {
   String info = "Test scores\n";
   for(int index = 0; index < number; ++index)
       info += scores[index] + "\n";
   info += "\nThe average of the above scores is " + average();
   io.writeInfo(info);
 }//END displayResults()
}//END Scores CLASS
```

The class includes all the data and method members just discussed. In addition, we have added a private constant data member for the maximum array size and a *StaugIO* class object for GUI I/O. To use this class, we must create an application that includes *main()* which must define a *Scores* class object and call the class methods. Here is the required application class code:

```
public class Action10_01
{
    public static void main(String[] args)
    {

    //DEFINE SCORES CLASS OBJECT
    Scores myScores = new Scores();
```

```
    //CALL METHODS TO SET ARRAY SCORES, CALCULATE AVERAGE
    //AND DISPLAY RESULTS
    myScores.setScores();              //CALL METHOD setScores()
    myScores.displayResults();         //CALL METHOD displayResults()

    //EXIT PROGRAM
    System.exit(0);
  }//END main()
 }//END Action10_01 CLASS
}//END Scores CLASS
```

That's it! You should not have any trouble understanding this code. Here is the final output the user would see for a sample set of test scores:

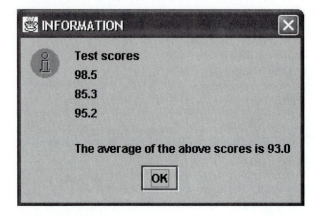

Notice how the information box shows all the test scores and the calculated average.

10.4   Arrays of Objects

Up to this point we have been dealing mostly with arrays of simple data types. In addition we can define arrays of more complex data, such as arrays of arrays and arrays of objects. In this section, we will deal with arrays of objects. Then, in Chapter 15, we will discuss arrays of arrays. Here is the format for creating an array of objects:

ARRAY OF OBJECTS FORMAT

```
className arrayName[ ] = new className[size];
```

As you can see, you simply use a class name rather than a primitive data type in the array definition. For example, consider the following definitions:

```
String names[] = new String[10];
Student students[] = new Student[number];
```

In the first example, an array of 10 *String* objects is defined. So, the *names[]* array will store 10 strings. In the second example, an array of *Student* objects is defined. The size of this array is *number*, where *number* must be an integer variable. To fill this array, objects must be defined for the *Student* class and filled with data. Let's pursue this idea. First, consider the following *Student* class declaration:

```
//DECLARE STUDENT DATA CLASS
class Student
{
    private String name = " ";
    private String number = " ";
    private String e_mail = " ";
    private double gpa = 4.0;
    private StaugIO io = new StaugIO();

    //PARAMETERLESS CONSTRUCTOR
    public Student()
    {
    }
    //END CONSTRUCTOR

    //SET STUDENT NAME
    public void setName()
    {
        name = io.readString("Enter the student name");
    }//END setName()

    //SET STUDENT NUMBER
    public void setNumber()
    {
        number = io.readString("Enter the student number");
    }//END setNumber()

    //SET STUDENT E_MAIL
    public void setEmail()
    {
        e_mail = io.readString("Enter the student's e-mail address");
    }//END setEmail()

    //SET STUDENT GPA
    public void setGPA()
    {
        gpa = io.readDouble("Enter the student's gpa");
    }//END getGPA()

    //GET STUDENT NAME
    public String getName()
    {
        return name;
    }//END getName()

    //GET STUDENT NUMBER
    public String getNumber()
    {
        return number;
    }//END getNumber()
```

```
//GET STUDENT E_MAIL
public String getEmail()
{
     return e_mail;
}//END getEmail()

//GET STUDENT GPA
public double getGPA()
{
     return gpa;
}//END getGPA()
}//END Student CLASS
```

Nothing new here. There is a *Student* class containing several student data members, and a set of *set()* and *get()* methods to access the data.

Now, consider the following code:

```
//READ NUMBER OF STUDENTS TO STORE
int number = io.readInt("How many students do you have to enter?");

//DYNAMICALLY DEFINE ARRAY OF STUDENT OBJECTS
Student students[] = new Student[number];

//DEFINE STUDENT OBJECTS AND FILL ARRAY OF OBJECTS
//WITH STUDENT DATA
for(int i = 0; i < number; ++i)
{
   students[i] = new Student();
   students[i].setName();
   students[i].setNumber();
   students[i].setEmail();
   students[i].setGPA();
}//END FOR
```

Here you see that we obtain the value of *number* from the user. This value is then used in the subsequent array definition to set the size of the array. The array is an array of *Student* objects, where *Student* is the class we just declared. Now, look at the `for` loop. You see that it ranges from 0 to *number*. Within each iteration, a *Student* object is defined for the array. For example, in the first iteration the *students[0]* object is defined. This object then calls its *set()* methods to set its student data. In the second iteration the *students[1]* object is defined and used to call its *set()* methods. In the last iteration the *students[number − 1]* object is defined and used to call its *set()* methods. When the loop terminates, the *students[]* array is filled with *Student* objects, each of which is filled with its respective student data entered by the user via the *set()* methods.

Next, consider the following:

```
//BUILD OUTPUT STRING FROM ARRAY OF STUDENT OBJECTS
//AND DISPLAY STUDENTS ONE AT A TIME
for(int i = 0; i < number; ++i)
```

```
{
   studentInfo = "STUDENT   " + (i+1) + "  DATA\n";
   studentInfo += "\nNAME: " + students[i].getName() + "\n"
             + "NUMBER: " + students[i].getNumber() + "\n"
             + "E-MAIL: " + students[i].getEmail() + "\n"
             + "GPA: " + students[i].getGPA() + "\n";
   //DISPLAY STUDENT DATA
   io.writeInfo(studentInfo);
}//END FOR
```

Here we have created another *for* loop to access our *students[]* array. This time, each loop iteration is used to build a string, called *studentInfo*, from the student data stored in the array. The string is used as an argument in the *writeInfo()* method at the end of the loop to display a given student's data in an information box. For example, in the first iteration the *students[0]* object calls its *get()* methods to build a string. The string is then used as an argument in the *writeInfo()* method to display the *student[0]* object data. Then, in the second iteration the *students[1]* object calls its *get()* methods to build a string and display its data. In the final iteration the *students[number − 1]* object calls its *get()* methods to build a string in order to display its data. Here is the output that you would see when the above code is placed in an application and executed using some sample data:

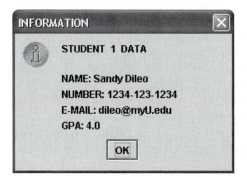

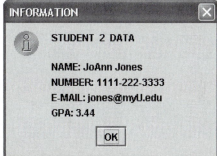

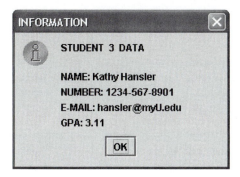

QUICK CHECK

1. True or false: An array cannot be defined using a variable for the size of the array.
2. Define an array called *employees[]* that will store 10 *Employee* objects.
3. Assume that the *Employee* class referred to in question 2 has three *set()* methods and three *get()* methods to set and get the employee's name, social security number, and department, respectively. Write a `for` loop to fill the array with the data for 10 employees.
4. Write a `for` loop to display the data for the 10 employees.

10.5   Passing Arrays and Array Elements to Methods

Some applications require that an array or one of its elements be passed to a class method from outside the class. You can pass an entire array to a method or pass single array elements to a method. The important thing to remember is that to pass the entire array, you must pass the address of the array. In Java, *the array name represents the address of the array*. So, by passing the array name you are actually passing the address of the array. Let's begin by looking at the required method header. Here is a typical header for passing a one-dimensional array to a method:

```
void weird(char array[])
```

Looking at the header, you see that the method does not return a value. There is one character array parameter called *array[]*. The square brackets specify an array parameter. Now, the array identifier "references" the address of the array, so the array is passed **by reference** to the method. A pass by reference means that you are actually passing the *address* of a variable or data structure to the method. Thus, any operations on the array within the method will affect the original array contents in the calling program because the method is operating on the data stored at the array address. Up to this point, you have been passing variables to methods **by value**. A pass by value passes a *copy* of the variable to the method. As a result, any operations on the variable within the method do not affect its original argument value because the method is simply operating on a copy.

Passing a variable by **value** passes a *copy* of the variable to a method. Any operations on the variable within the method do not affect the original argument value of the variable within the calling program. In Java, all variables are passed by value to methods. In Java, an array is passed by **reference** to a method. A pass by reference passes the *address* of the array to the method. Thus, any operations on the array within the method affect the original array values in the calling program.

Now, back to our *weird()* method. To call this method and pass an array, you simply use the following statement:

```
weird(name);
```

Of course, this call assumes that *name* is a character array in the calling program. (Remember that the argument identifier and the parameter identifier *can be and are often different.*) The call to *name* references the address of the array, so the array address is passed to the method rather than a copy of the array. Thus, any operations on the array within the method will affect the original array elements. Here's a complete program to consider:

```
class SpaceOdyssey
{
  //PARAMETERLESS CONSTRUCTOR
  public SpaceOdyssey()
  {
  }//END CONSTRUCTOR

  //THIS METHOD DECREMENTS EACH OF THE ARRAY ELEMENTS
  public void weird(char array[])
  {
   for(int index = 0; index < 3; ++index)
        --array[index];
  }//END weird()
}//END SpaceOdyssey

//APPLICATION CLASS
public class Foo
{
    public static void main(String[] args)
    {

    //DEFINE SPACE ODYSSEY OBJECT
    SpaceOdyssey arthurClarke = new SpaceOdyssey();

    //DEFINE CHARACTER ARRAY
    char name[] = {'I','B','M'};

    //DISPLAY ARRAY BEFORE METHOD CALL
    System.out.print("The contents of name[] before weird() is:  ");
    for(int index = 0;index < 3;++index)
        System.out.print(name[index]);

    //CALL METHOD weird()
    arthurClarke.weird(name);

    //DISPLAY ARRAY AFTER METHOD CALL
    System.out.print("\nThe contents of name[] after weird() is:  ");
    for(int index = 0;index < 3;++index)
        System.out.print(name[index]);

  }//END main()
}//END Foo
```

The array *name[]* is defined as an array of characters and initialized with the characters 'I', 'B', 'M' in *main()*. The characters stored in the array are displayed on the console screen using a `for` loop. Then, method *weird()* is called using the array name, *name*, as its argument. This passes the array to method *weird()*, where each of the elements in the array is decremented. After the method call, the array elements are displayed again. What do you suppose the user will see on the console screen after executing the program? Well, this is why things are "weird."

```
The contents of name[] before weird() is:  IBM
The contents of name[] after weird() is:  HAL
```

The point here is that the decrement operation within the method changed the original array elements. Thus, the word *IBM* was converted to the word *HAL*. Is there anything weird here? Recall that HAL was the artificially intelligent computer in the book and movie *2001: A Space Odyssey*. Is there a message here or is this just a coincidence? You will have to ask the author, Arthur C. Clarke, to find out.

One final point: You cannot pass the entire array by value to a method. If you do not want operations within the method to affect the array elements, you must pass the array to the method, make a temporary local copy of the array within the method using a `for` loop, and then operate on the temporary array, like this:

```
//THIS METHOD WILL NOT AFFECT THE PASSED ARRAY ELEMENTS
public void nonWeird(char array[])
{
  int temp[] = new int[SIZE];
  for(int index = 0; index < 3; ++index)
      temp[index] = array[index];
  for(int index = 0; index < 3; ++index)
      --temp[index];
}//END nonWeird()
```

Here you see that a character array, *array[]*, is accepted by the method. However, remember that any change to this array will change the contents of the array being passed to this method, because an array parameter is always a reference parameter. So, the first thing we have done in the method is to define a local temporary array called *temp[]* and used a `for` loop to copy the contents of the reference parameter array, *array[]*, into *temp[]*. Now, we can operate on *temp[]*, as shown in the second `for` loop, without affecting the contents of the array that was passed to the method.

DEBUGGING TIP

You must use the array bracket syntax within the method header when passing an array to a method. Thus, to pass a character array to method *weird()*, the header becomes

```
public void weird(char array[])
```

and not

```
public void weird(char array)   //THIS IS AN ERROR WHEN PASSING AN ARRAY
```

It is a common mistake to leave off the [ ] syntax. Here the compiler "thinks" that you are just passing a single character to the method. This will not cause an error until the method is called and you try to pass an array to the method.

Also, when calling a method and providing an array argument, you *do not* use the [ ] syntax. Rather, you simply provide the array name as the method argument like this:

```
weird(name);
```

A common mistake is to call the method using the [ ] syntax as follows:

```
weird(name[]);          //THIS IS AN ERROR
```

Passing Individual Array Elements to Methods

You can also pass individual array elements to a method. Look at the following method header:

```
public void passByValue(int arrayElement)
```

The header says that the method does not return any value and expects to receive a single integer value from the calling program. Suppose the method was called as follows:

```
passByValue(scores[0]);
```

   Notice that the argument in the method call is *scores[0]*. This is *not* an error, because the compiler "sees" *scores[0]* as a single integer element and the method expects to receive a single integer element when it is called. Thus, a copy of the element stored at *scores[0]* will be passed to the method by value. As a result, any operations on this element within the method will not affect the element value in the original *scores[]* array. Note that *scores* is the beginning address of the entire array in memory, while *scores[0]* is the single character stored at [0] of the array.

   You now have all the ingredients you need to write programs using the versatile one dimensional array. Next, you will learn how to search an array for a given element value as well as sort the elements in an array. What follows are some classic searching and sorting algorithms that are important for you to learn, regardless of the programming language that you are using. Of course, we will implement these classic algorithms using the Java language.

QUICK CHECK

1. True or false: An array name represents the address of index [1] of the array.
2. Write a header for a method called *sample()* that must accept and alter the following array:

   ```
   char characters[] = new char[15];
   ```

   Assume that the method does not return any values except the altered array.
3. Write a statement to call the *sample()* method in question 2 with an object called *myObject*. Pass the *characters[]* array defined in question 2 to the method.
4. Write a header for a method called *test()* that will accept a single array element from the array defined in question 2.
5. Write a statement that will call the *test()* method in question 4 with an object called *myObject*. Call the method and pass the element stored at index [5] of the *characters[]* array defined in question 2.

Problem Solving in Action: Searching an Array Using Iteration (Sequential Search)

Many applications require a program to search for a given element in an array. Two common algorithms used to perform this task are *sequential*, or *serial*, *search* and *binary search*. Sequential search is commonly used for unsorted arrays, and binary search is used on arrays that are already sorted. In this case study, you will learn about sequential search; then in a later case study, you will learn about binary search.

Problem

Develop a method that can be called to sequentially search an array of integers for a given element value, and return the index of the element if it is found in the array.

Defining the Problem

Because we are dealing with a method, the problem definition will focus on the method interface. As a result, we must consider what the method will accept and what the method will return. We will assume that the method must receive an array from outside the class in which it resides and, therefore, we must pass the array to the method. Let's call the method *seqSearch()*. Now, from the problem statement you find that the method must search an array of integers for a given element value. Thus, the method needs three things to do its job: (1) the array to be searched, (2) the size of the array to be searched, and (3) the element for which to search. These will be our method parameters.

Next, we need to determine what the method is to return to the calling program. From the problem statement you see that the method needs to return the index of the element being searched for if it is found in the array. All array indices in Java are integers, so the method will return an integer value. But, what if the element being searched for is not found in the array? We need to return some integer value that will indicate this situation. Because array indices in Java range from 0 to some finite positive integer, let's return the integer -1 if the element is not found in the array. Thus, we will use -1 to indicate the "not-found" condition because no array index in Java can have this value. Here is the method interface description:

Method *seqSearch()*: Searches an integer array for a given element value
Accepts: An array of integers, the size of the array, and the element for which to search
Returns: The array index of the element if found, or the value -1 if the element is not found

The preceding method interface description provides all the information required to write the method header:

```
int seqSearch(int array[], int SIZE, int element)
```

The header dictates that the method will accept three things: (1) an array of integer elements, (2) the size of the array, and (3) an integer value that will be the value for which to search.

The next task is to develop the sequential search algorithm.

Planning the Solution

Sequential search does exactly what it says: It *sequentially* searches the array from one element to the next, starting at the first array position and stopping when either the element is found or it reaches the end of the array. Thus, the algorithm must test the element stored in the first array position, then the second array position, then the third, and so on until the element is found or it runs out of array elements. This is obviously a repetitive task of testing an array element, moving to the next element, testing again, and so on. Consider the following algorithm that employs a `while` loop to perform the repetitive testing operation:

seqSearch() Algorithm

```
seqSearch()
BEGIN
  Set found = false.
  Set index = first array index.
  While (element is not found) AND (index <= last array index)
    If (array[index] == element)
      Set found = true.
    Else
      Increment index.
  If (found == true)
    Return index.
  Else
    Return −1.
END.
```

The idea here is to employ a Boolean variable, called *found*, to indicate if the element was found during the search. The variable *found* is initialized to `false`, and a variable called *index* is initialized to the index of the first element in the array. Notice the `while` loop test. Because of the use of the AND operation, the loop will continue as long as the element is not found *and* the value of *index* is less than or equal to the last index value of the array. Another way to say this is that the loop will repeat until the element is found *or* the value of *index* exceeds the last index value of the array. Think about it!

Inside the loop, the value stored at location [*index*] is compared to the value of *element*, received by the method. If the two are equal, the Boolean variable *found* is set to `true`. Otherwise, the value of *index* is incremented to move to the next array position. When the loop terminates, either the element was found or not found. If the element was found, the value of *found* will be `true`, and the value of *index* will be the array position, or index, at which the element was found. Thus, if *found* is `true`, the value of *index* is returned to the calling program. If the element was not found, the value of *found* will still be `false` from its initialized state, and the value −1 is returned to the calling program. That's all there is to it!

Coding the Program

We will code our *seqSearch()* method and place it into a class called *IntegerArrayProcessing*, as follows:

```
class IntegerArrayProcessing
{
  //PARAMETERLESS CONSTRUCTOR
  public IntegerArrayProcessing()
  {
  }//END CONSTRUCTOR

  //SEQUENTIAL SEARCH METHOD
  public int seqSearch(int array[], int SIZE, int element)
  {
    boolean found = false;     //INITIALIZE found TO false
    int index = 0;             //ARRAY INDEX VARIABLE
```

```
    //SEARCH ARRAY UNTIL FOUND OR REACH END OF ARRAY
    while((!found)&&(index < SIZE))
    {
      if(array[index] == element)    //TEST ARRAY ELEMENT
          found = true;              //IF EQUAL, SET found TO TRUE
      else                           //ELSE INCREMENT ARRAY INDEX
          ++index;
    }//END WHILE

    //IF ELEMENT FOUND, RETURN ELEMENT POSITION IN ARRAY
    //ELSE RETURN -1.
    if(found)
      return index;
    else
      return -1;
 }//END seqSearch()
}//END IntegerArrayProcessing CLASS
```

As you can see, this class contains only a parameterless constructor and our *seqSearch()* method. No class data is needed since the only purpose of the class will be to search an integer array supplied from outside the class. There should be no surprises in *seqSearch()* method code. At the top of the method, you see the header that is identical to the method interface developed earlier. The boolean variable *found* is defined and set to false. We will use the variable *index* as our array index variable. This variable is defined as an integer and set to the first array index, [0]. Remember that arrays in Java always begin with index [0]. The while loop employs the AND (&&) operator to test the values of *found* and *index*. The loop will repeat as long as the element is not found (!*found*) and the value of *index* is less than the size of the array, *SIZE*. Remember that when the size of the array is *SIZE*, the last array index is [*SIZE* − 1]. So, when *index* exceeds the maximum array index, [*SIZE* − 1], the loop breaks. When the loop is broken, the value of *found* is tested. If *found* is true, the value of *index* is returned; if *found* is false, the value −1 is returned to indicate that the element was not found in the array.

Finally, we need an application to test our solution. Here is one that will do the job:

```
public class Action10_02
{
    public static void main(String[] args)
    {
      //DEFINE ARRAY SIZE
      final int SIZE = 25;

      //DEFINE INTEGER ARRAY
      int values[] = new int[SIZE];

      //DEFINE ELEMENT VARIABLE
      int element = 0;

      //DEFINE POSITION VARIABLE
      int position = -1;

      //CREATE GUI OBJECT
      StaugIO io = new StaugIO();

      //CREATE A CLASS OBJECT
      IntegerArrayProcessing myTest = new IntegerArrayProcessing();
```

```
//FILL ARRAY WITH RANDOM VALUES
for(int i = 0;i < SIZE; ++i)
    values[i] = (int)(Math.random()*100);

//GET ELEMENT TO SEARCH FOR FROM USER
element = io.readInt("Enter an element between 0 and 100 "
                    + "for which to search");

//CALL seqSearch()
position = myTest.seqSearch(values,SIZE,element);

//DISPLAY ARRAY VALUES AND RESULTS IN AN INFO BOX
String info = "The random array values are\n";
for(int i = 0; i < SIZE; ++i)
  info += values[i] + " ";
if(position == -1)
  io.writeInfo(info + "\nThe element was not found in the array.");
else
  io.writeInfo(info + "\nThe element was found at position "
              + position + " of the array.");

//EXIT PROGRAM
    System.exit(0);
  }//END main()
}//END Action10_02
```

Here, we have defined an integer array called *values[]* of size, *SIZE*, and then filled it with random integer values using a `for` loop. Notice that the loop repeatedly calls the *Math* class *random()* method to fill the array with random integer values between 0 and 100. Once the array is filled, the user is asked to enter an integer value between 0 and 100. Our *seqSearch()* method is then called to search for this value in the random array. The array values are then displayed within an information box. Furthermore, the box notifies the user if the element was found in the array. If the element was found, its array position is displayed.

Here is what the user would see for a sample run:

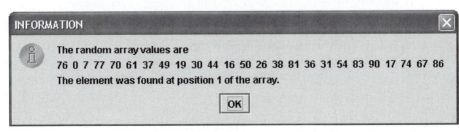

Problem Solving in Action: Sorting an Array Using Iteration (Insertion Sort)

To sort an array means to place the array elements in either ascending or descending order from the beginning to the end of the array. There are many common algorithms used for sorting. There is **insertion sort, bubble sort, selection sort, quick sort, merge sort**, and **heap sort**, just to mention a few. In a more advanced course, you will most likely learn about and analyze all of these sorting algorithms. In this problem, we will develop the **insertion sort** algorithm and code it as a method in Java.

Problem

Develop a method that can be called to sort an array of integers in ascending order using the **insertion sort** algorithm.

Defining the Problem

Again, we will code the algorithm as a Java method so that the problem definition will focus on the method interface, leading us to the method header. Let's call our method *insertSort()*. Think about what *insertSort()* needs to do its job. Well, it must receive an unsorted array of integers along with its size and return the same array as a sorted array, right? Does it need anything else? No. Additional data is not required by the method because the only thing being operated upon is the array itself. What about return values? Does the method need to return a single value? The method does not return any single value but must return the sorted array. Therefore, the return type of the method must be void, and the array must be a reference parameter. Remember that when arrays are passed to Java methods, they are always treated as reference parameters because the array name represents an address in memory. So, here's our *insertSort()* interface description:

Method *insertSort()*:   Sorts an array of integers in ascending order
Accepts: An unsorted array of integers and its size
Returns: A sorted array of integers

From the preceding description, the method interface is easily coded as

```
void insertSort(int array[], int SIZE)
```

The header says that *insertSort()* will receive an integer array. The return type is void because no single value is returned. However, because the entire array is being passed to the method, any sorting operations on the array within the method will be reflected in the calling program. Of course, if this method were in the same class as the array, the array would not be passed to the method because of their binding relationship. Now for the insertion sort algorithm.

Planning the Solution

Before we set up the algorithm, let's see how insertion sort works. Look at Figure 10-4. We will assume that we are going to sort a five-integer array in ascending order. Before getting into the details, look at the figure from top to bottom and from left to right. The beginning array is shown at the top of the figure, and the sorted array is shown at the bottom of the figure. We have started with an array that is sorted in descending order, which is the worst possible case if you wish to sort an array in ascending order. Now, notice that shading is employed in the figure to show the sorting process from top to bottom. As we proceed from the beginning array at the top, the shading

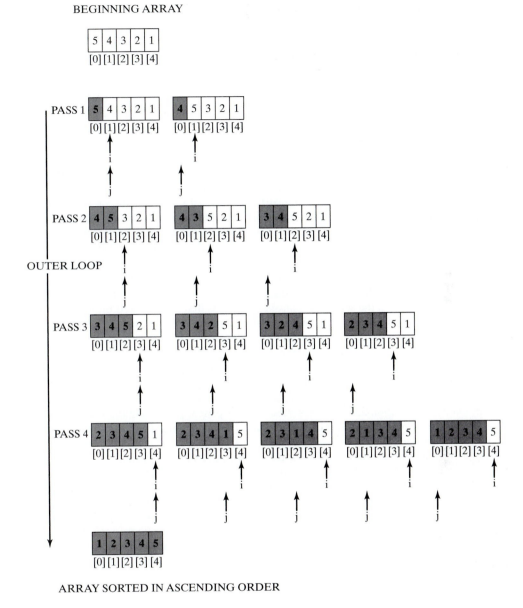

FIGURE 10-4 Insertion sort is a nested repetition process.

increases, showing the portion of the array that is sorted in ascending order, until the entire array is shaded at the bottom of the figure.

The top-to-bottom sequence shows that we will make four passes through the array to achieve the array sorted in ascending order shown at the bottom of the figure. With each pass, an element is placed into its sorted position *relative to the elements that occur before it* in the array. The first pass begins with the first element, 5, sorted as indicated by the shading. The single integer 5 is considered to be sorted by itself because it does not have any elements preceding it. Thus, the task in this first pass is to sort the second element, 4, relative to the integer 5 that precedes it. Since 4 is less than 5, the two elements are exchanged to place the 4 before the 5.

The second pass begins with the integers 4 and 5 sorted, as indicated by the shading. The task in this pass is to sort the third integer, 3, relative to these two integers. In the third pass, the elements 3, 4, and 5 are sorted, and the task is to sort the integer 2 relative to these integers. Remember, in each pass, the task is to sort the first element of the unsorted portion of the array relative to the elements that precede it in the sorted portion of the array. The process continues until all the elements are sorted, as shown at the bottom of the figure. With each pass, you are essentially repeating what was done in the previous pass. As a result, you can identify a repetitive process, from pass to pass, from the top to the bottom of the figure. This repetition will result in a loop structure in our algorithm.

Now, the question is: What happens during each pass to eventually sort the entire array? Well, during each pass, the first element in the unsorted (un-shaded) portion of the array is examined by comparing it to the sorted sequence of elements that precede it. If this element is less than the element preceding it, the two elements are exchanged. Once the element is exchanged with its predecessor, it is compared with its new predecessor element. Again, if it is less than its predecessor, the two elements are exchanged, and so on.

This process is repeated until one of two things happens: (1) the element is greater than or equal to its predecessor, or (2) the element is in the first position of the array (index [0]). In other words, the left-to-right compare/exchange process shown in Figure 10-4 ceases when the element under examination has been "inserted" into its proper position in the sorted portion of the array. This compare/exchange process represents repetition from left to right in the figure and will result in another loop structure in our algorithm. So, we can identify two repetitive processes in the figure: one from top to bottom, and one from left to right. How are the two repetitive processes related? Well, it seems that for each top-to-bottom pass through the array, the compare/exchange process is executed from left to right. Thus, the left-to-right process must be nested within the top-to-bottom process. This will be reflected in our algorithm by two loop structures: one controlling the left-to-right compare/exchange process that must be nested inside a second loop controlling the top-to-bottom process. Look at the figure again to make sure that you see this nested repetition. Now that you have an idea of how insertion sort works, here is the formal algorithm:

insertSort() **Algorithm**

```
insertSort()
BEGIN
  Set i = second array index.
  While  (i <= last array index)
      Set j = i.
      While ( (j > first array index) AND (array[j] < array[j − 1]) )
          Exchange array[j] and array[j − 1].
          Decrement j.
      Increment i.
END.
```

The variables *i* and *j* in the algorithm correspond to the *i* and *j* previously shown in Figure 10-4. The variable *i* controls the outer loop, and *j* controls the inner loop. Notice that *i* begins at the second array index. Why doesn't it begin at the first array index? Because the first element in the array is always sorted relative to any preceding elements, right? So, the first pass begins with the second array element. The first statement in the outer loop sets *j* equal to *i*. Thus, both *i* and *j* locate the first element in the unsorted portion of the array at the beginning of each pass. Now, the inner loop will exchange the element located by *j*, which is *array*[*j*], with its predecessor element, which is *array*[*j* − 1], as long as *j* is greater than the first array index, *and* element *array*[*j*] is less than element *array*[*j* − 1]. Once the exchange is made, *j* is decremented. This forces *j* to follow the element being inserted into the sorted portion of the array. The exchanges continue until either there are no elements preceding element *array*[*j*] that are greater than element *array*[*j*], or the element is inserted into the first element position.

Once the inner loop is broken, element *array*[*j*] is inserted in its correct position relative to the elements that precede it. Then, another pass is made by incrementing the outer loop control variable *i*, setting *j* to *i*, and executing the inner loop again. This nested looping process continues until *i* is incremented past the last array position.

Study the preceding algorithm and compare it to Figure 10-4 until you are sure that you understand *insertSort()*. Now for the Java code.

Coding the Program

We have already developed the *insertSort()* method header. The algorithm is easily coded as a method in Java, like this:

```java
public void insertSort(int array[], int SIZE)
{
   int i;        //OUTER LOOP CONTROL VARIABLE
   int j;        //INNER LOOP CONTROL VARIABLE
   int temp;     //CREATE TEMPORARY VARIABLE

   //SET i TO SECOND ARRAY INDEX
   i = 1;
   //MAKE SIZE - 1 PASSES THRU ARRAY
   while(i < SIZE)
   {
      //j LOCATES FIRST ELEMENT OF UNSORTED ARRAY PORTION
      j = i;

      //COMPARE/EXCHANGE array[j] AND array[j - 1]
      while((j > 0)&&(array[j] < array[j - 1]))
      {
         //EXCHANGE ARRAY ELEMENTS
         temp = array[j];
         array[j] = array[j-1];
         array[j-1] = temp;
         //MAKE j FOLLOW INSERT ELEMENT
         --j;
      }//END INNER WHILE
      //MAKE i LOCATE FIRST ELEMENT OF UNSORTED PORTION
      ++i;
   }//END OUTER WHILE
}//END insertSort()
```

The *insertSort()* code should be straightforward from the algorithm that we just analyzed. Study the code and compare it to the algorithm. You will find that they are identical from both a logical and structural point of view.

Next, we will place this method in our earlier *IntegerArrayProcessing* class which already contains the *seqSearch()* method. Here is the modified class code:

```
class IntegerArrayProcessing
{
  //PARAMETERLESS CONSTRUCTOR
  public IntegerArrayProcessing()
  {
  }//END CONSTRUCTOR

  //SEQUENTIAL SEARCH METHOD
  public int seqSearch(int array[], int SIZE, int element)
  {
    boolean found = false;          //INITIALIZE found TO false
    int index = 0;                  //ARRAY INDEX VARIABLE

    //SEARCH ARRAY UNTIL FOUND OR REACH END OF ARRAY
    while((!found)&&(index < SIZE))
    {
      if(array[index] == element)   //TEST ARRAY ELEMENT
        found = true;               //IF EQUAL, SET found TO TRUE
      else                          //ELSE INCREMENT ARRAY INDEX
        ++index;
    }//END WHILE

    //IF ELEMENT FOUND, RETURN ELEMENT POSITION IN ARRAY
    //ELSE RETURN -1.
    if(found)
      return index;
    else
      return -1;
}//END seqSearch()

public void insertSort(int array[], int SIZE)
{
 int i;        //OUTER LOOP CONTROL VARIABLE
 int j;        //INNER LOOP CONTROL VARIABLE
 int temp;     //CREATE TEMPORARY VARIABLE

 //SET i TO SECOND ARRAY INDEX
 i = 1;
 //MAKE SIZE - 1 PASSES THRU ARRAY
 while(i < SIZE)
 {
    //j LOCATES FIRST ELEMENT OF UNSORTED ARRAY PORTION
    j = i;
    //COMPARE/EXCHANGE array[j] AND array[j - 1]
    while((j > 0)&&(array[j] < array[j - 1]))
```

```
    {
        //EXCHANGE ARRAY ELEMENTS
        temp = array[j];
        array[j] = array[j-1];
        array[j-1] = temp;
        //MAKE j FOLLOW INSERT ELEMENT
        --j;
    }//END INNER WHILE
    //MAKE i LOCATE FIRST ELEMENT OF UNSORTED PORTION
    ++i;
  }//END OUTER WHILE
 }//END insertSort()
}//END IntegerArrayProcessing CLASS
```

Now we have a class that can be used to search or sort an integer array. Finally, we need an application to test our *insertSort()* method. Here is one that will do the job:

```java
public class Action10_03
{
    public static void main(String[] args)
    {
        //DEFINE ARRAY SIZE
        final int SIZE = 25;

        //DEFINE INTEGER ARRAY
        int values[] = new int[SIZE];

        //CREATE GUI OBJECT
        StaugIO io = new StaugIO();

        //CREATE A CLASS OBJECT
        IntegerArrayProcessing myTest = new IntegerArrayProcessing();

        //FILL ARRAY WITH RANDOM VALUES
        for(int i = 0;i < SIZE; ++i)
            values[i] = (int)(Math.random()*100);

        //DISPLAY UNSORTED ARRAY IN AN INFO BOX
        String info = "The un-sorted array is\n";
        for(int i = 0; i < SIZE; ++i)
            info += values[i] + " ";
        io.writeInfo(info);

        //CALL seqSearch()
        myTest.insertSort(values,SIZE);

        //DISPLAY SORTED ARRAY IN AN INFO BOX
        info = "The sorted array is\n";
        for(int i = 0; i < SIZE; ++i)
            info += values[i] + " ";
        io.writeInfo(info);
```

```
     //EXIT PROGRAM
     System.exit(0);
   }//END main()
}//END Action10_03
```

Again, we have filled the array with random values for testing purposes. Once filled, we display the unsorted array within an information box, call our *insertSort()* method, and display the sorted array in an information box. Here is what the user would see during a typical run:

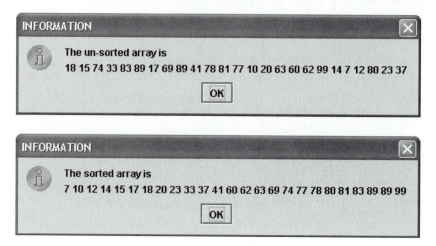

Problem Solving in Action: Searching an Array Using Recursion (Binary Search)

In this problem, we will develop another popular searching algorithm, called ***binary search***. The binary search algorithm that we will develop will employ recursion, although binary searching can also be done using iteration. One of the major differences between binary search and sequential search that you learned about earlier, is that binary search requires that the array be sorted prior to the search, whereas sequential search does not have this requirement. If, however, you have a sorted array to begin with, binary search is much faster than sequential search, especially for large arrays. For example, if you were to apply sequential search to an array of 1000 integers, the sequential search algorithm would make an *average* of 500 comparisons to find the desired element. Even worse, if the desired element is in the last array position, sequential search will make 1000 comparisons to find the element. On the other hand, a binary search would require a maximum of 10 comparisons to find the element, even if it is in the last array position! Of course, you must pay a price for this increased efficiency. The price you must pay is that the array must already be sorted.

Problem

Develop a Java method that can be called to search a sorted array of integers for a given element value and return the index of the element if it is found in the array. Employ a recursive binary search to accomplish this task.

We will be developing a Java method so our problem definition will again focus on the method header. However, before we can consider the method header, we must see how a recursive binary search works because the search algorithm will dictate our method parameters. So, let's first deal with the algorithm and then develop the method header.

Planning the Solution

Binary search represents a natural recursive operation. Remember that the idea behind recursion is to divide and conquer. You keep dividing a problem into simpler subproblems of exactly the same type, or clone the problem, until a terminating condition occurs. This is not the same as top-down software design, which divides problems into simpler subproblems. The idea with recursion is that the subproblems are clones of the original problem that operate on a different set of parameters. For example, suppose that you are searching for a name in a telephone book. Imagine starting at the beginning of the telephone book and looking at every name until you found the right one. This is exactly what sequential search does. Wouldn't it be much faster, on the average, to open up the book in the middle? Then, determine which half of the book contains the name that you are looking for, divide this section of the book in half, and so on, until you obtain the page on which the desired name appears. Of course, the book must be already sorted to do this, right? Here is an algorithm that describes the telephone book search just described.

A Recursive Telephone Book Search Algorithm

> *teleSearch()*
> BEGIN
>   If (the telephone book only contains one page)
>   Look for the name on the page.
>   Else
>   Open the book to the middle.
>   If (the name is in the first half)
>   *teleSearch*(first half of the book for the name).
>   Else
>   *teleSearch*(second half of the book for the name).
> END.

Do you see how this search is recursive? You keep performing the same basic operations until you come to the page that contains the name for which you are looking. In other words, the *teleSearch()* algorithm keeps calling itself in the nested `if/else` statement until the correct page is found. The reason that this is called a *binary* search process is that you must divide the book by 2 (*bi*) each time the algorithm calls itself.

Now, let's see how this process can be applied to searching an array of integers. We will call our recursive binary search method *binSearch()* and will develop our algorithm in several steps. Here is the first-level algorithm.

binSearch() **Algorithm: First Level**
binSearch()
BEGIN
  If (the array has only one element)
    Determine if this element is the element being searched for.
  Else
    Find the midpoint of the array.
    If (the element is in the first half)
        binSearch(first half).
    Else
        binSearch(second half).
END.

Notice how this algorithm is almost identical to the *teleSearch()* algorithm. Here, the recursive searching process continues until the array is reduced to one element that is tested against the element for which we are searching. Do you see how the search keeps calling itself until the terminating condition occurs? Although this algorithm provides the general binary search idea, we need to get more specific in order to code the algorithm. To do this, we must ask ourselves what data *binSearch()* needs to accomplish its task. Well, like sequential search, it needs an array to search and the element for which to search, right? However, sequential search deals with one array of a given size, whereas binary search needs to deal with arrays of different sizes as it keeps dividing the original array in half. Not only are these arrays of different sizes, but the first and last indices of each half are different. As a result, we must provide *binSearch()* with the boundaries of the array that it is dealing with at any given time. This can be done by passing the first and last indices of the given array segment to the method. Let's call these indices *first* and *last*.

We are now ready to write the method-interface description:

Method *binSearch()*:	Searches a sorted array of integers for a given value
Accepts:	An array of integers, an element for which to search, the first index of the array being searched, and the last index of the array being searched
Returns:	The array index of the element, if found, or the value −1 if the element is not found

This description gives us enough information to write the Java method header, as follows:

```
int binSearch(int array[], int element, int first, int last)
```

Here, *binSearch()* will return an integer value that represents the index of the element being searched for. Again, you will see that the value −1 will be returned if the element is not found in the array. The method receives the integer array being searched (*array[]*), the element being searched for (*element*), the first index of the array segment being searched (*first*), and the last index of the array segment being searched (*last*).

The next problem is to determine what the value of *first* and *last* will be for any given array segment during the search. Well, remember that we must divide any given array segment in half to produce two new array segments each time a recursive call to *binSearch()* is made. Given any array segment where the first index is *first* and the last index is *last*, we can determine the middle index, like this:

$$mid = (first + last)/2$$

By using this calculation, the first half of the array segment begins at *first* and ends at *mid* − 1, and the second half of the array segment begins at *mid* + 1 and ends at *last*. This idea is illustrated in Figure 10-5.

But, notice that neither half of the array contains the middle element. By using this technique, the two halves do not make a whole, right? So, before the split is made, suppose that we test the middle element to see if it is the element that we are looking for. The following test will do the job:

If (*array*[*mid*] == *element*)
Return *mid*.

If this test is true prior to the split, we have found the element we are looking for, and we can cease the recursive calls. Otherwise, the element stored in *array*[*mid*] is not the element we

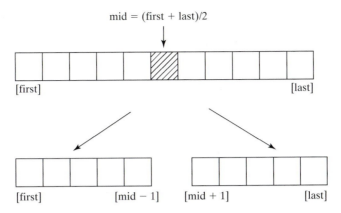

$$mid = (first + last)/2$$

[first]   [last]

[first]   [mid − 1]   [mid + 1]   [last]

FIGURE 10-5 Recursive binary search requires that an array be divided in half with each recursive call.

are looking for, and this array position can be ignored during the rest of the search. If this is the case, we will split the array segment and continue the recursive process. However, we have just added a second terminating condition to our recursive algorithm. Here are the two terminating conditions that we now have:

1. The array being searched has only one element.
2. $array[mid] == element$.

Either of these terminating conditions will cause the recursive calls to cease. Now, let's consider the first terminating condition more closely. How do we know if the array segment being searched has only one element? Well, as the recursive calls continue without finding the element, the array will eventually be reduced to a single element. If this is the element that we are looking for, the test *If array*[*mid*] $==$ *element* will be true, and the recursive calls will stop. If this is not the element that we are looking for, the value of *first* will become greater than the value of *last* on the next split. Why? Because if you think about the splitting action of the algorithm, you will realize that each recursive call causes *first* to increase and *last* to decrease. Thus, if the element is not in the array, the value of *first* will eventually become larger than the value of *last*. So, we can use this idea to test for the element not in the array, as well as use it for a terminating condition. Thus, we will replace the original terminating condition with the following statement:

$$If\ (first > last)$$
$$Return\ -1$$

If this condition occurs, the value −1 is returned, indicating that the element was not found, and the recursive calls cease.

Now, let's apply this knowledge to a second-level algorithm. Here it is:

binSearch() Algorithm: Second Level
binSearch(array, element, first, last)
BEGIN
  If (*first > last*)

```
        Return −1.
    Else
      Set mid = (first + last) / 2.
      If (array[mid] == element)
          Return mid.
      Else
        If (the element is in the first half)
              binSearch(array, element, first, mid − 1).
        Else
              binSearch(array, element, mid + 1, last).
    END.
```

It is much clearer now that our algorithm is performing recursion because the method is calling itself in either one of two places, depending on which half of the split array the element is likely to be found. Also, observe where the two terminating conditions are tested. If at the beginning of any recursive call, $first > last$, the element is not in the array, and the recursive calls will cease. In addition, if, after calculating *mid*, we find the element at $array[mid]$, the recursive calls will cease. In both cases, the method has finished executing, and a value is returned to the calling program. The last thing our algorithm needs is a way to determine if the element being searched for is likely to be in the first half or the second half of the split array. Here is where the requirement for a sorted array comes in. If the array is sorted, the element will likely be in the first half of the array when $element < array[mid]$; otherwise, the element is likely to be in the second half of the array. Notice that we are using the term "likely." We cannot guarantee that the element is in either half because it might not be in the array at all! All we can do is direct the search to the half where the element is likely to be, depending on the sorted ordering of elements. So, we can now complete our algorithm using this idea. Here is the final algorithm:

binSearch() Algorithm
```
binSearch(array, element, first, last)
BEGIN
If (first > last)
      Return −1.
Else
      Set mid = (first + last) / 2.
      If (array[mid] == element)
        Return mid.
      Else
        If (element < array[mid])
              binSearch(array, element, first, mid − 1).
        Else
              binSearch(array, element, mid + 1, last).
    END.
```

Notice how *elegant* the algorithm is. By elegant, we mean that the rather complicated binary search process is reduced to just a few statements. You *know* there is a lot going on here, but recursion allows us to express all of this processing in just a few statements. As you can see, recursive algorithms often provide simple solutions to problems of great complexity, where an equivalent iterative solution might be rather complex. This is not always the case because some recursive solutions are impractical relative to speed and memory efficiency. Remember the rule of thumb when considering recursion: Consider a recursive solution to a problem only when a simple iterative solution is not possible. You should be aware that binary search has a relatively simple iterative solution. You will code this solution for one of the problems at the end of the chapter.

Coding the Program

The required Java method now can be easily coded from the final algorithm. Here it is:

```java
public int binSearch(int array[], int element, int first, int last)
{
    int mid;                //ARRAY MIDPOINT
    if(first > last)        //IF ELEMENT NOT IN ARRAY
      return -1;            //RETURN -1, ELSE CONTINUE
    else
    {
      mid = (first + last) / 2;       //FIND MIDPOINT OF ARRAY
      if(element == array[mid])       //IF ELEMENT IS IN ARRAY[MID]
        return mid;                   //RETURN MID
      else                            //ELSE SEARCH APPROPRIATE HALF
        if(element < array[mid])
            return binSearch(array, element, first, mid - 1);
        else
            return binSearch(array, element, mid + 1, last);
    }//END OUTER ELSE
}//END binSearch()
```

You should not have any trouble understanding this code because it reflects the method header and algorithm just developed. The only difference here is that the recursive calls on *binSearch()* must be part of a `return` statement. Remember that Java requires that all execution paths of a non-void method lead to a `return` statement.

Now, we will add this final search method to our earlier *IntegerArrayProcessing* class, as follows:

```java
class IntegerArrayProcessing
{
  //PARAMETERLESS CONSTRUCTOR
  public IntegerArrayProcessing()
  {
  }//END CONSTRUCTOR

  //SEQUENTIAL SEARCH METHOD
  public int seqSearch(int array[], int SIZE, int element)
  {
    boolean found = false;        //INITIALIZE found TO false
    int index = 0;                //ARRAY INDEX VARIABLE

    //SEARCH ARRAY UNTIL FOUND OR REACH END OF ARRAY
    while((!found)&&(index < SIZE))
    {
      if(array[index] == element)     //TEST ARRAY ELEMENT
```

```
          found = true;                 //IF EQUAL, SET found TO TRUE
       else                             //ELSE INCREMENT ARRAY INDEX
          ++index;
    }//END WHILE

    //IF ELEMENT FOUND, RETURN ELEMENT POSITION IN ARRAY
    //ELSE RETURN -1.
    if(found)
      return index;
    else
      return -1;
}//END seqSearch()

public void insertSort(int array[], int SIZE)
{
 int i;        //OUTER LOOP CONTROL VARIABLE
 int j;        //INNER LOOP CONTROL VARIABLE
 int temp;     //CREATE TEMPORARY VARIABLE

 //SET i TO SECOND ARRAY INDEX
 i = 1;
 //MAKE SIZE - 1 PASSES THRU ARRAY
 while(i < SIZE)
 {
     //j LOCATES FIRST ELEMENT OF UNSORTED ARRAY PORTION
     j = i;

     //COMPARE/EXCHANGE array[j] AND array[j - 1]
     while((j > 0)&&(array[j] < array[j - 1]))
     {
         //EXCHANGE ARRAY ELEMENTS
          temp = array[j];
         array[j] = array[j-1];
         array[j-1] = temp;
         //MAKE j FOLLOW INSERT ELEMENT
         --j;
     }//END INNER WHILE
     //MAKE i LOCATE FIRST ELEMENT OF UNSORTED PORTION
     ++i;
 }//END OUTER WHILE
}//END insertSort()

public int binSearch(int array[], int element, int first, int last)
{
  int mid;            //ARRAY MIDPOINT
  if(first > last)    //IF ELEMENT NOT IN ARRAY
    return -1;        //RETURN -1, ELSE CONTINUE
  else
  {
    mid = (first + last) / 2;     //FIND MIDPOINT OF ARRAY
    if(element == array[mid])     //IF ELEMENT IS IN ARRAY[MID]
      return mid;                 //RETURN MID
```

```
        else                              //ELSE SEARCH APPROPRIATE HALF
          if(element < array[mid])
              return binSearch(array, element, first, mid - 1);
          else
              return binSearch(array, element, mid + 1, last);
    }//END OUTER ELSE
  }//END binSearch()
}//END IntegerArrayProcessing CLASS
```

Finally, we need an application class to test *binSearch()*. Here is the one we developed:

```
public class Action10_04
{
   public static void main(String[] args)
   {
     //DEFINE ARRAY SIZE
     final int SIZE = 25;

     //DEFINE INTEGER ARRAY
     int values[] = new int[SIZE];

     //DEFINE ELEMENT VARIABLE
     int element = 0;

     //DEFINE POSITION VARIABLE
     int position = -1;

     //CREATE GUI OBJECT
     StaugIO io = new StaugIO();

     //CREATE A CLASS OBJECT
     IntegerArrayProcessing myTest= new IntegerArrayProcessing();

     //FILL ARRAY WITH RANDOM VALUES
     for(int i = 0;i < SIZE; ++i)
         values[i] = (int)(Math.random()*100);

     //GET ELEMENT TO SEARCH FOR FROM USER
     element = io.readInt("Enter an element between 0 and 100 "
                          + "for which to search");

     //CALL insertSort() TO SORT ARRAY ELEMENTS
     myTest.insertSort(values,SIZE);

     //CALL binSearch() TO SEARCH FOR ELEMENT
     position = myTest.binSearch(values,element,0,SIZE-1);

     //DISPLAY ARRAY VALUES AND RESULTS IN AN INFO BOX
     String info = "The random array values are\n";
     for(int i = 0; i < SIZE; ++i)
       info += values[i] + " ";
```

```
   if(position == -1)
     io.writeInfo(info + "\nThe element was not found in the array.");
   else
     io.writeInfo(info + "\nThe element was found at position "
                   + position + " of the array.");
   //EXIT PROGRAM
   System.exit(0);
 }//END main()
}//END Action10_04
```

This code is almost identical to the code we used to test the *seqSearch()* method, with one important difference. Binary search requires that the array be sorted prior to the search, while sequential search does not have this requirement. As a result, we must make a call to our *insertSort()* method to sort the array prior to calling our *binSearch()* method.

So which is more efficient, sequential or binary search? Well, that depends. If an array is already sorted, like an array of names in a telephone book, then binary search is much more efficient than sequential search. However, if the array is completely random and unsorted, then sequential search is more efficient.

CHAPTER SUMMARY

An array is an important data structure used to locate and store elements of a given data type or class. The two components of any array are the elements that are stored in the array and the indices that locate the stored elements. Array elements can be any given data type or class, and array indices are always integers ranging from [0] to [$SIZE - 1$], where $SIZE$ is the number of elements in the array.

There are both one-dimensional arrays and multidimensional arrays. A one-dimensional array (list or vector) is a single row of elements and has a dimension of $1 \times SIZE$, where $SIZE$ is the number of elements in the array. In Java, the maximum index in any dimension is the size of the dimension ($SIZE$) minus 1.

Arrays can be initialized when they are defined by assigning initializing values and listing them within braces. When no initializing values are supplied, integer and floating-point arrays are initialized with zeros and character arrays are initialized with spaces.

To access array elements, you must use direct assignment statements, read/write statements, or loops. The `for` loop structure is the most common way of accessing multiple array elements.

Searching and sorting are common operations performed on arrays. Sequential search is an iterative search that looks for a given value in an array by sequentially comparing the value to the array elements, beginning with the first array element, until the value is found in the array or until the end of the array is reached. Binary search is a recursive process whereby the array is repeatedly divided into two (bi) smaller arrays until the search item is found or not found. Sequential search can be used to search both sorted and unsorted arrays, while binary search can only be used to search sorted arrays.

Many real-world applications require that information be sorted. There are several common sorting algorithms, including insertion sort, bubble sort, selection sort, and quick sort. All of these algorithms operate on arrays. The insertion sort algorithm is an iterative process that inserts a given element in the array in its correct place, relative to the elements that precede it in the array. You will be acquainted with bubble sort and selection sort in the chapter problems.

QUESTIONS AND PROBLEMS

Questions

1. What three things must be specified in order to define an array?

   Use the following array definition to answer questions 2–7.

   ```
   char characters[] = new char[15];
   ```

2. What is the index of the first array element?
3. What is the index of the last array element?
4. Write a statement that will place the character 'Z' in the third cell of the array.
5. Write a statement that will display the last array element on the console screen.
6. Write the code necessary to fill the array from keyboard entries. Make sure to prompt the user before each character entry.
7. Write a loop that will display all the array elements vertically on the console screen.
8. Show the contents of the following array:

   ```
   int integers[] = {1, 2, 3};
   ```

9. What is an array out-of-bounds error, and how does Java handle it?
10. Write a statement to define a `double` floating-point array of dimension $1 \times SIZE$ that will be initialized with all zeros.
11. Write a statement to define a character array of dimension $1 \times SIZE$ that will be initialized with all spaces.
12. What is wrong with the following definition?

    ```
    int numbers = {0, 1, 2, 3, 4};
    ```

13. Given the following array definition:

    ```
    int values[] = new int[10];
    ```

    Write a statement to place the product of the first and second array elements in the last element position.

    Use the following array definition to answer questions 14–16:

    ```
    String languages[] = {"Java", "C++", "COBOL", "Visual Basic"};
    ```

14. Write the header for a method called *stringLength()* that will receive the entire array and return the length of any string object in the array.
15. Write an implementation for method *stringLength()* that would be required to return the length of the last string in the array.
16. Write a *println()* statement to call the method in question 15 and pass the *languages* array to the method.
17. Write a header for a `void` method called *changeCharacters()* that will receive a character array.
18. Write a statement to call the method in question 17 and pass an array called *characters[]* to the method.
19. In general, what element position will be returned by the sequential search method developed in this chapter if there are multiple occurrences of the element in the array?
20. Revise the *insertSort()* algorithm to sort the array in descending order.

21. Why is binary search faster, on the average, than sequential search for sorted arrays?

22. When would sequential search be faster than binary search?

Problems

Least Difficult

1. Develop a class called *OddArray* to fill an array with all the odd integers from 1 to 50. Write one method to fill the array and another method to display the array, showing the odd integers across an information box separated by commas. Test your class via an application.

2. Develop a class called *StringArray* to read three stings from keyboard entries and place them in a string array. Provide one method to read the strings and another to display the strings in an information window. Test your class via an application.

3. Develop a class called *CharacterArray* to read a list of 10 character elements from a keyboard entry and display them in reverse order. Use one method to fill an array with the entered elements and another method to display the array within an information window in reverse order. Test your methods via an application.

4. Develop a class called *AddressArray* that uses a string array to store the user's name, street address, city, state, zip code, and telephone number. Provide one method to fill the array and another to display the array contents using proper addressing format within an information box. Test your methods via an application.

More Difficult

5. Another common iterative sorting algorithm is **bubble sort**. Here's the algorithm:

```
bubbleSort()
BEGIN
    Set passes = 1.
    Set exchange = true.
    While (passes < number of array elements) AND (exchange == true)
        Set exchange = false.
        For index = (first array index) To (last array index − passes)
            If array[index] > array[index + 1]
                Swap(array[index], array[index + 1]).
                Set exchange = true.
        Set passes = passes + 1.
END.
```

The bubble sort algorithm makes several passes through the array, comparing adjacent values during each pass. The adjacent values are exchanged if the first value is larger than the second value. The process terminates when $N - 1$ passes have been made (where N is the number of elements in the array), or when no more exchanges are possible.

Develop a class called *BubbleSort* that has three methods as follows:

- A method called *fillArray()* that will fill an integer array with 10 random values.
- A method called *displayArray()* that will display the array in an information box.
- A method called *bubbleSort()* that will sort the array using the bubble sort algorithm.

Write an application to test your class so that the user is able to examine the unsorted array followed by the sorted array.

6. Another common iterative sorting algorithm is ***selection sort.*** The algorithm goes like this:

```
selectionSort()
BEGIN
    For index1 = (first array index) To (last array index)
        Set position = index1.
        Set smallest = array[position].
        For index2 = (index1 + 1) To (last array index)
            If array[index2] < smallest
                Set position = index2.
                Set smallest = array[position].
        Set array[position] = array[index1].
        Set array[index1] = smallest.
END.
```

As with bubble sort, selection sort makes several passes through the array. The first pass examines the entire array and places the smallest element in the first array position. The second pass examines the array beginning at the second element. The smallest element in this array segment is found and placed in the second array position. The third pass examines the array beginning at the third element, finds the smallest element in this array segment, and places it in the third element position. The process continues until there are no more array segments left.

Develop a class called *SelectionSort* that has three methods as follows:

- A method called *fillArray()* that will fill an integer array with 10 random values.
- A method called *displayArray()* that will display the array in an information box.
- A method called *selectionSort()* that will sort the array using the selection sort algorithm.

Write an application to test your class so that the user is able to examine the unsorted array followed by the sorted array.

7. Here is an iterative solution for the binary search:

```
binarySearch()
BEGIN
    Set found = false.
    While ( !found AND first <= last)
        Set mid = (first + last) / 2.
        If (element == array[mid])
            Set found = true.
        Else
            If (element < array[mid])
                Set last = mid − 1.
            Else
                Set first = mid + 1.
    If (found)
        Return mid.
    Else
        Return −1.
END.
```

Develop a class called *BinarySearch* that will search for a given element in an integer array. Your class must have methods to fill an array with random values, display the array, sort the array, and apply binary search to find a given element in the array.

Write an application to test your class. Remember you must sort the array using a sorting method prior to calling the binary search method.

8. Develop a class called *MaxValue* that will take an *unsorted* integer array and find the location of the maximum value in the array. (*Hint:* Copy the array into another array and sort this second array to determine its maximum value. Then search the original array for this value.) Write an application to test your class.

9. A stack ADT is ideal to implement using a class because it must include the stack data elements, as well as the methods that operate on those elements in a tightly bound manner. As a result, object-oriented programming is perfect for implementing stacks. Here is a description for a *Stack* class:

Class: *Stack*

Data Members: An array to hold the stack elements

     An integer variable called *top* that locates

     the top of the stack

Method Members: *Stack()*: A method to initialize the stack

     clearStack(): A method to clear the stack

     emptyStack(): A method to determine if the stack is empty

     fullStack(): A method to determine if the stack is full

     push(element): A method to place *element* on the stack

     pop(): A method to remove an element from the stack

Assume the stack can hold *MAX* characters. A private member called *top* is declared to access the top element of the stack. Thus, *top* provides the array index of the top element in the stack. The stack is empty when *top* is -1, and the stack is full when *top* is $MAX-1$. Write the stack method implementations according to the following criteria:

- *Stack()* is a constructor that initializes *top* to -1.
- *clearStack()* sets *top* to -1.
- *emptyStack()* tests to see if $top = -1$.
- *fullStack()* tests to see if $top = MAX - 1$.
- *push(element)* checks to see if the stack is full by calling the *fullStack()* method. Then it must increment *top* and place *element* in the array at the index located by *top*.
- *pop()* checks to see if the stack is empty by calling the *emptyStack()* method. If the stack is not empty, it returns the character element located at the array index located by *top* and decrements *top*.

Write an application to test your stack class completely.

11

Graphical User Interfaces— GUIs Part I

OBJECTIVES

When you are finished with this chapter, you should have a good understanding of the following:

■ How to build event-driven programs

■ How to design and build a GUI

■ How to write an inner event handler class

■ How to use listener and adapter classes

■ The basic GUI components found in the Java *swing* package

■ The use of a layout manager to place GUI components onto a window

■ How to capture GUI component events using listeners and event handlers

■ How to write event handling logic

■ How to convert GUI input data from string data to numeric data for calculation

Introduction

Up to this point, you have been programming using simple dialog boxes generated by the *StaugIO* class methods. Although this provides somewhat of a GUI, there is much more that you can do with GUIs in Java. As you are aware, most commercial and Internet programs today are GUI programs. GUI design is a big area, not only in information systems, but in psychology and graphic arts as well. If this material interests you, you might want to take additional courses in these fields, as well as advanced graphics courses in computer information systems or computer science.

Until now, your programs have employed procedural control of the program logic, whereby control statements, such as decision

395

and loop statements, control the flow of the program. Even though your programs have been object-oriented programs, they have all employed procedural control. Windowed programs, on the other hand, are event-driven programs, whereby the flow of the program logic is dictated by external events. These events usually are the result of a mouse action, such as clicking or movement, or a keyboard stroke. ***Event-driven programs*** generate windows which provide any number of GUI components from which the user can choose to dictate the program behavior. For example, clicking on a button creates an event that dictates a specific program action. This chapter and the next are devoted to event-driven programming.

As you know, the background for a GUI component is the window. In Java, a window is referred to as a ***frame***. Java uses a ***frame*** as the basis for a container to hold GUI components. So, to build an application GUI in Java, we must first create a generic frame. Then, we will use this frame as a container which will contain our GUI components. The components will be added to the frame container using a ***layout manager***. A layout manager provides a standard, predefined way to lay out, or place, our components within a GUI container. Finally, we will add ***event handlers*** to our GUI code to capture and process events generated by the GUI components.

This chapter and the next will provide you with the basic techniques required to design and build GUIs. Make sure that you get plenty of practice by coding the examples in these chapters, doing the problems at the end of the chapters, and experimenting on your own. Most of the classes discussed in this chapter are provided in the GUI workshop in Appendix C. At this time, it would be a good idea to go through the workshop and experiment with the programs to become familiar with their "look and feel" before getting into the detailed discussions that follow. In this chapter, you will learn how to design and code your own GUIs using the components demonstrated within these workshop modules. The material in this text employs the Java *swing* package components which are a Java 2.0+ issue. So, to compile and execute the programs in this text you must have Java, version 2.0, or greater.

11.1   Frames—*JFrame*

As stated in the chapter introduction, a ***frame*** is the basis for a container used to hold GUI components. A frame is used to generate a generic window that inherits all the general characteristics of any window. These include a window title, window border, window sizing as well as window maximizing and minimizing. All graphical components in a Java *application* must be placed in a frame; however, this differs from the requirements of a Java applet. In a Java applet program, the applet itself acts as the container for GUI components. A window created from a frame is nothing more than an object of the standard *JFrame* class. The *JFrame* class is found in the *javax.swing* package. To create a simplified frame you must do three things as follows:

- Import the *javax.swing* package.
- Declare a subclass of the *JFrame* class.
- Write a constructor that sets the frame title.

Here is a simplified frame class that will get us started:

```
import javax.swing.*;           //FOR swing CLASSES

//INHERITS AND CUSTOMIZES FRAME CLASS TO ADD DESIRED FEATURES
class SimpleFrame extends JFrame
{
  //CONSTRUCTOR
  public SimpleFrame(String title)
  {
      //CALL SUPERCLASS CONSTRUCTOR
      super(title);
  }//END SimpleFrame() CONSTRUCTOR
}//END SimpleFrame CLASS
```

Here, we have created a *SimpleFrame* class that inherits, or extends, the standard *JFrame* class. Of course, we have to import the *javax.swing* package in order to inherit the *JFrame* class. All GUI containers and components are provided in the Java *javax.swing* package. Our *SimpleFrame* class only consists of a constructor to initialize the frame by calling the superclass constructor. Since the superclass is *JFrame*, a call to its constructor will pass a string, called *title,* required to set the frame title.

Now that we have a frame subclass, all we need to do is to place it in an application and use it. In the application, you must do three things, as follows:

- Create an object of your frame class, passing the frame title to the constructor.
- Set the size of the frame, or window, in pixels (picture elements).
- Show the frame to the user.

Here is the required code:

```
//APPLICATION CLASS TO TEST SimpleFrame CLASS
public class FrameTest
{
  public static void main(String[] args)
  {
    //DEFINE FRAME OBJECT
    SimpleFrame window = new SimpleFrame("SimpleFrame");

    //SET FRAME SIZE
    window.setSize(500,300);

    //MAKE FRAME VISIBLE
    window.show();
  }//END main()
}//END FrameTest
```

In the first line of code, we define our *SimpleFrame* object, called *window*. Notice that we have placed a string argument in the constructor. The string argument will be the frame, or window, title which will appear in the title bar at the top of the window.

In the second line of code our *window* object calls the *setSize()* method to set the size of the frame, in pixels. The first argument of *setSize()* is the width of the frame and the second argument is the height of the frame. Thus, the size of our frame is 500 pixels wide by 300 pixels high. The size of a typical display, in pixels, depends on your operating system platform as well as your system's display settings. We have used an 800 pixel by 600 pixel system setting for the graphical images shown in this text. However, your system settings might be different. Typical display settings are 640 × 480, 800 × 600, 1024 × 768, and 1280 × 1024, just to mention a few.

In the last line of *main()* we use our *window* object to call the *show()* method. This makes our frame visible to the user. The frame is not displayed until the *show()* method is called by the frame object. Here is the window produced by our *SimpleFrame* class:

If you execute the program, you will find that the window which it creates has all the features of a standard window, except for one important feature. You can maximize, minimize, resize, and close the window. However, there is one problem with this class. When you close the window, you would expect the *FrameTest.java* application to terminate, but it doesn't! Why, you ask? Because the *SimpleFrame* class does not detect the close *event*. To close the window you would normally click the close button in the upper right-hand corner, or select the close option in the control box menu in the upper left-hand corner. However, even though the close button and menu are part of the window, closing requires a window event. Our frame class does not yet include the code to handle such an event. Although the window will in fact close, the application is still running and must be stopped. In a Windows environment, you must hit *Ctrl-Alt-Delete* at this point and end the program task. In an Apple® Macintosh® environment, you end the task with *option-command-escape*. So, let's talk about how to handle events.

TABLE 11-1   Events Defined by Java

Event Class	Source Object(s)	User Action
WindowEvent	A frame	Window opened/closed
ActionEvent	A button	Click button
	A text field	Press Enter
	A text area	Press Enter
	A menu item	Select menu item
	A combo box	Select/deselect item
ItemEvent	A checkbox	Select/deselect item
	A radio button	Select/deselect item
ListSelection	A list box	Select/deselect item
KeyEvent	A key	Key pressed or released
MouseEvent	A mouse	Move or click mouse

Event Handling

As you know, windowed programs are event-driven programs, whereby the flow of the program logic is dictated by external events. These events usually are the result of a mouse action, such as clicking or movement, or a keyboard stroke.

Java defines several types of events, some of which are summarized in Table 11-1. Notice that each different type of event is associated with a given ***source object***. As its name implies, a source object is the object responsible for the event. Of course, each type of source object responds to a certain action by the user. These classes are found in the *java.awt.event* package and we must import this package into our GUI programs to detect user events.

Event Listeners   The event that we are interested in at this time is *WindowEvent*, because this event is associated with the closing of a window. Now, when an event occurs, the source object (frame object in the case of *WindowEvent*) triggers the predefined event. Thus, when the close button is clicked in a frame, the frame source object generates a *WindowEvent*. To detect the event, you need to add a ***listener*** for the frame. If a listener is not present, no event handling can occur. Adding a listener is accomplished with an associated *add_____Listener()* method. The blank, _____, in the foregoing method name is the type of event for which to listen from Table 11-1. For example, the *add<u>Window</u>Listener()* method is used to add a listener for a *WindowEvent* source object, the *add<u>Action</u>Listener()* method is used to add a listener for an *ActionEvent* source object, the *add<u>Item</u>Listener()* method is used to add a listener for an *ItemEvent* source object, and so on. Now when an event occurs, all the listeners will be notified. The listeners reference their respective listener class. For instance, a window listener references the *WindowListener* class, an action listener references the *ActionListener* class, and so on. Each class has one or more predefined abstract methods to handle the event. For example, the *WindowListener* class includes the *windowClosed()* method and the *ActionListener* class includes the *actionPerformed()* method. These methods are called automatically to handle the event. The listener classes and corresponding methods are listed in Table 11-2.

TABLE 11-2   Listener Classes and Corresponding Methods and Adapter Classes

Component	Listener Class	Method(s)	Adapter Class
Frame	WindowListener	windowClosing() windowOpened() windowClosed() windowIconified() windowDeiconified() windowActivated() windowDeactivated()	WindowAdapter
Button Combo Box Text Field Text Area	ActionListener	actionPerformed()	ActionAdapter
List Box	ListSelectionListener	valueChanged()	none
Check Box	ItemListener	itemStateChanged()	none
Radio Button	ItemListener	itemStateChanged()	none
Mouse	MouseListener	mousePressed() mouseReleased() mouseClicked()	MouseAdapter
	MouseMotionListener	mouseDragged() mouseMoved()	MouseMotionAdapter
Keyboard	KeyListener	keyPressed() keyReleased() keyTyped()	KeyAdapter

To detect an event, you must add a listener for the source event object. Once a listener is present, the corresponding listener class event method(s) will be called *automatically* to handle an event when it occurs on that source event object.

Remember, all the methods in Table 11-2 are abstract methods. Therefore, they are not implemented within their respective class. You must implement them in your GUI subclasses to handle a given type of event. If all of this sounds very complicated, it is! Maybe the flowcharts in Figures 11-1 and 11-2 will help. The flowchart in Figure 11-1 illustrates the programming process that you must go through in creating a GUI component object, adding a listener for the object, and processing an object event by implementing an event method. Notice from Figure 11-1 that you must first define an

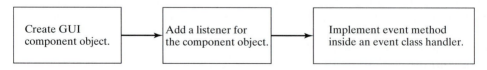

FIGURE 11-1   The steps required by you, the programmer, to create a GUI component and process the component event.

object for a GUI component class, then add a listener for the object, and then write the implementation code for one of the standard listener class methods to process, or handle, the event. All of this will be done inside your frame class.

   The flowchart in Figure 11-2 shows how Java detects and handles an event. Notice that the user action generates an event which is detected by a listener which has been added for the component object that generated the event. An event object is then passed to the event class method(s) called to handle the event.

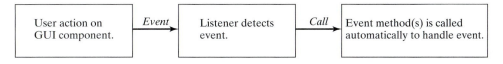

FIGURE 11-2   The event processing provided by Java.

   Let's look at some code that will allow us to handle a window closing event. Here is the frame class we developed earlier:

```java
import javax.swing.*;     //FOR FRAME CLASS
import java.awt.event.*; //FOR GUI EVENT HANDLERS

//INHERITS AND CUSTOMIZES FRAME CLASS TO ADD DESIRED FEATURES
class FrameWithClose extends JFrame implements WindowListener
{
  //CONSTRUCTOR
  public FrameWithClose(String title)
  {
      //CALL SUPERCLASS CONSTRUCTOR
      super(title);

      //ADD LISTENER FOR THIS FRAME
      addWindowListener(this);
  }//END FrameWithClose() CONSTRUCTOR

  public void windowClosing(WindowEvent e)
  {
    System.exit(0);     //EXIT TO OPERATING SYSTEM
  }//END windowClosing()

  public void windowClosed(WindowEvent e)
  {
  }
  public void windowDeiconified(WindowEvent e)
  {
  }
  public void windowIconified(WindowEvent e)
  {
  }
  public void windowActivated(WindowEvent e)
  {
  }
```

```
public void windowDeactivated(WindowEvent e)
{
}
public void windowOpened(WindowEvent e)
{
}
}//END FrameWithClose CLASS
```

The code that has been added is printed in bold type. Of course, the class name has been changed to *FrameWithClose* to reflect its new capability. First, notice that we have imported the *java.awt.event* package. This is where all the listener classes are located. Next, you see that the class header line includes the code implements WindowListener. This is required to use the *WindowListener* class. The *WindowListener* class is an **interface class.** Interface classes contain abstract methods that must be implemented in any class which uses the interface class. The next change that you see is the statement addWindowListener(this). This statement adds a listener for the object. But, which object? Well, "this" object. The this reference is used so that when an object is created for the class, a listener will be created for "this" object. Does *this* make sense? Finally you see that all of the *WindowListener* methods from Table 11-2 have been implemented. When a class defines several abstract methods, such as *WindowListener* does, you must implement all the methods in any subclass. Even though we do not need all the methods to process a window closing event, we must implement every method. Notice that only the *windowClosing()* method includes code, while the other methods do not. The code required in the *windowClosing()* method is simply System.exit(0).

Here's how it works: When a window event occurs, *WindowListener* calls *windowClosing()*, passing the event source object to the method. The event source object within the method is the method parameter, *e*. You can call the parameter anything you want, but standard Java convention is to call it simply *e*, for "event". The *windowClosing()* method executes, forcing the system to exit, thereby terminating any application that generated "this" frame. All the other *WindowListener* methods are also called, but do not perform any meaningful action in this application since they do not contain any code. Notice that we have not placed any code within the body of these methods. Now, here is an application that tests our new *FrameWithClose* class:

```
//CLASS TO TEST FrameWithClose CLASS
public class FrameWithCloseTest
{
  public static void main(String[] args)
  {

    //DEFINE FRAME OBJECT
    FrameWithClose window = new FrameWithClose("FrameWithClose");

    //SET FRAME SIZE
    window.setSize(500,300);
```

```
   //MAKE FRAME VISIBLE
  window.show();
 }//END main()
}//END FrameWithCloseTest
```

As you can see, our application class has not changed, except for its name.

Event Listeners and Handlers

Java uses what is called the ***event delegation model*** to process GUI events. The idea is that you create a GUI component object that can generate an event. Next, you create an event handler object that processes, or handles, the event. We say that the component object "delegates" the event handling task to the handler object. We have done this in a roundabout way in the foregoing *FrameWithClose* class. Now we will do it in a more direct way by creating an additional ***handler*** class, as follows:

```
private class WindowHandler extends WindowAdapter
{
  public void windowClosing(WindowEvent e)
  {
     System.exit(0);  //EXIT TO OPERATING SYSTEM
  }//END windowClosing()
}//END WindowHandler CLASS
```

Inner and Adapter Classes   Before we analyze this code, we need to discuss ***inner classes*** and ***adapter classes***. An inner class is simply a nested class. In other words, an inner class is a class contained inside of another class because it only serves the class in which it is contained. Therefore, it is usually designated as a `private` class as shown in our foregoing *WindowHandler* class code.

An ***inner class*** is a class which is nested, or contained, inside another class which is usually designated as a `private` class.

An ***adapter class*** is a standard class that implements all the methods in a given standard interface class.

An ***adapter class*** is a standard class that implements all the methods in a given standard interface class. The adapter classes associated with the standard listener classes are also listed in Table 11-2. For example, we said the *WindowListener* class is an interface class that contains several abstract methods as shown in Table 11-2. The associated *WindowAdapter* class provides an empty implementation for each of these methods so that you don't have to implement them in your code. By using an adapter class you only need to concern yourself with implementing the abstract method you need, like *windowClosing()* in our situation. This shortens the code we need for our program. So, you see that our foregoing *WindowHandler* class inherits, or extends, the *WindowAdapter* class. Then, inside this class we place our implementation for the *windowClosing()* method. That explains our *WindowHandler* class code. Now all we need to do is place this as an inner class within our *FrameWithClose* class, like this:

```java
import javax.swing.*;      //FOR FRAME CLASS
import java.awt.event.*;   //FOR GUI EVENT HANDLERS

//INHERITS AND CUSTOMIZES FRAME CLASS TO ADD DESIRED FEATURES
class FrameWithClose extends JFrame
{
  //CONSTRUCTOR
  public FrameWithClose(String title)
  {
    //CALL SUPERCLASS CONSTRUCTOR
    super(title);

    //ADD WINDOW LISTENER
    addWindowListener(new WindowHandler());
  }//END FrameWithClose() CONSTRUCTOR

  //WINDOW EVENT HANDLER CLASS
  private class WindowHandler extends WindowAdapter
  {
      public void windowClosing(WindowEvent e)
      {
        System.exit(0);   //EXIT TO OPERATING SYSTEM
    }//END windowClosing()
  }//END WindowHandler CLASS
}//END FrameWithClose CLASS
```

Here you see that all the empty code required to implement the *WindowListener* methods is gone and replaced by our inner *WindowHandler* class. There is one other change we need to point out. We have replaced the statement

```java
addWindowListener(this);
```

with the statement

```java
addWindowListener(new WindowHandler());
```

You see that we are still calling the *addWindowListener* method to add a listener for the frame. However, we have replaced `this` in the method argument with `new` WindowHandler(). What do you suppose this does? Well, anytime you see the keyword `new` you know an object is being created, right? So, we are creating an object for our inner *WindowHandler* class as an argument for the *addWindowListener()* method. This is our event object that is passed to the *windowClosing()* event method inside the class. Of course it is called *e* inside the method. This is a neat little trick. We actually create an object as a method argument. Why not, since we don't need to reference this object any other place. If we needed to reference it someplace else, we would give it a name and create it separately, using it as the method argument, like this:

```java
WindowHandler windowEvent = new WindowHandler();
addWindowListener(windowEvent);
```

As you can see, this little trick simply saved us one line of code. Now we have a class that generates a simple frame and allows us to close the frame and terminate the application in which the class is used. Of course, our frame is not very useful without anything on it. Think of it as an artist's canvas on which you can now add some functionality. How can you do this? You're right, by adding additional GUI components to allow for true event-driven applications. So our next task is to expand our frame discussion to a discussion of the most popular GUI components contained in Java. The various GUI component classes that we will cover in this text are listed in Table 11-3. These will provide you with the tools to build most of your GUIs. However, be aware that Java *swing* provides more components than are listed here. All these components are subclasses of the *JComponent* class. So, look under *JComponent* in your IDE help for a complete listing of GUI component classes with links to these classes. Once you learn how to deal with one component, all the others are similar. Let's begin with the simple button.

The methods used in this section and associated with the *JFrame* class are summarized in Table 11-4.

TABLE 11-3   Standard GUI Component Classes Provided by Java

Component Class	Component	Description
JButton	Button	An area that generates an event when clicked
JCheckBox	Check box	A Boolean component that can be selected or deselected
JComboBox	Combo box	A drop-down list from which the user can make a single choice
JLabel	Label	Non-editable, non-event text
JList	List	A list of selectable items with a scrollbar
JMenu	Menu	A set of selectable options located at the top of a window on a menu bar
JPanel	Panel	A container in which components can be placed and subsequently added to a frame container
JRadioButton	Radio button	A set of selectable buttons whereby only one button can be selected at any one time
JScrollPane	Scrollbar	A sliding bar to control position
JTextField	Text field	An editable or non-editable single line of text
JTextArea	Text area	An editable or non-editable area consisting of one or more lines of text

TABLE 11-4   Summary of Methods Used in this Section

Method	Description
addWindowListener()	Adds a listener for a frame
JFrame(String)	Creates new frame with *String* title
setSize(int, int)	Sets frame size to width by height in pixels
show()	Makes the frame visible to the user
windowClosing(WindowEvent)	Handles a window closing event

QUICK CHECK

1. What package must be imported into a program to use the GUI components available in *swing*?
2. The container used to hold GUI components in a Java application is the _____.
3. Write a statement to create a frame object called *myFrame* that will generate a window with a title of "This is my first frame".
4. Write a statement to set the size of *myFrame* to 450 by 250 pixels.
5. Write a statement to make *myFrame* visible.
6. What three things must you do as a programmer to set up a window component and process an event generated by that component?
7. What method is used to handle a window closing event?
8. Write a statement to add a listener for a frame that you have created.
9. What package must be imported into a program to handle a window event?
10. What is an inner class?
11. What is an adapter class?

11.2   Containers and Buttons—*Container* and *JButton*

An application GUI class is always a subclass of *JFrame* to which we will add GUI components and event handlers. Thus, when building a GUI class there are two major tasks to perform within the frame:

1. Create the GUI components and add listeners for them.
2. Create an event handler for each component.

The first task is always done within the frame class constructor, and the second task is done within an inner class. So, let's get to the coding details. To create a button, or any GUI component for that matter, we must first create a subclass of *JFrame* as we did earlier. We must then create a *container* to hold our button. Once we have a container we can create a button object and add it to the container. Here is the class we developed earlier, with the code required for a button shown in bold type:

```
import javax.swing.*;        //FOR SWING COMPONENT CLASSES
import java.awt.event.*;     //FOR EVENT HANDLING
import java.awt.*;           //FOR Container CLASS

//A FRAME CLASS WITH A SINGLE BUTTON
class FrameWithButton extends JFrame
{
   //DECLARE BUTTON OBJECT
   private JButton button;

   //CONSTRUCTOR
   public FrameWithButton(String title)
   {
      super(title);                          //CALL SUPERCLASS CONSTRUCTOR
```

```
    //CREATE A CONTAINER
    Container container = getContentPane();

    //DEFINE BUTTON OBJECT
    button = new JButton("Click Me, I'm a Button");

    //ADD BUTTON TO CONTAINER
    container.add(button);

    //ADD ACTION LISTENER AND BUTTON EVENT HANDLER
    button.addActionListener(new ButtonHandler());

    //ADD WINDOW LISTENER AND EVENT HANDLER
    addWindowListener(new WindowHandler());
  }//END FrameWithButton() CONSTRUCTOR

  //WINDOW EVENT HANDLER CLASS
  private class WindowHandler extends WindowAdapter
  {
    public void windowClosing(WindowEvent e)
    {
      System.exit(0);  //EXIT TO OPERATING SYSTEM
    }//END windowClosing()
  }//END WindowHandler CLASS

  //BUTTON EVENT HANDLER CLASS
  private class ButtonHandler implements ActionListener
  {
    //actionPerformed METHOD
    public void actionPerformed(ActionEvent e)
    {
      JOptionPane.showOptionDialog(null,
                        "Congratulations!\nYou Clicked Me",
                        "INFORMATION",
                        JOptionPane.INFORMATION_MESSAGE);

    }//END actionPerformed
  }//END ButtonHandler CLASS
}//END FrameWithButton CLASS
```

The first change you see is that we changed the class name to *FrameWithButton*. Next, you see that we have imported the *java.awt.** package. This is required for the *Container* class that we will use shortly. The first statement in the class declares a button object called *button* of the *JButton* class. Then the class constructor *FrameWithButton()* is coded. In building a GUI, you will always use the frame class constructor to perform the following tasks:

- Create a container to hold your GUI components.
- Define your GUI component objects.
- Add your GUI component objects to the container.
- Add a listener for each event-generating component.

So, it's the constructor that actually creates the GUI and gets it ready for an event. Well, isn't this the job of any constructor, to get things ready in preparation for using an object of the class? Here, after a call to super to display the frame title, our constructor creates a container object, called *container*, to hold our *button* object. Swing requires that all components be placed within a *Container* class content pane. The statement

```
Container container = getContentPane();
```

defines a *Container* class object and creates a content pane by calling the *getContentPane()* method.

The next statement instantiates the button object and calls a *JButton* constructor. This constructor takes a string argument which is used as the button label. So our button will have a label that says: "Click Me, I'm a Button". *(Be aware that the JButton class contains additional versions of the overloaded constructor for adding other things, like icons, to the button. See your IDE help for the use of these other versions.)*

Next, we need to add the *button* object to the container. This is accomplished by calling the *add()* method using our *container* object, and providing our *button* object as its argument using the statement

```
container.add(button);
```

Finally, we must add a listener for our *button* object. This is done with the statement

```
button.addActionListener(new ButtonHandler());
```

Notice that we use our *button* object to call the *addActionListener()* method providing a *ButtonHandler* object as an argument. Observe that all of this code is part of the frame constructor. As a result, both the frame and its button are created when an object is defined for our *FrameWithButton* class.

Now, we are almost there. From Table 11-2 you see that the *ActionListener* class has a single abstract method called *actionPerformed()*. So, we have created an inner class, called *ButtonHandler*, which implements the *ActionListener* interface class. This tells Java that our *ButtonHandler* class will "implement" the *actionPerformed()* event method and as you can see from the code, this is exactly what it does. We must implement this method to handle a button event. We did not use an adapter class here because *ActionListener* only has a single method and we must implement that method. So, our class simply *implements ActionListener*. You see that the *actionPerformed()* method receives an *ActionEvent* object, *e*. Inside the method, we are generating a dialog information box using the statement

```
JOptionPane.showMessageDialog(null,
                              "Congratulations!\nYou Clicked Me",
                              "INFORMATION",
                              JOptionPane.INFORMATION_MESSAGE);
```

USING THE JOptionPane CLASS

We have been using the *JOptionPane* class all along within our *StaugIO* class to display dialog boxes. We have used its *showMessageDialog()* method to generate information boxes, and its *showInputDialog()* method to prompt the user for input.

The *showMessageDialog()* method is overloaded, but the version that we have used here requires four arguments: `null`, a string which is the information to be displayed, a string which is the information box title, and a message icon constant. Here is an example:

```
JOptionPane.showMessageDialog(null,
                    "Hello World",
                    "INFORMATION",
                    JOptionPane.INFORMATION_MESSAGE);
```

This single statement creates the following dialog box:

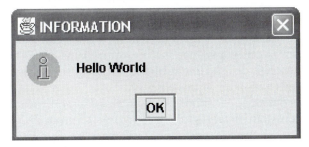

Here you see the two string arguments "Hello World" and "INFORMATION" displayed as the dialog box message and title, respectively. Notice that that icon is a colored circle with an "i" (for information) inside the circle. This is the INFORMATION_MESSAGE constant that is the last argument in the method call. Other constants that can be used are PLAIN_MESSAGE, QUESTION_MESSAGE, WARNING_MESSAGE, and ERROR_MESSAGE. Can you tell which constant is being used in each of the following?

The *showInputDialog()* method is used to obtain user input. Here's an example:

```
String input = JOptionPane.showInputDialog("Enter your name");
```

Here is the dialog box you would see as a result of this statement:

As you can see, the single string argument forms the user prompt. A text field is provided for the user to enter a string. The user entry is returned by the method as a string. If a numeric entry is desired, the returned string must be converted to a numeric value. More about this a bit later in this chapter.

Now, all we need is an application to test our new *FrameWithButton* class. Again, all this class needs to do within *main()* is to create an object for our *FrameWithButton* class, then use this object to call the *setSize()* and *show()* methods. Our *FrameWithButton* class does the rest of the work. Here is the required application:

```
//APPLICATION CLASS TO TEST FrameWithButton
public class FrameWithButtonTest
{
  public static void main(String[] args)
  {
    //DEFINE FRAME OBJECT
    FrameWithButton window = new FrameWithButton("FrameWithButton");

    //SET FRAME SIZE
    window.setSize(500,300);

    //MAKE FRAME VISIBLE
    window.show();
  }//END main()
}//END FrameWithButtonTest
```

Nothing is new here, except our application and frame class names. Method *main()* still creates a frame object, sets the size of the frame, and makes the frame visible just as before. The difference is that our frame now has a button component. Here is what the program would produce:

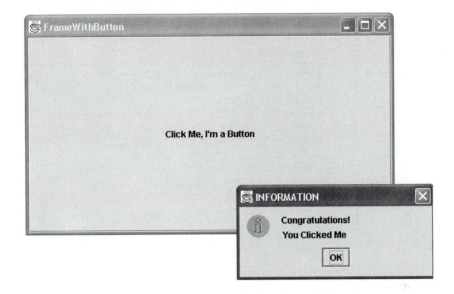

Wow, what a button! Our button fills up the entire window! It works fine, generating the dialog box when the button is clicked. However, do you suppose that we intended to fill up the entire window with a single button? Of course not! That brings us to our next section—layout managers. But before we go there, let's talk about one more button feature.

Tool Tips and Action Keys   We can add some pizzazz and features to our big button using a tool tip and an action key. A tool tip is a message that will appear when the mouse pointer is placed over the button, and an action key is a keystroke that will generate the button event, rather than clicking the mouse. For example, here is a tool tip and action key that we could create for our big button:

> This is a BIG Button ALT-C

This message would appear when the mouse passes over our button. Pressing the *Alt* key and the *C* key (ALT-C) at any time would generate the button event. To create this tool tip and action key, simply use the *button* object to call the *setToolTipText()* and *setMnemonic()* methods, like this:

```
//SET BUTTON TOOL TIP
button.setToolTipText("This is a BIG button");

//SET ACTION KEY
button.setMnemonic('C');
```

The methods used in this section and associated with the *JButton* class are summarized in Table 11-5.

TABLE 11-5   Summary of Methods Used in this Section

Method	Description
add(component)	Adds specified component to container
addActionListener()	Adds a listener for a calling object
actionPerformed()	Processes a button event
getContentPane()	Creates a content pane when called by a container object
JButton(String)	Creates a new button with *String* label
setToolTipText(String)	Sets a tool tip of *String* for a calling object
setMnemonic(char)	Sets an action key of *char* for a calling object
showInputDialog()	Generates an input dialog box
showMessageDialog()	Generates a information dialog box

QUICK CHECK

1. Write a statement to create a button called *myButton* with a label of "Store".
2. Write a statement to add the button in question 1 to a frame using a container object called *container*.
3. Write a statement to add a listener for the button in question 1 using an event handler class called *ButtonHandler*.
4. What method is used to handle a button event?
5. Write a statement to generate an error message dialog box that would display the message: "ERROR! ERROR! ERROR!"

11.3   Layout Managers and Panels

A layout manager does exactly what the name implies: it lays out the components within a frame. The layout managers provided by Java that we will discuss are listed in Table 11-6. We will discuss *FlowLayout*, *GridLayout*, and *BorderLayout* in this chapter, saving *CardLayout* and *BoxLayout* for the next chapter.

TABLE 11-6   Layout Managers Provided by Java

Layout Manager	Description
FlowLayout	Arranges components from left to right in the order they are added
GridLayout	Arranges components into rows and columns in the order they are added
BorderLayout	Arranges components into North, South, East, West, and Center areas within a container or panel (Default layout when none is specified)
CardLayout	Arranges components onto separate cards of a deck that can be displayed at different times
BoxLayout	Arranges components in a single row or column
GridBagLayout	Arranges components into rows and columns

Flow Layout—*FlowLayout*

All we need to do to our *FrameWithButton* class to make the button more manageable is to add the following statement to the *FrameWithButton()* constructor:

```
container.setLayout(new FlowLayout());
```

This single line invokes the *FlowLayout* manager to generate the following window:

Now, that's more like it! Here we have a single "Click Me, I'm a Button" button centered at the top of the window. So, what is this *FlowLayout* stuff anyway? Well, *FlowLayout* is one of several layout managers provided by Java. The *FlowLayout* manager arranges components sequentially, from left to right, as they are added to a container. There are three versions of the *FlowLayout* class constructor as follows:

```
//DEFAULT CENTER ALIGNMENT AND 5 PIXEL GAP
FlowLayout()

//CENTER, LEFT, or RIGHT ALIGN
FlowLayout(int alignment)

//CENTER, LEFT, or RIGHT ALIGN, HORIZONTAL GAP, VERTICAL GAP
FlowLayout(int alignment, int hGap, int vGap)
```

Each version of the constructor provides different component alignment and gapping options. Alignment relates to justification. Left alignment means that the components will be left-justified across the window, while right alignment means that the components will be right-justified across the window. Center alignment means the components will be justified equally left and right. Gapping is measured in pixels. You can set the horizontal gap between the components as well as the vertical component gap. The first constructor uses a default center alignment and default gapping of 5 pixels. The second constructor allows you to specify center, left, or right alignment. Finally, the third constructor allows you to specify both alignment and component gapping. Here is an example that will specify a left alignment, a horizontal gap of 10 pixels, and a vertical gap of 20 pixels:

```
container.setLayout(new FlowLayout(FlowLayout.LEFT,10,20));
```

Notice that the alignment must be specified using the standard *FlowLayout* class followed by a dot, followed by the constant *CENTER*, *LEFT*, or *RIGHT*. Here, a *FlowLayout* object is created and passed as an argument to the *setLayout()* method.

The *FlowLayout* manager forces components to wrap around the right side of the GUI if the window is resized smaller. Also, *FlowLayout* is the default layout manager for panels and applets.

More Buttons—*JButton*

Now, let's expand our single button class and develop a frame class that incorporates five buttons as follows:

```
import javax.swing.*;        //FOR SWING COMPONENT CLASSES
import java.awt.event.*;     //FOR EVENT HANDLING
import java.awt.*;           //FOR Container CLASS

//A FRAME CLASS WITH MULTIPLE BUTTONS
class FrameWithButtons extends JFrame
{
  //DECLARE BUTTON OBJECTS
  private JButton yellowButton;
  private JButton blueButton;
  private JButton cyanButton;
  private JButton redButton;
  private JButton greenButton;

  //CREATE A CONTAINER
  private Container container = getContentPane();

  //CONSTRUCTOR
  public FrameWithButtons(String title)
  {
    super(title);                       //CALL SUPERCLASS CONSTRUCTOR
    //SET FLOWLAYOUT, LEFT ALIGNMENT, 10 HORIZ. GAP, 20 VERT. GAP
    container.setLayout(new FlowLayout(FlowLayout.LEFT,10,20));

    //INSTANTIATE BUTTON OBJECTS
    yellowButton = new JButton("Yellow");
    blueButton = new JButton("Blue");
    cyanButton = new JButton("Cyan");
```

```
      redButton = new JButton("Red");
      greenButton = new JButton("Green");

      //ADD BUTTONS TO CONTAINER
      container.add(yellowButton);
      container.add(blueButton);
      container.add(cyanButton);
      container.add(redButton);
      container.add(greenButton);

      //DEFINE BUTTON HANDLER OBJECT
      ButtonHandler bHandler = new ButtonHandler();

      //ADD ACTION LISTENER WITH BUTTON EVENT HANDLER FOR THESE BUTTONS
      yellowButton.addActionListener(bHandler);
      blueButton.addActionListener(bHandler);
      cyanButton.addActionListener(bHandler);
      redButton.addActionListener(bHandler);
      greenButton.addActionListener(bHandler);

      //ADD WINDOW LISTENER WITH WINDOW EVENT HANDLER
      addWindowListener(new WindowHandler());
   }//END FrameWithButtons() CONSTRUCTOR

   //WINDOW EVENT HANDLER CLASS
   private class WindowHandler extends WindowAdapter
   {
     public void windowClosing(WindowEvent e)
     {
        System.exit(0);  //EXIT TO OPERATING SYSTEM
     }//END windowClosing()
   }//END WindowHandler CLASS

   //BUTTON EVENT HANDLER CLASS
   private class ButtonHandler implements ActionListener
   {
     //PROCESS EVENT
     public void actionPerformed(ActionEvent e)
     {
       //WHICH BUTTON CAUSED THE EVENT?
       if (e.getSource() == yellowButton)
         container.setBackground(Color.yellow);
       if (e.getSource() == blueButton)
         container.setBackground(Color.blue);
       if (e.getSource() == cyanButton)
         container.setBackground(Color.cyan);
       if (e.getSource() == redButton)
         container.setBackground(Color.red);
       if (e.getSource() == greenButton)
         container.setBackground(Color.green);
```

```
    }//END actionPerformed()
   }//END ButtonHandler CLASS
}//END FrameWithButtons CLASS
```

None of this code is really new to you. We have simply created a frame sub-class called *FrameWithButtons* that employs the *FlowLayout* manager. The button components will be left-justified across the frame, with horizontal spacing of 10 pixels and vertical spacing of 20 pixels. As you can see, five button objects have been defined and added to the frame. Also, an event listener has been added for each button object using the common *ButtonHandler* class. There is one subtle, but important, change we had to make. Notice that the *container* object is declared as a `private` member of the class, before the constructor. This is required so that we have access to it outside the constructor in the *actionPerformed()* method. If the *container* object was created within the constructor, it would not be visible outside of the constructor. So, in general, if a GUI item needs to be visible outside of the constructor, we will declare it as a `private` class member; otherwise, we will define it within the constructor.

If a GUI item needs to be visible outside of the constructor, then declare it as a `private` class member; otherwise, define it within the constructor.

Here is the window which is generated when an object is created for this class:

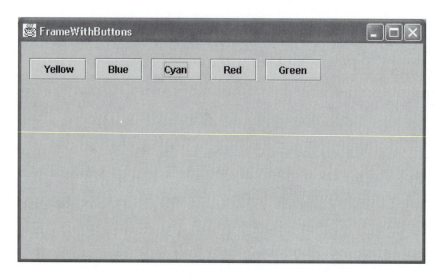

Now, the question is: If a button is clicked, which button is it? Well, to determine this we have added some logic to the *actionPerformed()* method as follows:

```
//PROCESS EVENT
public void actionPerformed(ActionEvent e)
{
```

```
   //WHICH BUTTON CAUSED THE EVENT?
   if(e.getSource() == yellowButton)
       container.setBackground(Color.yellow);
   if(e.getSource() == blueButton)
       container.setBackground(Color.blue);
   if(e.getSource() == cyanButton)
       container.setBackground(Color.cyan);
   if(e.getSource() == redButton)
       container.setBackground(Color.red);
   if(e.getSource() == greenButton)
       container.setBackground(Color.green);
 }//END actionPerformed()
```

Earlier we stated that the event object, *e*, carries with it information about the event. One thing that it "knows" is which particular component object generated the event. We can extract this information from the event object by using it to call the *getSource()* method. As you might expect, *getSource()* returns the object that triggered the event. We simply compare this returned object to all the button objects using a series of `if` statements. When a match is made, the background color of the container is set to a color that corresponds to the button label by calling the *setBackground()* method with our *container* object. In summary, once an event occurs, the *actionPerformed()* method is executed. The event object, *e*, is used to call the *getSource()* method which returns the object that caused the event. A series of `if` statements are used to determine which button generated the event and change the background color of the container accordingly.

Grid Layout—*GridLayout*

The next layout manager we need to discuss is the *GridLayout* manager. This layout manager places components in a grid with a specified number of rows and columns. You will use one of the following versions of the overloaded *GridLayout* constructor to specify the number of rows and columns in the grid:

```
//SINGLE ROW OF MULTIPLE COLUMNS
GridLayout();
```

```
//NUMBER ROWS, COLUMNS
GridLayout(int rows, int cols)
```

```
//NUMBER ROWS, COLUMNS, HORIZONTAL GAP, VERTICAL GAP
GridLayout(int rows, int cols, int hGap, int vGap)
```

The parameterless constructor simply places the components in a single row, from left to right. In the second version of the constructor, you simply specify the number of rows and columns desired for the grid. In the third version of the constructor, you specify the horizontal and vertical component gap in addition to the number of rows and columns. As an example, the following statement will set the container layout to *GridLayout* with 2 rows and 3 columns and horizontal and vertical gapping set to 10 pixels:

```
container.setLayout(new GridLayout(2,3,10,10));
```

If this statement were inserted into the previous *FrameWithButtons* class, here is what you would see when the application executes:

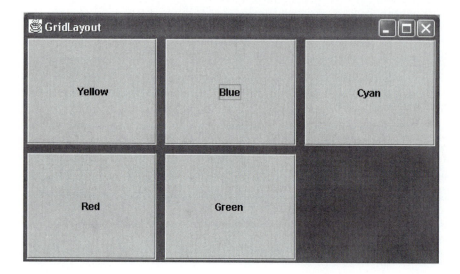

Notice that *GridLayout* forces all the buttons to be the same size.

  The *GridLayout* manager forces its GUI components to be the same size.

You should be aware that if you specify zero rows and columns, Java will throw an exception. However, if the number of rows and/or columns specified is too small for the number of components, Java will make room to accommodate all the components by adding more columns. The rows are always filled up first, then the columns. For instance, suppose we insert the following constructor into our *FrameWithButtons* class:

```
container.setLayout(new GridLayout(5,2,10,10));
```

This constructor specifies a grid of 5 rows and 2 columns, or 10 cells total. However, our *FrameWithButtons* class only contains five buttons. Here is what you would see when the program executes:

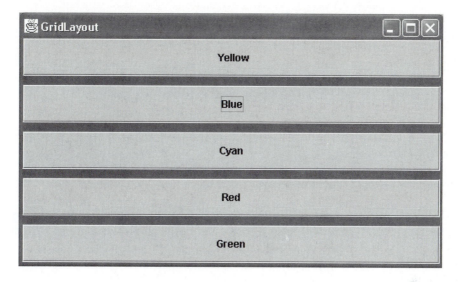

Observe that the rows are filled up first with our five buttons, and the second column in each row is not even used, or visible for that matter.

Border Layout—*BorderLayout*

The last layout manager that we will discuss in this chapter is *BorderLayout*. This layout manager divides the window into five predefined regions of *North*, *South*, *East*, *West*, and *Center* as illustrated in Figure 11-3.

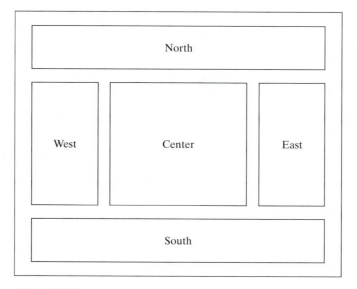

FIGURE 11-3   The *BorderLayout* manager divides the window into five predefined regions of *North*, *South*, *East*, *West*, and *Center*.

There are two versions of the overloaded *BorderLayout* constructor as follows:

```
//SET BORDER LAYOUT WITH NO GAP
BorderLayout()

//SET BORDER LAYOUT WITH HORIZONTAL, VERTICAL GAP
BorderLayout(int hGap, int vGap)
```

As an example, suppose we insert the following constructor into our *FrameWithButtons* class:

```
container.setLayout(new BorderLayout(10,10));
```

This constructor specifies *BorderLayout* with a 10-pixel horizontal and vertical gap. This means that there will be a 10 pixel gap between all the regions. Now, to use *BorderLayout* you must specify the region of the component when it is added to the container. Thus, we must modify the *add()* method arguments in our *FrameWithButtons* class like this:

```
//ADD BUTTONS TO CONTAINER
container.add(yellowButton,"North");
container.add(blueButton,"West");
container.add(cyanButton,"East");
container.add(redButton,"Center");
container.add(greenButton,"South");
```

As you can see, we must specify the component region as the second argument in the *add()* method. You can only place one component in a given region. Here is what you would see upon execution of an application containing this frame class:

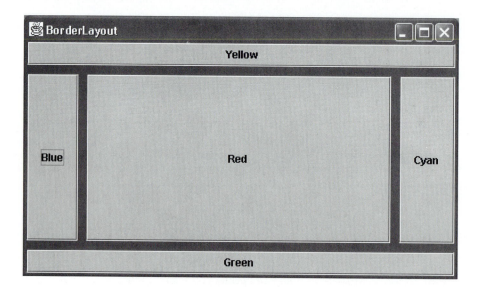

You see that the size of each component is governed by the size of the component region. The *North* and *South* components are as wide as the window, while the *East* and *West* components are as tall as the distance between the *North* and *South* components, minus any specified gap. The *Center* component fills in the space between the other four components, minus any specified gap. By the way, *BorderLayout* with no gapping is the default layout for a frame container when no layout is specified.

No Layout Manager

If you don't like the standard layout managers available in Java, you can choose not to use them and do your own layout. Take note, however, that this can be a bit tricky. Also, such layouts will not be consistent across different platforms or even different systems within a given platform. This is because you must specify your component positions and sizes in pixels. Not all platform monitors, or even monitors within a given platform for that matter, have the same number of pixels. In addition, if the window is resized smaller than its original frame size, cropping will occur.

 GUIs that do not employ a layout manager will not be consistent across different platforms. This is because you must specify your component positions and sizes in pixels. Not all platform monitors, or even monitors within a given platform for that matter, have the same number of pixels. In addition, if the window is resized smaller than its original frame size, cropping will occur.

To do your own layout, you must first tell Java that no standard layout manager is required. This is accomplished by setting the container layout to `null` as follows:

```
container.setLayout(null);
```

Then, you use the *setLocation()* and *setSize()* methods to set the component location and size, respectively, as desired. The interfaces for these methods are as follows:

```
//SETS COMPONENT LOCATION h PIXELS TO RIGHT, v PIXELS DOWN
public void setLocation(int hLoc, int vLoc)

//SETS COMPONENT SIZE w PIXELS WIDE BY h PIXELS HIGH
public void setSize(int w, int h)
```

The arguments in the *setLocation()* method provide the screen coordinates for the *upper left-hand corner* of the component. The point of reference is the top left-hand corner of the window, which has a coordinate of (0,0). Thus, a coordinate of (10,30) places the upper left-hand corner of the component 10 pixels to the right and 30 pixels down from the upper left-hand corner of the window. The arguments in the *setSize()* method provide the width and height measurements of the component in pixels. For example, consider the following code:

```
myComponent.setLocation(10,30);      //10 PIXELS TO RIGHT, 30 PIXELS DOWN
myComponent.setSize(50,20);          //50 PIXELS WIDE BY 20 PIXELS HIGH
```

The first statement tells Java to set the location of *myComponent* 10 pixels horizontal and 30 pixels vertical, placing the component in the upper left-hand corner of the window. (*Note*: For the component to be visible, it must be located below the window title bar. This is why a vertical coordinate of 30 pixels was used in the preceding example.) The second statement sets the size of *myComponent* to 50 pixels wide by 20 pixels high. Remember the five-button code developed earlier? Let's rewrite the class constructor to lay out the buttons without a layout manager. Consider the following:

```
//CONSTRUCTOR
public FrameWithButtons (String title)
{
   super(title);                      //CALL SUPERCLASS CONSTRUCTOR

   //SET LAYOUT MANAGER TO NULL
   container.setLayout(null);

   //INSTANTIATE BUTTON OBJECTS
   yellowButton = new JButton("Yellow");
   blueButton = new JButton("Blue");
   cyanButton = new JButton("Cyan");
   redButton = new JButton("Red");
   greenButton = new JButton("Green");

   //SET LOCATION AND SIZE OF EACH BUTTON
   yellowButton.setLocation(10,30);        //UPPER LEFT CORNER
   yellowButton.setSize(100,50);
   blueButton.setLocation(590,30);         //UPPER RIGHT CORNER
   blueButton.setSize(100,100);
   cyanButton.setLocation(10,370);         //LOWER LEFT CORNER
   cyanButton.setSize(100,150);
   redButton.setLocation(530,450);         //LOWER RIGHT CORNER
   redButton.setSize(100,20);
   greenButton.setLocation(300,140);       //CENTER
   greenButton.setSize(200,200);

   //ADD BUTTONS TO CONTAINER
   container.add(yellowButton);
   container.add(blueButton);
   container.add(cyanButton);
   container.add(redButton);
   container.add(greenButton);

   //DEFINE BUTTON HANDLER OBJECT
   ButtonHandler bHandler = new ButtonHandler();

   //ADD ACTION LISTENER WITH BUTTON EVENT HANDLER FOR THESE BUTTONS
   yellowButton.addActionListener(bHandler);
   blueButton.addActionListener(bHandler);
   cyanButton.addActionListener(bHandler);
   redButton.addActionListener(bHandler);
   greenButton.addActionListener(bHandler);
```

```
//ADD WINDOW LISTENER WITH WINDOW EVENT HANDLER
addWindowListener(new WindowHandler());
}//END FrameWithButtons() CONSTRUCTOR
```

First, you see that the layout manager is set to null. Next, you find the location and size of each button component explicitly set using the *setLocation()* and *setSize()* methods. The rest of the code is identical to that developed earlier. The resulting window is shown in Figure 11-4. The figure indicates the component coordinates and sizes specified in the constructor. Notice that the window size is 800 pixels wide by 600 pixels high. This is often the size of a PC screen. However, if the screen size were different, the layout would *not* be the same. So, be careful when doing your own layout. It might look fine on the system that you are using, and totally different on another system.

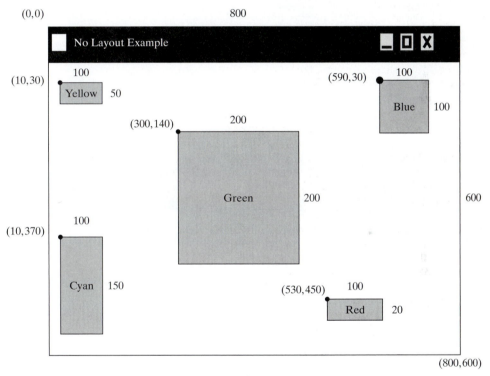

FIGURE 11-4   The window resulting from the *FrameWithButtons()* constructor that sets the location and size of the button components using coordinates in lieu of a layout manager.

Panels—*JPanel*

It is often difficult to get the look you desire using a single frame container. For this reason, *panels* are provided so that you can achieve presentable layouts. A panel is a container for components that does not create a window of its own. Rather, you place components on separate panels and then add the panels to a frame container to create a window.

A panel is a container for components that does not create a window of its own and must be placed in another container.

It's probably best at this point to just look at an example. Here is a window produced from a frame containing two easily identifiable panels. The top panel has three buttons and employs left-justified flow layout. The bottom panel has two buttons and employs center-justified flow layout. The frame employs border layout with the top panel located in the *Center* region, and the bottom panel located in the *South* region.

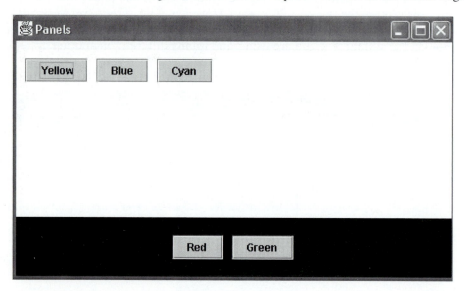

To create this window, we developed a frame subclass called *Panels* of the *JFrame* superclass. Here's the *Panels* class code:

```
import javax.swing.*;           //FOR SWING COMPONENT CLASSES
import java.awt.event.*;        //FOR EVENT HANDLING
import java.awt.*;              //FOR Container CLASS

class Panels extends JFrame
{
  //DECLARE BUTTON OBJECTS
  private JButton yellowButton;
  private JButton blueButton;
  private JButton cyanButton;
  private JButton redButton;
  private JButton greenButton;

  //DECLARE PANEL OBJECTS
  private JPanel centerPanel;
  private JPanel southPanel;

  //CONSTRUCTOR
  public Panels(String title)
```

```
{
   super(title);                           //CALL SUPERCLASS CONSTRUCTOR

   //CREATE A CONTAINER
   Container container = getContentPane();

   //DEFINE PANEL OBJECTS
   centerPanel = new JPanel();
   southPanel = new JPanel();

   //SET PANEL LAYOUT MANAGERS
   centerPanel.setLayout(new FlowLayout(FlowLayout.LEFT,10,20));
   southPanel.setLayout(new FlowLayout(FlowLayout.CENTER,10,20));

   //SET PANEL BACKGROUND COLORS
   centerPanel.setBackground(Color.white);
   southPanel.setBackground(Color.black);

   //INSTANTIATE BUTTON OBJECTS
   yellowButton = new JButton("Yellow");
   blueButton = new JButton("Blue");
   cyanButton = new JButton("Cyan");
   redButton = new JButton("Red");
   greenButton = new JButton("Green");

   //ADD BUTTONS TO PANELS
   centerPanel.add(yellowButton);
   centerPanel.add(blueButton);
   centerPanel.add(cyanButton);
   southPanel.add(redButton);
   southPanel.add(greenButton);

   //ADD PANELS TO CONTAINER
   container.add(centerPanel,"Center");
   container.add(southPanel,"South");

   //DEFINE BUTTON HANDLER OBJECT
   ButtonHandler bHandler = new ButtonHandler();

   //ADD ACTION LISTENER WITH BUTTON EVENT HANDLER FOR THESE BUTTONS
   yellowButton.addActionListener(bHandler);
   blueButton.addActionListener(bHandler);
   cyanButton.addActionListener(bHandler);
   redButton.addActionListener(bHandler);
   greenButton.addActionListener(bHandler);

   //ADD WINDOW LISTENER WITH WINDOW HANDLER
   addWindowListener(new WindowHandler());
}//END Panels()CONSTRUCTOR

//WINDOW EVENT HANDLER CLASS
private class WindowHandler extends WindowAdapter
```

```
{
  public void windowClosing(WindowEvent e)
  {
     System.exit(0);  //EXIT TO OPERATING SYSTEM
  }//END windowClosing()
}//END WindowHandler CLASS

//BUTTON EVENT HANDLER CLASS
private class ButtonHandler implements ActionListener
{
//PROCESS EVENT
public void actionPerformed(ActionEvent e)
{
    //WHICH BUTTON CAUSED THE EVENT?
    if (e.getSource() == yellowButton)
      centerPanel.setBackground(Color.yellow);
    if (e.getSource() == blueButton)
      centerPanel.setBackground(Color.blue);
    if (e.getSource() == cyanButton)
      centerPanel.setBackground(Color.cyan);
    if (e.getSource() == redButton)
      southPanel.setBackground(Color.red);
    if (e.getSource() == greenButton)
      southPanel.setBackground(Color.green);
  }//END actionPerformed()
 }//END ButtonHandler CLASS
}//END Panels CLASS
```

As before, the statements of interest are highlighted in bold type. You first see the panel objects, *centerPanel* and *southPanel*, declared as `private` members of the class just like our buttons. Next, you find the *Panels* class constructor. The first thing new within this constructor is the instantiation of our panel objects, and the setting of a layout manager for each of the panels. The *centerPanel* object is set to *FlowLayout* and left-justified, while *southPanel* is also set to *FlowLayout* but is center-justified. What you do not see in the code at all is the setting of the *container* layout manager. Remember that *BorderLayout* is the default layout manager. So, since no layout is set for our *container* object, it will default to *BorderLayout*.

After setting the panel layout managers, the background color of each panel is set when the respective panel object calls the *setBackground()* method. We have defined five button objects as before but, rather than adding them to the container, we have added the first three buttons to *centerPanel* and the last two buttons to *southPanel*. Finally, the panels are added to the container via the statements

```
//ADD PANELS TO CONTAINER
container.add(centerPanel,"Center");
container.add(southPanel,"South");
```

Notice that the first argument of the *add()* method is the panel object, and the second argument is the region of the frame container in which to add the panel. Remember, the container employs the *BorderLayout* manager by default. That's it for the constructor.

When an object is created for the *Panels* class in an application and made visible, you will see the window shown earlier. You might have noticed that as before, following the constructor we have implemented the *actionPerformed()* method as part of the inner *ButtonHandler* class to handle the button events. The only change here is the use of the panel objects to set the background color of their respective panels when a given button is clicked. Notice that the respective panel object must be used to call the *setBackground()* method to change the background color of the panel. This is why the panel objects had to be declared as private class members — so they could be accessible in the *actionPerformed()* method. Look over the above *Panels* class code again and make sure you understand all of its features. Here is the application code:

```
//APPLICATION TEST CLASS
public class PanelsTest
{
   public static void main(String[] args)
   {
      //DEFINE FRAME OBJECT
      Panels window = new Panels("Panels");

      //SET FRAME SIZE
      window.setSize(500,300);

      //MAKE FRAME VISIBLE
      window.show();
   }//END main()
}//END PanelsTest
```

There is nothing new here. We have just created an object for our *Panels* class called *window*, set the size of *window*, and made it visible. That's all there is to it! The new methods used in this section are summarized in Table 11-7.

TABLE 11-7   Summary of Methods Used in this Section

Method	Description
BorderLayout()	Creates border layout with no gaps
BorderLayout(int,int)	Creates border layout with *int* hGap and *int* vGap
FlowLayout()	Creates flow layout, center, and 5-pixel gap
FlowLayout(int)	Creates flow layout with *int* alignment
FlowLayout(int,int,int)	Creates flow layout with *int* alignment, *int* hGap, and *int* vGap
getSource()	Returns the object that caused this event
GridLayout()	Creates grid layout with one row
GridLayout(int,int)	Creates grid layout with *int* rows and *int* cols
GridLayout(int,int,int,int)	Creates grid layout with *int* rows, *int* cols., *int* hGap, and *int* vGap
JPanel()	Creates panel
JPanel(Layout Manager)	Creates panel with this layout manager
setLayout(Layout Manager)	Sets layout of a calling object to this layout manager
setLocation(int,int)	Sets component upper left corner to (*int x, int y*)
setSize(int,int)	Sets component size to *int* width, and *int* height

QUICK CHECK

1. The layout manager that arranges components from left to right within a container or panel in the order they are added is a(n) _____ layout manager.
2. The layout manager that arranges components into rows and columns within a container or panel in the order they are added is a(n) _____ layout manager.
3. Write a statement to set the layout for a panel called *topPanel* to flow layout, left-justified, with a 20-pixel horizontal gap and 10-pixel vertical gap.
4. What are the five regions designated by the *BorderLayout* manager?
5. Write a statement to designate no layout manager for a frame container called *container*.
6. Where is the origin, (0,0), of a window located?
7. Write a statement to locate a button called *myButton* at window coordinate (20,30).
8. Write a statement to set the size of a button called *myButton* to 50 pixels high and 25 pixels wide.
9. What method can be called by the event object to return the GUI component that caused the event?
10. Write a statement to set the layout for a panel called *bottomPanel* to border layout with 20-pixel gapping between all components.
11. Write a statement to place a panel, called *centerPanel*, in the center region of the panel in question 10.
12. True or false: The default layout manager is no layout.

11.4   Labels, Text Fields, and Text Areas—*JLabel*, *JTextField*, and *JTextArea*

You now have the basic concepts of frames, listeners, event handlers, and layout managers that are required to build GUIs in Java. All you need to learn about now are the additional components that are available in Java *swing*. All these additional components are handled much like the button component that you have already studied. So, let's see what additional components are available to build Java GUIs. In this section you will learn about labels, text fields, and text areas. The next chapter will continue this discussion with additional GUI components.

Labels—*JLabel*

A label is a non-editable text area that is used to label other components, usually text fields and text areas. There are two useful *JLabel* constructors, as follows:

```
//CREATES A LABEL WITH TEXT
public JLabel(String text);

//CREATES A LABEL WITH TEXT AND
//LEFT, RIGHT, OR CENTER ALIGNMENT
public JLabel(String text, int alignment);
```

The alignment in the second version of the constructor can be *JLabel.LEFT,* *JLabel.CENTER,* or *JLabel.RIGHT*. Here is a *Labels* class that we created to demonstrate the use of labels:

```java
import javax.swing.*;          //FOR SWING COMPONENT CLASSES
import java.awt.event.*;       //FOR EVENT HANDLING
import java.awt.*;             //FOR Container CLASS

class Labels extends JFrame
{
  //CONSTRUCTOR
  public Labels(String title)
  {
    super(title);                         //CALL SUPERCLASS CONSTRUCTOR

    //CREATE A CONTAINER
    Container container = getContentPane();

    //DEFINE LABEL OBJECTS
    JLabel nameLabel = new JLabel("Student name");
    JLabel numberLabel = new JLabel("Student Number");
    JLabel gpaLabel = new JLabel("GPA");

    //SET LABEL COLOR
    nameLabel.setForeground(Color.cyan);
    numberLabel.setForeground(Color.white);
    gpaLabel.setForeground(Color.blue);

    //SET CONTAINER LAYOUT MANAGER
    container.setLayout(new GridLayout(3,1));

    //ADD LABELS TO CONTAINER
    container.add(nameLabel);
    container.add(numberLabel);
    container.add(gpaLabel);

    //ADD WINDOW LISTENER WITH WINDOW EVENT HANDLER
    addWindowListener(new WindowHandler());
  }//END Labels() CONSTRUCTOR

  //WINDOW EVENT HANDLER CLASS
  private class WindowHandler extends WindowAdapter
  {
    public void windowClosing(WindowEvent e)
    {
      System.exit(0); //EXIT TO OPERATING SYSTEM
    }//END windowClosing()
  }//END WindowHandler CLASS
}//END Labels CLASS
```

We have simply created three labels and added them to the frame container. Notice, however, that the label objects are not declared as `private` members of the class.
Instead, they are defined totally within the constructor. This is OK, since a label cannot
generate an event and its object is only needed within the frame constructor to create
the GUI. As a rule of thumb, you do not need to make a GUI component object
`private` unless you must have access to it outside of the frame class constructor. Once
the label objects are defined, we have used the *setForeground()* method to set the color
of each label. Once the labels are ready, we created a container with *GridLayout* of 3
rows and 1 column so that the labels are displayed down the window. We then added the
label objects to the container. Finally, we don't need a label event handler since labels
don't generate events. They are simply used to "label" other GUI components, like text
fields and text areas, which we are about to discuss. That's all we have to say about labels
for now. Here is what you would see when the above class is tested in an application:

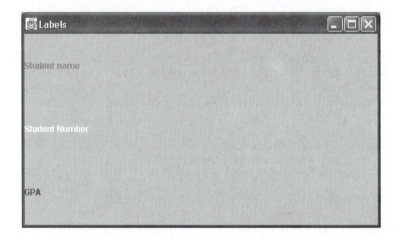

Text Fields and Text Areas—*JTextField* and *JTextArea*

A text field is a single line of text, while a text area is several lines of text. Text fields
and areas allow the user to enter string data into the system or to display text data. An
editable text field or area allows the user to enter data, while a non-editable text field
or area can only be used to display data. There are three *swing* classes that provide text
fields and areas: *JTextField*, *JPasswordField*, and *JTextArea*. A password field is simply
a text field that hides its contents with asterisks. In this section we will build a GUI
class that deals with all three. So, let's first look at the class constructors. There are
three versions of each class constructor as shown in Table 11-8.

Remember, a text field or password field is just one line of text, while a text area
is several lines of text. This is why two of the *JTextField()* and *JPasswordField* constructors allow you to specify the number of field columns (width), and two of the
JTextArea() constructors allow you to specify both the number of text area rows
(height) and columns (width). Also, you have the option of initializing both with a text
string. If you only supply a string, the field or area will be initialized to the size of the
string. You need to be aware that the width and height values supplied *are not* measured in pixels. They are measured in character rows and columns. So, for example,

TABLE 11-8   Summary Text Field and Text Area Constructors

Class	Constructor	Description
JTextField	*JTextField(int)*	Creates an empty text field with *int* columns
	JTextField(String)	Creates a text field initialized with *String*
	JTextField(String, int)	Creates a text field initialized with *String* and *int* columns
JPasswordField	*JPasswordField (int)*	Creates an empty password field with *int* columns
	JPasswordField (String)	Creates a password field initialized with *String*
	JPasswordField (String, int)	Creates a password field initialized with *String* and *int* columns
JTextArea	*JTextArea (int,int)*	Creates an empty text area with *int* rows and *int* columns
	JTextArea (String)	Creates a text area initialized with *String*
	JTextArea (String, int,int)	Creates a text area initialized with *String* with *int* rows and *int* columns

specifying a *JTextArea(5,10)* constructor will produce a text area that is 5 text characters high and 10 text characters wide.

Text fields and text areas are measured in character rows and columns, not pixels.

Now, look at the following GUI:

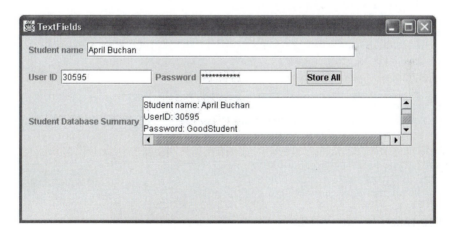

This window contains 4 labels, two text fields, a password field, a button, and a text area. Text fields and text areas do not come with labels like a button. Therefore, you have to add a separate label component for each field or area if needed. In addition, three panels are being used to hold these components. The top panel contains a label and a single text field. The middle panel contains two labels, a text field, a password field, and a button. The bottom panel contains a label and text area with scroll bars. The text fields are for user entry of the labeled student data. When the *Store All* button is clicked, the information entered in the text fields is simply displayed in the text area.

Now, here is the class that produced the foregoing GUI:

```
import javax.swing.*;          //FOR SWING COMPONENT CLASSES
import java.awt.event.*;       //FOR EVENT HANDLING
import java.awt.*;             //FOR Container CLASS

class TextFields extends JFrame
{
   //DECLARE COMPONENT OBJECTS
   private JTextField nameField;
   private JTextField userIDField;
   private JPasswordField userPassField;
   private JTextArea studentArea;
   private JButton storeButton;

  //CONSTRUCTOR
  public TextFields(String title)
  {
    //CALL SUPERCLASS CONSTRUCTOR
    super(title);

    //CREATE A CONTAINER
    Container container = getContentPane();

    //INSTANTIATE TEXT FIELD OBJECTS
    nameField = new JTextField(35);
    userIDField = new JTextField(12);
    userPassField = new JPasswordField(12);
    studentArea = new JTextArea(4,35);

    //INSTANTIATE BUTTON OBJECT
    storeButton = new JButton("Store All");

    //SET FRAME LAYOUT MANAGER
    container.setLayout(new FlowLayout(FlowLayout.LEFT));

    //DEFINE PANEL OBJECTS
    JPanel topPanel = new JPanel();
    JPanel middlePanel = new JPanel();
    JPanel bottomPanel = new JPanel();

    //SET PANEL LAYOUT MANAGERS
    topPanel.setLayout(new FlowLayout(FlowLayout.LEFT));
    middlePanel.setLayout(new FlowLayout(FlowLayout.LEFT));
    bottomPanel.setLayout(new FlowLayout(FlowLayout.LEFT));

    //DEFINE LABEL OBJECTS
    JLabel nameLabel = new JLabel("Student name");
    JLabel userIDLabel = new JLabel("User ID");
    JLabel userPassLabel = new JLabel("Password");
    JLabel summaryLabel = new JLabel("Student Database Summary");
```

```
//ADD COMPONENTS TO topPanel
topPanel.add(nameLabel);
topPanel.add(nameField);

//ADD COMPONENTS TO middlePanel
middlePanel.add(userIDLabel);
middlePanel.add(userIDField);
middlePanel.add(userPassLabel);
middlePanel.add(userPassField);
middlePanel.add(storeButton);

//ADD TEXT AREA LABEL TO BOTTOM PANEL
bottomPanel.add(summaryLabel);

//ADD TEXT AREA WITH SCROLL BARS TO BOTTOM PANEL
bottomPanel.add(new JScrollPane(studentArea));

//ADD PANELS TO CONTAINER
container.add(topPanel);
container.add(middlePanel);
container.add(bottomPanel);

  //ADD ACTION LISTENER WITH BUTTON EVENT HANDLER
  storeButton.addActionListener(new StoreButtonHandler());

  //ADD WINDOW LISTENER WITH WINDOW EVENT HANDLER
  addWindowListener(new WindowHandler());
}//END TextFields() CONSTRUCTOR

//WINDOW EVENT HANDLER
private class WindowHandler extends WindowAdapter
{
  public void windowClosing(WindowEvent e)
 {
    System.exit(0);  //EXIT TO OPERATING SYSTEM
 }//END windowClosing()
}//END WindowHandler CLASS

//BUTTON EVENT HANDLER
private class StoreButtonHandler implements ActionListener
{
//PROCESS EVENT
public void actionPerformed(ActionEvent e)
{
  studentArea.setText(" ");

  //DID THE STORE BUTTON CAUSE EVENT?
  if (e.getSource() == storeButton)
  {
    //DISPLAY TEXT FIELD DATA IN TEXT AREA
    studentArea.setText("This is an example of data stored"
                 + " in the student database.\n");
```

```
            studentArea.append("\nStudent name: " + nameField.getText());
            studentArea.append("\nUserID: " + userIDField.getText());
            studentArea.append("\nPassword: "
                               + new String(userPassField.getPassword()));
       }//END IF
     }//END actionPerformed()
   }//END StoreButtonHandler
}//END TextFields CLASS
```

We intend to discuss only those statements that are pertinent to text fields and text areas which are highlighted in bold. First you see the text fields and text area defined as `private` members of the class. They are defined here as `private` members, rather than within the class constructor, so that they will be visible to an event handler method later on. Next comes the *TextFields()* constructor which, as before, is responsible for displaying the window. We have used the text field and text area constructors that allow us to set the number of the text field columns and the number of text area rows and columns. The size of each should be consistent with the amount of data to be entered or displayed. Within the constructor, three panels are defined along with the other component objects (labels and button). Flow layout is employed for the container, as well as for the three panels. All the component objects, including the text field and text area objects, are added to their respective panel using the *add()* method as before. Notice how the text area is added using the following statement:

```
//ADD TEXT AREA WITH SCROLL BARS TO BOTTOM PANEL
bottomPanel.add(new JScrollPane(studentArea));
```

The *add()* method argument is actually a *JScrollPane* object created to hold our text area. Notice that our *studentArea* text area object is used as the argument for the *JScrollPane* constructor. This places our text area inside of scroll bars as you saw in the foregoing GUI. The scroll bars will automatically appear when the text exceeds the boundary of the text area. That's pretty cool! Without scroll bars, the text area would appear as just a white box. If the text displayed inside the text area became bigger than the specified text area size, the text area would actually expand to fit the text until the limits of the GUI were reached, at which time any additional text would be lost. This obviously might mess up the GUI and lose important information for the user. So, it's always a good idea to place your text areas inside of scroll bars using the *JScrollPane* class as we have done here.

Finally, the constructor adds the panels to the container, and a listener is added for the *storeButton* object using the *StoreButtonHandler* class. Nothing new here.

Now, look at the *actionPerformed()* method within the inner *StoreButtonHandler* class. As before, an `if` statement is used to test the event to see if it was caused by our button object. When a *storeButton* event occurs, the *studentArea* object calls the *setText()* and *append()* methods to write information into the text area. Both *setText()* and *append()* write string data to the text area when called by the text area object. The data to be written is formatted the same way that strings are formatted within the *println()* or *writeInfo()* methods. The *setText()* method must be called first to write the initial information, followed by calls to the *append()* method to "append" additional information to the text area. If you use *setText()* repeatedly, any information displayed previously is overwritten. Now, notice that within each *append()* call, there is a call to *getText()* by the respective text field object. The *getText()* method does exactly what it says—gets the text entered into the object text field. Thus, the statement

```
studentArea.append("\nStudent name: " + nameField.getText());
```

appends the *studentArea* text area with the string data obtained from the *nameField* text field. The last statement that gets the password field text needs some special explanation. Here is the statement:

```
studentArea.append("\nPassword: "
                    + new String(userPassField.getPassword()));
```

Notice that we are using the method *getPassword()* to obtain the password field data. If you go to your IDE help and read about *getPassword()* you would find that it returns a character array, not a string. However, the *append()* method requires a string. So, what we have done is to create the required string right inside the *append()* method argument listing. The code

```
new String(userPassField.getPassword()
```

calls a *String* class constructor that accepts a character array as its argument. It creates a string that represents the same sequence of characters as in the character array argument. Now the *append()* method has what it needs to display the contents of the password text field. Of course, you probably would not want to display a password in a real application. Rather, you might want to call the *getPassword()* method to verify the password. We only displayed it here for example purposes.

So, the user enters data into the student text fields, clicks the *Store All* button, and the data appears in the text area as shown in the GUI.

Text Events

In the foregoing program, the event we were looking for was a button event. If the user enters data and presses the ENTER key, nothing will happen. Wouldn't it be nice if we had this feature? Well, this would require that we detect a text field event. Is this possible? Of course, almost anything, within reason, is possible in Java. A text field event is triggered by pressing the ENTER key. Like a button, the *ActionEvent* class is also used to handle text field events. So, to handle a text field event we must provide additional logic within our event handler, and must add listeners for the text field objects using this handler. Here's the modified class code:

```
import javax.swing.*;        //FOR SWING COMPONENT CLASSES
import java.awt.event.*;     //FOR EVENT HANDLING
import java.awt.*;           //FOR Container CLASS
class TextFieldsEvent extends JFrame
{
    //DECLARE COMPONENT OBJECTS
    private JTextField nameField;
    private JTextField userIDField;
```

```java
  private JPasswordField userPassField;
  private JTextArea studentArea;
  private JButton storeButton;

//CONSTRUCTOR
public TextFieldsEvent (String title)
{
  //CALL SUPERCLASS CONSTRUCTOR
  super(title);

  //CREATE A CONTAINER
  Container container = getContentPane();

  //INSTANTIATE TEXT FIELD OBJECTS
  nameField = new JTextField(35);
  userIDField = new JTextField(12);
  userPassField = new JPasswordField(12);
  studentArea = new JTextArea(4,35);

  //INSTANTIATE BUTTON OBJECT
  storeButton = new JButton("Store All");

  //SET FRAME LAYOUT MANAGER
  container.setLayout(new FlowLayout(FlowLayout.LEFT));

  //DEFINE PANEL OBJECTS
  JPanel topPanel = new JPanel();
  JPanel middlePanel = new JPanel();
  JPanel bottomPanel = new JPanel();

  //SET PANEL LAYOUT MANAGERS
  topPanel.setLayout(new FlowLayout(FlowLayout.LEFT));
  middlePanel.setLayout(new FlowLayout(FlowLayout.LEFT));
  bottomPanel.setLayout(new FlowLayout(FlowLayout.LEFT));

  //DEFINE LABEL OBJECTS
  JLabel nameLabel = new JLabel("Student name");
  JLabel userIDLabel = new JLabel("User ID");
  JLabel userPassLabel = new JLabel("Password");
  JLabel summaryLabel = new JLabel("Student Database Summary");

  //ADD COMPONENTS TO topPanel
  topPanel.add(nameLabel);
  topPanel.add(nameField);
  //ADD COMPONENTS TO middlePanel
  middlePanel.add(userIDLabel);
  middlePanel.add(userIDField);
  middlePanel.add(userPassLabel);
  middlePanel.add(userPassField);
  middlePanel.add(storeButton);
```

```
    //ADD TEXT AREA LABEL TO BOTTOM PANEL
    bottomPanel.add(summaryLabel);

    //ADD TEXT AREA WITH SCROLL TO BOTTOM PANEL
    bottomPanel.add(new JScrollPane(studentArea));

    //ADD PANELS TO CONTAINER
    container.add(topPanel);
    container.add(middlePanel);
    container.add(bottomPanel);

      //ADD ACTION LISTENER WITH EVENT HANDLER FOR BUTTON AND TEXT FIELDS
      ButtonAndTextHandler handler = new ButtonAndTextHandler();
      storeButton.addActionListener(handler);
      nameField.addActionListener(handler);
      userIDField.addActionListener(handler);
      userPassField.addActionListener(handler);

      //ADD WINDOW LISTENER AND WINDOW EVENT HANDLER
      addWindowListener(new WindowHandler());
  }//END TextFieldsEvent() CONSTRUCTOR

//WINDOW EVENT HANDLER
private class WindowHandler extends WindowAdapter
{
   public void windowClosing(WindowEvent e)
  {
     System.exit(0);   //EXIT TO OPERATING SYSTEM
 }//END windowClosing()
}//END WindowHandler CLASS
//BUTTON AND TEXT EVENT HANDLER
private class ButtonAndTextHandler implements ActionListener
{
 //PROCESS EVENT
 public void actionPerformed(ActionEvent e)
 {
   studentArea.setText(" ");
   //DID THE STORE BUTTON CAUSE EVENT?
   //IF DISPLAY ALL
   if (e.getSource() == storeButton)
   {
     //DISPLAY TEXT FIELD DATA IN TEXT AREA
     studentArea.setText("This is an example of data stored"
                         + " in the student database.\n");
     studentArea.setText("This is an example of data stored"
                         + " in the student database.\n");
     studentArea.append("\nStudent name: " + nameField.getText());
     studentArea.append("\nUserID: " + userIDField.getText());
     studentArea.append("\nPassword: "
                         + new String(userPassField.getPassword()));
   }//END BUTTON IF
```

```
    //DID A TEXT FIELD CAUSE THE EVENT?
    //IF SO WHICH ONE?
    if(e.getSource() == nameField)
      studentArea.append("\nStudent name: " + nameField.getText());
    if(e.getSource() == userIDField)
      studentArea.append("\nUserID: " + userIDField.getText());
    if (e.getSource() == userPassField)
      studentArea.append("\nPassword: "
                          + new String(userPassField.getPassword()));
   }//END actionPerformed()
  }//END ButtonAndTextHandler CLASS
}//END TextFieldsEvent CLASS
```

We have highlighted the new code of interest in bold. The major change here is in the event handler. Besides changing its name to *ButtonAndTextHandler* to better reflect its purpose, you see that we have added a series of `if` statements to test each of the text field objects for an event. If a given text field object generates an event, its data is displayed within the text area. All the data is still displayed if a button event occurs. Of course, we had to add listeners for all the text field objects, and use our event class object as the argument for the *addActionListener()* method. Remember that a GUI object event cannot be processed, even by an event handler, unless a listener has been added for the object.

STYLE TIP

As your GUIs begin to get more complex, you will have several labels, fields, areas, etc., as part of a single frame. To make your code more readable and therefore less confusing, we suggest that you tag each component name with its component class. For instance, the text fields in the foregoing program are named *nameField*, *userIDField*, and *userPasswordField*, while the text area is named *studentArea*. The component class designation allows anyone reading the program to tell which type of component to which a given name refers. In addition, notice that the labels are named *nameLabel*, *userIDLabel*, and so on, to indicate which component the label belongs to, as well as that the component is a label component. This is much better than *Label1*, *Label2*, and so on.

QUICK CHECK

1. Write statements to create a "This is my label" label object called *myLabel* and add it to a panel called *myPanel*.
2. Write a statement to define a text field object called *myTextField* which is 20 columns wide.
3. Write a statement to define a text area object called *myTextArea* which is 10 rows high and 50 columns wide.
4. Write statements to add the objects in questions 2 and 3 to a panel called *myPanel*.

TABLE 11-9   Summary of Component Methods Used in This Section

Method	Description
append(String)	Appends *String* to text of calling text object
getText()	Returns text contained in calling text object
getPassword()	Returns a character array containing the characters in the calling password object field
JLabel(String)	Creates a label with *String* text
JLabel(String, int)	Creates a label with *String* text and specified alignment
setText(String)	Sets text of calling text object to *String*
JTextField(int)	Creates an empty text field with *int* columns
JTextField(String)	Creates a text field initialized with *String*
JTextField(String,int)	Creates a text field initialized with *String* and *int* columns
JPasswordField(int)	Creates an empty password field with *int* columns
JPasswordField (String)	Creates a password field initialized with *String*
JPasswordField (String,int)	Creates a password field initialized with *String* and *int* columns
JTextArea(int,int)	Creates an empty text area with *int* rows and *int* columns
JTextArea(String)	Creates a text area initialized with *String*
JTextArea(String,int, int)	Creates a text area initialized with *String* and *int* rows and *int* columns

Problem Solving in Action: Designing and Building Event-Driven Programs

Problem

In previous chapters, we have developed procedural programs. It's now time to develop event-driven programs. We will deal with a problem that has been dealt with before, so that we can concentrate, not on the problem itself, but on the user interface. The problem is that of determining monthly payments and interest on a consumer loan. Recall that we need the user to enter the loan amount, term of the loan, and loan interest rate. The program will then determine the monthly payments, total loan interest, and total loan amount.

Defining the Problem

Based on the problem statement, our problem definition addresses the input required to produce the output, the processing required to determine the output from the given input, and the output produced by the program, as follows:

Input:	Loan principal, term of the loan, and annual interest rate
Processing:	Calculate the following:
	$payment = principal * rate/(1 - (1 + rate)^{-term})$
	$interest = term * payment - principal$
	$total = principal + interest$
Output:	The monthly loan payment, total loan interest, and total loan amount, including interest

Planning the Solution

So far, nothing in our approach to problem solving is new. But here is where things change. We must now think of the problem in terms of a GUI interface and object-orientation. The first thing we must do is to visualize the interface. We can do this with a ***window layout chart*** like the one shown in Figure 11-5.

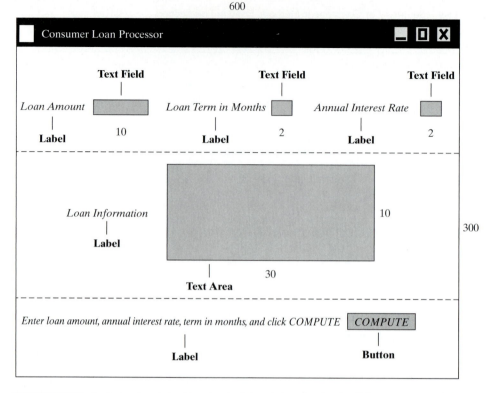

FIGURE 11-5 A window layout chart is a sketch of the window, showing the GUI components and their locations.

Notice that the window layout chart is simply a drawing, or sketch, of the GUI components and their layout, or location, on the window. In addition, each component is labeled as to
its type and size, if necessary. Notice also that the text of each label component is written just as
it will be seen by the user and coded by you, the programmer. Since no component coordinates
are shown, you can assume that we are going to use a layout manager. If you do not use a layout
manager, the window layout chart must show the component coordinates in addition to their
sizes. From the layout, you can visualize that three panels (indicated by dashed lines) are needed
if we use the flow layout manager. The text fields will go in the top panel, the text area will be
added to the middle panel, and the instruction label and compute button will go on the bottom
panel. It is also clear from the layout that the user will enter the text field data and click the
compute button. The calculated values will then be displayed in the text area. Window layout
charts are a must when developing GUIs. Don't be tempted to work without one. It's like anything else you try to build—you always need to start with a good plan.

Now, the algorithms we develop will relate not only to processing, but also to the construction of the GUI. There are three things we need, as follows:

- A *main()* method that will create a GUI object, set its size, and make it visible
- A frame class constructor that will create the GUI
- An event handler method that will process the GUI events

We will create a subclass of *JFrame* called *LoanProcessor* that will generate the GUI and process any component events. As you already know, the GUI will be generated by the constructor, *LoanProcessor()*, and the button event will be processed by the *actionPerformed()* method. Of course, *main()* will be used to define the frame object, set its size, and make it visible within an application. As a result, we must develop an algorithm for *main()*, the GUI class constructor, and the event handler method. Here is the first level of each:

Initial Algorithms
main()
BEGIN
   Define frame object.
   Set frame size.
   Make frame visible.
END.

LoanProcessor() Constructor
BEGIN
   Call superclass constructor and pass frame title.
   Create a container.
   Set container layout.
   Define panels.
   Set panel layout.
   Define components.
   Add components to panels.
   Add panels to container.
   Add event component listeners.
END.

actionPerformed() Event Handler
BEGIN
   Determine which component generated an event.
   Get event data.
   Process data.
   Generate any required output.
END.

Now, the foregoing algorithms are so general that they could be applied to any GUI program. The initial algorithm for *main()* is at a codeable level; however, the *LoanProcessor()* and *actionPerformed()* algorithms need some refinement. So, let's refine them to fit our program task, as follows:

First Level of Refinement
LoanProcessor() Constructor
BEGIN
   Call superclass constructor.
   Create a container.
   Set container layout to border layout.
   Define input panel.
   Define display panel.
   Define compute panel.

Set each panel to flow layout, center justified, with 10 pixel gapping.
Define user instruction label.
Define loan amount text field label.
Define loan term text field label.
Define loan interest rate text field label.
Define loan information text area label.
Instantiate text field and text area objects.
Instantiate button object.
Add loan amount, term, interest labels, and text fields to input panel.
Add text area label and text area to display panel.
Add user instruction label and compute button to compute panel.
Add all three panels to container.
Add a listener for the button object using a button event handler.
Add a frame listener using a window event handler.
END.

actionPerformed() Event Handler
BEGIN
    If the compute button caused the event
        Read *principal* from loan amount text field.
        Read *term* from term text field.
        Read *rate* from interest rate text field.
        Calculate $payment = principal * rate/(1-(1+rate)^{-term})$.
        Calculate $interest = term * payment - principal$.
        Calculate $total = principal + interest$.
        Append text area with *payment*.
        Append text area with *interest*.
        Append text area with *total*.
END.

Most of the steps within the *LoanProcessor()* constructor algorithm should be familiar to you and reflect the GUI layout diagram in Figure 11-5. Now, you should have no trouble coding the constructor algorithm at this point. Here's the code:

```
//CONSTRUCTOR
public LoanProcessor(String title)
{
    //CALL SUPERCLASS CONSTRUCTOR
    super(title);

    //DECLARE CONTAINER OBJECT AND GET CONTENT PANE
    Container container = getContentPane();

    //DEFINE THREE PANELS
    JPanel inputPanel = new JPanel();
    JPanel displayPanel = new JPanel();
    JPanel computePanel = new JPanel();
```

```java
//SET EACH PANEL TO FLOW LAYOUT, CENTER JUSTIFIED, 10 PT. GAPPING
inputPanel.setLayout(new FlowLayout(FlowLayout.CENTER,10,10));
displayPanel.setLayout(new FlowLayout(FlowLayout.CENTER,10,10));
computePanel.setLayout(new FlowLayout(FlowLayout.CENTER,10,10));

//DEFINE LABEL OBJECTS
Label userInstruction = new Label("Enter loan amount,"
                                + " annual interest rate, term in months,"
                                + " and click COMPUTE");
Label principalLabel = new Label("Loan Amount");
Label termLabel = new Label("Loan Term in Months");
Label rateLabel = new Label("Annual Interest Rate");
Label loanInfoLabel = new Label("Loan Information");

//INSTANTIATE TEXT FIELD OBJECTS
principalField = new JTextField(10);
termField = new JTextField(2);
rateField = new JTextField(2);
loanInfoArea = new JTextArea(10,30);

//INSTANTIATE BUTTON OBJECT
computeButton = new JButton("COMPUTE");

//ADD COMPONENTS TO PANELS
inputPanel.add(principalLabel);
inputPanel.add(principalField);
inputPanel.add(termLabel);
inputPanel.add(termField);
inputPanel.add(rateLabel);
inputPanel.add(rateField);
displayPanel.add(loanInfoLabel);
displayPanel.add(loanInfoArea);
computePanel.add(userInstruction);
computePanel.add(computeButton);

//ADD PANELS TO CONTAINER
container.add(inputPanel, "North");
container.add(displayPanel, "Center");
container.add(computePanel, "South");

//ADD ACTION LISTENER WITH BUTTON HANDLER
computeButton.addActionListener(new ButtonHandler());

   //ADD WINDOW LISTENER WITH WINDOW HANDLER
   addWindowListener(new WindowHandler());
}//END LoanProcessor() CONSTRUCTOR
```

Nothing new here—you have seen all of this before. Now for the *actionPerformed()* method. First, the algorithm looks pretty straightforward and you might suspect that it can be easily coded. In most programming languages this would be true; however, Java presents a problem when reading numerical data. Remember when we had to create a special *staugIO* package to read keyboard data? Well, we are now about to "unwrap" this package and explain some of the things that need to be done to get numerical data into your program. We will leave the *actionPerformed()* algorithm as is, assuming that it is at a codeable level. Here is how it must be coded in Java:

```java
public void actionPerformed(ActionEvent e)
{
      //DID A BUTTON CAUSE EVENT?
      if (e.getSource() == computeButton)
      {
        //IF SO, READ DATA AND CALCULATE LOAN INFORMATION
        //DEFINE WRAPPER CLASS OBJECTS AND GET TEXT FIELD DATA
        Double p = new Double(principalField.getText().trim());
        Double t = new Double(termField.getText().trim());
        Double r = new Double(rateField.getText().trim());

        //CONVERT Double TO double
        double principal = p.doubleValue();
        double term = t.doubleValue();
        double rate = r.doubleValue();

        //MAKE LOAN CALCULATIONS
        rate = rate/12/100;
        double payment = principal * rate/(1-Math.pow((1+rate), -term));
        double interest = term * payment - principal;
        double total = principal + interest;

        //DISPLAY IN TEXT AREA
        NumberFormat currency = NumberFormat.getCurrencyInstance();
        loanInfoArea.setText("CONSUMER LOAN AMOUNTS");
        loanInfoArea.append("\n\nMonthly Payment: "
                            + currency.format(payment));
        loanInfoArea.append("\nTotal Interest : "
                            + currency.format(interest));
        loanInfoArea.append("\nTotal Loan Amount: "
                            + currency.format(total));
      }//END IF
//END actionPerformed()
```

The first line should be familiar. We simply use an `if` statement to test for a *computeButton* object event. Then comes the problem: reading numeric data from the text fields. Java "sees" all input as string input. As a result, we must convert the text field strings to numeric values. To do this, we must first create a ***wrapper object*** for each value. Java includes several numeric wrapper classes that correspond to the primitive numeric data types. They are `Integer`, `Long`, `Float`, `Double`, `Character`, and `Boolean`. We say that the wrapper classes "wrap" a value of a primitive data type as an object. In other words, a wrapper class allows the storage of a primitive data type value within an object. Furthermore, the wrapper class contains methods that allow the primitive data type to be converted to and from a string. This is why we need a wrapper class for input. We want to read the string data from a text field, assign it to a `Double` wrapper object, and then convert the object to the primitive `double` data type so that we can use the value in a calculation. For example, consider the following line of code from our method:

```
Double p = new Double(principalField.getText().trim());
```

Here, we have created an object, *p*, of the `Double` wrapper class. In creating the object, the *Double()* class constructor is called. This constructor takes a string argument and converts it to a floating-point value, initializing the object with this value. Notice that the argument uses our *principalField* text field object to call the *getText()* method to get the text field string. The *trim()* method is a member of *String* class that "trims," or removes, any leading or trailing white space from the string. So, can this method be called here? Sure, since the code `principalField.get-Text()` returns a string object that is used to call the *trim()* method. At this point, our wrapper object, *p*, contains the floating-point representation of the string data obtained from the *principalField* text field. However, this object *cannot* be manipulated within an arithmetic expression because it is an object and not a primitive data type. It must first be converted to a `double` primitive data type. In other words, we need to convert `Double` to `double`. This is the purpose of the following statement:

```
double principal = p.doubleValue();
```

Here we have defined a primitive `double` floating-point variable, called *principal*, and assigned it the value returned from `p.doubleValue()`. The *doubleValue()* method is a member of the `Double` class that returns the `double` equivalent of the calling object value. Now, after all of this, the `double` variable *principal* contains a numerical floating-point value that can be used in an arithmetic expression. That's a lot of work just to read in a numeric value, but that's Java!

All Java I/O is string I/O. Therefore, you must convert between string data and primitive data when the data is used for calculation within a program. To convert input data, you must use the Java wrapper classes. Each primitive data type has a corresponding wrapper class (example `double` and `Double`). The wrapper class initializes a wrapper object with a given string value. The wrapper object is then used to call a conversion method, such as *doubleValue()* to convert the object value to a primitive data type value that can be arithmetically manipulated in a program.

So, you can see from the foregoing *actionPerformed()* method code that each text field string is read and converted to a `double` primitive data type variable in this manner. Then, the variables are used as before to make the required calculations. Here is what you would see for a sample run:

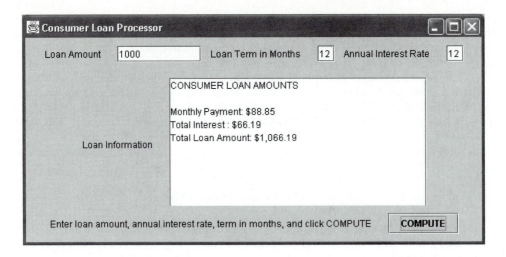

Notice the nice neat layout and the currency formatting. Now, let's put everything together in a complete program. Here it is:

```java
//ACTION 11-1  (ACTION11_01.JAVA)
//THIS PROGRAM WILL GENERATE AND PROCESS A GUI FOR THE
//CONSUMER LOAN PROBLEM
import javax.swing.*;         //FOR GUI COMPONENTS
import java.awt.*;            //FOR Container CLASS
import java.awt.event.*;      //FOR EVENT HANDLING
import java.text.NumberFormat;  //FOR CURRENCY FORMATTING

class LoanProcessor extends JFrame
{
   //DECLARE TEXT FIELD AND AREA OBJECTS AS PRIVATE CLASS DATA
   private JTextField principalField;
   private JTextField termField;
   private JTextField rateField;
   private JTextArea loanInfoArea;

   //DECLARE BUTTON OBJECT
   private JButton computeButton;

   //CONSTRUCTOR
   public LoanProcessor(String title)
   {
    //CALL SUPERCLASS CONSTRUCTOR
    super(title);

      //DECLARE CONTAINER OBJECT AND GET CONTENT PANE
      Container container = getContentPane();
```

```java
//DEFINE THREE PANELS
JPanel inputPanel = new JPanel();
JPanel displayPanel = new JPanel();
JPanel computePanel = new JPanel();
//SET EACH PANEL TO FLOW LAYOUT, CENTER JUSTIFIED, 10 PT. GAPPING
inputPanel.setLayout(new FlowLayout(FlowLayout.CENTER,10,10));
displayPanel.setLayout(new FlowLayout(FlowLayout.CENTER,10,10));
computePanel.setLayout(new FlowLayout(FlowLayout.CENTER,10,10));

//DEFINE LABEL OBJECTS
Label userInstruction = new Label("Enter loan amount,"
                         + " annual interest rate, term in months,"
                         + " and click COMPUTE");
Label principalLabel = new Label("Loan Amount");
Label termLabel = new Label("Loan Term in Months");
Label rateLabel = new Label("Annual Interest Rate");
Label loanInfoLabel = new Label("Loan Information");

//INSTANTIATE TEXT FIELD OBJECTS
principalField = new JTextField(10);
termField = new JTextField(2);
rateField = new JTextField(2);
loanInfoArea = new JTextArea(10,30);

//INSTANTIATE BUTTON OBJECT
computeButton = new JButton("COMPUTE");

//ADD COMPONENTS TO PANELS
inputPanel.add(principalLabel);
inputPanel.add(principalField);
inputPanel.add(termLabel);
inputPanel.add(termField);
inputPanel.add(rateLabel);
inputPanel.add(rateField);
displayPanel.add(loanInfoLabel);
displayPanel.add(new JScrollPane(loanInfoArea));
computePanel.add(userInstruction);
computePanel.add(computeButton);

//ADD PANELS TO CONTAINER
container.add(inputPanel,"North");
container.add(displayPanel,"Center");
container.add(computePanel,"South");

//ADD ACTION LISTENER WITH BUTTON HANDLER
computeButton.addActionListener(new ButtonHandler());
```

```
      //ADD WINDOW LISTENER WITH WINDOW HANDLER
      addWindowListener(new WindowHandler());
}//END LoanProcessor() CONSTRUCTOR


//WINDOW EVENT HANDLER
private class WindowHandler extends WindowAdapter
{
   public void windowClosing(WindowEvent e)
   {
      System.exit(0);   //EXIT TO OPERATING SYSTEM
   }//END windowClosing()
}//END WindowHandler CLASS


//BUTTON EVENT HANDLER CLASS
private class ButtonHandler implements ActionListener
{
   //PROCESS BUTTON EVENT
   public void actionPerformed(ActionEvent e)
   {
      //DID A BUTTON CAUSE EVENT?
      if (e.getSource() == computeButton)
      {
         //IF SO, READ DATA AND CALCULATE LOAN INFORMATION
         //DEFINE WRAPPER CLASS OBJECTS AND GET TEXT FIELD DATA
         Double p = new Double(principalField.getText().trim());
         Double t = new Double(termField.getText().trim());
         Double r = new Double(rateField.getText().trim());

         //CONVERT Double TO double
         double principal = p.doubleValue();
         double term = t.doubleValue();
         double rate = r.doubleValue();

         //MAKE LOAN CALCULATIONS
         rate = rate/12/100;
         double payment = principal * rate/(1-Math.pow((1+rate), -term));
         double interest = term * payment - principal;
         double total = principal + interest;

         //DISPLAY IN TEXT AREA
         NumberFormat currency = NumberFormat.getCurrencyInstance();
         loanInfoArea.setText("CONSUMER LOAN AMOUNTS");
         loanInfoArea.append("\n\nMonthly Payment: "
                           + currency.format(payment));
         loanInfoArea.append("\nTotal Interest : "
                           + currency.format(interest));
         loanInfoArea.append("\nTotal Loan Amount: "
                           + currency.format(total));
```

```
    }//END IF
  }//END actionPerformed()
 }//END ButtonHandler CLASS
}//END LoanProcessor CLASS

//APPLICATION CLASS TO TEST loanProcessor CLASS
public class Action11_01
{
  public static void main(String[] args)
  {
    //DEFINE FRAME OBJECT
    LoanProcessor window = new LoanProcessor("Consumer Loan Processor");
    //SET FRAME SIZE TO MAXIMIZE
    window.setSize(600,300);
    //MAKE FRAME VISIBLE
    window.show();
  }//END main()
}//END Action11_01 CLASS
```

As you can see, our *LoanProcessor* class appears first, along with its constructor. The text field, text area, and button objects are declared as private class members, then instantiated inside the constructor because they must be visible to the event handler class. The *LoanProcessor* class is followed by our standard *WindowHandler* class to handle the window closing event. Then comes our *ButtonHandler* class which contains *actionPerformed()* to handle our *computeButton* event. Of course, the program ends with an application test class called *Action11_01*. The application contains *main()*, which defines a frame object called *window*, sizes the frame, and makes the frame visible.

That's it! You should now be ready to design and build your own simple GUIs. Make sure that you do the programming problems that follow. The more practice you get, the better you will be at designing and building your own GUIs. You will find that it's a lot of fun.

CHAPTER SUMMARY

In this chapter you learned how to design and build your own simple graphical user interfaces, or GUIs, within a Java application. You found that the Java *javax.swing* package provides you with all the components necessary to build a GUI. The component classes in *javax.swing* allow you to create frames, buttons, labels, text fields, text areas, and more to come.

To design a GUI, you employ a window layout chart to lay out the components as they will appear on the window. You should indicate the type of component as well as its location and size, if applicable. Then, you employ algorithms and stepwise refinement to outline the steps required to create the GUI. Method *main()* in your application will create a frame object from your frame subclass, set the size of the frame, and make the frame visible. You create your own frame subclass by inheriting the standard *JFrame* class. Your GUI is actually created in the frame class constructor. You need to do the following within your frame subclass constructor to create a GUI:

- Call the superclass *JFrame* constructor and set the window title.
- Create a container.

- Set the container layout.
- Define any required panels.
- Set the layout for each panel.
- Define the GUI component objects.
- Add the GUI component objects to the panels.
- Add the panels to the container.
- Add a listener for a window closing event.
- Add listeners for any required event component objects.

To process a GUI component event, you must first add a listener for the component object in the constructor. Then, you create a `private` inner event handler class. Inside the event class you must implement your event logic within the required event method, such as *actionPerformed()* for action events. Each type of component is associated with a given event class and listener class. Each listener class contains its own abstract method(s) that must be implemented within your event handlers to process an event. When a listener class contains more than one event method, you can use an adapter class so you don't have to code those methods that you don't need to use. The following general tasks are normally performed within an event handler:

- Determine which component generated the event.
- Get the event data.
- Process the event data.
- Generate any required output.

Of course, these tasks must be stepwise refined to show the logic required to process a particular type of event.

QUESTIONS AND PROBLEMS

Questions

1. List the three tasks that must be performed within *main()* to create a visible frame in a Java application.
2. Explain why you must create your own subclass of the standard *JFrame* class to generate a window.
3. Explain the difference between procedural-controlled and event-driven programs.
4. List at least three GUI events defined by Java.
5. Explain the purpose of a listener.
6. Where is the event handling logic located for an action event?
7. The layout manager that arranges components into geographical regions is the _____ layout manager.
8. Write a statement to set the layout for a panel object, called *panel*, to grid layout, with 5 rows, and 3 columns.
9. Explain why using no layout manager can be a problem for portability.
10. Explain the purpose of a panel.

11. Most of the events handled in this chapter were handled by the *actionPerformed()* method because a button triggered the event. What GUI components generate events handled by the *itemStateChanged()* method?

12. Explain the functional difference between using *setText()* and *append()* when placing text in a text area.

13. Write the code required to perform the following tasks:

- Create a button object called *storeButton* with a label of "STORE".
- Create a "Midwestern States" label object called *statesLabel*.
- Add the label and button objects to a panel called *statesPanel*.

14. Suppose a GUI class contains the following button objects: *myButton*, *yourButton*, *hisButton*, *herButton*. Write an event handler class that will detect which button generated an event, and append the event button object name to a text area object called *textArea*.

15. Why must the button objects in question 14 be declared as `private` members of the GUI class?

Problems

Least Difficult

1. Write an application that contains the *FrameWithButtons* class developed in this chapter. Compile and execute your program. What happens when the various buttons are clicked?

Change the *FrameWithButtons* class developed in this chapter to employ different *FlowLayout* alignment and component gapping. Compile and execute your program and notice the effect of the different alignment and gapping.

Change the *FrameWithButtons* class developed in this chapter to employ different *GridLayout* cell arrangement (rows/columns) and component gapping. Compile and execute your program and notice the effect of the different cell arrangement and gapping.

2. Use the *PanelsTest* class given in this chapter to test the *Panels* class given in the chapter. Compile and execute your program and observe the effect of clicking the buttons. Change the *Panels* class code to employ different layouts, colors, etc., and observe the results by executing the program.

3. Code and execute the consumer loan processor GUI developed in this chapter to observe its behavior. This class can be found in the *Action11_01.java* file on the text CD.

More Difficult

4. Design and build a Banking GUI that will process a banking transaction. The GUI is to have the following components and capabilities, at a minimum:

- User instruction label(s)
- Text fields and associated labels for the user's personal identification number (PIN), and amount deposited or withdrawn
- Button to process the transaction
- Logic to calculate a new balance, assuming the initial balance was $1000.00
- A text area to display the new balance and a "Thank you" message, or a polite message, requesting the user enter a different amount if they attempt to withdraw more than $300

5. Design and build a loan application GUI. The GUI is to have the following components and capabilities, at a minimum:

- Text fields and associated labels that will allow the user to enter their name, address, telephone number, and social security number
- Text fields and associated labels that will allow the user to enter the amount of the loan and term for which they are applying
- Text field and associated label for annual income
- Text area to display the loan information
- A store/calculate button that will display the loan applicant information as well as monthly payment based on an interest rate of 10% in a text area, as well as "APPROVED" or "NOT APPROVED" based on the following criteria:

    - For loan amounts <= $1,000, annual income must be at least $10,000.
    - For loan amounts between $1,000 and $10,000, annual income must be at least $25,000.
    - For loan amounts between $10,000 and $25,000, annual income must be at least $50,000.
    - We do not make loans above $25,000.

12

Graphical User Interfaces— GUIs Part II

OBJECTIVES

When you are finished with this chapter, you should have a good understanding of the following:

- Combo and list boxes

- Check boxes and radio buttons

- Menus and submenus

- How to write event handlers to process combo and list box events

- How to use arrays to process list events

- How to write event handlers to process menu events

- How to use arrays to process menu events

- How to set the font of a GUI component and its contents

- The use of the *BoxLayout* and *CardLayout* layout managers

- How to generate different GUIs at different times under menu control

Introduction

This chapter is a continuation of the previous chapter. Here you will learn about some of the more advanced GUI components such as combo boxes, list boxes, and menus. In addition, you will learn how to use two more layout managers that will provide more flexibility when developing your own professional GUIs. We should mention, however, that there are even more GUI components and layout managers than discussed here. Java has a wealth of GUI-related classes that you will eventually want to learn if you do any commercial GUI programming. We have just covered the most common and useful ones in this text. If you haven't already done so, you might want to go through the parts of Appendix C that have to do with these components. Now, let's have some fun and get down to business.

12.1   **More GUI Components**

In order to develop professional looking GUIs, you need to learn about three more categories of GUI components. In this chapter, we will be discussing combo/list boxes, check boxes/radio buttons, and menus/submenus. We have grouped these components according to their similarity in client usage as well as programming. In addition, you need to learn about the *Font* class to dress up your GUIs and make them look more professional.

Combo and List Boxes

Combo boxes and list boxes are similar components in their appearance as well as the way in which they are handled in Java. Both a combo box and a list box are a listing of several selectable items. However, you can only select one item in a combo box, while one or more items can be selected in a list box.

A **combo box** allows you to select one of several items in a listing, while a **list box** allows you to select one or more items in a listing.

Combo Boxes—JComboBox   The following two screen shots show how a combo box works. Here, we see two labels, a combo box, a button, and a text area. The GUI on top shows how a combo box initially appears. Notice the arrow pointing down (▼) on the right side of "Accounting". This indicates that when the user clicks on the arrow, a drop-down box will appear as shown by the GUI on page 455.

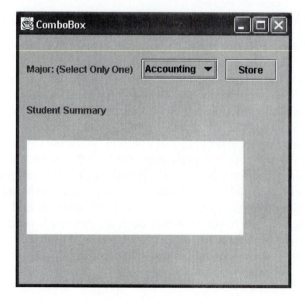

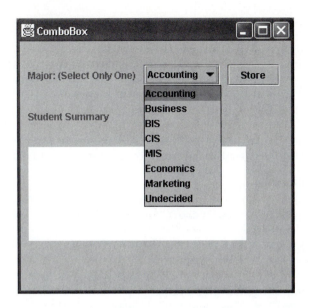

As you can see, the combo box provides a list of items for the user to select. Only the first item appears until the arrow is clicked. When the arrow is clicked, all possible choice items appear as shown in the screenshot above. When the user clicks on an item, that item is selected, the drop-down box disappears, and the selected item appears next to the arrow. The first thing we need to do to create our combo box is create an array of strings to hold the list of combo box items, like this:

```
//DEFINE ARRAY OF COMBO BOX ITEMS
String boxItems[] = {"Accounting", "Business", "BIS", "CIS", "MIS",
                     "Economics", "Marketing", "Undecided"};
```

Then, we use this array as an argument for the *JComboBox()* constructor, like this:

```
//DEFINE COMBO BOX OBJECT WITH boxItems[]
JComboBox majorsBox = new JComboBox(boxItems);
```

Once the combo box object is created, it can be added to a container or panel just like any other GUI component. Here is the class that created the combo box shown in the foregoing GUI:

```
import javax.swing.*;          //FOR SWING COMPONENT CLASSES
import java.awt.event.*;       //FOR EVENT HANDLING
import java.awt.*;             //FOR Container CLASS

class ComboBox extends JFrame
{
   //DECLARE COMPONENT OBJECTS
   private JComboBox majorsBox;      //COMBO BOX OBJECT
   private JTextArea studentArea;    //DISPLAY AREA OBJECT
   private JButton storeButton;      //STORE BUTTON OBJECT
```

```java
    //CONSTRUCTOR
    public ComboBox (String title)
    {
      super(title);                          //CALL SUPERCLASS CONSTRUCTOR

        //CREATE A CONTAINER
        Container container = getContentPane();

      //SET CONTAINER LAYOUT MANAGER
      container.setLayout(new FlowLayout(FlowLayout.LEFT,10,30));

      //DEFINE LABEL OBJECTS
      JLabel majorsLabel = new JLabel("Major: (Select Only One)");
      JLabel summaryLabel = new JLabel("Student Summary");

      //INSTANTIATE BUTTON OBJECT
      storeButton = new JButton("Store");

      //DEFINE ARRAY OF COMBO BOX ITEMS
      String boxItems[] = {"Accounting", "Business", "BIS", "CIS", "MIS",
                           "Economics", "Marketing", "Undecided"};

        //INSTANTIATE COMBO BOX OBJECT WITH boxItems[]
        majorsBox = new JComboBox(boxItems);

      //INSTANTIATE TEXT AREA OBJECT
      studentArea = new JTextArea(7,25);

      //ADD COMPONENTS TO CONTAINER
      container.add(majorsLabel);
      container.add(majorsBox);
      container.add(storeButton);
      container.add(summaryLabel);
      container.add(studentArea);

        //ADD ACTION LISTENER WITH BUTTON EVENT HANDLER
        storeButton.addActionListener(new ButtonHandler());

        //ADD WINDOW LISTENER WITH WINDOW EVENT HANDLER
        addWindowListener(new WindowHandler());
    }//END ComboBox() CONSTRUCTOR

  //WINDOW EVENT HANDLER CLASS
    private class WindowHandler extends WindowAdapter
    {
      public void windowClosing(WindowEvent e)
      {
        System.exit(0);  //EXIT TO OPERATING SYSTEM
      }//END windowClosing()
    }//END WindowAdapter CLASS
```

```
//BUTTON EVENT HANDLER CLASS
private class ButtonHandler implements ActionListener
{
//PROCESS BUTTON EVENT
public void actionPerformed(ActionEvent e)
{
  //CHECK FOR BUTTON EVENT
  if (e.getSource() == storeButton)
  {
    //CLEAR TEXT AREA
    studentArea.setText("");

    //DISPLAY IN COMBO BOX SELECTION IN TEXT AREA
    studentArea.append("\nMajor:\t" + majorsBox.getSelectedItem());
  }//END IF
 }//END actionPerformed()
 }//END ButtonHandler
}//END ComboBox CLASS
```

Again, we have highlighted the code of interest in bold. Notice that a *JComboBox* object is first declared as a `private` class member so that we can have access to it in an event handler. Then the object is instantiated within the class constructor. When the *majorsBox* object is instantiated, the *boxItems[]* array is passed as the *JComboBox()* constructor argument. The *majorsBox* object is added to the container just like any other GUI component. However, notice that a listener is added for the *storeButton* object, not the *majorsBox* object. As a result, we will process a combo box selection using a button event when the user clicks the *Store* button. Now, look at the *ButtonHandler* handler event class. Here is the combo box–related code we placed in *actionPerformed()*:

```
//DISPLAY IN COMBO BOX SELECTION IN TEXT AREA
studentArea.append("\nMajor:\t" + majorsBox.getSelectedItem());
```

This code appends the text area with the item chosen from the combo box. To do this, the *studentArea* object must call the *append()* method, which requires our *majorsChoice* object to call its *getSelectedItem()* method. The *getSelectedItem()* method is part of the *JComboBox* class and returns the string representation of the selected choice.

Detecting a Combo Box Event   Another way to process a combo box selection is to detect a combo box object event directly. A combo box object also generates an *ActionEvent*. Thus, to detect a combo box event, we must add a listener for the *majorsBox* object, like this:

```
//ADD LISTENER WITH COMBO BOX EVENT HANDLER
majorsBox.addActionListener(new BoxHandler());
```

Then, to handle a combo box event, we change our event handler method as follows:

```
//BOX EVENT HANDLER CLASS
private class BoxHandler implements ActionListener
```

```
{
  //PROCESS COMBO BOX EVENT
  public void actionPerformed(ActionEvent e)
  {
    //CHECK FOR COMBO BOX EVENT?
    if (e.getSource() == majorsBox)
    {
      //CLEAR TEXT AREA
      studentArea.setText("");
      //DISPLAY IN TEXT FIELD DATA IN TEXT AREA
      studentArea.append("\nMajor:\t" + majorsBox.getSelectedItem());
    }//END IF
  }//END actionPerformed()
}//END BoxHandler
```

Aside from the handler class name, the only change here is in the `if` statement that tests our combo box *majorsChoice* object for the event, rather than the *storeButton* button object. Here is the entire combo box class that has been altered to process a combo box event rather than a button event. The alterations are highlighted in bold.

```
import javax.swing.*;        //FOR SWING COMPONENT CLASSES
import java.awt.event.*;     //FOR EVENT HANDLING
import java.awt.*;           //FOR Container CLASS

class ComboBoxEvent extends JFrame
{
  //DECLARE COMPONENT OBJECTS
  private JComboBox majorsBox;      //COMBO BOX OBJECT
  private JTextArea studentArea;    //DISPLAY AREA OBJECT

  //CONSTRUCTOR
  public ComboBoxEvent(String title)
  {
    super(title);                   //CALL SUPERCLASS CONSTRUCTOR

    //CREATE A CONTAINER
    Container container = getContentPane();

    //SET CONTAINER LAYOUT MANAGER
    container.setLayout(new FlowLayout(FlowLayout.LEFT,10,30));

    //DEFINE LABEL OBJECTS
    JLabel majorsLabel = new JLabel("Major: (Select Only One)");
    JLabel summaryLabel = new JLabel("Student Summary");

    //DEFINE ARRAY OF COMBO BOX ITEMS
    String boxItems[] = {"Accounting", "Business", "BIS", "CIS", "MIS",
                         "Economics", "Marketing", "Undecided"};
```

```
      //INSTANTIATE COMBO BOX OBJECT WITH boxItems[]
      majorsBox = new JComboBox(boxItems);

      //INSTANTIATE TEXT AREA OBJECT
      studentArea = new JTextArea(7,25);

      //ADD COMPONENTS TO CONTAINER
      container.add(majorsLabel);
      container.add(majorsBox);
      container.add(summaryLabel);
      container.add(studentArea);

      //ADD LISTENER WITH COMBO BOX EVENT HANDLER
      majorsBox.addActionListener(new BoxHandler());

      //ADD WINDOW LISTENER WITH WINDOW EVENT HANDLER
      addWindowListener(new WindowHandler());
   }//END ComboBoxEvent() CONSTRUCTOR

   //WINDOW EVENT HANDLER CLASS
    private class WindowHandler extends WindowAdapter
    {
      public void windowClosing(WindowEvent e)
      {
        System.exit(0);   //EXIT TO OPERATING SYSTEM
      }//END windowClosing()
    }//END WindowAdapter CLASS

   //BOX EVENT HANDLER CLASS
    private class BoxHandler implements ActionListener
    {
    //PROCESS COMBO BOX EVENT
    public void actionPerformed(ActionEvent e)
    {
      //CHECK FOR COMBO BOX EVENT?
      if (e.getSource() == majorsBox)
      {
        //CLEAR TEXT AREA
        studentArea.setText("");
        //DISPLAY IN TEXT FIELD DATA IN TEXT AREA
        studentArea.append("\nMajor:\t" + majorsBox.getSelectedItem());
      }//END IF
    }//END actionPerformed()
   }//END BoxHandler
 }//END ComboBoxEvent CLASS
```

Here is the GUI produced by this class. Notice that the *Store* button is gone, and the event is detected by clicking on a combo box item. You might also notice that the drop-down box of items disappears and the selected item, *CIS* in this case, appears as the only visible item in the box when the item is selected.

List Boxes—JList A list box is like a combo box but allows the user to select one *or more* items within the item listing. Here is a GUI that contains a list box:

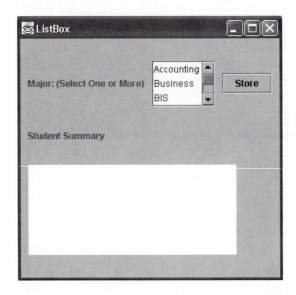

Notice that only three items are visible within the box. However, the box is associated with a scroll bar, indicating that more items are inside the box. Here is the class that created this GUI:

```
import javax.swing.*;       //FOR SWING COMPONENT CLASSES
import java.awt.event.*;    //FOR EVENT HANDLING
import java.awt.*;          //FOR Container CLASS
```

```java
class ListBox extends JFrame
{
    //DECLARE COMPONENT OBJECTS
    private JList majorsList;        //LIST OF MAJORS
    private JTextArea studentArea;   //SUMMARY AREA
    private JButton storeButton;     //STORE BUTTON OBJECT

    //DEFINE ARRAY OF LIST ITEMS
    private String listItems[] = {"Accounting", "Business", "BIS", "CIS",
                                  "MIS","Economics",
                                  "Marketing", "Undecided"};
    //CONSTRUCTOR
    public ListBox(String title)
    {
      //CALL SUPERCLASS CONSTRUCTOR
      super(title);

      //CREATE A CONTAINER
      Container container = getContentPane();

      //SET CONTAINER LAYOUT MANAGER
      container.setLayout(new FlowLayout(FlowLayout.LEFT,10,30));

      //DEFINE LABEL OBJECTS
      Label majorsLabel = new Label("Major: (Select One or More)");
      Label summaryLabel = new Label("Student Summary");

      //INSTANTIATE BUTTON OBJECT
      storeButton = new JButton("Store");

      //INSTANTIATE LIST BOX OBJECT WITH listItems[]
      majorsList = new JList(listItems);

      //SET VISIBLE ITEMS
      majorsList.setVisibleRowCount(3);

      //INSTANTIATE TEXT AREA OBJECT
      studentArea = new JTextArea(7,25);

      //ADD LIST LABEL TO CONTAINER
      container.add(majorsLabel);

      //ADD SCROLL BAR WITH LIST TO CONTAINER
      container.add(new JScrollPane(majorsList));

      //ADD STORE BUTTON TO CONTAINER
      container.add(storeButton);

      //ADD TEXT AREA LABEL TO CONTAINER
      container.add(summaryLabel);
```

```
     //ADD TEXT AREA TO CONTAINER
     container.add(studentArea);

     //ADD ACTION LISTENER WITH BUTTON EVENT HANDLER
     storeButton.addActionListener(new ButtonHandler());

     //ADD WINDOW LISTENER WITH WINDOW EVENT HANDLER
     addWindowListener(new WindowHandler());
  }//END ListBox() CONSTRUCTOR

//WINDOW HANDLER CLASS
 private class WindowHandler extends WindowAdapter
 {
   public void windowClosing(WindowEvent e)
   {
     System.exit(0);   //EXIT TO OPERATING SYSTEM
  }//END windowClosing()
 }//END WindowAdapter CLASS

//BUTTON HANDLER CLASS
 private class ButtonHandler implements ActionListener
 {
//PROCESS BUTTON EVENT
 public void actionPerformed(ActionEvent e)
 {
   //CHECK FOR storeButton EVENT
   if (e.getSource() == storeButton)
   {
     //GET SELECTED ITEM INDICES AND STORE IN ARRAY
     int selectedIndices[] = majorsList.getSelectedIndices();

     //DISPLAY HEADER
     studentArea.setText("\nMajor(s):\t");

     //DISPLAY SELECTED ITEMS
     for (int index = 0; index < selectedIndices.length; ++index)
     {
        studentArea.append(listItems[selectedIndices[index]]);
        studentArea.append("\n\t");
     }//END FOR
   }//END IF
  }//END actionPerformed()
 }//END ButtonHandler
}//END ListBox CLASS
```

Look at the `private` class members. We have declared a *JList* object called *majorsList* and defined a string array called *listItems[]*. We have defined these items as `private` so we can access them in our event handler. Looking inside the class constructor, you see that the *majorsList* object is instantiated using the following line of code:

```
//INSTANTIATE LIST BOX OBJECT WITH listItems[]
majorsList = new JList(listItems);
```

This is basically the same technique we used to set up a combo box. But, that's where the similarities end. Just after the *majorsList* object is instantiated, it is used to call its *setVisibleRowCount()* method, as follows:

```
//SET VISIBLE ITEMS
majorsList.setVisibleRowCount(3);
```

As you might suspect, the *setVisibleRowCount()* method sets the number of list items that will be visible within the list box at any one time. The next surprise is the use of the *JScrollPane* class to add scroll bars to the list when the list is added to the container with the following statement:

```
//ADD SCROLL BAR WITH LIST TO CONTAINER
container.add(new JScrollPane(majorsList));
```

The *add()* method argument is a *JScrollPane* object. So, we are actually adding a scroll pane to the container. But, the *JScrollPane()* constructor argument is our *majorList* object. In effect, this actually adds our *majorsList* to a scroll pane, which is added to the container. If we added our *majorList* object to the container without using *JScrollPane*, all the list items would appear without a scroll bar, even though we only set 3 items to appear.

Now to the event handler class, called *ButtonHandler*. The idea is that when the user clicks on the *Store* button, the selected list items will appear in the text area. Here is the handler class code:

```
//BUTTON HANDLER CLASS
private class ButtonHandler implements ActionListener
{
  //PROCESS BUTTON EVENT
  public void actionPerformed(ActionEvent e)
  {
    //CHECK FOR storeButton EVENT
    if (e.getSource() == storeButton)
    {
      //GET SELECTED ITEM INDICES AND STORE IN ARRAY
      int selectedIndices[] = majorsList.getSelectedIndices();

      //DISPLAY HEADER
      studentArea.setText("\nMajor(s):\t");

      //DISPLAY SELECTED ITEMS
      for (int index = 0; index < selectedIndices.length; ++index)
      {
        studentArea.append(listItems[selectedIndices[index]]);
        studentArea.append("\n\t");
      }//END FOR
    }//END IF
  }//END actionPerformed()
}//END ButtonHandler
```

This gets a little tricky, so stay with it. We have used *actionPerformed()* because we want to detect the *storeButton* event. When the event is detected, we define an integer array called *selectedIndices[]*. This array is initialized with the list item indices that were selected by the user when the *Store* button was clicked. (Remember that our list items are stored in an array and, therefore, have indices associated with them.) The selected indices are obtained by using our *majorsList* object to call its *getSelectedIndices()* method. This method returns an array of all the selected list item indices in increasing order. Now our program knows which items have been selected. The next task is to display those items in the text area. We have used a `for` loop to accomplish this task, as follows:

```
//DISPLAY SELECTED ITEMS
for (int index = 0; index < selectedIndices.length; ++index)
{
    studentArea.append(listItems[selectedIndices[index]]);
    studentArea.append("\n\t");
}//END FOR
```

The loop counter is tested against the value `selectedIndices.length`, which is the length of the *selectedIndices[]* array. Within the loop you see the following *append()* statement:

`studentArea.append(listItems[selectedIndices[index]]);`

Can you analyze this statement? We are appending the *studentArea* text area. The question is: How are we appending it? Well, the *append()* method argument references our original `private` array of list items, *listItems[]*. Then, the specific list item within this array that is appended is indexed by the *selectedIndices[]* array. For example, suppose the user selected the *Accounting* and *MIS* list items. These items have indices of [0] and [4], respectively, in our *listItems[]* array. Therefore, at this point in the program, our *selectedIndices[]* array would look like this:

selectedIndices[0,4]

Since the length of this array is 2, the `for` loop would execute two times. In the first iteration, the *append()* statement would break down as follows:

`studentArea.append(listItems[selectedIndices[index]]);`

which is equivalent to

`studentArea.append(listItems[selectedIndices[0]]);`

which is equivalent to

`studentArea.append(listItems[0]);`

which in turn is equivalent to

`studentArea.append("Accounting");`

During the second loop iteration, the *append()* statement would break down as follows:

```
studentArea.append(listItems[selectedIndices[index]]);
```

which is equivalent to

```
studentArea.append(listItems[selectedIndices[1]]);
```

which is equivalent to

```
studentArea.append(listItems[4]);
```

which in turn is equivalent to

```
studentArea.append("MIS");
```

Wow, isn't that cool? Here is what we will see when the user selects these two items and clicks the *Store* button:

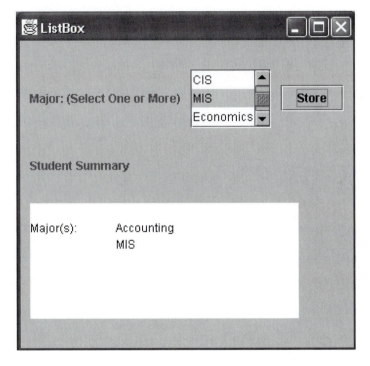

As is the convention of the selection process using a PC, the user must hold down the control (*Ctrl*) key to select multiple items. Also, the user can select a range of consecutive items by selecting the first item, holding down the *Shift* key, and then selecting the final item in the range.

Detecting a List Box Event   You might want to detect a list box object event directly, rather than using a button event. In order to do this, you must implement the *ListSelectionListener* class and not the *ActionPerformed* class. The *ListSelectionListener* class is contained in the *javax.swing.event* package and must be imported. This class has a single abstract method called *valueChanged()* that must be coded within your event handler.

The *ListSelectionListener* class is contained in the *javax.swing.event* package and must be imported. This class has a single abstract method called *valueChanged()* that must be implemented to handle *JList* events.

Here is our list box class again, with the altered code highlighted in bold:

```java
import javax.swing.*;          //FOR SWING COMPONENT CLASSES
import java.awt.*;             //FOR Container CLASS
import java.awt.event.*;       //FOR EVENT HANDLING
import javax.swing.event.*;    //FOR ListSelectionListener EVENT HANDLING

class ListBoxEvent extends JFrame
{
   //DECLARE COMPONENT OBJECTS
   private JTextArea studentArea; //SUMMARY AREA
   private JList majorsList;       //LIST OF MAJORS

   //DEFINE ARRAY OF LIST ITEMS
   private String listItems[] = {"Accounting", "Business", "BIS", "CIS",
                         "MIS","Economics", "Marketing", "Undecided"};
   //CONSTRUCTOR
   public ListBoxEvent(String title)
   {

     //CALL SUPERCLASS CONSTRUCTOR
     super(title);

     //CREATE A CONTAINER
     Container container = getContentPane();

     //SET CONTAINER LAYOUT MANAGER
     container.setLayout(new FlowLayout(FlowLayout.LEFT,10,30));

     //DEFINE LABEL OBJECTS
     Label majorsLabel = new Label("Major: (Select One or More)");
     Label summaryLabel = new Label("Student Summary");

     //INSTANTIATE LIST BOX OBJECT WITH listItems[]
     majorsList = new JList(listItems);

     //SET VISIBLE ITEMS
     majorsList.setVisibleRowCount(3);
```

```
        //INSTANTIATE TEXT AREA OBJECT
        studentArea = new JTextArea(7,25);

        //ADD LIST LABEL TO CONTAINER
        container.add(majorsLabel);

        //ADD SCROLL BAR WITH LIST TO CONTAINER
        container.add(new JScrollPane(majorsList));

        //ADD TEXT AREA LABEL TO CONTAINER
        container.add(summaryLabel);

        //ADD TEXT AREA TO CONTAINER
        container.add(studentArea);

        //ADD LIST LISTENER WITH LIST EVENT HANDLER
        majorsList.addListSelectionListener(new ListHandler());

        //ADD WINDOW LISTENER WITH WINDOW EVENT HANDLER
        addWindowListener(new WindowHandler());
    }//END ListBoxEvent() CONSTRUCTOR

//WINDOW EVENT HANDLER CLASS
private class WindowHandler extends WindowAdapter
{
    public void windowClosing(WindowEvent e)
   {
        System.exit(0);   //EXIT TO OPERATING SYSTEM
   }//END windowClosing()
}//END WindowAdapter CLASS

//LIST HANDLER CLASS
private class ListHandler implements ListSelectionListener
{
//PROCESS LIST EVENT
public void valueChanged(ListSelectionEvent e)
{
    //CHECK FOR LIST EVENT
    if (e.getSource() == majorsList)
    {
        //GET SELECTED ITEM INDICES AND STORE IN ARRAY
        int selectedIndices[] = majorsList.getSelectedIndices();

        //DISPLAY HEADER
        studentArea.setText("\nMajor(s):\t");

        //DISPLAY SELECTED ITEMS
        for (int index = 0; index < selectedIndices.length; ++index)
        {
            studentArea.append(listItems[selectedIndices[index]]);
            studentArea.append("\n\t");
```

```
    }//END FOR
   }//END IF
  }//END valueChanged()
 }//END ListHandler CLASS
}//END ListBoxEvent CLASS
```

First, you see the importation of all classes in the *javax.swing.event* package. This package contains the *ListSelectionListener* class. Our *majorsList* object is instantiated and added within a scroll bar to the container as before. Next, instead of adding a listener for a button object using the *addActionListener()* method with a button handler, we have added a listener for our *majorsList* object using the *addListSelectionListener()* method with a list handler. Our *ListHandler* class implements the *ListSelectionListener* class. Within our handler class we have implemented the abstract *valueChanged()* method. Notice that this method requires a *ListSelectionEvent* object parameter. The implementation code within the *valueChanged()* method is identical to that which we used earlier in the *actionPerformed()* method. Here is a sample run of this class:

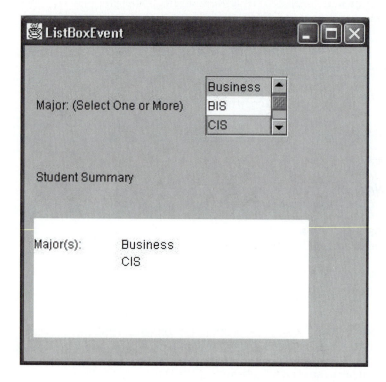

Notice that the *Store* button is gone and the user has selected the *Business* and *CIS* items, which appear highlighted in the list box and displayed within the text area. Clicking on any one item or range of items will generate a *ListSelectionEvent*, causing that item, or range of items, to be displayed within the text area.

Check Boxes and Radio Buttons

Check boxes and radio buttons are called *state buttons* because they can be turned on and off, representing one of two possible Boolean states, `true` or `false`. The difference between a check box and a radio button is that any number of check boxes within a group can be selected at a given time, while only one radio button within a group can be selected at any one time. Check boxes require the use of the *JCheckBox* class, while radio buttons employ the *JRadioButton* class. In addition, radio buttons also require the use of the *ButtonGroup* class, as you will see shortly.

Check Boxes—JCheckBox   Here is a GUI that shows four check boxes relating to student status:

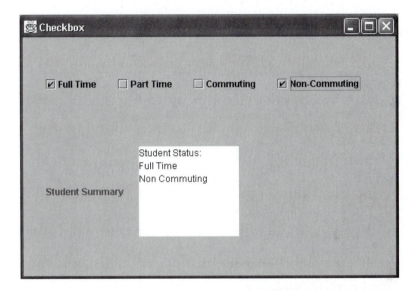

As you can see, the check boxes allow the user to select full time, part time, commuting, or non-commuting status. Here is the class that produced the foregoing GUI:

```
//CHECKBOX WITHOUT LABEL
public Checkbox();

import javax.swing.*;         //FOR SWING COMPONENT CLASSES
import java.awt.*;            //FOR Container CLASS
import java.awt.event.*;      //FOR EVENT HANDLING

class CheckBox extends JFrame
{
    //DECLARE CHECK BOX OBJECTS
    private JCheckBox fullTimeBox;
    private JCheckBox partTimeBox;
    private JCheckBox commutingBox;
    private JCheckBox nonCommutingBox;
```

```
//DECLARE TEXT AREA OBJECT
private JTextArea studentArea;

//CONSTRUCTOR
public CheckBox(String title)
{
//CALL SUPERCLASS CONSTRUCTOR
super(title);

//CREATE A CONTAINER
Container container = getContentPane();

//SET CONTAINER LAYOUT MANAGER
container.setLayout(new FlowLayout(FlowLayout.LEFT,10,30));

//DEFINE LABEL OBJECTS
JLabel summaryLabel = new JLabel("Student Summary");

//INSTANTIATE CHECK BOX OBJECTS
fullTimeBox = new JCheckBox("Full Time");
partTimeBox = new JCheckBox("Part Time");
commutingBox = new JCheckBox("Commuting");
nonCommutingBox = new JCheckBox("Non-Commuting");

//INSTANTIATE TEXT AREA OBJECT
studentArea = new JTextArea(7,25);

//DEFINE PANELS
JPanel topPanel = new JPanel();
JPanel bottomPanel = new JPanel();

//SET PANEL LAYOUT MANAGERS
topPanel.setLayout(new FlowLayout(FlowLayout.LEFT,20,20));
bottomPanel.setLayout(new FlowLayout(FlowLayout.LEFT,20,20));

//ADD COMPONENTS TO topPanel
topPanel.add(fullTimeBox);
topPanel.add(partTimeBox);
topPanel.add(commutingBox);
topPanel.add(nonCommutingBox);

//ADD TEXT AREA TO bottomPanel
bottomPanel.add(summaryLabel);
bottomPanel.add(studentArea);

//ADD PANELS TO FRAME
container.add(topPanel);
container.add(bottomPanel);

//CREATE HANDLER OBJECT
CheckBoxHandler checkHandler = new CheckBoxHandler();

//ADD ITEM LISTENER WITH CHECK BOX EVENT HANDLER
fullTimeBox.addItemListener(checkHandler);
partTimeBox.addItemListener(checkHandler);
```

```
   commutingBox.addItemListener(checkHandler);
   nonCommutingBox.addItemListener(checkHandler);

   //ADD WINDOW LISTENER WITH WINDOW EVENT HANDLER
   addWindowListener(new WindowHandler());
}//END CheckBox() CONSTRUCTOR

//WINDOW EVENT HANDLER CLASS
private class WindowHandler extends WindowAdapter
{
  public void windowClosing(WindowEvent e)
  {
    System.exit(0);  //EXIT TO OPERATING SYSTEM
  }//END windowClosing()
}//END WindowAdapter CLASS

//CHECK BOX HANDLER CLASS
private class CheckBoxHandler implements ItemListener
{
 //PROCESS CHECK BOX EVENT
 public void itemStateChanged(ItemEvent e)
 {
  //CLEAR TEXT AREA
  studentArea.setText("Student Status:");

  //DID A CHECK BOX CAUSE EVENT?
  if (e.getSource() instanceof JCheckBox)
  {
    //PROCESS CHECK BOXES
    if ((fullTimeBox.isSelected()) && (partTimeBox.isSelected()))
      studentArea.append("\nCANNOT SELECT BOTH FULL TIME\n"
                              + "AND PART TIME");
    else
    {
      if (fullTimeBox.isSelected())
        studentArea.append("\nFull Time");
      if (partTimeBox.isSelected())
        studentArea.append("\nPart Time");
    } //END ELSE

    if ((commutingBox.isSelected()) && (nonCommutingBox.isSelected()))
      studentArea.append("\nCANNOT SELECT BOTH COMMUTING\n"
                              + "AND NON-COMMUTING");
    else
    {
      if (commutingBox.isSelected())
        studentArea.append("\nCommuting");
      if (nonCommutingBox.isSelected())
        studentArea.append("\nNon Commuting");
    }//END ELSE
  }//END IF CHECK BOX
 }//END itemStateChanged()
}//END CheckHandler CLASS
}//END CheckBox CLASS
```

Here, we have declared four *JCheckBox* objects as `private` members of our *CheckBox* class. Within the *CheckBox()* class constructor, each object is instantiated using the *JCheckBox()* constructor, which requires a string argument. The string argument provides the label for the check box. No separate label needs to be provided when using this constructor. Next, the check box objects are added to a panel, and a listener is added for each object using the *addItemListener()* method. Notice that check boxes require the use of the *ItemListener* class. The *ItemListener* class has one abstract method, called *itemStateChanged()*, which must be implemented in our event handler class. Our event handler class is appropriately called *CheckBoxHandler*. Here is where all the work is done relative to the check boxes. The idea is simply to display the checked student status in the text area. To do this, our event handler must determine which check boxes are checked. In other words, since checking any of the check boxes generates an *ItemEvent,* the event handler must determine which specific check box generated the event. You see that our *CheckBoxHandler* class implements *ItemListener*, then provides the code for its single method, *itemStateChanged()*, which receives an *ItemEvent* object. Look at the first `if` statement in the event handler. It employs the `instanceof` operator. The statement:

```
if(e.getSource() instanceof JCheckBox)
```

uses the event object to call the *getSource()* method, which returns the source object that caused the event. If this object is an "instance of" the *JCheckBox* class, the `if` statement test expression will be `true`. Otherwise, it is `false`. The word `instanceof` is a keyword in Java. So, if any one of our check boxes generated the event, the statement will be `true` because we have added item listeners for all of our check box objects.

Now, we need some logic to process our check boxes. In this application, we will simply write the student status represented by the selected check boxes within the student summary text area when a given check box is checked. Now, think about the check box logic for a minute. It shouldn't be possible for the user to select both full time and part time status, right? Also, we need to prevent the user from selecting both commuting and non-commuting status. Any other combination of items is okay. This requires some `if/else` logic as follows:

```
if ((fullTimeBox.isSelected()) && (partTimeBox.isSelected()))
   studentArea.append("\nCANNOT SELECT BOTH FULL TIME\n"
                          + "AND PART TIME");
else
{
   if (fullTimeBox.isSelected())
      studentArea.append("\nFull Time");
   if (partTimeBox.isSelected())
      studentArea.append("\nPart Time");
} //END ELSE

if ((commutingBox.isSelected()) && (nonCommutingBox.isSelected()))
   studentArea.append("\nCANNOT SELECT BOTH COMMUTING\n"
                          + "AND NON-COMMUTING");

else
{
   if (commutingBox.isSelected())
```

```
    studentArea.append("\nCommuting");
  if (nonCommutingBox.isSelected())
    studentArea.append("\nNon Commuting");
}//END ELSE
```

The key ingredient here is the *isSelected()* method. This method is part of the *JCheckBox* class and returns the Boolean state of its calling check box object. In the first `if` statement, *isSelected()* is called by both the *fullTimeBox* and *partTimeBox* objects. If *isSelected()* returns `true` for both objects, the AND (&&) test is `true`, resulting in an error message being appended to the text area. Otherwise, the `else` clause is executed to determine which one, if any, of these two items have been selected. If either the full time or part time check box has been selected, but not both, the student status is appended to the text area. The same logic is then applied to the *commutingBox* and *nonCommutingBox* objects.

Here, we have handled the check boxes within the *itemStateChanged()* method since the primary event we are interested in handling is the checking of a check box. This triggers the *itemStateChanged()* method where all of our component processing logic appears. Of course, you could have also processed the check boxes using a *Store* button as we have done in the past. However, since a button is an *ActionEvent*, we would have to add an *ActionListener* for the button and implement the *actionPerformed()* method. This will be left as an exercise.

Radio Buttons—JRadioButton   Here is a GUI with two radio buttons to determine the undergraduate or graduate status of a student:

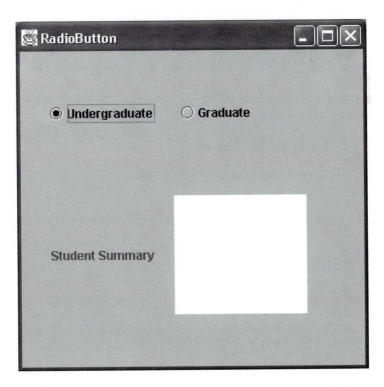

Here is the class that created this GUI:

```
import javax.swing.*;      //FOR SWING COMPONENT CLASSES
import java.awt.*;         //FOR Container CLASS
import java.awt.event.*;   //FOR EVENT HANDLING

class RadioButton extends JFrame
{
    //DECLARE RADIO BUTTON OBJECTS
    private JRadioButton undergraduate;;
    private JRadioButton graduate;

    //DECLARE TEXT AREA OBJECT
    private JTextArea studentArea;

  //CONSTRUCTOR
  public RadioButton(String title)
  {
    //CALL SUPERCLASS CONSTRUCTOR
    super(title);

    //CREATE A CONTAINER
    Container container = getContentPane();

    //SET CONTAINER LAYOUT MANAGER
    container.setLayout(new FlowLayout(FlowLayout.LEFT,10,30));

    //DEFINE LABEL OBJECTS
    JLabel summaryLabel = new JLabel("Student Summary");

    //CREATE RADIO BUTTON GROUP
    ButtonGroup graduateStatusGroup = new ButtonGroup();

    //INSTANTIATE RADIO BUTTON OBJECTS
    undergraduate = new JRadioButton("Undergraduate",true);
    graduate = new JRadioButton("Graduate",false);

    //ADD BUTTONS TO GROUP
    graduateStatusGroup.add(undergraduate);
    graduateStatusGroup.add(graduate);

    //INSTANTIATE TEXT AREA OBJECT
    studentArea = new JTextArea(7,12);

    //DEFINE PANELS
    JPanel topPanel = new JPanel();
    JPanel bottomPanel = new JPanel();
```

```
//SET PANEL LAYOUT MANAGERS
topPanel.setLayout(new FlowLayout(FlowLayout.LEFT,20,20));
bottomPanel.setLayout(new FlowLayout(FlowLayout.LEFT,20,20));

//ADD COMPONENTS TO topPanel
topPanel.add(undergraduate);
topPanel.add(graduate);

//ADD TEXT AREA TO bottomPanel
bottomPanel.add(summaryLabel);
bottomPanel.add(studentArea);

//ADD PANELS TO FRAME
container.add(topPanel);
container.add(bottomPanel);

//ADD ITEM LISTENER WITH RADIO BUTTON EVENT HANDLER
//ONLY NEED TO REGISTER LISTENER FOR ONE BUTTON OF GROUP
undergraduate.addItemListener(new RadioButtonHandler());

  //ADD WINDOW LISTENER WITH WINDOW EVENT HANDLER
  addWindowListener(new WindowHandler());
}//END RadioButton() CONSTRUCTOR

//WINDOW EVENT HANDLER CLASS
private class WindowHandler extends WindowAdapter
{
  public void windowClosing(WindowEvent e)
  {
    System.exit(0);  //EXIT TO OPERATING SYSTEM
  }//END windowClosing()
}//END WindowAdapter CLASS

//RADIO BUTTON HANDLER CLASS
private class RadioButtonHandler implements ItemListener
{
 //PROCESS RADIO BUTTON EVENT
 public void itemStateChanged(ItemEvent e)
 {
  //CLEAR TEXT AREA
  studentArea.setText("Student Status:");

    //APPEND TEXT AREA WITH BUTTON EVENT STATUS
    if (undergraduate.isSelected())
      studentArea.append("\nUndergraduate");
    else
      studentArea.append("\nGraduate");
  }//END itemStateChanged()
 }//END RadioButtonHandler CLASS
}//END RadioButton CLASS
```

First, you see that we declared our two radio button objects as `private` members of the class. The next thing you see in bold type is the definition of a *ButtonGroup* object, called *graduateStatusGroup*. Now, when a radio button object is added to this group, it becomes a member of the group such that only one of the buttons within the group can be "on" at any given time. After defining the *graduateStatusGroup*, the two radio button objects are instantiated and added to the group. Notice how the two radio button objects are instantiated. The *JRadioButton()* constructor that we are using requires a string argument followed by a Boolean argument. The string argument provides a label for the radio button, and the Boolean argument turns the button on (`true`) or off (`false`) when the GUI appears. This becomes the default selection status for the button. Of course, only one button within a group can be turned on at a time. Therefore, you want to set only one of the buttons to `true`. If you set more than one button to `true`, Java will turn the first button you set to `true` on, and all others will be turned off.

Radio buttons must be added to a group so that only one button within the group can be on at any given time. Of course, you can create as many different radio button groups as an application requires.

Radio buttons generate an item event directly. So, we have added an *ItemListener* for the *undergraduate* button. We only need to add a listener for one button within the group since the buttons are mutually exclusive. The logic required to handle the radio buttons is placed inside an event handler class called *RadioButtonHandler*. This class implements the *itemStateChanged()* method. The logic within this method is rather straightforward, as follows:

```
//APPEND TEXT AREA WITH BUTTON EVENT STATUS
if (undergraduate.isSelected())
  studentArea.append("\nUndergraduate");
else
  studentArea.append("\nGraduate");
```

All we need here is a single `if/else` statement because we are only dealing with two radio buttons. If one button is on, the other is off, and vice versa. If we had more than two buttons in our group, we would need nested `if/else` statements. You see that the *isSelected()* method is employed within the `if` test to determine the Boolean state of the *undergraduate* button.

Menus and Submenus—*JMenu, JMenuItem, JMenuBar*

A **menu** consists of a set of selectable options located at the top of a window within a **menu bar**. Menus are widely used in windowed applications because they make selection easier and don't clutter the GUI. Look at the *Color* menu on the following GUI:

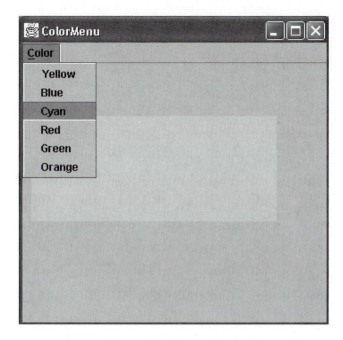

Notice the **menu bar** at the top of the window, just under the title bar. We have added a single *Color* menu to the menu bar. The color menu has six selectable color items. The purpose of the *Color* menu is to set the background color of the text area.

Here is what you have to do to create a menu:

- Define all main menu and submenu objects using *JMenu*.
- Define all menu item objects using *JMenuItem*.
- Add the menu items to the menus using *menu.add(menuItem)*.
- Add listeners for all the menu item objects using *menuItem.addActionListener()*.
- Add the submenus to the main menus using *mainMenu.add(submenu)*.
- Define a menu bar object using *JMenuBar*.
- Add the main menus to the menu bar using *menuBar.add(mainMenu)*.
- Set the menu bar on the frame, not the container, using *setJMenuBar(menuBar)*.

As you can see, there are three classes that control the creation and use of menus. They are *JMenu*, *JMenuItem*, and *JMenuBar*. Menu and submenu (a menu within a menu) objects must first be created using *JMenu*. Menu items are the selectable items that appear within a menu or submenu, and must be created using *JMenuItem*. All menus require a **menu bar**. The menu bar is a separate GUI component located under the title bar at the top of a window. The menu bar component is a container for menus and has its own separate class called *JMenuBar*. Let's see how we have applied the foregoing steps to create our *Color* menu GUI. The code that follows gets intense, applying many of the OOP and array concepts discussed in previous chapters, so stay with us. Here's the *ColorMenu* class code that produced the foregoing GUI:

```java
import javax.swing.*;            //FOR SWING COMPONENT CLASSES
import java.awt.*;               //FOR Container CLASS
import java.awt.event.*;         //FOR EVENT HANDLING

class ColorMenu extends JFrame
{
   //DECLARE MENU ITEM ARRAY
   private JMenuItem colorItems[];

   //DECLARE TEXT AREA OBJECT
   private JTextArea studentArea;

   //CONSTRUCTOR
   public ColorMenu(String Title)
   {
    //CALL SUPERCLASS CONSTRUCTOR
    super(Title);

    //CREATE A CONTAINER
    Container container = getContentPane();

    //SET CONTAINER LAYOUT MANAGER
    container.setLayout(new FlowLayout(FlowLayout.LEFT,10,60));

    //DEFINE MAIN MENU OBJECT
    JMenu colorMenu = new JMenu("Color");
    colorMenu.setMnemonic('C');                 //SET MENU MNEMONIC

    //DEFINE COLOR STRINGS FOR JMenuItem() CONSTRUCTOR
    String colors[] = {"Yellow","Blue","Cyan","Red","Green","Orange"};

    //INSTANTIATE COLOR ITEMS ARRAY
    colorItems = new JMenuItem[colors.length];

    //INSTANTIATE MENU ITEMS, ADD TO MENU, AND REGISTER AS LISTENERS
    for (int index = 0;index < colors.length;++index)
    {
       //INSTANTIATE MENU ITEM OBJECTS
       colorItems[index] = new JMenuItem(colors[index]);
       colorMenu.add(colorItems[index]);
       colorItems[index].addActionListener(new MenuHandler());
    }//END FOR

    //DEFINE MENU BAR OBJECT
    JMenuBar bar = new JMenuBar();

    //ADD MENU TO MENU BAR
    bar.add(colorMenu);

    //SET MENU BAR
    setJMenuBar(bar);
```

```
   //INSTANTIATE TEXT AREA OBJECT
   studentArea = new JTextArea(7,25);

   //ADD TEXT AREA TO CONTAINER
   container.add(studentArea);

   //ADD WINDOW LISTENER WITH WINDOW EVENT HANDLER
   addWindowListener(new WindowHandler());
}//END ColorMenu() CONSTRUCTOR

//WINDOW EVENT HANDLER CLASS
private class WindowHandler extends WindowAdapter
{
  public void windowClosing(WindowEvent e)
  {
    System.exit(0); //EXIT TO OPERATING SYSTEM
  }//END windowClosing()
}//END WindowAdapter CLASS

//MENU HANDLER CLASS
private class MenuHandler implements ActionListener
{
 //PROCESS MENU EVENT
 public void actionPerformed(ActionEvent e)
 {
  //DEFINE ARRAY OF Color OBJECTS
  Color textBackground[] = {Color.yellow,Color.blue,Color.cyan,
                            Color.red,Color.green,Color.orange};
  //LOOP THROUGH MENU ITEM ARRAY TO FIND EVENT ITEM
  for(int index = 0;index < colorItems.length; ++index)
  {
    //CHECK THIS ITEM FOR EVENT
    if(e.getSource() == colorItems[index])
      studentArea.setBackground(textBackground[index]);
  }//END FOR
 }//END actionPerformed()
}//END MenuHandler
}//END ColorMenu CLASS
```

The selectable items within a menu are what the user clicks to generate an event. So, our first task is to define a private *colorItems[]* array of the *JMenuItem* class. We will use this array to hold the menu item objects that make up the color menu. It must be a private class member, defined outside of the constructor, so that it is visible to our menu event handler. Within the constructor, you see the main color menu object defined as follows:

```
//DEFINE MAIN MENU OBJECT
JMenu colorMenu = new JMenu("Color");
colorMenu.setMnemonic('C');                    //SET MENU MNEMONIC
```

The *JMenu* class must be used to define a menu or submenu object. The class constructor argument is a string that is the menu label. Our *colorMenu* object is then used to call the *setMnemonic()* method to set a keyboard action key. Here, pressing the *Alt* key and the *C* key (ALT-C) at any time would open the menu list just the same as if you clicked on the menu label.

Next, we must create the menu items, add the items to the menu, and add listeners for each of the item objects. We have done all of this using the following lines of code:

```
//DEFINE COLOR STRINGS FOR JMenuItem() CONSTRUCTOR
String colors[] = {"Yellow","Blue","Cyan","Red","Green","Orange"};

//INSTANTIATE COLOR ITEMS ARRAY
colorItems = new JMenuItem[colors.length];

//INSTANTIATE MENU ITEMS, ADD TO MENU, AND REGISTER AS LISTENERS
for (int index = 0;index < colors.length;++index)
{
   //INSTANTIATE MENU ITEM OBJECTS
   colorItems[index] = new JMenuItem(colors[index]);
   colorMenu.add(colorItems[index]);
   colorItems[index].addActionListener(new MenuHandler());
}//END FOR
```

First, we have created an array of strings to hold the colors of our color menu items. You will see how this array is used shortly. Then, we instantiate the *colorItems[]* array that we declared earlier as a `private` class member. Remember that this array will hold our menu item objects. Don't forget that it is also an object by itself and must be instantiated in order to use it later on.

THINK!

A common mistake when using an array to hold menu item objects is to forget to instantiate the array object. Failure to do so will create a *NullPointerException* during runtime when you try to access the array in an event handler.

Now, look at the `for` loop. You see that the loop counter, *index*, ranges from 0 to the length of the previously defined *colors[]* array. The three statements inside this loop perform the following tasks:

- Define the color item objects and put them in the *colorItems[]* array.
- Add the color item objects to the *colorMenu*.
- Add a listener for each of the color item objects.

Let's trace the loop through its first two iterations. Here is what the compiler "sees" during the first iteration:

```
colorItems[index] = new JMenuItem(colors[index]);
colorMenu.add(colorItems[index]);
colorItems[index].addActionListener(new MenuHandler());
```

which, when *index = 0*, is equivalent to

```
colorItems[0] = new JMenuItem(colors[0]);
colorMenu.add(colorItems[0]);
colorItems[0].addActionListener(new MenuHandler());
```

which is equivalent to

```
colorItems[0] = new JMenuItem("Yellow");
colorMenu.add(colorItems[0]);
colorItems[0].addActionListener(new MenuHandler());
```

So, the first line of code creates a *JMenuItem* object with a "Yellow" label and places it in the *colorItems[]* array at index [0]. The second line adds this object (located at *colorItems[0]*) to the main *colorMenu*. The third line uses this menu item object to call the *addActionListener()* method to add a listener for the object. Here is what the compiler "sees" during the second iteration:

```
colorItems[index] = new JMenuItem(colors[index]);
colorMenu.add(colorItems[index]);
colorItems[index].addActionListener(new MenuHandler());
```

which, when *index = 1*, is equivalent to

```
colorItems[1] = new JMenuItem(colors[1]);
colorMenu.add(colorItems[1]);
colorItems[1].addActionListener(new MenuHandler());
```

which is equivalent to

```
colorItems[1] = new JMenuItem("Blue");
colorMenu.add(colorItems[1]);
colorItems[1].addActionListener(new MenuHandler());
```

Here, the first line of code creates a *JMenuItem* object with a "Blue" label and places it in the *colorItems[]* array at index [1]. The second line adds this object (located at *colorItems[1]*) to the main *colorMenu*. The third line uses this menu item object to call the *addActionListener()* method to add a listener for the object. The remaining iterations accomplish the same three tasks for each of the remaining colors in the *colors[]* array.

Now, we have almost created our GUI. All we have left to do is create a menu bar object, add the main menu to the menu bar, and set the menu bar on the frame. These three tasks are accomplished by the following code:

```
//DEFINE MENU BAR OBJECT
JMenuBar bar = new JMenuBar();

//ADD MENU TO MENU BAR
bar.add(colorMenu);

//SET MENU BAR
setJMenuBar(bar);
```

You see here that the *JMenuBar* class is used to create a menu bar object called *bar*. This object is then used to call the *add()* method to add our main *colorMenu* (which now contains all of its menu items) to the menu bar. The *setJMenuBar()* method is then used to set the *bar* object on the frame. Note that the menu is not set on a container. It must be set on the original window frame. This is why there is no *Container* class object calling the *setJMenuBar()* method. It does not need an object reference because it is being called within the original frame class constructor. Does this make sense?

 THINK!

A common mistake is to set a menu to a container. This will always create a compiler error since a menu must always be set to a frame.

Up to this point, we have only created a menu for the GUI. We must now develop the code to handle a menu event. A menu event occurs when one of the menu items is selected. Selection can occur by pointing and clicking the mouse on a menu item, by using the keyboard arrow and **ENTER** keys, or by using the action key if one has been set for the item. Either way, an *ActionEvent* is generated. So, we have created an event handler, appropriately called *MenuHandler*, that implements *actionPerformed()*, as follows:

```
//MENU HANDLER CLASS
private class MenuHandler implements ActionListener
{
 //PROCESS MENU EVENT
 public void actionPerformed(ActionEvent e)
 {

   //DEFINE ARRAY OF Color OBJECTS
   Color textBackground[] = {Color.yellow,Color.blue,Color.cyan,
                             Color.red,Color.green,Color.orange};
   //LOOP THROUGH MENU ITEM ARRAY TO FIND EVENT ITEM
   for(int index = 0;index < colorItems.length; ++index)
   {
     //CHECK THIS ITEM FOR EVENT
     if(e.getSource() == colorItems[index])
       studentArea.setBackground(textBackground[index]);
   }//END FOR
 }//END actionPerformed()
}//END MenuHandler
```

The purpose of the *ColorMenu* class is to set the background color of our GUI text area. Therefore, we have to determine which menu item generated the event. Once this is determined, we can set the background color of the text area to the color selected on the menu. As you know, the *setBackground()* method can be called by our *studentArea* object to set its background color. However, this method requires an argument from the standard *Color* class. Therefore, we have first created a *textBackground[]* array of the *Color* class to hold the same colors, in the same order, as our color menu items. These colors are predefined for the *Color* class. Table 12-1 lists the predefined *Color* class colors for your reference.

TABLE 12-1 Colors Available in the *Color* Class	
Color	**Code**
Black	*Color.black*
Blue	*Color.blue*
Cyan	*Color.cyan*
Dark Gray	*Color.darkGray*
Gray	*Color.gray*
Green	*Color.green*
Light Gray	*Color.lightGray*
Magenta	*Color.magenta*
Orange	*Color.orange*
Pink	*Color.pink*
Red	*Color.red*
White	*Color.white*
Yellow	*Color.yellow*

We cannot use strings here because, by definition, the *Color* class must contain its own predefined color constants. Once this array is created, a `for` loop is executed whose counter, *index*, ranges from 0 to the number of items we have in the *colorItems[]* array. The body of the loop contains an `if` statement to determine which menu item generated the event. Notice that the `if` statement is testing the source of the event against each of the menu items in the *colorItems[]* array with each loop iteration. When the event object is found, our *studentArea* object calls the *setBackground()* method to set the text color. The required argument is *textBackground[index]*, which is the color from the *textBackground[]* array that corresponds to the selected menu item color in the *colorItems[]* array, since they are both at the same array *index*.

Submenus   We will refer to the foregoing *Color* menu as a main menu because it appears on the menu bar. A **submenu** is a menu within a menu. You build submenus just as you build main menus. You must define a submenu object, add items to the submenu, and then add the submenu to a main menu. Let's suppose that we want to use a menu to control the type, style, and size of the character font within a text area as illustrated in the following set of screen shots.

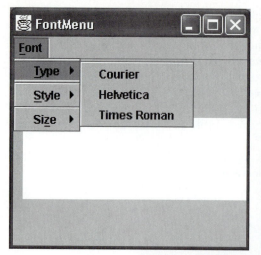

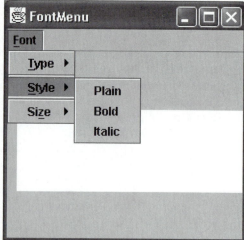

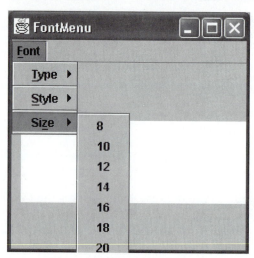

We have shown three screen shots of the GUI so that you can see all the submenu items. Notice that the main menu is *Font*, which contains three submenus called *Type*, *Style*, and *Size*. The font type is the font name, such as `Courier`, Helvetica, Times Roman, and so forth. The font style controls how a given font will appear, such as plain, *italic*, or **bold**. The font size controls the size of the font, like 8 point, 12 point, and so on. (*Note:* One point, abbreviated pt., is equivalent to 1/72 of an inch.) Most of this text is written in Times Roman, plain, 11 pt. font. The program code is written in 8 pt., plain, Courier font.) Now, our job is to create a class that will produce the main *Font* menu and submenus with the items shown. Here is a class that will do the job.

```
import javax.swing.*;          //FOR SWING COMPONENT CLASSES
import java.awt.*;             //FOR Container CLASS
import java.awt.event.*;       //FOR EVENT HANDLING
class FontMenu extends JFrame
{
```

```java
//DECLARE FONT SUBMENU ITEMS ARRAYS
private JMenuItem fontTypeItems[];
private JMenuItem fontStyleItems[];
private JMenuItem fontSizeItems[];

//DECLARE FONT STRINGS
private String fontTypes[] = {"Courier","Helvetica","Times Roman"};
private String fontStyles[] = {"Plain","Bold","Italic"};
private String fontSizes[] = {"8","10","12","14","16","18","20"};

//DECLARE TEXT AREA OBJECT
private JTextArea studentArea;

//CONSTRUCTOR
public FontMenu(String Title)
{
 //CALL SUPERCLASS CONSTRUCTOR
 super(Title);

 //CREATE A CONTAINER
 Container container = getContentPane();

 //SET CONTAINER LAYOUT MANAGER
 container.setLayout(new FlowLayout(FlowLayout.LEFT,10,60));

 //DEFINE MAIN MENU OBJECT AND SET MNEMONIC
 JMenu fontMenu = new JMenu("Font");
 fontMenu.setMnemonic('F');

 //DEFINE SUBMENU OBJECTS AND SET MNEMONICS
 JMenu fontTypeMenu = new JMenu("Type");
 fontTypeMenu.setMnemonic('T');
 JMenu fontStyleMenu = new JMenu("Style");
 fontStyleMenu.setMnemonic('S');
 JMenu fontSizeMenu = new JMenu("Size");
 fontSizeMenu.setMnemonic('z');
 //INSTANTIATE FONT SUBMENU ARRAY OBJECTS
 fontTypeItems = new JMenuItem[fontTypes.length];
 fontStyleItems = new JMenuItem[fontStyles.length];
 fontSizeItems = new JMenuItem[fontSizes.length];

 //INSTANTIATE TYPES SUBMENU ITEMS, ADD TO SUBMENU,
 //AND REGISTER AS LISTENERS
 for (int index = 0;index < fontTypes.length;++index)
 {
   //INSTANTIATE MENU ITEM OBJECTS
   fontTypeItems[index] = new JMenuItem(fontTypes[index]);
   fontTypeMenu.add(fontTypeItems[index]);
   fontTypeItems[index].addActionListener(new MenuHandler());
 }//END FOR

 //INSTANTIATE STYLES SUBMENU ITEMS, ADD TO SUBMENU,
 //AND REGISTER AS LISTENERS
```

```java
    for (int index = 0;index < fontTypes.length;++index)
    {
      //INSTANTIATE MENU ITEM OBJECTS
      fontStyleItems[index] = new JMenuItem(fontStyles[index]);
      fontStyleMenu.add(fontStyleItems[index]);
      fontStyleItems[index].addActionListener(new MenuHandler());
    }//END FOR

    //INSTANTIATE SIZES SUBMENU ITEMS, ADD TO SUBMENU,
    //AND REGISTER AS LISTENERS
    for (int index = 0;index < fontSizes.length;++index)
    {
      //INSTANTIATE MENU ITEM OBJECTS
      fontSizeItems[index] = new JMenuItem(fontSizes[index]);
      fontSizeMenu.add(fontSizeItems[index]);
      fontSizeItems[index].addActionListener(new MenuHandler());
    }//END FOR

    //ADD FONT SUBMENUS TO MAIN FONT MENU
    fontMenu.add(fontTypeMenu);        //ADD FONT TYPE SUBMENU
    fontMenu.addSeparator();           //ADD SEPARATOR BAR
    fontMenu.add(fontStyleMenu);       //ADD FONT STYLE SUBMENU
    fontMenu.addSeparator();           //ADD SEPARATOR BAR
    fontMenu.add(fontSizeMenu);        //ADD FONT STYLE SUBMENU

    //DEFINE MENU BAR OBJECT
    JMenuBar bar = new JMenuBar();

    //ADD MENU TO MENU BAR
    bar.add(fontMenu);

    //SET MENU BAR
    setJMenuBar(bar);

    //INSTANTIATE TEXT AREA OBJECT
    studentArea = new JTextArea(5,57);

    //ADD TEXT AREA TO CONTAINER
    container.add(studentArea);

    //ADD WINDOW LISTENER WITH WINDOW EVENT HANDLER
    addWindowListener(new WindowHandler());
  }//END FontMenu() CONSTRUCTOR

//WINDOW EVENT HANDLER CLASS
private class WindowHandler extends WindowAdapter
{
  public void windowClosing(WindowEvent e)
  {
     System.exit(0);  //EXIT TO OPERATING SYSTEM
  }//END windowClosing()
}//END WindowAdapter CLASS
```

```
//MENU HANDLER CLASS
private class MenuHandler implements ActionListener
{
//PROCESS MENU EVENT
public void actionPerformed(ActionEvent e)
{
  //DEFINE int ARRAY OF FONT STYLES
  int styles[] = {Font.PLAIN,Font.BOLD,Font.ITALIC};

  //DEFINE intARRAY OF FONT SIZES
  int sizes[] = {8,10,12,14,16,18,20};

  //GET CURRENT TEXT AREA FONT
  Font oldFont = studentArea.getFont();
  String fontType = oldFont.getName();   //GET CURRENT FONT TYPE NAME
  int fontStyle = oldFont.getStyle();    //GET CURRENT FONT STYLE
  int fontSize = oldFont.getSize();      //GET CURRENT FONT SIZE

  //LOOP THROUGH FONT TYPE ITEM ARRAY TO FIND EVENT ITEM
  for(int index = 0;index < fontTypeItems.length; ++index)
  {
    //CHECK THIS ITEM FOR EVENT AND SAVE
    if(e.getSource() == fontTypeItems[index])
      fontType = fontTypes[index];
  }//END FOR
  //LOOP THROUGH FONT STYLE ITEM ARRAY TO FIND EVENT ITEM
  for(int index = 0;index < fontStyleItems.length; ++index)
  {
    //CHECK THIS ITEM FOR EVENT AND SAVE
    if(e.getSource() == fontStyleItems[index])
      fontStyle = styles[index];
  }//END FOR

  //LOOP THROUGH FONT SIZE ITEM ARRAY TO FIND EVENT ITEM
  for(int index = 0;index < fontSizeItems.length; ++index)
  {
    //CHECK THIS ITEM FOR EVENT AND SAVE
    if(e.getSource() == fontSizeItems[index])
      fontSize = sizes[index];
  }//END FOR

  //CREATE A NEW FONT OBJECT
  Font newFont = new Font(fontType,fontStyle,fontSize);

  //SET THE NEW FONT ON THE TEXT AREA
  studentArea.setFont(newFont);

 }//END actionPerformed()
 }//END MenuHandler
}//END FontMenu CLASS
```

This looks a little overwhelming, but most of what we have done here is an extension of what we did in the *ColorMenu* class. Only the font stuff is really new. First you see that we declared three `private` *JMenuItem* arrays to hold the submenu item objects. Then we created three `private` *String* arrays to hold the submenu item labels. We will use these arrays when we instantiate the menu item objects with their respective labels. We will also use these arrays in our menu event handler. This is why they are declared as `private`. Now, let's examine the *FontMenu()* constructor. The first thing we have done here relative to menus is to create the main *fontMenu* object and the three submenu objects of *fontTypeMenu*, *fontStyleMenu*, and *fontSizeMenu*. Notice that the *JMenu* class is used to define both a main menu and a submenu object. After defining the menu objects, the menu item array objects are instantiated so that they can be used to hold the menu items. We then code three `for` loops, one for each submenu just like we did for our earlier *ColorMenu* class. Each loop instantiates the submenu items and places them in an array, adds the items to their respective submenu, and adds a listener for the items. Now that we have created all the submenus, we must add them to the main menu. This is easy using the following code:

```
//ADD FONT SUBMENUS TO MAIN FONT MENU
fontMenu.add(fontTypeMenu);       //ADD FONT TYPE SUBMENU
fontMenu.addSeparator();          //ADD SEPARATOR BAR
fontMenu.add(fontStyleMenu);      //ADD FONT STYLE SUBMENU
fontMenu.addSeparator();          //ADD SEPARATOR BAR
fontMenu.add(fontSizeMenu);       //ADD FONT STYLE SUBMENU
```

Here, the main menu object, *fontMenu*, is used to call the *add()* method that references the submenu object as its argument. In addition, we have used this object to call the *addSeparator()* method after each submenu. The *addSeparator()* method adds a **menu separator** which is the line that you can see between the submenus in the foregoing GUI. Once the main menu is created, we create a menu bar object, add the main menu to the menu bar, and set the bar to the frame using the following code:

```
//DEFINE MENU BAR OBJECT
JMenuBar bar = new JMenuBar();

//ADD MENU TO MENU BAR
bar.add(fontMenu);

//SET MENU BAR
setJMenuBar(bar);
```

The next task is to process a *fontMenu* event. Again, we will create an event handler that contains the *actionPerformed()* method to implement the logic required to handle a menu item event. The event handler controls the text area font, which leads us to our discussion of font control.

Font Control

The Java *Font* class can be used to control three main font properties within a GUI: the *font type* or *name*, the *font style*, and the *font size*. The font type can be any font supported by the operating system on which the program is running. Typical font types include Arial, Courier, Century Gothic, Helvetica, Sans Serif, and Times Roman, just to mention a few. In fact, some systems, such as Windows XP, support over 100 different font types, or names. The font styles provided within the *Font* class are plain, italic, and bold. These styles are declared as constants within the class and are accessed via *Font.PLAIN*, *Font.ITALIC*, and *Font.BOLD*. Finally, the font size is specified in **points**, where one point is 1/72 of an inch. Table 12-2 summarizes the properties of a font.

TABLE 12-2   Font Properties

Property	Description
type	Any font typeface supported by the underlying operating system
style	Font.PLAIN, Font.ITALIC, Font.BOLD
size	Specified in points, where one point is 1/72 of an inch

In our *actionPerformed()* method, we first create two arrays, as follows:

```
//DEFINE int ARRAY OF FONT STYLES
int styles[] = {Font.PLAIN,Font.BOLD,Font.ITALIC};
//DEFINE int ARRAY OF FONT SIZES
int sizes[] = {8,10,12,14,16,18,20};
```

The first array is used to hold the font style constants available in the *Font* class, while the second array holds the font sizes in our *fontSize* submenu. You will see how they are used shortly.

Next, we read the existing font characteristics from the text area, as follows:

```
//GET CURRENT TEXT AREA FONT
Font oldFont = studentArea.getFont();
String fontType = oldFont.getName();   //GET CURRENT FONT TYPE NAME
int fontStyle = oldFont.getStyle();    //GET CURRENT FONT STYLE
int fontSize = oldFont.getSize();      //GET CURRENT FONT SIZE
```

The first statement creates an object, called *oldFont*, of the Java *Font* class. When the *oldFont* object is created, it is assigned the current font name, style, and size of the *studentArea* text area from our GUI. Notice that the *studentArea* object is used to call the *getFont()* method. This method gets the font name, style, and size of the calling object. Since *oldFont* is a font object that now has the font properties of our *studentArea* object, we can extract the name, style, or size of the font from this object by calling *getName()*, *getStyle()*, or *getSize()*, respectively. The *getName()* method returns a string, while *getStyle()* and *getSize()* return integers. We need to store the old font properties because a given menu item event will only change one of the properties, right? The other two properties will not change and have to be saved in order for their values to remain constant when we set the new text area font.

Next we enter three `for` loops, one for each of our possible submenu events. For example, consider the `for` loop which processes the *Type* submenu, as follows:

```
//LOOP THROUGH FONT TYPE ITEM ARRAY TO FIND EVENT ITEM
for(int index = 0;index < fontTypeItems.length; ++index)
{
  //CHECK THIS ITEM FOR EVENT AND SAVE
  if(e.getSource() == fontTypeItems[index])
    fontType = fontTypes[index];
}//END FOR
```

This loop iterates through the *fontTypeItems[]* array, looking for the item that caused the event. If a given menu item in this array caused the event, the `if` test is `true` and the font type is set to the corresponding string in the *fontTypes[]* array. Next, the font style and font size are processed in the same way within their respective `for` loops.

When we come out of all the `for` loops, the menu item that caused the event has been detected and its corresponding font property has been changed. Now, all we need to do is write this new font property to the text area. So, we create a new font object called *newFont*, like this:

```
//CREATE A NEW FONT OBJECT
Font newFont = new Font(fontType,fontStyle,fontSize);
```

The *Font* class constructor sets the object properties to *fontType*, *fontStyle*, and *fontSize*. Remember, only one of these variables has changed due to the event. The other two have not changed and we have saved their values. Finally, the *studentArea* object is used to call the *setFont()* method which sets the text area font to the properties of the *newFont* object, like this:

```
//SET THE NEW FONT ON THE TEXT AREA
studentArea.setFont(newFont);
```

Table 12-3 summarizes some of the methods available in the *Font* class. See your Java IDE for more information on these and other font-related methods.

In addition to the font methods listed in Table 12-3, Table 12-4 summarizes the other methods used in this section.

TABLE 12-3   Font Methods

Method	Description
getFont()	Returns a font object representing the current font of the calling object
getName()	Returns a string which is the current font name
getSize()	Returns an integer which is the current font size
getStyle()	Returns an integer which represents the current font style
isBold()	Returns **true** if the font is bold
isItalic()	Returns **true** if the font is italic
isPlain()	Returns **true** if the font is plain
setFont()	Sets the font of the calling component object

TABLE 12-4   Summary of Methods Used in this Section

Method	Description
addItem(String)	Adds *String* item to calling combo box or list object
addItemListener()	Adds an *ItemListener* for the calling item object
addListSelectionListener()	Adds a *ListSelectionListener* for the calling object
getSource()	Gets the event source of the calling event object
getSelectedItem()	Returns selected item of calling combo box object
getSelectedItems()	Returns selected list items of calling list object in an array of strings
isSelected()	Returns the Boolean state of the calling state button object
JCheckbox(String)	Creates a check box with *String* label
JCheckbox(String, Boolean)	Creates a check box with *String* label set to a given Boolean state
JComboBox()	Creates an empty combo box
JList(listItems)	Creates a list box with items in *listItems[]* array
JMenu(String)	Creates a menu with *String* label
JMenuBar()	Creates a menu bar
JMenuItem(String)	Creates a menu item with *String* label
JScrollPane(component object)	Creates a scroll bar for the component argument object
setJMenuBar(JMenuBar)	Sets *JMenuBar* object to frame
setVisibleRowCount()	Sets the number of items that will be visible at any one time in the calling list box
valueChanged()	Returns `true` if the calling state button object is selected; otherwise returns `false`

QUICK CHECK

1. What is the difference between a combo box and a list box?
2. What method is used to determine the state of a check box or radio button?
3. What is the purpose of a menu bar?
4. Write a statement to create a menu bar called *myMenuBar*.
5. Write a statement to create a menu object called *myMenu* with a label of "My Menu".
6. Write a statement to add the menu in question 5 to the menu bar in question 4.
7. Write a statement to add the menu bar in question 4 to a frame.
8. What are the general properties associated with a font?
9. What is the size of a font point?
10. Write a statement to create a 16-point Arial bold font called *myFont*.
11. Write a statement to set the font of a text area called *myArea* to the font in question 10.

12.2   More Layout Managers

In this section, we will explore two additional layout managers: ***box layout*** and ***card layout***. The box layout manager is relatively simple and rigid, while the card layout manager is a bit more complex, but more flexible. Card layout is especially useful when you want to present different GUIs at different times. Both layout managers will be demonstrated using GUI classes that we have developed. Again, we encourage you to go through the GUI workshop in Appendix C and experiment with these layout managers. This is how you will really learn how to use them.

Box Layout—*Box* and *BoxLayout*

The *Box* class is used to implement the *BoxLayout* manager. A box is like a panel in that it's a container class that can be used to hold other GUI components. However, unlike a panel, you cannot set the layout manager for a box because it is always set to *BoxLayout*. The *BoxLayout* manager arranges GUI components from left to right in a single horizontal row, or from top to bottom in a single vertical column. It is really like a one-dimensional grid layout using a grid layout manager of either one row (horizontal) or one column (vertical). However, remember that *GridLayout* forces all of its components to be the same size. *BoxLayout*, on the other hand, displays components in their natural size. By natural size, we mean the size that Java determines for a given component. For example, the natural size of a button is the size it takes to include its label. Also, *BoxLayout* attempts to align the heights of horizontal components and the widths of vertical components. *BoxLayout* can be useful since it allows you to place boxes inside of boxes (box nesting). That is, you can nest multiple boxes and add components to get the arrangement you want.

The *BoxLayout* manager arranges GUI components from left to right in a single horizontal row, or from top to bottom in a single vertical column.

Here is a GUI that employs three boxes. There are two vertical boxes nested inside of a horizontal box. Do you see them? The left vertical box contains two text areas, and the right vertical box contains three text areas. The horizontal box contains the two vertical boxes and is set to the frame container.

Here's the class code that created this GUI:

```java
import javax.swing.*;          //FOR SWING COMPONENT CLASSES
import java.awt.event.*;       //FOR EVENT HANDLING
import java.awt.*;             //FOR Container CLASS

//A FRAME CLASS WITH MULTIPLE BUTTONS
class BoxLayout extends JFrame
{
  //CONSTRUCTOR
  public BoxLayout(String title)
  {
    super(title);                          //CALL SUPERCLASS CONSTRUCTOR

    //CREATE CONTAINER OBJECT
    Container container = getContentPane();

    //CREATE BOX CONTAINERS
    Box horizontalBox = Box.createHorizontalBox();
    Box leftVerticalBox = Box.createVerticalBox();
    Box rightVerticalBox = Box.createVerticalBox();

    //INSTANTIATE TEXT AREA OBJECTS
    JTextArea area1 = new JTextArea("My Area");
    JTextArea area2 = new JTextArea("Your Area");
    JTextArea area3 = new JTextArea("His Area");
    JTextArea area4 = new JTextArea("Her Area");
    JTextArea area5 = new JTextArea("Their Area");

    //SET AREA BACKGROUND COLORS
    //AREAS 1 AND 5 DEFAULT TO WHITE
    area2.setBackground(Color.lightGray);
    area3.setBackground(Color.gray);
    area4.setBackground(Color.darkGray);

    //SET AREA FOREGROUND COLORS
    //AREAS 1 AND 5 DEFAULT TO BLACK
    area2.setForeground(Color.red);
    area3.setForeground(Color.cyan);
    area4.setForeground(Color.white);

    //ADD TEXT AREAS TO LEFT AND RIGHT
    //VERTICAL BOXES
    leftVerticalBox.add(area1);
    leftVerticalBox.add(area2);
    rightVerticalBox.add(area3);
    rightVerticalBox.add(area4);
    rightVerticalBox.add(area5);

    //ADD TWO VERTICAL BOXES TO HORIZONTAL BOX
    horizontalBox.add(leftVerticalBox);
    horizontalBox.add(rightVerticalBox);
```

```
    //ADD HORIZONTAL BOX TO CONTAINER
    container.add(horizontalBox);

    //ADD WINDOW LISTENER WITH WINDOW EVENT HANDLER
    addWindowListener(new WindowHandler());
  }//END BoxLayout() CONSTRUCTOR

  //WINDOW EVENT HANDLER CLASS
  private class WindowHandler extends WindowAdapter
  {
    public void windowClosing(WindowEvent e)
    {
      System.exit(0);   //EXIT TO OPERATING SYSTEM
    }//END windowClosing()
  }//END WindowHandler CLASS
}//END BoxLayout CLASS
```

We have created three box objects, using the *Box* class, like this:

```
//CREATE BOX CONTAINERS
Box horizontalBox = Box.createHorizontalBox();
Box leftVerticalBox = Box.createVerticalBox();
Box rightVerticalBox = Box.createVerticalBox();
```

The *Box* class includes two static methods that are used to create a box object: *createHorizontalBox()* and *createVerticalBox()*. You have not seen an object created this way before and, as you might suspect, these two methods take care of both the object instantiation (`new`) and initialization (horizontal or vertical).

A **static method** is a class method that is called with a class reference, not an object reference.

Once the box objects are created, we created five text areas. Then we added two of the text areas to the left vertical box, and three of the text areas to the right vertical box, like this:

```
//ADD TEXT AREAS TO LEFT AND RIGHT
//VERTICAL BOXES
leftVerticalBox.add(area1);
leftVerticalBox.add(area2);
rightVerticalBox.add(area3);
rightVerticalBox.add(area4);
rightVerticalBox.add(area5);
```

To nest these two boxes inside the horizontal box, we called the *add()* method with the *horizontalBox* object, and used the *leftVerticalBox* and *rightVerticalBox* objects as arguments, as follows:

```
//ADD TWO VERTICAL BOXES TO HORIZONTAL BOX
horizontalBox.add(leftVerticalBox);
horizontalBox.add(rightVerticalBox);
```

Finally, we added the *horizontalBox* object to the frame container with this statement:

```
//ADD HORIZONTAL BOX TO CONTAINER
container.add(horizontalBox);
```

Another nice feature of the *Box* class is that the boxes it creates, as well as the components the boxes contain, are always sized proportionally to the size of the window. This way you will always see the GUI components at their same relative size and position regardless of the window size, as illustrated by the following screen shots:

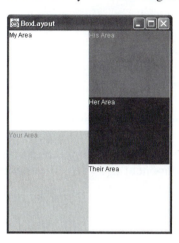

That's it for box layout. As you can see, it's pretty simple and straightforward to use.

Card Layout—*CardLayout*

Let's play a game of "card layout." Here's how: You take a deck of cards, mark one of the cards, and place it randomly in the deck so that your opponent can see its location. Now, pick another card in the deck as the "secret card" and do not tell your opponent its location. You lay the deck down with the first card face up and ask your opponent to make three moves to try to find the secret card. For any one move they can make one of the following choices:

1. Select the first card.
2. Select the next card.
3. Select the previous card.
4. Select the last card.
5. Select the marked card.

If they start with the first card and select the next card, the second card in the deck will appear. However, if they start with the first card and select the previous card, the last card in the deck will appear. So, it's as if the card deck is in a closed loop. Now, suppose they are at the second card in the deck. If they select the next card, the third card will appear. If they select the previous card, the first card will appear. Of course they can select the first, last, or marked card at any time. Here's the first GUI your opponent sees:

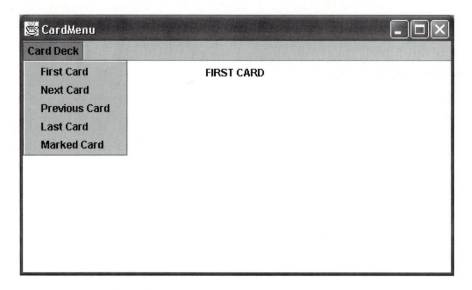

Notice that the first card appears on the GUI along with a menu of legal moves. Now, ask your opponent to make three consecutive menu selections. Suppose your opponent selected the following three moves:

Next card
Last card
Previous card

Here are the three consecutive GUIs that will appear for these moves:

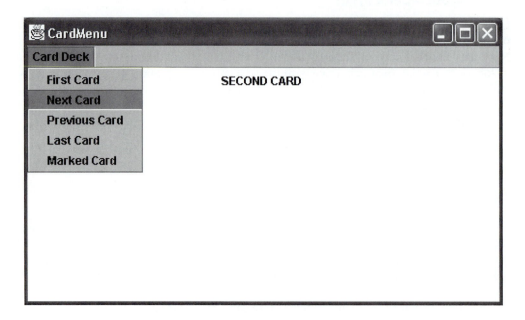

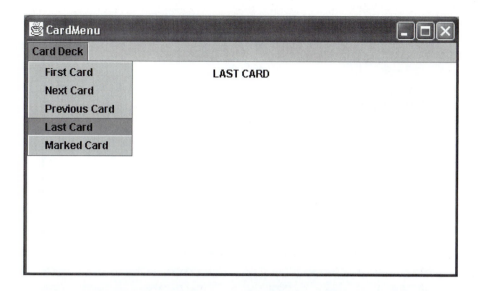

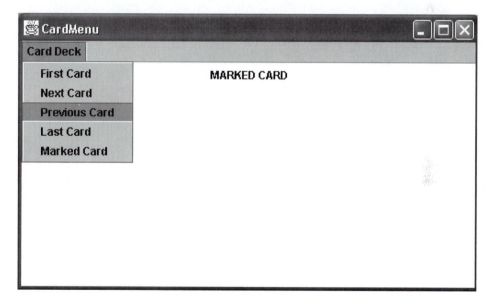

The secret card didn't appear in three moves. Therefore, your opponent loses and you win! If the deck consists of only five cards, where is the secret card?

Here is a series of moves that exposes the secret card:

Last card

Previous card

Previous card

Here is what the user will see with these moves:

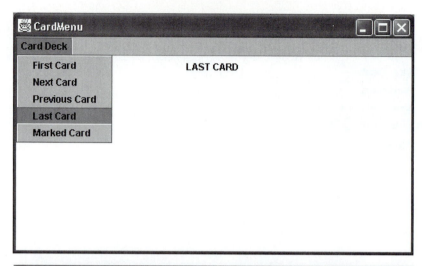

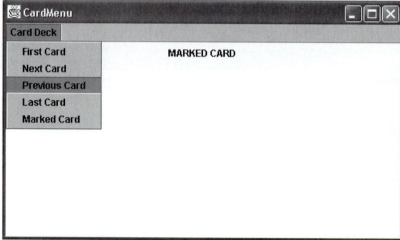

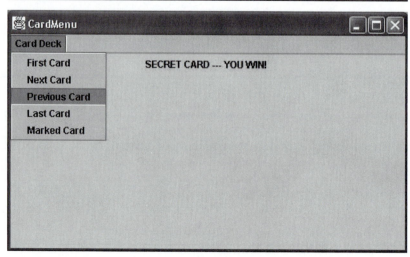

So, where was the secret card? You're right, it's the third card in the deck, just prior to the marked card. Before getting into the details, we should mention that the *CardLayout* manager is not provided just for writing card game programs. It is provided so that you can present different GUIs at different times, based upon an event. We just invented this simple card game to illustrate the use of this versatile layout manager. In fact, it illustrates all the possible moves within the *CardLayout* manager. *CardLayout* allows you to build a card deck as a panel, consisting of several unique GUI "cards" as panels. So the deck is a panel that contains the cards that are panels. When the card deck is first shown, the first card (panel) in the deck appears. From there you can display any of the other cards (panels) within the deck as a separate GUI, but you are restricted to the following five moves, just like in our card game:

Select the first card — *first()*

Select the next card — *next()*

Select the previous card — *previous()*

Select the last card — *last()*

Select the marked card — *show()*

Notice the method next to each move. The indicated method is the *CardLayout* class method that makes the given move. Here is the class that generated this simple card game using the *CardLayout* manager, with the code of interest highlighted in bold:

```
import javax.swing.*;        //FOR SWING COMPONENT CLASSES
import java.awt.event.*;     //FOR EVENT HANDLING
import java.awt.*;           //FOR Container CLASS

//A FRAME CLASS WITH A SINGLE BUTTON
class CardMenu extends JFrame
{
    //DECLARE CARD LAYOUT OBJECT
    private CardLayout cardSelector;

    //DECLARE CARD PANEL OBJECT
    private JPanel cardDeck;

    //DECLARE MENU ITEMS
    private JMenuItem firstCard;
    private JMenuItem nextCard;
    private JMenuItem previousCard;
    private JMenuItem lastCard;
    private JMenuItem markedCard;

  //CONSTRUCTOR
  public CardMenu(String title)
  {
    super(title);                       //CALL SUPERCLASS CONSTRUCTOR

    //CREATE A CONTAINER
    private Container container = getContentPane();
```

```
//INSTANTIATE MENU ITEM OBJECTS
firstCard = new JMenuItem("First Card");
nextCard = new JMenuItem("Next Card");
previousCard = new JMenuItem("Previous Card");
lastCard = new JMenuItem("Last Card");
markedCard = new JMenuItem("Marked Card");

//DEFINE MENU OBJECT
JMenu cardDeckMenu = new JMenu("Card Deck");

//ADD ITEM OBJECTS TO MENU
cardDeckMenu.add(firstCard);
cardDeckMenu.add(nextCard);
cardDeckMenu.add(previousCard);
cardDeckMenu.add(lastCard);
cardDeckMenu.add(markedCard);

//DEFINE MENU BAR OBJECT
JMenuBar bar = new JMenuBar();

//ADD MENU TO MENU BAR
bar.add(cardDeckMenu);

//SET MENU BAR
setJMenuBar(bar);

//INSTANTIATE CARD LAYOUT OBJECT
cardSelector = new CardLayout();
//INSTANTIATE PANEL OBJECT
cardDeck = new JPanel();

//SET LAYOUT OF CARD DECK PANEL TO CARD LAYOUT
cardDeck.setLayout(cardSelector);

//BUILD CARD DECK
JPanel card1 = new JPanel();
card1.setBackground(Color.white);
JLabel card1Label = new JLabel("FIRST CARD");
card1Label.setForeground(Color.black);
card1.add(card1Label);
cardDeck.add(card1,card1Label.getText());

JPanel card2 = new JPanel();
card2.setBackground(Color.white);
JLabel card2Label = new JLabel("SECOND CARD");
card2Label.setForeground(Color.black);
card2.add(card2Label);
cardDeck.add(card2,card2Label.getText());

JPanel card3 = new JPanel();
card3.setBackground(Color.cyan);
```

```
   JLabel card3Label = new JLabel("SECRET CARD --- YOU WIN!");
   card3Label.setForeground(Color.black);
   card3.add(card3Label);
   cardDeck.add(card3,card3Label.getText());

   JPanel card4 = new JPanel();
   card4.setBackground(Color.white);
   JLabel card4Label = new JLabel("MARKED CARD");
   card4Label.setForeground(Color.black);
   card4.add(card4Label);
   cardDeck.add(card4,card4Label.getText());
   //MAKE THIS CARD RANDOM ACCESS
   cardSelector.addLayoutComponent(card4,card4Label.getText());

   JPanel card5 = new JPanel();
   card5.setBackground(Color.white);
   JLabel card5Label = new JLabel("LAST CARD");
   card5Label.setForeground(Color.black);
   card5.add(card5Label);
   cardDeck.add(card5,card5Label.getText());

   //ADD CARD DECK TO CONTAINER
   container.add(cardDeck,"Center");

   //DEFINE MENU HANDLER OBJECT
   MenuHandler menuHandler = new MenuHandler();

   //ADD ACTION LISTENERS FOR MENU ITEMS
   firstCard.addActionListener(menuHandler);
   nextCard.addActionListener(menuHandler);
   previousCard.addActionListener(menuHandler);
   lastCard.addActionListener(menuHandler);
   markedCard.addActionListener(menuHandler);
   //ADD WINDOW LISTENER WITH WINDOW EVENT HANDLER
   addWindowListener(new WindowHandler());
}//END CardMenu()

//WINDOW HANDLER CLASS
private class WindowHandler extends WindowAdapter
{
  public void windowClosing(WindowEvent e)
 {
    System.exit(0);  //EXIT TO OPERATING SYSTEM
 }//END windowClosing()
}//END WindowHandler CLASS


//MENU EVENT HANDLER CLASS
private class MenuHandler implements ActionListener
{
  //PROCESS MENU EVENT
  public void actionPerformed(ActionEvent e)
  {
```

```
      //WHICH MENU ITEM CAUSED THE EVENT?
      if (e.getSource() == firstCard)
        cardSelector.first(cardDeck);
      if (e.getSource() == nextCard)
        cardSelector.next(cardDeck);
      if (e.getSource() == previousCard)
        cardSelector.previous(cardDeck);
      if(e.getSource() == lastCard)
        cardSelector.last(cardDeck);
      if(e.getSource() == markedCard)
        cardSelector.show(cardDeck,"MARKED CARD");
    }//END actionPerformed()
  }//END MENU HANDLER CLASS
}//END CardMenu CLASS
```

Remember that we need to create a card deck as a panel, then create separated cards as panels and add them to the card deck panel. So, the first `private` member of the class is *cardSelector,* which is declared as an object of the *CardLayout* class. The second `private` class member is our *cardDeck* panel object. Keep these two members in mind. The card game GUI contains a menu that displays all the legal game moves. The menu items are declared as `private` members of the class, then instantiated within the constructor and added to a menu object. A menu bar object is then created, the menu is added to the menu bar, and the bar is set to the frame. This is all review by now. After we set the menu bar to the frame, we instantiated the *cardDeck* panel object and the *cardSelector* layout object. Then we set the layout of the *cardDeck* panel to card layout using the *cardSelector* layout object, as follows:

```
//SET LAYOUT OF CARD DECK PANEL TO CARD LAYOUT
cardDeck.setLayout(cardSelector);
```

Not much is new here. You are simply setting the layout of a panel using a given layout manager, in this case, *CardLayout,* just like you have done in the past when setting other layout managers.

Next, we go about building the card deck. Here is the code we used to create the first card and add it to the deck:

```
JPanel card1 = new JPanel();
card1.setBackground(Color.white);
JLabel card1Label = new JLabel("FIRST CARD");
card1Label.setForeground(Color.black);
card1.add(card1Label);
cardDeck.add(card1,card1Label.getText());
```

You see that the card, *card1,* is simply a panel object. The panel background is set to white, and the foreground, to black. We then create a label object called *card1 Label* and add it to the *card1* panel. Finally, the *card1* panel is added to the *cardDeck* panel. The *add()* method requires two arguments. The first argument is the *card1* panel object, and the second argument is a string that identifies the card. Notice it's the label string that this panel (card) contains.

Each card is then sequentially created and added to the deck in the same way. There is one special line added to the *card4* code, as follows:

```
//MAKE THIS CARD RANDOM ACCESS
cardSelector.addLayoutComponent(card4,card3Label.getText());
```

Here, the *CardLayout* manager object, *cardSelector*, is calling its *addLayoutComponent()* method. This method identifies this particular card as a randomly accessible card, meaning that we can select this card using the *show()* method, at random, regardless of where it's located in the deck. The only other two cards that can be accessed directly are the first card and the last card using the *first()* and *last()* methods. All other cards must be accessed sequentially using the *next()* and *previous()* methods.

After our card deck is built, it's added to the frame container. Remember that the default layout manager for a *Container* object is *BorderLayout*. Therefore, we add the *cardDeck* panel object to the center of the *container* object using the statement

```
//ADD CARD DECK TO CONTAINER
container.add(cardDeck,"Center");
```

Now, look at the *actionPerformed()* method in our event handler. Here, we are looking for a menu item event. Therefore, we use a series of `if` statements to check for each possible menu item event, as follows:

```
if (e.getSource() == firstCard)
  cardSelector.first(cardDeck);
if (e.getSource() == nextCard)
  cardSelector.next(cardDeck);
if (e.getSource() == previousCard)
  cardSelector.previous(cardDeck);
if(e.getSource() == lastCard)
  cardSelector.last(cardDeck);
if(e.getSource() == markedCard)
  cardSelector.show(cardDeck,"MARKED CARD");
```

When a given menu item event occurs, our *CardLayout* manager object, *cardSelector*, is used to call one of five methods: *first()*, *next()*, *previous()*, *last()*, or *show()*. Notice that each method must reference the *cardDeck* object as its argument. In addition, the *show()* method must reference a string as its second argument. This string is a tag that identifies the card to be randomly shown. In our case, the string is the "MARKED CARD" label title we placed on this card.

Wow, that's a lot of stuff! You might want to read this section again to let it all sink in because you will surely need to use *CardLayout* at some point in your GUI programming career. The methods used in this section are summarized in Table 12-5 for future reference.

TABLE 12-5   Summary of Methods Used in this Section

Method	Description
CardLayout()	Creates a card layout object
creatHorizontalBox()	Creates a box container that displays its components from left to right
creatVerticalBox()	Creates a box container that displays its components from top to bottom
first(cardDeck)	Displays the first card of *cardDeck* object
last(cardDeck)	Displays the last card of *cardDeck* object
next(cardDeck)	Displays the next card of *cardDeck* object
previous(cardDeck)	Displays the previous card of *cardDeck* object
show(cardDeck, String)	Displays the card of *cardDeck* object with *String* tag

QUICK CHECK

1. What is the relationship between the *Box* class and the *BoxLayout* class?
2. Describe a box layout.
3. True or false: Components in a box layout will wrap around as the GUI window is resized.
4. Describe a card layout.
5. What methods are available to access the cards in a card deck?

CHAPTER SUMMARY

In this chapter you learned about some additional GUI components and layout managers. The combo (*JComboBox* class) and list box (*JList* class) components provide a means for the user to select items within a list. A combo box is a drop-down box that allows the user to select a single item. A list box is a scrolled list that allows the user to select one or more items. Combo and list box events can be processed by using an associated button event, or by detecting the combo or list box event directly. A combo box event is an *ActionEvent,* while a list box event is a *ListSelectionEvent.* The *javax.swing.event* package must be imported to use this event class. You must register a list box object as a listener using the *addListSelectionListener()* method. Processing list box events requires an event handler that implements an abstract *ListSelectionListener* class method called *valueChanged().* Event detection requires the use of arrays and the *getSelectedIndices()* method of the *JList* class.

Check boxes (*JCheckBox* class) and radio buttons (*JRadioButton* class) are called state buttons because they are in one of two states, on or off, represented internally by `true` or `false`. Check boxes are not grouped like radio buttons. Any check box on a GUI can be selected, while only one radio button within a group can be selected. As a result, radio button objects must be part of a radio button group that is created using the *ButtonGroup* class. Check boxes and radio buttons both generate an *ItemEvent.* To handle such events, listeners must be added using the *addItemListener()* method, and events processed in an event handler that implements an abstract *ItemListener* class method called *itemStateChanged().* Since check boxes and radio buttons are state buttons, event processing is controlled by nested `if/else` logic.

Menus and submenus require the use of the *JMenu, JMenuItem,* and *JMenuBar* classes. You must perform the following tasks to create menus and submenus:

- Define all main menu and submenu objects using *JMenu.*
- Define all menu item objects using *JMenuItem.*
- Add the menu items to the menus using *menu.add(menuItem).*
- Add listeners for the menu item objects using *menuItem.addActionListener().*
- Add the submenus to the main menus using *mainMenu.add(submenu).*
- Define a menu bar object using *JMenuBar.*
- Add the main menus to the menu bar using *menuBar.add(mainMenu).*
- Set the menu bar on the frame, not the frame container, using *setJMenuBar().*

Submenus must be added to main menus, which are added to a menu bar, which is added to the original GUI frame, not a frame container. Menu and submenu item selections generate an *ActionEvent.* Therefore, you must add an *ActionListener* for each of the menu items and implement the *actionPerformed()* method to detect a menu item event. Arrays are used to hold the items of a menu or submenu; therefore, event processing involves array processing.

The *Box* class is a container class that implements the *BoxLayout* manager to achieve simple, but flexible, GUI layouts. The *BoxLayout* manager arranges GUI components in a single horizontal row from left to right, or single vertical column from top to bottom. The *CardLayout* manager is a very flexible layout manager that allows you to generate different GUIs at different times. To use it, you must create a card deck panel and several card panels. The card panels are then added to the card deck panel which is added to the frame container. The first, last, and designated marked cards can be accessed directly using the *first(), last(),* and *show()* methods, respectively. All other cards must be accessed sequentially using the *next()* and *previous()* methods.

QUESTIONS AND PROBLEMS

Questions

1. What is the difference between a combo box and a list box?
2. What event listener class and method must be used to process a combo box event directly?
3. What event listener class and method must be used to process list box events directly?
4. Why are check boxes and radio buttons similar?
5. What is the difference between a check box and a radio button?
6. What event listener class and method must be used to process check box events directly?
7. What event listener class and method must be used to process radio button events directly?
8. Write the code required to perform the following tasks:
   - Create a "Midwestern States" label object called *statesLabel.*
   - Create a combo box object called *midStatesChoice* that contains the following choice items: "Arkansas", "Missouri", "Iowa", and "Kansas".
   - Add the label and combo box objects to a panel called *statesPanel.*
9. Write the statements required to determine if a combo box event has occurred and, if so, determine which choice item in question 8 was selected.
10. List the things you must do to create a menu.
11. How are menu item objects stored for event handling?

12. What event listener class and method must be used to process menu item events?

13. What are the three attributes of a font?

14. Describe the layouts possible with the *BoxLayout* manager.

15. What is the function of the *Box* class?

16. What feature of the *CardLayout* manager makes it useful for certain applications?

17. Explain how to create and access a deck of cards using the *CardLayout* manager.

Problems

Least Difficult

Use the following *StudentGUITest* application code for problems 1–5. This application can be found on the text CD.

```java
import java.awt.*;        //FOR Container CLASS
import java.awt.event.*;  //FOR EVENT HANDLING
import javax.swing.*;     //FOR SWING COMPONENTS

class StudentGUI extends JFrame
{
  //DECLARE TEXT FIELD OBJECTS AND BUTTON OBJECT
  private JTextField nameField;
  private JTextField numberField;
  private JTextField gpaField;
  private JTextArea studentArea;
  private JButton storeButton;

  //CONSTRUCTOR
  public StudentGUI (String title)
  {
    //CALL SUPERCLASS CONSTRUCTOR
    super(title);
    //CREATE A CONTAINER
    Container container = getContentPane();

    //SET CONTAINER LAYOUT MANAGER
    container.setLayout(new FlowLayout(FlowLayout.LEFT));

    //INSTANTIATE TEXT FIELD OBJECTS
    nameField = new JTextField(35);
    numberField = new JTextField(13);
    gpaField = new JTextField(4);
    studentArea = new JTextArea(4,20);

    //INSTANTIATE BUTTON OBJECT
    storeButton = new JButton("STORE");

    //DEFINE PANELS
    JPanel panel1 = new JPanel();
    JPanel panel2 = new JPanel();
    JPanel panel3 = new JPanel();
```

```
//SET PANEL LAYOUT MANAGERS
panel1.setLayout(new FlowLayout(FlowLayout.LEFT));
panel2.setLayout(new FlowLayout(FlowLayout.LEFT));
panel3.setLayout(new FlowLayout(FlowLayout.LEFT));

//DEFINE LABEL OBJECTS
JLabel nameLabel = new JLabel("Student name");
JLabel numberLabel = new JLabel("Student Number");
JLabel gpaLabel = new JLabel("GPA");
JLabel summaryLabel = new JLabel("Student Summary");

 //ADD COMPONENTS TO panel1
panel1.add(nameLabel);
panel1.add(nameField);

//ADD COMPONENTS TO panel2
panel2.add(numberLabel);
panel2.add(numberField);
panel2.add(gpaLabel);
panel2.add(gpaField);
panel2.add(storeButton);

//ADD COMPONENTS TO panel3
panel3.add(summaryLabel);
panel3.add(new JScrollPane(studentArea));

//ADD PANELS TO CONTAINER
container.add(panel1);
container.add(panel2);
container.add(panel3);

//REGISTER BUTTON LISTENER
storeButton.addActionListener(new ButtonHandler());

 //ADD WINDOW LISTENER WITH WINDOW EVENT HANDLER
 addWindowListener(new WindowHandler());
}//END StudentGUI() CONSTRUCTOR
//WINDOW EVENT HANDLER CLASS
private class WindowHandler extends WindowAdapter
{
  public void windowClosing(WindowEvent e)
  {
    System.exit(0);  //EXIT TO OPERATING SYSTEM
 }//END windowClosing()
}//END WindowHandler CLASS

//BUTTON EVENT HANDLER CLASS
private class ButtonHandler implements ActionListener
{
  //PROCESS BUTTON EVENT
  public void actionPerformed(ActionEvent e)
```

```
    {
    //DID A BUTTON CAUSE EVENT?
    if (e.getSource() == storeButton)
    {
      //DISPLAY TEXT FIELD DATA IN TEXT AREA
      studentArea.setText("This is an example of data stored"
                        + " in the student data base.\n");
      studentArea.append("\nStudent name: " + nameField.getText());
      studentArea.append("\nStudent Number: " + numberField.getText());
      studentArea.append("\nGPA: " + gpaField.getText());
    }//END IF
  }//END actionPerformed()
  }//END ButtonHandler CLASS
}//END StudentGUI

//APPLICATION TEST CLASS
public class StudentGUITest
{
  public static void main(String[] args)
  {
    //DEFINE FRAME OBJECT
    StudentGUI window = new StudentGUI("StudentGUI");

    //SET FRAME SIZE
    window.setSize(500,300);

    //MAKE FRAME VISIBLE
    window.show();
  }//END main()
}//END TEST CLASS
```

1. Compile and execute the *StudentGuiTest.java* application given above. Fill in the given text fields and press the *STORE* button to observe its execution. This file can be found on the text CD.

   Place the *ListBox* class code given in this chapter within the *StudentGUI* class code. Compile and execute the program. Make sure it displays the selected majors.

   Place the *CheckBox* class code given in this chapter within the *StudentGUI* class code. Compile and execute the program. Make sure it displays the checked student status.

   Place the *RadioButton* class code given in this chapter within the *StudentGUI* class code. Compile and execute the program. Make sure it displays the selected student graduate status.

   Place the *ColorMenu* class code given in this chapter within the *StudentGUI* class code. Compile and execute the program. Make sure it displays the text area background with the selected color.

   Place the *FontMenu* class code given in this chapter within the *StudentGUI* class code. Compile and execute the program. Make sure it displays the text area font in the selected font type, style, and size.

More Difficult

2. Add a menu to the *Action11_01.java* consumer loan processor GUI developed in the last chapter that will allow the user to select the color of the text appearing in the text area. This class can be found in the *Action11_01.java* file on the text CD.

Add a menu to the *Action11_01.java* consumer loan processor GUI developed in the last chapter that will allow the user to select the font type, style, and size of the text area.

Most Difficult

3. Design and build a *BankingTransaction* class that will process a banking transaction. The GUI is to have the following components and capabilities, at a minimum:

- User instruction label(s)
- Text fields and associated labels for the user's personal identification number (PIN), and amount deposited or withdrawn
- Radio buttons to select between a checking or savings account transaction
- Button to process the transaction
- Logic to calculate a new balance, assuming the initial balance was $1000
- A text area to display the new balance and a "Thank you" message, or a polite message, requesting the user enter a different amount if he or she attempts to withdraw more than $300.00

(*Note: This problem is an extension of Problem 4 in Chapter 11.*)

4. Design and build a *LoanApplication* class. The GUI is to have the following components and capabilities, at a minimum:

- Text fields and associated labels that will allow the user to enter their name, address, telephone number, and social security number
- Text fields and associated labels that will allow the user to enter the amount of the loan and term for which he or she is applying
- Text field and associated label for annual income
- Radio buttons for married/single status
- Text area to display the loan information
- Menu to set the text area font type, style, and size
- A store/calculate button that will display the loan applicant information as well as monthly payment based on an interest rate of 10% in a text area as well as "APPROVED" or "NOT APPROVED" based on the following criteria:
  - For loan amounts <= $1,000, annual income must be at least $10,000.
  - For loan amounts between $1,000 and $10,000, annual income must be at least $25,000.
  - For loan amounts between $10,000 and $25,000, annual income must be at least $50,000.
  - We do not make loans above $25,000.

(*Note: This problem is an extension of Problem 5 in Chapter 11.*)

5. Design and build a *StockTransaction* class. The GUI is to have the following components and capabilities, at a minimum:

- Text fields and associated labels for account number, trading password, stock "ticker" symbol, number of shares to buy/sell, and price per share
- Radio button group for type of transaction: buy or sell
- Radio button group for type of order: market or limit order. A market order is an order to buy or sell at the current market price. A limit order becomes a market order when the stock price reaches the price you specify in an associated text field

- Combo box for items "good for a day" or "good until canceled"
- Buttons to preview order, place order, or cancel order
  - If preview order is selected, a text area must display the type of transaction, quantity of shares, stock symbol, and total price which includes a $19.95 commission. If the order is a "buy" order, the commission is added to the total price of the order. If the order is a "sell" order, the commission is subtracted from the gross proceeds realized from the sale. For a market order, assume the price is $25.00 per share. For a limit order, the price per share is the amount entered by the user in the text field associated with the limit order radio button.
  - If place order is selected, display the same information as a preview order and make a statement confirming that the order has been placed.
  - If cancel order is selected, clear the text area and make a statement confirming that the order is canceled.
- Do not accept an order if either the account number or trading password is not correct.

6. Combine the classes developed in problems 3, 4, and 5 to build a *Financial* e-commerce class that will allow users to select a banking transaction, stock transaction, or apply for a consumer loan at different times, depending on their needs.

13

Applets and Graphics

OBJECTIVES

When you are finished with this chapter, you should have a good understanding of the following:

- Java applets versus applications
- How to create applets
- The use of the *paint()* method
- The graphical components contained within the Java *Graphics* class
- How to create graphical images using rectangles, ovals, arcs, lines, and strings
- How to use graphics in both applets and applications
- How to add components and process events within an applet
- The use of panels in an applet

Introduction

As you are now aware, you can build **applications** or **applets** in Java. Although Java's current popularity has to do with creating applications, it was initially popular because of its ability to create little applications, called applets, that could be run within a Web page. The term "applet" denotes a "little application," just as the term "piglet" denotes a "little pig." The term "applet" has nothing to do with the Apple computer company. Applications are created for general systems and shrink-wrapped commercial software, while applets are created to run on the Internet when called by a HyperText Markup Language, or HTML, page. As a result, applets are designed to be run from a "Java-enabled" Web browser. An applet provides for dynamic user interaction and graphical animation on a Web page through its graphical user interface. Without applets, static HTML Web pages would be very boring.

Everything that you have learned to date can be applied to applets, except for frames. This is because a frame is a container for GUI components within an application, while the applet itself is a container for GUI components within an applet. Like frames in applications, applets are used as containers to hold GUI components. When you create an applet, it is, by definition, a GUI program. Furthermore, a Java application has a *main()* method which is called when the program starts. Applets, on the other hand, do not have a *main()* method. Rather, applets rely on the Web browser to call certain other methods that we will discuss shortly.

13.1   Applets

Here is what a do-nothing applet looks like:

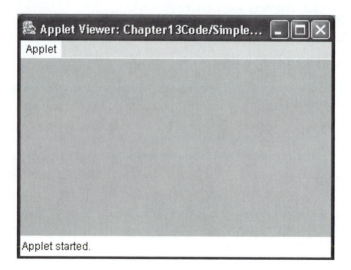

Not very exciting, is it? However, it does have the attributes and behavior that you would expect with any window. It has a title bar and borders. Also, notice it has a unique attribute called a ***status bar*** at the bottom of the window. Here, the status bar indicates that the applet has started running. You can resize the applet window, minimize it, maximize it, and even close it. These are its simple behaviors. Here is the code that produced the foregoing applet:

```
import javax.swing.*;          //FOR JApplet CLASS

public class SimpleApplet extends JApplet
{
  //AUTOMATICALLY CALLED WHEN APPLET STARTS
  public void init()
```

```
   {
   }//END init()
}//END APPLET
```

Wow, what a simple program! In fact, it's completely empty. Notice that the standard Java *javax.swing* package is imported. This package includes a class called *JApplet*, which we extend to create our own applet subclass, called *SimpleApplet*. All the work of creating this generic window is being done by the inherited *JApplet* superclass methods. An applet is like a frame that provides a window for GUI components; however, unlike a frame, an applet includes a status bar at the bottom of the window and the window close feature. Recall that the window closing feature had to be added to a simple frame. It doesn't have to be added for an applet. Notice that our *SimpleApplet* class has a single method, called *init()*. The *init()* method is called automatically when the applet is executed. It is used to "initialize" the applet. The *init()* method in our *SimpleApplet* class is empty to keep it as simple as possible.

Now, think about what you do *not* see in the above applet code. You do not see *main()*. You do not see an object created for the applet class. All you see is the applet class by itself. Applets never use *main()* and never have objects created for them. The applet class executes and calls *init()* automatically when it is referenced within an HTML page.

In this text we are using the *JApplet* class within the Java *javax.swing* package to construct our applets. Be aware that older browsers do not support Java *javax.swing* and, therefore, would not execute our *JApplet* class code. Older browsers support the non-*Swing*, *Applet* class which is in the Java *awt* package. Make sure you have the latest version of Netscape or Explorer as well as the Java plug-in if you intend to execute your applets through a browser rather than the applet viewer in your Java IDE.

The *init()* method is used to initialize an applet. It is called automatically by the applet container when the applet is executed.

HTML

HTML is used to create Web pages. It allows you to create pages of text and images that can be viewed through a Web browser regardless of the computer platform that you are using. An HTML file is simply a text document that includes a series of *tags* that tell the browser what to do, just like a movie script tells an actor or actress what to do. Here is the HTML file that was used to run the foregoing *SimpleApplet* class. The file name is *SimpleApplet.html*.

```
<HTML>
<HEAD>
    <TITLE>Chapter13Code/SimpleApplet</TITLE>
</HEAD>
<BODY>
```

```
<APPLET codebase=.. code="Chapter13Code/SimpleApplet.class"
                      width=350 height=200>
</APPLET>
</BODY>
</HTML>
```

The HTML tags are coded within angle brackets, < >, are case sensitive, and always come in pairs. Every time you use a tag, such as <HTML>, you must close it with another tag, such as </HTML>, where a forward slash, /, is placed before the tag name. Thus, a pair of tags frame the information that is pertinent to that pair.

An HTML page always begins with the <HTML> tag and ends with the </HTML> tag. The header, <HEAD> and </HEAD> tags, frame information about the page, such as the Web page title. Notice that the title is framed within the <TITLE> and </TITLE> tags which specify a title for the window title bar. So, within the header tags we have the title "Chapter13Code/SimpleApplet" that will appear on the title bar of the Web page.

Everything that appears on the Web page itself must be enclosed within the <BODY> and </BODY> tags. The sole purpose of our *SimpleApplet.html* file is to execute the *SimpleApplet.class* file. Therefore, there is only one set of meaningful tags within the body of our page, <APPLET> and </APPLET>. These are the applet tags that invoke the built-in Java interpreter to translate and execute the byte codes contained in our *SimpleApplet.class* file. Notice that we must specify the *.class* byte-code file and not the *.java* source code file. A Java compiler must first be used to translate the *.java* file to the *.class* file before it can be tagged within an HTML page. Here is the applet tag code we used:

```
<APPLET codebase=.. code="Chapter13Code/SimpleApplet.class"
                      width=350 height=200>
</APPLET>
```

You see here that the required syntax of `codebase=..  code=` is followed by the applet class path within quotation marks. The working directory path that was used to compile the applet must be specified here. In addition to the applet class path, you must specify the width and height of the area in which the applet is to be displayed. The applet call, as well as the width and height specification, must appear before the right angle bracket, >, of the <APPLET> tag as shown.

You can create your own HTML file to execute an applet using any simple text editor, such as *Notepad*. Your IDE editor can also be used for this purpose. Once the HTML file is created, you simply open it within the *File* menu of your browser. However, you might have noticed that your IDE automatically creates an associated HTML file when you compile an applet. So, when you execute an applet through your IDE, it invokes a built-in *Applet Viewer* program to open the HTML file and execute the applet.

Now, back to our discussion of applets. Here is another applet. Notice that a string is displayed within the window and a status bar message is displayed at the bottom of the window.

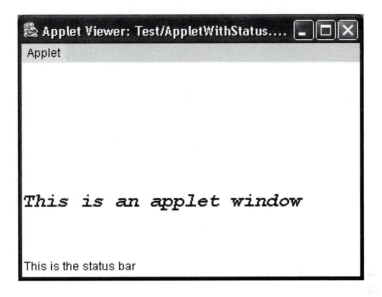

Here is the code that produced this applet:

```java
import javax.swing.*;   //FOR JApplet CLASS
import java.awt.*;      //FOR Graphics CLASS

public class AppletWithStatus extends JApplet
{
   public void init()
   {
   }//END init()

   public void paint(Graphics g)
   {

      //DEFINE FONT OBJECT AND SET FONT
      Font f = new Font("Courier",Font.ITALIC + Font.BOLD,20);
      g.setFont(f);

      //SET COLOR
      g.setColor(Color.blue);

      //DRAW STRING
      g.drawString("This is an applet window",0,150);

      //DISPLAY STATUS MESSAGE
      showStatus("This is the status bar");
   }//END paint()
}//END APPLET
```

This applet also has an empty *init()* method and a method called *paint()*. The *paint()* method is also called automatically (after *init()*) during the execution of an applet and is used to draw strings and graphical shapes. The *paint()* method is not called again, unless the applet is resized or the user leaves and then returns to the HTML page containing the applet. You cannot call the *paint()* method directly within your program. However, you can call it indirectly by calling the *repaint()* method when you need to refresh the applet window. Furthermore, the *paint()* method is not used to display GUI components; it is only used to display strings and graphical shapes. You will learn how to display GUI components in an applet shortly. The *paint()* method always has a single parameter which is an object of the standard *Graphics* class. This object is used within *paint()* to call methods of the *Graphics* class, such as *setColor()*, *setFont()*, and *drawString()* as shown in the program. The *setFont()* method sets the font for all subsequent text operations to the font object specified in its argument. Note that we have defined a font object, *f*, which is passed to the *setFont()* method. The *setColor()* method of the *Graphics* class sets the color of all subsequent graphical objects to the color specified in its argument. Here we have specified a color of blue. The *drawString()* method draws the text of the specified string using the current font and color. The first character of the string is placed at the coordinate specified in the method. Here, the *drawString()* method places the first character of the string at coordinate (0,150). The applet title bar requires about 20 pixels. When painting strings, the point of reference is (0,0) which is the top left-hand corner of the applet window. The first number is its horizontal position in pixels, while the second number is its vertical position in pixels. Many display screens are 800 pixels wide by 600 pixels high. So, the coordinate of the lower right-hand corner of the window is (800,600). Finally, the *showStatus()* method is used to display a string in the status bar at the bottom of the window. This method is a member of the *JApplet* class, not the *Graphics* class and, therefore, is called directly and not with a graphics object.

The *paint()* method is used to display graphical components and is called automatically after *init()*. The *paint()* method receives a *Graphics* object that is used to call methods to "paint" graphical components. The Java *AWT* (Advanced Window Toolkit) package must be imported to use the *Graphics* class.

QUICK CHECK

1. When must you write a Java applet versus a Java application?
2. What package must be imported to use the *JApplet* class?
3. True or false: You must implement the window closing feature of an applet, just like you do for a frame.
4. What feature does an applet have at the bottom of a window that an application frame does not?
5. What method is executed first and automatically for an applet?
6. What method is used to paint graphical components within an applet?
7. What parameter must always be included in the method referred to in question 6?
8. Write the HTML code required to execute an applet called *myApplet*.

13.2   Graphics

In this section you will use the Java *Graphics* class with the *paint()* method to implement graphical components. These components include rectangles, ovals, arcs, lines, and
strings. Here is an applet that has several graphical components. It is made up of rectangles, ovals, arcs, lines, and strings. See if you can identify each of these components.

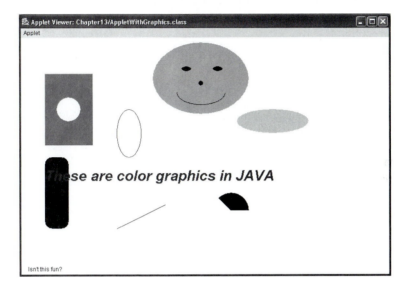

Wow, what an applet! The graphics you see in this applet window are composed
of several graphical components, as follows:

- A filled 3D rectangle, implemented by method *fill3DRect()*
- A filled rounded rectangle, implemented by method *fillRoundRect()*
- A filled oval, implemented by method *fillOval()*
- An unfilled oval, implemented by method *drawOval()*
- An arc, implemented by method *drawArc()*
- A line, implemented by method *drawLine()*
- A filled arc, implemented by method *fillArc()*

See if you can identify each of these graphics in the applet. Here is the code that
produced the applet:

```
1    import javax.swing.*;          //FOR JApplet CLASS
2    import java.awt.*;             //FOR Graphics CLASS
3    public class AppletWithGraphics extends JApplet
4    {
5       //RGB COLOR
6       private int red = 100;
7       private int green = 150;
```

```
8          private int blue = 250;
9          public void init()
10         {
11         }//END init()
12         public void paint(Graphics g)
13         {
14           //RGB COLOR
15           g.setColor(new Color(red,green,blue));

16           //RECTANGLES
17           //FILL 3D RECTANGLE
18           g.fill3DRect(50,75,100,150,true);

19           //SET COLOR TO BLACK
20           g.setColor(Color.black);

21           //FILL ROUNDED RECTANGLE
22           g.fillRoundRect(50,250,50,150,30,30);

23           //OVALS
24           //FILL WHITE OVAL
25           g.setColor(Color.white);
26           g.fillOval(75,125,50,50);

27           //DRAW BLUE OVAL
28           g.setColor(Color.blue);
29           g.drawOval(200,150,50,100);

30           //FILL CYAN OVAL
31           g.setColor(Color.cyan);
32           g.fillOval(450,150,150,50);

33           //DRAW SMILING FACE
34           //USE FILLED OVAL FOR FACE
35           g.setColor(Color.lightGray);        //SET FACE COLOR TO LIGHT GRAY
36           g.fillOval(275,10,200,150);

37           //USE FILLED OVAL FOR EYES
38           g.setColor(Color.black);
39           g.fillOval(335,60,20,10);           //LEFT EYE
40           g.fillOval(400,60,20,10);           //RIGHT EYE

41           //USE FILLED OVAL FOR NOSE
42           g.fillOval(370,90,10,10);

43           //ARCS
44           //USE ARC FOR MOUTH OF SMILING FACE
45           g.drawArc(325,90,100,50,0,-180);
```

```
46              //FILLED ARC
47              g.fillArc(400,325,75,75,0,135);

48              //LINES
49              //DRAW A LINE
50              g.drawLine(200,400,300,350);

51              //FONTS AND STRINGS
52              //DRAW BLUE FONT STRING
53              g.setColor(Color.blue);
54              g.setFont(new Font("Helvetica",Font.ITALIC + Font.BOLD,30));
55              g.drawString("These are color graphics in JAVA",50,300);

56              //SHOW APPLET STATUS
57              showStatus("    Isn't this fun?");
58          }//END paint()
59      }//END APPLET
```

The preceding code is divided into sections for each major type of graphic as indicated by the comment lines. We have also added line number references to facilitate our discussion.

RGB Color

Again, we have an empty *init()* method and a *paint()* method. All the graphics work is being done within the *paint()* method. The *paint()* method receives a *Graphics* class object that we call *g*. The standard *Graphics* class contains a wealth of methods that can be used to draw geometric shapes. The first thing you see in lines 6–8 of the program are three private class members called *red*, *green*, and *blue*. These members control the amount of red, green, and blue color for a filled rectangle with a circle inside of it in the upper left-hand side of the applet window. Each color value can range from 0 to 255. If all three colors have a value of 0, you get black. If all three have a value of 255 you get white. Any color is possible with the proper combination of *red*, *green*, and *blue* (*RGB*) values. The larger the value for a given color, the larger the amount of that color is added to the image.

To set the color of a graphical component, you simply use the *Graphics* class object, *g*, to call the *setColor()* method as in line 15 or 20. This method sets the color of any *subsequent* graphical components to the color specified within its argument as an RGB value, or one of the thirteen constant colors defined by Java. (Reference Table 13-1.) In line 15, we have defined a *Color* class object as the *setColor()* method argument. Notice that our *red*, *green*, and *blue* variables are used as arguments for the *Color* class constructor when the object is created. In line 20, we simply reference the constant *Color.black* to generate the desired black color. You can set the color of the graphics object either way, but you have much more control over the color by using RGB values, rather than one of the thirteen fixed color constants in the *Color* class.

TABLE 13-1 Constant Colors of the *Color* Class

Color	Code
Black	Color.black
Blue	Color.blue
Cyan	Color.cyan
Dark gray	Color.darkGray
Gray	Color.gray
Green	Color.green
Light gray	Color.lightGray
Magenta	Color.magenta
Orange	Color.orange
Pink	Color.pink
Red	Color.red
White	Color.white
Yellow	Color.yellow

Rectangles

In line 18 of the program, you see that the rectangle is produced by using the graphics object, *g*, to call the *fill3DRect()* method. This method produces a raised (or sunken) rectangle to give it a 3D look. Here is the header for this method:

```
public void fill3DRect(int x,              //HORIZONTAL COOR.
                       int y,              //VERTICAL COOR.
                       int width,          //RECT. WIDTH
                       int height,         //RECT. HEIGHT
                       boolean raised)     //RAISED OR SUNKEN
```

The first two method arguments are the horizontal and vertical, (*x*,*y*), coordinates for the *upper left-hand corner* of the rectangle, as shown in Figure 13-1. The next two arguments are the width and height of the rectangle, in pixels. The last argument produces a *raised* 3D rectangle with a value of `true,` and a *sunken* 3D rectangle with a value of `false`.

The position of any graphical component is controlled by specifying the (*x*,*y*) coordinates of the upper left-hand corner of an imaginary bounding rectangle.

In line 20, you see that the color of the graphics object, *g*, is set to black rather than an *RGB* color. Line 22 calls the *fillRoundRect()* method of the *Graphics* object. This creates the filled, rounded, black rectangle in the lower left-hand corner of the foregoing applet window. Notice that the corners of the rectangle are rounded. This is why it's called a "rounded" rectangle.
Here is the header for this method:

```
public void fillRoundRec(int x,            //HORIZONTAL COOR.
                         int y,            //VERTICAL COOR.
                         int width,        //RECT WIDTH
```

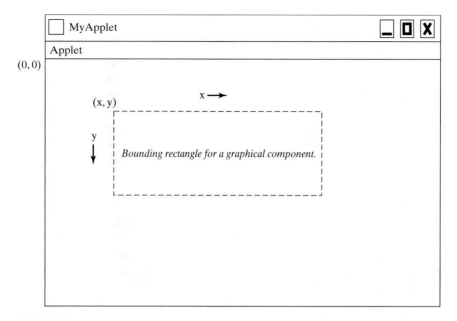

FIGURE 13-1   The position of any graphical component is controlled by specifying the (x,y) coordinates of the upper left-hand corner of an imaginary bounding rectangle.

```
int height,        //RECT HEIGHT
int arcWidth,      //CORNER HORIZ. DIAM.
int arcHeight)     //CORNER VERT. DIAM.
```

The method requires six arguments. The first two values represent the horizontal and vertical coordinates of the upper left-hand corner of the rectangle. The next two arguments control the width and height of the rectangle. The last two arguments control the amount of roundness of the rectangle corners. The first of these sets the horizontal diameter of the arc at the four corners, while the second sets the vertical diameter of the arc at the four corners. There is another method called *drawRoundRect()* that employs the same arguments as the *fillRoundRect()* method, but paints an empty, unfilled, rectangle.

 Several of the *Graphics* class methods allow you to "fill" or "draw" a graphical component. When the "fill" method is called, the component is filled with the color that has been set for the graphics object, g. When the "draw" method is called, the object appears as a cartoon-like line drawing whose outline is the color of the graphics object and whose interior is the color of the applet background.

Ovals

In lines 25 and 26 of the program, a white-filled oval is added to the applet inside the rectangle in the upper left corner of the window. This time the color is set to white in line 25 using the *Color* class. The filled oval is created by calling the *fillOval()* method in line 26 with the graphics object. In lines 28 and 29, a blue unfilled oval is added to the applet. This time the color is set to blue in line 28 using the *Color* class. The oval is created by calling the *drawOval()* method in line 29 with the graphics object. In lines 31 and 32, a cyan-filled oval is added to the applet. This oval is created by calling the *fillOval()* method with the graphics object. Can you tell which oval is which?

Ovals are created using two methods from the *Graphics* class: *fillOval()* and *drawOval()*. As with rectangles, a filled oval created by *fillOval()* is filled with the color set for the *Graphics* class object, while an unfilled oval, created by *drawOval()*, is simply a line drawing with the line reflecting the color of the *Graphics* class object. Here are the headers for these methods:

```
public abstract void fillOval(int x,        //HORIZONTAL COOR.
                              int y,        //VERTICAL COOR.
                              int width,    //OVAL WIDTH
                              int height)   //OVAL HEIGHT


public abstract void drawOval(int x,        //HORIZONTAL COOR.
                              int y,        //VERTICAL COOR.
                              int width,    //OVAL WIDTH
                              int height)   //OVAL HEIGHT
```

Here you see that the first two arguments for both methods provide the (*x,y*) pixel coordinate for the oval. Imagine the oval contained within a rectangle as shown in Figure 13-2. The (*x,y*) coordinate for the oval is the upper left-hand corner of this rectangle. The length and width of the rectangle provide the size and shape of the oval.

When the width and height of the oval are the same, you will get a circle, as in the white oval created in line 26 of the program.

Now, how do you suppose we constructed the smiling face in the applet window? You are right if you thought mostly with ovals. The face itself, as well as the eyes and

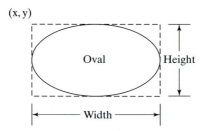

FIGURE 13-2   Imagine an oval inside of a rectangle where the upper left-hand corner of the rectangle provides the oval coordinate, and the width and height of the rectangle provide the size and shape of the oval.

nose are all filled ovals created in lines 35–42 of the program. The mouth, however, was created with an arc using the *drawArc()* method in line 45. Can you correlate the oval code with the graphic components it creates?

Arcs

Like rectangles and ovals, arcs can be filled or unfilled. Filled arcs, like the one in the bottom right side of the applet window, are created using the *fillArc()* method, while unfilled arcs, like the mouth on the smiling face, are created using the *drawArc()* method. Here are the headers of each:

```
public abstract void fillArc(int x,         //HORIZONTAL COOR.
                             int y,         //VERTICAL COOR.
                             int width,     //ARC WIDTH
                             int height     //ARC HEIGHT
                             int start,     //START ANGLE
                             int arcAngle)  //ARC ANGLE FROM START

public abstract void drawArc(int x,         //HORIZONTAL COOR.
                             int y,         //VERTICAL COOR.
                             int width,     //ARC WIDTH
                             int height     //ARC HEIGHT
                             int start,     //START ANGLE
                             int arcAngle)  //ARC ANGLE FROM START
```

Notice that both arc headers are the same. To see how an arc works, imagine that the arc is bounded by a rectangle, as shown in Figure 13-3.

The first pair of arguments specify the (x,y) coordinates of the upper left-hand corner of the bounding rectangle. The second pair of arguments specify the bounding rectangle width and height, which would be the actual arc width and height if the arc swept 360° to form a complete circle. The third pair of arguments control the arc angle based on a polar coordinate system where 0° is at the three o'clock position. The first argument in this pair is called the ***start angle*** and specifies where the arc will start within this coordinate system. The second argument in the pair is called the ***arc angle*** and specifies how many degrees the arc will sweep from its starting point. A *positive arc angle* will force the arc to be swept in a *counterclockwise* direction, while a *negative arc angle* will force the arc to be swept in a *clockwise* direction. In Figure 13-3a, the arc starts at 0° and has a +90° counterclockwise arc angle. Thus, the start angle argument would be 0 and the arc angle argument would be 90. The arc in Figure 13-3b starts at 0° and has a −90° clockwise arc angle. Therefore, the start angle argument would be 0 and the arc angle argument would be −90. By changing the arc width, height, start angle, and arc angle, you can achieve just about any filled or unfilled arc you desire.

An unfilled arc is used to create the mouth of the smiling face in the foregoing applet window. Look at the *drawArc()* method code that was used to create the mouth arc in line 45 of the program. A filled arc is shown in the lower right side of the applet window. This arc is created by the *fillArc()* method in line 47 of the program. Notice that the arc is *swept counterclockwise* about 135° beginning at the three o'clock position.

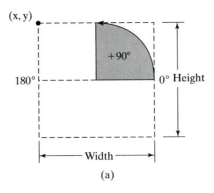

(a)

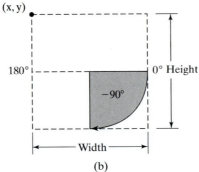

(b)

FIGURE 13-3   Imagine an arc inside a rectangle where the upper left-hand corner of the rectangle provides the arc coordinate, and the width and height of the rectangle provide the size of the arc. The arc in (a) has a start angle of 0° and an arc angle of 90°. The arc in (b) has a start angle of 0° and an arc angle of −90°.

Lines

In the bottom center of our applet window, you find a simple line. The line is created from the *drawLine()* method in line 50 of the program. This method has the following header:

```
public abstract void drawLine(int x1,       //X COOR. OF START OF LINE
                             int y1,        //Y COOR. OF START OF LINE
                             int x2,        //X COOR. OF END OF LINE
                             int y2)        //Y COOR. OF END OF LINE
```

You see that the first pair of method arguments specify the coordinate for the start of the line, while the second pair of arguments specify the coordinate for the end of the line.

Strings

The last graphic that we need to talk about in our applet window is the string. The string that is drawn will take on the font and color to which the graphics object has been set. The color and font of the string are set in lines 53 and 54 of the program. The string is drawn by using the graphics object to call the *drawString()* method in line 55 of the program. Here you see that the string text is the first argument of the method. What do you suppose the second pair of arguments represent? The *drawString()* method has the following header:

```
public abstract void drawString(String text,      //TEXT OF STRING
                                int x,             //X COOR. OF STRING
                                int y)             //Y COOR. OF STRING
```

The *drawString()* header is straightforward. The only thing you might note is that the last two arguments specify the coordinate of the **baseline**, or bottom, of the string. If you imagine the string contained within a rectangle, then the *string coordinate is the lower left-hand corner of the rectangle*.

By the way, you can also use the *paint()* method in an application just like we did here in an applet. This is the topic of the next section.

Polygons

A polygon graphic in Java is simply a multisided rectangle which can be viewed as a series of lines connecting a series of (x,y) coordinates in a rectangular plane, as shown in Figure 13-4.

Here, our "bow-tie" polygon begins and ends at coordinate $(x0, y0)$. The polygon is painted in the numeric order of the coordinates so that first the line from $(x0,y0)$ to $(x1,y1)$ is painted, then the line from $(x1,y1)$ to $(x2,y2)$ is painted, and so on.

If we place this polygon within an applet or frame, we must determine values for the (x,y) coordinates in terms of pixels, as shown in Figure. 13-5.

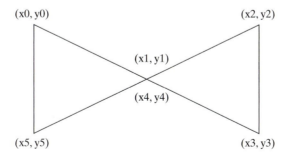

FIGURE 13-4   A polygon graphic in Java is simply a multisided rectangle that can be viewed as a series of lines connecting a series of (x,y) coordinates in a rectangular plane.

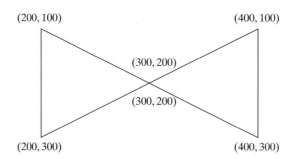

FIGURE 13-5   Polygon coordinate values for placement within an applet or frame.

Here is how our polygon bow tie might appear within an applet window:

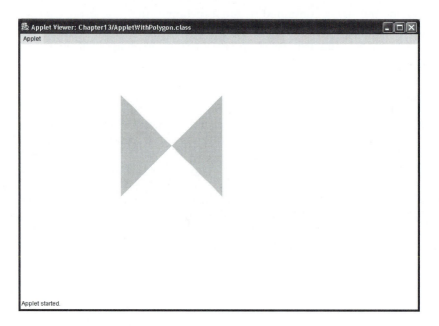

Here is the applet code that produced the polygon:

```
1    import javax.swing.*;          //FOR JApplet CLASS
2    import java.awt.*;             //FOR Graphics CLASS

3    public class AppletWithPolygon extends JApplet
4    {
5      public void init()
6      {
7      }//END init()
8
9      public void paint(Graphics g)
```

```
10              {
11                 //DEFINE POLYGON COORDINATES
12                 int x[] = {200,300,400,400,300,200};  //X-COORDINATES
13                 int y[] = {100,200,100,300,200,300};  //Y-COORDINATES

14                 //SET GRAPHICS OBJECT COLOR
15                 g.setColor(Color.cyan);

16                 //PAINT FILLED POLYGON
17                 g.fillPolygon(x,y,6);
18                 }//END paint()
19              }//END APPLET
```

Notice in lines 12 and 13 that two arrays are initialized with the coordinate values. The first value in each array forms the $(x0,y0)$ coordinate of the polygon, the second value in each array forms the $(x1,y1)$ coordinate, and so on. The polygon is painted in line 17 using these arrays as arguments within the *fillPolygon()* method. Here is the header for this method:

```
public void fillPolygon(int[] x,      //x COORDINATES
                        int[] y,      //y COORDINATES
                        int n)        //NUMBER OF POINTS
```

The method requires two array arguments, one for the *x*-coordinates and one for the *y*-coordinates, plus a third argument that specifies the number of coordinates to use from the two arrays in constructing the polygon. The (x,y) coordinates supply the vertices of the polygon perimeter in the order in which they appear within the arrays. Thus, the first pair of (x,y) values provides the point of origin for the polygon perimeter. A line is drawn from this point to a point defined by the second pair of (x,y) values. Then, a line is drawn from this second point to a point defined by the third pair of (x,y) values, and so on. Finally, a line is drawn from the last specified point to the point of origin to complete the polygon perimeter. Of course, the *fillPolygon()* method fills the polygon with the color of the graphics object.

The three methods available to construct polygons are *fillPolygon()*, *drawPolygon()*, and *drawPolyline()*. They all have the same header, except for their names. The *fillPolygon()* method constructs a filled polygon, while the *drawPolygon()* method constructs an unfilled polygon. Both of these methods construct a complete polygon, where a connecting line is drawn from the last specified coordinate to the point of origin, which is the first coordinate specified. However, the *drawPolyline()* method constructs an unfilled polygon but does not connect the last coordinate to the point of origin.

Graphics in Applications

Graphics can also be included within a frame in an application. Here are the same graphics, now produced within a frame by a Java application:

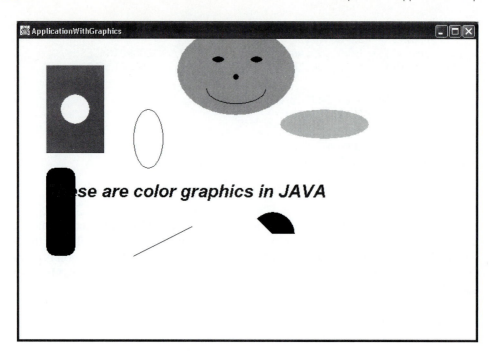

Here is the program that produced the application window:

```java
import java.awt.*;                        //FOR FRAME CLASS
import javax.swing.?;                     //FOR SWING COMPONENTS

class GraphicsDemo extends JFrame
{
  //CONSTRUCTOR
  public GraphicsDemo(String title)
  {
    //CALL SUPERCLASS CONSTRUCTOR
    super(title);
    //CALL paint() VIA repaint() TO GENERATE GRAPHICS
    repaint();
  }//END GraphicsDemo()

  public void paint(Graphics g)
  {
    //RGB COLOR AND RECTANGLES
    //SET RGB COLOR
    int red = 100;
    int green = 150;
    int blue  = 250;

    g.setColor(new Color(red,green,blue));
```

```
//FILL 3D RECTANGLE
g.fill3DRect(50,75,100,150,true);

//SET COLOR TO BLACK
g.setColor(Color.black);

//FILL ROUNDED RECTANGLE
g.fillRoundRect(50,250,50,150,30,30);

//OVALS
//FILL WHITE OVAL
g.setColor(Color.white);
g.fillOval(75,125,50,50);

//DRAW BLUE OVAL
g.setColor(Color.blue);
g.drawOval(200,150,50,100);

//FILL CYAN OVAL
g.setColor(Color.cyan);
g.fillOval(450,150,150,50);

//DRAW SMILING FACE
//USE FILLED OVAL FOR FACE
g.setColor(Color.lightGray);        //SET FACE COLOR TO LIGHT GRAY
g.fillOval(275,10,200,150);

//USE FILLED OVAL FOR EYES
g.setColor(Color.black);
g.fillOval(335,60,20,10);           //LEFT EYE
g.fillOval(400,60,20,10);           //RIGHT EYE

//USE FILLED OVAL FOR NOSE
g.fillOval(370,90,10,10);

//ARCS
//USE ARC FOR MOUTH OF SMILING FACE
g.drawArc(325,90,100,50,0,-180);

//FILLED AN ARC
g.fillArc(400,325,75,75,0,135);

//LINES
//DRAW A LINE
g.drawLine(200,400,300,350);

//FONTS AND STRINGS
//DRAW BLUE FONT STRING
g.setColor(Color.blue);
```

```
    g.setFont(new Font("Helvetica",Font.ITALIC + Font.BOLD,30));
    g.drawString("These are color graphics in JAVA",50,300);
  }//END paint()
}//END FRAME SUBCLASS


//APPLICATION CLASS TO TEST GraphicsDemo CLASS
public class ApplicationWithGraphics
{
  public static void main(String[] args)
  {
    //DEFINE FRAME OBJECT
    GraphicsDemo window = new GraphicsDemo("AppliationWithGraphics");

    //SET FRAME BACKGROUND COLOR TO WHITE FOR MAXIMUM CONTRAST
    window.setBackground(Color.white);

    //SET FRAME SIZE
    window.setSize(500,300);

    //MAKE FRAME VISIBLE
    window.show();
  }//END main()
}//END ApplicationWithGraphics
```

You see that we have created a *JFrame* subclass called *GraphicsDemo* and included the *paint()* method as a method within this class. However, we have eliminated the call to the *showStatus()* method at the end of *paint()* since frames don't have a status bar, and therefore don't support the *showStatus()* method. The test class which includes *main()* simply defines a frame object, sets that size of the frame, sets the frame background color, and makes the frame visible. Within the frame constructor, a call is made to the *repaint()* method, which calls the *paint()* method within our *GraphicsDemo* class. Remember, you cannot call *paint()* directly. You must call *repaint()* which indirectly calls *paint()*. That's all there is to it!

 An applet's *paint()* method is called automatically when it is executed. In an application, the *paint()* method must be called indirectly by calling the *repaint()* method.

You might notice a slight difference between the graphical windows produced by the applet versus the application. The obvious difference is that the applet contains a status bar, while the frame does not. Another difference is the frame coordinate system places (0,0) at the upper left-hand corner of the frame, or window, while the applet coordinate system places (0,0) just below the title bar of the applet. Notice how the head of the smiling face is cut off slightly by the title bar in the application window. This is because the (0,0) origin is at the corner of the frame, and not below the title bar, so the same component coordinates produce a slightly different vertical positioning of the components within a frame versus an applet.

QUICK CHECK

1. What package must be imported to use the *Graphics* class?
2. What is the difference between a graphical "fill" method and a "draw" method in Java?
3. What graphical component is generally used to generate circles?
4. What RGB value will generate black?
5. True or false: Once the color of the *Graphics* class object is set, all subsequent graphical components painted by that object will be the same color.
6. What is the difference between a "3D" rectangle and one that is not "3D"?
7. What do the (*x,y*) coordinates of an oval specify?
8. The 0° position of an arc is the _____ o'clock position.
9. True or false: A positive arc angle will force the arc to be swept in a clockwise direction.
10. What data structure must be used to specify the vertices of a polygon?
11. What is the difference between a polygon and a polyline in Java?
12. What method must be used in an application to call the *paint()* method?

13.3   Applets with GUI Components

In Chapter 12, you learned how to create application GUIs. Almost everything you learned about application GUIs can be applied to creating GUIs for applets, with the exception of using a frame. In an application, the *JFrame* class is inherited to produce a generic window for the GUI components that make up a window. In an applet, the *JApplet* class is extended to produce a generic window for the GUI components.

By definition, an applet is a GUI. You simply cannot create a non-GUI applet, as you can an application. Of course, an applet can only be executed from a Java IDE or a Java-enabled Web browser and, therefore, is primarily an Internet-based program. All Java programs for non-Internet applications must be Java applications. A classic example of when an application is required over an applet is when the program must operate on disk files. Since an applet is primarily created for use over the Internet, Java applets do not even support file handling. This is part of the inherent security built into Java. Would you want someone else's applet to have access to your disk files?

In this section, you will learn about applets that contain GUI components. You will see the use of layout managers, font control, and GUI components used within an applet.

There are several standard methods that are called automatically when an applet is run. They are the *init(), start(), paint(), stop(),* and *destroy()* methods, in this order. All of these methods are summarized in Table 13-2.

TABLE 13-2   Standard Methods Called by an Applet

Method	Description
public void init()	Called when the applet is first loaded for execution and also when the applet is reloaded. Used to initialize variables and GUI components.
public void start()	Called after *init()* and when the applet is reactivated, or when the user moves back to the HTML page containing the applet. Used to "start" any tasks, such as animation, that must be started each time the HTML page containing the applet is revisited.
public void paint(Graphics g)	Called automatically after *init()* and by *repaint()* when the applet must be repainted. Receives an object from the standard *Graphics* class to create applet graphics. Used to "paint" graphical components.
public void stop()	Called when the user leaves the HTML page containing the applet. Used to "stop" any actions, such as animation, being performed by the applet.
public void destroy()	Called after *stop()* only when an applet is being removed from memory such as when the use of the browser is terminated. Used to release any system resources that were allocated by the applet.

Now, look at this applet window. Doesn't it look familiar from Chapter 12?

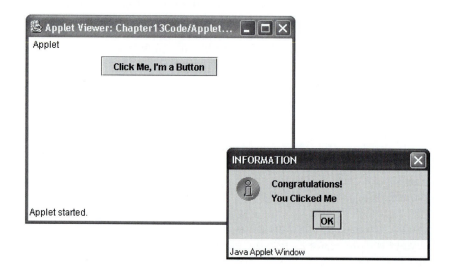

Here is the code that produced the applet window:

```
1    import java.awt.*;         //FOR LAYOUT MANAGER AND RELATED METHODS
2    import java.awt.event.*;   //FOR EVENT PROCESSING
3    import javax.swing.*;      //FOR JApplet CLASS GUI COMPONENT CLASSES

4    public class AppletWithButton extends JApplet
5    {
6      //DECLARE BUTTON OBJECT
7      private JButton button;

8      //INITIALIZE APPLET
9      public void init()
10     {
11       //CREATE A CONTAINER
12       Container container = getContentPane();

13       //SET CONTAINER LAYOUT
14       container.setLayout(new FlowLayout());

15       //DEFINE BUTTON OBJECT
16       button = new JButton("Click Me, I'm a Button");

17       //ADD BUTTON TO CONTAINER
18       container.add(button);

19       //ADD EVENT LISTENER THIS BUTTON
20       button.addActionListener(new ButtonHandler());
21     }//END init()

22     //BUTTON EVENT HANDLER CLASS
23     private class ButtonHandler implements ActionListener
24     {
25       //actionPerformed METHOD
26       public void actionPerformed(ActionEvent e)
27       {
28       JOptionPane.showMessageDialog(null,
                                 "Congratulations!\nYou Clicked Me",
                                 "INFORMATION",
                                 JOptionPane.INFORMATION_MESSAGE);

29       }//END actionPerformed
30     }//END ButtonHandler CLASS

31     //SET BACKGROUND BACK TO WHITE ON RESTART
32     public void start()
33     {
34       setBackground(Color.white);
35     }//END start()
36   }//END APPLET CLASS
```

Recall that, in an application, the GUI was constructed as part of a frame constructor since the constructor is the first thing executed when a frame object is created. In an applet, the GUI should be constructed within the *init()* method since the *init()* method is the first thing executed within an applet. So, to construct GUI components within an applet, you simply place all your GUI component code within *init()* since it acts as the constructor for the applet class. Event handling is identical to that of an application. Look at lines 8 – 21 and you will find that we have instantiated our button object, added the button object to the applet container, then added an event listener just like we have done in the past, but all within the *init()* method.

Following the *init()* method we have coded the *actionPerformed()* method within an event handler in lines 22 through 30. Here, we simply call the *showMessageDialog()* method to display a dialog box the same way we did in the last chapter.

When you minimize and then restore the applet, you restart the applet. Whenever an applet is restarted like this, or revisited as you might if you go back and forth between Web pages, the applet automatically calls its *start()* method if one exists. The *start()* method that we coded in lines 31 through 35 simply sets the applet background color to white when it is restored.

Here is an applet with several buttons:

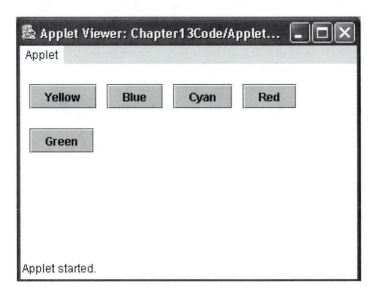

If you click any of the buttons, the applet background color is changed accordingly. Then, if you minimize then restore the window, the restored window will appear with a white background. Here is the code that produced this applet window:

```
1    import javax.swing.*;     //FOR JApplet CLASS GUI COMPONENT CLASSES
2    import java.awt.*;         //FOR LAYOUT MANAGER AND RELATED METHODS
3    import java.awt.event.*;   //FOR EVENT PROCESSING

4    public class AppletWithButtons extends JApplet
5        {
```

```
6       //DECLARE BUTTON OBJECTS
7       private JButton yellowButton;
8       private JButton blueButton;
9       private JButton cyanButton;
10      private JButton redButton;
11      private JButton greenButton;

12      //CREATE A CONTAINER
13      private Container container = getContentPane();

14      //APPLET INITIALIZATION METHOD
15      public void init()
16      {
17        //SET FLOWLAYOUT, LEFT ALIGNMENT, 10 HORIZ. GAP, 20 VERT. GAP
18        container.setLayout(new FlowLayout(FlowLayout.LEFT,10,20));

19        //INSTANTIATE BUTTON OBJECTS
20        yellowButton = new JButton("Yellow");
21        blueButton = new JButton("Blue");
22        cyanButton = new JButton("Cyan");
23        redButton = new JButton("Red");
24        greenButton = new JButton("Green");

25        //ADD BUTTONS TO CONTAINER
26        container.add(yellowButton);
27        container.add(blueButton);
28        container.add(cyanButton);
29        container.add(redButton);
30        container.add(greenButton);

31        //DEFINE BUTTON HANDLER OBJECT
32        ButtonHandler bHandler = new ButtonHandler();

33        //ADD ACTION LISTENER WITH BUTTON EVENT HANDLER FOR BUTTONS
34        yellowButton.addActionListener(bHandler);
35        blueButton.addActionListener(bHandler);
36        cyanButton.addActionListener(bHandler);
37        redButton.addActionListener(bHandler);
38        greenButton.addActionListener(bHandler);
39      }//END init()

40      //BUTTON EVENT HANDLER CLASS
41      private class ButtonHandler implements ActionListener
42      {
43        //PROCESS EVENT
44        public void actionPerformed(ActionEvent e)
45        {
46          //WHICH BUTTON CAUSED THE EVENT?
47          if (e.getSource() == yellowButton)
                  container.setBackground(Color.yellow);
48          if (e.getSource() == blueButton)
```

```
                     container.setBackground(Color.blue);
49              if (e.getSource() == cyanButton)
                     container.setBackground(Color.cyan);
50              if (e.getSource() == redButton)
                     container.setBackground(Color.red);
51              if (e.getSource() == greenButton)
                     container.setBackground(Color.green);
52          }//END actionPerformed()
53       }//END ButtonHandler CLASS

54       //SET BACKGROUND BACK TO WHITE ON RESTART
55       public void start()
56       {
57          container.setBackground(Color.white);
58       }//END start()
59    }//END APPLET
```

In this applet, we have first defined five button objects as private members of the applet class. The buttons are defined outside the *init()* method as private class members because we must have access to them in the subsequent *actionPerformed()* method. The *init()* method simply defines a container object and sets the layout manager of the container to *FlowLayout* the same way that we set the layout manager in an application. In fact, applets support any of the layout managers that are supported by frames, including no layout. The buttons are then added to the container, and a listener is added for each button using the *addActionListener()* method. The *actionPerformed()* method processes the button events as you have seen in the past. The *start()* method is used as before to reset the background color to white when the applet is restarted for any reason.

QUICK CHECK

1. What five methods are called automatically when an applet runs?
2. Which of the methods referred to in question 1 must be used to create a GUI?
3. Which of the methods referred to in question 1 must be used to halt any actions being performed by an applet when the user leaves the HTML page containing the applet?
4. True or false: A container object is required to hold the GUI components of an applet the same way it is required in an application.
5. True or false: GUI events are handled within an applet the same way they are handled within an application.
6. True or false: Panels and layout managers cannot be used in an applet.

Problem Solving in Action: E-Commerce

Most likely you have seen a stock market Web site where you can set up an account and make stock transactions. Here is a typical screen you might see at such a site. This GUI was produced by an applet and, at this point, you should be able to identify all of the GUI components contained within the applet.

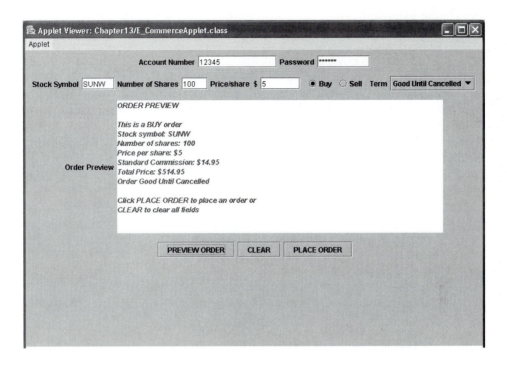

Here is the code that generated the stock transaction GUI:

```
1    import javax.swing.*;      //FOR JApplet AND GUI COMPONENT CLASSES
2    import java.awt.*;         //FOR LAYOUT MANAGER AND RELATED METHODS
3    import java.awt.event.*;   //FOR EVENT PROCESSING

4    public class E_CommerceApplet extends JApplet
5    {
6      //DECLARE BUTTON OBJECTS
7      private JButton previewButton;
8      private JButton cancelButton;
9      private JButton orderButton;

10     //DECLARE TEXT FIELD OBJECTS
11     private JTextField accountNumberField;
12     private JTextField stockSymbolField;
13     private JTextField numberSharesField;
14     private JTextField priceField;
15     private JPasswordField passwordField;
16     private JTextArea previewArea;

17     //DECLARE COMBO BOX OBJECT
18     private JComboBox termChoice;
```

```
19      //DECLARE RADIO BUTTON OBJECTS
20      private JRadioButton buy;
21      private JRadioButton sell;

22      //INITIALIZE APPLET WITH GUI COMPONENTS
23      public void init()
24      {
25        //CREATE A CONTAINER
26        Container container = getContentPane();

27        //SET CONTAINER LAYOUT MANAGER
28        container.setLayout(new FlowLayout());

29        //INSTANTIATE JButton OBJECTS
30        previewButton = new JButton("PREVIEW ORDER");
31        cancelButton = new JButton("CLEAR");
32        orderButton = new JButton("PLACE ORDER");

33        //INSTANTIATE TEXT FIELD AND TEXT AREA OBJECTS
34        accountNumberField = new JTextField(12);
35        stockSymbolField = new JTextField(5);
36        numberSharesField = new JTextField(4);
37        priceField = new JTextField(6);
38        passwordField = new JPasswordField(8);
39        previewArea = new JTextArea(14,50);

40        //INSTANTIATE COMBO BOX OBJECT
41        termChoice = new JComboBox();

42        //INSTANTIATE RADIO BUTTON GROUP AND OBJECTS
43        ButtonGroup transactionGroup = new ButtonGroup();
44        buy = new JRadioButton("Buy",false);
45        sell = new JRadioButton("Sell",true);
46        transactionGroup.add(buy);
47        transactionGroup.add(sell);

48        //DEFINE TEXT AREA FONT AND COLOR
49        Font f = new Font("Helvetica",Font.BOLD + Font.ITALIC,12);
50        previewArea.setFont(f);
51        previewArea.setForeground(Color.blue);

52        //DEFINE PANELS
53        JPanel panel1 = new JPanel();
54        JPanel panel2 = new JPanel();
55        JPanel panel3 = new JPanel();
56        JPanel panel4 = new JPanel();
57        JPanel panel5 = new JPanel();

58        //SET PANEL LAYOUT MANAGERS
59        panel1.setLayout(new FlowLayout(FlowLayout.LEFT));
```

```
60    panel2.setLayout(new FlowLayout(FlowLayout.LEFT));
61    panel3.setLayout(new FlowLayout(FlowLayout.LEFT));
62    panel4.setLayout(new FlowLayout(FlowLayout.LEFT));
63    panel5.setLayout(new FlowLayout(FlowLayout.LEFT));

64    //DEFINE JLabel OBJECTS
65    JLabel acctNumLabel = new JLabel("Account Number",JLabel.RIGHT);
66    JLabel passwordLabel = new JLabel("Password",JLabel.RIGHT);
67    JLabel stockLabel = new JLabel("Stock Symbol",JLabel.RIGHT);
68    JLabel numLabel = new JLabel("Number of Shares",JLabel.RIGHT);
69    JLabel priceLabel = new JLabel("Price/share  $",JLabel.RIGHT);
70    JLabel termLabel = new JLabel("Term",JLabel.RIGHT);
71    JLabel previewLabel = new JLabel("Order Preview",JLabel.RIGHT);

72    //ADD ITEMS TO CHOICE BOX
73    termChoice.addItem("Good For a Day");
74    termChoice.addItem("Good Until Cancelled");

75    //ADD COMPONENTS TO panel1
76    panel1.add(acctNumLabel);
77    panel1.add(accountNumberField);
78    panel1.add(passwordLabel);
79    panel1.add(passwordField);

80    //ADD COMPONENTS TO panel2
81    panel2.add(stockLabel);
82    panel2.add(stockSymbolField);
83    panel2.add(numLabel);
84    panel2.add(numberSharesField);
85    panel2.add(priceLabel);
86    panel2.add(priceField);

87    //ADD COMPONENTS TO panel3
88    panel3.add(buy);
89    panel3.add(sell);
90    panel3.add(termLabel);
91    panel3.add(termChoice);

92    //ADD COMPONENTS TO panel4
93    panel4.add(previewLabel);
94    panel4.add(previewArea);

95    //ADD COMPONENTS TO panel5
96    panel5.add(previewButton);
97    panel5.add(cancelButton);
98    panel5.add(orderButton);

99    //ADD PANELS TO CONTAINER
100   container.add(panel1);
101   container.add(panel2);
102   container.add(panel3);
```

```java
103          container.add(panel4);
104          container.add(panel5);

105          //REGISTER LISTENERS
106          previewButton.addActionListener(new ButtonHandler());
107          orderButton.addActionListener(new ButtonHandler());
108          cancelButton.addActionListener(new ButtonHandler());
109      }//END init()

110      //BUTTON HANDLER CLASS
111      private class ButtonHandler implements ActionListener
112      {
113        //PROCESS JButton EVENT
114        public void actionPerformed(ActionEvent e)
115        {
116          //PREVIEW ORDER?
117          if(e.getSource() == previewButton)
118          {
119            previewArea.setText("ORDER PREVIEW\n");

120            //BUY OR SELL?
121            if (buy.isSelected())
122              previewArea.append("\nThis is a BUY order");
123            else
124              previewArea.append("This is a SELL order");

125            //DISPLAY ORDER INFO
126            previewArea.append("\nStock symbol: "
                                    + stockSymbolField.getText());
127            previewArea.append("\nNumber of shares: "
                                    + numberSharesField.getText());
128            previewArea.append("\nPrice per share: $"
                                    + priceField.getText());
129            previewArea.append("\nStandard Commision: $14.95");

130            //GET PRICE AND NUMBER OF SHARES AND CONVERT TO DOUBLE
131            Double price = new Double(priceField.getText().trim());
132            double p = price.doubleValue();
133            Double shares = new
                 Double(numberSharesField.getText().trim());
134            double s = shares.doubleValue();

135            //CALCULATE AND DISPLAY TOTAL
136            double total = p*s + 14.95;
137            previewArea.append("\nTotal Price: $"
                                    + String.valueOf(total));

139            previewArea.append("\nOrder " +
                 termChoice.getSelectedItem());
140            previewArea.append("\n\nClick PLACE ORDER to place an order"
                                    + " or\nCLEAR to clear all fields");
141          }//END IF PREVIEW
```

```
142          //CANCEL ORDER?
143          if(e.getSource() == cancelButton)
144          {
145            accountNumberField.setText("");
146            stockSymbolField.setText("");
147            numberSharesField.setText("");
148            priceField.setText("");
149            passwordField.setText("");
150            previewArea.setText("");
151          }//END IF CANCEL

             //PLACE ORDER?
152          if(e.getSource() == orderButton)
153          {
154            previewArea.setText("ORDER PLACED");
155          }//END IF ORDER
156        }//END actionPerformed()
157      }//END ButtonHandler CLASS
158    }//END APPLET
```

As you can see, most of the GUI code resides in the *init()* method, which is called when the applet is initially started. In an application GUI, this code would be placed within the frame subclass constructor. Of course, any component object that must be accessed outside the *init()* method must be defined as a member of the applet subclass. This is why all the component objects, except the labels, are defined as private class members. These objects must be visible in the *actionPerformed()* method. You should be able to understand most of the code at this point. Here are a few features of which you might want to take note:

- Applets support panels just as frames do in applications.
- The text area font is set in lines 48–51.
- The number of shares and price per share are converted to a primitive double data type in lines 130–134 so that they can be used to calculate the total order price in line 136.
- The resulting price is converted to a string in line 137 using the *valueOf()* method for display within the text area.
- All the text fields and the text area are set with a blank string in lines 143 through 150 if the user clicks the *CLEAR* button.

CHAPTER SUMMARY

In this chapter you learned about applets and graphics. You found that an applet does not require a *main()* method, but does require an HTML file to execute. Upon execution, the applet's *init()* method is called automatically, just like an application class calls its constructor automatically when an object is defined for it. Therefore, to build an applet GUI, the GUI is created in the applet *init()* method.

Standard graphical components from the *Graphics* class can be "painted" within an applet or application. The graphical methods must be called with a *Graphics* class object within the *paint()* method. The *paint()* method is called automatically, after *init()* for an applet, but must be called using *repaint()* in an application. You can paint rectangles, ovals, arcs, lines, and polygons of just about any color using the standard *Graphics* methods.

Event-driven applications can be easily converted to applets by placing the application constructor code within the applet *init()* method, and eliminating the window listener registration and associated window handler code that a frame requires for closing the window.

QUESTIONS AND PROBLEMS

Questions

1. True or false: An applet contains a constructor just like an application.

2. True or false: A window listener and associated window handler class must be coded in an applet to provide for window closing just as in an application.

3. When constructing the GUI for an applet, the GUI is created within the _____ method just as it is created within the constructor in an application.

4. What tags are used within an HTML file to execute an applet?

5. The Java file that must be specified to execute an applet within an HTML file is the _____ file.

6. True or false: In an applet, the *paint()* method is called automatically after the *init()* method.

7. What applet method must be used to begin any tasks, such as animation, when an HTML page containing the applet is revisited within a Web browser?

8. What method is called within an applet to display a message at the bottom of the applet window?

9. What parameter must always be present in the *paint()* method?

10. What RGB value would create a color of white?

11. Write a line of code to draw a circle that is 100 pixels in diameter at coordinate (200,300) using a graphics object called *g*.

12. Write a line of code to paint a filled arc at coordinate (100,300) that would appear as a half-moon of an arbitrary size using a *Graphics* object called *g*.

13. Write a line of code to draw a line from the upper left corner of an applet window to the lower right corner of the window. Assume that your screen resolution is 800 × 600 pixels.

14. How must you specify the vertices of a polygon?

15. True or false: Graphics cannot be used in applications.

16. True or false: Panels and layout managers can be used within an applet just as in an application.

17. True or false: It would be relatively easy to convert an event-driven application to an applet.

Problems

All Challenging

1. Design and build a *BankingTransaction* applet that will process a banking transaction. The applet is to have the following components and capabilities, at a minimum:

   - User instruction label(s)
   - Text fields and associated labels for the user's personal identification number (PIN), and amount deposited or withdrawn

- Radio buttons to select between a checking or savings account transaction
- Button to process the transaction
- Logic to calculate a new balance, assuming the initial balance was $1000.00
- A text area to display the new balance and a "Thank you" message, or a polite message, requesting the user enter a different amount if he/she attempts to withdraw more than $300.00

(*Note: This problem is an extension of Problem 3 in Chapter 12.*)

2. Design and build a *LoanApplication* applet. The applet is to have the following components and capabilities, at a minimum:

- Text fields and associated labels that will allow the user to enter his/her name, address, telephone number, and social security number
- Text fields and associated labels that will allow the user to enter the amount of the loan and term for which he/she is applying
- Text field and associated label for annual income
- Radio buttons for married/single status
- Text area to display the loan information
- Menu to set the text area font type, style, and size
- A store/calculate button that will display the loan applicant information as well as monthly payment based on an interest rate of 10% in a text area and "APPROVED" or "NOT APPROVED" based on the following:

  - For loan amounts <= $1,000, annual income must be at least $10,000.
  - For loan amounts between $1,000 and $10,000, annual income must be at least $25,000.
  - For loan amounts between $10,000 and $25,000, annual income must be at least $50,000.
  - We do not make loans above $25,000.

(*Note: This problem is an extension of Problem 4 in Chapter 12.*)

3. Design and build a *StockTransaction* applet. The applet is to have the following components and capabilities, at a minimum:

- Text fields and associated labels for account number, number of shares to buy/sell, stock "ticker" symbol, and trading password
- Radio button group for type of transaction: buy or sell
- Radio button group for price: market or limit order (A market order is an order to buy or sell at the current market price. A limit order becomes a market order when the stock price reaches the price you specify in an associated text field.)
- Combo box for items of "good for a day" or "good until canceled"
- Buttons to preview order or cancel order. If preview order is clicked, a text area must display the type of transaction, quantity of shares, stock symbol, and total price which includes a $14.95 commission. If the order is a "buy" order, the commission is added to the total price of the order. If the order is a "sell" order, the commission is subtracted

from the gross proceeds realized from the sale. For a market order, assume the price is $25.00 per share. For a limit order, the price per share is the amount entered by the user in the text field associated with the limit order radio button.

- Do not accept an order if either the account number or trading password is not entered.

4. Combine the classes developed in Problems 1, 2, and 3 to build a *Financial* e-commerce Web site that will allow users to select an online banking transaction, stock transaction, or apply for a consumer loan at different times, depending on their needs.

14

File I/O and Exception Handling

OBJECTIVES

When you are finished with this chapter, you should have a good understanding of the following:

- The difference between a binary file and a text file
- How to use the Java file stream classes to create, or open, disk files
- How to use Java classes to read and write both binary and text files
- The concept of streams and the role they play in communicating with I/O devices

- How to handle I/O errors, which generate exceptions in Java
- The use of `try` and `catch` in your program to handle exceptions
- How to provide for exception handling when reading and writing files

Introduction

In data processing applications, a ***file*** is a collection of related ***records***. Each record is made up of related ***fields*** that contain the file information. We implement a record in Java using the class, whose `private` members represent the fields of the record. For example, a student record might consist of a student name field, a student number field, a GPA field, and so on. All of these fields encapsulated together for a given student form a record. Several student records stored together on a disk form a file. In a typical college computer center you might find student files, faculty files, staff files, inventory files, transcript files, and so on. Several related files form a ***database***. For example, a college employee database might consist of faculty files, staff files, and administrator files.

All the data types and structures you have learned about so far have provided a means of organizing and storing data in primary memory. However, recall that primary memory is relatively small and, more importantly, volatile. In other words, when the system is turned off or power is lost for any reason, all information stored in primary memory goes to "bit heaven." The obvious solution to this problem is to store any long-term data in secondary memory because secondary memory is nonvolatile. Furthermore, secondary memory provides a means of storing data between program runs. A file is a secondary memory storage structure.

In this chapter, you will learn how to create and manipulate your own disk files in Java. There are three basic operations that you will need to perform when working with disk files:

- Open the file for input or output.
- Process the file, by reading from or writing to the file.
- Close the file.

In addition, since working with files requires that you communicate with a peripheral device, there is always the possibility that something unexpected could happen such as a disk could be write-protected during a write operation, a disk file might not exist during a read operation, and so on. To protect your program from terminating prematurely during file operations, you must learn how to handle such events. This, together with the aforementioned file operations, forms the topics of this chapter.

14.1   Fundamental Concepts and Ideas

 A *file* is a data structure that consists of a sequence of components.

A file is a *sequence* of components. This means that the data elements, called **components**, are arranged within the file sequentially, or serially, from the first component to the last component. As a result, when accessing files, the file components must be accessed in a sequential manner from one component to the next. A common analogy for a file is an audiocassette tape. Think of the songs on the tape as the file components. How are they stored on the tape? You're right, sequentially from the first song to the last. How must you access a given song? Right again, by sequencing forward or backward through the tape until the desired song is found. Thus, like a cassette tape, a file is a sequential, or serial, storage medium. This makes file access relatively slow as compared to other random-access storage mediums, like primary memory.

You might be tempted to think of a file as a one-dimensional array, but there are some important differences. First, files provide a means for you to store information within a program run, as you do with arrays. But, unlike arrays, files also allow you to store information between program runs. Second, many compilers require you to access the file components in sequence, starting with the first file component. You cannot jump into the middle of a file as you can an array to access a given component. However, Java does provide a means of semi-random direct access using *seek* operations.

Third, files are not declared with a specific dimension as are arrays. Once you create a file, its size is theoretically unlimited. Of course, the file size is actually limited by the amount of storage space available in secondary memory, such as a disk.

Text versus Binary Files

There are two general types of files you need to learn about: *text* files and **binary** files. A text, or character-based, file stores information using ASCII/Unicode character representations. As you learned in Chapter 3, the Unicode system assigns a unique 16-bit code to the digits 0 through 9, each alphabetic character, and symbols like the decimal point, comma, semicolon, dollar sign, etc. The ASCII system assigns an 8-bit character code to the English character set. For these characters, the Unicode code is simply the ASCII code appended with eight leading zeros. For example, the Unicode code for the character 'A' is 0000 0000 0100 0001, while the ASCII code for the character 'A' is 0100 0001. Notice that the Unicode code simply appends 8 leading 0s to the ASCII code to get 16 bits. This is consistent for all the characters in the English character set. Text files usually store the ASCII character codes so that any given text file can be easily read and displayed using any word processing program or text editor, like your Java IDE editor. So, using the Unicode table provided in Appendix F, the string "Price $3.14" would be stored in a text file as the sequence of codes shown in Table 14-1.

The Unicode table in Appendix F provides decimal character codes for human consumption and convenience. The 8-bit ASCII equivalent of these codes is what is actually used by the machine and stored in the file, as shown in Table 14-1. However, storing numeric data as a sequence of characters presents a problem when the program must perform arithmetic operations on the data. The character-based numeric data must be converted to its equivalent internal binary machine representation before it can be added, subtracted, multiplied or divided. Then it must be converted back to the ASCII character representation prior to being stored in a text file. To eliminate these conversions when reading and writing files, you can use a binary file. A binary file stores numerical values using the internal numeric binary format specified by the language in use, in our case a 32-bit or 64-bit format specified by the Institute of Electrical and Electronics

TABLE 14-1   Text File Codes for the Value 3.14

Character	Unicode Decimal	Unicode Binary	ASCII Binary
'P'	80	00000000 01010000	01010000
'r'	114	00000000 01110010	01110010
'i'	105	00000000 01101001	01101001
'c'	99	00000000 01100011	01100011
'e'	101	00000000 01100101	01100101
SPC (blank)	32	00000000 00100000	00100000
'$'	36	00000000 00100100	00100100
'3'	51	00000000 00110011	00110011
'.'	46	00000000 00101110	00101110
'1'	49	00000000 00110001	00110001
'4'	52	00000000 00110100	00110100

Engineers (IEEE) standard #754-1985. We will not bore you by discussing this complicated standard. Just keep in mind that when using this format, a Java program can read a binary file to get numeric data, manipulate the data arithmetically, and write the data to a binary file without any intermediate conversions. Of course, you cannot read and display a binary file using a word processing program or text editor like you can a text file.

In this chapter, you will learn how to read and write both binary and text files in Java.

File Streams

In Java, all I/O, including file I/O, is based on the concept of *streams*.

 A *stream* provides a connection between your program and the outside world.

In general, a file stream provides a channel for the flow of data from some source to some destination. Think about what happens when you are typing characters on the keyboard when prompted by a program. You can think of the characters as flowing, or streaming, from the keyboard into the program. Likewise, when your program generates a character display, you can easily visualize the characters streaming from the program to the display monitor. Java provides standard streams for the keyboard and monitor. However, you must create separate streams to read and write disk files.

All program I/O is supported by predefined classes in Java that operate on files. The familiar *System* class that you have been using in your programs for console output is a class included in Java that provides for standard input and output. When you called the *print()* or *println()* methods to display something, you called either method using the code *System.out*. Here, *System* references the *System* class in package *java.lang*, and *out* specifies the standard output stream. This "standard" output stream is connected, by default, to the system monitor. Likewise, you can use the *System* class for keyboard input, although it is awkward to do so. In this case, you would call a standard keyboard input method, such as *read()*, using the code *System.in.read()*. Again, *System* references the standard *System* class in package *java.lang*, and *in* specifies the standard input stream, which is connected, by default, to the system keyboard. Thus, we say that standard input is read from the *System.in* stream, and standard output is written to the *System.out* stream. Of course, the only files that you can access conveniently with *System.in* and *System.out* are the keyboard and monitor that are connected to these streams. You will also use predefined classes to access binary and text files in Java. Each type of file (binary or text) requires a different set of classes, as shown in Table 14-2 and Table 14-3 . All of these classes are part of the *java.io* package which must be imported into your program when working with files.

The first two classes in each table are used to open a file by creating input and output file streams. The remaining classes in each table are used to actually read from and write to the file. Be aware that there are a wealth of file stream classes provided by the *java.io* package to support other types of file access, such as semi-random access. Check your IDE help or Java reference material for these additional classes since they will not be covered in this text.

TABLE 14-2   Binary File Stream Classes

Class	Purpose
FileInputStream	To open a binary input stream and connect it to a physical disk file
FileOutputStream	To open a binary output stream and connect it to a physical disk file
DataInputStream	To read binary data from a stream
DataOutputStream	To write binary data to a stream

TABLE 14-3   Text File Stream Classes

Class	Purpose
FileReader	To open a character input stream and connect it to a physical disk file
FileWriter	To open a character output stream and connect it to a physical disk file
BufferedReader	To provide buffering and to read data from an input stream
BufferedWriter	To provide output buffering
PrintWriter	To write character data to an output stream

QUICK CHECK

  1. True or false: A file is a random-access data structure.
  2. What is the Unicode code for the character 'c' if the ASCII code is 01100011?
  3. What is the problem with using text files to store numeric data?
  4. A connection where data can flow between your Java program and the outside world is called a(n) _____.
  5. Standard output in Java is written to the _____ file stream.
  6. What class is used to create an input binary file stream and connect it to a disk file?
  7. What class is used to write data to a binary file?
  8. What class is used to create an output character file stream and connect it to a disk file?
  9. What class is used to write data to a text file?
 10. What standard Java package must be imported to use the file classes?

14.2   Opening Binary Files

The first thing that must be done to process a file is to open it. In Java, you open a file by creating a file stream object. A unique file stream object is required for each file that your program uses. If your program both reads and writes a file, you must create both an input and output stream object. To create a binary file stream, you must do two things:

  1. Using the *FileInputStream* or *FileOutputStream* class, create a file stream and *connect* it to a physical disk file to *open* the file.
  2. Define a file stream object for the *DataInputStream* or *DataOutputStream* class.

The *FileInputStream* and *FileOutputStream* classes contain a constructor to create a file stream and connect it to a physical disk file, as illustrated in Figure 14-1. The

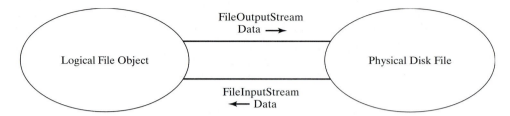

FIGURE 14-1   The *FileOutputStream* and *FileInputStream* classes are used to create file streams that connect a logical program object to a physical binary disk file.

constructor requires a string argument which is the name of the disk file to be read or written. For example, the statement

```
FileOutputStream out = new FileOutputStream("student.dat");
```

will create an output file stream called *out* and connect it to the *student.dat* disk file, while the statement

```
FileInputStream in = new FileInputStream(myFile);
```

will create an input file stream called *in* and connect it to the disk file represented by the string object *myFile*. Of course, this assumes that *myFile* has been previously defined as a string object and contains a valid file name.

The *DataInputStream* and *DataOutputStream* classes contain methods that allow you to read and write a binary file. As a result, an object must be created for one of these classes in order to call the methods required to read or write the file. The *DataInputStream* constructor requires a *FileInputStream* object, while the *DataOutputStream* constructor requires a *FileOutputStream* object. Thus, the statements

```
FileOutputStream out = new FileOutputStream("student.dat");
DataOutputStream outFile = new DataOutputStream(out);
```

create an object called *outFile* and prepare it to write data to the *out* file stream connected to the *student.dat* disk file. Likewise the statements

```
FileInputStream in = new FileInputStream(myFile);
DataInputStream inFile = new DataInputStream(in);
```

create an object called *inFile* and prepare it to read data from the *in* file stream connected to the disk file name contained in the *myFile* string object. Notice that, in each of the above cases, a *FileStream* object is provided to the *DataStream* constructor. We can streamline the coding by actually creating the *FileStream* object within the *DataStream* constructor argument, as follows:

```
DataOutputStream outFile =
              new DataOutputStream(new FileOutputStream("student.dat"));

DataInputStream inFile = new DataInputStream(new FileInputStream(myFile));
```

This saves a line of code and is referred to as the **chaining**, or **wrapping**, of objects. Wrapping of objects simply means that the constructor of one class calls the constructor of another class as its argument to create an object. Here, the physical disk file name is supplied to the *FileStream* constructor, which supplies an object for the *DataStream* constructor, which is used to create an object that can be manipulated within a program. Thus, a communication path is established between the *logical* program object and the *physical* disk file (see Figure 14-1). We say that this process **opens** a file for processing.

Let's incorporate the foregoing file stream definitions into methods for opening binary input or output files. We will name these methods *openInputFile()* and *openOutputFile()*, respectively. Here is the code:

```
//CREATE AN OUTPUT STREAM AND CONNECT IT TO A PHYSICAL DISK FILE
public void openOutputFile(String s)
{
   DataOutputStream outFile =
                         new DataOutputStream(new FileOutputStream(s));
}//END openOutputFile()


//CREATE AN INPUT STREAM AND CONNECT IT TO A PHYSICAL DISK FILE
public void openInputFile(String s)
{
   DataInputStream inFile = new DataInputStream(new FileInputStream(s));
}//END openInputFile()
```

Here, we have simply placed our *inFile* and *outFile* object definitions inside two methods so that the files can be easily opened by calling a method. Each method receives a string object, *s*, which is the disk file to be opened. But, what if the file, *s*, doesn't exist for whatever reason? In the case of an input file, a nonexistent file would cause an **exception**, or error, to be generated, and might result in a program crash if the exception was not *caught* by the program. Here is where Java forces you to protect yourself from such errors. In fact, neither of the above methods will compile. An error message such as "*unreported exception … must be caught or declared to be thrown*" would be generated by the Java compiler. So we must add some error protection to our file opening methods. Such protection is called **exception handling**, and is the topic of the next section.

Example 14-1

Write statements to open the following binary files:

a. A file called *sample.dat* that will be read using an object called *read*

b. A file whose name is stored in a string named *fileName* that will be written using an object called *write*

Solution

```
a. DataInputStream read =
        new DataInputStream(new FileInputStream("sample.dat"));
b. DataOutputStream write =
        new DataOutputStream(new FileOutputStream(fileName));
```

QUICK CHECK

1. What happens when a disk file is opened?
2. Write a statement to open a binary disk file for output by creating an object called *myFile*. Assume that the file name is *"myFile.dat"*. Use object wrapping to form a single statement that will open the file.
3. Write a statement to open a binary disk file for input by creating an object called *yourFile*. Assume that the file name is stored in a string called *yourFileName*. Use object wrapping to form a single statement that will open the file.

14.3   Exception Handling

We have put off a discussion of exception handling long enough. Now Java is really forcing us to provide it to protect our programs from crashing when working with files. Exception handling has to do with error handling. To handle an error, the error condition must first be detected, and then control must be transferred from the point where the error occurred, to an error handling routine that can deal with error. What types of errors might you want to deal with? Well, user input is always a possible source of error. Users do not always enter data the way the program expects to see it. Another general source of error is when you exceed the storage capacity of things such as primary memory or disk space. However, one of the most common sources of error is related to I/O devices. I/O errors occur when an I/O device presents the program with an unexpected condition. A printer could be off-line or run out of paper, a disk could be write-protected during a write operation, or a disk file might not exist during a read operation, and so on.

When an error occurs at run time, a Java method can ***throw*** an exception. When an exception is thrown, Java has detected an error condition. In order to prevent program failure, an exception that is thrown must be ***caught***. When an exception is caught, control is transferred to a routine that can deal with the error. This throwing and catching of exceptions is referred to as ***exception handling***. If a thrown exception is not caught, an error message is displayed and the program might terminate.

PROGRAMMING NOTE

An exception that is not caught might cause abnormal termination of a program. The one "exception" to this rule is a Java applet or application employing a GUI. If a thrown exception is not caught in a GUI program, an error message is generated but the program is not terminated and control returns to normal event processing. In a non-GUI application, an exception that is not caught usually results in a program crash.

To throw and catch exceptions, you must include statements that have the potential of throwing an exception within a `try` statement block. A `try` block consists of a framed block of code appearing after the keyword `try`. The `try` block is followed immediately with one or more `catch` blocks of code. A `catch` statement block consists of a framed block of code appearing after the keyword `catch`. Any code required to handle the exception(s) is contained within the `catch` block(s). Thus, the `catch` blocks are referred to as **exception handlers**. The `catch` blocks can be followed by an optional `finally` statement block. A `finally` block is a framed block of code appearing after the keyword `finally`. A `finally` block always executes, whether or not an exception is thrown within the `try` block or handled within a `catch` block. Here's the general format for the `try`/`catch`/`finally` sequence:

```
try
{
    //STATEMENTS THAT MIGHT THROW EXCEPTIONS
}

catch (ExceptionClass exceptionObject)
{
    //STATEMENTS TO HANDLE EXCEPTIONS THROWN BY try BLOCK
}

finally
{
    //STATEMENTS THAT WILL EXECUTE WHETHER OR NOT EXCEPTION IS
    //THROWN OR CAUGHT
}
```

You place statements that might throw exceptions within the `try` block. Then you code one or more `catch` blocks that contain statements required to handle any exceptions thrown by the `try` block. Each `catch` block specifies the type of exception that it will catch. You cannot have a `try` block without a corresponding `catch` block, unless you have a `finally` block. When an exception is thrown within the `try` block, Java searches for a `catch` block that will handle that type of exception. In the search, Java tries to match the type of exception thrown with the exception parameter listed in one of the `catch` blocks. When the correct exception parameter is found, control is transferred to the respective `catch` block and its code is executed. A compiler error results if a match is not found, unless you have a `finally` block of code. A `finally` block is always executed, regardless of whether an exception is thrown or not.

As a practical example, let's revise the foregoing *openInputFile()* method code to include exception handling. One of the most common errors associated with opening an input file is a *file-not-found* error. We can use a `try` block when opening the file and a corresponding `catch` block to catch a file-not-found exception as follows:

```
//CREATE AN INPUT STREAM AND CONNECT IT TO A PHYSICAL DISK FILE
public void openInputFile(String s)
{
    //TRY TO OPEN FILE BY CONNECTING INPUT STREAM TO A DISK FILE
    try
```

```
  {
     DataInputStream inFile = new DataInputStream(new FileInputStream(s));
     textArea.setText("FILE OPEN");
  }//END try()


  //CATCH EXCEPTION IF FILE CANNOT BE OPENED
  catch(IOException io)
  {
     textArea.setText("\n\nFILE NOT FOUND ERROR\n" + io.toString());
  }//END catch()
}//END openInputFile()
```

When the file to be opened cannot be found for whatever reason, the *FileInputStream()* constructor throws an *IOException* object. This is a predefined exception, called a ***checked*** exception, in Java. To prevent the program from terminating, we have placed the statement that creates our *inFile* object within a `try` block. Then, if the file is not found, the *FileInputStream()* constructor throws an *IOException* object. Notice that the `catch` block of code has an *IOException* object as its parameter. Since the thrown object matches this exception parameter, the object is caught and control passes to the `catch` block. The caught object takes on the name *io* within the `catch` block. Within the `catch` block, an error message is displayed within a text area of the program GUI. In addition, notice that the *io* object is used to call the *toString()* method. The thrown object carries with it information about the error that can be converted to a string by using it to call the *toString()* method. So, the code `io.toString()` concatenates more information about the exception to the error message already being displayed. At this point, control is passed back to the GUI. The user has been notified that a file-not-found error has occurred and can take corrective action before attempting to open the file again.

Now, what happens if an error does not occur and an exception is not thrown? Well, the statement that will cause an exception to be thrown is the first statement within the `try` block that defines our *inFile* object. If this generates an exception, control is passed to the `catch` block immediately, without executing the remaining statements within the `try` block. However, if opening the file does not generate an exception, the remaining statements within the `try` block are executed and the `catch` block is skipped. If an exception is not generated, the foregoing `try` block simply displays a "FILE OPEN" message in the GUI text area.

 PROGRAMMING NOTE

Once an exception is thrown from within a `try` block, control is passed immediately out of the `try` block without executing the remaining statements in the `try` block. Control *never* returns to the `try` block, whether the exception is caught or not.

Next, let's expand our *openOutputFile()* method to include exception handling. Here's the expanded code:

```
//CREATE AN OUTPUT STREAM AND CONNECT IT TO A PHYSICAL DISK FILE
public void openOutputFile(String s)
{
   //TRY TO OPEN FILE BY CONNECTING OUTPUT STREAM TO A DISK FILE
   try
   {
     DataOutputStream outFile =
                          new DataOutputStream(new FileOutputStream(s));
     textArea.setText("FILE OPEN");
   }//END try()

   //CATCH EXCEPTION IF FILE CANNOT BE OPENED
   catch(IOException io)
   {
     textArea.append("\n\nFILE NOT FOUND ERROR\n"+ io.toString() );
   }//END catch() IOException
 }//END openOutputFile
```

Here again, we have included our file opening statement within a `try` block. A `catch` block is again coded to catch an *IOException* object and notify the user if there is any problem opening the file. We will be using exception handling throughout our discussion of files because errors often occur when working with files. You should be aware, however, that Java includes a wealth of checked exceptions that you can use to prevent programs from terminating prematurely, some of which are listed in Table 14-4. Check your IDE help for more information on these and other checked exceptions.

Notice from Table 14-4 that there is a *FileNotFoundException* that we could have used within our file open methods. The *FileNotFoundException* class is a subclass of the *IOException* class. The *FileInputStream* class constructor throws a *FileNotFoundException*

TABLE 14-4   Checked Exceptions Provided by Java

Exception	Description
ArithmeticException	Thrown when an arithmetic error has occurred, such as division by zero
ArrayIndexOutOfBoundsException	Thrown when an array has been accessed with an index which is negative or greater than or equal to the size of the array
Exception	Thrown for any checked exception
EOFException	Thrown when the end of a file has been reached
FileNotFoundException	Thrown when a file cannot be found
InterruptedIOException	Thrown when an I/O operation has been interrupted
IOException	Thrown when an I/O error has occurred
NullPointerException	Thrown when a program tries to use `null` when an object is required. Often occurs when you try to use an object that has not been instantiated.
NumberFormatException	Thrown when a program tries to convert a string to a numeric data type when the string doesn't have the correct format.
StringIndexOutOfBoundsException	Thrown by *String* class methods when a string has been accessed with an index which is negative or greater than or equal to the size of the string

exception directly when a problem is encountered opening an input file. We could have caught this exception in place of the *IOException* and accomplished the same goal. However, the *FileOutputStream* class constructor throws an *IOException* directly, and a *FileNotFoundException* indirectly. This is because the *IOException* class is a superclass to the *FileNotFoundException* class. As a result, to catch a *FileNotFoundException* we must also catch an *IOException*. This would require two catch blocks in our *openOutputFile()* method. It is just simpler to catch an *IOException*, knowing it had to be the result of a file not being found for whatever reason.

PROGRAMMING NOTE

Through inheritance, it is possible that several types of exceptions will be thrown for the same error condition. For instance, a file-not-found error will cause a *FileNotFoundException* as well as an *IOException* to be thrown when opening a file for output, since the *FileNotFoundException* class is a subclass of the *IOException* class. If a `catch` block is coded to catch the subclass exception, it must also be coded before the superclass exception `catch` block. If it is not, the subclass `catch` block will be unreachable and result in a compiler error. Thus, a *FileNotFoundException* `catch` block must be coded before an *IOException* `catch` block.

There is one "catch-all" exception called *Exception*. The *Exception* class is the superclass of all exception classes. Thus, the following `catch` block will catch any checked exception:

```
catch(Exception e)
{
    // STATEMENTS TO HANDLE ANY CHECKED EXCEPTION
}
```

Of course, if you catch this exception, you might not know what type of exception has occurred. Therefore, you should always catch one of the more specific subclass exceptions if possible. If you catch this exception in addition to any of its subclass exceptions, you must catch it after all `catch` blocks that catch the subclass exceptions, or a syntax error will occur.

QUICK CHECK

1. The process of throwing and catching exceptions is known as _____.
2. Why is exception handling required when opening files?
3. A predefined exception in Java is referred to as a(n) _____ exception.
4. True or false: An exception that is not caught in a non-GUI program will cause the program to terminate prematurely.
5. True or false: An exception that is not caught in a GUI program will cause the program to terminate prematurely.
6. To handle a checked exception, you must place any statements that have the potential of generating an exception within a(n) _____ block.

7. True or false: You can have more than one `catch` block for a given `try` block.
8. What Java exception is thrown for a divide-by-zero exception?
9. True or false: A `finally` block only executes when an exception is thrown and no `catch` block is found for the exception.
10. True or false: A subclass exception handler must always be coded before its superclass exception handler.

14.4   Reading and Writing Binary Files

We have a lot to talk about here, so make yourself comfortable. In order to effectively demonstrate file operations, we will wrap our file handling within two GUI classes, one called *WriteStudentFile* that will write student records to a file, and another called *ReadStudentFile* that will read student records from a sequential file. Before we begin, take a look at Figures 14-2 and 14-3. These figures show the GUIs created by the two classes just mentioned. Notice that both classes generate a GUI that requires the user to enter the file name and click an *Open File* button.

To create a file, the user will use the *WriteStudentFile* class and enter the student name, student number, and gpa in the appropriate text fields, and then click the *Store*

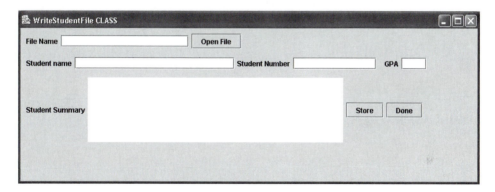

FIGURE 14-2   The GUI created by the *WriteStudentFile* class.

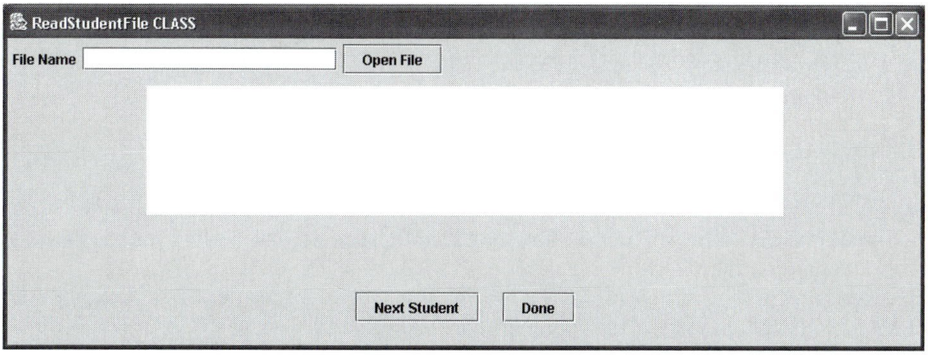

FIGURE 14-3   The GUI created by the *ReadStudentFile* class.

button shown in Figure 14-2. When the *Store* button is clicked, the student data will be written to the file. In addition, the student data will be displayed in the text area and the text fields will be blanked to allow another student record entry. The user can enter as many student records as desired, entering the data in the text fields, and clicking the *Store* button for each entry. When there are no more records to enter, the user must click the *Done* button. This event **closes** the file and terminates the program. You will learn shortly that *all* files should be explicitly closed after they have been processed.

To read a file, the user will use the *ReadStudentFile* class. Again, the user must enter the file name to read and click the *Open File* button. Once the file is open, the user simply clicks the *Next Student* button, which displays each student record, one at a time, within the text area. The program will terminate when the end of the file is reached or the *Done* button is clicked.

Now, you already have a pretty good idea of how to build the GUIs shown in Figures 14-2 and 14-3, so, let's concentrate on the file stuff. First the files must be opened when a file name is entered by the user and the *Open File* button is clicked. We have used the two open methods discussed in the last section to accomplish this task within each respective file class. Here's the method code we developed earlier:

```java
//CREATE AN OUTPUT STREAM AND CONNECT IT TO A PHYSICAL DISK FILE
public void openOutputFile(String s)
{
    //TRY TO OPEN FILE BY CONNECTING OUTPUT STREAM TO A DISK FILE
    try
    {
        DataOutputStream outFile =
                            new DataOutputStream(new FileOutputStream(s));
        studentArea.setText("FILE OPEN, BEGIN STORING RECORDS");
    }//END try()

    //CATCH EXCEPTION IF FILE CANNOT BE OPENED
    catch(IOException io)
    {
        studentArea.append("\n\nFILE NOT FOUND ERROR\n" + io.toString() );
    }//END catch() IOException
}//END openOutputFile

//CREATE AN INPUT STREAM AND CONNECT IT TO A PHYSICAL DISK FILE
public void openInputFile(String s)
{
    //TRY TO OPEN FILE BY CONNECTING INPUT STREAM TO A DISK FILE
    try
    {
        DataInputStream inFile = new DataInputStream(new FileInputStream(s));
        studentArea.setText("FILE OPEN, PRESS Next Student BUTTON");
    }//END try()
    //CATCH EXCEPTION IF FILE CANNOT BE OPENED
    catch(IOException io)
    {
```

```
      studentArea.setText("\n\nFILE NOT FOUND ERROR\n" + io.toString());
   }//END catch()
 }//END openInputFile()
```

As you might suspect, each method is called when an event is generated by the user clicking the *Open File* button within its respective GUI. There is nothing new here.

When a file is open for output via the *FileOutputStream* class, its contents are destroyed and will be replaced by any subsequent data written to the file.

Next, we must develop methods to write student records to a file and read student records from a file. We have chosen to call these methods *writeStudentRecord()* and *readStudentRecord()*, respectively. Of course, the *writeStudentRecord()* method will appear in the *WriteStudentFile* class, and the *readStudentRecord()* method will appear in the *ReadStudentFile* class. Let's examine the *writeStudentRecord()* method first. Here's its code:

```
//METHOD TO WRITE A STUDENT RECORD TO AN OPENED DISK FILE
public void writeStudentRecord()
{
  //TRY TO WRITE STUDENT RECORD TO FILE
  try
  {
    outFile.writeUTF(nameField.getText());
    outFile.writeUTF(numberField.getText());
    outFile.writeDouble(
                   (new Double(gpaField.getText().trim())).doubleValue());
  }//END try() TO WRITE RECORD

  //CATCH NUMBER FORMAT EXCEPTION FOR GPA FIELD
  catch (NumberFormatException nfe)
  {
    studentArea.append("\n\nWRITE FILE ERROR\n"
                          + "MAKE SURE GPA IS CORRECT\n"
                          + nfe.toString());
  }//END NumberFormatcatch()

  //CATCH ANY EXCEPTIONS WRITING TO FILE
  catch (IOException io)
  {
    studentArea.append("\nWRITE FILE ERROR\n" + io.toString());
  }  //END IO catch()

  //CLEAR TEXT FIELDS
  numberField.setText("");
  nameField.setText("");
  gpaField.setText("");
}//END writeStudentRecord()
```

TABLE 14-5   *DataOutputStream* Methods for Writing Files

Method	Description
writeBoolean(boolean b)	Writes a Boolean value to the output stream as a 1-byte value
writeByte(byte b)	Writes a `byte` to the output stream
writeChar(char c)	Writes a Unicode `char` to the output stream as a 2-byte value, high byte first
writeDouble(double f)	Writes a `double` to the output stream as an 8-byte value, high byte first
writeFloat(float f)	Writes a `float` to the output stream as a 4-byte value, high byte first
writeInt(int i)	Writes an `int` to the output stream as a 4-byte value, high byte first
writeLong(long l)	Writes a `long` to the output stream as an 8-byte value, high byte first
writeShort(short s)	Writes a `short` to the output stream as a 2-byte value, high byte first
writeUTF(String s)	Writes a string to the output stream using UTF-8 encoding

The first thing you see is a `try` block which contains three statements that write the student name, student number, and gpa, respectively, to the opened file. We include these statements within a `try` block since there is a potential for an I/O error when writing to a file. Here, we use our *outFile* object to call two standard methods: *writeUTF()* and *writeDouble()*. These methods are members of the *DataOutputStream* class of which our object was created in the *openOutputFile()* method. Remember that the *DataOutputStream* class was used so that binary data could be written to the output file stream. Other methods contained in this class are listed in Table 14-5. The *writeUTF()* method is used to write a string to the output stream using UTF-8 character encoding format. This is a byte-oriented character coding format that is a machine-independent format for writing to files. Notice that the argument for the method is simply the string obtained from a given text field using the *getText()* method. The *writeDouble()* method writes a `double` floating-point value to the output file stream. However, the *gpaField* object contains a string that must be converted to a `double` before it is written to the binary file. Remember, you are writing to a binary file, not a text file. So, strings representing numeric data must be converted to their numeric binary representation. As a result, you see that the *writeDouble()* method contains an argument of

```
(new Double(gpaField.getText().trim())).doubleValue()
```

Remember doing this conversion in the GUI chapter case study? Just to review, the *gpaField* object is used to call the *getText()* method which returns the string contained in the GPA text field. The *trim()* method of the *String* class is called to "trim," or remove, any white space from the string. The resulting string is used as an argument for the *Double()* class constructor. Recall that the constructor takes a string argument and creates a `Double` floating-point object. At this point, we have a `Double` floating-point wrapper object that contains the floating-point representation of the string data obtained from the *gpaField* text field. However, this object *cannot* be written directly to the output stream using the *writeDouble()* method, because this method requires a primitive data type of `double` as its argument. In other words, we need to convert `Double` to `double`. So, the *doubleValue()* method is called by the new `Double` object, resulting in a `double` value. Now we have something that can be used by the *writeDouble()* method.

You see two `catch` blocks in the *writeStudentRecord()* method. The first block catches a *NumberFormatException*, while the second block catches an *IOException*. The *Double* class constructor throws a *NumberFormatException*. The exception is thrown if its argument does not contain a valid string. For example, a blank field or a string containing any alphabetic characters would cause a *NumberFormatException* to be thrown since our *gpa* string must represent a number. Notice that our `catch` block notifies the user that the *gpa* text field could have a problem. The second `catch` block is used to catch a general *IOException* generated by the *writeUTF()* or *writeDouble()* methods. Such an exception will be generated if there are any errors writing to the file.

The *readStudentRecord()* method code is as follows:

```
//METHOD TO READ A STUDENT RECORD FROM AN OPENED DISK FILE
public void readStudentRecord()
{
  //TRY TO READ FILE
  try
  {
    //DISPLAY STUDENT RECORD DATA IN TEXT AREA
    studentArea.append("\n\nStudent Name: " + inFile.readUTF());
    studentArea.append("\nStudent Number: " + inFile.readUTF());
    studentArea.append("\nGPA:  " + String.valueOf(inFile.readDouble()));
  } //END try() READ

  //CATCH UTF EXCEPTION
  catch (UTFDataFormatException utf)
  {
    studentArea.append("\nINCORRECT DATA IN FILE");
    System.exit(1);
  }//END CATCH UTF

  //CATCH NO RECORD TO READ EXCEPTION
  catch (NullPointerException np)
  {
    studentArea.append("\nREAD ERROR, MAKE SURE FILE IS OPEN\n");
  }//END CATCH NULL POINTER

  //CATCH END OF FILE EXCEPTION
  catch (EOFException eof)
  {
    studentArea.append("\n\nTHERE ARE NO MORE RECORDS IN FILE");
  }//END CATCH EOF

  //CATCH GENERAL READ EXCEPTION AND EXIT PROGRAM
  catch (IOException io)
  {
    studentArea.append("\n\nGENERAL FILE READ ERROR");
    System.exit(1);
  }//END CATCH IO
}//readStudentRecord()
```

Again, you see that all the file action is coded within a `try` block. However, this time we are using our *inFile* object to call the *readUTF()* and *readDouble()* methods. These methods, along with others listed in Table 14-6, are part of the *DataInputStream* class. You see that the *DataInputStream* methods listed in Table 14-6 are simply the counterparts of the *DataOutputStream* methods listed in Table 14-5. Now, note from the foregoing program that the *readUTF()* and *readDouble()* methods are called as part of an argument for the text area *append()* method so that the values read from the file will be appended to the GUI text area.

The *readUTF()* method is the counterpart of the *writeUTF()* method. This method will read a string in UTF-8 format and convert it to a Unicode Java string. The method is called twice in succession to read the student name and student number strings stored previously in the file via our *writeStudentRecord()* method. The *readDouble()* method is the counterpart of the *writeDouble()* method. It reads a `double` value. However, this value must be converted to a string before it can be appended to the text area. This is why the *valueOf()* method is called within the argument of the *append()* method.

Note that there are four `catch` blocks in our method. The first block is used to catch a *UTFDataException*. This exception is thrown by the *readUTF()* method when the data it reads is not in proper UTF format. Such a situation might occur if the user opened the wrong file. Notice that the handler appends an error message to the text area then terminates the program via the statement `System.exit(1)`. A call to the *System.exit()* method terminates program execution. A nonzero argument within the *exit()* method notifies the operating system of an abnormal termination due to an error, while an argument of zero indicates a normal termination. The second `catch` block is used to catch a *NullPointerException*. This exception is thrown by the *readUTF()* or *readDouble()* methods when there is no value to read. This will happen when the user tries to read data before opening the file. Notice that the handler notifies the user to open the file and try again. The third block catches an *EndOfFileException*. This exception is thrown when the end of the file is reached, indicating that no more records are available. The handler notifies the user of this condition by appending a message to the text area. Finally, the last block catches a general *IOException*. This block is required because both the *readUTF()* and *readDouble()* methods throw an *IOException*. If a general *IOException* occurs, the handler will exit the program, notifying the operating system of an abnormal termination.

TABLE 14-6 *DataInputStream* Methods for Reading Files

Method	Description
readBoolean()	Reads a Boolean value from the data input stream
readByte()	Reads a signed 8-bit value from the data input stream
readChar()	Reads a Unicode character from the data input stream
readDouble()	Reads a `double` from the data input stream
readFloat()	Reads a `float` from the data input stream
readInt()	Reads an `int` from the data input stream
readLong()	Reads a `long` from the data input stream
readShort()	Reads a `short` from the data input stream
readUTF()	Reads a UTF string from the data input stream

Closing a Binary File

The last thing that needs to be done is to develop methods to close both our input and output files. You should always close a file when the file processing is complete, otherwise you cannot ensure the integrity of the file for future processing. Our two file closing methods are similar. One is called *closeOutputFile()*, while the other is called *closeInputFile()*. These methods are executed when the user clicks the *Done* button in Figures 14-2 and 14-3, respectively. Here they are:

```
//CLOSE OUTPUT FILE
public void closeOutputFile()
{
  //TRY TO CLOSE FILE
  try
  {
    outFile.flush();
    outFile.close();
    studentArea.append("\nFILE CLOSED");
    System.exit(0);
  }//END try()

  //CATCHES EXCEPTION OF NO FILE EXISTS TO CLOSE
  catch (NullPointerException np)
  {
    studentArea.append("\nNO FILE TO CLOSE\n" +  np.toString());
  }  //END CATCH NULL POINTER

  //CATCH GENERAL IO EXCEPTION
  catch(IOException io)
  {
    studentArea.append("\nFILE CLOSING ERROR\n" +  io.toString());
    System.exit(1);
  }//END CATCH IO
}//END closeOutputFile()

//CLOSE INPUT FILE
public void closeInputFile()
{

  //TRY TO CLOSE FILE
  try
  {
    inFile.close();
    studentArea.append("\nFILE CLOSED");
    System.exit(0);
  }//END try()

  //CATCH NO FILE TO CLOSE EXCEPTION
  catch(NullPointerException np)
  {
    studentArea.append("\nNO FILE TO CLOSE\n" +  np.toString());
  }//END CATCH NULL POINTER
```

```
  //CATCH CLOSE EXCEPTION
  catch(IOException io)
  {
    studentArea.append("\nFILE CLOSING ERROR\n" + io.toString());
    System.exit(1);
  }//END CATCH GENERAL IO
}//END closeInputFile()
```

As you can see, both methods attempt to close the file within a `try` block. Both methods use their respective objects to call the standard *close()* method available in the *FileStream* classes. In addition, notice that the *closeOutputFile()* method calls the *flush()* method prior to closing the file. The *FileOutputStream* class inherits the *flush()* method from the *OutputStream* class. This method "flushes" the output stream, causing any internally buffered data to be written to the file. Both file closing methods call the *exit()* method with an argument of zero to terminate the program normally.

Each closing method has two identical `catch` blocks. The first block catches a *NullPointerException* that will occur if the user tries to close a file that has not been opened. The second block catches a general *IOException* that will occur if the operating system has trouble closing the file for any reason. If this happens, the handler terminates the program abnormally.

Putting Everything Together in Classes

Now we have all the ingredients for our binary file processing classes. The *WriteStudentFile* class contains the *openOutputFile()*, *writeStudentRecord()*, and *closeOutputFile()* methods, and the *ReadStudentFile* class contains the *openInputFile()*, *readStudentRecord()*, and *closeInputFile()* methods. Of course these classes must also contain all of the respective GUI code.

A Class to Write a Binary File   Encapsulating the file write methods and GUI code into a single class gives us the following:

```
import javax.swing.*;      //FOR GUI COMPONENTS
import java.awt.*;         //FOR Container CLASS
import java.awt.event.*;   //FOR EVENT HANDLING
import java.io.*;          //FOR FILE CLASSES

//CLASS TO WRITE A STUDENT FILE
class WriteStudentFile extends JFrame
{
   //DECLARE OUTPUT FILE STREAM OBJECT
   private DataOutputStream outFile;

   //DECLARE BUTTON OBJECTS AS PRIVATE MEMBERS
   private JButton openFileButton;
   private JButton storeButton;
   private JButton doneButton;

   //DECLARE TEXT FIELD OBJECTS AS PRIVATE CLASS DATA
   private JTextField nameField;
```

```java
private JTextField numberField;
private JTextField gpaField;
private JTextField fileNameField;
private JTextArea studentArea;

//CONSTRUCTOR
public WriteStudentFile(String Title)
{
//CALL SUPERCLASS CONSTRUCTOR
super(Title);

//DEFINE CONTAINER OBJECT
Container container = getContentPane();
//SET FRAME LAYOUT MANAGER
container.setLayout(new FlowLayout(FlowLayout.LEFT));

//INSTANTIATE PRIVATE OBJECTS
openFileButton = new JButton("Open File");
storeButton = new JButton("Store");
doneButton = new JButton("Done");
nameField = new JTextField(25);
numberField = new JTextField(13);
gpaField = new JTextField(4);
fileNameField = new JTextField(20);
studentArea = new JTextArea(7,40);

//DEFINE PANELS
JPanel panel1 = new JPanel();
JPanel panel2 = new JPanel();
JPanel panel3 = new JPanel();
JPanel panel4 = new JPanel();

//SET PANEL LAYOUT MANAGERS
panel1.setLayout(new FlowLayout(FlowLayout.LEFT));
panel2.setLayout(new FlowLayout(FlowLayout.LEFT));
panel3.setLayout(new FlowLayout(FlowLayout.LEFT));
panel4.setLayout(new FlowLayout(FlowLayout.LEFT));

//DEFINE LABEL OBJECTS
JLabel nameLabel = new JLabel("Student name");
JLabel numberLabel = new JLabel("Student Number");
JLabel gpaLabel = new JLabel("GPA");
JLabel summaryLabel = new JLabel("Student Summary");
JLabel fileNameLabel = new JLabel("File Name");

//ADD COMPONENTS TO panel1
panel1.add(fileNameLabel);
panel1.add(fileNameField);
panel1.add(openFileButton);

//ADD COMPONENTS TO panel2
panel2.add(nameLabel);
panel2.add(nameField);
```

```java
      panel2.add(numberLabel);
      panel2.add(numberField);
      panel3.add(gpaLabel);
      panel3.add(gpaField);

      //ADD COMPONENTS TO panel3
      panel4.add(summaryLabel);
      panel4.add(studentArea);
      panel4.add(storeButton);
      panel4.add(doneButton);

      //ADD PANELS TO CONTAINER
      container.add(panel1);
      container. add(panel2);
      container.add(panel3);
      container.add(panel4);

      //REGISTER LISTENERS
      openFileButton.addActionListener(new ButtonHandler());
      storeButton.addActionListener(new ButtonHandler());
      doneButton.addActionListener(new ButtonHandler());

      //ADD LISTENER FOR THIS FRAME
      addWindowListener(new WindowHandler());
   }//END WriteStudentFile()

   //WINDOW EVENT HANDLER
   private class WindowHandler extends WindowAdapter
   {
      public void windowClosing(WindowEvent e)
      {
         System.exit(0);//EXIT TO OPERATING SYSTEM
      }//END windowClosing()
   }//END WindowHandler CLASS

//PRIVATE HANDLER CLASS
private class ButtonHandler implements ActionListener
{
//PROCESS EVENT
public void actionPerformed(ActionEvent e)
{

      //DID OPEN FILE BUTTON CAUSE EVENT?
      if (e.getSource() == openFileButton)
      {
         //IF SO, OPEN FILE
         openOutputFile(fileNameField.getText());
      }//END IF OPEN FILE

      //DID STORE BUTTON CAUSE EVENT?
      if (e.getSource() == storeButton)
      {
```

```
            //DISPLAY IN TEXT FIELD DATA IN TEXT AREA
            studentArea.setText("");
            studentArea.append("\nStudent name: " + nameField.getText());
            studentArea.append("\nStudent Number: " + numberField.getText());
            studentArea.append("\nGPA: " + gpaField.getText());

            //CALL METHOD TO WRITE STUDENT RECORD
            writeStudentRecord();
        }//END IF STORE BUTTON

        //DID DONE BUTTON CAUSE EVENT?
        if (e.getSource() == doneButton)
        {
          closeOutputFile();
        }//END IF DONE BUTTON
    }//END actionPerformed()
}//END ButtonHandler CLASS

//CREATE AN OUTPUT STREAM AND CONNECT IT TO A PHYSICAL DISK FILE
public void openOutputFile(String s)
{
 //TRY TO OPEN FILE BY CONNECTING OUTPUT STREAM TO A DISK FILE
 try
 {
   outFile = new DataOutputStream(new FileOutputStream(s));
   studentArea.setText("FILE OPEN, BEGIN STORING RECORDS");
 }//END try()

 //CATCH EXCEPTION IF FILE CANNOT BE OPENED
 catch(IOException io)
 {
     studentArea.append("\n\nFILE NOT FOUND ERROR\n" + io.toString() );
 }//END catch() IOException
}//END openOutputFile

public void writeStudentRecord()
{
 //TRY TO WRITE STUDENT RECORD TO FILE
 try
 {
  outFile.writeUTF(nameField.getText());
  outFile.writeUTF(numberField.getText());
  outFile.writeDouble(
                 (new Double(gpaField.getText().trim())).doubleValue());
 } //END try() TO WRITE RECORD

 //CATCH NUMBER FORMAT EXCEPTION FOR GPA FIELD
 catch (NumberFormatException nfe)
 {
   studentArea.append("\n\nWRITE FILE ERROR\n"
                        + "MAKE SURE GPA IS CORRECT\n"
                        + nfe.toString());
 }//END NumberFormatcatch()
```

```
//CATCH ANY EXCEPTIONS WRITING TO FILE
catch (IOException io)
{
   studentArea.append("\nWRITE FILE ERROR\n" + io.toString());
}  //END IO catch()

//CLEAR TEXT FIELDS
numberField.setText("");
nameField.setText("");
gpaField.setText("");
}//writeStudentRecord

//CLOSE OUTPUT FILE
public void closeOutputFile()
{
 //TRY TO CLOSE FILE
 try
 {
    outFile.flush();
    outFile.close();
    studentArea.append("\nFILE CLOSED");
    System.exit(0);
 }//END try()

 //CATCHES EXCEPTION OF NO FILE EXISTS TO CLOSE
 catch (NullPointerException np)
 {
  studentArea.append("\nNO FILE TO CLOSE\n" +  np.toString());
 }//END CATCH NULL POINTER

 //CATCH GENERAL IO EXCEPTION
 catch(IOException io)
 {
  studentArea.append("\nFILE CLOSING ERROR\n" +  io.toString());
  System.exit(1);
 }//END CATCH IO
}//END closeOutputFile()
}//writeStudentFile CLASS
```

   The only thing we have changed here from our previous discussions is to declare our *DataOutputStream* object, *outFile*, as a `private` class member, then instantiate it within the *openOutputFile()* method. This makes our *outFile* object visible to the other methods in the class. Of course, we had to import the *java.io* package to get access to the file stream classes.

A Class to Read a Binary File   Encapsulating the file read methods and GUI code into a single class gives us the following:

```java
import javax.swing.*;        //FOR GUI COMPONENTS
import java.awt.*;           //FOR Container CLASS
import java.awt.event.*;     //FOR EVENT HANDLING
import java.io.*;            //FOR FILE CLASSES

//CLASS TO READ A STUDENT FILE
class ReadStudentFile extends JFrame
{
    //DECLARE INPUT FILE STREAM OBJECT
    private DataInputStream inFile;

    //DECLARE PRIVATE GUI OBJECTS
    private JTextField fileNameField;
    private JTextArea studentArea;
    private JButton openFileButton;
    private JButton nextStudentButton;
    private JButton doneButton;

    //CONSTRUCTOR
    public ReadStudentFile(String Title)
    {
     //CALL SUPERCLASS CONSTRUCTOR
     super(Title);

        //DEFINE CONTAINER OBJECT
        Container container = getContentPane();

        //SET FRAME LAYOUT MANAGER
        container.setLayout(new BorderLayout());

        //INSTANTIATE PRIVATE OBJECTS
        fileNameField = new JTextField(20);
        studentArea = new JTextArea(7,50);
        openFileButton = new JButton("Open File");
        nextStudentButton = new JButton("Next Student");
        doneButton = new JButton("Done");

        //DEFINE PANELS
        JPanel panel1 = new JPanel();
        JPanel panel2 = new JPanel();
        JPanel panel3 = new JPanel();

        //SET PANEL LAYOUT MANAGERS
        panel1.setLayout(new FlowLayout(FlowLayout.LEFT));
        panel2.setLayout(new FlowLayout(FlowLayout.CENTER));
        panel3.setLayout(new FlowLayout(FlowLayout.CENTER,20,20));

        //DEFINE LABEL OBJECTS
        JLabel fileNameLabel = new JLabel("File Name");

        //ADD COMPONENTS TO panel1
        panel1.add(fileNameLabel);
```

```
      panel1.add(fileNameField);
      panel1.add(openFileButton);

      //ADD COMPONENTS TO panel2
      panel2.add(studentArea);

      //ADD COMPONENTS TO panel3
      panel3.add(nextStudentButton);
      panel3.add(doneButton);

      //ADD PANELS TO CONTAINER
      container.add(panel1,"North");
      container.add(panel2,"Center");
      container.add(panel3,"South");

   //REGISTER LISTENERS
   openFileButton.addActionListener(new ButtonHandler());
   nextStudentButton.addActionListener(new ButtonHandler());
   doneButton.addActionListener(new ButtonHandler());

   //ADD LISTENER FOR THIS FRAME
   addWindowListener(new WindowHandler());
}//END ReadStudentFile() CONSTRUCTOR

 //WINDOW EVENT HANDLER
 private class WindowHandler extends WindowAdapter
 {
   public void windowClosing(WindowEvent e)
   {
      System.exit(0);//EXIT TO OPERATING SYSTEM
  }//END windowClosing()
}//END WindowHandler CLASS

 //BUTTON HANDLER CLASS
 private class ButtonHandler implements ActionListener
 {
 //PROCESS BUTTON EVENT
 public void actionPerformed(ActionEvent e)
 {
    //DID OPEN FILE BUTTON CAUSE EVENT?
    if (e.getSource() == openFileButton)
    {
       //IF SO, OPEN FILE
       openInputFile(fileNameField.getText());
    }//END IF OPEN FILE

    //DID NEXT STUDENT BUTTON CAUSE EVENT?
    if (e.getSource() == nextStudentButton)
    {
      readStudentRecord();
    }//END IF NEXT STUDENT
```

```java
  //DID DONE BUTTON CAUSE EVENT?
  if (e.getSource() == doneButton)
  {
    closeInputFile();
  }//END IF DONE
 }//END actionPerformed()
}//END ButtonHandler CLASS

//CREATE AN INPUT STREAM AND CONNECT IT TO A PHYSICAL DISK FILE
public void openInputFile(String s)
{
  //TRY TO OPEN FILE BY CONNECTING INPUT STREAM TO A DISK FILE
  try
  {
    inFile = new DataInputStream(new FileInputStream(s));
    studentArea.setText("FILE OPEN, PRESS Next Student BUTTON");
  }//END try().

  //CATCH EXCEPTION IF FILE CANNOT BE OPENED
  catch(IOException io)
  {
     studentArea.setText("\n\nFILE NOT FOUND ERROR\n" + io.toString());
  }//END catch()
 }//END openInputFile()

 public void readStudentRecord()
 {
   //TRY TO READ FILE
   try
   {
     //DISPLAY STUDENT RECORD DATA IN TEXT AREA
     studentArea.append("\n\nStudent Name: " + inFile.readUTF());
     studentArea.append("\nStudent Number: " + inFile.readUTF());
     studentArea.append("\nGPA:   "
                          + String.valueOf(inFile.readDouble()));
   }//END try() READ

   //CATCH UTF EXCEPTION
   catch (UTFDataFormatException utf)
   {
     studentArea.append("\nINCORRECT DATA IN FILE");
     System.exit(1);
   }//END CATCH UTF

   //CATCH NO RECORD TO READ EXCEPTION
   catch (NullPointerException np)
   {
     studentArea.append("\nREAD ERROR, MAKE SURE FILE IS OPEN\n");
   }//END CATCH NULL POINTER

   //CATCH END OF FILE EXCEPTION
   catch (EOFException eof)
```

```
      {
        studentArea.append("\nTHERE ARE NO MORE RECORDS IN THIS FILE");
      }//END CATCH EOF

      //CATCH GENERAL READ EXCEPTION AND EXIT PROGRAM
      catch (IOException io)
      {
        studentArea.append("\n\nGENERAL FILE READ ERROR");
        System.exit(1);
      }//END CATCH IO
    }//END readStudentRecord()

    //CLOSE INPUT FILE
    public void closeInputFile()
    {
      //TRY TO CLOSE FILE
      try
      {
        inFile.close();
        studentArea.append("\nFILE CLOSED");
        System.exit(0);
      }//END try()

      //CATCH NO FILE TO CLOSE EXCEPTION
      catch(NullPointerException np)
      {
        studentArea.append("\nNO FILE TO CLOSE\n" +  np.toString());
      }//END CATCH NULL POINTER

      //CATCH CLOSE EXCEPTION
      catch(IOException io)
      {
        studentArea.append("\nFILE CLOSING ERROR\n" +  io.toString());
        System.exit(1);
      }//END CATCH GENERAL IO
    }//END closeInputFile()
}//END ReadStudentFile CLASS
```

Notice that we have declared our *DataInputStream* object, *inFile*, as a private class member, then instantiated it within the *openInputFile()* method. This makes our *inFile* object visible to the other methods in the class. Again, we had to import the *java.io* package to get access to the file stream classes.

There you have it. Take a close look at each class and make sure you understand all of the details. You now have the knowledge required to read/write your own sequential binary disk files. Now you need to learn how to read/write text files.

QUICK CHECK

1. True or false: The *DataInputStream* class provides methods to write binary data to files.
2. What method was used in this text to write a string to a binary file?

3. Write a statement that will obtain a string from a text field object called *myName* and write it to a binary file connected to an object called *myOutputFile*.

4. Write a statement to read a string from a binary file connected to an object called *myInputFile* and display it in a text area called *displayText*.

5. Write a statement that will obtain a string from a text field called *myAge*, convert it to an `int`, and write it to a binary file connected to an object called *myOutputFile*.

6. Write a statement to read an `int` from a binary file connected to an object called *myInputFile* and display it in a text area called *displayText*.

7. The last thing that needs to be done when processing a disk file is to _____ the file.

8. What is the purpose of calling the *flush()* method when closing an output file?

14.5   Opening Text Files

To work with text files, you must do the same things you did with binary files, except that you must use the *FileReader* and *FileWriter* classes to create the character file stream, and the *BufferedReader*, *BufferedWriter*, and *PrintWriter* classes to read and write character data from/to the file. The *FileReader* and *FileWriter* classes contain constructors to create a file stream. The *BufferedReader* and *BufferedWriter* classes provide input and output buffering, which allows for increased system performance when reading and writing files. The *PrintWriter* class contains a wealth of methods to facilitate writing to text files. By wrapping the required file classes, we can open a text file for output with one statement, as follows:

```
PrintWriter outFile =
              new PrintWriter((new BufferedWriter(new FileWriter(s))));
```

This statement will create an output file stream object called *outFile* and connect it to a disk file name stored in the string object *s*. Notice how a *FileWriter* object is created as an argument for the *BufferedWriter* constructor, which creates a *BufferedWriter* object as the argument of the *PrintWriter* constructor. Here, the *FileWriter* object creates an output stream and connects it to the file designated by *s*. The *BufferedWriter* object creates an **output buffer** to temporarily store the data as it is being written to the file. This is why we are using a **buffered stream**, as illustrated in Figure 14-4. Buffering increases system performance by allowing the CPU to write the data to the buffer at CPU speed (nanoseconds) versus disk speed (milliseconds). An operating system device driver then transfers the data from the buffer to the disk file at disk speed.

Our final *PrintWriter* class object, *outFile*, is created to call methods that will allow us to write text data to the buffer and ultimately to the file.

Likewise, a text file can be opened for input using the *FileReader* and *BufferedReader* classes, as follows:

```
BufferedReader inFile = new BufferedReader(new FileReader(s));
```

This statement will create an input file stream object called *inFile* and connect it to the disk file represented by the string object *s*. Again, wrapping is used such that a *FileReader* object is created as an argument for the *BufferedReader* class. The *FileReader* object

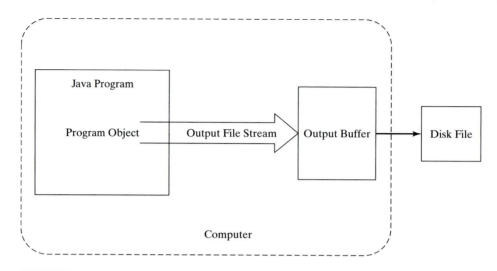

FIGURE 14-4 A buffered stream "buffers," or stores, the data as it is being transferred from the program to the file to increase system performance.

creates an input file stream which connects to the file designated by *s*. The *BufferedReader* class creates an **input buffer** to temporarily store the data as it is being read from the file to increase system performance during the read operation. The input buffer works just like the output buffer shown in Figure 14-5, but in reverse. Our *BufferedReader* object, called *inFile*, will be used to call methods that read text data from the input buffer which has been transferred to the buffer by an operating system device driver.

     Placing the foregoing file stream object definitions into methods for opening text files and providing the required exception handling, we get

openOutputTextFile() Method To Open a Text File for Output

```java
//CREATE AN OUTPUT STREAM AND ATTACH IT TO A PHYSICAL DISK FILE
public void openOutputTextFile(String s)
{
  //TRY TO OPEN FILE BY ATTACHING OUTPUT STREAM TO A DISK FILE
  try
  {
    PrintWriter outFile =
              new PrintWriter((new BufferedWriter(new FileWriter(s))));
    fileNameField.setText("FILE OPEN: BEGIN TYPING TEXT");
  }//END try()

  //CATCH EXCEPTION IF FILE CANNOT BE OPENED
  catch(IOException io)
  {
     textArea.append("\n\nFILE NOT FOUND ERROR\n" + io.toString() );
  }//END catch() IOException
}//END openOutputTextFile
```

openInputTextFile() Method To Open a Text File for Input

```
//CREATE AN INPUT STREAM AND ATTACH IT TO A PHYSICAL DISK FILE
public void openInputTextFile(String s)
{
  //TRY TO OPEN FILE BY ATTACHING INPUT STREAM TO A DISK FILE
  try
  {
    BufferedReader inFile = new BufferedReader(new FileReader(s));
    textArea.setText("FILE OPEN, PRESS Read "
                    + "File BUTTON TO READ FILE CONTENTS");
  }//END try()

  //CATCH EXCEPTION IF FILE CANNOT BE OPENED
  catch(IOException io)
  {
    textArea.setText("\n\nFILE NOT FOUND ERROR\n" + io.toString());
  }//END catch()
}//END openInputTextFile()
```

You now have all the necessary knowledge to understand these methods. Our next task is to develop methods to read and write a text file.

QUICK CHECK

1. Write a statement to open a text file for output by creating an object called *myFile*. Assume that the file name is *"myFile.txt"*. Use object wrapping to form a single statement that will open the file.
2. Write a statement to open a text file for input by creating an object called *yourFile*. Assume that the file name is stored in a string called *yourFileName*. Use object wrapping to form a single statement that will open the file.

14.6   Reading and Writing Text Files

Now all we have to do is use our *inFile* and *outFile* objects to call the appropriate methods to read and write a text file. Remember that our *outFile* object is an object of the *PrintWriter* class. The methods contained in the *PrintWriter* class are listed in Table 14-7.

TABLE 14-7   *PrintWriter* Methods for Writing Text Files

Method	Description
close()	Close an output file stream
flush()	Flush an output stream buffer
print(any data type or object)	Writes any type of data to a text file without a newline character termination
println(any data type or object)	Writes any type of data to a text file with a newline character termination

Look familiar? Sure they do! These are some of the same methods we used to provide console output using the standard *System.out* stream and they are used in exactly the same way. So, everything you know about *print()* and *println()* for writing to console screens using *System.out* will apply to writing text files using a *PrintWriter* file stream object.

Here is a method that uses the *print()* method to write the text obtained from a GUI text area to our buffered *outFile* stream:

```
public void writeTextFile()
{
//TRY TO WRITE LINE TO FILE
try
{
  outFile.print(textArea.getText());
} //END try() TO WRITE LINE

//CATCHES EXCEPTION OF NO FILE EXISTS
catch (NullPointerException np)
{
    textArea.append("\nNO FILE \n" + np.toString());
}  //END CATCH NULL POINTER

//CLEAR TEXT FIELDS
textArea.setText("");
}//writeTextFile
```

That's all there is to it! No special data conversions are required, as in a binary file stream, since the text area contains text data that is being written to a text file. You shouldn't have any trouble understanding this code at this point.

Next, we will use our *inFile* object to call methods contained in the *BufferedReader* class to read a text file. These methods are listed in Table 14-8. As you can see, we can read a single character from the buffer using *read()*, or an entire line from the buffer using *readLine()*. What defines a line? Of course, a newline character defines a line.

Here is a method that uses the *readLine()* method to read the text obtained from our buffered *inFile* stream and write it to a text area:

```
public void readTextFile()
{
  String line;              //STRING TO STORE LINE OF TEXT

  //CLEAR TEXT AREA
  textArea.setText("");
```

TABLE 14-8 *BufferedReader* Methods for Reading Text Files

Method	Description
close()	Close an input file stream
read()	Reads and returns a single character from the input buffer
readLine()	Reads and returns a single line (delimited by a newline character) from the input buffer

```
//TRY TO READ FILE
try
{
  while((line = inFile.readLine()) != null)
    textArea.append(line + '\n');
} //END try() READ

//CATCH NO RECORD TO READ EXCEPTION
catch (NullPointerException np)
{
  textArea.append("\nREAD ERROR, MAKE SURE FILE IS OPEN\n");
}//END CATCH NULL POINTER

//CATCH END OF FILE EXCEPTION
catch (EOFException eof)
{
  textArea.append("\nTHERE ARE NO MORE RECORDS IN THIS FILE");
}//END CATCH EOF

//CATCH GENERAL READ EXCEPTION AND EXIT PROGRAM
catch (IOException io)
{
  textArea.append("\n\nGENERAL FILE READ ERROR");
  System.exit(1);
}//END CATCH IO
}//readTextFile()
```

Notice how we used a `while` loop to read all the lines in the text file until a `null` reference is encountered. The word `null` is a keyword in Java. Java equates the end-of-file marker as a `null` reference. Every file has an end-of-file marker known as EOF to "mark" the end of the file. Without it, your program could not determine where one file ends and another begins. Also, notice that no special data conversions are required because we are reading text data from a text file and writing it to a text area. Of course, conversions would be required if we must arithmetically manipulate any of the text data.

Closing a Text File

The last thing that needs to be done is to develop methods to close both our input and output text files. We can close our text files just like we closed our binary files using the *close()* method, as follows:

Method to Close an Output Text File

```
//CLOSE OUTPUT FILE
public void closeOutputFile()
{
  //TRY TO CLOSE FILE
  try
  {
    outFile.flush();
```

```
        outFile.close();
        textArea.append("\nFILE CLOSED");
        System.exit(0);
    }//END try()


    //CATCHES EXCEPTION OF NO FILE EXISTS TO CLOSE
    catch (NullPointerException np)
    {
        textArea.append("\nNO FILE TO CLOSE\n" + np.toString());
    } //END CATCH NULL POINTER
}//END closeOutputFile()
```

Method to Close an Input Text File

```
//CLOSE INPUT FILE
public void closeInputFile()
{
  //TRY TO CLOSE FILE
  try
  {
    inFile.close();
    textArea.append("\nFILE CLOSED");
    System.exit(0);
  }//END try()

  //CATCH NO FILE TO CLOSE EXCEPTION
  catch(NullPointerException np)
  {
    textArea.append("\nNO FILE TO CLOSE\n" + np.toString());
  }//END CATCH NULL POINTER

  //CATCH CLOSE EXCEPTION
  catch(IOException io)
  {
    textArea.append("\nFILE CLOSING ERROR\n" + io.toString());
    System.exit(1);
  }//END CATCH GENERAL IO
}//END closeInputFile()
```

Putting Everything Together in Classes

Now we have all the ingredients needed to create a set of classes to process text files. We will create a class called *WriteTextFile* that contains the *openOutputTextFile()*, *writeTextFile()*, and *closeOutputFile()* methods, and a class called *ReadTextFile* contains the *openInputTextFile()*, *readTextFile()*, and *closeInputFile()* methods. Of course, these classes must also contain the required GUI code.

A Class to Write a Text File   Encapsulating the file write methods and GUI code into a single class gives us the following:

```
import javax.swing.*;       //FOR GUI COMPONENTS
import java.awt.*;          //FOR Container CLASS
```

```java
import java.awt.event.*;   //FOR EVENT HANDLING
import java.io.*;          //FOR FILE CLASSES

//CLASS TO WRITE A TEXT FILE
class WriteTextFile extends JFrame
{
    //DECLARE OUTPUT FILE STREAM OBJECT
    private PrintWriter outFile;

    //DECLARE BUTTON OBJECTS AS PRIVATE MEMBERS
    private JButton openFileButton;
    private JButton storeButton;
    private JButton doneButton;

    //DECLARE TEXT FIELD OBJECTS AS PRIVATE CLASS DATA
    private JTextField fileNameField;
    private JTextArea textArea;

  //CONSTRUCTOR
  public WriteTextFile(String Title)
  {
  //CALL SUPERCLASS CONSTRUCTOR
  super(Title);

  //DEFINE CONTAINER OBJECT
  Container container = getContentPane();

  //SET FRAME LAYOUT MANAGER
  container.setLayout(new FlowLayout(FlowLayout.LEFT));

  //INSTANTIATE PRIVATE OBJECTS
  openFileButton = new JButton("Open File");
  storeButton = new JButton("Store");
  doneButton = new JButton("Done");
  fileNameField = new JTextField(20);
  textArea = new JTextArea(7,40);

  //DEFINE PANELS
  JPanel panel1 = new JPanel();
  JPanel panel2 = new JPanel();
  JPanel panel3 = new JPanel();
  JPanel panel4 = new JPanel();

  //SET PANEL LAYOUT MANAGERS
  panel1.setLayout(new FlowLayout(FlowLayout.LEFT));
  panel2.setLayout(new FlowLayout(FlowLayout.LEFT));
  panel3.setLayout(new FlowLayout(FlowLayout.LEFT));
  panel4.setLayout(new FlowLayout(FlowLayout.LEFT));

  //DEFINE LABEL OBJECTS
  JLabel fileNameLabel = new JLabel("File Name");
  JLabel summaryLabel = new JLabel("Text Area");
```

```java
        //ADD COMPONENTS TO panel1
        panel1.add(fileNameLabel);
        panel1.add(fileNameField);
        panel1.add(openFileButton);

        //ADD COMPONENTS TO panel3
        panel2.add(summaryLabel);
        panel2.add(new JScrollPane(textArea));
        panel2.add(storeButton);
        panel2.add(doneButton);

        //ADD PANELS TO CONTAINER
        container.add(panel1);
        container. add(panel2);

        //REGISTER LISTENERS
        openFileButton.addActionListener(new ButtonHandler());
        storeButton.addActionListener(new ButtonHandler());
        doneButton.addActionListener(new ButtonHandler());

        //ADD LISTENER FOR THIS FRAME
        addWindowListener(new WindowHandler());
    }//END WriteTextFile()

    //WINDOW EVENT HANDLER
    private class WindowHandler extends WindowAdapter
    {
       public void windowClosing(WindowEvent e)
       {
          System.exit(0);  //EXIT TO OPERATING SYSTEM
       }//END windowClosing()
    }//END WindowHandler CLASS

//PRIVATE HANDLER CLASS
private class ButtonHandler implements ActionListener
{
 //PROCESS EVENT
 public void actionPerformed(ActionEvent e)
 {
     //DID OPEN FILE BUTTON CAUSE EVENT?
     if (e.getSource() == openFileButton)
     {
        //IF SO, OPEN FILE
        openOutputTextFile(fileNameField.getText());
     }//END IF OPEN FILE
     //DID STORE BUTTON CAUSE EVENT?
     if (e.getSource() == storeButton)
     {
      //CALL METHOD TO WRITE A LINE TO THE FILE
       writeTextFile();
     }//END IF STORE BUTTON
```

```java
      //DID DONE BUTTON CAUSE EVENT?
      if (e.getSource() == doneButton)
      {
        closeOutputFile();
      }//END IF DONE BUTTON
   }//END actionPerformed()
}//END ButtonHandler CLASS

   //CREATE AN OUTPUT STREAM AND ATTACH IT TO A PHYSICAL DISK FILE
   public void openOutputTextFile(String s)
   {
     //TRY TO OPEN FILE BY ATTACHING OUTPUT STREAM TO A DISK FILE
     try
     {
       outFile = new PrintWriter((new BufferedWriter(new FileWriter(s))));
       fileNameField.setText("FILE OPEN: BEGIN TYPING TEXT");
     }//END try()

     //CATCH EXCEPTION IF FILE CANNOT BE OPENED
     catch(IOException io)
     {
       textArea.append("\n\nFILE NOT FOUND ERROR\n" + io.toString());
     }//END catch() IOException
   }//END openOutputTextFile

   public void writeTextFile()
   {
   //TRY TO WRITE LINE TO FILE
   try
   {
     outFile.print(textArea.getText());
   } //END try() TO WRITE LINE

   //CATCHES EXCEPTION OF NO FILE EXISTS
   catch (NullPointerException np)
   {
       textArea.append("\nNO FILE \n" +  np.toString());
   }   //END CATCH NULL POINTER
   //CLEAR TEXT FIELDS
   textArea.setText("");
   }//writeTextFile

//CLOSE OUTPUT FILE
public void closeOutputFile()
{
   //TRY TO CLOSE FILE
   try
   {
      outFile.flush();
      outFile.close();
      textArea.append("\nFILE CLOSED");
      System.exit(0);
   }//END try()
```

```
    //CATCHES EXCEPTION OF NO FILE EXISTS TO CLOSE
    catch (NullPointerException np)
    {
        textArea.append("\nNO FILE TO CLOSE\n" + np.toString());
    }   //END CATCH NULL POINTER
 }//END closeOutputFile()
}//writeTextFile CLASS
```

Again, the only thing we have changed here from our previous discussions is to declare our *PrintWriter* object, *outFile*, as a `private` class member then instantiate it within the *openOutputFile()* method. This makes our *outFile* object visible to the other methods in the class. Of course, we had to import the *java.io* package to get access to the file stream classes.

A Class to Read a Text File   Encapsulating the file read methods and GUI code into a single class gives us the following:

```
import javax.swing.*;       //FOR GUI COMPONENTS
import java.awt.*;          //FOR Container CLASS
import java.awt.event.*;    //FOR EVENT HANDLING
import java.io.*;           //FOR FILE CLASSES

//CLASS TO READ A STUDENT FILE
class ReadTextFile extends JFrame
{
   //DECLARE INPUT FILE STREAM OBJECT
   private BufferedReader inFile;

   //DECLARE PRIVATE GUI OBJECTS
   private JTextField fileNameField;
   private JTextArea textArea;
   private JButton openFileButton;
   private JButton readFileButton;
   private JButton doneButton;

   //CONSTRUCTOR
   public ReadTextFile(String Title)
   {
    //CALL SUPERCLASS CONSTRUCTOR
    super(Title);

    //DEFINE CONTAINER OBJECT
    Container container = getContentPane();

    //SET FRAME LAYOUT MANAGER
    container.setLayout(new BorderLayout());

    //INSTANTIATE PRIVATE OBJECTS
    fileNameField = new JTextField(20);
```

```java
        textArea = new JTextArea(7,50);
        openFileButton = new JButton("Open File");
        readFileButton = new JButton("Read File");
        doneButton = new JButton("Done");

        //DEFINE PANELS
        JPanel panel1 = new JPanel();
        JPanel panel2 = new JPanel();
        JPanel panel3 = new JPanel();

        //SET PANEL LAYOUT MANAGERS
        panel1.setLayout(new FlowLayout(FlowLayout.LEFT));
        panel2.setLayout(new FlowLayout(FlowLayout.CENTER));
        panel3.setLayout(new FlowLayout(FlowLayout.CENTER,20,20));

        //DEFINE LABEL OBJECTS
        JLabel fileNameLabel = new JLabel("File Name");

        //ADD COMPONENTS TO panel1
        panel1.add(fileNameLabel);
        panel1.add(fileNameField);
        panel1.add(openFileButton);

        //ADD COMPONENTS TO panel2
        panel2.add(new JScrollPane(textArea));

        //ADD COMPONENTS TO panel3
        panel3.add(readFileButton);
        panel3.add(doneButton);

        //ADD PANELS TO CONTAINER
        container.add(panel1,"North");
        container.add(panel2,"Center");
        container.add(panel3,"South");

      //REGISTER LISTENERS
      openFileButton.addActionListener(new ButtonHandler());
      readFileButton.addActionListener(new ButtonHandler());
      doneButton.addActionListener(new ButtonHandler());

      //ADD LISTENER FOR THIS FRAME
      addWindowListener(new WindowHandler());
  }//END ReadTextFile() CONSTRUCTOR

  //WINDOW EVENT HANDLER
  private class WindowHandler extends WindowAdapter
  {
    public void windowClosing(WindowEvent e)
    {
      System.exit(0); //EXIT TO OPERATING SYSTEM
    }//END windowClosing()
  }//END WindowHandler CLASS
```

```java
//BUTTON HANDLER CLASS
private class ButtonHandler implements ActionListener
{
//PROCESS BUTTON EVENT
public void actionPerformed(ActionEvent e)
{
    //DID OPEN FILE BUTTON CAUSE EVENT?
    if (e.getSource() == openFileButton)
    {//IF SO, OPEN FILE
       openInputTextFile(fileNameField.getText());
    }//END IF OPEN FILE

    //DID NEXT STUDENT BUTTON CAUSE EVENT?
    if (e.getSource() == readFileButton)
    {
      readTextFile();
    }//END IF NEXT STUDENT

    //DID DONE BUTTON CAUSE EVENT?
    if (e.getSource() == doneButton)
    {
      closeInputFile();
    }//END IF DONE
  }//END actionPerformed()
}//END ButtonHandler CLASS

  //CREATE AN INPUT STREAM AND ATTACH IT TO A PHYSICAL DISK FILE
  public void openInputTextFile(String s)
  {
    //TRY TO OPEN FILE BY ATTACHING INPUT STREAM TO A DISK FILE
    try
    {
      inFile = new BufferedReader(new FileReader(s));
      textArea.setText("FILE OPEN, PRESS Read File BUTTON"
                       + "TO READ FILE CONTENTS");
    }//END try()

    //CATCH EXCEPTION IF FILE CANNOT BE OPENED
    catch (IOException io)
    {
      textArea.setText("\n\nFILE NOT FOUND ERROR\n" + io.toString());
    }//END catch()
  }//END openInputTextFile()

  public void readTextFile()
  {
    String line;          //STRING TO STORE LINE OF TEXT
    //CLEAR TEXT AREA
    textArea.setText("");

    //TRY TO READ FILE
    try
    {
```

```java
      while((line = inFile.readLine()) != null)
        textArea.append(line + '\n');
    } //END try() READ

    //CATCH NO RECORD TO READ EXCEPTION
    catch (NullPointerException np)
    {
      textArea.append("\nREAD ERROR, MAKE SURE FILE IS OPEN\n");
    }//END CATCH NULL POINTER

    //CATCH END OF FILE EXCEPTION
    catch (EOFException eof)
    {
      textArea.append("\nTHERE ARE NO MORE RECORDS IN THIS FILE");
    }//END CATCH EOF

    //CATCH GENERAL READ EXCEPTION AND EXIT PROGRAM
    catch (IOException io)
    {
      textArea.append("\n\nGENERAL FILE READ ERROR");
      System.exit(1);
    }//END CATCH IO
  }//readTextFile()

  //CLOSE INPUT FILE
  public void closeInputFile()
  {
    //TRY TO CLOSE FILE
    try
    {
      inFile.close();
      textArea.append("\nFILE CLOSED");
      System.exit(0);
    }//END try()

    //CATCH NO FILE TO CLOSE EXCEPTION
    catch(NullPointerException np)
    {
      textArea.append("\nNO FILE TO CLOSE\n" +  np.toString());
    }//END CATCH NULL POINTER

    //CATCH CLOSE EXCEPTION
    catch(IOException io)
    {
      textArea.append("\nFILE CLOSING ERROR\n" +  io.toString());
      System.exit(1);
    }//END CATCH GENERAL IO
  }//END closeInputFile()
}//END ReadTextFile CLASS
```

An application can now be coded to create objects of these classes that will read and write text files using a GUI environment. Here is what the user would see when running the application:

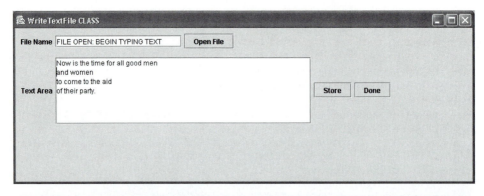

Notice that the text entered in the *WriteTextFile* GUI text area appears in the *ReadTextFile* GUI text area.

QUICK CHECK

1. True or false: The *PrintWriter* class provides methods to write data to text files.
2. True or false: The *print()* and *println()* methods are used to write data to a text file just like they are used to write data to the console screen.
3. Write a statement that will obtain the text from a text area object called *myText* and write it to a text file connected to an object called *myTextFile*.
4. Write a statement to read all the text in a text file connected to an object called *myTextFile* and display it in a text area called *myText*.
5. What is the difference between the *read()* and *readLine()* methods when reading text files?
6. Why should buffered I/O be used when reading and writing text files?
7. What classes provide for buffered I/O when reading and writing text files?

CHAPTER SUMMARY

In data processing applications, a file is a collection of related records, or classes. Each record is made up of related fields, or members, that contain the file information. A file can be viewed as a data structure that consists of a sequence of components. Files provide a means for your program to communicate with the outside world. Any I/O operations performed by your program, even keyboard input and display output, are handled via file streams. A file stream provides a connection between your program and the outside world.

There are binary files and text files. A binary file stores numerical values using the internal numeric binary format specified by the language in use. As a result, a Java program can read a binary file to get numeric data, manipulate the data arithmetically, and write the data to a binary file without an intermediate conversion. A text, or character-based, file stores information using ASCII character representations. This allows a text file to be easily read and displayed using any word processing program or text editor, like your Java IDE editor.

There are three basic operations that you will need to perform when working with disk files:

- Open the file for input or output.
- Process the file, by reading from or writing to the file.
- Close the file.

Working with files requires that your program communicate with a peripheral device. When communicating with a peripheral device, there is always the possibility that something unexpected could happen such as a disk could be write-protected during a write operation, a disk file might not exist during a read operation, and so on. As a result, you must provide exception handling to protect your program from terminating prematurely during file operations, as well as other possible sources of error. Exception handling in Java is provided by coding any statements that have a potential of causing an error within a `try` block. One or more `catch` blocks are then coded to catch and handle any exception thrown from within the `try` block.

You will encapsulate your file opening, processing, and closing methods along with the required exception handling and GUI code into classes to read or write a given file. Although they look complex, such classes are easy to build once you understand the basics of file I/O, exception handling, and GUI construction. You now have this knowledge.

QUESTIONS AND PROBLEMS

Questions

1. List the three major operations that must be performed in order to process files.
2. What is a file stream?
3. What is the purpose of opening a file?
4. What classes does Java provide to create a binary file stream and connect it to a physical disk file?
5. What classes does Java provide to read from and write to binary files?
6. Write a statement to create a file stream object called *fileIn* that will read a binary file called *mydata.dat*.
7. Write a statement to create a file stream object called *fileOut* that will write to a binary file whose name is stored in a string called *fileName*.
8. Statements that have the potential for throwing an exception are placed within a(n) _____ block.
9. When an exception is thrown, it must be caught by a(n) _____ block in order to handle the exception.
10. List and describe at least four checked exceptions that are defined in Java.
11. True or false: Once an exception is caught and processed by the handler, control returns to the `try` block that threw the exception.

12. True or false: A subclass exception handler must be coded prior to its superclass exception handler.

13. What problem is encountered when catching the generic *Exception* class exception to catch any and all exceptions?

14. What happens in a non-GUI program when an exception is thrown, but not caught?

15. What happens in a GUI program when an exception is thrown, but not caught?

16. True or false: You can have more than one `catch` block for a given `try` block.

17. Write a `catch` block to notify the user that a divide-by-zero error has occurred.

18. Write a statement that gets a string from a text field called *doubleField* and converts it to a primitive `double` data type.

19. What is UTF format and what type of data uses this format for binary file I/O?

20. What exception must be caught when reading data in UTF format?

21. Write a statement to close a file connected to a file object called *myFile*.

22. What exception should be caught when closing a file?

23. What *DataInputStream* method would you use to read a character from a binary disk file?

24. Write a statement that will obtain a string from a text field called *employeeSalary*, convert it to a `double`, and write it to a file connected to an object called *employeeFile*.

25. Write a statement to read a `double` from a file connected to an object called *employeeFile* and display it in a text area called *employeeData*.

26. What classes does Java provide to create a text file stream and connect it to a physical disk file?

27. What classes does Java provide to create buffered I/O for text files?

28. What classes does Java provide to read from and write to character files?

29. Write a statement to create a file stream object called *fileIn* that will read a buffered text file called *myText.txt*.

30. Write a statement to create a file stream object called *fileOut* that will write to a buffered text file whose name is stored in a string called *fileName*.

31. Write a statement to read a string from the file stream created in question 29 and display it on the console screen.

32. Write a statement to write "This text is great!" to the file stream created in question 30.

Problems

Least Difficult

1. Place the *WriteStudentFile* and the *ReadStudentFile* classes discussed in this chapter inside two separate applications. The class source code can be found on the CD that accompanies this book. All the application class needs to do is create an object for the given class, then use this object to set the size of the GUI frame and make it visible. Execute your applications and experiment with the classes by writing then reading disk files. Make sure to test the exception handling features of the classes.

2. Place the *WriteTextFile* and the *ReadTextFile* classes discussed in this chapter inside two separate applications. The class source code can be found on the CD that accompanies this book. All the application class needs to do is create an object for the given class, then use this object to set the size of the GUI frame and make it visible. Execute your applications and experiment with the classes by writing then reading disk files. Make sure to test the exception handling features of the classes.

More Difficult

Refer to the student database GUI shown in Figure 14-5 for Problems 3 through 5.

3. Add a student majors list box similar to the one shown in Figure 14-5 to the *WriteStudentFile* GUI. Modify the *WriteStudentFile* and *ReadStudentFile* classes given in this chapter to read/write the student's major(s) selected from the added list box.

4. Add student status check boxes similar to those shown in Figure 14-5 to the *WriteStudentFile* GUI. Modify the *WriteStudentFile* and *ReadStudentFile* classes given in this chapter to read/write the student's full-time/part-time and commuting status selected from the added check boxes.

5. Add student status radio buttons similar to those shown in Figure 14-5 to the *WriteStudentFile* GUI. Modify the *WriteStudentFile* and *ReadStudentFile* classes given in this chapter to read/write the student's undergraduate/graduate status selected from the added radio buttons.

Most Difficult

6. Using the techniques discussed in this chapter, develop classes that will process a parts inventory file of the following information:

   - Part name
   - Part number
   - Part price
   - Quantity on hand

   Develop one class that will allow a user to create the parts inventory file and another class that will read and display the file. Make sure to provide a GUI interface for both classes. Place your classes in two separate applications to execute and test your code.

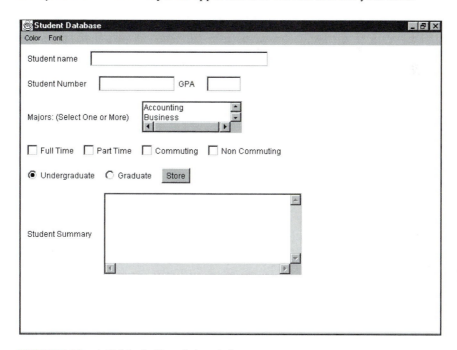

FIGURE 14-5 A GUI for Problems 3 through 5.

7. Using the techniques discussed in this chapter, develop classes that will process an employee file containing the following information:

- Employee name
- Employee number
- Employee type: salaried, commissioned, or hourly
- Employee gender: male or female
- Employee wage: annual salary, commission rate, or hourly rate

Develop one class that will allow a user to create the employee file, and another class that will read and display the file. Make sure to provide a GUI interface for both classes. Place your classes in two separate applications to execute and test your code.

15

Multidimensional Arrays

OBJECTIVES

When you are finished with this chapter, you should have a good understanding of the following:

■ How to define multidimensional arrays in Java

■ How to access multidimensional arrays using direct assignment, reading/writing, and loops

■ How to construct a program that uses multidimensional arrays to solve simultaneous equations using Cramer's rule

Introduction

A multidimensional array is simply an extension of a one-dimensional array. Rather than storing a single row of elements, you can think of a multidimensional array as storing multiple rows of elements. For instance, a two-dimensional array stores rows in a two-dimensional table format of rows and columns, where each row is a one-dimensional array. The rows provide the vertical dimension of the array, and the columns provide the horizontal array dimension. A three-dimensional array stores elements in a three-dimensional format of rows, columns, and planes, where each plane is a two-dimensional array. The rows provide the vertical dimension, the columns provide the horizontal dimension, and the planes provide the depth dimension of the array.

In this chapter, you will learn about two- and three-dimensional arrays: Arrays larger than this are seldom needed in programming. The chapter will conclude with a comprehensive problem-solving exercise employing two-dimensional arrays to solve sets of simultaneous equations using Cramer's rule, something you probably learned in an algebra class.

15.1   Two-Dimensional Arrays

The most common multidimensional array is the ***two-dimensional*** array shown in Figure 15-1. Here, you see that a two-dimensional array contains multiple rows. It's as if several one-dimensional arrays are combined to form a single rectangular structure of data. As a result, you can think of this rectangular data structure as a ***table*** of elements.

Observe that the two-dimensional array in Figure 15-1 is composed of elements that are located by rows and columns. The rows are labeled on the vertical axis and range from 0 to m. The columns are labeled on the horizontal axis and range from 0 to n. How many rows and columns are there? Each dimension starts with index [0], so there must be $m + 1$ rows and $n + 1$ columns, right? As a result, we say that this two-dimensional array has a dimension, or size, of $m + 1$ rows by $n + 1$ columns, written as $(m + 1) \times (n + 1)$.

How many elements are in the array? You're right: $m + 1$ times $n + 1$ elements! How do you suppose a given element is located? You're right again: by specifying its row and column index values. For instance, the element in the upper left-hand corner is located at the intersection of row 0 and column 0, or index [0][0]. Likewise, the element in the lower right-hand corner is located where row m meets column n, or index $[m][n]$.

The ***dimension*** of an array is a measure of its size. Thus, the dimension of an array tells you how many elements an array can store.

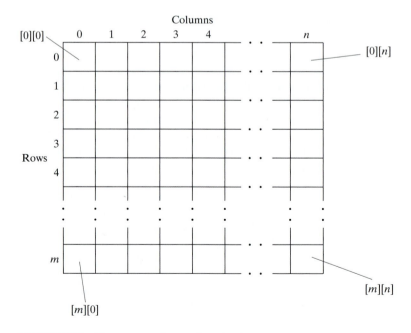

FIGURE 15-1   The structure of a two-dimensional array.

Defining Two-Dimensional Arrays in Java

You define a two-dimensional array in Java in almost the same way as you define a one-dimensional array. Here's the general format:

TWO-DIMENSIONAL ARRAY DEFINITION FORMAT

```
elementType arrayName[][] = new elementType[rows][columns];
```

The only difference between this definition and one required for a one-dimensional array is found within the size specification. You must specify two open sets of brackets after the array name and both the row and column sizes, as shown.

Example 15-1

Given the following two-dimensional array definitions, describe the array structures relative to the given definitions.

a. `double salesTaxTable[][] = new double[5][7];`

b. `final int ROWS = 5;`
    `final int COLS = 7;`
    `double salesTaxTable[][] = new double[ROWS][COLS];`

c. `final int PERCENT = 101;`
    `final int INCOME = 1001;`
    `double bonusPayTable[][] = new double[PERCENT][INCOME];`

d. `final int WEEKS = 6;`
    `final int DAYS = 7;`
    `int may[][] = new int[WEEKS][DAYS];`

e. `final int ROW = 57;`
    `final int SEAT = 10;`
    `boolean theaterSeat[][] = new boolean[ROW][SEAT];`

Solution

a. This is a two-dimensional array, or table, whose rows range from 0 to 4 and columns range from 0 to 6. Remember that because array indices start with [0], the last index in a given array dimension is one less than its size. The array name is *salesTaxTable* and will store `double` floating-point values of sales tax information, which would most likely be sales tax percentages versus amount of sales.

b. This array is identical to the first array. The only difference here is the way in which the array is defined. Notice that the row and column indices are defined as [*ROWS*][*COLS*], where *ROWS* and *COLS* are defined as constants.

c. Here, the rows are called *PERCENT* and range from 0 to 100. The array columns are labeled *INCOME* and range from 0 to 1000. The array name is *bonusPayTable*, and it will store `double` floating-point elements. Obviously, the array will store the bonus values corresponding to percentage values from 0 to 100 and income values from 0 to 1000. So, what would be the bonus value stored at index [10,100]? You're right if you thought 10.00.

d. This array is constructed to store the dates for the month of May, just like a calendar. Look at a common calendar if you have one handy. Isn't a given month simply a table of integers whose values are located by a given week and a given day within that week? The array structure duplicates a monthly calendar. The rows are labeled 0 through 5, representing the six possible weeks in any given month. The columns of the array are labeled 0 through 6, representing the seven days of the week.

e. This last array also has a practical application. Can you determine what it is from the definition? Notice that it is an array of Boolean elements. The rows range from 0 to 56, and the columns range from 0 to 9, as shown. The array name is *theaterSeat*. Suppose that you use this array to store Boolean values of `true` and `false`. Then, this array could be used in a reservation program for a theater to indicate whether or not a given seat is reserved or not reserved.

Example 15-2

How many elements will each of the arrays in Example 15-1 store, and what type of elements will they store?

Solution

a. This array will store 5 × 7, or 35 elements. The elements will be `double` floating-point values.

b. This array will also store 5 × 7, or 35 `double` floating-point elements.

c. This array has 101 rows and 1001 columns and, therefore, will store 101 × 1001 = 101,101 `double` floating-point elements.

d. This array has 6 rows and 7 columns and, therefore, will store 6 × 7 = 42 integer elements.

e. This array has 57 rows and 10 columns and will store 57 × 10 = 570 Boolean elements.

Accessing Two-Dimensional Arrays

You access two-dimensional array elements in much the same way as one-dimensional array elements. The difference is that to locate the elements in a two-dimensional array, you must specify a row index and a column index.

You can access the array elements using direct assignment, reading/writing, or looping.

Direct Assignment   The general format for direct assignment of element values is as follows:

TWO-DIMENSIONAL ARRAY DIRECT ASSIGNMENT FORMAT (inserting elements)

`arrayName[rowIndex][columnIndex] = elementValue;`

TWO-DIMENSIONAL ARRAY DIRECT ASSIGNMENT FORMAT (copying elements)

`variableName = arrayName[rowIndex][columnIndex];`

First, you see the format for inserting elements into a two-dimensional array, followed by the format for copying elements from the array. Notice that in both instances you must specify a row and column index to access the desired element position. The row index is specified first, followed by the column index. By using the arrays defined in Example 15-1, possible direct assignments for insertion might be

```
salesTaxTable[2][3] = 0.06;
bonusPayTable[2][175] = 3.5;
may[1][3] = 8;
theaterSeat[5][0] = true;
```

In the first case, the floating-point value 0.06 is placed in row [2], column [3] of the *salesTable* array. This might represent a sales tax of $0.06 using a sales tax of 2% on a sales amount of $3.00. In the second case, a value of 3.5 is inserted into row [2], column [175] of the *bonusPayTable* array. This bonus value, in dollars and cents, corresponds to a bonus percentage value of 2% on an income value of $175.00. In the third case, a value of 8 is placed in row [1], column [3] of the *may* array. Thus, the fourth day of the second week is the 8th of May. Think about it! Finally, the last case assigns the Boolean value true to row [5], column [0] of the *theaterSeat* array. Therefore, the first seat of the sixth row in the theater is reserved.

By using the same arrays, direct assignment statements to copy elements might be

```
tax = salesTaxTable[0][0];
bonus = bonusPayTable[5][100];
today = may[2][4];
tomorrow = may[2][5];
reserved = theaterSeat[3][3];
```

In each of these statements, the element value stored at the row/column position within the respective array is assigned to a variable identifier. Of course, the variables must be defined as the same type as the array element being assigned to it.

Remember that copy operations have no effect on the array elements. In other words, the elements are not actually removed from the array; they are simply "copied" to the assigned variable.

Reading and Writing   Read statements can be used to insert two-dimensional array elements, and *writeInfo()* or *print()/printlln()* statements can be used to copy array elements, like this:

```
salesTaxTable[1][1] = io.readDouble("Enter a tax value");
io.writeInfo("The sales tax on this item is "  + salesTaxTable[1][1]);
bonusPayTable[5][20] = io.readDouble("Enter a bonus pay value");
io.writeInfo("Your bonus pay is " + bonusPayTable[5][20]);
may[1][3] = io.readInt("Enter the date for week 2, day 4");
io.writeInfo("Today is May " + may[1][3]);
if (theaterSeat[3][1])
    System.out.println("Seat reserved");
else
    System.out.println("Seat not reserved");
```

Again, you can see that both a row and a column index must be specified. The *read()* statements will insert elements obtained from a keyboard entry. The *writeInfo()* and *println()* statements will then copy the array element just inserted and simply "echo" the user entry back to the display. Notice that the last *println()* statement is contained within an `if/else` statement to determine if the element is a Boolean `true` or `false` value. This statement will produce a "Seat reserved" or "Seat not reserved" message on the console screen, depending on the contents of location [3][1] of the *theaterSeat* array.

Using Loops   As you know, loops provide a more efficient way to access arrays, especially when working with large multidimensional arrays. The thing to remember with multidimensional arrays is that *a separate loop is required for each dimension of the array*. In addition, the loops must be nested. Thus, a two-dimensional array requires two nested loops.

Look at the calendar pictured in Figure 15-2. As you have seen, this calendar can be stored in memory using a two-dimensional array. How do you suppose you might go about filling the calendar with the dates required for a given month? A logical approach would be to fill in all of the dates of week 0, from *Sun* to *Sat*, then go to week 1 and fill in its dates, then fill in the week 2 dates, and so on.

May

	Sun [0]	Mon [1]	Tue [2]	Wed [3]	Thu [4]	Fri [5]	Sat [6]
week [0]							1
week [1]	2	3	4	5	6	7	8
week [2]	9	10	11	12	13	14	15
week [3]	16	17	18	19	20	21	22
week [4]	23	24	25	26	27	28	29
week [5]	30	31					

FIGURE 15-2   The calendar for any given month, such as May, is simply a two-dimensional array of integers.

Think about what the array indices must do to perform this filling operation. The week index would start at [0], and then the days index would begin at [0] and increment through the days of the week to [6]. This will fill the first week. To fill the second week, the week index must be incremented to 1, with the days index starting at [0] and incrementing to [6] all over again. To fill the third week, the week index is incremented to 2, and the days index incremented from [0] to [6] again. In other words, you are filling in the dates week by week, one week at a time. Each time the week index is incremented, the days index starts at [0] and increments to [6], before the week index is incremented to the next week.

Does this suggest two loops, one to increment the week index and a second to increment the days index? Moreover, doesn't this process suggest that the days loop must be nested within the week loop, because the days must run through its entire range for each week?

Here's the general loop structure for accessing elements in a two-dimensional array.

LOOPING FORMAT FOR ACCESSING TWO-DIMENSIONAL ARRAY ELEMENTS

```
for(int row index = 0; row index < row size; ++row index)
   for(int col index = 0; col index < col size; ++col index)
              Process array[row index][col index]
```

You see that the column index loop is nested within the row index loop. Thus, the column loop runs through all of its iterations for each iteration of the row loop. The actual array processing takes place within the column loop. Let's look at an example to get the idea.

Example 15-3

Write a method using loops to fill a calendar array for the month of *May*. Write another method to display the *May* calendar. Assume that these methods are part of a class called *MayCalendar*.

Solution

We will begin by defining the month array as before.

```
final int WEEKS = 6;
final int DAYS = 7;
int may[][] = new int[WEEKS][DAYS];
```

Now, we must write a method to fill the array with the dates for May. But first, we must consider the method interface. The method must receive the array, get the dates from the user, and return the filled array to the calling program. This will be easy since we will assume that the array is a `private` member of the *MayCalendar* class. Thus, the method-interface description becomes as follows:

Method *fillMay()*:   Obtains dates of the month of May from the user and fills a
                        two-dimensional integer array
Accepts: Nothing
Returns: Nothing

(*Note:* If this array were not part of the same class as the method, it would have to be passed to and from the method because there would be no binding relationship between the array and the method.)

Now, here's a method that will do the job:

```
//THIS METHOD  WILL FILL A 2-DIM ARRAY FOR MAY
public void fillMay()
{
   //DEFINE I/O OBJECT
   StaugIO io = new StaugIO();

   //DISPLAY INFO BOX TO USER
   io.writeInfo("Enter the dates of the month,"
            + "\nbeginning with Sunday of the first"
```

```
                    + "\nweek in the month"
                    + "\nEnter a 0 if there is no date for a given
                        day");

//READ MAY DATES FROM USER
for (int week = 0; week < WEEKS; ++week)
    for (int day = 0; day < DAYS; ++day)
        may[week][day] = io.readInt("Enter the date for week "
                                        + (week + 1)
                                        + " day "
                                        + (day + 1));
}//END fillMay()
```

The first *writeInfo()* information box provides a few simple directions to the user. The array-filling operation takes place within the two `for` loops. Notice that the *week* loop is the outer loop, and the *day* loop is the inner loop. Here's how it works. The *week* counter begins with 0, and the *day* counter begins with 0. As a result, the first date is inserted into *may*[0][0], corresponding to Sunday of week 0 in the month. After an element is read into *may*[0][0], the inner `for` loop increments the *day* counter to 1, and an element is read into *may*[0][1]. Notice that the *week* counter remains the same. What is the next array position to be filled? You're right: *may*[0][2]. In summary, the inner *day* loop will increment from 0 to 6 for each iteration of the outer *week* loop. Thus, the first iteration of the outer *week* loop will fill:

may[0][0]
may[0][1]
may[0][2]
may[0][3]
may[0][4]
may[0][5]
may[0][6]

The second iteration of the outer *week* loop will fill the second week, like this:

may[1][0]
may[1][1]
may[1][2]
may[1][3]
may[1][4]
may[1][5]
may[1][6]

This filling process will continue for weeks 2, 3, 4, and 5. The looping is terminated when a value is read into the last array position, *may*[5][6].

Now, let's look at a similar method to display our May calendar once it has been filled. Again, consider the following method interface description:

Method *displayMay()*: Displays the two-dimensional May array
Accepts: Nothing
Returns: Nothing

Here is the completed method:

```
//THIS METHOD  WILL DISPLAY THE MAY ARRAY
void displayMay()
{
  //DEFINE I/O OBJECT
  StaugIO io = new StaugIO();

  //DEFINE INFORMATION STRING
  String info = "          CALENDAR FOR MAY"
             + "\n  Sun   Mon   Tue   Wed   Thur   Fri
                  Sat\n";

  //CONCATENATE ARRAY ELEMENTS TO INFORMATION STRING
  for (int week = 0; week < WEEKS; ++week)
  {
    info += '\n';
    for (int day = 0; day < DAYS; ++day)
      info += "          " + may[week][day];
  }//END WEEK FOR

  //DISPLAY INFORMATION STRING WITHIN AN INFORMATION BOX
  io.writeInfo(info);
}//END displayMay()
```

The first part of the method statement defines a string, called *info*, and initializes it with some header information required for the calendar. Then, the nested `for` loops are executed to concatenate the array contents to the *info* string, which is displayed by the *writeInfo()* statement at the end of the method. The basic loop structures are the same as those we discussed for the filling operation: The *day* counter is incremented from 0 through 6 for every iteration of the *week* loop. Thus, the array contents are displayed in a row-by-row, or week-by-week, fashion.

Now, putting everything together, here is the entire class:

```
//THIS CLASS WILL FILL AND DISPLAY A 2-DIM ARRAY FOR A CALENDAR
import staugIO.StaugIO;    //FOR I/O

class MayCalendar
{
  //ARRAY CONSTANTS
  private final int WEEKS = 6;
  private final int DAYS = 7;

  //MAY ARRAY DEFINITION
  private int may[][] = new int[WEEKS][DAYS];

  //THIS METHOD  WILL FILL A 2-DIM ARRAY FOR MAY
  public void fillMay()
```

```
   {
     //DEFINE I/O OBJECT
     StaugIO io = new StaugIO();

     //DISPLAY INFO BOX TO USER
     io.writeInfo("Enter the dates of the month,"
             + "\nbeginning with Sunday of the first"
             + "\nweek in the month"
             + "\nEnter a 0 if there is no date for a given day");

     //READ MAY DATES FROM USER
     for (int week = 0; week < WEEKS; ++week)
       for (int day = 0; day < DAYS; ++day)
         may[week][day] = io.readInt("Enter the date for week "
                                       + (week + 1)
                                       + " day "
                                       + (day + 1));
   }//END fillMay()

   //THIS METHOD  WILL DISPLAY THE MAY ARRAY
   void displayMay()
   {
     //DEFINE I/O OBJECT
      StaugIO io = new StaugIO();

     //DEFINE INFORMATION STRING
     String info = "          CALENDAR FOR MAY"
                  + "\n    Sun    Mon    Tue    Wed    Thur    Fri
                     Sat\n";

     //CONCATENATE ARRAY ELEMENTS TO INFORMATION STRING
     for (int week = 0; week < WEEKS; ++week)
     {
       info += '\n';
       for (int day = 0; day < DAYS; ++day)
         info += "          " + may[week][day];
     }//END WEEK FOR

     //DISPLAY INFORMATION STRING WITHIN AN INFORMATION BOX
      io.writeInfo(info);
   } //END displayMay()
}//END MayCalendar CLASS
```

First, you see that *WEEKS*, *DAYS*, and *may* have been defined as private class members so that all methods have access to them. Then you see the two methods we developed. Here is an application class to test our *mayCalendar* class:

```
public class Example15_3
{
    public static void main(String[] args)
    {
```

```
                //DEFINE SCORES CLASS OBJECT
                MayCalendar may = new MayCalendar();

                //CALL METHODS TO FILL AND DISPLAY ARRAY
                //AND DISPLAY RESULTS
                may.fillMay();          //CALL METHOD fillMay()
                may.displayMay();       //CALL METHOD displayMay()

                //EXIT PROGRAM
                System.exit(0);
           }//END main()
       }//END TEST CLASS
```

Assuming that the user executes this program and keys in the proper dates for May, the program will generate the following calendar display within an information box:

CALENDAR FOR MAY

Sun	Mon	Tue	Wed	Thur	Fri	Sat
0	0	0	0	0	0	1
2	3	4	5	6	7	8
9	10	11	12	13	14	15
16	17	18	19	20	21	22
23	24	25	26	27	28	29
30	31	0	0	0	0	0

Notice that 0's have been entered for those days that do not exist in this month.

QUICK CHECK

1. Given the following two-dimensional array definition:

   ```
   double sample[][] = new double[10][15];
   ```

   What is the maximum row index? What is the maximum column index?
2. What is the dimension of the array in question 1 and how many elements will it store?
3. Write a statement that will read a value from the keyboard and place it in the first row and last column of the array defined in question 1.
4. Write a statement that will display the value stored in the second row and third column of the array defined in question 1 on the console screen.
5. Write the code, using **for** loops, that will display the elements of the array defined in question 1 in row/column format on the console screen.

15.2   Arrays of More than Two Dimensions

Arrays of more than two dimensions are required for some applications. In this text, we will only consider three-dimensional arrays because few common applications require larger arrays. The easiest way to picture a three-dimensional array is to imagine a cube such as that shown in Figure 15-3. Think of a three-dimensional array as several two-dimensional arrays combined to form a third dimension, depth. The cube is made up of rows (vertical dimension), columns (horizontal dimension), and planes (depth dimension). A given element within the cube array is located by specifying its plane, row, and column. The plane indice is specified first, followed by the row indice, followed by the column indice. See if you can verify for yourself the element positions indicated in Figure 15-3.

Now, let's look at a practical example of a three-dimensional array so you can see how one is defined and accessed in Java. Think of this excellent textbook as a three-dimensional array where each page of the book is a two-dimensional array made up of rows and columns. The combined pages then form the planes within a three-dimensional array that make up the book. Let's suppose there are 45 lines on each page that form the rows for the array, and 80 characters per line that form the columns of the array. If there are 1000 pages in the book, there are 1000 planes in the array. Thus, this book array is a 45 × 80 × 1000 array. What are the array elements, and how many are there? Well, the array elements must be characters, because characters form the words within a page. In addition, there must be 45 × 80 × 1000 = 3,600,000 of them, including spaces, because this is the size of the book in terms of rows, columns, and pages.

How might our book array be defined in Java? How about this:

```
final int PAGES = 1000;
final int LINES = 45;
final int COLUMNS = 80;
char textBook[][][] = new char [PAGES][LINES][COLUMNS];
```

You should be able to understand this definition from your work with one- and two-dimensional arrays. There are three dimensions—[*PAGES*], [*LINES*], and

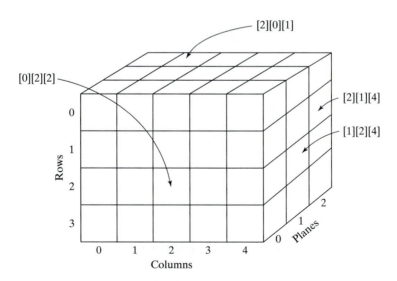

FIGURE 15-3 A 3 × 4 × 5 three-dimensional array.

[*COLUMNS*]—that define the size of the *textBook* array. The array data type is char because the elements are characters. Of course, additional arrays could be used to create
arrays for other books of the same general dimensions, right? Well, theoretically yes, but
just one of these book arrays would be too large for some PC systems. In most systems,
the definition would result in a *array size too big* error when the program is compiled.

Next, how do you suppose you might access the book information? The easiest
way is to use nested loops. How should the loops be nested? Well, think of how you
read a book. You first access the book page-by-page, then read line-by-line, and character-
by-character. As a result, the page loop should be the outermost loop, the line loop
should be nested inside of the page loop, leaving the column loop as the innermost
loop, nested inside of the line loop. Translating this to our book array, we get

```
for (int page = 0; page < PAGES; ++page)
        for (int line = 0; line < LINES; ++line)
                for (int column = 0; column < COLUMNS; ++column)
                        Process textBook[page][line][column]
```

By using this nesting approach, the column loop is executed 80 times for each iteration of the line loop, which is executed 45 times for each iteration of the page loop.
Of course, the page loop is executed 1,000 times. This for loop structure would process
elements one line at a time for a given page. Notice the use of the variables *page*, *line*,
and *column* as the loop counters. These variables must be different from the constants
(*PAGES, LINES, COLUMNS*) used to define the array, because they are local to the
for loops.

 **CAUTION**

When you define an array, Java actually sets aside enough primary memory to store the array
during program execution. This memory is reserved exclusively for the defined array and cannot
be used for other programming or system chores. In other words, a large array "eats up" a lot of
memory. For instance, the foregoing book array contains 3,600,000 character elements. Each
character requires 2 bytes of memory to store, so Java will allocate about 6.9MB of user memory for the book array. If the array is defined too big, it might create a "memory overflow" error
during execution, often resulting in a program crash. So be careful that your arrays don't get too
big for your system to store. There are other, more memory efficient ways to store large
amounts of data—dynamic linked list, tree, or graph structures. You would most likely study
these in a data structures course.

Example 15-4

Given the foregoing *textBook* array definition:

  a. Write a program segment that could be used to fill the book from user entries.
  b. Write a program segment that could be used to display the entire book on a console
  screen.
  c. Write a program segment that could be used to display page 2 of the book on a console screen.

Solution:

a.   Using the three foregoing nested loops, you could fill the book, like this:

```
for (int page = 0; page < PAGES; ++page)
    for (int line = 0; line < LINES; ++line)
        for (int column = 0; column < COLUMNS; ++column)
            textBook[page][line][column]
                            = io.readChar("Enter a character");
```

The innermost loop employs a *readChar()* method to read one character at a time and place it in the indexed position. Wow, this is a lot of work! Wouldn't it be better to just read a file containing the book?

b.   A *print()* method is employed in the innermost loop to display the book on the console screen.

```
for (int page = 0; page < PAGES; ++page)
    for (int line = 0; line < LINES; ++line)
    {
        System.out.println();
        for (int column = 0; column < COLUMNS; ++column)
            System.out.print(textBook[page][line][column]);
    }//END MIDDLE FOR
```

Notice the single empty *println()* statement used in the middle loop to provide a newline after a given line has been displayed.

c.   You need only two loops to display a given page number, as follows:

```
for (int line = 0; line < LINES; ++line)
{
    System.out.println();
    for (int column = 0; column < COLUMNS; ++column)
        System.out.print(textBook[1][line][column]);
} //END FOR
```

Observe that the *page* index is fixed at [1] within the *print()* statement in order to print page 2 of the book. (Remember that the first page of the book is actually at page index [0].) How could this segment be modified to print any page desired by the user? Think about it! This will be left as an exercise at the end of the chapter.

QUICK CHECK

1. What problem might be encountered when defining large multidimensional arrays?

2. Define a three-dimensional array of integers that has 10 planes, 15 rows, and 3 columns.

3. How many bytes of storage are occupied by the array that you defined in question 2, if each integer requires 4 bytes of storage?

4. Write the code necessary to display the contents of the array that you defined in question 2, one plane at a time, on the console screen.

Problem Solving in Action: Easy Equation Solution

Many real world problems, including business problems, require the solution of a set of simultaneous equations. Remember from algebra that a set of simultaneous equations exists when you have two or more equations with two or more common unknowns. For instance, consider the following:

$$7x - 5y = 20$$

$$-5x + 8y = -10$$

Here you have two equations and two unknowns. To solve the equations, you must find both x and y. This is impossible using just one of the equations alone, but does not present a problem when both equations are solved "simultaneously," or together. One thing you might remember from algebra class is that in order to solve simultaneous equations, there must be at least as many equations as there are unknowns. This is why you cannot solve for two unknowns using a single equation. However, two unknowns can be solved using two or more equations. Wouldn't it be nice if you had a program to solve this problem? Well, that's what you're about to get. Don't let the algebra scare you, because it is not hard. It is, however, an excellent problem to illustrate and learn how to manipulate multidimensional arrays.

Determinants

A common way to solve simultaneous equations is by using determinants. You might recall from algebra that a **determinant** is simply a *square array*. By a square array, we mean an array that has the same number of rows and columns. Here is a simple 2×2, called an **order** 2, determinant:

$$\begin{vmatrix} A_1 & B_1 \\ A_2 & B_2 \end{vmatrix}$$

The elements are A_1, B_1, A_2, and B_2. (*Note:* These elements will be numeric values when we actually use determinants to solve simultaneous equations.) Notice the vertical "bars" on the left and right sides of the array. These bars are used to indicate that the array is a determinant. This determinant is called an order 2 determinant because it has two rows and two columns. There are also order 3, order 4, order 5, and so on, determinants. In each case, the determinant is a square array. Here is an order 3 determinant:

$$\begin{vmatrix} A_1 & B_1 & C_1 \\ A_2 & B_2 & C_2 \\ A_3 & B_3 & C_3 \end{vmatrix}$$

Expansion of a Determinant

A determinant is said to be expanded when you replace the array with a single value. An order 2 determinant expansion is the simplest. To get the idea, look at the following:

$$\begin{vmatrix} A_1 & B_1 \\ A_2 & B_2 \end{vmatrix} = A_1 B_2 - A_2 B_1$$

Imagine the two diagonals in the determinant. There is one diagonal running from the top left corner to the bottom right corner. We will call this the *down diagonal*, which forms the product $A_1 B_1$. The second diagonal runs from bottom left to top right. We will call this the *up diagonal*, which forms the product $A_2 B_1$. In the expansion on the right side of the equals sign, you see that the up-diagonal product is subtracted from the down-diagonal product.

Example 15-5

Expand the following determinants:

a. $\begin{vmatrix} 20 & -5 \\ -10 & 8 \end{vmatrix}$

b. $\begin{vmatrix} 7 & 20 \\ -5 & -10 \end{vmatrix}$

c. $\begin{vmatrix} 7 & 5 \\ -5 & 8 \end{vmatrix}$

Solution:

a. $\begin{vmatrix} 20 & -5 \\ -10 & 8 \end{vmatrix} = (20)(8) - (-10)(-5) = 160-50 = 110$

b. $\begin{vmatrix} 7 & 20 \\ -5 & -10 \end{vmatrix} = (7)(-10) - (-5)(20) = -70 - (-100) = -70 + 100 = 30$

c. $\begin{vmatrix} 7 & 5 \\ -5 & 8 \end{vmatrix} = (7)(8) - (-5)(5) = 56-(-25) = 56 + 25 = 81$

Expansion of an order 3 determinant is a bit more challenging. Here is a general order 3 determinant again:

$$\begin{vmatrix} A_1 & B_1 & C_1 \\ A_2 & B_2 & C_2 \\ A_3 & B_3 & C_3 \end{vmatrix}$$

To manually expand this determinant, you must rewrite the first two columns to the right of the determinant, and then use the diagonal method, as follows:

$$\begin{matrix} A_1 & B_1 & C_1 & A_1 & B_1 \\ A_2 & B_2 & C_2 & A_2 & B_2 \\ A_3 & B_3 & C_3 & A_3 & B_3 \end{matrix} = \begin{matrix} A_1B_2C_3 + B_1C_2A_3 + C_1A_2B_3 - A_3B_2C_1 \\ - B_3C_2A_1 - C_3A_2B_1 \end{matrix}$$

Here, you create three down diagonals that form the products $A_1B_2C_3$, $B_1C_2A_3$, and $C_1A_2B_3$, and three up diagonals that form the products $A_3B_2C_1$, $B_3C_2A_1$, and $C_3A_2B_1$. The three up-diagonal products are subtracted from the sum of the three down-diagonal products. This is called the "method of diagonals" for expanding order 3 determinants. We should caution you, however, that the method of diagonals does not work for determinants larger than order 3. To expand determinants larger than order 3, you must use the method of *cofactors*. We will not discuss this method here since it is not required in any of our solutions.

Example 15-6

Expand the following order 3 determinant:

$$\begin{vmatrix} 6 & -2 & -4 \\ 15 & -2 & -5 \\ -4 & -5 & 12 \end{vmatrix}$$

Solution

Rewriting the first two columns to the right of the determinant, you get:

$$\begin{array}{ccccc} 6 & -2 & -4 & 6 & -2 \\ 15 & -2 & -5 & 15 & -2 \\ -4 & -5 & 12 & -4 & -5 \end{array}$$

Now, multiplying the diagonal elements and adding/subtracting the diagonal products, you get:

$$+(6)(-2)(12) + (-2)(-5)(-4) + (-4)(15)(-5)$$
$$-(-4)(-2)(-4) - (-5)(-5)(6) - (12)(15)(-2)$$

Finally, performing the required arithmetic gives you:

$$+(-144) + (-40) + (300)$$
$$-(-32) - (150) - (-360)$$

$$= -144 - 40 + 300 + 32 - 150 + 360$$

$$= 358$$

As you can see from the preceding example, expanding an order 3 determinant can get a bit tricky! You have to pay particular attention to the signs. One simple sign error during your arithmetic will result in an incorrect expansion. Wouldn't it be nice if a computer program could be written to perform the expansion? This is an ideal application for a non-void Java method because the expansion operation returns a single value.

Cramer's Rule

Cramer's rule allows you to solve simultaneous equations using determinants. Let's begin with two equations and two unknowns.

An equation is said to be in **standard form** when all the variables are on the left-hand side of the equals sign, and the constant term is on the right-hand side of the equals sign. Here is a general equation containing two variables in standard form:

$$Ax + By = C$$

This equation has two variables, x and y. The x-coefficient is A and the y-coefficient is B. The constant term is C.

Here is a set of two general simultaneous equations in standard form:

$$A_1x + B_1y = C_1$$
$$A_2x + B_2y = C_2$$

The common variables between the two equations are x and y. Subscripts 1 and 2 denote the coefficients and constants of equations 1 and 2, respectively. Cramer's rule allows you to solve for x and y using determinants, like this:

$$x = \frac{\begin{vmatrix} C_1 & B_1 \\ C_2 & B_2 \end{vmatrix}}{\begin{vmatrix} A_1 & B_1 \\ A_2 & B_2 \end{vmatrix}} \qquad y = \frac{\begin{vmatrix} A_1 & C_1 \\ A_2 & C_2 \end{vmatrix}}{\begin{vmatrix} A_1 & B_1 \\ A_2 & B_2 \end{vmatrix}}$$

As you can see, the determinants are formed using the coefficients and constants from the two equations. Do you see a pattern? First, look at the denominator determinants. They are identical and are formed using the x- and y-coefficients directly from the two equations. However, the numerator determinants are different. When solving for x, the numerator determinant is formed by replacing the x-coefficients with the constant terms. When solving for y, the numerator determinant is formed by replacing the y-coefficients with the constant terms. Here's an example:

Example 15-7

Solve the following set of simultaneous equations using Cramer's rule:

$$x + 2y = 3$$

$$3x + 4y = 5$$

Solution:

Forming the required determinants, you get:

$$x = \frac{\begin{vmatrix} 3 & 2 \\ 5 & 4 \end{vmatrix}}{\begin{vmatrix} 1 & 2 \\ 3 & 4 \end{vmatrix}} \qquad y = \frac{\begin{vmatrix} 1 & 3 \\ 3 & 5 \end{vmatrix}}{\begin{vmatrix} 1 & 2 \\ 3 & 4 \end{vmatrix}}$$

Expanding the determinants and dividing gives you x and y.

$$x = \frac{(3)(4) - (5)(2)}{(1)(4) - (3)(2)} = \frac{2}{-2} = -1 \qquad y = \frac{(1)(5) - (3)(3)}{(1)(4) - (3)(2)} = \frac{-4}{-2} = 2$$

Implementing Cramer's Rule in Java

We will create a class called *CramersRule* to solve two equations and two unknowns using Cramer's rule. Our class will use two-dimensional arrays to store the original equation values and the values for each required determinate. How many arrays do you suppose we need? Well, we can store the coefficients and constant terms for the two equations in a single 2 × 3 array. Then, using this array we can form three 2 × 2 arrays to store the x-, y-, and common denominator determinates.

Now, think about the "methods" you just went through using Cramer's rule to solve the previous set of simultaneous equations in Example 15-7. There are three major tasks to be performed:

- *Task 1*: Obtain the equation coefficients and constants.
- *Task 2*: Form the determinants.
- *Task 3*: Expand the determinants.

So, we can implement these tasks using five methods within our class, as follows:

Task 1: A method to fill a 2 × 3 equations array with the coefficients and constant terms of the two equations

Task 2: A method to form the three 2 × 2 determinate arrays from the values in the 2 × 3 equations array

Task 3: Three methods to expand each of the three determinate arrays

Thus, the specification for our *CramersRule* class becomes:

Class: *Scores*

   Data Members: *equations array*

   x-determinate array

   y-determinate array

   denominator determinate array

   Method Members: *fill()*

   formDet()

   expandX()

   expandY()

   expandD()

An associated UML class diagram is shown in Figure 15-4.

```
+---------------------------------------------------+
|                   CramersRule                     |
+---------------------------------------------------+
| -equations[2][3]:double                           |
|                                                   |
| -x[2][2]:double                                   |
|                                                   |
| -y[2][2]:double                                   |
|                                                   |
| -D[2][2]:double                                   |
+---------------------------------------------------+
| +CramersRule()                                    |
|                                                   |
| +fill()                                           |
|                                                   |
| +formDet()                                        |
|                                                   |
| +expandX():double                                 |
|                                                   |
| +expandY():double                                 |
|                                                   |
| +expandD():double                                 |
+---------------------------------------------------+
```

FIGURE 15-4 The *CramersRule* class consists of four `private` arrays to hold the equation and determinate values, and methods to fill and manipulate the arrays as required by Cramer's rule.

We can now develop Java methods to accomplish the required tasks.

Task 1: Obtain the Equation Coefficients and Constants

To perform Task 1, we must write a method that will obtain the coefficients and constants of the equations to be solved. There are two equations and three items (two coefficients and a constant) that must be obtained for each equation. Does this suggest any particular data structure? Of course, it suggests a 2 × 3 array! So, let's write a method to fill a 2 × 3 array from coefficient and constant terms of the two equations that will be entered by the user. Here it is:

```
//THIS METHOD  WILL FILL AN ARRAY WITH THE EQUATION COEFFICIENTS
public void fill()
{
 //ROW LOOP
 for(int row = 0; row < 2; ++row)
 {
     //USER PROMPT
     io.writeInfo("Enter the values for equation " + (row + 1)
                 + "\nThe equation must be in standard form");

     //COLUMN LOOP
     for(int col = 0; col < 3; ++col)
     {
         //READ COEFFICIENT OR CONSTANT
        if (col == 2)
          equations[row][col]
          = io.readDouble("Enter the constant term:  ");
        else
          equations[row][col]
          = io.readDouble("Enter the coefficient for variable "
                          + (col + 1) + ":  ");
     }//END COLUMN LOOP
  }//END ROW LOOP
}//END fill()
```

Such a method should not be new to you because it simply employs nested `for` loops to fill an array. The method name is *fill()*. It fills an array called *equations* that must be defined as a `private` member of the same class. Given the following two general equations in standard form:

$$A_1x + B_1y = C_1$$

$$A_2x + B_2y = C_2$$

The *fill()* method will fill the 2 × 3 array, like this:

$$\begin{array}{ccc} A_1 & B_1 & C_1 \\ A_2 & B_2 & C_2 \end{array}$$

As you can see, the first equation coefficients and constant term are inserted into the first row of the array. The second row of the array stores the coefficients and constant term of the second equation. Of course, the method assumes that the user will enter the coefficients and constants in their proper order.

Task 2: Form the Determinants

To accomplish Task 2, we will develop a method to form the determinants from the equation coefficients and constants. How can we obtain the coefficients and constants? You're right: from the 2×3 *equations* array that was just filled! Now, how many unique determinants does Cramer's rule require to solve two equations and two unknowns? Three are required: a numerator determinant for the *x* unknown, a numerator determinant for the *y* unknown, and a denominator determinant that is the same for both the *x* and *y* unknowns. All of the determinants must be order 2, right?

So, our method must fill three 2×2 arrays that will form the two numerator and one denominator determinant required by Cramer's rule. Since all the arrays involved are members of our class, they do not need to be passed to/from the method. Here's the method code:

```
//THIS METHOD  WILL FORM THE DETERMINANTS
public void formDet()
{
 for(int row = 0;  row < 2;  ++row)
 {
   for(int col = 0;  col < 2;  ++col)
   {
     x[row][col] = equations[row][col];
     y[row][col] = equations[row][col];
     D[row][col] = equations[row][col];
   }//END COLUMN LOOP
   x[0][0] = equations[0][2];
   x[1][0] = equations[1][2];
   y[0][1] = equations[0][2];
   y[1][1] = equations[1][2];
 }//END ROW LOOP
}//END formDet()
```

The first two columns of the equation array are copied into each of the determinant arrays using `for` loops. Then, the constant terms are inserted into the *x* and *y* determinant arrays at the required positions using direct assignment. The formation pattern results from Cramer's rule. Notice that in all instances, the determinants are formed using the elements from the 2×3 *equations* array of coefficients and constants generated by the *fill()* method.

Task 3: Expand the Determinants

Now we must write three Java methods to expand each of the three order 2 determinants. We will assume that the elements in the determinant are stored in a 2×2 array. Since all of the arrays are `private` members of our class, we do not need to pass them to their respective method. However, each method must evaluate its respective array and return a single expansion value. Here is the method interface description:

Method *expand()*: Expands an order 2 determinant
Accepts: Nothing if a member of the same class as the array; otherwise a 2×2 array
Returns: The expansion value

By using this interface description, the method header becomes

```
double expand();
```

The method name is *expand()*. The data type of the returned expansion value is `double`. Now, the *determinant* array has row indices that range from [0] to [1], and column indices that range from [0] to [1]. Here is the array showing the row/column index layout:

[0] [0]   [0] [1]

[1] [0]   [1] [1]

Remember that these are only the array indices and not the elements stored in the array. Recall that to expand the determinant, the up diagonal must be subtracted from the down diagonal. Thus, the product of indices [1] [0] and [0] [1] must be subtracted from the product of [0] [0] and [1] [1]. Using this idea in our method, we get a single `return` statement, as follows:

```
return element[0][0] * element[1][1] - element[1][0] * element[0][1];
```

That's all there is to it! But, we need a separate method to expand each determinant, *x*, *y*, and *D*. Here are the required methods using the interface and expansion ideas we just developed:

```
//THIS METHOD  WILL EXPAND THE X-DETERMINANT
public double expandX()
{
   return  x[0][0] * x[1][1] - x[1][0] * x[0][1];
}//END expandX()

//THIS METHOD  WILL EXPAND THE Y-DETERMINANT
public double expandY()
{
   return  y[0][0] * y[1][1] - y[1][0] * y[0][1];
}//END expandY()

//THIS METHOD  WILL EXPAND THE D-DETERMINANT
public double expandD()
{
   return  D[0][0] * D[1][1] - D[1][0] * D[0][1];
}//END expandD()
}//END CramersRule CLASS
```

Writing a method to expand an order 3 determinant will be left as an exercise at the end of the chapter. Now we have all the ingredients for a Java program that will solve two equations and two unknowns using Cramer's rule. Combining our *fill()* method, our *formDet()* method, and our expansion methods into a single program, we get the following:

```
/*
 * Action15_01.java
```

```
  *
  * Created on August 18, 2002, 7:31 AM
  */


/**
  *
  * @author  Andrew C. Staugaard, Jr.
  * @version 1.0
  */

import staugIO.StaugIO;          //FOR GUI I/O

class CramersRule
{
    //CREATE I/O OBJECT
    private StaugIO io = new StaugIO();

    //ARRAY DEFINITIONS
    private double equations[][] = new double[2][3]; //EQUATIONS ARRAY
    private double x[][] = new double[2][2];         //x-DETERMINANT
    private double y[][] = new double[2][2];         //y-DETERMINANT
    private double D[][] = new double[2][2];         //DENOMINATOR DETERMINANT

    //PARAMETERLESS CONSTRUCTOR
    CramersRule()
    {
    }//END CramersRule()

    //THIS METHOD  WILL FILL AN ARRAY WITH THE EQUATION COEFFICIENTS
    public void fill()
    {
        //ROW LOOP
        for(int row = 0; row < 2; ++row)
        {
            //USER PROMPT
            io.writeInfo("Enter the values for equation " + (row + 1)
                       + "\nThe equation must be in standard form");
            //COLUMN LOOP
            for(int col = 0; col < 3; ++col)
            {
                //READ COEFFICIENT OR CONSTANT
                if (col == 2)
                  equations[row][col]
                  = io.readDouble("Enter the constant term:  ");
                else
                  equations[row][col]
                  = io.readDouble("Enter the coefficient for variable "
                                + (col + 1) + ":  ");
```

```
      }//END COLUMN LOOP
     }//END ROW LOOP
  }//END fill()

  //THIS METHOD  WILL FORM THE DETERMINANTS
  public void formDet()
  {
   for(int row = 0; row < 2; ++row)
   {
     for(int col = 0; col < 2; ++col)
     {
       x[row][col] = equations[row][col];
       y[row][col] = equations[row][col];
       D[row][col] = equations[row][col];
     }//END COLUMN LOOP
     x[0][0] = equations[0][2];
     x[1][0] = equations[1][2];
     y[0][1] = equations[0][2];
     y[1][1] = equations[1][2];
    }//END ROW LOOP
   }//END formDet()

  //THIS METHOD  WILL EXPAND THE X-DETERMINANT
  public double expandX()
  {
     return  x[0][0] * x[1][1] - x[1][0] * x[0][1];
  }//END expandX()

  //THIS METHOD  WILL EXPAND THE Y-DETERMINANT
  public double expandY()
  {
     return  y[0][0] * y[1][1] - y[1][0] * y[0][1];
  }//END expandY()

  //THIS METHOD  WILL EXPAND THE D-DETERMINANT
  public double expandD()
  {
     return  D[0][0] * D[1][1] - D[1][0] * D[0][1];
  }//END expandD()
 }//END CramersRule CLASS

public class Action15_01
{
  public static void main(String args[])
  {
    //CREATE CramersRule OBJECT
    CramersRule cramer = new CramersRule();
```

```
//CREATE I/O OBJECT
StaugIO io = new StaugIO();


//CALL METHOD TO FILL EQUATION ARRAY
cramer.fill();


//CALL METHOD TO FORM DETERMINANTS
cramer.formDet();


//IF DENOMINATOR = 0, WRITE ERROR MESSAGE.
//ELSE CALCULATE x AND y
if(cramer.expandD() == 0)
    io.writeInfo("Denominator = 0.  Equations are unsolvable.");
else
    io.writeInfo("The value of the first variable is: "
                        + cramer.expandX()/cramer.expandD()
                        + "\nThe value of the second variable is: "
                        + cramer.expandY()/cramer.expandD());
} //END main()
} //END Action15_01 CLASS
```

Observe that all the arrays are defined as `private` class members. The *equations* array is a 2 × 3 array that will store the coefficients and constants of the two equations. This is followed by definitions for the three 2 × 2 determinant arrays.

Now, look at the statement section of *main()*. The *fill()* method is called first to obtain the coefficient and constant terms of the two equations. Next, the *formDet()* method is called to form the required determinants.

Finally, look at how the expansion methods are called. The *expandD()* method is first called as part of an `if/else` statement to see if the denominator determinant value is zero. If it is, the equations cannot be solved using Cramer's rule because division by zero is undefined. If the denominator determinant is not zero, the *expandX()* and *expandD()* methods are called to calculate the first unknown (x) within a *writeInfo()* statement like this: *expandX() / expandD()*. This expands the x determinant, expands the common denominator determinant, and divides the two returned expansion values to obtain the value of the first unknown (x). Then the *expandY()* and *expandD()* methods are called to find the second unknown (y).

Given the following two equations:

$$x + 2y = 3$$

$$3x + 4y = 5$$

Here is the series of windows you would see when the program is executed:

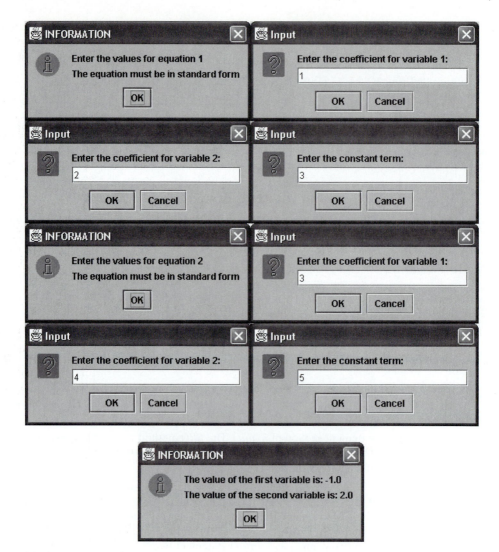

Do you think that you could develop a similar program to solve a set of three simultaneous equations? You now have all the required knowledge! Guess what you will be doing in the programming exercises at the end of the chapter?

CHAPTER SUMMARY

A two-dimensional array, or table, is a combination of two or more element rows. It has dimension $m \times n$, where m is the number of rows in the array, and n is the number of array columns. A three-dimensional array is the combination of two or more two-dimensional arrays. It is comprised of rows, columns, and planes. Thus, a three-dimensional array has dimension $p \times m \times n$, where p is the number of planes in the array, m is the number of array rows, and n is the number of columns.

A separate `for` loop is required to access each array dimension. In addition, the loops must be nested when accessing multidimensional arrays. Thus, to access a three-dimensional array, the column loop is nested in the row loop, which is nested in the plane loop.

There are many technical applications for arrays. A common use of an array is to store determinants that are used to solve systems of simultaneous equations using Cramer's rule.

QUESTIONS AND PROBLEMS

Questions

Use the following array definitions to answer questions 1–10:

```
final int MULTIPLIER = 12;
final int MULTIPLICAND = 20;
int product[][] = new int[MULTIPLIER][MULTIPLICAND];

boolean cube[][][] = new boolean[3][7][4];
```

1. Describe each array structure.
2. List the identifiers that must be used to access each array.
3. What are the dimensions of each array?
4. How many elements will each array store?
5. List all of the possible element values in the *cube* array.
6. Write a Java statement that will display the element in the fourth row and second column of the *product* array on the console screen.
7. Write a Java statement that will assign any legal element to the second row and last column of the *product* array.
8. Write the Java code required to fill each array from keyboard entries using the *StaugIO* class, if needed, for input.
9. Write the Java code required to display each array on the console screen.

Problems

Least Difficult

1. Write a program to read 15 integers from the keyboard and store them in a 3 × 5 array. Once the integers have been read, display them as a 5 × 3 array. (*Hint:* Reverse the rows and columns.)
2. Write a method that will display any given page of the book array used in Example 15-4. Assume that the user will enter the page number to be displayed.
3. Write a program that employs two methods to fill and print a calendar for the current month.

More Difficult

Employ the program developed in the chapter case study to solve Problems 4 and 5. Modify the program to meet the given application.

4. Look at the lever in Figure 15-5. If you know one of the weights and all the distances of the weights from the fulcrum, you can calculate the other two weights using two simultaneous equations. The two equations have the following general form:

$$w_1 d_1 + w_2 d_2 = w_3 d_3$$

FIGURE 15-5   A lever/fulcrum
arrangement for Problem 4.

where:

w_1, w_2, and w_3 are the three weights

d_1, d_2, and d_3 are the distances the three weights are located from the fulcrum, respectively

Using this general equation format, you get two equations by knowing two balance points. Suppose weight w_3 is 5 pounds, and you obtain a balance condition for the following distance values:

Balance point 1:

$$d_1 = 3 \text{ in.}$$
$$d_2 = 6 \text{ in.}$$
$$d_3 = 36 \text{ in.}$$

Balance point 2:

$$d_1 = 5 \text{ in.}$$
$$d_2 = 4 \text{ in.}$$
$$d_3 = 30 \text{ in.}$$

Find the two unknown weights, w_1 and w_2.

5. The following equations describe the tension, in pounds, of two cables supporting an object. Find the amount of tension on each cable (T_1 and T_2).

$$0.5T_2 + 0.93T_1 - 120 = 0$$
$$0.42T_1 - 0.54T_2 = 0$$

Most Difficult

6. Write a method to fill a 3 × 4 array with the coefficients and constant terms from three simultaneous equations, expressed in standard form. Assume that the user will enter the array elements in the required order.

7. Write a method to display the equation array in problem 6.

8. Using Cramer's rule, write a method to form 3 × 3 determinants from the 3 × 4 equation array you filled in problem 6.

9. Write a method to expand an order 3 determinant using the method of diagonals.

10. Employ the methods you developed in problems 6 through 9 to write a program that will solve a set of three simultaneous equations.

11. Suppose the perimeter of a triangle is 14 inches. The shortest side is half as long as the longest side, and 2 inches more than the difference of the two longer sides. Find the length of each side using the program you developed in problem 10.

12. Assume the following table represents the monthly rental price of six resort cabins over a five-year period.

		YEAR				
		FIRST	**SECOND**	**THIRD**	**FOURTH**	**FIFTH**
	1	200	210	225	300	235
	2	250	275	300	350	400
CABIN	3	300	325	375	400	450
	4	215	225	250	250	275
	5	355	380	400	404	415
	6	375	400	425	440	500

Write a program that employs methods to perform the following tasks:

- Fill a two-dimensional array with the table.
- Compute the total rental income for each cabin by year, and store the yearly totals in a second array.
- Compute the percentage increase/decrease in price between adjacent years for each cabin, and store the percentages in a third array.
- Generate a report showing all three arrays in table form with appropriate row/column headings.

A

Jump Start: *Sun ONE Studio* and *JBuilder*

Introduction

Sun ONE Studio (Forte)
  Community Edition

JBuilder Personal Edition

Conclusion

Introduction

Who Should Use This Appendix?

Before you attempt to program, you should have a working knowledge of a windowed environment. Knowing how to launch programs and use standard menus, buttons, etc. is a minimum requirement for programming. Having a general knowledge of the file structures (i.e., how and where files are stored) will also help you out. You can often pick up these basics simply by surfing the Internet, or even by playing a few simple games of solitaire in Microsoft® Windows. Once you have the basics down, you will be well equipped to begin this tutorial.

It helps to know Java before trying to master an ***Integrated Development Environment (IDE)***, like *Sun ONE Studio* or *JBuilder*. Likewise, it is easier to learn Java if you are already familiar with an IDE. This puts the beginner in a distinct "catch-22" situation. This tutorial is written with the beginner in mind. It attempts to give the new user some insight into an IDE environment, without addressing Java concepts. Like the title says, this appendix is here to provide you a "jump start" in using a given IDE. The drawback is that a new user will probably not gain much knowledge about the Java language just by doing the tutorial. In order to truly understand how to program using the Java language, you must go through the entire textbook using your IDE to write and execute programs.

What Is in This Appendix?

We will cover how to use the *Sun ONE Studio* (*Forte*) and *JBuilder* environments. Java concepts are not presented. You should use this tutorial in conjunction with the material presented in this text. It is possible to read through all the sections and go through all the examples of this appendix without knowing anything about Java, but you will probably not gain anything from it.

Why *Sun ONE Studio* (formally *Forte*) and *JBuilder*?

Both *Sun ONE Studio* and *JBuilder* are excellent IDEs and provide free download versions of a basic Java development environment after a required registration. *Sun ONE Studio* (formally *Forte*) is manufactured by Sun Microsystems, Inc. (*http://www.java.sun.com*), and *JBuilder* is manufactured by Borland Software Corporation (*http://www.borland.com*). The free download versions are *Sun ONE Studio Community* edition and *JBuilder Personal* edition. If you choose the *Sun ONE Studio Community* edition, make sure you download it as a bundle with *J2SE*. If you choose the *JBuilder Personal* edition, make sure you download the related document package. In this appendix, we will cover the basic use of these IDEs. You will learn how to enter, compile, and execute a simple "Hello World" program. You will be referred to Sun's or Borland's Web site for more advanced information and tutorials on these products.

Sun ONE Studio (Forte) Community Edition

Getting Started

This tutorial was written around *Sun ONE Studio, version 4.1*. Other editions or versions of *Sun ONE Studio* might be slightly different from what you see here, but should be similar. We will assume that you have already installed *Sun ONE Studio, Community Edition*. Launch *Sun ONE Studio* from your system. If your screen has a "Welcome ..." dialog box, click on the *Close* button and you will be left with a screen similar to the one shown in Figure A-1.

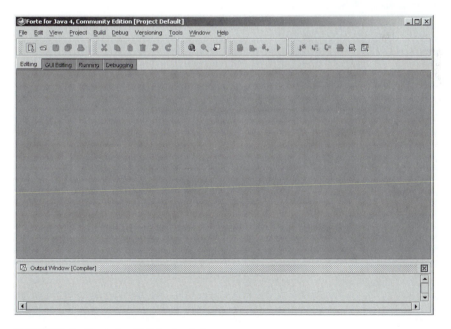

FIGURE A-1 Empty *Sun ONE Studio* window.

Your First *Sun ONE Studio* Program

This section will take you through building a simple program. You will begin by creating a new Java source file, and then you will type in a very simple program. Finally, you will compile and run the program.

Create a New Java Source File   The first step is to create a new Java source file. Click on the *File* menu, then click on *New...* in the dropdown menu. The *New Wizard* window that is shown in Figure A-2 will appear.

Select the *Classes* template from the template listings by double clicking on the word "Classes". Several *Classes* templates will appear, including *Applet*, *Class*, *Empty*, *Main*, and so on. Select the *Empty* class template. This template generates an "empty" Java source file. Click on the *Next* button at the bottom of the wizard window. A *Target Location* window will appear similar to the one shown in Figure A-3.

The default package is the one created when you installed *Sun ONE Studio* and should appear at the top of the *Filesystems* listing. Select this package. Now, drag your mouse over *<default name>* that appears in the *Name* text box at the top of the window, and type *Hello* into the text box. (*Note*: You can specify another directory for your program by typing its path into the *Package* text box.) Click on the *Finish* button at the bottom of the window. The window shown in Figure A-4 will appear, showing an empty source editor panel with the cursor blinking in the upper left corner of the panel.

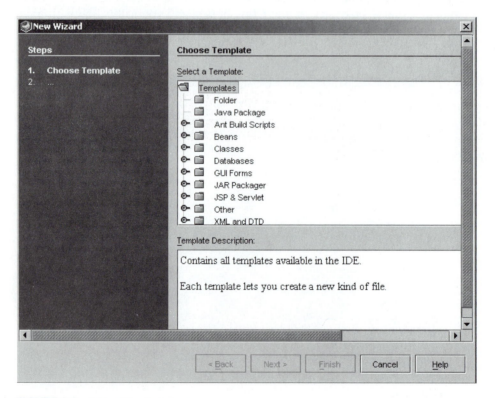

FIGURE A-2   *A New Wizard window.*

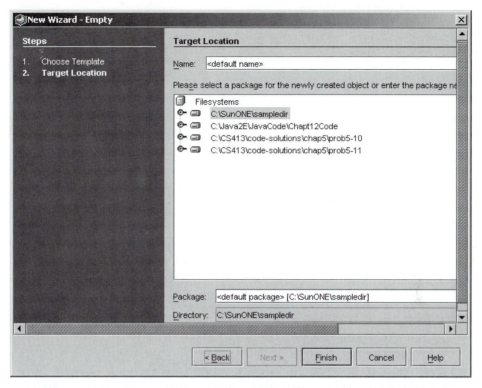

FIGURE A-3   The *Target Location* window in the *New Wizard* window.

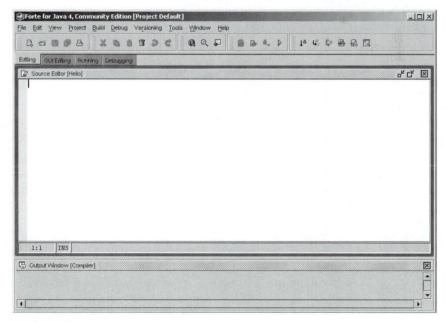

FIGURE A-4   An empty source editor window.

Type in the Code   Now you are ready to type in your first Java program. Type the following code exactly as it is shown. However, add today's date after "Created on:" and your name after "Author:".

```
/*
* Hello.java
*
* Created on:
*
* Author:
* Version: 1.0
*/


public class Hello
{//BEGIN CLASS


    public static void main(String args[])
    {//BEGIN main()
     System.out.println("HELLO WORLD!"); //DISPLAY HELLO WORLD MESSAGE
    }//END main()
}//END Hello CLASS
```

Notice that *Sun ONE Studio* shows the Java language code in black, blue, and red, while coloring the program comments in gray. This is called ***syntax highlighting***. Syntax highlighting is one of the many features that *Sun ONE Studio* provides to make writing programs simpler.

Compile the Program   Now we need to compile the program. First, save your file. Either click on the *File* menu then select *Save* from the dropdown menu, or simply type *Ctrl+s* (hold down the *Ctrl* key and type *s*). Now click on the *Build* menu, and then select *Compile* from the dropdown menu (or press the *F9* key, which is the "hot key" for the *Compile* command).

Your screen should now look similar to Figure A-5. If any error messages appear in the *Output Window*, make sure that your code is typed in correctly. If you are sure your code is correct, you might want to ask someone to double-check it for you. It is very easy to miss something when copying code, especially if you are not familiar with Java. Once your code compiles successfully, the message "Finished Hello" will appear in the *Output Window* as shown in Figure A-5.

In the event that your code is right and you are still getting an error, you should look for other problems. Your first step should be to quit *Sun ONE Studio*, then reopen it and try to compile your program again. If that doesn't help, try rebooting your computer. If you still have trouble, it is possible that *Sun ONE Studio* is not installed properly. It is also possible that you do not have the file permissions within the operating system required to write to the directory where your program is located. If you

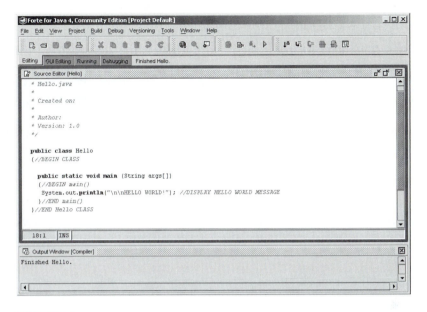

FIGURE A-5 *Sun ONE Studio* window with a Java source file and successful compile.

have placed your program on a floppy disk, you may not have enough disk space to build the program. You may need to consult your computer and software manuals and/or technical support.

Explore the Environment   In general, your program will compile without any problems and you will be ready to execute it. Before running the program, take a moment to explore the *Sun ONE Studio* environment now that you have an active program.

At the top of the window, just below the tool bar, there are four tabs. The *Editing* tab should be active at this time. When this tab is active, you will see your Java program and be able to edit it. The next tab is the *GUI Editing* tab and is used to create and edit GUIs (graphical user interfaces). See the IDE help if you want to use this feature in the future. The *Running* tab will produce the *Output Window* so that you can watch any console output produced by your program. Finally, the *Debugging* tab will produce a *Debugger Window* that is used for program debugging. Consult the IDE help if you want to use this feature in the future. Pressing the *F1* key at any time will produce the IDE help window. You will want to do this at some time in the future to explore the help features of the IDE.

Another useful feature of the IDE is the *Open File* tool bar button which appears as an open folder icon just above the *Editing* tab. Clicking this button will generate an *Open* window that allows you to browse your system and open an existing Java program file.

Run the Program Make sure your program appears in the *Source Editor* window. If not, click the *Editing* tab. Click on the *Build* menu and select the *Execute* menu item at the bottom of the menu (or press the *F6* key, which is the "hot key" for the *Execute* command). The *Running* tab will activate automatically, showing the *Output Window*. The words "HELLO WORLD!" should appear in the *Output Window* as shown in Figure A-6. Congratulations! You have just created your first program with *Sun ONE Studio*.

To see your program again, simply click the *Editing* tab. Once your cursor is placed within the editing window, the green arrow tool button will become active. Clicking this button will both compile and execute your program.

Here is a summary of the steps you just performed:

1. Created a new Java source file (*File*→*New...*→*Classes*→*Empty*→*Target Location* (select project directory location)→*Name* (enter program file name)

2. Typed in the code

3. Compiled the program (*Build*→*Compile)*

4. Ran the program (*Build*→*Execute*)

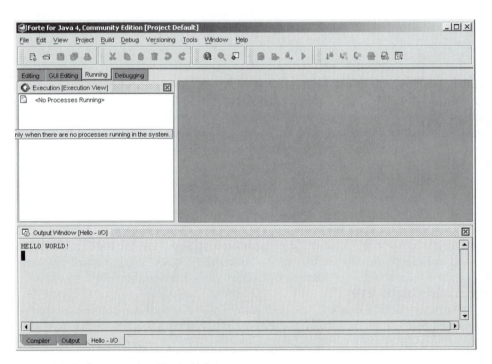

FIGURE A-6 Output produced by the *Hello.java* program.

Dealing with Errors in *Sun ONE Studio*

Syntax Errors

Syntax errors occur when you do not follow the rules of a programming language correctly. For instance, if you forget a semicolon at the end of a line, or if you mistype a keyword or a variable name, the compiler will generate a syntax error. A program will not compile if it has syntax errors. As a result, these are the first errors you will have to fix. However, most of the time they are easy to find and fix. *Sun ONE Studio* does an excellent job of finding and helping you fix syntax errors. With most errors, it stops just short of fixing them for you.

Let's create a syntax error in your *hello* program to see how Java handles it. Click on the *Editing* tab so that your program appears. Delete the semicolon from the end of the line that begins with "System." Your code should now look like this:

```
/*
* Hello.java
*
* Created on:
*
* Author:
* Version: 1.0
*/


public class Hello
{//BEGIN CLASS

   public static void main(String args[])
   {//BEGIN main()
    System.out.println("HELLO WORLD!")      //DISPLAY HELLO WORLD MESSAGE
   }//END main()
}//END Hello CLASS
```

Now press *Ctrl+s* to save the file, and then push *F9* to compile the program. The line in the *Output Window* should now show:

```
Hello.java [15:1] ';' expected
    System.out.println("\n\nHELLO WORLD!")ʌ //DISPLAY HELLO WORLD MESSAGE
```

The message indicates that a ';' was "expected" at the end of the *System.out. print-ln()* statement, as indicated by the caret symbol, ^, at the end of the statement. The caret shows where the compiler expects to find the semicolon. Click anywhere on the line that shows the error message (the one that is blue and underscored, like a link). You will be pleasantly surprised to see what happens. Your screen should look similar to Figure A-7. The line in which *Sun ONE Studio* "thinks" the error is located will be highlighted in red.

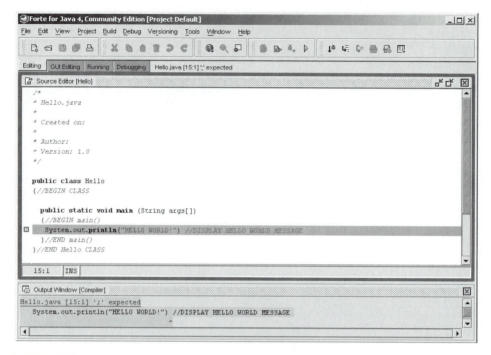

FIGURE A-7   *Sun ONE Studio* window with syntax error highlighted.

In a large program this error-finding ability will speed up program development tremendously. From here, you can fix the error and then recompile and run your program. Take some time to play around. Delete things, add things—play around with the program and get a feel for the syntax error reporting capability in *Sun ONE Studio*.

Using the Debugger

Syntax errors in code are the least of your worries. Logic errors are much harder to find. A logic error occurs when the computer does what you tell it to do via your program, but does not do what you want or meant it to do. These errors do not keep your program from compiling or running (although sometimes they cause your program to crash), and the compiler will not find them for you. A debugger, however, is a great tool for finding these errors.

The *Sun ONE Studio* IDE contains a rather sophisticated debugger. Sun has created an excellent tutorial on how to use this debugger. The tutorial is built right into your IDE help system. Rather than duplicate much of this material here, we suggest that you take this tutorial to learn how to use the debugger and some other features of the IDE. To get there, simply click on the *Help* menu and select *Contents*. You should now see the window shown in Figure A-8. You can begin the tutorial by clicking the *Creating the ColorSwitch Application* link.

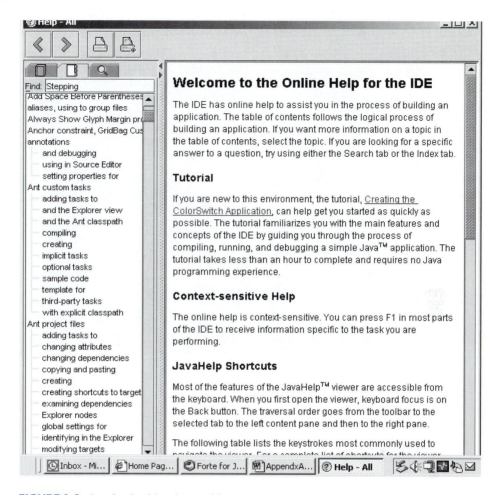

FIGURE A-8   Locating the debugging tutorial.

JBuilder Personal Edition

Getting Started

This tutorial was written around *JBuilder Personal Edition, version 8.0.* Other editions or versions of *JBuilder* might be slightly different from what you see here, but should be similar. We will assume that you have already installed *JBuilder Personal* edition. Launch *JBuilder* and you will see a screen that looks similar to that in Figure A-9. If your screen has a dialog box showing the "Tip of the Day", click on the *Close* button and you will be left with the screen shown in Figure A-9. Next, click on the *View* menu and select the *Messages* item. You should see a white message panel appear at the bottom of the window containing the words "No messages".

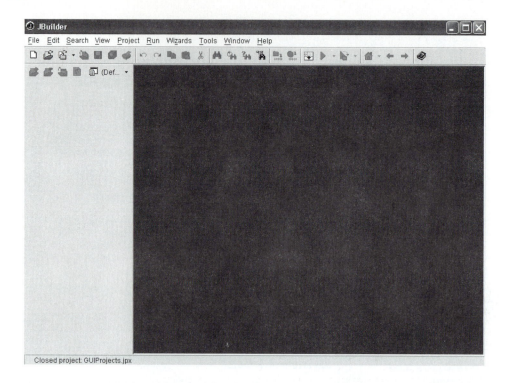

Closed project: GUIProjects.jpx

FIGURE A-9   Empty *JBuilder* window.

Your First *JBuilder* Program

This section will take you through building a simple console program. You will begin by creating a new Java project and source file, and then you will type in a very simple program. Finally, you will compile and run the program. In *JBuilder*, you must have a *project* in order to compile a program.

Create a New Java Project   Click on the *File* menu, then click on *New Project...* in the dropdown menu. The window that is shown in Figure A-10 will appear.

Select a directory where you would like your project placed. You can type in a directory path in the text field labeled *Directory*, or browse and select a directory using the associated ellipses (...) button.

Once you select a directory path, type *Hello* into the text field labeled *Name* in place of anything that might be there.

Click the *Finish* button and you should see the project window shown in Figure A-11.

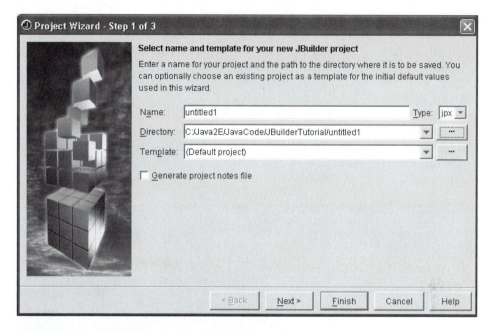

FIGURE A-10   A *New Project* window.

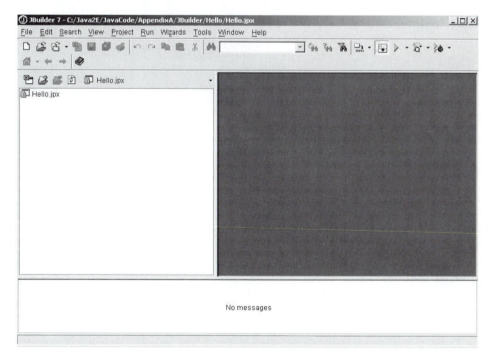

FIGURE A-11   A *New* window (*Files* tab).

Add a New Source File to the Project   Click on the *Project* menu and select the *Add Files/Packages …* menu item. A window will appear with a directory tree. You should see your *Hello* package directory within this tree. If you do not see it, browse the tree until you find it. Click on the *Hello* directory.

Once you have selected the *Hello* directory, type *Hello.java* in the *File name* text field. Click the *OK* button and you should see a window like the one shown in Figure A-12. If you are asked to create a new file, click *OK*.

The window panel on the left shows your *Hello.jpx* project, which contains your empty *Hello.java* source file. Double-click on the *Hello.java* source file name, and the edit panel on the right should turn white with the cursor blinking in the upper left corner of the panel.

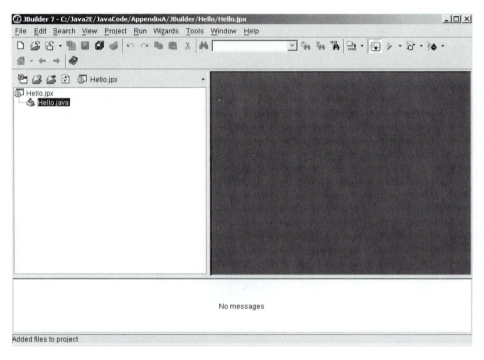

FIGURE A-12   The project window with an empty *Hello.java* source file opened.

Type in the Code   Now you are ready to type in your first Java program. Type the following code exactly as it is shown. However, add today's date after "Created on:" and your name after "Author:".

```
/*
 * Hello.java
 *
 * Created on:
 *
 * Author:
 * Version: 1.0
 */
```

```
public class Hello
{//BEGIN CLASS

   public static void main(String args[])
   {//BEGIN main()
    System.out.println("HELLO WORLD!"); //DISPLAY HELLO WORLD MESSAGE
   }//END main()
}//END Hello CLASS
```

Notice that *JBuilder* shows the Java language code in black and blue colors, while coloring the program comments in green. This is called ***syntax highlighting***. Syntax highlighting is one of the many features that *JBuilder* provides to make writing programs simpler.

Compile the Program   Now we need to compile (make) and run the program. First, save your file. Either click on the *File* menu and then select *Save "Hello.java"* from the dropdown menu, or simply type *Ctrl+s* (hold down the *Ctrl* key and type *s*). Now click on the *Project* menu, and then select *Make Project "Hello.jpx"* from the dropdown menu (or type the *Ctrl+F9* key, which is the "hot key" for the *Make* command).

Your screen should now look similar to Figure A-13. Now look at the status bar at the bottom of the window. It should say something like, "Build succeeded with 1 file built. Build took 0 seconds."

If any error messages appear in the message panel, make sure that your code is typed in correctly then try to compile the program again. If you are sure your code is correct, you might want to ask someone to double-check it for you. It is very easy to miss something when copying code, especially if you are not familiar with Java.

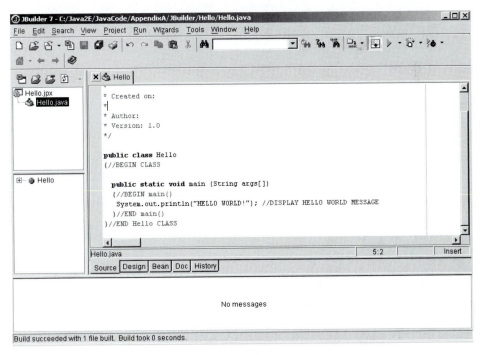

FIGURE A-13   *JBuilder* window with active project and Java source file.

In the event that your code is right and you are still getting an error, you should look for other problems. Your first step should be to quit *JBuilder*, then reopen it and try to compile your program again. If that doesn't help, try rebooting your computer. If you still have trouble, it is possible that *JBuilder* is not installed properly. It is also possible that you do not have the file permissions within the operating system to write in the directory where your project is located. If you have built your project on a floppy disk, you may not have enough disk space to build the project. You may need to consult your computer and software manuals and/or technical support.

Explore the Environment   In general, your program will compile without any problems and you will be ready to execute it. Before running the program, take a moment to explore the *JBuilder* environment now that you have an active project.

At the left side of the screen is a window containing two panels. The top panel shows the contents of your *Hello.jpx* project, which is your *Hello.java* program. The bottom left panel shows the classes contained in your *Hello.jpx* project. You see here that the *Hello* class is part of the project. If a plus sign is present, click on it and *main(String[] args)* will appear underneath the *Hello* class. This means that method *main()* is part of your *Hello* class. If you click on *main()* or the icon next to it, the line in your program containing *main()* will become highlighted, thus locating this method within your program.

Run the Program   Make sure the message panel appears at the bottom of the window. If not, click the *View* menu and select the *Messages* item. Now, click on the *Project* menu and select the *Project Properties* … item towards the bottom of the menu. You should see a screen similar to that shown in Figure A-14.

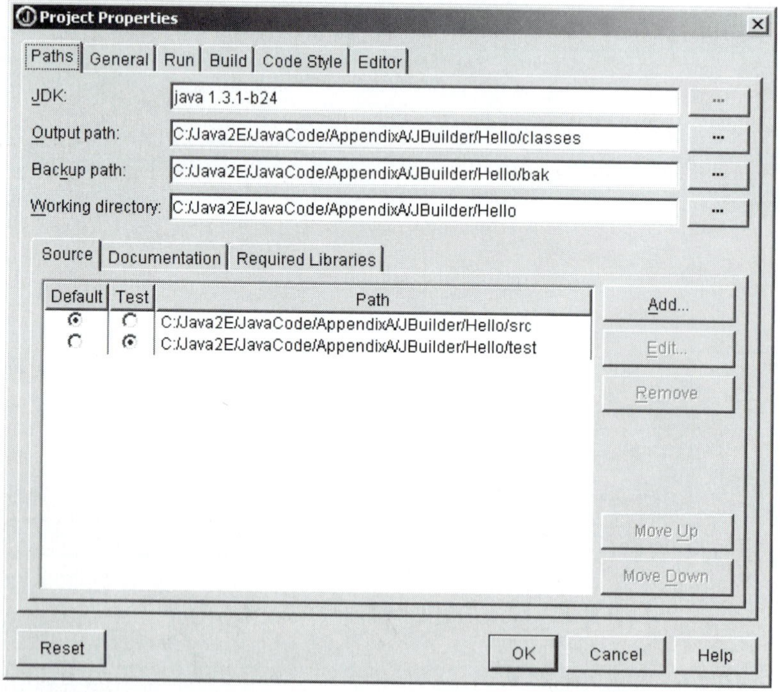

FIGURE A-14   General project properties window.

Click the *Run* tab and the window shown in Figure A-15 will appear. (*Note:* If your *JBuilder* is earlier than version 7.0, you will get the *Runtime Properties* window shown in Figure A-16.) Now click the *Edit...* (or *New...* if the window is empty) button and the window shown in Figure A-16 will appear. Make sure that "*Application*" is high-lighted in the <u>*Type*</u> box as shown in Figure A-16, then click the ellipses (...) button to the right of the *Main class* text field. Another window will appear with a *Search for* (*Class name* for earlier versions) text field at the top of the window. Type *Hello* in this text field, and then click the *OK* button at the bottom of the window. The *Runtime Properties* window shown in Figure A-16 should reappear with your *Hello* class shown in the *Main class* text field. Click the *OK* button at the bottom of this window. Now click the *OK* button at the bottom of the *Project Properties* window.

 PROGRAMMING NOTE

You must set the *Runtime Properties Main class* name to your application or applet class name in this manner each time you want to run a different program.

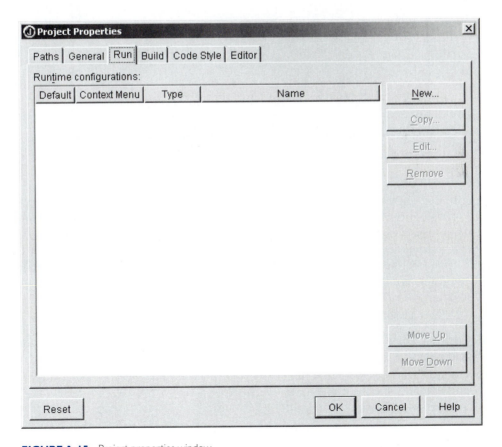

FIGURE A-15 Project properties window.

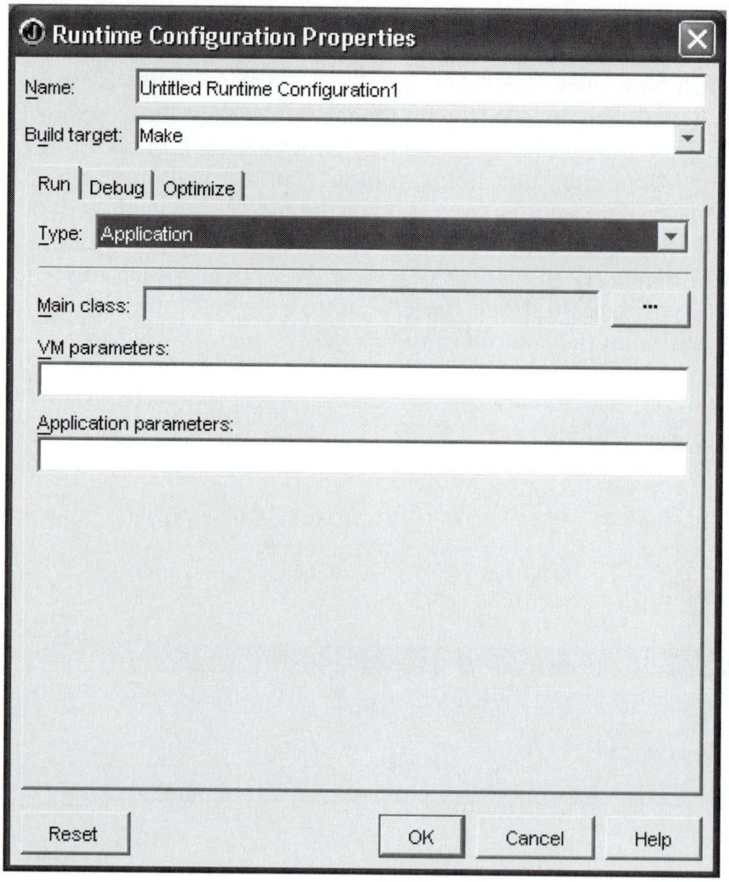

FIGURE A-16   Runtime properties window.

You are now ready to run your program. Click on the *Run* menu, and then select the *Run Project* option. You can alternatively press the *F9* hot key or click directly on the green arrow icon on the tool bar to run a program. This will also compile (make) the program automatically if it needs to be compiled. The words "HELLO WORLD!" should appear in the message panel at the bottom of the window showing the output of your program, as shown in Figure A-17. Congratulations! You have just created your first program with *JBuilder*.

Here is a summary of the steps you just performed:

1. Created a new Java project (*File→New Project…*, enter project directory location and name)
2. Created a new Java source file (*Project→Add Files/Packages…*, select directory and enter source file name)
3. Typed in the code
4. Made the program by compiling it (*Project→Make Project*)

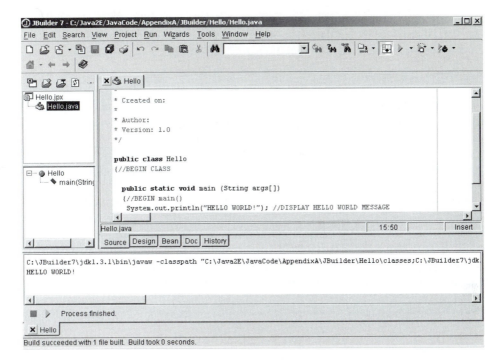

FIGURE A-17 Output produced by the *Hello.java* program.

5. Set the runtime properties (*Project→Project Properties→Run→Edit…→Application→ … →Search→*(type in the source file name) *OK→OK→OK*
6. Ran the program (*Run→Run Project*)

Dealing with Errors in *JBuilder*

Syntax Errors

Syntax errors occur when you do not follow the rules of a programming language correctly. For instance, if you forget a semicolon at the end of a line, or if you mistype a keyword or a variable name, the compiler will generate a syntax error. A program will not compile if it has syntax errors. As a result, these are the first errors you will have to fix. However, most of the time they are easy to find and fix. *JBuilder* does an excellent job of finding and helping you fix syntax errors. With most errors, it stops just short of fixing them for you.

Let's create a syntax error in your *Hello* program to see how Java handles it. Delete the semicolon from the end of the line that begins with "System …". Your code should now look like this:

```
public class Hello
{//BEGIN CLASS
```

```
public static void main(String args[])
{//BEGIN main()
 System.out.println("HELLO WORLD!") //DISPLAY HELLO WORLD MESSAGE
}//END main()
}//END Hello CLASS
```

Now push *Ctrl+S* to save the file, and then push *Ctrl+F9* to compile the project. The line in the message window should now show ""Hello.java": Error #: 200 : ';' expected at line 15, column 38." Click anywhere on the line that shows the error message. You will be pleasantly surprised to see what happens. Your screen should look similar to Figure A-18. The error line in the message window will be highlighted in blue, and the line in which *JBuilder* "thinks" the error is located will be highlighted in red. Notice also that the error is indicated in the class panel to the left using an exclamation symbol within a red circle.

In a large program this error-finding ability will speed up program development tremendously. From here, you can fix the error and recompile your program. Take some time to play around. Delete things, add things—play around with the program and get a feel for the syntax error reporting capability in *JBuilder*.

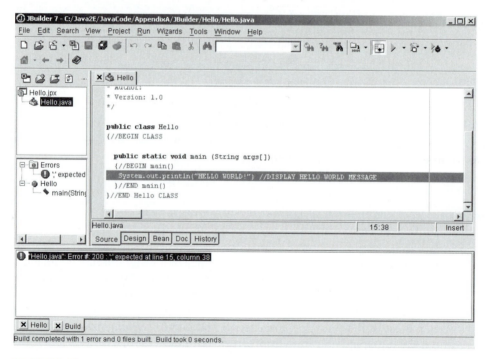

FIGURE A-18   *JBuilder* window with compile error.

Using the Debugger

Syntax errors in code are the least of your worries. *Logic* errors are much harder to find. A logic error occurs when the computer does what you tell it to do via your program, but does not do what you want or meant it to do. These errors do not keep your program from compiling or running (although sometimes they cause your program to crash), and the compiler will not find them for you. A debugger, however, is a great tool for finding these errors.

The *JBuilder* IDE contains a rather sophisticated debugger. Borland has created an excellent tutorial on how to use this debugger. The tutorial is built right into your IDE help system as long as you have downloaded the supporting documentation file. (*Note:* The documentation file is a separate download and installation from *JBuilder Personal.*) Rather than duplicate much of this material here, we suggest that you take this tutorial to learn how to use the debugger. To get there, simply click on the *Help* menu and select *JBuilder Tutorials.* Then select the *Basic Tutorials* link, followed by the *Compiling, running, and debugging* link. Now, scroll down and click on the *Debugging Java Programs* link. You should now see the window shown in Figure A-19. You can begin the tutorial using the scrollbar.

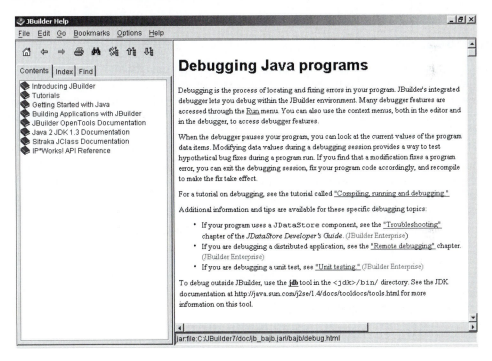

FIGURE A-19   Locating the debugging tutorial.

Conclusion

It is beyond the scope of this tutorial to cover every aspect of *Sun ONE Studio* and *JBuilder*, but you should have a good working knowledge of the environment after going through it. There are several features of each IDE that have not even been mentioned here; however, everything you need to get started using *Sun ONE Studio* or *JBuilder* to create programs is here. Enjoy!

A Systems Engineering Tutorial with UML

Introduction

This appendix provides a series of learning modules that have been written to acquaint you with systems and software engineering. As you go through the modules, you will follow a team of programmers from the *Foo.com* company as they progress from a poorly designed "build-it, fix-it" customer billing system (that wreaked havoc with their customers and bank), through a structured design of the system, until they finally reach an object-oriented design of their system. You will want to pay special attention to the topic of UML™ class diagrams in the last module because they are used extensively within this text. Before we get started, we need to address *systems engineering* versus *software engineering*. The differences between the two are often obscure. People that have this expertise are sometimes called *systems analysts* and at other times called *software engineers*, often depending on the job title imposed by the organization that employs them. In either case, such people have often spent several years "in the trenches" as programmers developing software specified by other systems analysts or software engineers. Many of them also have graduate degrees in computer science, computer information systems, or software engineering. With this in mind, let's begin with a brief overview and history of the discipline.

SE101: SYSTEMS AND SOFTWARE ENGINEERING: HISTORY AND OVERVIEW

OBJECTIVES

When you are finished with this module, you should have a good understanding of the following:

- The importance of software engineering
- The purpose of software engineering
- The six major steps of the software development life cycle, or SDLC

Introduction

There is a story about a new *Foo.com* company whose programmers developed an accounting software system. Although the accounting system performed most tasks without any problems, the programmers did not test the customer billing software for the case when a customer's account balance was $0.00. So, at the end of each month, the system would automatically send a statement requesting a minimum payment of $0.00 to each customer with a $0.00 balance. When a customer would complain, the *Foo.com* customer service department instructed the customer to simply send a check for $0.00 to avoid penalties and bad credit reports. (Of course, you could probably imagine how this went over with the customer!) Several customers did as instructed and sent their checks for $0.00. One day, the *Foo.com* accounting department received a call from their bank, complaining that the checks they deposited for $0.00 totally crashed their banking system! Of course, the accounting department, along with the customer relations department, immediately requested that their programmers fix the problem.

This type of problem often occurs when problem solving and software development is left completely to programmers, without direction from experienced software engineers, sometimes called systems analysts. Such scenarios are not uncommon in today's world. In most cases, the problems they create are not catastrophic and are corrected with little loss. But, what if such a software "glitch" occurred in our national defense system or in the laser system that is performing surgery on your eye? This is where software engineering comes into play. Software engineering is an attempt to solve problems *before* they happen. Specifically, software engineering is a discipline whose goal is to produce error-free software that considers all the what-if scenarios, is cost-effective, and meets all the client's needs. The term *software engineering* was coined in 1967 by NATO to describe software development as an engineering process that attempts to head off problems through engineering-like activities *before* the software is released to the client.

The renowned computer scientist Grace Hopper stated in her 1988 address to the ACM conference in Atlanta, that we *must* put the systems analyst back into the software development cycle. She further stated that we must walk all the way around a problem, considering all the what-if scenarios. As in the foregoing story, what if the customer's balance is $0.00? She also stressed that the human being must be kept within the processing loop, citing what happened to the stock market in October 1987 when we human beings were left out of the trading loop. In October 1987, the market crashed over 1000 points in a few seconds through accelerated computer trading. As a result, the Securities and Exchange Commission (SEC), has since stipulated that all computer trading must cease after any market swing of 200 points or more, thus placing us humans back in the loop. Fortunately, most of the computer industry took her words of wisdom seriously and have since placed more emphasis on software engineering.

Software engineering is a discipline whose goal is to produce error-free software that considers all the what-if scenarios, is cost-effective, and meets all the client's needs.

The Software Development Life Cycle (SDLC)

Software engineering is concerned with the entire life of a software project, often referred to as the *software development life cycle* or simply *SDLC*, from initial problem definition through the eventual retirement of the software. The software development life cycle is formalized by a set of phases which describe a logical process used by software engineers to develop fault-free, cost-effective software that meets all the client's needs. Most texts identify six phases to the life cycle as follows:

- *Survey phase*
- *Analysis phase*
- *Design phase*
- *Construction phase*
- *Maintenance phase*
- *Retirement phase*

Keep in mind that up to the retirement phase, SDLC is an iterative process. As systems requirements change and needs for system improvements and efficiencies are identified, the software development life cycle will be repeated until the system is retired.

The Survey Phase

This phase is sometimes called the *feasibility* phase or the *requirements* phase. The primary purpose of this phase is to investigate the problems, opportunities, and directives that have triggered the need for a software solution to a problem. Its purpose is to determine what the client *needs*, not what the client *wants*. In addition, the software engineer/analyst attempts to define the scope, size, and preliminary timetable for the project. And finally, the engineer must answer the question: "Is the project both technically and economically feasible?".

The primary purpose of the survey phase is to investigate the problems, opportunities, and directives that have triggered the need for a software solution to a problem.

The survey phase usually begins with a series of meetings between the engineering team and the major players and users within the client organization. Interviews are then scheduled with key client personnel. These interviews can be structured with pre-planned, closed-ended questions, or unstructured with open-ended questions which encourage the interviewee to speak out. Simple questionnaires can also be used to ascertain information about the needs of the client. The engineering team will also perform a preliminary look at the various manual and automated forms that are used within the target area of the project.

The outcome of this phase will be an initial feasibility report addressing the project scope and timetable, and conclude with a go/no-go recommendation.

The Analysis Phase

The analysis phase, sometimes called the *study* phase, is a continuation of the survey phase. Most engineers agree that this phase is probably the most important phase in the software development life cycle, since it attempts to model and formalize the current system. Notice we said the *current* system and *not* the future system. The current system might be a manual or an automated system. In fact, it might be a new system entirely. In order to develop a new system, the engineer must completely understand the current system. Modeling the current system provides the analyst with a more thorough understanding of the problems, opportunities, and directives that created the system request. The analysis phase also attempts to define the requirements and priorities for a new or improved system.

 The purpose of the analysis phase is to model the current system, whether it be a manual or automated system, and to determine *what* the new or improved system is supposed to do. It also attempts to define the requirements and priorities for a new or improved system.

Further interviews, observations, and questionnaires are conducted. The results are formalized using a visual (graphical) modeling technique, depending on whether a structured or object-oriented analysis is being performed. ***Structured analysis*** uses ***logical data flow diagrams*** (***LDFDs***) to model the flow of data within the current system. An LDFD is a graphic that shows the logical movement of data within the system, and the processes being performed on that data without regard to the physical software or hardware devices that are operating on the data. ***Object-oriented analysis*** (***OOA***) employs case and class modeling to describe the current, as well as future, system in terms of existing objects and new or modified objects. A ***CASE*** (***Computer-Aided Systems Engineering***) ***tool*** is often used to generate the required graphics with either the structured or object-oriented approach. CASE tools are software products that automate the phases of the software development life cycle. Both structured analysis and OOA will be explored in future software engineering modules in this appendix.

At this point, some engineers might employ rapid prototyping, especially for simple projects. A prototype is a quickly built software package that models the target system. Rapid application development (RAD) tools, such as Visual BASIC, are often used for this purpose. The idea is to allow the client users to experiment with the prototype system, while the engineers observe, ask questions, and record their observations.

A rapid prototype allows the engineers and the client to quickly agree on what the software should do, since it resembles the basic functionality of the target system.

The outcome of the analysis phase is a comprehensive **systems requirements statement** which includes the graphical models, prototypes, and supporting documentation such as interview, observation, and questionnaire summaries. A refined timetable as well as another go/no-go recommendation is also normally included in the document.

The Design Phase

The purpose of the design phase is to determine *how* the new system will satisfy the client's needs. Thus, the engineer must convert the analysis requirements statement to a specification for a new or modified system.

The purpose of the design phase is to determine *how* the new system will satisfy the client's needs. Thus, the engineer must convert the analysis requirements statement to a specification for a new or modified system.

Here, alternative solutions are first identified and evaluated based on technical, economical, and schedule feasibility. Alternative solutions often include doing nothing, modifying the current system, buying canned software, or developing new software, or some combination of these. Based on the alternative analysis, a target solution is recommended to the client and, if acceptable, the actual system design begins.

The design of new software can be a **structured design** or an **object-oriented design (OOD)**. A structured design requires formalization of the new process models in the form of **physical data flow diagrams (PDFDs)**. A PDFD depicts actual physical entities of the proposed system such as a "Java *xyz* method", not just logical entities like a process as in the LDFD of the analysis phase. Structured design also employs **entity relationship diagrams (ERDs)** to formalize data relationships in order to build any required system databases. An OOD requires formalization of detailed class and class interaction diagrams. Again, a CASE tool is used to automate the design process, whether it be a structured or OOD. In addition to the graphical design, algorithms are developed for the various processes defined for the system. These algorithms will later be converted to code, such as Java methods. System prototypes are again often employed to get user feedback on input and output design specifications.

The outcome of the design phase is a system specification consisting of the alternative analyses, system recommendation, graphical models and algorithms for the proposed system, prototypes, and a refined timetable. A final cost-benefit analysis is sometimes included to determine if the proposed system is still economically feasible. Of course, the engineer also makes another go/no-go recommendation at this point.

The Construction Phase

The construction phase, sometimes called the *implementation* phase, is pretty straightforward. This is when the various design components are coded and tested individually, then integrated together and tested as a system. The system components will include the classes (OOP), processes (algorithms), databases, and interfaces specified in the design phase. In addition, the system must be fully documented in terms of user and reference manuals.

The purpose of the construction phase is to code and test the individual system components, as well as the complete integrated system.

The outcome of this phase is a completed software system, ready for delivery to the client.

The Maintenance Phase

The maintenance phase is where any future changes and enhancements to the system are made. Two types of maintenance are *corrective maintenance* and *enhancement maintenance*. Corrective maintenance is the removing of any software bugs found by the system developers or the user, without requiring any changes to the software specification developed in the design phase. Enhancement maintenance involves updating the software with new or improved features. When enhancements are made, the software specifications are changed first, then the changes are implemented by changing or adding the system code. By the way, studies have shown that over the complete life cycle of the system, the maintenance phase accounts for over 50% of the total cost of the system.

The purpose of the maintenance phase is to perform both corrective and enhancement maintenance on the system until it is retired.

The Retirement Phase

The retirement phase is when the system software is "retired" from service. However, even a human retiree might do some work at a part time job. Software systems do as well, since various components of the system might be used in newer systems, especially with object-oriented systems that employ inheritance and polymorphism. Some say that old systems never die, they just keep getting enhanced or converted. We have thought for years that the old COBOL and RPG systems would be retired, but many of them have not been retired yet. Rather than getting retired, they get converted using a newer paradigm and language, like object-orientation using Java or C++.

You should now have a good overall perspective of systems/software engineering and its role in the software development life cycle. Future modules will address both the structured and object-oriented paradigms in more detail.

SE102: SOFTWARE PARADIGMS

OBJECTIVES

When you are finished with this module, you should have a good understanding of the following:

- ■ The concept of a paradigm
- ■ The history of software paradigms
- ■ The idea behind the structured paradigm
- ■ The idea behind the object-oriented paradigm
- ■ The software development life cycle applied using the structured versus the object-oriented paradigm

Introduction

When the chief information officer (CIO) of *Foo.com* heard about the problems in their billing software, he became so upset that he summoned his programmers. With his past experience as a programmer and systems analyst, he just could not believe that his programmers did not follow the software development life cycle. As a result, he directed all of them to learn about the life cycle and how it must be applied using a modern programming paradigm. Many of them decided to take a course in software engineering or systems analysis/design at a local university to learn the latest software engineering techniques.

In this module, you will find out what they learned about different programming paradigms, and how the life cycle differs when applied to these paradigms. Then, in future *SE* modules, you will follow their analysis and design of a new billing system.

A Historical Perspective

First, we should define what we mean by a "paradigm." Webster defines a paradigm as "a pattern, example, or model." Another way to say it is that a paradigm is a way of thinking of things. In religion, for example, there is the Jewish paradigm, the Christian paradigm, and the Islamic paradigm, among others. In software engineering, there are primarily two ways of thinking of things: the structured paradigm and the object-oriented paradigm. Prior to these paradigms, there was no software engineering at all. The prevailing paradigm was "build it and fix it," without any formal analysis or design specifications. Due to a lack of any formal software development paradigm, the idea was to solve the problem at the keyboard, test it, and fix it until the client was satisfied. This approach will probably work to solve simple problems using small programs, but is totally unworkable for today's complex problems requiring complex software solutions. Remember folks, all the simple problems have been solved! Today's problems are extremely complex, requiring thousands and even millions of lines of code. The build-it, fix-it model just doesn't cut the mustard when dealing with today's real-world problems. This is why this book is striving to teach you good software development techniques, even though the problems you are solving are relatively simple and could be solved at the keyboard using the build-it, fix-it approach. The intent of this book is to get you into good software development habits so that you will be able to deal with the complex problems that you will encounter in the real world. This short module will provide an overview and comparison of the two most common paradigms in use today: the structured paradigm and the object-oriented paradigm. Then, later modules will explore these two paradigms in more detail, from a software engineering perspective.

A **paradigm** is a model that provides a way of thinking of things.

In the mainframe days of the 1960s, it became clear that the build-it, fix-it paradigm was not sufficient to manage the increasing complexity of software systems. Many programs written in these days resulted in "spaghetti code" which became totally unreadable, and therefore, impossible to maintain. How can you deal with complexity? One way is to break a complex problem down into smaller subproblems which are more manageable than the original complex problem. Then, employ teams of programmers to solve the individual subproblems. This is the essence of the structured paradigm which was developed in the early 1970s to deal with ever-increasing complexity.

The **structured paradigm** employs a top/down functional decomposition methodology that breaks the original complex problem down into smaller, more manageable subproblems.

As complexity continued to increase exponentially during the 1970s and early 1980s, it became apparent that the structured paradigm needed to be replaced. This realization led to the object-oriented paradigm which was developed in the late 1970s through the early 1990s. The object-oriented paradigm employs objects and object interaction to attack complex problems in a natural way, like we humans tend to think about things. So, both paradigms are attempts to deal with the increasing complexity of the software projects and resulting systems. When we talk about software complexity, we usually associate it with the number of lines of code required to solve a problem. The structured paradigm was developed to handle systems with hundreds and thousands of lines of code. But when systems begin to grow beyond 100,000 lines of code, the structured paradigm becomes inadequate to manage the increased complexity. The object-oriented paradigm was developed to manage systems with hundreds of thousands, and even millions of lines of code. Yes, some of today's software products require millions of lines of code! We feel that it is important that you know both paradigms so that you can deal with either when needed. In fact, you will find that the object-oriented paradigm contains many elements of its predecessor, the structured paradigm.

The **object-oriented paradigm** employs objects and object interaction to attack complex problems in a natural way, like we humans tend to think about things in terms of attributes and behavior.

The Structured versus the Object-Oriented Paradigm

The primary difference between the structured paradigm and the object-oriented paradigm is that the structured paradigm is either *data-oriented* or *action-oriented*, but not both. In the structured paradigm, the program data structures are designed and coded separately, but work in conjunction with the program algorithms (methods). In the object-oriented paradigm, the program data structures and related algorithms are combined into well-defined independent units, called objects. Objects represent the application system more naturally because they reflect the way we humans think about the system. For example, consider an ATM machine. We don't think of the data (money) it contains separately from the operations, or actions, that it performs on the data. We look at it as one *encapsulated* and independent unit that dispenses its data (money) in connection with a related action, such as a withdrawal.

In the *SE101* module, you were introduced to the software development life cycle in general. There are minor, but important, differences when the life cycle is applied using the structured versus the object-oriented paradigm. Here are the general life cycle phases we discussed in *SE101*:

- *Survey phase*
- *Analysis phase*
- *Design phase*
- *Construction phase*
- *Maintenance phase*
- *Retirement phase*

The general phases are still the same, but let's consider one additional level of refinement. Here is a refinement of the life cycle when applied to the structured paradigm:

- *Survey phase*
  Initial feasibility study and report
- *Analysis phase*
  Detailed analysis of the current system using logical DFDs to produce a requirements statement that specifies what the new system is supposed to do
- *Design phase*
  Determination of how the new system will satisfy the client's needs through physical DFDs and functional decomposition
  Also, the developing of any algorithms required for the methods
- *Construction phase*
  Code the data structures and algorithms separately, then combine
- *Maintenance phase*
  Perform corrective and enhancement maintenance
- *Retirement phase*

Now, here is the life cycle when applied to the object-oriented paradigm:

- *Survey phase*
  Initial feasibility study and report

- *Analysis phase*
  Detailed analysis of the current system to produce a requirements statement that specifies what the new system is supposed to do
  Identification of the system objects
- *Design phase*
  Determination of how the new system will satisfy the client's needs by constructing object interaction and class diagrams
- *Construction phase*
  Code the data and related algorithms together as objects
- *Maintenance phase*
  Perform corrective and enhancement maintenance
- *Retirement phase*

The major difference that you see if you compare the two cycles is that the analysis phase is extended in the object-oriented paradigm to include identification of the objects, thus addressing the software structure, or *architecture*, of the system early during the analysis phase, *before* the design phases. In the structured paradigm, the system architecture is not addressed until the design phase, when the functional decomposition takes place. Since the object-oriented paradigm addresses the system architecture during the analysis phase, the design phase deals with the required object interaction to satisfy the client's needs. This approach introduces the primary system component, the object, earlier in the life cycle and makes for an easier transition from the analysis to the design phase, thus managing complexity in a more natural and cohesive way.

Also, notice that in the construction phase, the data structures and algorithms are coded separately, then combined using the structured paradigm. However, in the object-oriented paradigm, the data structures and related algorithms are coded *together* to form the program objects. The objects are then combined in an application program as specified by the object interaction, which was determined in the design phase. Again, this makes for an easier transition from the design phase to the construction phase.

Now that you are familiar with the fundamental differences between the two paradigms, future *SE* modules will deal with the details of each as related to software engineering.

SE103: THE STRUCTURED PARADIGM

OBJECTIVES

When you are finished with this module, you should have a good understanding of the following:

- Structured analysis and design
- Context diagrams
- Logical data flow diagrams
- Physical data flow diagrams
- The difference between a logical and a physical data flow diagram
- Functional decomposition diagrams

Introduction

At the direction of their CIO, the *Foo.com* programmers took a course in software engineering at their local university. After learning about the general software development life cycle, they applied the life cycle using both the structured paradigm and the object-oriented paradigm. This *SE* module provides an overview of their structured analysis and design, while the next *SE* module looks at their object-oriented analysis and design.

Structured Analysis

From *SE101*, you learned that the purpose of the analysis phase is to model the current system, whether it be a manual or automated system, to determine *what* the new or improved system is supposed to do. This analysis is done by studying the current system and documenting the system relative to the flow of data within the system, using graphical models called ***logical data flow diagrams***, or ***LDFDs***. Graphical CASE tools are used to produce the LDFDs. Since the structured paradigm is a top/down approach to problem solving, the data flow diagrams produced by structured analysis depict a top/down hierarchy of several levels. At the top level is the ***context*** diagram. The context diagram shows the entire system as *one* process and the ***external entities*** with which the system must interact. An external entity is a person, organization, or system that interacts with the system being studied. Thus, a context diagram defines the boundaries of the system. The context diagram developed by the *Foo.com* programmers for their billing system is shown in Figure B-1.

A ***context diagram*** shows the entire system as one process and what external entities with which the system must interact. Thus, a context diagram defines the boundaries of the system.

At this level, there is only one process which represents the system being analyzed. Notice that the process symbol is a rounded rectangle. At the top of the rectangle

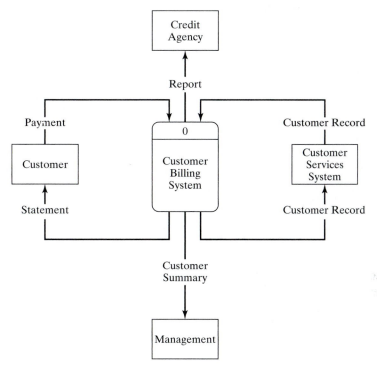

FIGURE B-1   The context diagram produced by the *Foo.com* programmers for the billing process.

is the level of the process. The context diagram is always labeled as level 0 because it is at the top of the process hierarchy. The external entities are represented with a standard, non-rounded, rectangle. As you can see, the *Foo.com* billing system interacts with four external entities—the customer, management, credit agency, and the customer services system. The external entities depict the input and output to and from the system, thereby defining the scope and boundary of the system. The data flows to/from the system process are shown using arrows, labeled with the data/information that they represent.

Next, using a classic structured approach, the context diagram is refined to one or more levels. The *Foo.com* programmers identified four processes within the billing system, as shown in Figure B-2.

The process refinements should be self-explanatory. Notice, however, that each process has a key number associated with it. In addition, you can see here that a *data store* is central to the entire system. A data store can be a manual location to store data, such as a file cabinet, or an automated location, such as a disk file or database. We don't really care during the analysis. We are only concerned with modeling the *current* system, and how/where data moves within this system. As you can see, the LDFD represents a data store with an open-ended rectangle.

Since this problem is relatively simple, the processes do not need any more levels of refinement. If they did, we would simply expand any processes needing further

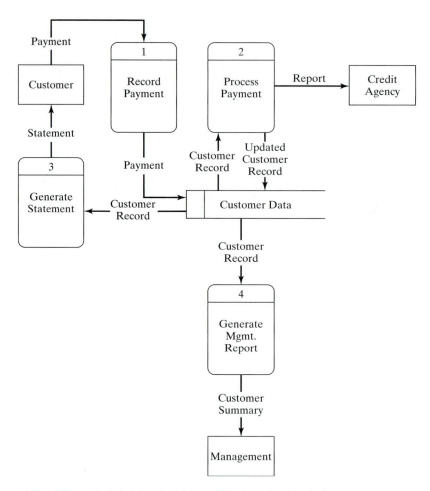

FIGURE B-2   The logical data flow diagram (LDFD) produced by the *Foo.com* programmers for the billing process.

refinement. The labeling technique would be consistent with the refinement. So, if process 1 needed refinement, we would refine it into processes 1.1, 1.2, 1.3, and so on. If further refinement of process 1.2, for example, was needed, we would refine it into processes 1.2.1, 1.2.2, 1.2.3, and so on. Hopefully, you can visualize the top/down hierarchy inherent in the structured paradigm.

Now, it's on to see how the *Foo.com* programmers performed their system design.

Structured Design

During the structured design phase, the engineers must determine how the new system will satisfy the client's needs through a physical DFD and a functional decomposition diagram. Algorithms are also developed for any methods identified in the functional decomposition diagram.

One of the first tasks at this phase is to convert the logical DFD developed in the analysis phase to a physical DFD. Remember, a logical DFD only depicts the logical processing and storage of data, without regard to *how* the data are to be processed or stored. A physical DFD addresses the *physical* things, like programs, files, and database tables that are used to process and store the data. So, the *Foo.com* programmers took their logical DFD from Figure B-2 and converted it to the physical DFD shown in Figure B-3.

Here you see that each data flow, process, and data store has been labeled with the *physical* way in which it will be implemented in the *new* system. The data flows are labeled with the form in which the data will take. In addition, if the data flow involves a data store, it is shown as a *read*, *write*, *update*, or *delete* operation depending on its action on the data store involved.

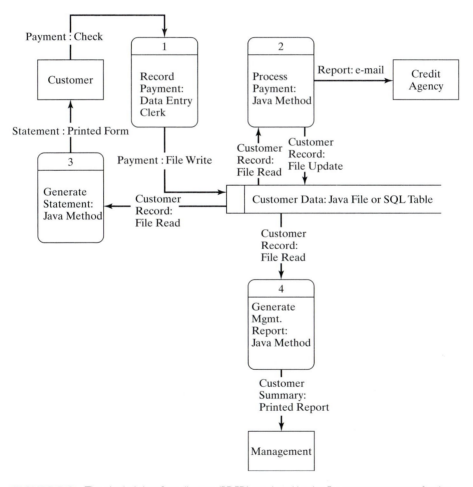

FIGURE B-3   The physical data flow diagram (PDFD) produced by the *Foo.com* programmers for the billing process.

The processes will be labeled according to who or what will be implementing the process in the new system. If the process is a manual process, it is labeled with the title of the person performing the process, as in process 1 of Figure B-3. If the process is an automated process, it is labeled with the type of software unit performing the process, as in processes 2, 3, and 4 of Figure B-3.

The data stores are labeled according to the type of data storage unit being proposed. A manual data store will usually be labeled as a file cabinet. An automated data store might be labeled as a disk file or database table.

The physical DFD leads directly to a functional decomposition diagram, as shown in Figure B-4.

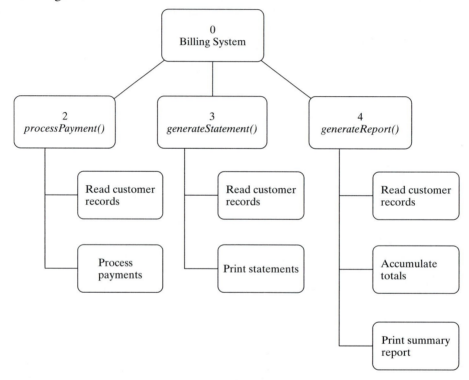

FIGURE B-4   A functional decomposition diagram developed from the physical DFD in Figure B-3.

Look familiar? Notice that the functional decomposition diagram looks very much like the problem solving diagrams that we have been developing during our case studies. Here you see each method identified by its process number, as well as the major tasks to be performed within each method. Notice that process 1 from Figure B-3 is not included here because it is a manual process.

The final task is to translate each method identified in the functional decomposition diagram to an algorithm. Here are the algorithms developed by the *Foo.com* programming team:

```
processPayment()
BEGIN
    While (read customer record from customer database)
```

Subtract *payment* from *balance*.
Calculate *interest* and add to *balance*.
 If *payment* late or *payment* < *minimumPayment*
   Generate report to credit agency.
   Add late charge to *balance*.
   Set *minimumPayment* to 10% of *balance*.
 If *balance* == 0
   Set *minimumPayment* to 0.
 Else
   Set *minimumPayement* to 5% of *balance*.
END.

generateStatement()
BEGIN
   While (read customer record from customer database)
      Write *balance*, *minimumPayment*, and *interest* to customer statement.
      Print customer statement.
END.

generateReport()
BEGIN
   While (read customer record from customer database)
      Add *balance* to *balanceTotals*.
      Add *interest* to *interestTotals*.
      If *payment* late
         Increment *latePayments* counter.
      If *payment* < *minimumPayment*
         Increment *lowPayments* counter.
   Write *balanceTotals*, *interestTotals*, *latePayments*, and *lowPayments* to summary report.
   Print summary report.
END.

   In each of the algorithms you see that a *While* loop is required to read the customer records from the customer database. Each customer record is processed within the *While* loop. Look at the logic in the *processPayment()* algorithm and you will see that the *Foo.com* programmers now have solved the $0.0 balance problem that they created when they first attempted to "design the system at the keyboard" using the build-it, fix-it paradigm. They now have a system that has been fully analyzed, designed, and documented.

   You should now have a good idea of what goes on during the analysis and design phases of the software development life cycle using the structured paradigm. Be aware, however, that alternative solution analysis, feasibility analysis, database design, prototyping, and other activities also take place during the structured design phase. We have only scratched the surface here with the major tasks directly related to the program design.

   The next *SE* module will discuss how the life cycle is applied using the object-oriented paradigm.

SE104: THE OBJECT-ORIENTED PARADIGM USING UML

OBJECTIVES

When you are finished with this module, you should have a good understanding of the following:

- The basics of object-oriented analysis and design using the *Unified Modeling Language*, or **UML**
- A brief history of the UML
- Use case modeling
- Use case diagrams
- Use case scenarios
- Object identification using noun extraction
- Object interaction diagrams
- Class diagrams and corresponding UML notation

Introduction

In the *SE103* module, you learned about the structured analysis and design performed by the *Foo.com* programmers on their billing system. In this module, you will learn about their object-oriented analysis/design. We should mention that we cannot do object-oriented analysis and design justice in just one short module. The intent here is to give you a "look and feel" for it, using a simple example. Only the basic concepts and procedures employed by this paradigm will be covered here. You will need to take advanced courses in object-oriented analysis and design to become a competent software engineer using this paradigm.

We will implement the object-oriented analysis/design paradigm using the *Unified Modeling Language (UML)*. So, let's begin this module with an introduction to UML.

Unified Modeling Language, UML

The Unified Modeling Language, or UML, is *not* a computer language at all. The word "language" is used to mean a notation, or syntax. Furthermore, you see the word "modeling" in UML. This means that the UML is a *language*, or notation, for *modeling* systems. More specifically, the UML provides techniques to specify, visualize, construct, and document object-oriented systems. The UML can be used for non-software business system modeling, as well as software system modeling.

A Little History

The UML was developed at Rational Software Corporation when three pioneers of object-oriented engineering joined forces to "unify" their methods to produce an industry standard for object-oriented system modeling. These three pioneers are Grady

Booch, Jim Rumbaugh, and Ivar Jacobson. Booch developed his *Booch Technique* at Rational, Rumbaugh developed his *Object Modeling Technique*, or *OMT*, at General Electric, while Jacobson developed his methodology, called *Object-Oriented Software Engineering*, or *OOSE*, at his Objectory company. All three methodologies were gaining popularity and, in fact, began evolving independently towards each other. So, it just made sense to combine their efforts to produce a common methodology that would become an industry standard. Rumbaugh joined Booch at Rational in 1994 and began to develop what they called the *Unified Methodology*, or *UM*. In 1995, Jacobson joined the effort to merge his OOSE method into UM. This trio has become known as "the three amigos". Their combined efforts, named the UML, is an industry standard for modeling object-oriented systems. You can get more information on the UML by going to the *UML Resource Center* within the Rational Web site at *www.rational.com/uml*.

Object-Oriented Analysis, OOA

Remember from the *SE102* module how object-oriented analysis, or OOA, differs from structured analysis? Well, one of the goals of OOA is to identify the objects of the proposed system, thus addressing the software structure, or architecture, of the system early during the analysis phase, *before* the design phases. The structured paradigm does not address the software architecture until the design phase during functional decomposition. To identify the system objects, and thus perform the object-oriented analysis, you perform the following tasks:

- Develop *use case* models of the system.
- Write *scenarios* for the use cases.
- Extract the nouns from the use case scenarios.
- Identify object candidates from the foregoing noun extraction.

Use Case Modeling

A *use case* model attempts to graphically depict the system users, called *actors*, and actions, called *use cases*. It also defines the system boundaries. Remember from structured analysis that the system boundaries were defined using a context diagram. So, to begin, the *Foo.com* programmers employed their billing system context diagram shown again in Figure B-5.

From the context diagram, the programmers identified three actors: the customer, management, and the customer services system. An *actor* represents anything that must interact with the system. An actor can be a person, an organization, or another system. Actors usually initiate a system activity. Here, the customer actor is a person that initiates an activity by sending a payment to the system. The management actor represents an individual or organization that initiates an activity by making a request for a customer summary report. The customer service system actor is another system that interacts with the billing system by providing customer information.

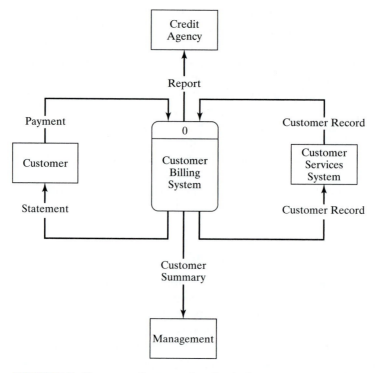

FIGURE B-5   The context diagram produced by the *Foo.com* programmers for
the billing process.

 An **actor** represents anything that must interact with the system. An actor can be a person, an organization, or another system.

Once the actors are identified from the context diagram, the engineer must attempt to define the actions, called ***use cases***, performed by the system as the result of requests by the actors. A ***use case*** represents a pattern of behavior exhibited by the system as the result of a dialogue between the system and an actor. The collection of all the system use cases specifies all the ways in which to *use* the system.

 A ***use case*** represents a pattern of behavior exhibited by the system as the result of a dialogue between the system and an actor. The collection of all the system use cases specifies all the ways in which to use the system.

Use cases are created by examining the actors and defining everything a given actor can do with the system. The *Foo.com* programmers created two use cases for their billing system: *make payment,* which is initiated by the customer actor, and *request summary,* which is initiated by the management actor. No use case was defined for the customer services actor since its only purpose is to supply customer records to the system. The resulting ***use case diagram*** is shown in Figure B-6.

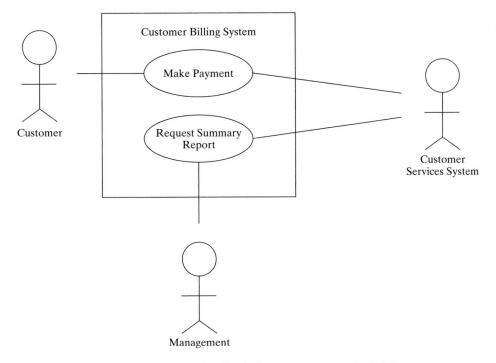

FIGURE B-6   The use case diagram produced by the *Foo.com* programmers for the billing process.

Here you see the UML symbols used for the actors, use cases, and interaction. The actors are placed outside the system and the use cases within the system, thus defining the system boundary. The lines between the actors and use cases simply depict the actor interaction with one or more use cases.

Use Case Scenarios

Remember that each use case represents a system behavior. Thus, the next task is to define this behavior via a *use case scenario*. A use case scenario is simply the sequence of tasks that are performed for each use case behavior.

  A *use case scenario* is the sequence of tasks that are performed for a given use case.

Here are the scenarios developed by the *Foo.com* programmers for their two use cases:

Make Payment Scenario

  1. Receive payment on customer account.
  2. Customer record is read from customer services system.

3. Payment is subtracted from customer balance.
4. Customer interest is calculated and added to customer balance.
5. Payment is checked for late payment.
6. Payment is checked for less than minimum payment.
7. Customer balance is checked for $0.00 and minimum payment is calculated.
8. Customer statement is printed.

Request Summary Report Scenario

1. Receive summary report request from management.
2. Customer record is read from customer services system.
3. Customer balance is added to total balance for all customers.
4. Customer interest is added to total interest for all customers.
5. If payment was late, increment late payments.
6. If payment was less than minimum payment, increment low payments.
7. Summary report is printed.

Take a close look at each scenario so that you are familiar with each use case behavior. The next step is to extract the nouns from the scenarios.

Noun Extraction

Usually, a noun represents a person, place, or thing. But a noun can also represent an action, such as *fishing*, a quality, such as *beauty*, or an idea, such as *love*. Nouns suggest potential objects within the system. All that needs to be done here is to underline the nouns in each use case, then compile a list of the nouns which were identified. Here are the use cases again, showing the nouns underlined by the *Foo.com* programmers.

Make Payment Scenario

1. Receive payment on customer account.
2. Customer record is read from customer services system.
3. Payment is subtracted from customer balance.
4. Customer interest is calculated and added to customer balance.
5. Payment is checked for late payment.
6. Payment is checked for less than minimum payment.
7. Customer balance is checked for $0.00 and minimum payment is calculated.
8. Customer statement is printed.

Request Summary Report Scenario

1. Receive summary report request from management.
2. Customer record is read from customer services system.
3. Customer balance is added to total balance for all customers.

4. <u>Customer interest</u> is added to <u>total interest</u> for all customers.
5. If <u>payment</u> was late, increment <u>late payments</u>.
6. If <u>payment</u> was less than <u>minimum payment</u>, increment <u>low payments</u>.
7. <u>Summary report</u> is printed.

The nouns are then extracted and placed in a noun extraction table which shows the potential system objects, as follows:

Noun Extraction (Potential Object List)

Payment
Customer account
Customer record
Customer services system
Customer balance
Customer interest
Late
Late payment
Minimum payment
Customer statement
Summary report
Management
Total balance
Total interest
Late payments
Low payments

Object Identification

The last step in the OOA is to identify object candidates from the noun extraction process. To accomplish object identification, you must eliminate any nouns that meet the following criteria:

- Synonyms (words of similar meaning)
- Nouns outside the system boundary
- Abstract nouns that represent an action (*fishing*), a quality (*beauty*), or an idea (*love*)
- Nouns that are attributes of other higher-level object candidates
- Nouns that are interface items, such as something coming from an actor

Here is a table that the *Foo.com* programmers developed which lists all the nouns from the foregoing noun extraction table, and shows which are potential object candidates and which are not, along with the reason why a given noun is not an object candidate:

Accept as Object?	Potential Object	Reason for not Accepting
√	Customer account	
	Payment	Interface item
	Record	Part of file or database
	Customer services system	Outside boundary
	Customer balance	Attribute of customer account
	Customer interest	Attribute of customer account
	Late	Abstract noun
	Late payment	Attribute of customer account
	Minimum payment	Attribute of customer account
	Customer statement	Attribute of customer account
√	Summary report	
	Management	Outside boundary
	Total balance	Attribute of summary report
	Total interest	Attribute of summary report
	Late payments	Attribute of summary report
	Low payments	Attribute of summary report

Notice that two object candidates have been identified: a customer account object and a summary report object. Do you understand why the other nouns are not object candidates from the reasons given? These object candidates will actually become classes in our design. That's it! The potential system objects/classes have been identified and the OOA is complete.

Object-Oriented Design, OOD

The purpose of the OOD is to determine how the new system is to satisfy the client's needs through the construction of object interaction and class diagrams, as well as other UML tools such as sequence and collaboration diagrams. In this module we will discuss two of these tasks, as follows:

- Construction of object interaction diagrams for each identified object that show the interaction of objects within the system
- Construction of class diagrams that show the class attributes (data) and behavior (methods)

Object Interaction Diagrams

Object interaction diagrams are used to show system objects and the *relationships* among them. If two objects need to "talk", there must be a relationship between them. Object relationships are determined by examining the use case diagram and scenarios developed in the OOA phase. The object interaction diagram developed by the *Foo.com* programmers for their billing system is shown in Figure B-7.

FIGURE B-7 The object interaction diagram produced by the *Foo.com* programmers for the billing process.

Here, you see both objects represented by rectangles. Notice the UML syntax used for the object name. The syntax *:CustomerAccount* (notice the colon preceding the class name) means that this rectangle represents an object of the *CustomerAccount* class. We could have given the object a name such as *myAccount*. Then the rectangle designation would have been *myAccount:CustomerAccount*, referring specifically to the *myAccount* object of the *CustomerAccount* class. An object name is optional, and we chose not to use one here to make our interaction diagram more generic. The divisions within each object rectangle, called ***compartments***, will become apparent shortly. With UML, a bi-directional line between two objects represents a relationship.

The relationship shown in Figure B-7 is called an ***association*** because it represents a pathway of communication between two objects. The association in Figure B-7 is labeled to show how many objects on each side of the association participate in the relationship. This is called ***multiplicity***. Each end of the association is labeled. In our billing system the *:SummaryReport* object end of the association is label with a **1**, while the *:CustomerAccount* end of the association is labeled with a **1..***. This means that one (1) *:SummaryReport* object will communicate with one or more (1..*) *:CustomerAccount* objects. Thus, a *:SummaryReport* object must interact with one or more *:CustomerAccount* objects to prepare its report. There are other possible association labels, such as ***roles*** and ***aggregations***. These are beyond the scope of our simple billing system example and this book.

Another type of relationship is an ***inheritance*** relationship which shows how one object shares the attributes and behavior of another object. You will see this relationship used in the text.

Once the interaction diagram is complete, it is time to construct the class diagrams.

Class Diagrams

Remember that a class provides a model for its objects. It defines the attributes and behavior common to all of these objects. A class diagram shows both the data which provide the attributes of the class, and the methods which provide the class behavior. Thus, using UML, a class diagram consists of three compartments, one for the class name, one for the data, and one for the methods.

Here are the UML class diagrams developed by the *Foo.com* programmers for their billing system:

```
┌──────────────────────────────────────────┐
│               CustomerAccount              │
├──────────────────────────────────────────┤
│ -accountNumber:string                      │
│                                            │
│ -balance:double                            │
│                                            │
│ -interest:double                           │
│                                            │
│ -minPayment:double                         │
│                                            │
│ -latePayment:bool                          │
│                                            │
│ -lessThanMin:bool                          │
├──────────────────────────────────────────┤
│ +setCustData()                             │
│                                            │
│ +subtractPayment(in payment:double)        │
│                                            │
│ +addInterest()                             │
│                                            │
│ +checkLatePayment()                        │
│                                            │
│ +checkMinPayment()                         │
│                                            │
│ +calculateMinPayment()                     │
│                                            │
│ +getInterest():double                      │
│                                            │
│ +getBalance():double                       │
│                                            │
│ +getLatePayment():bool                     │
│                                            │
│ +getLessThanMin():bool                     │
│                                            │
│ +printStatement()                          │
└──────────────────────────────────────────┘
```

```
┌─────────────────────────────────────────┐
│              SummaryReport               │
├─────────────────────────────────────────┤
│                                          │
│  -accountNumber:string                   │
│                                          │
│  -totalBalance:double                    │
│                                          │
│  -totalInterest:double                   │
│                                          │
│  -latePayments:int                       │
│                                          │
│  -lowPayments:int                        │
│                                          │
├─────────────────────────────────────────┤
│                                          │
│  +addTotalBalance()                      │
│                                          │
│  +addTotalInterest()                     │
│                                          │
│  +checkLatePayment()                     │
│                                          │
│  +checkLowPayment()                      │
│                                          │
│  +printReport()                          │
│                                          │
└─────────────────────────────────────────┘
```

The class name is placed in the top compartment of the diagram. Then, the data is placed in the second compartment of the diagram, while the methods are placed in the third compartment. Next, notice that each member is labeled with a minus (–) or a plus (+) sign. A minus sign is used to denote a `private` member, while a plus sign is used to denote a `public` member. Notice that all the data are `private`, while all the methods are `public` in these classes.

Looking at the data in the second compartment, you see the attribute name, followed by a colon, followed by the type or class of the data attribute. Looking at the methods in the third compartment, you find the method name, followed by a parameter listing. If parameters are required, they are listed as *in*, *out*, or *inout* followed by the parameter name, followed by a colon, followed by the data type or class of the parameter value. For instance, in the *subtractPayment()* method you see a single parameter specified as *in payment : double*. This means that the method will accept (*in*) a parameter whose name is *payment* and is a *double* floating-point value. A specification of *out* would signify that the parameter is being returned by the method. A specification *inout* would signify that the parameter is being accepted and returned by the method, as in the case of a reference parameter. The default label is *in* if none is specified.

If the method returns a value, a colon follows the parameter listing, followed by the return data type, as in the *getInterest()* and *getBalance()* methods shown.

That completes the object-oriented analysis and design performed by the *Foo.com* programmers for their billing system. The only thing they have to do now is develop individual algorithms for the methods, and code the classes and the application. However, they must still study more about object-oriented software engineering because there is much more to learn. A more complex problem would have required a more in-depth analysis and design, employing *collaboration diagrams* and *sequence diagrams*, as well as other activities. With this simple example, you and they have just been exposed to "the tip of the iceberg".

C

A GUI Workshop with Swing

Introduction

*A **graphical user interface***, or ***GUI***, is a window-based program whereby input and output are handled via ***graphical components***. Components include menus, buttons, check boxes, text fields, and radio buttons, just to mention a few. Windowed programs are event-driven programs, whereby the flow of the program logic is dictated by events. These events usually are the result of a mouse action, such as clicking or movement, or a keyboard stroke.

In this appendix, you will be acquainted with the topic of graphical user interfaces, or GUIs, through a series of hands-on "***GUI 10X***" modules. These modules will familiarize you with the components and related Java code that are required to build a GUI. The prewritten Java programs that you will use are located on the CD that accompanies this book. You will be asked to load a given program, execute the program, and exercise the GUI. In some cases you will be asked to modify the program code and observe the effect on the GUI and its components. Don't worry about how to design your own GUIs yet—this is covered in Chapters 11 and 12 of the text. For now, it is only important that you get acquainted with GUIs in general, along with some GUI terminology and behavior. So, crank-up your Java IDE and have some fun. Don't be afraid to change the code given here and just experiment. This is how you learn.

GUI 101: GRAPHICAL USER INTERFACES

PURPOSE

- *To become familiar with loading and executing a Java program*
- *To demonstrate a typical graphical user interface, or GUI*
- *To identify the various components which are used to build a GUI*
- *To observe the behavior of GUI components*

Procedure

1. The GUI in Figure C-1 is what you would see in a Windows environment, while the one in Figure C-2 is a Mac GUI. However, the same Java program produced both GUIs! This is one of the reasons that Java is so popular, because it is totally **portable** across all platforms. The program that produced the GUI in Figures C-1 and C-2 is included on your text CD as the file *GUI101.java*. Compile, run, and exercise this program via your Java development environment.

2. Resize the window by grabbing and moving the window borders.

3. Fill in your student name, student number, and GPA.

4. Select one or more majors from the list of majors.

5. Check any student status items that apply: full-time, part-time, commuting, or non-commuting.

6. The GUI is already set for an undergraduate student; click the graduate student button if it applies. Notice that clicking the *Graduate* button turns the *Undergraduate* button off, and vice versa.

7. Click the *Store* button and notice that the student information you entered now appears in the *Student Summary* area. To see all the information you will have to use the scrollbars which appear around the *Student Summary* area when the data is displayed.

8. Click on the *Color* menu and select a color. Notice that the *Student Summary* area changes its background color to the color you selected.

9. Click on the *Font* menu and select the *Font Type* submenu. Select a font from this menu and notice that the text in the *Student Summary* area changes to the selected font.

10. Click on the *Font* menu and select the *Font Style* submenu. Select a style from this menu and notice that the text in the *Student Summary* area changes to the selected font style, while keeping the same type of font.

11. Click on the *Font* menu and select the *Font Size* submenu. Select a size from this menu and notice that the text in the *Student Summary* area changes to the selected font size, while keeping the same type and style of font.

12. Change the student information and click the *Store* button again. Notice that the *Student Summary* area reflects any changes you made.

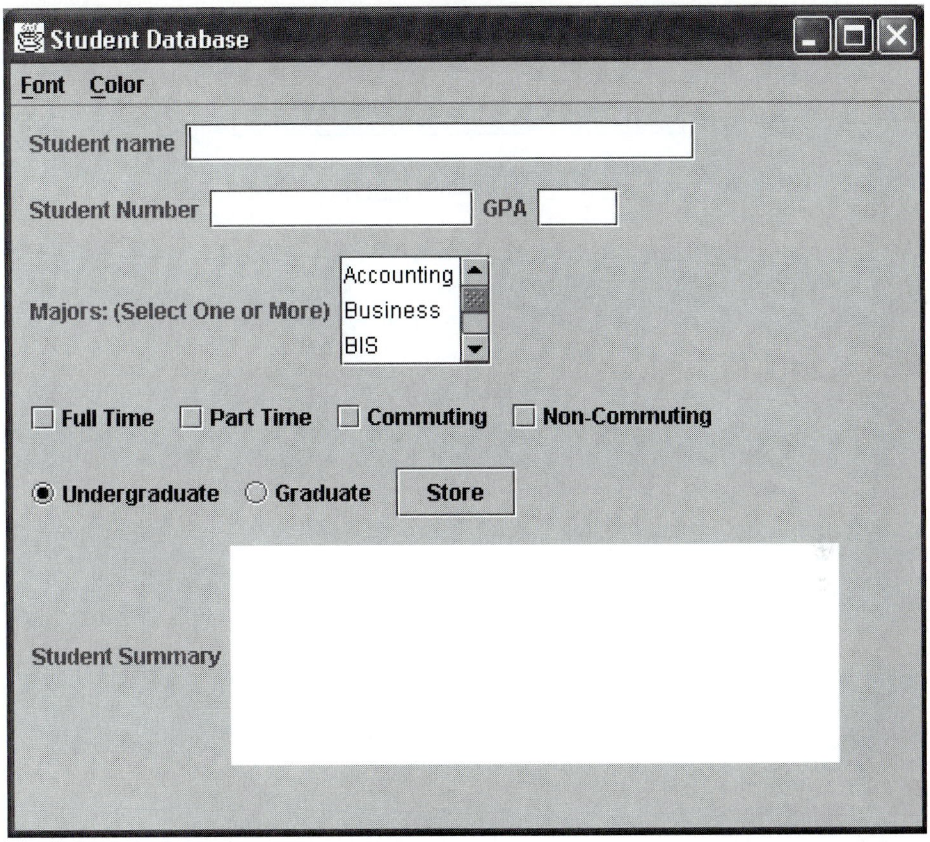

FIGURE C-1 The student database GUI generated by the *GUI101.java* program in a Windows environment.

13. Check both the full-time and part-time student status and click the *Store* button. Notice that an error message appears in the *Student Summary Area* since you cannot be a full-time and a part-time student at the same time.

14. See if you can identify the following components of the GUI:

- Title bar
- Scrollbars
- Close button
- Menu bar
- Menu
- Submenu
- Labels
- Button
- Text field
- Text area

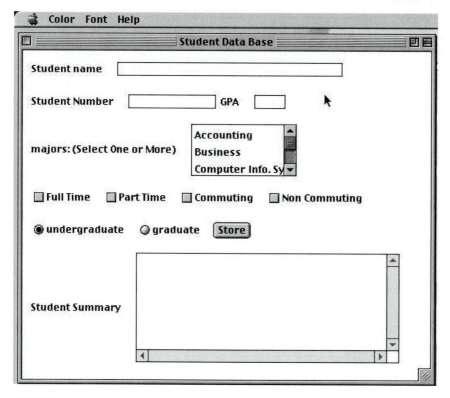

FIGURE C-2   The student database GUI generated by the *GUI101.java* program in a Mac environment.

- List Box
- Check box
- Radio button

Discussion

The GUI that you just exercised contains most of the components required for any GUI. First, you observed a standard window that contained a title bar with title and window borders just like any other window. The window could be maximized, minimized, resized, and closed. These features are common to all windows, and any GUI we create will "inherit" these basic features. This is the beauty of object-oriented programming (OOP). You *inherit* things, like standard window features, from other things that have already been developed. You do not have to reinvent the wheel each time you want to create a new GUI. In Java applications, windows are created by a GUI component called a *frame*. A frame is the basis for a GUI in all Java applications and is used as a container to hold the GUI components.

The areas where you type in information are called *text fields*. There is a *label* designation, or name, for each text field such as *Student Name*. When you selected one or more majors, you were selecting from a *list box*. When you checked student status, you were using *check boxes*. When you selected undergraduate or graduate, you were using *radio buttons*. The *Store* button is a Java component called a *button*. When you selected a color and font, you were using a *menu* component. Finally, all the student information was displayed in a *text area*. All these things are components of a GUI.

The *GUI 10X* modules that follow will deal with each of these components independently. You will not really learn how to design and build your own GUI in these modules since they have only been provided to get you somewhat acquainted with GUI component attributes and behavior. The details of designing and building GUIs are covered in Chapters 11 and 12 of the text. So, be patient. Read on and have fun playing with our GUI modules.

GUI 102: FRAMES AND CONTAINERS

PURPOSE

- *To become familiar with Java frames*
- *To demonstrate that frames have all the generic window features, except the closing feature*
- *To show how to set the title of a frame/window*
- *To show how to set the initial size of a frame/window*

Introduction

The *frame* is the basis for a GUI in all Java applications. Frames are used as containers to hold GUI components. When you build a GUI in a Java application, you will first create a frame, then add the desired components to the frame. In this module, you will load and execute a Java program that produces a frame. You will modify the code and observe the effect on the window generated by the frame.

Procedure

1. Compile and execute the *GUI102_1.java* program contained on the CD that accompanies this book. You should observe the window shown in Figure C-3 if you are in a Windows environment, or Figure C-4 if you are in a Mac environment.

2. Resize the window to different sizes by grabbing and moving the window borders.

3. If you are in a Windows environment, minimize the window by clicking the *Minimize* button in the upper right-hand corner of the window. Restore the window by switching to the *GUI102_1.java* task (*Alt+Tab*).

4. Try to close the window by clicking the *Close* button in the upper right-hand corner of the window (Windows), or upper left-hand corner of the window (Mac). Now, although you think you closed the window because it disappeared, it is still running in background. What? You can't stop the application from executing? That's right, this program does not include the code necessary to terminate the application. You will have to manually terminate its execution by going to the execution window/panel of your IDE to stop the process. (In *JBuilder*, click the red square just below the *JBuilder* message window. In *Sun ONE Studio*, select *Execution Window* from the *View* menu. Right-click on *GUI102_1* in the *Execution* window, then click *Terminate Process*.)

5. Compile and execute the *GUI102_2.java* program. You should see the same window as before except for the window title.

6. Now try to close the window by clicking the *Close* button. You should find that the window closes fine, and the program task ends.

7. Here is the Java code that produced the frame window with the closing feature:

```
1   import javax.swing.*;       //FOR FRAME CLASS
2   import java.awt.event.*;    //FOR EVENT HANDLING
3
```

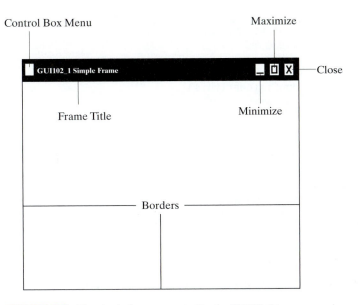

FIGURE C-3 The simple frame generated by the *GUI102_1.java* program in a Windows environment.

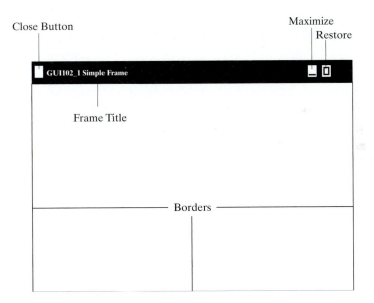

FIGURE C-4 The simple frame generated by the *GUI102_1.java* program in a Mac environment.

```
4    //INHERITS AND CUSTOMIZES FRAME CLASS TO ADD DESIRED FEATURES
5    class FrameWithClose extends JFrame implements WindowListener
6    {
7      //CONSTRUCTOR
8      public FrameWithClose(String title)
```

```
 9     {
10       //CALL SUPERCLASS CONSTRUCTOR
11       super(title);
12
13       //ADD LISTENER FOR THIS FRAME
14       addWindowListener(this);
15     }//END FrameWithClose()
16
17     public void windowClosing(WindowEvent e)
18     {
19       System.exit(0);     //EXIT TO OPERATING SYSTEM
20     }//END windowClosing()
21
22     public void windowClosed(WindowEvent e)
23     {
24     }
25     public void windowDeiconified(WindowEvent e)
26     {
27     }
28     public void windowIconified(WindowEvent e)
29     {
30     }
31     public void windowActivated(WindowEvent e)
32     {
33     }
34     public void windowDeactivated(WindowEvent e)
35     {
36     }
37     public void windowOpened(WindowEvent e)
38     {
39     }
40 }//END FrameWithClose
41
42 //CLASS TO TEST FrameWithClose CLASS
43 public class GUI102_2
44 {
45   public static void main(String[] args)
46   {
47   //DEFINE FRAME OBJECT
48   FrameWithClose window = new FrameWithClose("GUI102_2 Frame With
     Close");
49
50   //SET FRAME SIZE
51   window.setSize(500,300);
52
53   //MAKE FRAME VISIBLE
54   window.show();
55
56
57
58 }//END main()
59 }//END GUI102_2
```

8. Wow, what a program! Don't be overwhelmed and worry about all the coding details now. You will learn them in time. We will just focus on a few statements that are pertinent to our window frame. Change the "GUI102_2 Frame With Close" phrase in line 48 to: "This Is My First Frame." Do not change anything else in this line. Recompile, and then execute the program again. Notice that the title in the window title bar has changed.

9. Close the window and change the statement in line 51 to:

```
window.setSize(100,200);
```

Notice that there is a dot (period) between the words *window* and *setSize,* and a semicolon ends the statement. Recompile, and then execute the program again. Notice that the window is now smaller, but it can still be resized, minimized, maximized, or closed.

10. Try different values in line 51. You should find the first value controls the width of the frame, and the second value controls the frame height. Of course, if you exceed the size of your monitor screen, the frame is maximized.

11. Add the following statement on line 55:

```
FrameWithClose win = new FrameWithClose("My Frame With Close");
```

12. Add the following statement on line 56:

```
win.setSize(500,300);
```

13. Add the following statement on line 57:

```
win.show();
```

14. Recompile, then execute the program again. Observe that two windows are produced. Notice that you can switch back and forth between these multiple frames. Close the windows.

Discussion

The two applications that you just ran create a Java frame which, when executed, each creates a window. A Java frame is created from the standard *JFrame* class available in the *javax.swing* package. This is why we imported this package at the beginning of the program in line 1. Packages contain Java classes. The *javax.swing* package contains all the components necessary to build a GUI. Here, we are using the *JFrame* class in the *javax.swing* package to create the GUI frame. In the first program, the window closing feature is not operable because a frame by itself is not able to handle this **event**. The second program imports the *java.awt.event* package in line 2, and adds additional code to handle the window closing event when it occurs.

When you changed line 48, you found that you changed the window title in the title bar. The window title will reflect whatever **string** is placed within the parentheses of line 48. A string is simply a collection of characters and recognized by Java by enclosing them within double quotation marks.

When you changed line 51, you changed the *initial* size of the frame. Of course, the frame could still be resized after it appeared. The first value, called an **argument**, is the initial frame width, in **pixels** (picture elements), while the second argument is the initial frame height, in pixels.

In steps 11-13 you created a new frame **object** called *win*, set the size of the *win* frame, and made the *win* frame visible by using the *win* object to call the *show()* method. This added a second frame to the program, thus creating multiple windows, or frames, when the program was executed.

GUI 103: BUTTONS AND LAYOUT MANAGERS

PURPOSE

- ■ *To become familiar with the GUI button component*
- ■ *To show how buttons are added to a frame container*
- ■ *To demonstrate the purpose of a listener*
- ■ *To experiment with frame background and foreground color*
- ■ *To become familiar with a frame layout manager*
- ■ *To demonstrate the flow layout manager*
- ■ *To show how component alignment and gapping can be set within a frame*

Introduction

The **button** is one of the most common components found in a GUI. Buttons are often used to trigger, or signal, an event, such as a calculation or store event. In this module, you will load and execute a Java application that produces a frame with a single button. Then, you will load an application that produces a frame with several buttons. You will modify the code and observe the effect on the windows generated by the application.

Procedure

1. Compile and execute the *GUI103_1.java* program contained on the CD that accompanies this book. You should observe the window shown in Figure C-5. What you see here is one BIG button covering the entire frame. Notice that the button has a label which says "Click Me, I'm a Button." In addition, there is a *tool tip* associated with the button. A tool tip is one of those annoying little boxes that pop up when you pass the mouse pointer over a GUI component. Placing the mouse pointer over any part of our BIG button will produce the tool tip shown. This tool tip has a purpose because it notifies the user that they can press the *Alt* and *C* (*Alt+C*) keys simultaneously to activate the button.
   Here is the Java code that produced the window you see in Figure C-5.

```
1    import javax.swing.*;      //FOR SWING COMPONENT CLASSES
2    import java.awt.event.*;   //FOR EVENT HANDLING
3    import java.awt.*;         //FOR Container CLASS
4
5    //A FRAME CLASS WITH A SINGLE BUTTON
6    class FrameWithButton extends JFrame
7    {
8      //DECLARE BUTTON OBJECT
9      private JButton button;
10
11     //CONSTRUCTOR
12     public FrameWithButton(String title)
13     {
14       super(title);           //CALL SUPERCLASS CONSTRUCTOR
15
```

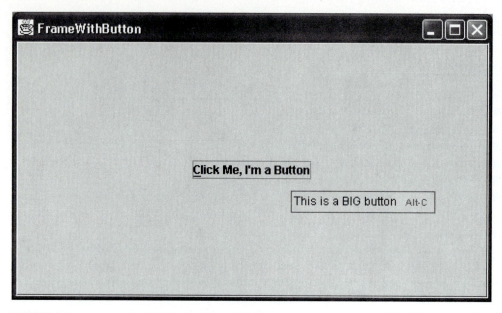

FIGURE C-5   A frame with a single button and no layout manager.

```
16        //CREATE A CONTAINER
17        Container container = getContentPane();
18
19
20        //SET CONTAINER BACKGROUND COLOR
21        container.setBackground(Color.black);
22
23        //DEFINE BUTTON OBJECT
24        button = new JButton("Click Me, I'm a Button");
25
26        //SET BUTTON FOREGROUND COLOR
27        button.setForeground(Color.black);
28
29        //SET BUTTON TOOL TIP
30        button.setToolTipText("This is a BIG button");
31        //SET ACTION KEY
32        button.setMnemonic('C');
33
34        //ADD BUTTON TO CONTAINER
35        container.add(button);
36
37        //ADD EVENT HANDLER FOR THIS BUTTON
38        button.addActionListener(new ButtonHandler());
39
40        //ADD LISTENER FOR THIS FRAME
41        addWindowListener(new WindowHandler());
42   }//END FrameWithButton()
```

```
43
44      private class WindowHandler extends WindowAdapter
45      {
46        public void windowClosing(WindowEvent e)
47        {
48          System.exit(0);  //EXIT TO OPERATING SYSTEM
49        }//END windowClosing()
50      }//END WindowAdapter CLASS
51
52      private class ButtonHandler implements ActionListener
53      {
54        //actionPerformed METHOD
55        public void actionPerformed(ActionEvent e)
56        {
57          JOptionPane.showMessageDialog(null,
58                            "Congratulations!\nYou Clicked Me",
59                            "INFORMATION",
60                            JOptionPane.INFORMATION_MESSAGE);
61        }//END actionPerformed
62      }//END ButtonHandler
63    }//END FrameWithButton CLASS
64
65  //APPLICATION CLASS TO TEST CLASS
66  public class GUI103_1
67  {
68    public static void main(String[] args)
69    {
70      //DEFINE FRAME OBJECT
71      FrameWithButton window = new FrameWithButton("FrameWithButton");
72
73      //SET FRAME SIZE
74      window.setSize(500,300);
75
76      //MAKE FRAME VISIBLE
77      window.show();
78    }//END main()
79  }//END GUI103_1
```

2. Again, don't be overwhelmed and worry about all the coding details now. The details are covered in the text. We will just focus on a few statements that are pertinent to our frame. Click the button and you should see a dialog box appear, as shown in Figure C-6.

3. Click the OK button on the dialog box and close the button window.

4. Look at the code in lines 29 through 32. This is where the tool tip and mnemonic are created. Change the tool tip message in line 30 and the tool tip mnemonic in line 32, and execute the program again. You should see your new message and mnemonic in the tool tip box. Activate the button by simultaneously pressing the *Alt* key plus the mnemonic character you chose. The information box should appear again. Click OK on the information box and close the button window.

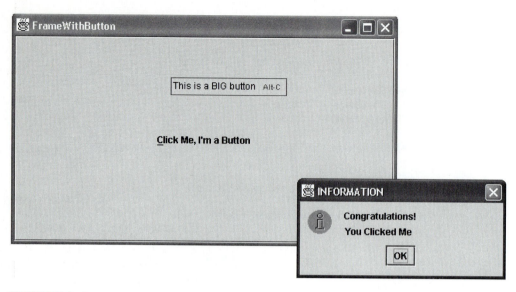

FIGURE C-6   The button event generates an information box as shown.

5. Change the color in line 21 from "black" to "cyan". Recompile, and then execute the program again. Observe that nothing has changed because this statement sets the background color of the frame container. Again, our giant button is covering the entire frame. As a result, there is no background visible. Close the window.

6. Change the color in line 27 from "black" to "blue". Recompile, and then execute the program again. Observe the color of the button label has changed to blue. This is the foreground color of the button. Close the window.

7. Add the following statement on line 18 of the program:

```
container.setLayout(new FlowLayout());
```

8. Execute the program again. You should observe a window similar to the one shown in Figure C-7. Now, this is much better. We now have a window with a single manageable button. The window background color should be cyan and the button foreground color should be blue. Close the window.

Discussion

First, look at line 6 in the program. This line tells Java that this class is named *FrameWithButton*, and it extends the standard *JFrame* class. The *FrameWithButton* class in this module **inherits** the attributes and behaviors of the *JFrame* class so that we do not have to rewrite the code to produce a window. Why rewrite this code if it is already available? The concept of **inheritance** is one of the cornerstones of OOP. Inheritance allows the reuse of code that has already been developed.

Now, back to the window in Figure C-5. The background color of a frame container is the color visible behind any components in the container. The foreground

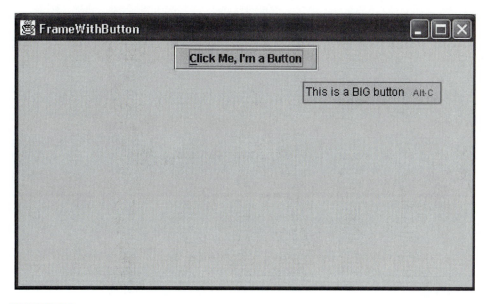

FIGURE C-7   A frame with a single button using the flow layout manager.

color of a button is the color of any labeling on a GUI component. In steps 5 and 6, you changed the container background and the button foreground colors. There are 13 different standard colors available in Java, as follows:

- black
- blue
- cyan
- darkGray
- gray
- green
- lightGray
- magenta
- orange
- pink
- red
- white
- yellow

Try experimenting with these different colors in lines 21 and 27 of the program.

The first button you generated was so big that it covered the entire frame. The reason this happened is because the frame did not use a *layout manager*. A layout manager controls the placement of the components within a container. In step 7, you set the frame layout to the *FlowLayout* manager. This layout manager places components

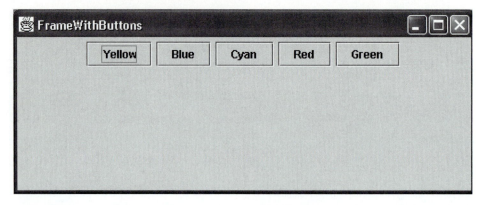

FIGURE C-8   A frame with five buttons using the flow layout manager.

on the container, from left to right, and centers them within the container. This is why you observed a single button in the middle of the frame, just below the title bar.

Procedure (continued)

9. Compile and execute the *GUI103_2.java* program contained on the CD that accompanies this book. You should observe the window shown in Figure C-8. Here, you see five buttons centered across the top of the frame.

10. Click on the buttons and notice that the frame background color changes to the color indicated by the button label. Here is the program that generated the five-button frame:

```
1    import javax.swing.*;       //FOR SWING COMPONENT CLASSES
2    import java.awt.event.*;    //FOR EVENT HANDLING
3    import java.awt.*;          //FOR Container CLASS
4
5    //A FRAME CLASS WITH MULTIPLE BUTTONS
6    class FrameWithButtons extends JFrame
7    {
8      //DECLARE BUTTON OBJECTS
9      private JButton yellowButton;
10     private JButton blueButton;
11     private JButton cyanButton;
12     private JButton redButton;
13     private JButton greenButton;
14
15     //CREATE A CONTAINER
16     private Container container = getContentPane();
17
18     //CONSTRUCTOR
19     public FrameWithButtons(String title)
20     {
21       super(title);   //CALL SUPERCLASS CONSTRUCTOR
22
```

```
23      //SET LAYOUT MANAGER
24      container.setLayout(new FlowLayout());
25
26      //INSTANTIATE BUTTON OBJECTS
27      yellowButton = new JButton("Yellow");
28      blueButton = new JButton("Blue");
29      cyanButton = new JButton("Cyan");
30      redButton = new JButton("Red");
31      greenButton = new JButton("Green");
32
33      //ADD BUTTONS TO CONTAINER
34      container.add(yellowButton);
35      container.add(blueButton);
36      container.add(cyanButton);
37      container.add(redButton);
38      container.add(greenButton);
39
40      //DEFINE BUTTON HANDLER OBJECT
41      ButtonHandler bHandler = new ButtonHandler();
42
43      //ADD LISTENERS AND EVENT HANDLER FOR THESE BUTTONS
44      yellowButton.addActionListener(bHandler);
45      blueButton.addActionListener(bHandler);
46      cyanButton.addActionListener(bHandler);
47      redButton.addActionListener(bHandler);
48      greenButton.addActionListener(bHandler);
49
50      //ADD LISTENER FOR THIS FRAME
51      addWindowListener(new WindowHandler());
52   }//END FrameWithButtons()
53
54   private class WindowHandler extends WindowAdapter
55   {
56     public void windowClosing(WindowEvent e)
57     {
58       System.exit(0);  //EXIT TO OPERATING SYSTEM
59     }//END windowClosing()
60   }//END WindowAdapter CLASS
61
62   private class ButtonHandler implements ActionListener
63   {
64   //PROCESS EVENT
65   public void actionPerformed(ActionEvent e)
66   {
67       //WHICH BUTTON CAUSED THE EVENT?
68       if (e.getSource() == yellowButton)
69         container.setBackground(Color.yellow);
70       if (e.getSource() == blueButton)
71         container.setBackground(Color.blue);
72       if (e.getSource() == cyanButton)
73         container.setBackground(Color.cyan);
74       if (e.getSource() == redButton)
```

```
75           container.setBackground(Color.red);
76         if (e.getSource() == greenButton)
77           container.setBackground(Color.green);
78       }//END actionPerformed()
79     }//END ButtonHandler
80 }//END FrameWithJButtons CLASS
81
82 //APPLICATION CLASS TO TEST FrameWithButton
83 public class GUI103_2
84 {
85   public static void main(String[] args)
86   {
87     //DEFINE FRAME OBJECT
88     FrameWithButtons window = new
89       FrameWithButtons("FrameWithButtons");
90
91     //SET FRAME SIZE
92     window.setSize(500,200);
93
94     //MAKE FRAME VISIBLE
95     window.show();
96   }//END main()
   }//END GUI103_2
```

11. Change line 24 to the following:

```
container.setLayout(new FlowLayout(FlowLayout.LEFT));
```

Notice that there is a dot between the words FlowLayout and LEFT in the above statement. Execute the program and notice that the buttons are left-justified within the window.

12. Change line 24 to the following:

```
container.setLayout(new FlowLayout(FlowLayout.RIGHT));
```

Recompile, then execute the program and notice that the buttons are right-justified within the window.

13. Change line 24 to the following:

```
container.setLayout(new FlowLayout(FlowLayout.CENTER));
```

Recompile, then execute the program and notice that the buttons are centered within the window.

14. Change line 24 to the following:

```
container.setLayout(new FlowLayout(FlowLayout.CENTER,10,50));
```

Recompile, then execute the program and notice that the buttons are centered, but placed farther down the window.

15. Change line 24 to the following:

```
container.setLayout(new FlowLayout(FlowLayout.CENTER,50,50));
```

Recompile, then execute the program and notice that the buttons are center-justified toward the top of the window, but with more of a gap between them.

Discussion

The *GUI103_2.java* program contains a *FrameWithButtons* class that creates a frame with five buttons using the *FlowLayout* manager. Notice that the *FlowLayout* manager centered the buttons, from left to right, in the order in which they were *added* to the frame in lines 34 through 38 of the program. The frame background defaulted to gray, and the frame foreground (button labels) defaulted to black. When a given button was clicked, the button generated an **event** which was "handled" by the program to change the frame background color. This program also employs a `private` *WindowHandler* class to handle the window closing event.

When you changed the statement in line 24, you changed the way in which the *FlowLayout* manager was set. You found that you could direct the layout manager to left-justify, right-justify, or center the buttons within the window. This is referred to as **component alignment** in Java. The default alignment is center. Then, you changed line 24 to add two integer values toward the end of the statement. The first value controls the horizontal gapping of the components within the frame, while the second value controls the vertical gapping of components within the frame. When the statement included the values 10, 50 the buttons were relatively close together, due to a horizontal gapping value of 10, but displaced farther down the window, due to a vertical gapping value of 50. When the statement included the values 50, 50, the buttons were placed farther apart horizontally because the horizontal gapping value changed from 10 to 50.

Procedure (continued)

16. Comment out line 38 by placing two forward slashes, //, at the beginning of the line. Recompile, then execute the program and notice that the green button does not appear on the frame. Why?

17. Comment out line 44 by placing two forward slashes, //, at the beginning of the line. Recompile, then execute the program and click the yellow button. Notice that nothing happens. Why?

Discussion

When you commented out line 38, you commented out the statement that added the *green* button to the frame. A component must be added to a frame using the *add()* method, or else it will not appear on the resulting window.

When you commented out line 44, you commented out the statement that added an *ActionListener* for the *yellow* button. A **listener** must be added for a component if the GUI is to respond to an event generated by the component. A listener is added for

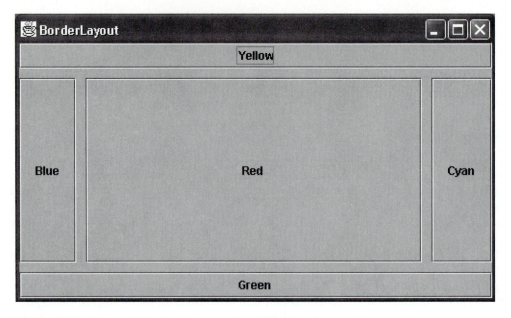

FIGURE C-9   A frame with five buttons using the border layout manager.

a button component using the *addActionListener()* method. When you commented line 44, you commented out the line that added the *Yellow* button as a listener. As a result, the GUI did not respond to the clicking event.

Procedure (continued)

18. Compile and execute the *GUI103_3.java* program contained on the CD that accompanies this book. You should observe the window shown in Figure C-9.

19. Click on any of the buttons and you should see that the frame container background color is changed to that respective color.

Discussion

The only change in this program from the previous program is the use of *BorderLayout* rather than *FrameLayout*. Look at the program code and you will find the following statement at the beginning of the constructor:

```
//SET LAYOUT MANAGER
container.setLayout(new BorderLayout(10,10));
```

As you might suspect, this line of code sets the layout manager of the container to *BorderLayout* with a 10 pixel horizontal and vertical gapping. Now, look further down within the constructor and you will find the following code:

```
//ADD BUTTONS TO CONTAINER
container.add(yellowButton,"North");
```

```
container.add(blueButton,"West");
container.add(cyanButton,"East");
container.add(redButton,"Center");
container.add(greenButton,"South");
```

Here you see that each button is added to a specific region defined by *BorderLayout*. The available regions are *North*, *West*, *East*, *Center*, and *South*. The remaining parts of the *GUI103_3* program are identical to the *GUI103_2* program that employed *FlowLayout*. Even the event handling is identical.

GUI 104: LABELS, TEXT FIELDS, AND TEXT AREAS

PURPOSE

- *To become familiar with the GUI label and text components*
- *To demonstrate how to set the length of a text field*
- *To show how to initialize a text field with text*
- *To demonstrate the use of panels*
- *To demonstrate the order in which components are added to a frame*

Introduction

The **label** is a GUI component that is normally used to label other components within a window. A **text field** is a GUI component that displays a single line of text, or allows the user to enter a single line of text. A **text area** is a GUI component that allows the user to enter multiple lines of text or display multiple lines of text. It can be set to allow user editing, or placed in a read-only mode such that it cannot be edited. In this module, you will load and execute a Java program that produces a frame with labels, text fields, and a text area. In addition, you will use panels to arrange your components more conveniently on the container. You will modify the code and observe the effect on the window generated by the program.

Procedure

1. Compile and execute the *GUI104_1.java* program contained on the CD that accompanies this book. You should see a window similar to the one shown in Figure C-10. Here, you see three text fields. The first text field contains the text "This is a text field," while the second and third text fields do not contain any text. Press the *Tab* key on the keyboard and notice that the window cursor will move from one text field to the next each time you press *Tab*. Place the cursor in the first text field and edit the text in the field. This text field is called an editable text field since you can edit the text within it. Move the cursor to the other two text fields and enter some text into these fields. Notice that these are also editable text fields. All text fields are editable by default in Java, even if they are initialized with text by the program. Now press the *Store All* button and observe that the text you entered appears in the *Student Database Summary* text area. Notice the value you entered into the *Password* field was hidden by *s. However, the actual value appeared in the text area when it was read and displayed by the program.

2. Edit the contents of a text field and press the **ENTER** key after you type the text. Notice that the GUI will not respond to the **ENTER** key event. You must click on the *Store All* button for the text area to reflect the edited text.
   Here is the Java code that produced the frame in Figure C-10:

```
1   import javax.swing.*;        //FOR SWING COMPONENT CLASSES
2   import java.awt.event.*;     //FOR EVENT HANDLING
3   import java.awt.*;           //FOR Container CLASS
4
```

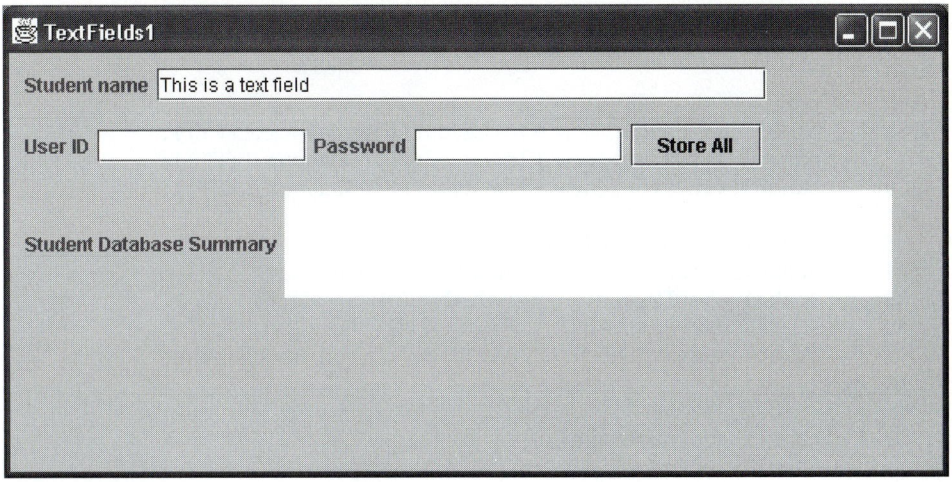

FIGURE C-10 A frame with three text fields.

```
5    class TextFields1 extends JFrame
6    {
7       //DECLARE COMPONENT OBJECTS
8       private JTextField nameField;
9       private JTextField userIDField;
10      private JPasswordField userPassField;
11      private JTextArea studentArea;
12      private JButton storeButton;
13
14      //CREATE A CONTAINER
15      private Container container = getContentPane();
16
17   //CONSTRUCTOR
18   public TextFields1 (String title)
19      {
20       //CALL SUPERCLASS CONSTRUCTOR
21       super(title);
22
23       //INSTANTIATE TEXT FIELD OBJECTS
24       nameField = new JTextField("This is a text field",35);
25       userIDField = new JTextField(12);
26       userPassField = new JPasswordField(12);
27       studentArea = new JTextArea(4,35);
28
29       //INSTANTIATE BUTTON OBJECT
30       storeButton = new JButton("Store All");
31
32       //SET FRAME LAYOUT MANAGER
33       container.setLayout(new FlowLayout(FlowLayout.LEFT));
34
35       //DEFINE PANEL OBJECTS
36       JPanel panel1 = new JPanel();
```

```
37      JPanel panel2 = new JPanel();
38      JPanel panel3 = new JPanel();
39
40      //SET PANEL LAYOUT MANAGERS
41      panel1.setLayout(new FlowLayout(FlowLayout.LEFT));
42      panel2.setLayout(new FlowLayout(FlowLayout.LEFT));
43      panel3.setLayout(new FlowLayout(FlowLayout.LEFT));
44
45      //DEFINE LABEL OBJECTS
46      JLabel nameLabel = new JLabel("Student name");
47      JLabel userIDLabel = new JLabel("User ID");
48      JLabel userPassLabel = new JLabel("Password");
49      JLabel summaryLabel = new JLabel("Student Database Summary");
50
51      //ADD COMPONENTS TO panel1
52      panel1.add(nameLabel);
53      panel1.add(nameField);
54
55      //ADD COMPONENTS TO panel2
56      panel2.add(userIDLabel);
57      panel2.add(userIDField);
58      panel2.add(userPassLabel);
59      panel2.add(userPassField);
60      panel2.add(storeButton);
61
62      //ADD COMPONENTS TO panel3
63      panel3.add(summaryLabel);
64      panel3.add(studentArea);
65
66      //ADD PANELS TO CONTAINER
67      container.add(panel1);
68      container.add(panel2);
69      container.add(panel3);
70
71       //ADD LISTENER AND EVENT HANDLER FOR THE STORE BUTTON
72       storeButton.addActionListener(new StoreButtonHandler());
73
74       //ADD LISTENER FOR THIS FRAME
75       addWindowListener(new WindowHandler());
76    }//END TextFields1()
77
78    //WINDOW EVENT HANDLER
79    private class WindowHandler extends WindowAdapter
80    {
81       public void windowClosing(WindowEvent e)
82       {
83          System.exit(0);  //EXIT TO OPERATING SYSTEM
84       }//END windowClosing()
85    }//END WindowAdapter CLASS
86
87    //BUTTON EVENT HANDLER
88    private class StoreButtonHandler implements ActionListener
```

```
89  {
90     //PROCESS EVENT
91     public void actionPerformed(ActionEvent e)
92     {
93       //DID THE STORE BUTTON CAUSE EVENT?
94       if (e.getSource() == storeButton)
95       {
96         //DISPLAY TEXT FIELD DATA IN TEXT AREA
97         studentArea.setText("This is an example of data stored"
98                           + " in the student database.\n");
99         studentArea.append("\nStudent name: " + nameField.getText());
100        studentArea.append("\nUserID: " + userIDField.getText());
101        studentArea.append("\nPassword: "
102                          + new String(userPassField.getPassword()));
103      }//END IF
104    }//END actionPerformed()
105  }//END StoreButtonHandler
106 }//END TextFields1 CLASS
107
108 //APPLICATION TEST CLASS
109 public class GUI104_1
110 {
111   public static void main(String[] args)
112   {
113     //DEFINE FRAME OBJECT
114     TextFields1 window = new TextFields1("TextFields1");
115
116     //SET FRAME SIZE
117     window.setSize(600,300);
118
119     //MAKE FRAME VISIBLE
120     window.show();
121   }//END main()
122 }//END GUI104_1
```

3. Close the window and change the text within the quotation marks in line 24 to something different. Recompile, then execute the program again, and notice that the first text field is initialized with the new text.

4. Close the window and change the values at the end of lines 24, 25, and 26 to different values, and execute the program again. Notice that the length of each text field changes in proportion to the value entered.

5. Our text area object, called *studentArea*, is defined in line 27 of the program. Notice that there are two values within parentheses at the end of the statement in line 27. These two values define the number of rows and number of columns, respectively, of the text area. Close the window and change these values to define a different size text area. Recompile, then execute the program and observe the resulting text area.

6. Close the window and add the following statement in line 28 of the program:

```
studentArea.setEditable(false);
```

Execute the program and try to type some text in the text area. You should find that the text area is now non-editable.

Discussion

The foregoing program produced three text field components within the frame. A text field is a single editable line of text. When a text field is created, its length in columns across the screen must be set to the anticipated length of text to be entered by the user. In addition, the field can be optionally initialized with a text string. A standard text field is created by the *JTextField* class, while a password field is created by the *JPasswordField* class. A password field places *s in the field as the user enters a value to hide the entry. However, the actual value entered can be read and stored by the program. A text area is a rectangular area used to display text. The two values passed to the *JTextArea()* constructor in line 27 specify its horizontal and vertical dimensions, respectively, in character units, not pixel units. You must define the size of a text area when its object is instantiated in a program. When you changed these values, you observed a different size text area in the resulting window. In step 6, you added a line to the program which called the *setEditable()* method to make the text area non-editable. An argument of `false` in this method makes the text area non-editable, while an argument of `true` makes it editable. Of course, a text area is editable by default.

Unlike buttons, text fields and text areas do not have a built-in label associated with them. In order to label a text field or text area, you must add a ***label*** component to the frame adjacent to the text field or text area.

Procedure (continued)

7. Four label objects are created in lines 46 through 49 of the program. Notice that the text which forms the label is passed to the *JLabel()* constructor in each case. Close the window and change the text. Execute the program again and you should find that the label text has changed accordingly.
8. Notice how the text fields and labels are added to panels in lines 51 – 64. (A *panel* is a container that can be used to hold GUI components.) A label is added, then its associated text field, then another label, followed by its text field, and so on. Remember that components are placed into a container in the order in which they are added within the program. Close the window, change the order, recompile, execute the program, and observe the results.
9. Notice also that we are using three panels, one for the *Student Name* field, one for the *User ID* field, *Password* field and *Store* button, and one for the *Student Database Summary* text area. The panels are created in lines 36 – 38 and added to the frame container in lines 67 through 69. Close the window and change the order in which the panels are added to the container in lines 67 through 69. You should observe a redistribution of the GUI components according to the new order in which you added the panels.
10. Close the *GUI104_1* window.

Discussion

When label objects are created, the label text must be provided within the object definition; otherwise there is no visible label. When components are added to a panel or frame container, they will appear in the order in which they are added. This program employs the *FlowLayout* manager for the frame container as well as the panels. As a result, GUI components are placed within their respective panels, from left to right, and the panels are placed within the frame container from left to right.

Procedure (continued)

11. Compile and execute the *GUI104_2.java* program contained on the CD that accompanies this book.

12. At first glance it appears the same as the *GUI104_1* window. However, its behavior has been modified. Enter your name in the *Student name* text field and press the **ENTER** key when you are done. Notice that your name appears in the text area as the student name. Enter your student ID and a password in the same manner and notice that as soon as you press the **ENTER** key, the information appears in the text area.

13. Go back and edit any of the text field information, pressing the **ENTER** key after your editing of a given field is complete. You should observe that the new information appears in the text area. You can also click on the *Store All* button at any time to display all the text field information at one time.

Discussion

In this program you entered information into a text field, then pressed the **ENTER** key. What do you suppose triggered the event that generated the information in the text area? You're right if you thought, the **ENTER** key. The **ENTER** key can be used to generate a text field event. Here is the *GUI104_2.java* code.

```
1    import javax.swing.*;       //FOR SWING COMPONENT CLASSES
2    import java.awt.event.*;    //FOR EVENT HANDLING
3    import java.awt.*;          //FOR Container CLASS
4
5    class TextFields2 extends JFrame
6    {
7       //DECLARE COMPONENT OBJECTS
8       private JTextField nameField;
9       private JTextField userIDField;
10      private JPasswordField userPassField;
11      private JTextArea studentArea;
12      private JButton storeButton;
13
14      //CREATE A CONTAINER
15      private Container container = getContentPane();
16
17   //CONSTRUCTOR
```

```
18     public TextFields2(String title)
19     {
20      //CALL SUPERCLASS CONSTRUCTOR
21       super(title);
22
23       //INSTANTIATE TEXT FIELD OBJECTS
24       nameField = new JTextField(35);
25       userIDField = new JTextField(12);
26       userPassField = new JPasswordField(12);
27       studentArea = new JTextArea(4,35);
28
29     //INSTANTIATE BUTTON OBJECT
30     storeButton = new JButton("Store All");
31
32     //SET FRAME LAYOUT MANAGER
33     container.setLayout(new FlowLayout(FlowLayout.LEFT));
34
35     //DEFINE PANEL OBJECTS
36     JPanel panel1 = new JPanel();
37     JPanel panel2 = new JPanel();
38     JPanel panel3 = new JPanel();
39
40     //SET PANEL LAYOUT MANAGERS
41     panel1.setLayout(new FlowLayout(FlowLayout.LEFT));
42     panel2.setLayout(new FlowLayout(FlowLayout.LEFT));
43     panel3.setLayout(new FlowLayout(FlowLayout.LEFT));
44
45     //DEFINE LABEL OBJECTS
46     JLabel nameLabel = new JLabel("Student name");
47     JLabel userIDLabel = new JLabel("User ID");
48     JLabel userPassLabel = new JLabel("Password");
49     JLabel summaryLabel = new JLabel("Student Database Summary");
50
51     //ADD COMPONENTS TO panel1
52     panel1.add(nameLabel);
53     panel1.add(nameField);
54
55     //ADD COMPONENTS TO panel2
56     panel2.add(userIDLabel);
57     panel2.add(userIDField);
58     panel2.add(userPassLabel);
59     panel2.add(userPassField);
60     panel2.add(storeButton);
61
62     //ADD COMPONENTS TO panel3
63     panel3.add(summaryLabel);
64     panel3.add(studentArea);
65
66     //ADD PANELS TO CONTAINER
67     container.add(panel1);
68     container.add(panel2);
69     container.add(panel3);
```

```
70
71      //ADD LISTENERS AND EVENT HANDLER FOR BUTTON AND TEXT FIELDS
72      ButtonAndTextHandler handler = new ButtonAndTextHandler();
73      storeButton.addActionListener(handler);
74      nameField.addActionListener(handler);
75      userIDField.addActionListener(handler);
76      userPassField.addActionListener(handler);
77
78      //ADD LISTENER FOR THIS FRAME
79      addWindowListener(new WindowHandler());
80   }//END TextFields2()
81
82   //WINDOW EVENT HANDLER
83   private class WindowHandler extends WindowAdapter
84   {
85     public void windowClosing(WindowEvent e)
86     {
87        System.exit(0);  //EXIT TO OPERATING SYSTEM
88     }//END windowClosing()
89   }//END WindowAdapter CLASS
90
91   //BUTTON AND TEXT EVENT HANDLER
92   private class ButtonAndTextHandler implements ActionListener
93   {
94   //PROCESS EVENT
95   public void actionPerformed(ActionEvent e)
96   {
97     //DID THE STORE BUTTON CAUSE EVENT?
98     //IF DISPLAY ALL
99     if (e.getSource() == storeButton)
100    {
101      //DISPLAY TEXT FIELD DATA IN TEXT AREA
102      studentArea.setText("This is an example of data stored"
103                     + " in the student database.\n");
104      studentArea.append("\nStudent name: " + nameField.getText());
105      studentArea.append("\nUserID: " + userIDField.getText());
106      studentArea.append("\nPassword: " + new
              String(userPassField.getPassword()));
107    }//END BUTTON IF
108
109     //DID THE TEXT FIELDS CAUSE THE EVENT?
110     //IF SO WHICH ONE?
111     if(e.getSource() == nameField)
112       studentArea.append("\nStudent name: " + nameField.getText());
113     if(e.getSource() == userIDField)
114       studentArea.append("\nUserID: " + userIDField.getText());
115     if (e.getSource() == userPassField)
116       studentArea.append("\nPassword: " + new
              String(userPassField.getPassword()));
117    }//END actionPerformed()
118   }//END ButtonAndTextHandler
119 }//END TextFields2 CLASS
```

```
120
121 //APPLICATION TEST CLASS
122 public class GUI104_2
123 {
124   public static void main(String[] args)
125   {
126     //DEFINE FRAME OBJECT
127     TextFields2 window = new TextFields2("TextFields2");
128
129     //SET FRAME SIZE
130     window.setSize(600,300);
131
132     //MAKE FRAME VISIBLE
133     window.show();
134   }//END main()
135 }//END GUI104_2
```

Notice that in lines 74 through 76, each text field object has a listener *added* for an action event. A component object must always add a listener if an event is to be processed for that object. If you comment out any of these lines, the GUI will not respond to a text entry for the respective field.

Next, look at lines 95 through 117. This code forms the *actionPerformed()* method, which is required to process a text field event. You see that the method consists of a series of if statements that determine which GUI component generated the event. The first if statement checks to see if the *storeButton* object caused the event. If so, all the text field information is written to the text area. The next series of if statements check each text field object for an event. When a given text field event is recognized, its information is appended to the text area using the standard *append()* method.

GUI 105: COMBO AND LIST BOXES

PURPOSE

- To become familiar with the GUI combo and list box components
- To understand the differences between combo and list boxes
- To add items to combo and list boxes
- To experiment with list box object definitions
- To demonstrate a list box event

Introduction

A **combo box** is a GUI component that allows the user to choose one of several items in a *drop-down* menu listing. A **list box** allows the user to choose one *or more* items within a *scrolled* item listing. In this module, you will first load and execute a Java program that produces a combo box and a text area. You will experiment with the combo box by adding items to it, and displaying selected items in the text area when the item is clicked. Then, you will compile and execute a program that produces a list box and a text area. You will experiment with the list box by selecting multiple items, and displaying the selected items in the text area when the items are clicked. You will add items to the list box and set the number of visible items.

Procedure

1. Compile and execute the *GUI105_1.java* program contained on the CD that accompanies this book. You should see a window similar to the one shown in Figure C-11. The window contains a combo box and a text area.

2. Notice that the combo box shows the single visible item, "Accounting". This item is highlighted, indicating that it is selected, by default. Click the drop down arrow next to the *Accounting* major, and notice that a list of selectable items appears.

3. Click on any of the items and notice that the list disappears and the item you selected appears highlighted within the combo box. Also, the selected item is reflected within the text area.

4. Try to select more than one item in the box. You will find that this is not possible because a combo box only allows you to select a single item. Here is the Java code that produced the window in Figure C-11:

```
1    import javax.swing.*;       //FOR SWING COMPONENT CLASSES
2    import java.awt.event.*;    //FOR EVENT HANDLING
3    import java.awt.*;          //FOR Container CLASS
4
5
6    class ComboBoxEvent extends JFrame
7    {
8        //DECLARE COMPONENT OBJECTS
9        private JComboBox majorsBox;  //COMBO BOX OBJECT
```

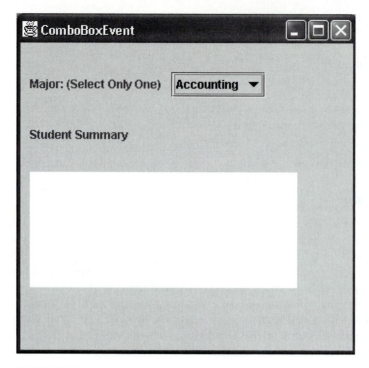

FIGURE C-11   A window with a combo box and a text area.

```
10      private JTextArea textArea;    //DISPLAY AREA OBJECT
11
12  //CONSTRUCTOR
13  public ComboBoxEvent (String title)
14  {
15    super(title);                //CALL SUPERCLASS CONSTRUCTOR
16
17    //CREATE A CONTAINER
18    Container container = getContentPane();
19
20    //SET CONTAINER LAYOUT MANAGER
21    container.setLayout(new FlowLayout(FlowLayout.LEFT,10,30));
22
23    //DEFINE LABEL OBJECTS
24    JLabel majorsLabel = new JLabel("Major: (Select Only One)");
25    JLabel summaryLabel = new JLabel("Student Summary");
26
27    //DEFINE ARRAY OF COMBO BOX ITEMS
28    String boxItems[]={"Accounting", "Business", "BIS", "CIS", "MIS",
29                       "Economics", "Marketing", "Undecided"};
30
31    //INSTANTIATE COMBO BOX OBJECT WITH boxItems[]
32    majorsBox = new JComboBox(boxItems);
33
```

```
34      //INSTANTIATE TEXT AREA OBJECT
35      textArea = new JTextArea(7,25);
36
37      //ADD COMPONENTS TO CONTAINER
38      container.add(majorsLabel);
39      container.add(majorsBox);
40      container.add(summaryLabel);
41      container.add(textArea);
42
43      //ADD LISTENER WITH COMBO BOX EVENT HANDLER
44      majorsBox.addActionListener(new BoxHandler());
45
46      //ADD WINDOW LISTENER WITH WINDOW EVENT HANDLER
47      addWindowListener(new WindowHandler());
48   }//END ComboBoxEvent() CONSTRUCTOR
49
50   //WINDOW EVENT HANDLER CLASS
51     private class WindowHandler extends WindowAdapter
52     {
53       public void windowClosing(WindowEvent e)
54       {
55         System.exit(0);  //EXIT TO OPERATING SYSTEM
56     }//END windowClosing()
57     }//END WindowAdapter CLASS
58
59
60     //BOX EVENT HANDLER CLASS
61     private class BoxHandler implements ActionListener
62     {
63     //PROCESS COMBO BOX EVENT
64     public void actionPerformed(ActionEvent e)
65     {
66       //CHECK FOR COMBO BOX EVENT?
67       if (e.getSource() == majorsBox)
68       {
69         //CLEAR TEXT AREA
70         textArea.setText("");
71         //DISPLAY IN TEXT FIELD DATA IN TEXT AREA
72         textArea.append("\nMajor:\t" + majorsBox.getSelectedItem());
73       }//END IF
74     }//END actionPerformed()
75     }//END BoxHandler
76   }//END ComboBoxEvent CLASS
77
78   //APPLICATION TEST CLASS
79   public class GUI105_1
80   {
81     public static void main(String[] args)
82     {
83       //DEFINE FRAME OBJECT
84       ComboBoxEvent window = new ComboBoxEvent("ComboBoxEvent");
85
```

```
86        //SET FRAME SIZE
87        window.setSize(350,350);
88
89        //MAKE FRAME VISIBLE
90        window.show();
91    }//END main()
92  }//END  GUI105_1 CLASS
```

5. In line 9 of the program, we declare a combo box object called *majorsBox* and in-stantiate it in line 32. The *JComboBox()* constructor requires an array argument. The array must be an array of strings that stores the combo box items. We have defined an array called *boxItems[]* and initialized it with the required string items in lines 28 and 29. Now, close the window and add another combo box item to the array in lines 28 and 29.

6. Recompile, then execute the program again, and verify that the item you added in line 29 appears in the combo box and is a selectable item. Select the new item to assure it generates an event and appears in the text area. Close the window.

Discussion

A combo box provides a drop-down menu of choices. In Java, combo boxes are pro-vided by the *JComboBox* class. Items may be added to the box by the *JComboBox()* constructor when an array of strings is provided as the constructor argument. A combo box generates an action event which is handled using the *actionPerformed()* method. In line 72 of this method, you see the *getSelectedItem()* method being called by the *majorsBox* object to return the item that was selected. This item is appended to the text area. By definition, a combo box can only be used to select a single item. But, what if you need to select more than one item, such as more than one major in a majors' item listing? Well, to select more than one item you need a list box.

Procedure (continued)

7. Compile and execute the *GUI105_2.java* program contained on the CD that accom-panies this book. You should see a window similar to the one shown in Figure C-12. The window contains a list box and a text area.

8. Notice that the list box shows three visible items, none of which is highlighted. In addition, notice the scrollbar to the right of the item listing. Scroll through the items and select two or more items by clicking on the items. Each time you select an item, the item will be highlighted within the listing.

9. Now, hold the *Ctrl* key down and click two or more items. All the items you select should appear in the text area as you click them.

10. You can deselect an item by clicking on it after it has been selected (highlighted). Hold the *Ctrl* key down again and select two or more items. Continue to hold the *Ctrl* key down after the items are selected and click on one of the selected items again. This should deselect the item and remove it from the text area.

11. Finally, hold the *Shift* key down and select an item. Then select another item sev-eral items away. All the items between the two selected items should be highlighted

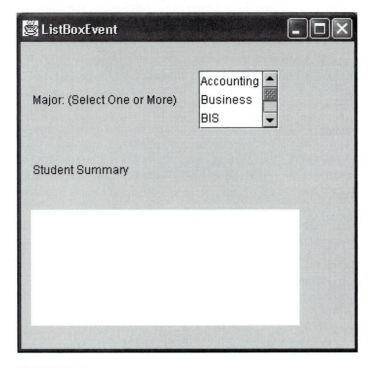

FIGURE C-12   A window with a list box and a text area.

and appear in the text area. Here is the Java code that produced the window in Figure C-12:

```
1    import javax.swing.*;        //FOR SWING COMPONENT CLASSES
2    import java.awt.*;           //FOR Container CLASS
3    import java.awt.event.*;     //FOR EVENT HANDLING
4    import javax.swing.event.*;  //FOR ListSelectionListener HANDLING
5
6    class ListBoxEvent extends JFrame
7    {
8      //DECLARE COMPONENT OBJECTS
9      private JTextArea textArea;    //SUMMARY AREA
10     private JList majorsList;      //LIST OF MAJORS
11
12     //DEFINE ARRAY OF LIST ITEMS
13     private String listItems[] = {"Accounting", "Business", "BIS",
14                 "CIS","MIS","Economics", "Marketing", "Undecided"};
15
16     //CONSTRUCTOR
17     public ListBoxEvent(String title)
18     {
19       //CALL SUPERCLASS CONSTRUCTOR
20       super(title);
21
```

```
22      //CREATE A CONTAINER
23      Container container = getContentPane();
24
25      //SET CONTAINER LAYOUT MANAGER
26      container.setLayout(new FlowLayout(FlowLayout.LEFT,10,30));
27
28      //DEFINE LABEL OBJECTS
29      Label majorsLabel = new Label("Major: (Select One or More)");
30      Label summaryLabel = new Label("Student Summary");
31
32      //INSTANTIATE LIST BOX OBJECT WITH listItems[]
33      majorsList = new JList(listItems);
34
35      //SET VISIBLE ITEMS
36      majorsList.setVisibleRowCount(3);
37
38      //INSTANTIATE TEXT AREA OBJECT
39      textArea = new JTextArea(7,25);
40
41      //ADD LIST LABEL TO CONTAINER
42      container.add(majorsLabel);
43
44      //ADD SCROLL BAR WITH LIST TO CONTAINER
45      container.add(new JScrollPane(majorsList));
46
47      //ADD TEXT AREA LABEL TO CONTAINER
48      container.add(summaryLabel);
49
50      //ADD TEXT AREA TO CONTAINER
51      container.add(textArea);
52
53      //ADD LIST LISTENER WITH LIST EVENT HANDLER
54      majorsList.addListSelectionListener(new ListHandler());
55
56      //ADD WINDOW LISTENER WITH WINDOW EVENT HANDLER
57      addWindowListener(new WindowHandler());
58   }//END ListBoxEvent() CONSTRUCTOR
59
60   //WINDOW EVENT HANDLER CLASS
61   private class WindowHandler extends WindowAdapter
62   {
63      public void windowClosing(WindowEvent e)
64      {
65         System.exit(0);   //EXIT TO OPERATING SYSTEM
66      }//END windowClosing()
67   }//END WindowAdapter CLASS
68
69   //LIST HANDLER CLASS
70   private class ListHandler implements ListSelectionListener
71   {
72   //PROCESS LIST EVENT
73   public void valueChanged(ListSelectionEvent e)
```

```
74    {
75        //CHECK FOR LIST EVENT
76        if (e.getSource() == majorsList)
77        {
78          //GET SELECTED ITEM INDICES AND STORE IN ARRAY
79          int selectedIndices[] = majorsList.getSelectedIndices();
80
81          //DISPLAY HEADER
82          textArea.setText("\nMajor(s):\t");
83
84          //DISPLAY SELECTED ITEMS
85          for (int index = 0; index < selectedIndices.length; ++index)
86          {
87              textArea.append(listItems[selectedIndices[index]]);
88              textArea.append("\n\t");
89          }//END FOR
90        }//END IF
91      }//END valueChanged()
92    }//END ListHandler CLASS
93  }//END ListBoxEvent CLASS
94
95  //APPLICATION CLASS TO TEST ListBoxEvent CLASS
96  public class GUI105_2
97  {
98    public static void main(String[] args)
99    {
100       //DEFINE FRAME OBJECT
101       ListBoxEvent window = new ListBoxEvent("ListBoxEvent");
102
103       //SET FRAME SIZE
104       window.setSize(350,350);
105
106       //MAKE FRAME VISIBLE
107       window.show();
108     }//END main()
109 }//END GUI105_2 CLASS
```

12. In line 33 of the program, we instantiated a list box object called *majorsList* with list items contained in the *listItems[]* array defined in lines 13 and 14. Close the window and add another item to the list array in lines 13 and 14.

13. Recompile, then execute the program again. Verify that the item you added appears in the list box and is a selectable item. Close the window.

14. The number of visible items in the list was set in line 36 as follows:

```
majorsList.setVisibleRowCount(3);
```

Change this line of code, as follows:

```
majorsList.setVisibleRowCount(2);
```

Recompile, then execute the program again and observe the window. You should find that only the first two list items are visible. Why?

Discussion

A list box provides a scrollable list of items from which to select. A list box allows more than one item to be selected by holding down the *Ctrl* key or the *Shift* key and selecting the desired items or range of items. In Java, list boxes are provided via the *JList* class and include an active scrollbar when the number of items in the list exceeds the visible portion of the list box. The items are added to the box by the *JList()* constructor. An array of string items must be created and provided as the constructor argument to add the items. A list box generates a *ListSelectionEvent* and, therefore, is handled using the *valueChanged()* method. This method is implemented to handle a list event in lines 73 – 91 of the program. The visible portion of the list box is set by using the list box object to call the *setVisibleRowCount()* method, and by supplying the desired number of visible items as the method argument. At first, the number of visible items was set to 3. Then, you changed the method argument and set the number of visible items to 2.

GUI 106: CHECK BOXES AND RADIO BUTTONS

PURPOSE

- To become familiar with the GUI check box and radio button components
- To understand the differences between a check box and a radio button
- To learn how to define check box and radio button objects
- To learn how to process check box and radio button events

Introduction

Both the **check box** component and **radio button** component are referred to as **state buttons** because they represent a Boolean state of `true`/`false`. A **check box** is a GUI component that allows the user to select one of two possible states: checked or unchecked. The user clicks the box, placing a checkmark inside of it, or once checked, clicks the box to remove the checkmark. Any number of check boxes can be checked at any given time since checking one box has no effect on another, unless underlying logic is developed to prevent multiple selection. Class *JCheckBox* is used to create check boxes.

A **radio button** is also a type of check box and is created using the *JRadioButton* class. However, radio buttons are grouped using the *ButtonGroup* class so that only one radio button within the group can be on, or `true`, at any given time. Selecting one radio button within a group turns all other radio buttons within that group off, or `false`.

In this module, you will compile and execute a program that produces several check boxes. You will experiment with the check boxes by selecting/deselecting them and displaying the check box status in a text area. You will also create an additional check box for the GUI. Next, you will compile and execute a program that produces a group of radio buttons. Again, you will experiment by selecting/deselecting them and displaying the radio button status within a text area. You will create an additional radio button for the group and add logic to process the additional button.

Procedure

1. Compile and execute the *GUI106_1.java* program contained on the CD that accompanies this book. You should see a window similar to the one shown in Figure C-13. The window includes four check boxes and a text area.

2. Notice that each check box has a label that indicates a student's status when the box is checked. Select a box and notice that a checkmark appears inside the box, indicating that it is selected. Deselect the same box and notice that the checkmark disappears.

3. Select any number of boxes. You should see the student status information represented by the selected boxes within the text area, unless you selected both full time and part time, or both commuting and non-commuting. A student cannot be both full time and part time, or both commuting and non-commuting, right?

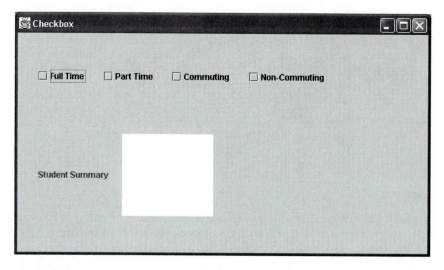

FIGURE C-13   A window with four check boxes and a text area.

We have added logic to our event processing code that displays a message to the user if these pairs of check boxes are selected. Close the window. Here is the class code that produced the GUI and processes the event:

```
1   import javax.swing.*;          //FOR SWING COMPONENT CLASSES
2   import java.awt.*;             //FOR Container CLASS
3   import java.awt.event.*;       //FOR EVENT HANDLING
4
5   class Check box extends JFrame
6   {
7       //DECLARE CHECK BOX OBJECTS
8       private JCheckBox fullTimeBox;
9       private JCheckBox partTimeBox;
10      private JCheckBox commutingBox;
11      private JCheckBox nonCommutingBox;
12
13      //DECLARE TEXT AREA OBJECT
14      private JTextArea textArea;
15
16   //CONSTRUCTOR
17   public Check box(String title)
18   {
19   //CALL SUPERCLASS CONSTRUCTOR
20   super(title);
21
22   //CREATE A CONTAINER
23   Container container = getContentPane();
24
25   //SET CONTAINER LAYOUT MANAGER
26   container.setLayout(new FlowLayout(FlowLayout.LEFT,10,30));
27
```

```
28        //DEFINE LABEL OBJECTS
29        JLabel summaryLabel = new JLabel("Student Summary");
30
31        //INSTANTIATE CHECK BOX OBJECTS
32        fullTimeBox = new JCheckBox("Full Time");
33        partTimeBox = new JCheckBox("Part Time");
34        commutingBox = new JCheckBox("Commuting");
35        nonCommutingBox = new JCheckBox("Non-Commuting");
36
37        //INSTANTIATE TEXT AREA OBJECT
38        textArea = new JTextArea(7,12);
39
40        //DEFINE PANELS
41        JPanel topPanel = new JPanel();
42        JPanel bottomPanel = new JPanel();
43
44        //SET PANEL LAYOUT MANAGERS
45        topPanel.setLayout(new FlowLayout(FlowLayout.LEFT,20,20));
46        bottomPanel.setLayout(new FlowLayout(FlowLayout.LEFT,20,20));
47
48        //ADD COMPONENTS TO topPanel
49        topPanel.add(fullTimeBox);
50        topPanel.add(partTimeBox);
51        topPanel.add(commutingBox);
52        topPanel.add(nonCommutingBox);
53
54        //ADD TEXT AREA TO bottomPanel
55        bottomPanel.add(summaryLabel);
56        bottomPanel.add(textArea);
57
58        //ADD PANELS TO FRAME
59        container.add(topPanel);
60        container.add(bottomPanel);
61
62        //CREATE HANDLER OBJECT
63        Check boxHandler checkHandler = new Check boxHandler();
64
65        //ADD ITEM LISTENER WITH CHECK BOX EVENT HANDLER
66        fullTimeBox.addItemListener(checkHandler);
67        partTimeBox.addItemListener(checkHandler);
68        commutingBox.addItemListener(checkHandler);
69        nonCommutingBox.addItemListener(checkHandler);
70
71         //ADD WINDOW LISTENER WITH WINDOW EVENT HANDLER
72         addWindowListener(new WindowHandler());
73     }//END Check box() CONSTRUCTOR
74
75     //WINDOW EVENT HANDLER CLASS
76     private class WindowHandler extends WindowAdapter
77     {
78       public void windowClosing(WindowEvent e)
79       {
```

```
 80        System.exit(0);  //EXIT TO OPERATING SYSTEM
 81     }//END windowClosing()
 82    }//END WindowAdapter CLASS
 83
 84    //CHECK BOX HANDLER CLASS
 85    private class Check boxHandler implements ItemListener
 86    {
 87     //PROCESS CHECK BOX EVENT
 88     public void itemStateChanged(ItemEvent e)
 89     {
 90      //CLEAR TEXT AREA
 91      textArea.setText("Student Status:");
 92
 93      //DID A CHECK BOX OBJECT CAUSE EVENT?
 94      if (e.getSource() instanceof JCheckBox)
 95      {
 96        //PROCESS CHECK BOXES
 97
 98
 99        if ((fullTimeBox.isSelected()) && (partTimeBox.isSelected()))
100          textArea.append("\nCANNOT SELECT BOTH FULL TIME\n"
101                          + "AND PART TIME");
102        else
103        {
104          if (fullTimeBox.isSelected())
105            textArea.append("\nFull Time");
106          if (partTimeBox.isSelected())
107            textArea.append("\nPart Time");
108        } //END ELSE
109
110        if((commutingBox.isSelected()) &&
           (nonCommutingBox.isSelected()))
111          textArea.append("\nCANNOT SELECT BOTH COMMUTING\n"
112                            + "AND NON-COMMUTING");
113        else
114        {
115          if (commutingBox.isSelected())
116            textArea.append("\nCommuting");
117          if (nonCommutingBox.isSelected())
118            textArea.append("\nNon Commuting");
119        }//END ELSE
120      }//END IF CHECK BOX
121    }//END itemStateChanged()
122   }//END CheckHandler CLASS
123  }//END Check boxes CLASS
124
125 //APPLICATION TEST CLASS
126  public class GUI106_1
127 {
128   public static void main(String[] args)
129   {
130     //DEFINE FRAME OBJECT
```

```
131      Check box window = new Check box("Check box");
132
133      //SET FRAME SIZE
134      window.setSize(500,350);
135
136      //MAKE FRAME VISIBLE
137      window.show();
138    }//END main()
139 }//END GUI106_1 CLASS
```

4. You see that our four check box objects are declared as `private` class members in lines 8 – 11 and instantiated in lines 32 – 35. Notice that the check box label is provided as the argument to the *JCheckBox()* constructor. As a result, check boxes do not need a separate label object to identify them as do text fields and text areas. Declare an additional check box object in line 12 and instantiate it in line 36 to add a "My Box" check box to the GUI. Name your object *myBox*.

5. Recompile, then execute the program again, and verify that the check box you added appears on the GUI. What? It isn't there? The reason it's not there is because it was not placed in the panel with the other check boxes. Close the window and add your check box to *topPanel* in line 53, using the same syntax that you see for the other check boxes added in lines 49 – 52.

6. Recompile, then execute the program again. Notice that your check box appears as the last check box within the group.

7. Select your new check box and observe that its status is not reflected within the text area. Why? Close the window.

8. Add the following line of code at line 70:

```
myBox.addItemListener(checkHandler);
```

9. Add the following statement at lines 97 and 98:

```
if(myBox.isSelected())
    textArea.append("\nMy Box Selected");
```

10. Recompile, then execute the program again and select your check box. You should see its status reflected in the text area.

Discussion

A check box allows the user to select one of two possible states: checked or unchecked, which represents `true`/`false`. Any number of check boxes can be selected at any given time, unless there is underlying logic that prevents multiple selections. This is exactly what we did in lines 99 – 120 in the foregoing program. Notice that the `if/else` logic prevents both the full time and part time, or commuting and non-commuting boxes to be selected at the same time. Look at the logic and convince yourself that this is the case. Notice that to get the Boolean state of a given check box, you call its *isSelected()*

method. The *isSelected()* method returns `true` if the object's check box is selected, or `false` if the object's check box is deselected.

    A check box object is created using the *JCheckBox* class. You added a new check box object, but found that it did not appear unless the object was added to the frame container via a panel. Then, you found that selecting your check box had no effect until you added it as a listener in line 70. Finally, you added an `if` statement in lines 97 and 98 of the *itemStateChanged()* method to get the state of the check box, and append its status to the text area. Check boxes generate an *ItemEvent* which is handled by the *itemStateChanged()* method.

Procedure (continued)

11. Compile and execute the *GUI106_2.java* program contained on the CD that accompanies this book. You should see a window similar to the one shown in Figure C-14. The window contains two radio buttons and a text area.

12. First, notice that a radio button appears differently than a check box. The radio button is round, and is either filled in or not filled in. A filled in radio button means that it is selected. Observe that the *Undergraduate* button has been selected and the *Graduate* button is not selected in Figure C-14. However, the undergraduate student status does not appear in the text area yet because an event has not been generated.

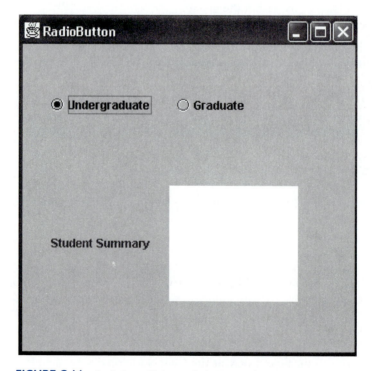

FIGURE C-14   A window with two radio buttons and a text area.

13. Click the *Graduate* button and notice that it becomes filled in, while the *Undergraduate* button does not. This demonstrates that only a single radio button can be selected at any given time. In addition, the graduate student status appears in the text area. Close the window.

Here is the class code that produced the GUI and processes the button event:

```
1    import javax.swing.*;        //FOR SWING COMPONENTS CLASS
2    import java.awt.*;           //FOR Container CLASS
3    import java.awt.event.*;     //FOR EVENT HANDLING
4
5    class RadioButton extends JFrame
6    {
7       //DECLARE RADIO BUTTON OBJECTS
8       private JRadioButton undergraduate;;
9       private JRadioButton graduate;
10
11      //DECLARE TEXT AREA OBJECT
12      private JTextArea textArea;
13
14     //CONSTRUCTOR
15     public RadioButton(String title)
16     {
17      //CALL SUPERCLASS CONSTRUCTOR
18      super(title);
19
20      //CREATE A CONTAINER
21      Container container = getContentPane();
22
23      //SET CONTAINER LAYOUT MANAGER
24      container.setLayout(new FlowLayout(FlowLayout.LEFT,10,30));
25
26      //DEFINE LABEL OBJECTS
27      JLabel summaryLabel = new JLabel("Student Summary");
28
29      //CREATE RADIO BUTTON GROUP
30      ButtonGroup graduateStatusGroup = new ButtonGroup();
31
32      //INSTANTIATE RADIO BUTTON OBJECTS
33      undergraduate = new JRadioButton("Undergraduate",true);
34      graduate = new JRadioButton("Graduate",false);
35
36      //ADD BUTTONS TO GROUP
37      graduateStatusGroup.add(undergraduate);
38      graduateStatusGroup.add(graduate);
39
40      //INSTANTIATE TEXT AREA OBJECT
41      textArea = new JTextArea(7,12);
42
43      //DEFINE PANELS
44      JPanel topPanel = new JPanel();
45      JPanel bottomPanel = new JPanel();
```

```
46
47       //SET PANEL LAYOUT MANAGERS
48       topPanel.setLayout(new FlowLayout(FlowLayout.LEFT,20,20));
49       bottomPanel.setLayout(new FlowLayout(FlowLayout.LEFT,20,20));
50
51       //ADD COMPONENTS TO topPanel
52       topPanel.add(undergraduate);
53       topPanel.add(graduate);
54
55       //ADD TEXT AREA TO bottomPanel
56       bottomPanel.add(summaryLabel);
57       bottomPanel.add(textArea);
58
59       //ADD PANELS TO FRAME
60       container.add(topPanel);
61       container.add(bottomPanel);
62
63       //ADD ITEM LISTENER WITH RADIO BUTTON EVENT HANDLER
64       undergraduate.addItemListener(new RadioButtonHandler());
65       graduate.addItemListener(new RadioButtonHandler());
66
67        //ADD WINDOW LISTENER WITH WINDOW EVENT HANDLER
68        addWindowListener(new WindowHandler());
69     }//END RadioButton() CONSTRUCTOR
70
71     //WINDOW EVENT HANDLER CLASS
72     private class WindowHandler extends WindowAdapter
73     {
74       public void windowClosing(WindowEvent e)
75       {
76         System.exit(0);   //EXIT TO OPERATING SYSTEM
77       }//END windowClosing()
78     }//END WindowAdapter CLASS
79
80     //RADIO BUTTON HANDLER CLASS
81     private class RadioButtonHandler implements ItemListener
82     {
83      //PROCESS RADIO BUTTON EVENT
84      public void itemStateChanged(ItemEvent e)
85      {
86       //CLEAR TEXT AREA
87       textArea.setText("Student Status:");
88
89       //APPEND TEXT AREA WITH BUTTON EVENT STATUS
90       if(undergraduate.isSelected())
91         textArea.append("\nUndergraduate");
92       if(graduate.isSelected())
93         textArea.append("\nGraduate");
94
95
96      }//END itemStateChanged()
97     }//END RadioButtonHandler CLASS
```

```
98    }//END RadioButton CLASS
99
100 //APPLICATION TEST CLASS
101  public class GUI106_2
102  {
103    public static void main(String[] args)
104    {
105      //DEFINE FRAME OBJECT
106      RadioButton window = new RadioButton("RadioButton");
107
108      //SET FRAME SIZE
109      window.setSize(350,350);
110
111      //MAKE FRAME VISIBLE
112      window.show();
113    }//END main()
114 }//END GUI106_2 CLASS
```

Add the following radio button object declaration in line 10:

```
private JRadioButton myButton;
```

14. Instantiate the *myButton* component in line 35, like this:

```
myButton = new JRadioButton("My Button",false);
```

115. Add the *myButton* component to the *graduateStatusGroup* in line 39, as follows:

```
graduateStatusGroup.add(myButton);
```

16. Add the *myButton* component to *topPanel* in line 54, as follows:

```
topPanel.add(myButton);
```

17. Add an item listener for the *myButton* component in line 66, as follows:

```
myButton.addItemListener(new RadioButtonHandler());
```

18. Recompile, then execute the program. Notice that a third radio button, called *My Button*, appears on the GUI.

19. Select *My Button*. What's this? You selected the *My Button*, but its status does not appear in the text area. There must be something wrong with the event logic, right?

20. Look at the logic in lines 90 – 93. Notice that the *undergraduate* and *graduate* objects are being tested for an event, but your new *myButton* object is not being tested. So, more logic must be added to handle our new *myButton* object. Close the window and add an `if` statement in lines 94 and 95 to test for a *myButton* event.

21. Recompile, then execute the program again, and select any of the radio buttons. You should observe the selected button status reflected in the text area.

Discussion

You see that the two original radio button objects are declared in lines 8 and 9 and instantiated in lines 33 and 34 using the *JRadioButton* class. Notice that the radio button label is part of the object instantiation. As a result, radio buttons, like check boxes, do not need a separate label object to identify the button. A radio button object needs to be set to a Boolean state of `true` or `false`. A `true` state means that the respective button is selected, by default. A `false` state means the button is deselected by default. Of course, only one button within a group can be initially set to `true`. So we set the *undergraduate* object to `true`, and the *graduate* object to `false`. Lastly, a radio button object needs to know the *ButtonGroup* to which it belongs. A radio button needs to belong to a button group so that only one button within the group can be selected at any given time. Notice that, in line 30, the *ButtonGroup* class is used to define a *graduateStatusGroup* object. Our radio button objects are then added to this group in lines 37 and 38. You added code to define a third radio button object called *myButton*. This object was set to a `false` state and added to the same *graduateStatusGroup* group as the other two button objects. After adding the *myButton* object to the GUI, you found that an `if` statement had to be added within the *itemStateChanged()* method to detect any event generated by this object. Like a check box, a radio button generates an *itemEvent* which must be handled by the *itemStateChanged()* method.

GUI 107: MENUS AND FONT CONTROL

PURPOSE

- To become familiar with menus
- To understand the purpose of a menu bar
- To learn how to add menu items to a menu
- To learn how to add menus to a menu bar
- To understand the logic required to process menu events
- To demonstrate and experiment with font control
- To learn how to set the foreground and background color of a text area

Introduction

A *menu* consists of a set of selectable options located at the top of a window within a *menu bar*. Menus are widely used in window applications because they make selection easier and do not clutter up the GUI. Menus are created in Java by creating menu objects. Selectable items are added to the menu object and the menu is added to a menu bar object, which is set in a frame. Thus, a frame is a container for a menu bar, which is a container for one or more menus.

Java allows you to control the *font* for a text component. A font consists of a *font name*, *font style*, and *font size*. The font name is the type of font, such as Courier, Helvetica, or Times Roman. There are literally hundreds of different fonts available within the computer industry. The fonts that are available for a given Java program are those that are supported within the host operating environment. As long as the host operating environment, like Windows XP or Mac®, supports it, a given font is available to a Java program running within that environment. The font style can be plain, *italic*, or **bold**. In addition ***bold-italic*** can be generated by combining **bold** with *italic*. The font size is measured in points, where one point is approximately 1/72 of an inch. For example, the font that you are now reading is Times New Roman, plain, 11 point. Java allows you to set the font name, style, and size for a text component, such as a text area.

In this module, you will compile and execute a program that produces a menu bar with a font menu. The font menu will allow you to set the font type for any text displayed within a text area. You will experiment with the menu by selecting different font types, and observing the selected font within a text area. You will also create an additional font type and add it to the menu. Then, you will experiment with different styles and sizes of font. Finally, you will experiment with setting the foreground and background color of a text area.

Procedure

1. Compile and execute the *GUI107_1.java* program contained on the CD that accompanies this book. You should see a window similar to the one shown in Figure C-15. At the top of the window you see a menu bar with a *Font type* menu. A text area appears in the middle of the window.

FIGURE C-15   A window with a single menu and text area.

2. Click on the *Font Types* menu and notice that it drops down, providing several se-
    lectable menu items. Click on any of the font types and observe the font dis-
    played within the text area. The selected font will be displayed along with a
    message that indicates the name, style, and size of the font being displayed. Also
    notice that once a given font is selected, the menu disappears.
3. Select the *Font Types* menu again with your mouse, then use the up/down arrow
    keys on your keyboard to highlight a given font type. Press the **ENTER** key to se-
    lect the highlighted font. Close the window.

Here is the program code that produced the GUI in Figure C-15 and processes a menu
event:

```
1    import javax.swing.*;          //FOR SWING COMPONENTS CLASS
2    import java.awt.*;             //FOR Container CLASS
3    import java.awt.event.*;       //FOR EVENT HANDLING
4
5    class FontMenu extends JFrame
6    {
7        //DECLARE MENU ITEMS
8        private JMenuItem courier;
9        private JMenuItem helvetica;
10       private JMenuItem timesRoman;
11
12       //DECLARE TEXT AREA OBJECT
13       private JTextArea textArea;
14
15       //CONSTRUCTOR
16       public FontMenu(String Title)
17       {
18        //CALL SUPERCLASS CONSTRUCTOR
19        super(Title);
20
```

```
21      //CREATE A CONTAINER
22      Container container = getContentPane();
23
24      //SET FRAME LAYOUT MANAGER
25      container.setLayout(new FlowLayout(FlowLayout.LEFT,10,60));
26
27
28      //INSTANTIATE MENU ITEM OBJECTS
29      courier = new JMenuItem("Courier");
30      helvetica = new JMenuItem("Helvetica");
31      timesRoman = new JMenuItem("Times Roman");
32
33      //DEFINE MENU OBJECT
34      JMenu fontNameMenu = new JMenu("Font Types");
35
36      //ADD ITEM OBJECTS TO MENU
37      fontNameMenu.add(courier);
38      fontNameMenu.add(helvetica);
39      fontNameMenu.add(timesRoman);
40
41      //DEFINE MENU BAR OBJECT
42      JMenuBar bar = new JMenuBar();
43
44      //ADD MENU TO MENU BAR
45      bar.add(fontNameMenu);
46
47      //SET MENU BAR
48      setJMenuBar(bar);
49
50      //INSTANTIATE TEXT AREA OBJECT
51      textArea = new JTextArea(5,57);
52
53      //ADD TEXT AREA TO CONTAINER
54      container.add(textArea);
55
56      //REGISTER MENU ITEM OBJECTS AS LISTENERS
57      courier.addActionListener(new MenuHandler());
58      helvetica.addActionListener(new MenuHandler());
59      timesRoman.addActionListener(new MenuHandler());
60
61      //ADD WINDOW LISTENER WITH WINDOW EVENT HANDLER
62      addWindowListener(new WindowHandler());
63   }//END FontMenu() CONSTRUCTOR
64
65   //WINDOW EVENT HANDLER CLASS
66   private class WindowHandler extends WindowAdapter
67   {
68     public void windowClosing(WindowEvent e)
69     {
70       System.exit(0);  //EXIT TO OPERATING SYSTEM
71     }//END windowClosing()
72   }//END WindowAdapter CLASS
```

```
73
74    //MENU EVENT HANDLER CLASS
75    private class MenuHandler implements ActionListener
76    {
77
78    //PROCESS MENU EVENT
79    public void actionPerformed(ActionEvent e)
80    {
81      //DID MENU CAUSE EVENT?
82      if (e.getSource() == courier)
83      {
84          //CREATE NEW COURIER FONT OBJECT
85          Font newFont = new Font("Courier",Font.PLAIN,12);
86          //SET TEXT AREA TO NEW FONT
87          textArea.setFont(newFont);
88          //DISPLAY NEW FONT IN TEXT AREA
89          textArea.setText("\n\nTHE FONT IS NOW:\n"
90                          + newFont.toString());
91      }//END IF COURIER
92
93      //CHECK FOR HELVETICA ITEM
94      if (e.getSource() == helvetica)
95      {
96          //CREATE NEW HELVETICA FONT OBJECT
97          Font newFont = new Font("Helvetica",Font.PLAIN,18);
98          //SET TEXT AREA TO NEW FONT
99          textArea.setFont(newFont);

100          //DISPLAY NEW FONT IN TEXT AREA
101          textArea.setText("\n\nTHE FONT IS NOW:\n"
102                          + newFont.toString());
103      }//END IF HELVETICA
104
105      //CHECK FOR TIMES ROMAN ITEM
106      if (e.getSource() == timesRoman)
107      {
108          //CREATE NEW TIMES ROMAN FONT OBJECT
109          Font newFont = new Font("TimesRoman",Font.PLAIN,22);
110          //SET TEXT AREA TO NEW FONT
111          textArea.setFont(newFont);
112          //DISPLAY NEW FONT IN TEXT AREA
113          textArea.setText("\n\nTHE FONT IS NOW:\n"
114                          + newFont.toString());
115      }//END IF TIMES ROMAN
116
117
118
119
120
121
122
123
124
```

```
125
126
127    }//END actionPerformed()
128   }//END MenuHandler
129 }//END FontMenu CLASS
130
131 //APPLICATION CLASS TO TEST FrameWithButton
132 public class GUI107_1
133 {
134   public static void main(String[] args)
135   {
136     //DEFINE FRAME OBJECT
137     FontMenu window = new FontMenu("Font Menu");
138
139     //SET FRAME SIZE
140     window.setSize(640,300);
141
142     //MAKE FRAME VISIBLE
143     window.setVisible(true);
144   }//END main()
145 }//END GUI107_1 CLASS
```

4. You see that a font menu object called *fontNameMenu* is defined in line 34. The menu title appears in quotation marks as an argument for the constructor. The menu item objects are declared in lines 8 through 10, and instantiated in lines 29 through 31. Declare a *bookman* menu item object in line 11, and instantiate this object in line 32 using similar code.

5. In lines 37 – 39 you see the code that adds the menu item objects to the menu. Add your *bookman* item object to the menu in line 40 using similar code.

6. Recompile, then execute the program again, click the menu, and notice that the *Bookman* option appears at the bottom of the menu. Select the *Bookman* font type. What? It isn't displayed within the text area? Why?

7. Look at lines 79 – 127 in the program. This is where the menu items are processed as part of the *actionPerformed()* method. A series of if statements is used to determine which menu item was selected, and to set the text area font accordingly. However, we have not added any code to process the *Bookman* menu item. Add the following statements in lines 116 – 126:

```
//CHECK FOR BOOKMAN
if (e.getSource() == bookman)
{
    //CREATE NEW BOOKMAN FONT OBJECT
    Font newFont = new Font("Bookman",Font.PLAIN,22);
    //SET TEXT AREA TO NEW FONT
    textArea.setFont(newFont);
    //DISPLAY NEW FONT IN TEXT AREA
    textArea.setText("\n\nTHE FONT IS NOW:\n"
                    + newFont.toString());
}//END IF BOOKMAN
```

8. Recompile, then execute the program again and select the *Bookman* menu item. What, the *Bookman* font still does not appear? Why? Well, we added the required event logic in *actionPerformed()*; however, we neglected to add a listener for the *Bookman* menu item object. Any GUI component that generates an event *must* have a listener added for the event object if the event is to be detected and processed. Close the window and add the following statement in line 60:

```
bookman.addActionListener(new MenuHandler());
```

9. Recompile, then execute the program again and select the *Bookman* menu item. You should now see it is reflected in the text area. Close the window.

10. Notice that within each menu item `if` statement, there is a statement that creates a *newFont* object. This statement sets the font name to the type of font selected in the menu. In addition, the font style and font size are set within this statement. For example, notice that in line 85, the *newFont* object is set to "Courier" with a style of plain, and a size of 12 points. Then, in line 87 the text area is set with the *newFont* object by calling the *setFont()* method. This changes the font of the text area to the font selected on the menu. Now, change the style and/or size of any font within its respective *newFont* object definition statement. To change the font style you must use the syntax `Font.PLAIN`, `Font.ITALIC`, or `Font.BOLD`. Note that there is a dot between the word `Font` and its style. The style must be in all caps.

11. Recompile, then execute the program again, click the menu items whose font style and/or size you changed, and observe the changes within the text area. Close the window.

12. Change one of the font styles to `Font.BOLD + Font.ITALIC`.

13. Recompile then execute the program again, and select the font that you changed. Observe the style of this font is now ***bold-italic***.

14. Close the window.

Discussion

A menu is a GUI component located at the top of a window that contains several user-selectable menu items. A menu bar is a container for menus. Menu objects are created with the *JMenu* class, menu items are created with the *JMenuItem* class, and menu bar objects are created using the *JMenuBar* class. Once a menu object is created, items are added to the menu using the *JMenuItem* class. A menu is made part of a window by adding the menu object to a menu bar object using the *add()* method, then placing the menu bar object on the frame using the *setMenuBar()* method. Menu events are processed by adding a listener for the menu item object and handling the event within the *actionPerformed()* method.

Font objects are created using the *Font* class. A font object has three characteristics: its name, or type, its style, and its size. The font name can be any type of font supported by the operating environment. The font style can be plain, **bold**, *italic*, or ***bold-italic***. The font size can be any reasonable value and is measured in points, where

FIGURE C-16   A window with a Color menu and a text area.

one point is approximately 1/72 of an inch. Once a font object is created, it can be applied to a text component such as a text field or text area using the *setFont()* method.

Procedure (continued)

15. Compile and execute the *GUI107_2.java* program contained on the CD that accompanies this book. You should see a window similar to the one shown in Figure C-16. This window contains a *Color* menu and a text area.

16. Select a color from the *Color* menu. You should find that the text area background color is set to the color you selected.

17. Select a different color and notice that the text reflects the selected color.

Here is the class code that produced the GUI in Figure C-16 and processes the menu:

```
1    import javax.swing.*;          //FOR SWING COMPONENTS CLASS
2    import java.awt.*;             //FOR Container CLASS
3    import java.awt.event.*;       //FOR EVENT HANDLING
4
5    class ColorMenu extends JFrame
6    {
7        //DECLARE MENU ITEM ARRAY
```

```
8        private JMenuItem colorItems[];
9
10       //DECLARE TEXT AREA OBJECT
11       private JTextArea textArea;
12
13       //CONSTRUCTOR
14       public ColorMenu(String Title)
15       {
16        //CALL SUPERCLASS CONSTRUCTOR
17        super(Title);
18
19        //CREATE A CONTAINER
20        Container container = getContentPane();
21
22        //SET CONTAINER LAYOUT MANAGER
23        container.setLayout(new FlowLayout(FlowLayout.LEFT,10,60));
24
25        //DEFINE MAIN MENU OBJECT
26        JMenu colorMenu = new JMenu("Color");
27
28        //SET MENU MNEMONIC
29        colorMenu.setMnemonic('C');
30
31        //DEFINE COLOR STRINGS FOR JMenuItem() CONSTRUCTOR
32        String colors[] =
           {"Yellow","Blue","Cyan","Red","Green","Orange"};
33
34        //INSTANTIATE COLOR ITEMS ARRAY
35        colorItems = new JMenuItem[colors.length];
36
37        //INSTANTIATE MENU ITEMS, ADD TO MENU, AND REGISTER LISTENERS
38        for (int index = 0;index < colors.length;++index)
39        {
40          //INSTANTIATE MENU ITEM OBJECTS
41          colorItems[index] = new JMenuItem(colors[index]);
42          colorMenu.add(colorItems[index]);
43          colorItems[index].addActionListener(new MenuHandler());
44        }//END FOR
45
46        //DEFINE MENU BAR OBJECT
47        JMenuBar bar = new JMenuBar();
48
49        //ADD MENU TO MENU BAR
50        bar.add(colorMenu);
51
52        //SET MENU BAR
53        setJMenuBar(bar);
54
55        //INSTANTIATE TEXT AREA OBJECT
56        textArea = new JTextArea(7,25);
57
```

```
58      //ADD TEXT AREA TO CONTAINER
59      container.add(textArea);
60
61      //ADD WINDOW LISTENER WITH WINDOW EVENT HANDLER
62      addWindowListener(new WindowHandler());
63    }//END ColorMenu() CONSTRUCTOR
64
65    //WINDOW EVENT HANDLER CLASS
66    private class WindowHandler extends WindowAdapter
67    {
68      public void windowClosing(WindowEvent e)
69      {
70        System.exit(0);  //EXIT TO OPERATING SYSTEM
71      }//END windowClosing()
72    }//END WindowAdapter CLASS
73
74    //MENU HANDLER CLASS
75    private class MenuHandler implements ActionListener
76    {
77     //PROCESS MENU EVENT
78     public void actionPerformed(ActionEvent e)
79     {
80      //DEFINE ARRAY OF Color OBJECTS
81      Color textBackground[] = {Color.yellow,Color.blue,Color.cyan,
82                                Color.red,Color.green,Color.orange};
83      //LOOP THROUGH MENU ITEM ARRAY TO FIND EVENT ITEM
84      for(int index = 0;index < colorItems.length; ++index)
85      {
86        //CHECK THIS ITEM FOR EVENT
87        if(e.getSource() == colorItems[index])
88          textArea.setBackground(textBackground[index]);
89      }//END FOR
90     }//END actionPerformed()
91    }//END MenuHandler
92  }//END ColorMenu CLASS
93
94  //APPLICATION TEST CLASS
95  public class GUI107_2
96  {
97    public static void main(String[] args)
98    {
99      //DEFINE FRAME OBJECT
100     ColorMenu window = new ColorMenu("ColorMenu");
101
102     //SET FRAME SIZE
103     window.setSize(350,350);
104
105     //MAKE FRAME VISIBLE
106     window.show();
107   }//END main()
108 }//END GUI107_2 CLASS
```

There are 13 different standard colors available in the Java *Color* class, as follows:

- black
- blue
- cyan
- darkGray
- gray
- green
- lightGray
- magenta
- orange
- pink
- red
- white
- yellow

18. Close the window and add a new color to the *colors[]* array in line 32. Make sure to use one of the 13 standard colors listed above, and place it within double quotation marks at the end of the array.

19. Recompile, then execute the program again and select the *Color* menu. Notice that the color you added appears at the bottom of the menu. Select the new color. Why didn't the text area reflect the new color? You're right! We have not added any logic to process the new color in the *actionPerformed()* method. In fact when you selected the new color, Java generates an *ArrayIndexOutOfBoundsException* exception in the console window.

20. Close the window and add the new color to the *textBackground[]* array in line 82 using the same syntax that you see for the other colors.

21. Recompile, then execute the program again, and select your new color from the *Color* menu. Notice that the text area now reflects your new font color.

22. Close the window.

Discussion

The color of a GUI component can be set using any of the 13 standard colors available in the Java *Color* class. The foreground of a component object is set using the *setForeground()* method, while its background is set using the *setBackground()* method. The default foreground color is black, while the default background color is white.

First, we had to create an array of strings to hold the colors of our color menu items. The color item objects are then instantiated within a `for` loop using the color strings. To handle a menu item event, we created a *textBackground[]* array of the *Color* class to hold the same colors, in the same order, as our color menu items. These colors are predefined for the *Color* class. We cannot use strings here because, by definition, the *Color* class contains its own predefined color constants. Once this array is created, a `for` loop is executed whose counter, *index*, ranges from 0 to the number of items we have in the *colorItems[]* array. The body of the loop contains an `if` statement to determine which menu item generated the event. Notice that the `if` statement is testing the source of the event against each of the menu items in the *colorItems[]* array with each loop iteration. When the event object is found, our *textArea* object calls the *setBackground()* method to set the text area color. The required argument is *textBackground[index]*, which is the color from the *textBackground[]* array that corresponds to the selected menu item color in the *colorItems[]* array since they are both at the same array *index*.

D

Database Connectivity Using JDBC

Introduction

It could be said that the world today is one big database, networked by the Internet. Databases are almost everywhere you look, from the address book in your cell phone to your account at the bank. In fact, most commercial business programs today store and retrieve data from a database instead of using sequential file access.

There are four fundamental tasks that we need to discuss relative to database connectivity. They are:

- Loading the database driver
- Making the database connection
- Generating a result set
- Retrieving a record
- Closing the connection

Each of these tasks will be discussed and coded as a method in order to connect to and query a Microsoft Access database called *Alumni.mdb*. The methods will be coded as part of a class called *AlumniConnect* and tested using an application called *AlumniConnectTest*. The *Alumni.mdb* database and *AlumniConnectTest.java* application can be found on the text CD.

Loading the Database Driver

Java facilitates accessing a database with its ***Java Database Connectivity (JDBC)***™ set of classes. The JDBC classes, called an application program interface (API), and associated methods allow you to connect to and access data in many different types of databases. JDBC is an industry standard that allows a Java program to connect with almost any database, even those written in other languages such as ***Structured Query Language*** (*SQL*). The Java language includes the JDBC API, as well as a ***JDBC driver*** called the ***JDBC-to-ODBC*** bridge driver. ODBC stands for ***Open Database Connectivity***, and is Microsoft's version of an interface designed to handle different database formats. We will use the JDBC-to-ODBC bridge driver in this text. In general, a database driver is a software package that handles the communication between your Java program and a given commercial database. Companies that develop database software will provide the required JDBC driver for their database. In addition, there are JDBC drivers generally available for sale or free download to support just about any commercial database.

> A ***database driver*** is a software package that handles the communication between your Java program and a given commercial database.

The Java 2 SDK provides the JDBC-to-ODBC bridge driver as part of the `sun.jdbc.odbc.JdbcOdbcDriver` class. The standard *forName()* method from the standard *Class* class must be used to load the driver. The *forName()* method requires a path to the driver class as its argument. Thus, to load the driver we will use the statement

```
//LOAD SUN DRIVER
Class.forName("sun.jdbc.odbc.JdbcOdbcDriver");
```

When dealing with a database, you must deal with physical unknowns just like you do when working with files. As a result, you must provide some degree of protection against unforeseen errors, such as a non-existing database. As with file handling, you provide this protection in your program by implementing exception handling via `try` and `catch` blocks. We will place a set of `try/catch` blocks within a method called *loadDriver()* to load the required driver, as follows:

```
private void loadDriver()
{
    //TRY LOADING SUN DRIVER
    try
    {
      //LOAD SUN DRIVER
      Class.forName ("sun.jdbc.odbc.JdbcOdbcDriver");
    }//END try

    //DRIVER NOT FOUND, REPORT ERROR
    catch (ClassNotFoundException err)
    {
      JOptionPane.showMessageDialog(null,"Could not load Sun driver");
      System.exit(1);
    }//END catch
}//END loadDriver()
```

Notice that the `try` block attempts to load the driver. If this fails, a *ClassNotFoundException* is thrown which is caught by the corresponding `catch` block. The `catch` block reports an error within an information window and exits the program.

Making the Database Connection

In order to connect to the physical database, we must create a logical object of the *Connection* class. This object will be used to communicate with the database via *SQL* (structured query language) statements. Here is our object declaration:

```
//DECLARE CONNECTION OBJECT
Connection alumni;
```

Structured Query Language, referred to as **SQL** or simply **sequel**, is an industry standard language for communicating with relational databases. The JDBC driver uses SQL to query the database when building a result set. (*Note:* We do not intend to discuss SQL extensively in this appendix. We will only cover those SQL statements needed to access our database. For more information on SQL, you can look in your IDE Help or go to the companion Web site and click on the related links.)

Now we will use this object to make a "connection" between the object and a given database. This is done using the *getConnection()* method of the standard *DriverManager* class, like this:

```
//CONNECT TO DATABASE
alumni = DriverManager.getConnection("jdbc:odbc:Alumni");
```

The *getConnection()* method requires a string that specifies the driver, bridge, and associated database name. Since our driver bridge is *JDBC-to-ODBC* and our database name is *Alumni*, the required string argument is `"jdbc:odbc:Alumni"`. Notice that the string syntax is in *URL* (Universal Resource Locator) format. The URL address helps the program locate the database (which might be somewhere on a network) via the JDBC-to-ODBC driver connection. The *getConnection()* method will return a *Connection* class object which we have assigned to our *alumni* object. Now all we need to do is to place this statement inside a `try` block. If, for any reason, the connection cannot be made, the *getConnection()* method will throw a *SQLException* which we will handle with an associated `catch` block. Placing this code in a method called *connectDatabase()*, we get the following:

```
private void connectDatabase()
{
  try
  {
    //CONNECT TO DATABASE
    alumni = DriverManager.getConnection("jdbc:odbc:Alumni");
  }//END try
  catch(SQLException error)
  {
    JOptionPane.showMessageDialog(null,"Error connecting to database:\n"
                          + error.toString());
  }//END catch
}//END connectDatabase()
```

We are now ready to retrieve information from our *Alumni* database.

Generating a Result Set

A *result set* is used to hold information returned from a SQL query on a database. The Java *ResultSet* interface class is used for this purpose and the *Statement* interface class is used to generate SQL statements to the database. Figure D-1 shows the *AlumniTBL* table created in our *Alumni.mdb* database.

Last Name	First Name	Address	City	State	Zip	E-mail
Barber	Sue	12 Iris Ln.	Platte City	MO	64079	sbarber@foo.com
Fisher	John	4 Elm St.	Branson	MO	65616	jfisher@yafoo.com
Jones	Sam	43 Sun Blvd.	New York	NY	00234	sjones@foo.com
Simmons	Andy	5 Ocean Blvd.	Myrtle Beach	SC	23645	as@yafoo.com
Gordon	Jim	25 Hunter St.	Bozeman	MT	84567	jg@yafoo.com

FIGURE D-I   The *AlumniTBL* table in the *Alumni.mdb* database.

Here you see that the table consists of five alumni records, each containing seven fields. To read this table from the database we must create two objects: one for the *ResultSet* interface and one for the *Statement* interface, as follows:

```
//DECLARE RESULT SET OBJECT
ResultSet alumniRS;
```

```
//DECLARE STATEMENT OBJECT
Statement alumniStmt;
```

The *ResultSet* object, called *alumniRS*, will be used to hold the database information returned from a SQL query. The *Statement* object, called *alumniStmt*, is required to submit *SQL* queries to the database. Once these objects are declared, they are used to read the *AlumniTBL* table and generate a result set, as follows:

```
//CREATE A STATEMENT OBJECT FOR THE ALUMNI CONNECTION
alumniStmt = alumni.createStatement();
```

```
//EXECUTE A SQL STATEMENT TO RETURN A RESULT SET
alumniRS = alumniStmt.executeQuery("Select * from AlumniTBL;");
```

Here you see our *alumni* connection object (declared earlier) is used to call the *createStatement()* method. This method creates a *Statement* object for our alumni connection, which is assigned to our *alumniStmt* object. Next, you see the *alumniStmt* object calling the *executeQuery()* method. The *executeQuery()* method requires a SQL query statement as its argument and returns a *ResultSet* object that contains the queried data. The returned object is assigned to our *alumniRS* object. The SQL statement `"Select * from AlumniTBL;"` says to "`Select` all (`*`) records `from` the `AlumniTBL` table." Thus, our *alumniRS* result set object receives all the records stored in this table. Finally, we will place these statements within a `try` block as part of a method called *generateResultSet()*, as follows:

```
private void generateResultSet()
{
  try
  {
    //CREATE A STATEMENT OBJECT FOR THE ALUMNI CONNECTION
    alumniStmt = alumni.createStatement();

    //EXECUTE A SQL STATEMENT TO RETURN A RESULT SET
    alumniRS = alumniStmt.executeQuery("Select * from AlumniTBL;");
  }
  catch (SQLException error)
  {
    JOptionPane.showMessageDialog(null,"Error connecting to database:\n"
                             + error.toString());
  }//END catch
}//END generateResultSet()
```

Notice that the catch block will handle a *SQLException* which will be thrown by either the *createStatement()* or *executeQuery()* method if an error occurs when creating the statement object or reading the table. Now that we have read the database table and stored it in our *alumniRS* result set object, our next task is to retrieve and display the table records. We will use this result set to retrieve all the alumni last names and add them to a GUI combo box using a method we call *getNames()*, like this:

```
private void getNames()
{
  //GET DATABASE NAMES AND ADD TO COMBO BOX ITEM LIST
  try
  {
    //GET LAST NAMES FROM DATABASE AND ADD TO COMBO BOX
    while (alumniRS.next())
    {
      namesBox.addItem(alumniRS.getString("LastName"));
    }//END while
  }//END try
  catch (SQLException error)
  {
    JOptionPane.showMessageDialog(null,"Error reading database names");
  }//END catch
}//END getNames()
```

Notice the `while` loop test. When the result set was created, a *record cursor* was created and positioned just *before* the first row (record) in the table. Thus, the first call to method *next()* positions the cursor to the first record, the second call positions the cursor to the second record, and so on. The *next()* method also returns a Boolean value of `false` when no more records are available, thus breaking the loop. Once the cursor is positioned to a given record, the result set object (*alumniRS*) is used to call its *getString()* method to read the *LastName* field in the record. The name is used as an argument for the *addItem()* method which adds it to the list of items in our combo box object, called *namesBox*. Of course, we have placed our loop within `try`/`catch` blocks to handle any SQL exceptions that might occur. You will see this code embedded in a method called *createGUI()* that will be discussed shortly.

Retrieving a Record

Now, at this point we will assume that we have a GUI with a combo box that contains all the last names of the alumni that are in our database. The program user will select a name from the combo box and the associated alumni record will be displayed in a text area. To do this, we must detect a combo box event and retrieve the record associated with the selected alumni name. We have developed a method to retrieve and display a given record, as follows:

```java
private void retrieveRecord()
{
  try
  {
  alumniRS = alumniStmt.executeQuery(
            "Select * from AlumniTBL where [LastName] = '"
            + namesBox.getSelectedItem() + "';");

    //READ AND DISPLAY ALUMNI INFO
    if(alumniRS.next())        //CHECK FOR A RECORD
    {
      alumniRecordArea.setText(alumniRS.getString("LastName"));
      alumniRecordArea.append(", " + alumniRS.getString("FirstName"));
      alumniRecordArea.append("\n" + alumniRS.getString("Address"));
      alumniRecordArea.append("\n" + alumniRS.getString("City"));
      alumniRecordArea.append(", " + alumniRS.getString("State"));
      alumniRecordArea.append("  " + alumniRS.getString("Zip"));
      alumniRecordArea.append("\n" + alumniRS.getString("E-Mail"));
    }//END if
    else
      alumniRecordArea.setText("Record not found");
    }//END try
    catch(SQLException error)
    {
      JOptionPane.showMessageDialog(null,"Error reading record");
  }//END catch
}//END retrieveRecord()
```

Upon entering this method, we do not know where the desired record is located in the result set. So we must build a new result set by generating a SQL query that selects only the record associated with the name selected in the combo box, as follows:

```java
//CREATE RESULT SET FOR SELECTED ALUMNI NAME
alumniRS = alumniStmt.executeQuery(
                    "Select * from AlumniTBL where [LastName] = '"
                    + namesBox.getSelectedItem() + "';");
```

Notice the SQL statement, which is interpreted as: "Select all (*) records from the AlumniTBL where the LastName field is namesBox.getSelectedItem(). In other words, the record(s) associated with the name selected in the combo box is selected and placed in the result set. Once the desired record is in the result set, we can access its individual fields. This is accomplished in our method within an `if/else` statement, as follows:

```
//READ AND DISPLAY ALUMNI INFO
if(alumniRS.next())        //CHECK FOR A RECORD
{
  alumniRecordArea.setText(alumniRS.getString("LastName"));
  alumniRecordArea.append(", " + alumniRS.getString("FirstName"));
  alumniRecordArea.append("\n" + alumniRS.getString("Address"));
  alumniRecordArea.append("\n" + alumniRS.getString("City"));
  alumniRecordArea.append(", " + alumniRS.getString("State"));
  alumniRecordArea.append("  " +alumniRS.getString("Zip"));
  alumniRecordArea.append("\n" + alumniRS.getString("E-Mail"));
}//END if
else
  alumniRecordArea.setText("Record not found");
```

Here, we use our result set object, *alumniRS*, to call the *next()* method as part of an `if` test. This call does two things: it positions the cursor at the first (and only) record and returns a Boolean value of `false` if there is no record available, at which time the associated `else` will display a "Record not found" message in the GUI text field. If there is a record available, the *next()* method returns the value `true` and the record fields are individually retrieved by calling the *getString()* method using our result set object. Notice that the *getString()* method argument is the field name we wish to retrieve. The retrieved field data is then appended to the GUI text area.

Closing the Connection

To insure the integrity of the database, we must close the database connection. This is a simple task using our database *Connection* class object, *alumni*, to call the *close()* method. We have created a method called *closeConnection()* to accomplish this task, as follows:

```
private void closeConnection()
{
 try
 {
   //CLOSE CONNECTED
   alumni.close();
}//END try
catch(SQLException error)
{
  JOptionPane.showMessageDialog(null,"Cannot disconnect database');
 }//END catch
}//END closeConnection()
```

Of course, we must place the close statement within a `try` block just in case there is a problem. The *close()* method will throw a *SQLException* error if there is a problem closing the database, which we will report within an information window. We will call our *closeConnection()* method within the *windowClosing()* method, which is executed when the user closes the GUI window.

Putting It All Together

Now, putting all the pieces together, we get the following *AlumniConnect* class:

```java
import java.sql.*;          //FOR SQL
import javax.swing.*;       //FOR SWING COMPONENTS CLASS
import java.awt.event.*;    //FOR EVENT HANDLING
import java.awt.*;          //FOR Container CLASS

class AlumniConnect extends JFrame
{
   //DECLARE DATABASE OBJECTS
   private Connection alumni;        //CONNECTS TO DATABASE
   private Statement alumniStmt;     //USED TO SUBMIT SQL STATEMENTS
   private ResultSet alumniRS;       //USED TO HOLD RESULT SET

   //DECLARE GUI COMPONENT OBJECTS
   private JComboBox namesBox;
   private JTextArea alumniRecordArea;

   //CREATE A CONTAINER
   private Container container = getContentPane();

   //CONSTRUCTOR
   public AlumniConnect(String title)
   {
     super(title);
     loadDriver();
     connectDatabase();
     generateResultSet();
     createGUI();
   }//END CONSTRUCTOR

   private void loadDriver()
   {
       //TRY LOADING SUN DRIVER
       try
       {
         //LOAD SUN DRIVER
         Class.forName ("sun.jdbc.odbc.JdbcOdbcDriver");
       }//END try

       //DRIVER NOT FOUND, REPORT ERROR
       catch (ClassNotFoundException err)
       {
         JOptionPane.showMessageDialog(null,"Could not load Sun driver");
         System.exit(1);
```

```java
      }//END catch
   }//END loadDriver()

   private void connectDatabase()
   {
      try
      {
         //CONNECT TO DATABASE
         alumni = DriverManager.getConnection("jdbc:odbc:Alumni");
      }//END try
      catch(SQLException error)
      {
       JOptionPane.showMessageDialog(null,"Error connecting to database:\n"
                                + error.toString());
      }//END catch
   }//END connectDatabase()

   private void generateResultSet()
   {
      try
      {
         //CREATE A STATEMENT OBJECT FOR THE ALUMNI CONNECTION
         alumniStmt = alumni.createStatement();

         //EXECUTE A SQL STATEMENT TO RETURN A RESULT SET
         alumniRS = alumniStmt.executeQuery("Select * from AlumniTBL;");
      }
      catch(SQLException error)
      {
       JOptionPane.showMessageDialog(null,"Error connecting to database:\n"
                                + error.toString());
      }//END catch
   }//END generateResultSet()

   private void createGUI()
   {
      //SET FLOWLAYOUT, LEFT ALIGNMENT, 10 HORIZ. GAP, 20 VERT. GAP
      container.setLayout(new FlowLayout(FlowLayout.LEFT,10,20));

      //INSTANTIATE COMBO BOX OBJECT
       namesBox    = new JComboBox();

      getNames();

      //INSTANTIATE TEXT AREA OBJECT
       alumniRecordArea  = new JTextArea(4,20);

      //ADD GUI COMPONENTS TO CONTAINER
      container.add(new JLabel("Names"));
      container.add(namesBox);
      container.add(new JLabel("Alumni Record"));
      container.add(alumniRecordArea);
```

```
  //ADD LISTENER WITH COMBO BOX EVENT HANDLER
  namesBox.addActionListener(new BoxHandler());

  //ADD LISTENER AND EVENT HANDLER FOR THIS FRAME
  addWindowListener(new WindowHandler());
}//END createGUI()

//WINDOW EVENT HANDLER CLASS
private class WindowHandler extends WindowAdapter
{
  public void windowClosing(WindowEvent e)
  {
    closeConnection();              //CLOSE DATABASE CONNECTION
    System.exit(0);    //EXIT TO OPERATING SYSTEM
  }//END windowClosing()
}//END WindowHandler CLASS

//BOX EVENT HANDLER CLASS
private class BoxHandler implements ActionListener
{
  //PROCESS COMBO BOX EVENT
  public void actionPerformed(ActionEvent e)
  {
    //CHECK FOR LIST EVENT
    if (e.getSource() == namesBox)
    {
      retrieveRecord();
    }//END if
  }//END actionPerformed()
}//END BoxHandler CLASS

private void getNames()
{
  //GET DATABASE NAMES AND ADD TO COMBO BOX ITEM LIST
  try
  {
    //GET LAST NAMES FROM DATABASE AND ADD TO COMBO BOX
    while(alumniRS.next())
    {
      namesBox.addItem(alumniRS.getString("LastName"));
    }//END while
  }//END try
  catch (SQLException error)
  {
    JOptionPane.showMessageDialog(null,"Error reading database names");
  }//END catch
}//END getNames()

private void retrieveRecord()
{
  try
```

```java
  {
    alumniRS = alumniStmt.executeQuery(
            "Select * from AlumniTBL where [LastName] = '"
            + namesBox.getSelectedItem() + "';");
    //READ AND DISPLAY ALUMNI INFO
    if(alumniRS.next())        //CHECK FOR A RECORD
    {
      alumniRecordArea.setText(alumniRS.getString("LastName"));
      alumniRecordArea.append(", " + alumniRS.getString("FirstName"));
      alumniRecordArea.append("\n" + alumniRS.getString("Address"));
      alumniRecordArea.append("\n" + alumniRS.getString("City"));
      alumniRecordArea.append(", " + alumniRS.getString("State"));
      alumniRecordArea.append("  " + alumniRS.getString("Zip"));
      alumniRecordArea.append("\n" + alumniRS.getString("E-Mail"));
    }//END if
    else
      alumniRecordArea.setText("Record not found");
    }//END try
    catch(SQLException error)
    {
      JOptionPane.showMessageDialog(null,"Error reading record");
    }//END catch
  }//END retrieveRecord()
  private void closeConnection()
  {
   try
   {
     //CLOSE CONNECTED
     alumni.close();
   }//END try
   catch(SQLException error)
   {
     JOptionPane.showMessageDialog(null,"Cannot disconnect database");
   }//END catch
  }//END closeConnection()
}//END AlumniConnect CLASS

public class AlumniConnectTest
{
  public static void main(String args[])
  {
   //DEFINE OBJECT
   AlumniConnect test = new AlumniConnect("Alumni Database");
   test.setSize(300,250);
   test.show();
  }//END main()
}//END TEST CLASS
```

Here is a screen shot of what the user will see when executing this application:

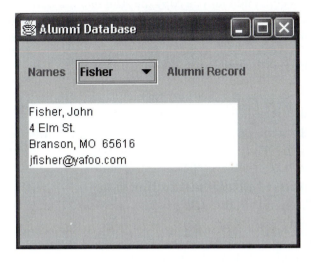

FIGURE D-1 The *AlumniTBL* table in the *Alumni.mdb* database.

Now, let's analyze the application code. We have called our classes *AlumniConnect* and *AlumniConnectTest*. The first line of code imports the *java.sql* package. This package includes classes, interfaces, and methods for making database connections, sending SQL statements to a database, retrieving and updating query results, and providing exception handling. In particular, it contains the *Connection*, *Statement*, and *ResultSet* interface classes that we need at the beginning of the program to declare our *alumni*, *alumniStmt*, and *alumniRS* objects referred to in previous discussions. After these objects are declared, we declare our GUI objects: *namesBox* and *alumniRecordArea*. The *AlumniConnect* constructor then calls the *loadDriver()*, *connectDatabase()*, and *generateResultSet()* methods discussed earlier. As you recall, these methods do exactly what their names imply. The next method called by the constructor is the *createGUI()* method. In this method, you see that we first create our container and combo box objects, then call the *getNames()* method discussed earlier to get the alumni names from the database and add them to the combo box. We then add the combo box to the GUI along with a text area and add the combo box object as a listener. Our combo box event handler is the *BoxHandler* class which implements *actionPerformed()*. Inside *actionPerformed()* we simply test to see that the event source was our *namesBox* object and, if so, call our *retrieveRecord()* method which retrieves the record associated with the selected combo box name and displays the record fields within the GUI text area. Finally, we call our *closeConnection()* method within the *windowClosing()* method of the *WindowHandler* class to close the database connection.

Your Turn

At this point, we recommend that you copy the *Alumni.mdb* database file from the CD to your IDE working directory. If you are using Windows 95, 98, 2000, or XP, you must set up a data source name (DSN) which registers this database in your operating system. The DSN is the database name that you used in your program. In our case, the DSN is *Alumni*. Here is how you must set up this DSN:

- Select the *Control Panel* from the *Start* menu.
- Double-click on the *Administrative Tools* icon.
- Double-click on the *Data Sources (ODBC)* icon in the *Administrative Tools* window.
- Select the *User DSN* tab and click the *Add* button.
- Select the *Microsoft Access (.mdb)* driver.
- Click *Finish* and the *ODBC Microsoft Access Setup* window will appear.
- Enter "Alumni" in the *Data Source Name* field.
- Click the *Select* button and browse to locate the *Alumni.mdb* file that you saved on your computer. Click on the file then click *OK*.
- Now, click OK to close the *ODBC Microsoft Access Setup* window, then *OK* to close the *ODBC Data Source Administrator* window.

Now that you have set up a DSN, load, compile, and run the *AlumniDatabase-Test.java* application using your IDE. This file can be found on the text CD.

Answers to Quick-Check Questions

Chapter I

Section 1-1

1. CPU, memory, and I/O
2. microprocessor
3. arithmetic: addition, subtraction, multiplication, division
4. logic: equal to, not equal to, less than, greater than, less than or equal to, greater than or equal to
5. arithmetic logic unit (ALU), control unit, and internal registers
6. 134,217,728
7. firmware

Section 1-2

1. Java is strictly an object-oriented language, while C++ is a hybrid structured and object-oriented language.
2. machine language, assembly language, high-level language
3. to manage the resources of the system
4. Java is object-oriented, simple, portable, secure, a network language, supports multithreading, growing, cheap, and is for business.
5. true
6. Oak
7. Sun

Section 1-3

1. enter/edit, save, compile, correct errors, translate Java byte code to machine code
2. Java byte code is a low-level code which is generic and not specific to any particular CPU.
3. The generic byte codes generated by the Java compiler make Java an extremely portable language.
4. Java applications are designed to be run on a computer, just like any other application software. Java applets are designed only to be run using an Internet Web browser.
5. A compiler translates the entire program into machine code all at one time, before execution by the CPU. An interpreter translates, then executes, one high-level program statement at a time.
6. source code
7. import and class
8. `import myPackage.*;`
9. method
10. Inventory.java
11. d. two forward slashes like this `//COMMENT`.
12. At a minimum, the program should include the following comments:

    The beginning of the program should be commented with the programmer's name, date the program was written, date the program was last revised, and the name of the person doing the revision. In other words, a brief ongoing maintenance log should be commented at the beginning of the program.

    The beginning of the program should be commented to explain the purpose of the program, which includes the problem definition. This provides an overall perspective by which anyone, including you, the programmer, can begin debugging or maintaining the program.

    Import statements should be commented as to their purpose.

    Constants, variables, and objects should be commented as to their purpose.

    Major sections of the program should be commented to explain the overall purpose of the respective section.

    Individual program lines should be commented when the purpose of the code is not obvious relative to the application.

    All major subprograms (methods in Java) should be commented just like the main program method.

    The end of each program block (right curly brace) should be commented to indicate what the brace is ending.

Chapter 2

Section 2-1

1. pseudocode
2. What output is needed?

What input is needed?

What processing is needed to produce the output from the input?

3. Desk-check, compile, debug using a debugger, and run the program.

4. Commenting explains what the program does and self-documents the program, making it easier to read and maintain.

5. A syntax error is any violation of the rules of the programming language.

6. A logic error is an error made by the programmer relative to the way in which the program will execute. A logic error occurs when the program does what you tell it to do, but is not doing what you meant it to do.

Section 2-2

1. To define what steps are needed to produce the desired final result. An algorithm keeps you from "spinning your wheels" at the keyboard.

2. sequence, decision, and iteration

3. The three decision operations are *if*, *if/else*, and *switch/case*.

4. The three iteration operations are *while*, *do/while*, and *for*.

Section 2-3

1. Abstraction allows you to "see the forest over the trees," because it permits you to initially concentrate on the problem at hand, without agonizing over the implementation details of a computer language.

2. Stepwise refinement begins with the initial abstract algorithm, and step by step divides it into one or more refined algorithms that provide more and more implementation detail.

3. A codeable level of an algorithm is reached when all the statements have been reduced to the pseudocode operations listed in Table 2-1.

Chapter 3

Section 3-1

1. class

2. standard classes

3. An abstract data type, or ADT, describes the data attributes and behavior of its objects.

4. primitive data types, standard classes, and programmer-defined classes

5. Behavior, as related to classes and ADTs, describes how the ADT or class will act and react to a given operation.

6. A method is a subprogram in Java, usually associated with an algorithm of some kind.

7. Because a class allows you to build your own ADTs in a programming language. Classes contain data to provide the ADT attributes, and methods to provide the ADT behavior.

Section 3-2

1. approximately −2 billion to +2 billion
2. an overflow error
3. fixed decimal or exponential
4. the character 'a'
5. the character 'a'
6. 28 characters (including blanks) @ two bytes per character = 56 bytes
7. `boolean`

Section 3-3

1. The two reasons for defining constants and variables in a Java program are as follows:

   • The compiler must know the value of a constant before it is used, and must reserve memory locations to store variables.
   • The compiler must know the data type of constants and variables to determine their data attributes and behavior.

2. `final char  PERIOD = '.';`
3. `final String  BOOK  = "Information Systems Programming with Java";`
4. `int age = 0;`
5. `String  course = "Accounting";`
6. `int length = 0;`
   `length = course.length();`
7. `course = course.toUpperCase();`
8. true

Section 3-4

1. A class provides the foundation for creating specific objects, each of which shares the general attributes and behavior of the class.
2. An object is an instance, or specimen, of a given class. An object of a given class has the structure and behavior defined by the class that is common to all objects of the same class.
3. By a class defining the behavior of its objects, we mean that the class defines how its objects act and react when they are accessed via the class methods.
4. true
5. `CheckingAccount myAccount = new CheckingAccount();`
6. `Truck myPickup = new Truck();`
7. `Automobile myConvertible = new Automobile();`

Section 3-5

1. `StaugIO myIO = new StaugIO();`
2. `myIO.writeInfo("THIS STUFF IS GREAT!");`
3. `myIO.writeInfo("THIS STUFF \n IS GREAT!");`
4. `double gpa = 0.0;`

   `gpa = myIO.readDouble("Enter your grade point average: ");`
5. `myIO.writeNumber(gpa);`
6. `import java.text.*;`

   `NumberFormat currency = NumberFormat.getCurrencyInstance();`

   `io.writeInfo(currency.format(mySalary));`
7. The *NumberFormat* class provides for true currency formatting in dollars and cents, which includes a $ sign, commas where required, and trailing 0's.

Section 3-6

1. `System.out.println("Andrew C. Staugaard, Jr.");`
2. `System.out.println(name);`
3. `\t`
4. `\r`
5. The *println()* method generates a newline after its output to place the cursor on the next line, while the *print()* method does not generate a newline.

Chapter 4

Section 4-1

1. The order in which Java performs arithmetic operations is as follows:

   `( ) * / % + -`

   Any operations inside of parentheses are performed first, then (from left to right) multiplication, division, and modulus, and then (from left to right) addition and subtraction.
2. The value of x is even.
3. The value of y is divisible by 17.
4. 0
5. 0
6. 1
7. `--x; or x--;`
8. False, because this happens only when *both* the numerator and denominator operands are integers.
9. The difference between using the preincrement operator versus the postincrement operator on a variable is that a preincrement operator increments the

variable before any expression involving the variable is evaluated, and a post-increment operator increments the variable after any expression involving the variable is evaluated.

10. The result of 10/100 is 0 because both operands are integers, and the / operator generates an integer result when both operands are integers.

11. `System.out.println(Math.random()*100);`

12. `System.out.println(Math.tan(45*Math.PI/180);`

13. `Math.PI;`

14. The answer to this question depends on your particular Java compiler. Press the *F1* key for *JBuilder* and *Shift+F1* for *Sun ONE Studio (Forte)*.

Section 4-2

1. `x+=5;`

2. `x/=10;`

3. This expression cannot be written using a compound assignment operator.

4. Because *x* can never be equal to itself plus 5 in math class, but you can add 5 to *x* and assign the sum to *x* in Java.

Chapter 5

Section 5-1

1. relational operators

2. The difference between the = operator and the == operator in Java is that the = operator assigns the value on the right to the variable on the left, and the == operator compares two quantities to determine if they are equal.

3. the Boolean value `true`

4. The Boolean value `false` is generated, because (`5!=5`) is `false`, making the entire AND statement `false`.

5. because string values are represented as objects, not primitive data types

Section 5-2

1. False, because the logical opposite of greater than is less than *or equal to*.

2. False, because the `if` statements are executed when the test expression is `true`.

3. The test expression needs to be a comparison, not an assignment. The correct `if` statement is:

```
if(x == y)
    System.out.println("There is a problem here");
```

4. The && (AND) operator must be employed to test if all conditions are `true`.

5. The !&& (NOT AND) operators must be employed to test if one or more of several conditions is `false`.

6. The ¦¦ (OR) operator must be employed to test if one of several conditions is `true`.

7. for all values of *x* that are less than or equal to 50

Section 5-3

1. True, an `else` must always have a corresponding `if`.

2. Because, without an `else` statement, both strings, "It's payday" and "It's not payday", would be written when the `if` test is true.

3. True, framing can be eliminated when an `if` or `else` has only a single statement, but it is not advisable to do so.

4. subtract

5. False, *compareTo()* returns an integer value that must be tested against 0.

6. True, the *equals()* method returns a Boolean value.

Section 5-4

1. Indentation is important when operations are nested for code readability, and to be able to see at a glance which statements belong to which `if` or `if/else` statement.

2. misplaced, or dangling, `else`

3. "Red" will be written when the value is greater than −50 and less than 50.

4. "White" will be written when the value is less than or equal to −50.

5. "Blue" will be written when the value is greater than or equal to 50.

6. The equivalent `if-else-if-else` logic is:

If *Value* >= 50
    Write ("Blue")
else
    If *Value* <= −50
        Write ("White")
    else
        Write ("Red")

Section 5-5

1. matching

2. If you have *n* cases in a `switch` statement and there are no `break` statements in any of the cases, all of the subsequent cases will be executed sequentially when a match is made on any given case.

3. False, because there may be times when several subsequent cases need to be executed as the result of a match to a given case.

4. `default`

5. for menu-driven programs

Chapter 6

Section 6-1

1. False, because a `while` loop repeats until the test expression is `false`.
2. False, because a `while` loop is a pretest loop not a posttest loop.
3. The `while` loop statements need to be framed because without the framing, the value of *x* is never changed and you will have an infinite loop.
4. The correct code is:

```
x = 10;
while (x > 0)
{
    System.out.println( "This is a while loop");
    --x;
}//END WHILE
```

5. The loop will never execute because the loop test is `false` the first time it is tested. Notice that *x* is initialized to 1 and is never < = 0.
6. Without the limitations of the computer, the loop will execute infinitely because *x* starts out greater than 0 and is incremented inside of the loop. But, considering the physical limitations of the computer, it will execute about 2 billion times before wrapping around to a negative value, causing the test to be `false`.

Section 6-2

1. False, because a do/while loop repeats until the test expression is `false`.
2. true
3. The value of *x* is never changed within the loop, thereby creating an infinite loop.
4. The correct code is:

```
x = 10;
do
{
    System.out.println("This is a do/while loop");
    --x;
} //END DO/WHILE
while (x > 0);
```

5. The loop will execute once because a do/while loop is a posttest loop.
6. Without the limitations of the computer, the loop will execute infinitely because *x* starts out greater than 0 and is incremented inside of the loop. But, considering the physical limitations of the computer, it will execute about 2 billion times before wrapping around to a negative value, causing the test to be false.

Section 6-3

1. The three things that must appear in the first line of a `for` loop structure are:
   - The loop counter initialization
   - The loop test expression
   - The changing of the counter value

2. true
3. true, as long as the `while` loop counter is changed at the end of the loop body
4. The loop will execute zero times because the test condition is `false` the first time.
5. The loop will execute 11 times.
6. The `for` loop statements must be framed when there is more than one statement to be executed within the loop.
7. The inner loop will execute 5 times for every outer loop iteration. Thus, there are 5 × 10, or 50, total iterations.
8. decremented

Section 6-4

1. `continue`
2. `if`
3. The loop will execute twice. When x is incremented to 1 at the end of the first iteration, the `if(x>0)` statement will be `true` in the second iteration, causing the `break` statement to execute and terminate the loop.

Chapter 7

Section 7-1

1. Methods eliminate the need for duplicate statements in a program.
   Methods make the program easier to design.
   Methods make the program easier to code and test.
   Methods allow for software reusability.
   Methods make the program more clear and readable.
   Methods provide the basis for classes in OOP.
2. non-void, void
3. header, body
4. `return`
5. what the method accepts and what the method returns to the calling program
6. The method header provides the data interface for the method.
7. optional modifiers, return type, method name, and parameter list
8. parameter

9. to return both a value and control to the calling program

10. An argument is used in the method call, whereas a parameter is used in the method header and receives the value of the corresponding argument when the method is called.

11. `public double loanPayment(double amount, double interestRate, double term)`

12. `public int wheels()`

13. The term *message* is used to describe a call to an instance method with the idea that when we are calling a method, we are sending a message to the class object in which it is defined.

Section 7-2

1. `void`

2. what the method accepts and what the method returns to the calling program

3. by listing the method name and any required arguments as a statement within the calling program and calling it with an object reference if it is a `public` method of a class

4. False, a non-void method can be called with an assignment operator, not a void method.

5. to return control to the calling program

6. `public void displayEmployee()`

Section 7-3

1. In the class from which the object calling the method was created.

2. just after the opening brace of *main()*, or any place prior to the method call in *main()*

3. just after the opening brace of the method, or any place prior to their use within the method

4. Two, the class in which the method is defined and the application test class that contains *main()*.

5. The file must have the same name as the application class name, with a *.java* extension.

Section 7-4

1. the number or types of arguments provided in the method call

2. so that the same operation can behave differently depending on what arguments are provided

3. False, the compiler can only distinguish between parameter lists of overloaded methods.

4. polymorphism

Section 7-5

1. False, because Java supports recursion, which allows a method to call itself.
2. We can describe recursion as a "winding" and "unwinding" process because recursion "winds up" when it places information onto a stack, and "unwinds" by removing information from the stack until the terminating condition is reached.
3. a terminating condition
4. If n is 0
    $$factorial(n) = 1.$$
    Else
    $$factorial(n) = n * factorial(n - 1)$$
5. false, because recursion uses large amounts of memory to keep track of each recursive call in a memory stack
6. true
7. stack
8. last-in, first-out, or LIFO

Chapter 8

Section 8-1

1. By a class defining the behavior of its objects, we mean how an object of a given class acts and reacts when it is accessed via one of its methods.
2. False, because encapsulation dictates only that the data and/or methods are packaged together in a well-defined unit. Encapsulation does ensure information hiding in an OO language, but not in other, non-OO languages.
3. true
4. encapsulation with information, or data, hiding
5. true
6. `private`
7. implementation

Section 8-2

1. constructor
2. The constructor has the same name as the class and has no return value.
3. false, because constructors must not have a return type, not even `void`
4. A class constructor is called automatically when an object is defined for that class.
5. false, because any method can be overloaded, including a constructor
6. You call a non-constructor `public` method of a class by listing the class object name, a dot, and the method name with any required arguments.

7. `public MyClass(int value1, int value2)`
8. `MyClass myObject = new MyClass(5,6);`

Chapter 9

Section 9-1

1. superclass
2. subclass
3. family of classes
4. Two reasons for using inheritance are:

   - Inheritance allows you to reuse code without having to start from scratch.
   - Inheritance allows you to build a family hierarchy among classes.

5. IS-A
6. false, because a line IS NOT A point
7. true, because a pixel IS-A point
8. true, because a pickup truck IS-A truck

Section 9-2

1. true
2. `super`
3. false, because a `protected` member is inherited by any subclasses of the class in which it resides
4. A `private` member is only visible within the class in which it is defined.
   A `protected` member is visible in any subclasses of the class in which it is defined.
   A `public` member is visible anywhere the class object is visible.
5. The reason that the *Savings* class should not be derived from the *InterestChecking* class is that a saving account is *not* a form of checking account. Such a derivation would violate the IS-A principle.
6. *AndrewStaugaard:*   *accountNumber* = "0000:
                               name = " "
                               balance = 0.0
                               minimum = 500.0
                               charge = 0.5
   MichaelJordan: *accountNumber* = "0010"
                               name = "Michael Jordan"
                               balance = 10000.0
                               minimum = 500.0
                               charge = 0.5
   PaulAllen: *accountNumber* = "0020"
                               name = "Paul Allen"

$$balance = 100000.0$$
$$minimum = 100.0$$
$$charge = 0.25$$

Section 9-3

1. true
2. false, because overloaded methods are statically bound at compile time.
3. true
4. statically
5. dynamically
6. run, or execution, time
7. An abstract class is a superclass for which no objects will ever be created. A concrete class is a subclass for which objects will always be created.
8. true
9. In the subclasses of the class in which the abstract method header appears.

Chapter 10

Section 10-1

1. index and elements
2. false, because the elements within a given array must all be of the same data type or class
3. 1×11

Section 10-2

1. `double testScores[] = new double[15];`
2. 1×15
3. [0]
4. [14]
5. 26, because the first element index is [0]
6. `int values[] = { -3,-2,-1,0,1,2,3};`
7. 1×7
8. `String family[] = {"Andy","Janet","Ron","David","Zane","Andrew"};`
9. zeros
10. blanks

Section 10-3

1. ```
for(int index = 0; index < 15; ++ index)
    characters[index] = io.readChar();
```

   (Assumes that *io* has been defined as an object of the *StaugIO* class.)
```

2. `for (int index = 0; index < 15; ++index)`
       `info += characters[index] + "\n";`
   `io.writeInfo(info);`
   (assumes that *io* has been defined as an object of the *StaugIO* class)

Section 10-4

1. False, an array can be defined using a variable for the size of the array.
2. `Employee employees[] = new Employee[10];`
3. `for(int i = 0; i < 10; ++i)`
   `{`
       `employees[i] = new Employee();`
       `employees[i].setName();`
       `employees[i].setNumber();`
       `employees[i].setDept();`
   `}//END FOR`
4. `for(int i = 0; i < 10; ++i)`
   `{`
       `employInfo = "EMPLOYEE  " + (i+1) + "  DATA\n";`
       `employInfo += "\nNAME: " + employees[i].getName() + "\n"`
                    `+ "NUMBER: " + employees[i].getNumber() + "\n"`
                    `+ "DEPARTMENT: " + employees[i].getDept() + "\n";`
           `io.writeInfo(studentInfo);`
   `}//END FOR`

Section 10-5

1. true
2. `public void sample(char array[])`
3. `myObject.sample(characters);`
4. `public void test(char arrayElement)`
5. `myObject.test(characters[5]);`

Chapter 11

Section 11-1

1. *javax.swing*
2. a container created from the *Container* class which has been placed on a frame created from the *JFrame* class
3. `JFrame myFrame = new JFrame("This is my first frame");`
4. `myFrame.setSize(450,250);`
5. `myFrame.show();`

6. Create a GUI component object, add a listener for the object, and implement the corresponding event method to process an event generated by the object.

7. *windowClosing()*

8. addWindowListener(this); or addWindowListener(new WindowHandler());
   if a *WindowHandler* class is being used.

9. *java.awt.event*

10. An **inner class** is a class which is nested, or contained, inside another class which is usually designated as a private class.

11. An **adapter class** is a standard class that implements all the methods in a given standard abstract class.

Section 11-2

1. JButton myButton = new JButton("Store");

2. container.add(myButton);

3. myButton.addActionListener(new ButtonHandler());

4. *actionPerformed()*

5. JOptionPane.showMessageDialog(null,

                                 "ERROR! ERROR! ERROR!",

                                 "INFORMATION",

                                 JOptionPane.INFORMATION_MESSAGE);

Section 11-3

1. *FlowLayout*

2. *GridLayout*

3. topPanel.setLayout(new FlowLayout(FlowLayout.LEFT,20,10);

4. North, South, East, West, Center

5. container.setLayout(null);

6. at the top left-hand corner of the window

7. myButton.setLocation(20,30);

8. myButton.setSize(50,25);

9. *getActionCommand()*

10. bottomPanel.setLayout(new BorderLayout(20,20));

11. bottomPanel.add(centerPanel,"Center");

12. False, the default layout manager is *BorderLayout*.

Section 11-4

1. JLabel myLabel = new JLabel("This is my label");
   myPanel.add(myLabel);

2. JTextField myTextField = new JTextField(20);

3. `JTextArea myTextArea = new JTextArea(10,50);`
4. `myPanel.add(myTextField);`
   `myPanel.add(myTextArea);`

Chapter 12

Section 12-1

1. A combo box only allows for one item selection, while a list box allows for multiple item selection, when enabled.
2. *isSelected()*
3. to act as a container for menu objects
4. `JMenuBar myMenuBar = new JMenuBar();`
5. `JMenu myMenu = new JMenu("My Menu");`
6. `myMenuBar.add(myMenu);`
7. `setJMenuBar(myMenuBar);`
8. the font type, or name, the font style, and the font size
9. Approximately 1/72 inch.
10. `Font myFont = new Font("Arial", Font.BOLD, 16);`
11. `myTextArea.setFont(myFont);`

Section 12-2

1. The *Box* class is used to implement the *BoxLayout* manager. A box is like a panel in that it is a container class that can be used to hold other GUI components.
2. *BoxLayout* arranges GUI components from left to right in a single horizontal row, or from top to bottom in a single vertical column.
3. False, components in a box will not wrap around when the GUI window is resized.
4. A card layout allows you to build a card deck as a panel, consisting of several unique GUI "cards" as panels. When the card deck is first shown, the first card (panel) in the deck appears. From there you can display any of the other cards (panels) within the deck as a separate GUI.
5. *first(), next(), previous(), last(), show()*

Chapter 13

Section 13-1

1. when the program must run from a Web browser
2. *javax.swing*
3. False, you do not implement the window closing feature of an applet since it is implemented within *JApplet*.

4. a status bar

5. *init()*

6. *paint()*

7. an object of the *Graphics* class

8. `<APPLET codebase=.. code="myApplet.class" width=350 height=200>`
`</APPLET>`

Section 13-2

1. *java.awt*

2. When the "fill" method is called, the component is filled with the color that has been set for the graphics object, *g*. When the "draw" method is called, the object appears as a cartoon-like line drawing whose outline is the color of the graphics object, and whose interior is the color of the applet background.

3. oval

4. $R = 0, G = 0, B = 0$

5. true

6. A "3D" rectangle appears either raised or sunken.

7. the upper left corner of an imaginary bounding rectangle

8. three

9. true

10. two arrays, one to store the *x*-coordinates and one to store the *y*-coordinates

11. Unlike a polygon, a polyline does not connect the last coordinate to the point of origin.

12. *repaint()*

Section 13-3

1. *init()*, *paint()*, *start()*, *stop()*, and *destroy()*

2. *init()*

3. *stop()*

4. true

5. true

6. False, panels and layout managers can be used in an applet just like they are used in an application.

Chapter 14

Section 14-1

1. false, because a file is a sequential access data structure

2. 00000000 01100011

3. When a numeric value is stored in a text file, it must be converted to its machine representation before it can be manipulated arithmetically, after being read by a program.

4. stream

5. *System.out*

6. *FileInputStream*

7. *DataOutputStream*

8. *FileWriter*

9. *PrintWriter*

10. *java.io*

Section 14-2

1. A communication path, or stream, is established between the logical program object and the physical disk file.

2. `DataOutputStream myFile =`
   `        new DataOutputStream(new FileOutputStream("myFile.dat"));`

3. `DataInputStream yourFile =`
   `        new DataInputStream(new FileInputStream(yourFileName));`

Section 14-3

1. exception handling

2. Exception handling is required when opening files to catch a file-not-found or general I/O error.

3. checked

4. true

5. false, because exceptions that are not caught do not cause GUI programs to terminate prematurely

6. `try`

7. true

8. *ArithmeticException*

9. false, because a `finally` block always executes regardless of whether or not an exception is thrown or caught.

10. true

Section 14-4

1. false, because the *DataInputStream* method provides methods to *read* binary files.

2. *writeUTF()*

3. `myOutputFile.writeUTF(myName.getText));`

4. `displayText.append(myInputFile.readUTF());`

5. `myOutputFile.writeInt((new`
   `Integer(myAge.getText().trim())).intValue());`
6. `displayText.append(String.valueOf(myInputFile.readInt()));`
7. close
8. The *flush()* method flushes the output stream causing any internally buffered data to be written to the file.

Section 14-5

1. `PrintWriter myFile = new PrintWriter((`
   `                  new BufferedWriter(`
   `                  new FileWriter("myFile.txt"))));`
2. `BufferedReader yourFile =`
   `                  new BufferedReader(new FileReader(yourFileName));`

Section 14-6

1. true
2. true
3. `myTextFile.print(myText.getText());`
4. `String line;`
   `while((line = myTextFile.readLine()) != null)`
   `      myText.append(line + '\n');`
5. The *read()* method returns a single character, while the *readln()* method returns a string.
6. Because buffered I/O increases system performance.
7. *BufferedReader* and *BufferedWriter*.

Chapter 15

Section 15-1

1. The maximum row index is 9, and the maximum column index is 14.
2. The arrays dimension is 10×15 and it will store 150 `double` floating-point elements.
3. `sample[0][14] = io.readDouble("Enter a decimal value ");`
4. `System.out.print(sample[1][2]);`
5. `for(int row = 0; row < 10; ++row)`
   `{`
   `      for(int col = 0; col < 15; ++col)`
   `                  System.out.print(sample[row][col] + " ");`
   `      System.out.println();`
   `}//END row FOR`

Section 15-2

1. A problem that might be encountered when defining large multidimensional arrays is the *array size too big error*. This means that you are attempting to set aside more memory for the array than a particular computer system can allocate.

2. ```
int myArray[][][] = new int [10][15][3];
```

3. $10 \times 15 \times 3 \times 4 = 1800$ bytes

4. ```
for(int plane = 0; plane < 10; ++plane)
{
    for(int row = 0; row < 15; ++row)
    {
        for(int col = 0; col < 3; ++col)
            System.out.print(myArray[plane][row][col]);
        System.out.println();
    }//END row FOR
}//END plane FOR
```

ASCII/Unicode Character Table

Dec	Char	Dec	Char	Dec	Char	Dec	Char
0	Null	32	Space	64	@	96	`
1	Start of Header	33	!	65	A	97	a
2	Start of Text	34	''	66	B	98	b
3	End of Text	35	#	67	C	99	c
4	End of Trans	36	$	68	D	100	d
5	Enquiry	37	%	69	E	101	e
6	Acknowledge	38	&	70	F	102	f
7	Bell	39	'	71	G	103	g
8	Back Space	40	(	72	H	104	h
9	Horizontal Tab	41	)	73	I	105	i
10	Line Feed	42	*	74	J	106	j
11	Vertical Tab	43	+	75	K	107	k
12	Form Feed	44	,	76	L	108	l
13	Carriage Return	45	-	77	M	109	m
14	Shift Out	46	.	78	N	110	n
15	Shift In	47	/	79	O	111	o
16	Data Link Esc	48	0	80	P	112	p
17	Device Ctrl 1	49	1	81	Q	113	q
18	Device Ctrl 2	50	2	82	R	114	r
19	Device Ctrl 3	51	3	83	S	115	s
20	Device Ctrl 4	52	4	84	T	116	t
21	No Acknowledge	53	5	85	U	117	u
22	Sync. Idle	54	6	86	V	118	v
23	End of Block	55	7	87	W	119	w
24	Cancel	56	8	88	X	120	x
25	End of Medium	57	9	89	Y	121	y
26	Substitute	58	:	90	Z	122	z
27	Escape	59	;	91	[	123	{
28	File Separator	60	<	92	\	124		
29	Group Separator	61	=	93	]	125	}
30	Record Separator	62	>	94	^	126	~
31	Unit Separator	63	?	95	--	127	Delete

Glossary

Abstract class   A superclass for which objects will never be created.

Abstract data type (ADT)   A collection of data and related operations.

Abstract method   A polymorphic method in a superclass whose behavior will be defined in the subclasses.

Abstraction   Looking at things in general terms, ignoring detail.

Accessor method   A get method used to return the value(s) of a private class member(s).

Action key   A keystroke that will generate the button event, rather than clicking the mouse.

Actor   In object-oriented analysis, an actor represents anything that must interact with the system. An actor can be a person, an organization, or another system.

Adapter class   A standard class that implements all the methods in a given standard abstract class.

Address   A value that designates the memory location of a data element.

Algorithm   A series of step-by-step instructions that produce a solution to a problem.

Applet   A Java program designed only to be run over the Internet using a Web browser.

Application   A Java program designed to be run on a computer, just like any other computer program written in any other language.

Arc angle   The amount of traversal, in degrees, from the start angle of an arc method of the *Graphics* class. A positive angle forces a counterclockwise traversal, while a negative angle forces a clockwise traversal.

Argument   A value used within a method call.

Arithmetic and logic unit (ALU)   That part of the CPU that performs all arithmetic and logic operations.

Array   An indexed data structure that is used to store data elements of the same data type or class.

ASCII   American Standard Code for Information Interchange. An 8-bit code used to represent the English language character set.

Assembler   A program that translates assembly language into machine language for a given CPU.

Assembly language   A language that employs alphabetic abbreviations called mnemonics that are easily remembered by you, the programmer.

Association   A relationship in an object-interaction diagram that represents a pathway of communication between two objects.

Attribute of a class   The data members that make up a class provide the class attributes, or characteristics.

Base class   A class from which one or more other classes are derived. Also called a *superclass*.

Baseline   The bottom of a string drawn by the *drawString()* method of the *Graphics* class.

Behavior   Used to describe how an ADT, or class object, will act and react for a given operation.

Binary file   A file that stores values using the internal binary format specified by the language in use.

Block scope   The accessibility, or visibility, of a local variable defined in a given block of code, such as a method.

Buffer   A temporary storage area used to improve system performance as in file input and output buffers.

Bus   A signal path within a computer system.

Button   A GUI component that, when clicked, generates an event.

Byte code   A binary code generated by the Java compiler that is a low-level program, similar to machine language but generic and not specific to any particular CPU. Any given computer will have its own Java interpreter that translates the generic byte code into machine language for that CPU.

Cache   High-speed RAM that is usually contained within the same chip as the CPU. Instructions waiting to be processed are fetched from primary memory and placed in the cache so that they are ready for execution when the CPU needs them.

Calling program   The program that calls, or invokes, a method.

CASE (Computer-Aided Systems Engineering) tool   Software products that automate the phases of the software development life cycle, and are used to generate the required graphics with either the structured or object-oriented paradigms.

Casting   Temporarily converting one type of data to another, as in type casting.

Checkbox   A GUI component that allows the user to select one of two possible states: checked or unchecked.

Checked exception   A predefined exception class in Java.

Circular array   An array that wraps around such that the first element of the array follows the last element of the array.

Class (abstract level)   Provides the foundation for creating specific objects, each of which shares the same attributes and behavior.

Class (implementation level)   A syntactical unit that describes a set of data and related operations that are common to its objects.

Class diagram   Used in object-oriented design to show both the private data members which provide the attributes of the class, and the method members which provide the class behavior.

Class method   A method that is not called with an object reference. A `static` modifier declares a method as a class method.

Combo box   A GUI component that allows the user to choose one of several items in a pop-down menu listing.

Compiler   A program that translates an entire program into machine code all at one time, before it is executed by the CPU.

Compiling   The process of translating source code to machine, or object, code.

Component   An item of meaningful data within a file. A graphical object within a GUI such as a button, text field, rectangle, oval, and so on.

Compound statement   Several statements framed by curly braces.

Concrete class   A subclass for which objects will always be created.

Console screen   A non-GUI screen that you see in a text-based environment.

Constructor   A special class method that is used to initialize the data members of an object automatically when the object is defined.

Container A windowing object, such as a frame or applet, that is used to hold GUI components.

Context diagram A graphic that shows the entire system as one process and the external entities with which the system must interact. A context diagram defines the system boundaries.

Control structure A pattern for controlling the flow of a program module.

Control unit That part of the CPU that directs and coordinates the activities of the entire system.

Cramer's rule A method for solving systems of simultaneous equations using determinants (two-dimensional arrays).

Dangling else An else that is not associated with a corresponding if. A dangling, or misplaced, else problem often occurs when improper framing is used within nested if/else logic.

Data abstraction That property of an ADT that allows you to work with the data elements without concern for how the data elements are stored inside the computer, or how the data operations are performed inside the computer.

Data hiding That property of a programming entity, such as a class object, that shields private data from operations that are not predefined to operate on the data.

Data type A particular category of data elements.

Database A collection of related records and/or files.

Declaration Specifies the name and attributes of a programming entity, but does not reserve storage.

Definition Specifies the name and attributes of a variable or object, and also reserves storage.

Derived class An inherited, or subclass, class that will include its own members and also include members inherited from its superclass.

Determinant A two-dimensional array that has as single value.

Dimension The size of an array, such as $m \times n$, where m is the number of rows and n is the number of columns in the array.

Dynamic binding Dynamic binding occurs when a polymorphic method is defined for several classes in a family, but the actual code for the method is not attached, or bound, until execution time.

Editor A program that allows you to enter, save, and edit a source code program.

Element A data value; in particular, one stored within an array.

Encapsulation To package data and/or operations into a single well-defined programming unit.

Entity relationship diagram (ERD) A diagram which shows data relationships required to build a system database.

Escape sequence A special formatting character for text output.

Event An action generated by a program user activating a GUI component, such as clicking a button.

Event handler A method used to process a GUI event.

Event listener An object that has been registered to generate an event within a GUI.

Exception An error generated within a Java program.

Exception handler A Java program segment that is used to catch and handle errors as they occur during the execution of a Java program.

Exception handling The process of handling an exception.

Family A group of classes related through inheritance.

Fetch/execute cycle The basic cycle that takes place when a program is executed by a CPU. The four basic operations of the cycle are *fetch*, *decode*, *execute*, and *store*.

Fibonacci sequence A sequence of numbers such that the first two numbers in the sequence are 0 and 1. Then, each additional number is the sum of the two previous numbers in the sequence.

Field   An area used to store a meaningful collection of characters, such as your name.

FIFO   First-in, first-out; FIFO is associated with queues.

File   A data structure that consists of a sequence of components usually associated with program I/O. A means by which the program communicates with the "outside world"; a sequence of components stored in secondary memory; a collection of related records.

File stream   A channel for data to flow between the program and the outside world.

Firmware   Software stored in ROM.

Fixed repetition loop   A loop that will be executed a predetermined number of times.

Font   The name, style, and size of text as in `Courier`, **bold/italic**, 10 point.

Frame   A graphical container used to hold GUI components in a Java application program.

Get method   An accessor method used to return the value(s) of a private class member(s).

Global identifier   A constant, variable, object, or data structure that is visible to the entire program.

Graphical component   A graphical object within a graphical user interface, such as a button, text field, choice box, and so on. Also, a graphical image such as a rectangle, oval, arc, line, string, or polygon.

Graphical user interface, GUI   A window-based program whereby input and output are handled via graphical components, and program control is event driven via the components.

Header   The first line of a method that specifies the method return type, name, and parameter listing. Also referred to as a method interface.

Helper method   A private method used to perform tasks internal to a class. Also called a utility method.

High-level language   A language consisting of instructions, or statements, that are similar to English and common mathematical notation.

HyperText Markup Language (HTML)   Used to create Web pages. HTML allows you to create pages of text and images that can be viewed through a Web browser, regardless of the computer platform that you are using. An HTML file is simply a text document which includes a series of tags that tell the browser what to do.

Identifier   A symbolic name associated with a constant, variable, method, data structure, class, object, and so on.

Implementation   The body of a method.

Index   An integer that locates an element within an array.

Information hiding   Accomplished when there exists a binding relationship between the information, or data, and its related operations so that operations outside an encapsulated unit cannot affect the information inside the unit.

Inheritance   That property of object-oriented programming that allows one class, called a subclass, or derived class, to share the structure and behavior of another class, called a superclass, or base class.

Inner class   A class which is nested, or contained, inside another class which is usually designated as a private class.

Instance   In object-oriented programming, an example, or specimen, of a class. We say that an object is an *instance* of a class.

Instance method   A nonstatic method which must be called with an object reference.

Instance variable   A private data member of a class. A variable that will be created for any given object of the class.

Instruction set   The set of machine instructions designed for a given CPU.

Interface   Something that forms a common boundary, or barrier, between two systems.

In the case of a method, the method interface, or header, dictates what the method will accept by way of its parameters, and what the method will return by the way of its return type.

Interface of a class The set of all public method headers that forms a boundary to a class.

Interface of a method The header of a method that forms a common boundary between the method and its calling program.

Internal registers That part of the CPU that provides temporary storage areas for program instructions and data.

Interpreter A program that translates and executes one high-level statement at a time. Once a given statement has been executed, the interpreter then translates and executes the next statement, and so on, until the entire program has been executed.

IS-A The link between a subclass class and its superclass.

Iteration A control structure, also called looping, that causes the program flow to repeat a finite number of times.

Java A state-of-the-art object-oriented programming language.

Java Virtual Machine (JVM) Translates the generic bytecode generated by a Java compiler into the machine language for a given CPU.

Keyword A word that is predefined and recognized by a programming language.

Label A line of noneditable text used to identify GUI components.

Layout chart A graphical aid in laying out text output for a display screen or the components within a GUI window.

Layout manager Standard classes in Java that lay out GUI components within a frame or applet so that they can be easily managed within the GUI.

LIFO Last-in, first-out; LIFO is associated with stacks.

Linking The process of combining object files needed for a program execution to form an executable file.

List Another name for a one-dimensional array.

List box A GUI component that allows the user to choose one or more items within a scrolled item listing.

Listener An object that has been registered to generate an event within a GUI.

Local variable A variable that is defined within a given block of code, such as a method. Local variables have block scope.

Logic error An error created when the computer does what you tell it to do, but that is not what you meant it to do. Such an incidence usually results from an error in thinking on the programmer's part.

Logical data flow diagram (LDFD) Used to model the flow of data within the current system during structured analysis. An LDFD is a graphic that shows the logical movement of data within the system, and the processes being performed on that data without regard to the physical software or hardware devices that are operating on the data.

Loop control variable A variable that is tested with each loop iteration to determine whether or not the loop will continue.

Machine language A binary code, called machine code, that forms the instruction set for a given CPU.

Main memory *See* primary memory.

Member Any item declared in a class.

Menu A set of user-selectable options.

Menu bar A container on the top of a frame for holding menus.

Menu item A selectable item within a menu.

Menu separator A line between two menu items.

Message A call to an object method.

Method A procedure designed to perform specific tasks, such as those performed by an algorithm. In other programming languages, methods might be referred to as subprograms, functions, or subroutines.

Method body The statement section, or implementation, of a method.

Method header The first line of a method. The header dictates the method interface that forms a common boundary between the method and its calling program.

Microprocessor A single integrated-circuit (IC) chip that contains the entire central processing unit (CPU).

Misplaced else An `else` that is not associated with a corresponding `if`. The misplaced, or dangling, `else` problem often occurs when improper framing is used within nested `if/else` logic.

Mnemonic An assembly language instruction abbreviation.

Multidimensional array An array with more than one dimension.

Multiple inheritance Multiple inheritance occurs when the inherited class members can be traced back to more than one superclass. Java does not support multiple inheritance directly.

Multiplicity Used in an object interaction diagram to show how many objects on each side of an association participate in the relationship.

Nested looping Looping structures that are located within other looping structures.

Newline A non-printable character that forces the cursor to the next line on the monitor. Sometimes referred to as a carriage-return line-feed (CFLF) character.

Nonvoid method A method that returns a single value to the calling program.

Object An instance, or specimen, of a given class. An object of a given class has the attributes and behavior described by the class that is common to all objects of the same class.

Object interaction diagram In object-oriented design, they are used to show the relationships between the system objects.

Object program The binary machine-language program generated by a compiler; usually has a file extension of *.obj*.

Object-oriented analysis (OOA) Employs use-case and class modeling to describe the current as well as future system in terms of existing objects and new or modified objects.

Object-oriented design (OOD) The process of determining how the new system is to satisfy the client's needs through the construction of object interaction and class diagrams, as well as other UML tools such as sequence and collaboration diagrams.

Object-oriented paradigm A software engineering methodology that employs objects and object interaction to attack complex problems in a natural way, like we humans tend to think about things.

Object-oriented programming (OOP) A form of programming whereby data and related operations are specified as classes whose instances are objects. The data and related operations are bound so tightly that only those operations defined for a class can affect the class data. This idea of encapsulation and information hiding allows the easy formation of ADTs.

One-dimensional array An array with one row and n columns that has a dimension of $1 \times n$.

Operating system (OS) A collection of software programs dedicated to managing the resources of the system.

Overflow error An error that occurs when a numeric data type value exceeds its predefined range.

Overloaded method A method that has different behavior depending on the number and/or class of arguments that it receives. An overloaded method is statically bound at compile time.

Package A set, or family, of related classes contained within a unique directory.

Panel A GUI component container that, when added to a frame or applet, allows you to achieve presentable layouts.

Paradigm A model that provides a way of thinking of things. In software, the structured paradigm versus the object-oriented paradigm.

Parameter A variable, or object, appearing in a method header that receives an argument value when the method is called.

Parameterless constructor A constructor that does not contain any parameters.

Physical data flow diagram (PDFD) A diagram that depicts actual physical entities of the proposed system such as a "Java *xyz* method" during structured design, not just logical entities like a process, as in the LDFD of the structured analysis phase.

Pixel A picture element which is a point of illumination on a display screen.

Point A unit of font measurement, approximately 1/72 inch.

Pointer A direct program reference to an actual physical address in memory. Java uses pointers extensively to implement programs but does not allow you, the programmer, to use pointers.

Polymorphic method A method that has the same name but different behavior for different classes within the same family. Polymorphic methods are dynamically bound at run time.

Polymorphism Occurs when a method has the same name but different behavior within a program. Both overloaded and polymorphic methods exhibit polymorphism in Java.

Portability That feature of a language that allows programs written for one type of computer to be used on another type of computer, with few or no changes to the program source code.

Posttest loops A loop that tests a condition *after* each loop iteration, as in the do/while loop structure.

Present value (PV) A measure of the value of a future expenditure in today's dollars.

Pretest loops A loop that tests a condition each time *before* a loop is executed, as in the while and for loop structures.

Primary memory Used to store programs and data while they are being "worked," or executed, by the CPU.

Private member A member of a class that is accessible only to the public methods of the same class. Private members of a superclass are *not* inherited by a subclass.

Problem abstraction Provides for generalization in problem solving by allowing you to view a problem in general terms, without worrying about the details of the problem solution.

Program A set of software instructions that tells the computer what to do.

Program development life cycle (PDLC) A systematic method that will make you a good problem solver, and therefore a good programmer. The phases of the life cycle include defining the problem, planning the solution, coding the solution, testing/debugging the code, documentation, and maintenance.

Programmer-defined method A block of statements, or a subprogram, that is written to perform a specific task required by you, the programmer.

Project file A file that identifies the files that need to be compiled and linked to create a workable Java program.

Project manager A program development tool which links several packages and classes together to build a complete workable program.

Protected member A member that is accessible to both a superclass and any subclasses of the superclass in which it is declared. Thus, a protected member of a superclass is accessible to any descendent subclass within the family, but not accessible to things outside the class family.

Pseudocode An informal set of English-like statements that are generally accepted within the computer industry to denote common computer programming operations. Pseudocode statements are used to describe the steps in a computer algorithm.

Public member   A member of a class that is accessible outside the class within the scope of the class. A public member of a superclass is inherited by any subclasses of the superclass.

Queue   A primary memory storage structure that consists of a list, or sequence, of data elements. All insertions of elements into the queue are made at one end of the queue, called the *rear* of the queue, and all deletions of elements from the queue are made at the other end of the queue, called the *front* of the queue. A queue operates on the *first-in, first-out*, or *FIFO*, principle.

Radio button   A state (on/off) button within a group of buttons that can be selected or deselected. Only one button within the group can be selected at any given time.

Random-access memory (RAM)   Volatile, read/write memory.

Read-only memory (ROM)   Nonvolatile system memory that contains firmware.

Reading   The process of obtaining data from something such as an input device or a data structure; a copy operation. A read operation is usually a nondestructive operation.

Record   A collection of related fields.

Recursion   A process whereby an operation calls, or clones, itself until a terminating condition is reached.

Recursive method   A method that calls itself.

Reference parameter   A method parameter that provides two-way communication between the calling program and the method. An array name is a reference parameter.

Return value   A value returned by a non-void method. The value replaces the method call in the calling program.

Root class   The class at the top of a class hierarchy. The root class in Java is the *Object* class.

Run-time error   An error that occurs during the execution of a program.

Scope   The largest block in which a given constant, variable, object, data structure, or method is accessible, or visible within a program.

Search   The process of finding a given data element. In particular, searching for a given element within an array.

Secondary memory   Nonvolatile memory, such as disk memory, used to store programs and data between program runs.

Selection   A control structure where the program selects, or decides, between one of several routes depending on the conditions that are tested.

Sentinel controlled loop   A loop that terminates when a given sentinel value is entered by the user.

Sentinel value   A value that terminates a sentinel controlled loop.

Sequence   A control structure where statements are executed sequentially, one after another, in a straight-line fashion.

Set method   A method used to set the value(s) of a private class member(s).

Side effect   The process of altering the value of a global variable.

Software development life cycle (SDLC)   A set of phases which describe a logical process used by systems engineers to develop fault-free, cost-effective software that meets all the client's needs.

Sort   The process of placing data elements in order. In particular, sorting the elements within an array.

Source code program   The program that you write in the Java language that normally has a file extension of *.java*.

Source object   In GUI event handling, the object responsible for an event.

Stack   A primary memory storage structure that consists of a list, or sequence, of data elements where all the insertions and deletions of elements to and from the stack are made at one end of the stack called the *top*. A stack operates on the *last-in, first-out principle*, or *LIFO*.

Standard method   A predefined operation that the Java compiler will recognize and evaluate to return a result or perform a given task.

Start angle   The angle of beginning for an arc method of the *Graphics* class, where 0 degrees is the 3:00 position.

State button   A GUI component, such as a checkbox or radio button, that has two possible states, on or off.

Static binding   Occurs when a method is defined with the same name, but with different headers and implementations. The actual code for the method is attached, or bound, at compile time. Overloaded methods are statically bound.

Static method   A class method that is called with a class reference, not an object reference.

Status bar   A bar that contains a line of text at the bottom of an applet window.

Stepwise refinement   The process of gradually adding detail to a general problem solution until it easily can be coded in a computer language.

Stream   A connection for data to flow between your program and the outside world.

String   A collection of characters.

Structured analysis   Employs logical data flow diagrams (LDFDs) to model the flow of data within the current system using a top/down methodology.

Structured design   A methodology that requires software to be designed using a top/down modular approach. A structured design requires formalization of the new process models in the form of physical data flow diagrams (PDFDs) and functional decomposition.

Structured paradigm   A software engineering methodology that employs top/down functional decomposition that breaks the original complex problem down into smaller, more manageable subproblems.

Structured programming   Structured programming allows programs to be written using well-defined control structures and independent program modules.

Subclass   An inherited, or derived, class that will include its own members, and also include members inherited from its superclass.

Submenu   A menu within a menu.

Superclass   A class from which one or more other classes are derived. Also called a *base class*.

Swing   A class of lightweight GUI components contained in the *javax.swing* package.

Syntax   The grammar of a programming language.

Syntax error   An error created by violating the required syntax, or grammar, of a programming language.

System memory   ROM firmware that stores system-related programs and data.

System requirements statement   Outcome of the analysis phase which includes the graphical models, prototypes, and supporting documentation such as interview, observation, and questionnaire summaries. A refined timetable as well as another go/no-go recommendation is also normally included in the document.

Terminating condition   A known condition that terminates a recursive method call.

Text area   Several lines of editable or noneditable text.

Text field   A single line of editable text on a GUI.

Text file   A character-based ASCII file that is viewable using a word processor or simple text editor.

this   A pointer reference to "this" object.

Tool tip　A message that will appear when the mouse pointer is placed over a button.

Truth table　A table that shows the results of a logic operation on Boolean values.

Type cast　Converts data of one type to a different type, temporarily.

Unicode　An international 16-bit code used by Java to represent international language characters. The first 128 values of the code represent the common ASCII character codes used in the U.S.A, Canada, and the U.K.

Unified Modeling Language (UML)　A language, or notation, for modeling systems that provides techniques to specify, visualize, construct, and document systems. The UML can be used for non-software business system modeling, as well as software system modeling.

Use case　Used in object-oriented analysis. A use-case represents a pattern of behavior exhibited by the system as the result of a dialogue between the system and an actor. The collection of all the system use cases specifies all the ways in which to use the system.

Use case scenario　A sequence of tasks that are performed for a given use case.

Utility method　A private method used to perform tasks internal to a class. Also called a helper method.

Value parameter　A parameter that allows for one-way communication of data from the calling program to the method.

Venn diagram　A class family diagram that illustrates the common members within the family.

Void method　A method that performs some procedural task or operates directly on class data, rather than returning a single value to the calling program.

Virtual memory　Hard-disk memory that is being used by the CPU as RAM when no more actual RAM is available.

Visibility　That part of the program code in which a constant, variable, object, data structure, or method is accessible.

Whitespace　Non-printable characters such as blanks, tabs, newlines, form feeds, and so on, are all forms of whitespace.

Wrapper class　A class that encapsulates a primitive data type along with methods that allow for conversion of the data type to/from strings, as well as other methods useful in dealing with the primitive data type.

Wrapper object　An object of a wrapper class.

Writing　The process of generating data to a display monitor, printer, or file. In addition, data can be written to data structures such as arrays. A write operation is usually a destructive operation.

Index

Java™ 2 Platform, SDK Standard Edition Version 1.4.1_X License Agreement

Sun Microsystems, Inc.
Binary Code License Agreement

READ THE TERMS OF THIS AGREEMENT AND ANY PROVIDED SUPPLEMENTAL LICENSE TERMS (COLLECTIVELY "AGREEMENT") CAREFULLY BEFORE OPENING THE SOFTWARE MEDIA PACKAGE. BY OPENING THE SOFTWARE MEDIA PACKAGE, YOU AGREE TO THE TERMS OF THIS AGREEMENT. IF YOU ARE ACCESSING THE SOFTWARE ELECTRONICALLY, INDICATE YOUR ACCEPTANCE OF THESE TERMS BY SELECTING THE "ACCEPT" BUTTON AT THE END OF THIS AGREEMENT. IF YOU DO NOT AGREE TO ALL THESE TERMS, PROMPTLY RETURN THE UNUSED SOFTWARE TO YOUR PLACE OF PURCHASE FOR A REFUND OR, IF THE SOFTWARE IS ACCESSED ELECTRONICALLY, SELECT THE "DECLINE" BUTTON AT THE END OF THIS AGREEMENT.

1. **LICENSE TO USE.** Sun grants you a non-exclusive and non-transferable license for the internal use only of the accompanying software and documentation and any error corrections provided by Sun (collectively "Software"), by the number of users and the class of computer hardware for which the corresponding fee has been paid.

2. **RESTRICTIONS.** Software is confidential and copyrighted. Title to Software and all associated intellectual property rights is retained by Sun and/or its licensors. Except as specifically authorized in any Supplemental License Terms, you may not make copies of Software, other than a single copy of Software for archival purposes. Unless enforcement is prohibited by applicable law, you may not modify, decompile, or reverse engineer Software. Licensee acknowledges that Licensed Software is not designed or intended for use in the design, construction, operation or maintenance of any nuclear facility. Sun Microsystems, Inc. disclaims any express or implied warranty of fitness for such uses. No right, title or interest in or to any trademark, service mark, logo or trade name of Sun or its licensors is granted under this Agreement.

3. **LIMITED WARRANTY.** Sun warrants to you that for a period of ninety (90) days from the date of purchase, as evidenced by a copy of the receipt, the media on which Software is furnished (if any) will be free of defects in materials and workmanship under normal use. Except for the foregoing, Software is provided "AS IS". Your exclusive remedy and Sun's entire liability under this limited warranty will be at Sun's option to replace Software media or refund the fee paid for Software.

4. **DISCLAIMER OF WARRANTY.** UNLESS SPECIFIED IN THIS AGREEMENT, ALL EXPRESS OR IMPLIED CONDITIONS, REPRESENTATIONS AND WARRANTIES, INCLUDING ANY IMPLIED WARRANTY OF MERCHANTABILITY, FITNESS FOR A PARTICULAR PURPOSE OR NON-INFRINGEMENT ARE DISCLAIMED, EXCEPT TO THE EXTENT THAT THESE DISCLAIMERS ARE HELD TO BE LEGALLY INVALID.

5. **LIMITATION OF LIABILITY.** TO THE EXTENT NOT PROHIBITED BY LAW, IN NO EVENT WILL SUN OR ITS LICENSORS BE LIABLE FOR ANY LOST REVENUE, PROFIT OR DATA, OR FOR SPECIAL, INDIRECT, CONSEQUENTIAL, INCIDENTAL OR PUNITIVE DAMAGES, HOWEVER CAUSED REGARDLESS OF THE THEORY OF LIABILITY, ARISING OUT OF OR RELATED TO THE USE OF OR INABILITY TO USE SOFTWARE, EVEN IF SUN HAS BEEN ADVISED OF THE POSSIBILITY OF SUCH DAMAGES. In no event will Sun's liability to you, whether in contract, tort (including negligence), or otherwise, exceed the amount paid by you for Software under this Agreement. The foregoing limitations will apply even if the above stated warranty fails of its essential purpose.

6. **Termination.** This Agreement is effective until terminated. You may terminate this Agreement at any time by destroying all copies of Software. This Agreement will terminate immediately without notice from Sun if you fail to comply with any provision of this Agreement. Upon Termination, you must destroy all copies of Software.

7. **Export Regulations.** All Software and technical data delivered under this Agreement are subject to US export control laws and may be subject to export or import regulations in other countries. You agree to comply strictly with all such laws and regulations and acknowledge that you have the responsibility to obtain such licenses to export, re-export, or import as may be required after delivery to you.

8. **U.S. Government Restricted Rights.** If Software is being acquired by or on behalf of the U.S. Government or by a U.S. Government prime contractor or subcontractor (at any tier), then the Government's rights in Software and accompanying documentation will be only as set forth in this Agreement; this is in accordance with 48 CFR 227.7201 through 227.7202-4 (for Department of Defense (DOD) acquisitions) and with 48 CFR 2.101 and 12.212 (for non-DOD acquisitions).

9. **Governing Law.** Any action related to this Agreement will be governed by California law and controlling U.S. federal law. No choice of law rules of any jurisdiction will apply.

10. **Severability.** If any provision of this Agreement is held to be unenforceable, this Agreement will remain in effect with the provision omitted, unless omission would frustrate the intent of the parties, in which case this Agreement will immediately terminate.

11. **Integration.** This Agreement is the entire agreement between you and Sun relating to its subject matter. It supersedes all prior or contemporaneous oral or written communications, proposals, representations and warranties and prevails over any conflicting or additional terms of any quote, order, acknowledgment, or other communication between the parties relating to its subject matter during the term of this Agreement. No modification of this Agreement will be binding, unless in writing and signed by an authorized representative of each party.

JAVA™ 2 SOFTWARE DEVELOPMENT KIT (J2SDK), STANDARD EDITION, VERSION 1.4.1_X
SUPPLEMENTAL LICENSE TERMS

These supplemental license terms ("Supplemental Terms") add to or modify the terms of the Binary Code License Agreement (collectively, the "Agreement"). Capitalized terms not defined in these Supplemental Terms shall have the same meanings ascribed to them in the Agreement. These Supplemental Terms shall supersede any inconsistent or conflicting terms in the Agreement, or in any license contained within the Software.

1. **Software Internal Use and Development License Grant.** Subject to the terms and conditions of this Agreement, including, but not limited to Section 4 (Java Technology Restrictions) of these Supplemental Terms, Sun grants you a non-exclusive, non-transferable, limited license without fees to reproduce internally and use internally the binary form of the Software complete and unmodified for the sole purpose of designing, developing and testing your Java applets and applications intended to run on the Java platform ("Programs").

2. **License to Distribute Software.** Subject to the terms and conditions of this Agreement, including, but not limited to Section 4 (Java Technology Restrictions) of these Supplemental Terms, Sun grants you a non-exclusive, non-transferable, limited license without fees to reproduce and distribute the Software, provided that (i) you distribute the Software complete and unmodified (unless otherwise specified in the applicable README file) and only bundled as part of, and for the sole purpose of running, your Programs, (ii) the Programs add significant and primary functionality to the Software, (iii) you do not distribute additional software intended to replace any component(s) of the Software (unless otherwise specified in the applicable README file), (iv) you do not remove or alter any proprietary legends or notices contained in the Software, (v) you only distribute the Software subject to a license agreement that protects Sun's interests consistent with the terms contained in this Agreement, and (vi) you agree to defend and indemnify Sun and its licensors from and against any damages, costs, liabilities, settlement amounts and/or expenses (including attorneys' fees) incurred in connection with any claim, lawsuit or action by any third party that arises or results from the use or distribution of any and all Programs and/or Software. (vi) include the following statement as part of product documentation (whether hard copy or electronic), as a part of a copyright page or proprietary rights notice page, in an "About" box or in any other form reasonably designed to make the statement visible to users of the Software: "This product includes code licensed from RSA Security, Inc.", and (vii) include the statement, "Some portions licensed from IBM are available at *http://oss.software.ibm.com/icu4j/*".

3. **License to Distribute Redistributables.** Subject to the terms and conditions of this Agreement, including but not limited to Section 4 (Java Technology Restrictions) of these Supplemental Terms, Sun grants you a non-exclusive, non-transferable, limited license without fees to reproduce and distribute those files specifically identified as redistributable in the Software "README" file ("Redistributables") provided that: (i) you distribute the Redistributables complete and unmodified (unless otherwise

specified in the applicable README file), and only bundled as part of Programs, (ii) you do not distribute additional software intended to supersede any component(s) of the Redistributables (unless otherwise specified in the applicable README file), (iii) you do not remove or alter any proprietary legends or notices contained in or on the Redistributables, (iv) you only distribute the Redistributables pursuant to a license agreement that protects Sun's interests consistent with the terms contained in the Agreement, (v) you agree to defend and indemnify Sun and its licensors from and against any damages, costs, liabilities, settlement amounts and/or expenses (including attorneys' fees) incurred in connection with any claim, lawsuit or action by any third party that arises or results from the use or distribution of any and all Programs and/or Software, (vi) include the following statement as part of product documentation (whether hard copy or electronic), as a part of a copyright page or proprietary rights notice page, in an "About" box or in any other form reasonably designed to make the statement visible to users of the Software: "This product includes code licensed from RSA Security, Inc.", and (vii) include the statement, "Some portions licensed from IBM are available at *http://oss.software.ibm.com/icu4j/*".

4. **Java Technology Restrictions.** You may not modify the Java Platform Interface ("JPI", identified as classes contained within the "java" package or any subpackages of the "java" package), by creating additional classes within the JPI or otherwise causing the addition to or modification of the classes in the JPI. In the event that you create an additional class and associated API(s) which (i) extends the functionality of the Java platform, and (ii) is exposed to third party software developers for the purpose of developing additional software which invokes such additional API, you must promptly publish broadly an accurate specification for such API for free use by all developers. You may not create, or authorize your licensees to create, additional classes, interfaces, or subpackages that are in any way identified as "java", "javax", "sun" or similar convention as specified by Sun in any naming convention designation.

5. **Notice of Automatic Software Updates from Sun.** You acknowledge that the Software may automatically download, install, and execute applets, applications, software extensions, and updated versions of the Software from Sun ("Software Updates"), which may require you to accept updated terms and conditions for installation. If additional terms and conditions are not presented on installation, the Software Updates will be considered part of the Software and subject to the terms and conditions of the Agreement.

6. **Notice of Automatic Downloads.** You acknowledge that, by your use of the Software and/or by requesting services that require use of the Software, the Software may automatically download, install, and execute software applications from sources other than Sun ("Other Software"). Sun makes no representations of a relationship of any kind to licensors of Other Software. TO THE EXTENT NOT PROHIBITED BY LAW, IN NO EVENT WILL SUN OR ITS LICENSORS BE LIABLE FOR ANY LOST REVENUE, PROFIT OR DATA, OR FOR SPECIAL, INDIRECT, CONSEQUENTIAL, INCIDENTAL OR PUNITIVE DAMAGES, HOWEVER CAUSED REGARDLESS OF THE THEORY OF LIABILITY, ARISING OUT OF OR RELATED TO THE USE OF OR INABILITY TO USE OTHER SOFTWARE, EVEN IF SUN HAS BEEN ADVISED OF THE POSSIBILITY OF SUCH DAMAGES.

7. **Distribution by Publishers.** This section pertains to your distribution of the Software with your printed book or magazine (as those terms are commonly used in the industry) relating to Java technology ("Publication"). Subject to and conditioned upon your compliance with the restrictions and obligations contained in the Agreement, in addition to the license granted in Paragraph 1 above, Sun hereby grants to you a non-exclusive, nontransferable limited right to reproduce complete and unmodified copies of the Software on electronic media (the "Media") for the sole purpose of inclusion and distribution with your Publication(s), subject to the following terms: (i) You may not distribute the Software on a stand-alone basis; it must be distributed with your Publication(s); (ii) You are responsible for downloading the Software from the applicable Sun web site; (iii) You must refer to the Software as JavaTM 2 Software Development Kit, Standard Edition, Version 1.4.1; (iv) The Software must be reproduced in its entirety and without any modification whatsoever (including, without limitation, the Binary Code License and Supplemental License Terms accompanying the Software and proprietary rights notices contained in the Software); (v) The Media label shall include the following information: Copyright 2002, Sun Microsystems, Inc. All rights reserved. Use is subject to license terms. Sun, Sun Microsystems, the Sun logo, Solaris, Java, the Java Coffee Cup logo, J2SE , and all trademarks and logos based on Java are trademarks or registered trademarks of Sun Microsystems, Inc. in the U.S. and other countries. This information must be placed on the Media label in such a manner as to only apply to the Sun Software; (vi) You must clearly identify the Software as Sun's product on the Media holder or Media label, and you may not state or imply that Sun is responsible for any third-party software contained on the Media;

(vii) You may not include any third party software on the Media which is intended to be a replacement or substitute for the Software; (viii) You shall indemnify Sun for all damages arising from your failure to comply with the requirements of this Agreement. In addition, you shall defend, at your expense, any and all claims brought against Sun by third parties, and shall pay all damages awarded by a court of competent jurisdiction, or such settlement amount negotiated by you, arising out of or in connection with your use, reproduction or distribution of the Software and/or the Publication. Your obligation to provide indemnification under this section shall arise provided that Sun: (i) provides you prompt notice of the claim; (ii) gives you sole control of the defense and settlement of the claim; (iii) provides you, at your expense, with all available information, assistance and authority to defend; and (iv) has not compromised or settled such claim without your prior written consent; and (ix) You shall provide Sun with a written notice for each Publication; such notice shall include the following information: (1) title of Publication, (2) author(s), (3) date of Publication, and (4) ISBN or ISSN numbers. Such notice shall be sent to Sun Microsystems, Inc., 4150 Network Circle, M/S USCA12-110, Santa Clara, California 95054, U.S.A , Attention: Contracts Administration.

8. **Trademarks and Logos.** You acknowledge and agree as between you and Sun that Sun owns the SUN, SOLARIS, JAVA, JINI, FORTE, and iPLANET trademarks and all SUN, SOLARIS, JAVA, JINI, FORTE, and iPLANET-related trademarks, service marks, logos and other brand designations ("Sun Marks"), and you agree to comply with the Sun Trademark and Logo Usage Requirements currently located at *http://www.sun.com/policies/trademarks*. Any use you make of the Sun Marks inures to Sun's benefit.

9. **Source Code.** Software may contain source code that is provided solely for reference purposes pursuant to the terms of this Agreement. Source code may not be redistributed unless expressly provided for in this Agreement.

10. **Termination for Infringement.** Either party may terminate this Agreement immediately should any Software become, or in either party's opinion be likely to become, the subject of a claim of infringement of any intellectual property right.

For inquiries please contact: Sun Microsystems, Inc., 4150 Network Circle, Santa Clara, California 95054, U.S.A
(LFI#120080/Form ID#011801)

Sun™ ONE Studio 4 update 1, Community Edition
License Agreement

Sun Microsystems, Inc.
Binary Code License Agreement

READ THE TERMS OF THIS AGREEMENT AND ANY PROVIDED SUPPLEMENTAL LICENSE TERMS (COLLECTIVELY "AGREEMENT") CAREFULLY BEFORE OPENING THE SOFTWARE MEDIA PACKAGE. BY OPENING THE SOFTWARE MEDIA PACKAGE, YOU AGREE TO THE TERMS OF THIS AGREEMENT. IF YOU ARE ACCESSING THE SOFTWARE ELECTRONICALLY, INDICATE YOUR ACCEPTANCE OF THESE TERMS BY SELECTING THE "ACCEPT" BUTTON AT THE END OF THIS AGREEMENT. IF YOU DO NOT AGREE TO ALL THESE TERMS, PROMPTLY RETURN THE UNUSED SOFTWARE TO YOUR PLACE OF PURCHASE FOR A REFUND OR, IF THE SOFTWARE IS ACCESSED ELECTRONICALLY, SELECT THE "DECLINE" BUTTON AT THE END OF THIS AGREEMENT.

1. **LICENSE TO USE.** Sun grants you a non-exclusive and non-transferable license for the internal use only of the accompanying software and documentation and any error corrections provided by Sun (collectively "Software"), by the number of users and the class of computer hardware for which the corresponding fee has been paid.

2. **RESTRICTIONS.** Software is confidential and copyrighted. Title to Software and all associated intellectual property rights is retained by Sun and/or its licensors. Except as specifically authorized in any Supplemental License Terms, you may not make copies of Software, other than a single copy of Software for archival purposes. Unless enforcement is prohibited by applicable law, you may not modify, decompile, or reverse engineer Software. You acknowledge that Software is not designed, licensed

or intended for use in the design, construction, operation or maintenance of any nuclear facility. Sun disclaims any express or implied warranty of fitness for such uses. No right, title or interest in or to any trademark, service mark, logo or trade name of Sun or its licensors is granted under this Agreement.

3. **LIMITED WARRANTY.** Sun warrants to you that for a period of ninety (90) days from the date of purchase, as evidenced by a copy of the receipt, the media on which Software is furnished (if any) will be free of defects in materials and workmanship under normal use. Except for the foregoing, Software is provided "AS IS". Your exclusive remedy and Sun's entire liability under this limited warranty will be at Sun's option to replace Software media or refund the fee paid for Software.

4. **DISCLAIMER OF WARRANTY.** UNLESS SPECIFIED IN THIS AGREEMENT, ALL EXPRESS OR IMPLIED CONDITIONS, REPRESENTATIONS AND WARRANTIES, INCLUDING ANY IMPLIED WARRANTY OF MERCHANTABILITY, FITNESS FOR A PARTICULAR PURPOSE OR NON-INFRINGEMENT ARE DISCLAIMED, EXCEPT TO THE EXTENT THAT THESE DISCLAIMERS ARE HELD TO BE LEGALLY INVALID.

5. **LIMITATION OF LIABILITY.** TO THE EXTENT NOT PROHIBITED BY LAW, IN NO EVENT WILL SUN OR ITS LICENSORS BE LIABLE FOR ANY LOST REVENUE, PROFIT OR DATA, OR FOR SPECIAL, INDIRECT, CONSEQUENTIAL, INCIDENTAL OR PUNITIVE DAMAGES, HOWEVER CAUSED REGARDLESS OF THE THEORY OF LIABILITY, ARISING OUT OF OR RELATED TO THE USE OF OR INABILITY TO USE SOFTWARE, EVEN IF SUN HAS BEEN ADVISED OF THE POSSIBILITY OF SUCH DAMAGES. In no event will Sun's liability to you, whether in contract, tort (including negligence), or otherwise, exceed the amount paid by you for Software under this Agreement. The foregoing limitations will apply even if the above stated warranty fails of its essential purpose.

6. **Termination.** This Agreement is effective until terminated. You may terminate this Agreement at any time by destroying all copies of Software. This Agreement will terminate immediately without notice from Sun if you fail to comply with any provision of this Agreement. Upon Termination, you must destroy all copies of Software.

7. **Export Regulations.** All Software and technical data delivered under this Agreement are subject to US export control laws and may be subject to export or import regulations in other countries. You agree to comply strictly with all such laws and regulations and acknowledge that you have the responsibility to obtain such licenses to export, re-export, or import as may be required after delivery to you.

8. **U.S. Government Restricted Rights.** If Software is being acquired by or on behalf of the U.S. Government or by a U.S. Government prime contractor or subcontractor (at any tier), then the Government's rights in Software and accompanying documentation will be only as set forth in this Agreement; this is in accordance with 48 CFR 227.7201 through 227.7202-4 (for Department of Defense (DOD) acquisitions) and with 48 CFR 2.101 and 12.212 (for non-DOD acquisitions).

9. **Governing Law.** Any action related to this Agreement will be governed by California law and controlling U.S. federal law. No choice of law rules of any jurisdiction will apply.

10. **Severability.** If any provision of this Agreement is held to be unenforceable, this Agreement will remain in effect with the provision omitted, unless omission would frustrate the intent of the parties, in which case this Agreement will immediately terminate.

11. **Integration.** This Agreement is the entire agreement between you and Sun relating to its subject matter. It supersedes all prior or contemporaneous oral or written communications, proposals, representations and warranties and prevails over any conflicting or additional terms of any quote, order, acknowledgment, or other communication between the parties relating to its subject matter during the term of this Agreement. No modification of this Agreement will be binding, unless in writing and signed by an authorized representative of each party.

Sun™ ONE STUDIO 4 UPDATE 1, COMMUNITY EDITION SUPPLEMENTAL LICENSE TERMS

These supplemental license terms ("Supplemental Terms") add to or modify the terms of the Binary Code License Agreement (collectively, the "Agreement"). Capitalized terms not defined in these Supplemental Terms shall have the same meanings ascribed to them in the Agreement. These Supplemental Terms shall supersede any inconsistent or conflicting terms in the Agreement, or in any license contained within the Software.

1. **Software Internal Use and Development License Grant.** Subject to the terms and conditions of this Agreement, including, but not limited to Section 4 (Java Technology Restrictions) of these Supplemental Terms, Sun grants you a non-exclusive, non-transferable, limited license to reproduce internally and use internally the binary form of the Software complete and unmodified for the sole purpose of designing, developing and testing your applets and applications ("Programs"). To the extent that you are designing, developing and testing Java applets and applications for a particular version of the Java platform, any executable output generated by a compiler that is contained in the Software must (a) only be compiled from source code that conforms to the corresponding version of the OEM Java Language Specification; (b) be in the class file format defined by the corresponding version of the OEM Java Virtual Machine Specification; and (c) execute properly on a reference runtime, as specified by Sun, associated with such version of the Java platform.

2. **License to Distribute Software.** Subject to the terms and conditions of this Agreement, including, but not limited to Section 4 (Java Technology Restrictions) of these Supplemental Terms, Sun grants you a non-exclusive, non-transferable, limited license to reproduce and distribute the Software in binary code form only, provided that (i) you distribute the Software complete and unmodified, (ii) you do not distribute additional software intended to replace any component(s) of the Software, (iii) if you are distributing Java applets and applications for a particular version of the Java platform, any executable output generated by a compiler that is contained in the Software must (a) only be compiled from source code that conforms to the corresponding version of the OEM Java Language Specification; (b) be in the class file format defined by the corresponding version of the OEM Java Virtual.

   Machine Specification; and (c) execute properly on a reference runtime, as specified by Sun, associated with such version of the Java platform, (iv) you do not remove or alter any proprietary legends or notices contained in the Software, (v) you only distribute the Software subject to a license agreement that protects Sun's interests consistent with the terms contained in this Agreement, and (vi) you agree to defend and indemnify Sun and its licensors from and against any damages, costs, liabilities, settlement amounts and/or expenses (including attorneys' fees) incurred in connection with any claim, lawsuit or action by any third party that arises or results from the use or distribution of any and all Programs and/or Software.

3. **License to Distribute Redistributables.** Subject to the terms and conditions of this Agreement, including but not limited to Section 4 (Java Technology Restrictions) of these Supplemental Terms, Sun grants you a non-exclusive, non-transferable, limited license to reproduce and distribute the binary form of those files specifically identified as redistributable in the Software "RELEASE NOTES" file ("Redistributables") provided that: (i) you distribute the Redistributables complete and unmodified (unless otherwise specified in the applicable RELEASE NOTES file), and only bundled as part of Programs, (ii) you do not distribute additional software intended to supersede any component(s) of the Redistributables, (iii) you do not remove or alter any proprietary legends or notices contained in or on the Redistributables, (iv) if you are distributing Java applets and applications for a particular version of the Java platform, any executable output generated by a compiler that is contained in the Software must (a) only be compiled from source code that conforms to the corresponding version of the OEM Java Language Specification; (b) be in the class file format defined by the corresponding version of the OEM Java Virtual Machine Specification; and (c) execute properly on a reference runtime, as specified by Sun, associated with such version of the Java platform, (v) you only distribute the Redistributables pursuant to a license agreement that protects Sun's interests consistent with the terms contained in the Agreement, and (v) you agree to defend and indemnify Sun and its licensors from and against any damages, costs, liabilities, settlement amounts and/or expenses (including attorneys' fees) incurred in connection with any claim, lawsuit or action by any third party that arises or results from the use or distribution of any and all Programs and/or Software.

4. **Java Technology Restrictions.** You may not modify the Java Platform Interface ("JPI", identified as classes contained within the "java" package or any subpackages of the "java" package), by creating additional classes within the JPI or otherwise causing the addition to or modification of the classes in the JPI. In the event that you create an additional class and associated API(s) which (i) extends the functionality of the Java platform, and (ii) is exposed to third party software developers for the purpose of developing additional software which invokes such additional API, you must promptly publish broadly an accurate specification for such API for free use by all developers. You may not create, or authorize your licensees to create, additional classes, interfaces, or subpackages that are in any way identified as "java", "javax", "sun" or similar convention as specified by Sun in any naming convention designation.

5. **Java Runtime.** Availability. Refer to the appropriate version of the Java Runtime Environment binary code license (currently located at *http://www.java.sun.com/jdk/index.html*) for the availability of runtime code which may be distributed with Java applets and applications.

6. **Distribution by Publishers.** This section pertains to your distribution of the Software with your printed book or magazine (as those terms are commonly used in the industry) relating to Java technology ("Publication"). Subject to and conditioned upon your compliance with the restrictions and obligations contained in the Agreement, in addition to the license granted in Paragraph 1 above, Sun hereby grants to you a non-exclusive, nontransferable limited right to reproduce complete and unmodified copies of the Software on electronic media (the "Media") for the sole purpose of inclusion and distribution with your Publication(s), subject to the following terms: (i) you may not distribute the Software on a stand-alone basis; it must be distributed with your Publication(s); (ii) you are responsible for downloading the Software from the applicable Sun web site; (iii) you must refer to the Software as Sun ONE Studio 4, Community Edition; (iv) the Software must be reproduced in its entirety and without any modification whatsoever (including, without limitation, the Binary Code License and Supplemental License Terms accompanying the Software and proprietary rights notices contained in the Software); (v) the Media label shall include the following information: Copyright 2002, Sun Microsystems, Inc., 4150 Network Circle, Santa Clara, CA 95054. Java and SUN One and all trademarks and logos based on Java and SUN One are trademarks or registered trademarks of Sun Microsystems, Inc. in the U.S. and other countries. This information must be placed on the Media label in such a manner as to only apply to the Sun Software; (vi) you must clearly identify the Software as Sun's product on the Media holder or Media label, and you may not state or imply that Sun is responsible for any third-party software contained on the Media; (vii) you may not include any third party software on the Media which is intended to be a replacement or substitute for the Software or which directly competes with the Software; (viii) you shall indemnify Sun for all damages arising from your failure to comply with the requirements of this Agreement. In addition, you shall defend, at your expense, any and all claims brought against Sun by third parties, and shall pay all damages awarded by a court of competent jurisdiction, or such settlement amount negotiated by you, arising out of or in connection with your use, reproduction or distribution of the Software and/or the Publication. Your obligation to provide indemnification under this section shall arise provided that Sun: (i) provides you prompt notice of the claim; (ii) gives you sole control of the defense and settlement of the claim; (iii) provides you, at your expense, with all available information, assistance and authority to defend; and (iv) has not compromised or settled such claim without your prior written consent; (ix) you shall provide Sun with a written notice for each Publication; such notice shall include the following information: (1) title of Publication, (2) author(s), (3) date of Publication, and (4) ISBN or ISSN numbers. Such notice shall be sent to Sun Microsystems, Inc., 4150 Network Circle, M/S USCA12-110, Palo Alto, CA 94303-4900, Attention: Contracts Administration; and (x) you shall provide Sun with quarterly written reports regarding the number of copies of the Software distributed during the prior quarter; such reports shall be sent to Sun Microsystems, Inc., 4150 Network Circle, Santa Clara, CA, 95054, Attn.: Sun ONE Studio Product Management Group, M/S UOAK01.

7. **Trademarks and Logos.** You acknowledge and agree as between you and Sun that Sun owns the SUN, SOLARIS, JAVA, JINI, FORTE, and iPLANET trademarks and all SUN, SOLARIS, JAVA, JINI, FORTE, and iPLANET-related trademarks, service marks, logos and other brand designations ("Sun Marks"), and you agree to comply with the Sun Trademark and Logo Usage Requirements currently located at *http://www.sun.com/policies/trademarks*. Any use you make of the Sun Marks inures to Sun's benefit.

8. **Source Code.** Software may contain source code that is provided solely for reference purposes pursuant to the terms of this Agreement. Source code may not be redistributed unless expressly provided for in this Agreement.

9. **Termination for Infringement.** Either party may terminate this Agreement immediately should any Software become, or in either party's opinion be likely to become, the subject of a claim of infringement of any intellectual property right.

For inquiries please contact:
Sun Microsystems, Inc.
4150 Network Circle, Santa Clara, California 95054.
(LFI#117241/Form ID#011801)

Pearson Prentice Hall License Agreement and Limited Warranty

READ THE FOLLOWING TERMS AND CONDITIONS CAREFULLY BEFORE OPENING THIS SOFTWARE PACKAGE. THIS LEGAL DOCUMENT IS AN AGREEMENT BETWEEN YOU AND

PEARSON EDUCATION, INC. (THE "COMPANY"). BY OPENING THIS SEALED SOFTWARE PACKAGE, YOU ARE AGREEING TO BE BOUND BY THESE TERMS AND CONDITIONS. IF YOU DO NOT AGREE WITH THESE TERMS AND CONDITIONS, DO NOT OPEN THE SOFT-WARE PACKAGE. PROMPTLY RETURN THE UNOPENED SOFTWARE PACKAGE AND ALL ACCOMPANYING ITEMS TO THE PLACE YOU OBTAINED THEM FOR A FULL REFUND OF ANY SUMS YOU HAVE PAID.

1. **GRANT OF LICENSE:** In consideration of your purchase of this book, and your agreement to abide by the terms and conditions of this Agreement, the Company grants to you a nonexclusive right to use and display the copy of the enclosed software program (hereinafter the "SOFTWARE") on a single computer (i.e., with a single CPU) at a single location so long as you comply with the terms of this Agreement. The Company reserves all rights not expressly granted to you under this Agreement.

2. **OWNERSHIP OF SOFTWARE:** You own only the magnetic or physical media (the enclosed media) on which the SOFTWARE is recorded or fixed, but the Company and the software developers retain all the rights, title, and ownership to the SOFTWARE recorded on the original media copy(ies) and all subsequent copies of the SOFTWARE, regardless of the form or media on which the original or other copies may exist. This license is not a sale of the original SOFTWARE or any copy to you.

3. **COPY RESTRICTIONS:** This SOFTWARE and the accompanying printed materials and user man-ual (the "Documentation") are the subject of copyright. The individual programs on the media are copyrighted by the authors of each program. Some of the programs on the media include separate licensing agreements. If you intend to use one of these programs, you must read and follow its accom-panying license agreement. You may not copy the Documentation or the SOFTWARE, except that you may make a single copy of the SOFTWARE for backup or archival purposes only. You may be held legally responsible for any copying or copyright infringement which is caused or encouraged by your failure to abide by the terms of this restriction.

4. **USE RESTRICTIONS:** You may not network the SOFTWARE or otherwise use it on more than one computer or computer terminal at the same time. You may physically transfer the SOFTWARE from one computer to another provided that the SOFTWARE is used on only one computer at a time. You may not distribute copies of the SOFTWARE or Documentation to others. You may not reverse engi-neer, disassemble, decompile, modify, adapt, translate, or create derivative works based on the SOFT-WARE or the Documentation without the prior written consent of the Company.

5. **TRANSFER RESTRICTIONS:** The enclosed SOFTWARE is licensed only to you and may not be transferred to any one else without the prior written consent of the Company. Any unauthorized trans-fer of the SOFTWARE shall result in the immediate termination of this Agreement.

6. **TERMINATION:** This license is effective until terminated. This license will terminate automatically without notice from the Company and become null and void if you fail to comply with any provisions or limitations of this license. Upon termination, you shall destroy the Documentation and all copies of the SOFTWARE. All provisions of this Agreement as to warranties, limitation of liability, remedies or damages, and our ownership rights shall survive termination.

7. **MISCELLANEOUS:** This Agreement shall be construed in accordance with the laws of the United States of America and the State of New York and shall benefit the Company, its affiliates, and assignees.

8. **LIMITED WARRANTY AND DISCLAIMER OF WARRANTY:** The Company warrants that the SOFTWARE, when properly used in accordance with the Documentation, will operate in substantial conformity with the description of the SOFTWARE set forth in the Documentation. The Company does not warrant that the SOFTWARE will meet your requirements or that the operation of the SOFTWARE will be uninterrupted or error-free. The Company warrants that the media on which the SOFTWARE is delivered shall be free from defects in materials and workmanship under normal use for a period of thirty (30) days from the date of your purchase. Your only remedy and the Company's only obligation under these limited warranties is, at the Company's option, return of the warranted item for a refund of any amounts paid by you or replacement of the item. Any replacement of SOFTWARE or media under the warranties shall not extend the original warranty period. The limited warranty set forth above shall not apply to any SOFTWARE which the Company determines in good faith has been subject to misuse, neglect, improper installation, repair, alteration, or damage by you. EXCEPT FOR THE EXPRESSED WARRANTIES SET FORTH ABOVE, THE COMPANY DISCLAIMS ALL WARRANTIES, EXPRESS OR IMPLIED, INCLUDING WITHOUT LIMITATION, THE IMPLIED WARRANTIES OF MERCHANTABILITY AND FITNESS FOR A PARTICULAR PURPOSE. EXCEPT FOR THE EXPRESS WARRANTY SET FORTH ABOVE, THE COMPANY DOES NOT WARRANT, GUARANTEE, OR MAKE ANY REPRESENTATION REGARDING

THE USE OR THE RESULTS OF THE USE OF THE SOFTWARE IN TERMS OF ITS CORRECTNESS, ACCURACY, RELIABILITY, CURRENTNESS, OR OTHERWISE.

IN NO EVENT, SHALL THE COMPANY OR ITS EMPLOYEES, AGENTS, SUPPLIERS, OR CONTRACTORS BE LIABLE FOR ANY INCIDENTAL, INDIRECT, SPECIAL, OR CONSEQUENTIAL DAMAGES ARISING OUT OF OR IN CONNECTION WITH THE LICENSE GRANTED UNDER THIS AGREEMENT, OR FOR LOSS OF USE, LOSS OF DATA, LOSS OF INCOME OR PROFIT, OR OTHER LOSSES, SUSTAINED AS A RESULT OF INJURY TO ANY PERSON, OR LOSS OF OR DAMAGE TO PROPERTY, OR CLAIMS OF THIRD PARTIES, EVEN IF THE COMPANY OR AN AUTHORIZED REPRESENTATIVE OF THE COMPANY HAS BEEN ADVISED OF THE POSSIBILITY OF SUCH DAMAGES. IN NO EVENT SHALL LIABILITY OF THE COMPANY FOR DAMAGES WITH RESPECT TO THE SOFTWARE EXCEED THE AMOUNTS ACTUALLY PAID BY YOU, IF ANY, FOR THE SOFTWARE.

SOME JURISDICTIONS DO NOT ALLOW THE LIMITATION OF IMPLIED WARRANTIES OR LIABILITY FOR INCIDENTAL, INDIRECT, SPECIAL, OR CONSEQUENTIAL DAMAGES, SO THE ABOVE LIMITATIONS MAY NOT ALWAYS APPLY. THE WARRANTIES IN THIS AGREEMENT GIVE YOU SPECIFIC LEGAL RIGHTS AND YOU MAY ALSO HAVE OTHER RIGHTS WHICH VARY IN ACCORDANCE WITH LOCAL LAW.

ACKNOWLEDGMENT

YOU ACKNOWLEDGE THAT YOU HAVE READ THIS AGREEMENT, UNDERSTAND IT, AND AGREE TO BE BOUND BY ITS TERMS AND CONDITIONS. YOU ALSO AGREE THAT THIS AGREEMENT IS THE COMPLETE AND EXCLUSIVE STATEMENT OF THE AGREEMENT BETWEEN YOU AND THE COMPANY AND SUPERSEDES ALL PROPOSALS OR PRIOR AGREEMENTS, ORAL, OR WRITTEN, AND ANY OTHER COMMUNICATIONS BETWEEN YOU AND THE COMPANY OR ANY REPRESENTATIVE OF THE COMPANY RELATING TO THE SUBJECT MATTER OF THIS AGREEMENT.

Should you have any questions concerning this Agreement or if you wish to contact the Company for any reason, please contact in writing at the address below.

Robin Short
Pearson Prentice Hall
One Lake Street
Upper Saddle River, New Jersey 07458